Nashua Public Library

34517010118052

DISCARDED

Enjoy this book!

Please remember to return it on time.
so that others may enjoy it too.

Manage your library account and
discover all we offer by visiting us
online at www.nashualibrary.org.

Love your library? Tell a friend!

GREAT ATHLETES

GREAT ATHLETES

Volume 8

Unser–Zurbriggen
Appendices
Indexes

Edited by
The Editors of Salem Press

Special Consultant
Rafer Johnson

SALEM PRESS, INC.
Pasadena, California   Hackensack, New Jersey

Ref
796.092
G
NPL

Editor in Chief: Dawn P. Dawson

Managing Editor: R. Kent Rasmussen
Manuscript Editor: Lauren Mitchell
Production Editor: Cynthia Beres
Photograph Editor: Philip Bader
Assistant Editors: Andrea Miller
Elizabeth Slocum

Research Supervisor: Jeffry Jensen
Acquisitions Editor: Mark Rehn
Page Design and Layout: James Hutson
Additional Layout: William Zimmerman
Eddie Murillo

Cover Design: Moritz Design, Los Angeles, Calif.

Copyright © 1992, 1994, 2002, by Salem Press, Inc.

All rights in this book are reserved. No part of this work may be used or reproduced in any manner whatsoever or transmitted in any form or by any means, electronic or mechanical, including photocopy, recording, or any information storage and retrieval system, without written permission from the copyright owner except in the case of brief quotations embodied in critical articles and reviews. For information address the publisher, Salem Press, Inc., P.O. Box 50062, Pasadena, California 91115.

© 2002 *Great Athletes, Revised*
© 1994 *The Twentieth Century: Great Athletes, Supplement* (3 volumes)
© 1992 *The Twentieth Century: Great Athletes* (20 volumes)

∞ The paper used in these volumes conforms to the American National Standard for Permanence of Paper for Printed Library Materials, Z39.48-1992 (R1997).

Library of Congress Cataloging-in-Publication Data

Great athletes / edited by the editors of Salem Press ; Rafer Johnson, special consultant.—Rev.
p. cm.
Includes bibliographical references and index.
ISBN 1-58765-007-X (set : alk. paper) — ISBN 1-58765-008-8 (v. 1 : alk. paper) — ISBN 1-58765-009-6 (v. 2 : alk. paper) — ISBN 1-58765-010-X (v. 3 : alk. paper) — ISBN 1-58765-011-8 (v. 4 : alk. paper) — ISBN 1-58765-012-6 (v. 5 : alk. paper) — ISBN 1-58765-013-4 (v. 6 : alk. paper) — ISBN 1-58765-014-2 (v. 7 : alk. paper) — ISBN 1-58765-015-0 (v. 8 : alk. paper)
1. Athletes—Biography—Dictionaries. I. Johnson, Rafer, 1935- . II. Salem Press

GV697.A1 G68 2001
796′.092′2—dc21

2001042644

First Printing

PRINTED IN THE UNITED STATES OF AMERICA

Contents

page

Al Unser 2853
Bobby Unser. 2856
Gene Upshaw 2859

Fernando Valenzuela 2862
Marco van Basten 2866
Norm Van Brocklin 2869
Steve Van Buren. 2872
Dazzy Vance 2875
Pieter van den Hoogenband 2878
Amy Van Dyken 2881
Harry Vardon 2884
Glenna Collett Vare 2887
Greg Vaughn 2890
Mo Vaughn 2893
Peter Vidmar 2896
Guillermo Vilas 2899
Jacques Villeneuve 2902
Dave Villwock 2905
Chuck Vinci 2908
Lasse Viren 2911

Rube Waddell 2914
Virginia Wade 2917
Honus Wagner 2920
Lisa Wagner 2923
Greta Waitz 2925
Doak Walker. 2928
Herschel Walker. 2931
John Walker 2934
Rusty Wallace 2937
Bobby Walthour. 2940
Bill Walton. 2943
Charlie Ward 2947
Paul Warfield 2950
Cornelius Warmerdam 2953
Kurt Warner. 2955
Bob Waterfield 2958
Tom Watson 2961
Chris Webber 2964
Dick Weber 2967
Johnny Weissmuller. 2970
Buddy Werner. 2973
Jerry West 2976

	page
Peter Westbrook	2979
Byron "Whizzer" White	2981
Randy White	2984
Reggie White	2987
Mal Whitfield	2990
Simon Whitfield	2993
Kathy Whitworth	2996
Deena Wigger	2999
Lones Wigger	3002
Hazel Wightman	3006
Mats Wilander	3009
Hoyt Wilhelm	3012
Lenny Wilkens	3015
David Wilkie	3018
Dominique Wilkins	3021
Mac Wilkins	3024
Laura Wilkinson	3027
Billy Williams	3029
Esther Williams	3032
Natalie Williams	3035
Ricky Williams	3038
Serena Williams	3040
Ted Williams	3043
Venus Williams	3046
Walter Ray Williams, Jr.	3049
Maury Wills	3051
Hack Wilson	3054
Larry Wilson	3057
Dave Winfield	3059
Hans Winkler	3062
Katarina Witt	3065
Willie Wood	3068
Lynette Woodard	3070
John Wooden	3073
Cynthia Woodhead	3076
Tiger Woods	3079
Charles Woodson	3083
Gump Worsley	3086
James Worthy	3089
Billy Wright	3092
Mickey Wright	3095
Early Wynn	3098
Kristi Yamaguchi	3101
Yasuhiro Yamashita	3104
Cale Yarborough	3107
Ivan Yarygin	3110
Lev Yashin	3113

page

Carl Yastrzemski . . . 3116
Cy Young . . . 3119
Sheila Young . . . 3122
Steve Young . . . 3125
Robin Yount . . . 3128
Steve Yzerman . . . 3131

Babe Didrikson Zaharias . . . 3134
Emil Zatopek . . . 3137
Jan Zelezny . . . 3140
Kim Zmeskal . . . 3143
Steve Zungul . . . 3146
Pirmin Zurbriggen . . . 3149

Resources

Select Bibliography of Notable Sports Books . . . 3155
Sports Resources on the World Wide Web . . . 3159
Timeline . . . 3166
Glossary . . . 3188

All-Time Great Athletes Lists

AP Top Athletes of the Twentieth Century . . . 3217
ESPN SportsCentury 100 Greatest Athletes of the Twentieth Century . . . 3219
Major League Baseball's All-Time Team . . . 3221
National Basketball Association's Fifty Greatest Players . . . 3222

Athlete-of-the-Year Awards

ABC *Wide World of Sports* Athlete of the Year . . . 3225
Associated Press Athlete of the Year . . . 3226
CNN/*Sports Illustrated* Sportsman of the Year . . . 3228
ESPY Outstanding Athlete of the Year . . . 3229
James E. Sullivan Memorial Award . . . 3230
Jesse Owens International Trophy . . . 3231
Sporting News Sportsman of the Year . . . 3232
USOC Sportsman and Sportswoman of the Year . . . 3233

Halls of Fame

Hockey Hall of Fame . . . 3237
International Boxing Hall of Fame . . . 3240
International Gymnastics Hall of Fame . . . 3241
International Soccer Hall of Champions . . . 3242
International Swimming Hall of Fame . . . 3243
International Tennis Hall of Fame . . . 3246
International Women's Sports Hall of Fame . . . 3248
Naismith Memorial Basketball Hall of Fame . . . 3250
National Baseball Hall of Fame . . . 3252
National Track and Field Hall of Fame . . . 3255
Pro Football Hall of Fame . . . 3257

page

U.S. Olympic Hall of Fame 3259
World Golf Hall of Fame 3261
World Skating Hall of Fame 3262

Indexes
Sport Index III
Country Index XIII
Name Index XXI

GREAT ATHLETES

AL UNSER

Sport: Auto racing

Born: May 29, 1939
Albuquerque, New Mexico

Early Life

Al Unser was born on May 29, 1939, in Albuquerque, New Mexico, into a racing family. His father, Jerry Sr., and his older brothers, Jerry, Louis, and Bobby, were all racers. His father ran a garage and allowed the boys to tinker with an old pickup truck, which they finally got to run. Informal races and driving around the desert gave Al his earliest contact with driving. The neighborhood was a rough one, with clashes between Hispanics and Anglos and between newcomers and old-time residents. Working in the family business and on the family racing team gave Al a constructive outlet for his energy.

The Unser family was involved in the annual Pikes Peak road race, and this event gave Al his racing groundwork. He also gained experience

Courtesy of Amateur Athletic Foundation of Los Angeles

with stock cars and sprint cars. During these years, Al was somewhat in the shadow of his older brother, Bobby, who was rapidly establishing a racing reputation for himself.

The Road to Excellence

In 1967, Al had his first success in an Indianapolis 500 race by finishing second. His brother Bobby won the race the next year, so Al was still struggling for recognition, which came for him in 1970.

During the qualifying events for the Indianapolis 500, it appeared a close race was shaping up. At least four drivers were very close in speed, and Al won the pole position by only two and one-half feet over a 10-mile race. In the actual race, both Unser brothers were at the front of the pack by lap 3. Their driving skill was enhanced by their pit crews, Al's crew consistently getting his car back on the track in about 20 seconds on each of his stops. This combined effort helped Al build a 32-second lead by the end of the race.

The Emerging Champion

The next year, 1971, Indianapolis was marked by problems from the first. The pace car crashed into a photographers' stand as it was leaving the track. Early in the race, three drivers wrecked, leading to 17 laps under the caution flag. Other cars dropped out with mechanical problems and, after 118 laps, Al was in the lead to stay. Late in the race, a final fiery crash took out yet more cars and strewed the track with burning gas and wreckage. Still, Al steered clear and ended the race with a new track speed record, an average of 157.735 miles per hour. Al joined a select group of only three other back-to-back Indy winners.

The 1972 season saw Al's career slow down. He won some races, but not on a consistent basis, frequently plagued with breakdowns and penalties. He was involved in a controversy with fans and other drivers about the tactics he used to win the 1973 Texas 200 race. In 1975 and 1976, Al had to work out problems with a new type of car, a Cosworth Ford eight-cylinder turbocharged engine, a powerful engine that won races when it did not break down. In addition to his racing problems, Al's mother died in 1975.

Continuing the Story

The years of 1976 and 1977 were better racing years, but Al still was not winning the big races such as the Indy 500 or taking the United States Auto Club (USAC) Championship. In 1978, however, all the pieces came together. After spending several years developing the new engine, Al simply ran away with the Indy 500. This win was aided by car designer Jim Hall, whose ground-effects design caused the car to hug the ground more closely and so take the corners at a higher speed. Al became one of only three peo-

CART AND OTHER VICTORIES

1964-65, 1983	Pikes Peak Hill Climb
1968	Nazareth 100
1969	Phoenix 200
1969-70	Duquoin 100
1969-70, 1976	Milwaukee 200
1970	Indianapolis Raceway Park 150 Springfield 100 Trenton 300 USAC National Champion
1970-71, 1976, 1979, 1985	Phoenix 150
1970-71, 1978, 1987	Indianapolis 500
1970, 1972, 1975	Tony Bettenhausen 100
1970-73	Hoosier 100
1971	Milwaukee 150
1973	Texas 200 Valvoline/USAC Silver Crown Series Champion
1974	Michigan 250
1976, 1978	Pocono 500
1977-78	California 500
1980	Can-Am Challenge Cup Race (Laguna Seca)
1983	Cleveland Grand Prix Cleveland 500 kilometers
1983, 1985	PPG Indy Car World Series Championship

HONORS, AWARDS, AND RECORDS

1967	USAC Rookie of the Year
1970	Jerry Titus Memorial Award
1970, 1978	Martini & Rossi Driver of the Year
1986	Inducted into Indianapolis Motor Speedway Hall of Fame
1987	One of only three drivers to capture the Indianapolis 500 four times At forty-seven years and eleven months of age, the oldest driver in history to capture the Indianapolis 500
1991	Inducted into Motorsports Hall of Fame of America

ple to have won at Indianapolis three times. Less than a month later, Al won the Pocono 500 race in the same car.

Al, along with several other drivers, was very dissatisfied with the way USAC regulated racing, so, at the end of 1978, twenty racing teams formed their own association to sponsor races, the Championship Auto Racing Teams (CART). It touched off a controversy between the two sponsoring groups that eventually had to be settled in court.

In 1979, Al again changed racing teams, this time joining Bobby Hillin's Chaparral Racing Team because the car designer attended races to see the car perform and to identify problems. Although this change was successful, Al soon found himself facing a new competitor, his son Al, Jr.

Although father and son were in competition, they worked together, as in the 1983 Indianapolis 500, when Al, Jr., blocked driver Tom Sneva for 10 laps in an unsuccessful attempt to protect his father's lead.

In 1985 Al, Sr., and Al, Jr., came into the last race of the season virtually tied for the championship. Although an excellent driver, Al, Sr., had started the year with a contract for only three races. He consistently finished in the top five and came to the final race on the verge of the championship. Al, Jr., needed to beat Al, Sr., by two places to win the championship for himself. Almost at the end, Al, Sr., charged past another driver, and, although finishing the race behind his son, won the championship by one point.

Perhaps the zenith of Al's career came in 1987, when he went to Indianapolis without a car to drive. The injury of another driver during the qualifying events gave him his chance. His skill and experience gave him the victory for the fourth time and made him the oldest person ever to win the Indy 500. With age beginning to take its toll, Al finished his racing career with a third-place finish in 1992 and a twelfth-place finish in his final race of 1993.

Summary

Al Unser is both relaxed and competitive, with a rural manner of speaking and a wry sense of humor. Noted for clean living, sticking to his work, and finishing almost every race he enters, he enjoys his children's company and his relationship with his racing "family."

Michael R. Bradley

Additional Sources:

Bentley, Karen. *The Unsers.* New York: Chelsea House, 1996.

Berger, Phil, and Larry Bortstein. *The Boys of Indy.* New York: Corwin Books, 1977.

Orr, Frank. *World's Great Race Drivers.* New York: Random House, 1972.

Sakkis, Tony. *Indy Racing Legends.* Osceola, Wis.: Motorbooks International, 1996.

Taylor, Rich. *Indy: Seventy-Five Years of Racing's Greatest Spectacle.* New York: St. Martin's Press, 1991.

BOBBY UNSER

Sport: Auto racing

Born: February 20, 1934
Albuquerque, New Mexico

Courtesy of Amateur Athletic Foundation of Los Angeles

Early Life

Robert William Unser was born on February 20, 1934, not far from Albuquerque, New Mexico, and moved into town at age three when his parents, Jerry, Sr., and Mary, opened an automobile repair garage there. Bobby had twin brothers, Jerry and Louis, older than he and a younger brother, Al.

Bobby grew up during the later years of the Great Depression, so money for the Unser family was hard to come by. Also, the boys were newcomers to town and had to fend for themselves against the more established youth.

The boys' father allowed them to rebuild an old pickup truck when Bobby was nine, so he learned about mechanics at an early age. Indeed, the entire family became involved in racing. Their father drove racers; one uncle did also. Jerry, Jr., was a United States Auto Club (USAC) stock car champion in 1957 and was killed in an auto race at Indianapolis in 1959. Louis won the Pikes Peak Hill Climb twice before being confined to a wheelchair by multiple sclerosis. Younger brother Al was also a racer, as is his son Al, Jr.

At age fifteen, Bobby began racing in Albuquerque and soon established a reputation. In 1953, Bobby entered the Air Force but managed to combine his duties with auto racing. He was discharged in 1957 because of the death of his father. At that point, Bobby began to concentrate fully on his racing in the Pikes Peak Hill Climb.

The Road to Excellence

In 1963, Bobby drove for the first time in the Memorial Day race at Indianapolis, Indiana. This race was not a long one for Bobby because he crashed his car on the third lap. In 1966, Bobby was back, finishing eighth, and in 1968 he hit the big time.

Turbine cars were supposed to win the Indy 500 in 1968, but with his mother Mary and second wife Norma watching from the same spot where his brother had been killed in 1959, Bobby stayed on the tail of these cars as, one after the other, they broke down. Coming into lap 191 of the 200 laps in the race, Bobby was still trailing when the last turbine sputtered to a stop, and he sprinted ahead. Because of his immense popularity on the race circuit, the fans cheered wildly.

In winning the race, Bobby had set a new track record of 152.8 miles per hour.

With money from his prize and with an established reputation, Bobby began to attract sponsors who would make available money, automobile parts, and backing. Bobby began an association with Roger Penske that would last many years. Each season after 1968, Bobby did a little better, winning more of the big races. By 1972, he held speed records at seventeen of the eighteen race tracks on the United States Auto Club (USAC) circuit.

The Emerging Champion

Bobby did not confine himself to Indy-style cars. In 1974, he set a new speed record in the Pikes Peak Hill Climb in a stock car. This twelve-and-one-half mile race climbs to the top of Pikes Peak, 14,100 feet in height, over a road that makes more than five hundred turns. This race is almost an Unser family possession, because various family members have won it twenty-eight times.

On Memorial Day in 1975, Bobby was back in Indianapolis. This time, there was no concern about turbo cars, but other drivers, such as archrival A. J. Foyt, were out to give Bobby a run for the money. Again, someone else led for most of the race, but as the race neared its end, several drivers pulled into the pit to take on gas. Bobby had planned better and had taken on gas earlier and began to take the lead. Suddenly, the skies opened up in a heavy downpour. With Bobby ahead, the starter waved the checkered flag after only 174 laps. This win in the rain was Bobby's second Indy win.

Wins and championships continued to come to Bobby, and he kept on pushing hard. As he put it, he did what came naturally and was the easiest thing for him—going fast.

Continuing the Story

A third Indy win came to Bobby in 1981, but only after a month-long period of controversy. During the race, Bobby dueled with Mario Andretti and, as the race reached the three-quarters point at lap 148, both men pulled into the pits under a yellow flag to take fuel. Under a yellow flag, no driver is supposed to improve his position. As Bobby left the pit, he reentered the track in a way not clearly covered by the rules. At the end of the race, Bobby was ahead, but Andretti filed a protest. The next day, the USAC board upheld the protest and declared Andretti the winner. Bobby then protested because the rules called for a one-lap penalty to be assessed immediately. In October, 1981, the USAC agreed and officially awarded the race to Bobby. He became the oldest driver ever to win the Indianapolis 500 (a record later broken by younger brother Al).

The controversy and its worry and tension caused Bobby to lose some of his enthusiasm for racing, and he decided to retire. He had won almost three million dollars and had three victories at Indianapolis and two national championships. Retirement did not mean completely giving up racing because two of his sons, Robbie and Bobby, Jr., continued to drive racers, and Bobby himself still occasionally drove stock cars and four-wheel-drive dirt road races.

NASCAR AND STOCK CAR VICTORIES

1950	New Mexico Modified Stock Car Championship
1956, 1958-62, 1966, 1968-69, 1974, 1976	Pikes Peak Hill Climb
1965	Stardust 150
1968, 1972, 1976	Phoenix 150
1968, 1974	USAC National Driving Champion
1968, 1975, 1981	Indianapolis 500
1969-70	Langhorne 150
1971	Marlboro 300 Milwaukee 200 Trenton 200 Tony Bettenhausen 200
1972-73	Milwaukee 150
1974	Michigan 200
1974, 1976, 1979-80	California 500
1979	Michigan 126 Michigan 150
1980	Pocono 500

Summary

Bobby Unser paid a price for success. For years, he risked his life in every race. He spent more time away from his family than with it, and he suffered the physical injuries that are a part of race car driving. Bobby had a strong personal motivation, however: "There is no such thing as a slow day in the life of Bobby Unser and I will go fast until the day I die."

Michael R. Bradley

HONORS, AWARDS, AND RECORDS	
1974	Martini & Rossi Driver of the Year
1976	Made the fastest pit stop ever, using only four seconds to refuel on lap ten of the Indianapolis 500
1990	Inducted into Indianapolis Motor Speedway Hall of Fame Inducted into International Motorsports Hall of Fame

Additional Sources:

Bentley, Karen. *The Unsers.* New York: Chelsea House, 1996.

Hickok, Ralph. *A Who's Who of Sports Champions: Their Stories and Records.* Boston: Houghton Mifflin, 1995.

Sakkis, Tony. *Indy Racing Legends.* Osceola, Wis.: Motorbooks International, 1996.

Scalzo, Joe. *The Bobby Unser Story.* Garden City, N.Y.: Doubleday, 1979.

Taylor, Rich. *Indy: Seventy-Five Years of Racing's Greatest Spectacle.* New York: St. Martin's Press, 1991.

GENE UPSHAW

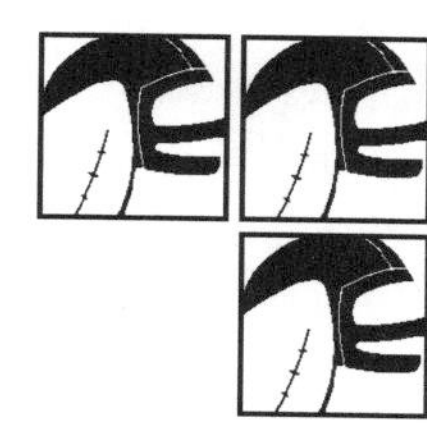

Sport: Football

Born: August 15, 1945
Robstown, Texas

Early Life

Eugene Upshaw was born in the small Texas town of Robstown on August 15, 1945. His father, Eugene Sr., worked in the oil fields near Robstown and instructed his two boys, Gene and Marvin, in discipline, charity, and racial tolerance. Cora Upshaw, Gene's mother, worked as a maid for white families. The family was poor, and the two boys worked picking cotton for $1.25 per one hundred pounds. It was backbreaking labor under the hot Texas sun.

When Gene and his brother were not in the fields, they were spending their days in the four-room schoolhouse in Robstown. During recess and after school they would play baseball. They were good players, but their strict father continually warned them not to sacrifice their education for sports.

The Road to Excellence

Gene and his brother stayed in school and applied themselves to their studies. While Marvin, Gene's younger brother, grew large and strong enough to star on the high school football team, Gene remained small for his age. At football games he stood on the sidelines holding the first-down chains.

By his senior year, Gene had developed into a fine athlete. At 5 feet 10 inches and 185 pounds, he became a genuine professional prospect as a baseball pitcher. Football would become his sport of choice, however, when he enrolled at Texas A&I College. At Texas A&I, Gene added seven inches to his height and filled out to a strong 255 pounds. Yet, in spite of his size, he was a failure at offensive positions such as fullback and tight end. Even on defense he appeared to be uncoordinated, playing three straight games without making one tackle.

In his typical late-bloomer fashion, however, by the end of his senior season Gene had distinguished himself as an offensive lineman and was projected as a third-round National Football League (NFL) draft pick. In the Senior Bowl, play-

AP/Wide World Photos

Gene Upshaw of the Oakland Raiders in 1981.

ing aggressively against All-Americans from Michigan State University, the University of Notre Dame, and the University of Southern California, Gene suddenly became first-round material.

The Emerging Champion

Impressed by his speed, strength, and intelligence, the Oakland Raiders selected Gene in the first round of the 1967 American Football League (AFL)/National Football League draft. Soon the Raiders became one of the league's most dominant teams. They played the Green Bay Packers in Super Bowl II, losing 33-14. Despite this loss, the Raiders missed the playoffs only four times in the years Gene anchored their offensive line at left guard.

Sending running backs to the left, behind Gene and his monstrous teammate, Art Shell, became an Oakland Raiders trademark play. Gene loved it whenever a sweep to the left was called. "That's my play," Gene told Robert Oates in *The Winner's Edge* (1980). "A wide receiver wants to catch a long touchdown pass. A defensive lineman wants to break in to sack the quarterback. I get my satisfaction pulling to lead those sweeps. That's a play where it comes down to just me and the defensive back. If I get him clean, we're going to make a long gain. If I miss him, we don't get a yard."

His success at his position helped guide the Raiders to two Super Bowl championships and earned him the honor of playing on four All-Pro teams and six American Football Conference (AFC) All-Star teams, and of being named AFC Lineman of the Year in 1973 and 1974 and NFL Lineman of the Year in 1977. In his sixteen-season career, Gene played in 209 consecutive games out of a total of 217 games.

Continuing the Story

Gene was known for his outspokenness both on and off the field. Playing the guard position, he would call out to teammates, directing their moves. As a member of the NFL Players Association (NFLPA), he represented league players at the bargaining table. A member of the Executive Committee of the Players Association since 1976, Gene was elected its president in 1980. In 1982, when contract negotiations broke down and a strike ensued, Gene helped maintain the players' morale in the face of intense criticism from fans and the press. He actively served on the Player-Club Relations Committee, the NFLPA/Bert Bell Retirement Board, the NFL's Competition Committee, and the NFLPA's Committee on Institutional Discrimination.

After his retirement as a player, Gene went on to become the executive director of the NFLPA in June of 1983. In his new post, Gene sought to increase player confidence in the union, improve the public's understanding of the union's goals, enhance communication between players and management, and improve the financial situation for players.

At the time the only visible African American labor official in the United States, Gene also engaged in a variety of public charities and was the recipient of the NFLPA's Byron Whizzer White Humanitarian Award for his services to his former team, his community, and the country in 1980. In 1982, he was presented with the A. Phillip Randolph Award in recognition of his significant accomplishments as one of the outstanding black leaders in America. Gene also accepted a position to serve as a National Vice President for the Muscular Dystrophy Association and as a member of the National Committee on Drug Prevention, a program sponsored by the U.S. Drug Enforcement Administration.

In addition to receiving his bachelor of science degree from Texas A&I University in 1968, he has also done postgraduate studies at both Golden Gate University and Lincoln University.

HONORS AND AWARDS

1967	Senior Bowl All-Star Team
1967-69	*Sporting News* AFL All-Star Team
1969	AFL All-Star Team
1970-71, 1977	*Sporting News* AFC All-Star Team
1973-74	AFC Lineman of the Year
1973-78	NFL Pro Bowl Team
1977	NFL Lineman of the Year
1980	NFL All-Pro Team of the 1970's NFLPA Byron Whizzer White Humanitarian Award
1987	Inducted into Pro Football Hall of Fame
1994	NFL 75th Anniversary All Time Team

Summary

Gene Upshaw, one of the greatest offensive linemen in the history of the NFL, blossomed as a player in his senior year at Texas A&I and went on to become a Super Bowl captain and champion. He was a perennial All-Star team selection, was named to six Pro Bowl teams, was chosen as AFC Lineman of the Year twice and the NFL's best lineman once (he was the NFL runner-up for that distinction in 1980). Gene is the only player to participate in Super Bowl games in the 1960's, the 1970's, and the 1980's. He was elected to the Pro Football Hall of Fame in Canton, Ohio, in 1987—his first year of eligibility. In 1994 Gene was selected as a member of the NFL's 75th Anniversary All Time Team. As a high-ranking labor official, Gene became a spokesman for the rights of NFL players and earned the respect of the league's players and management.

Rustin Larson

Additional Sources:

Attner, Paul. "NFL: Football's One Hundred Greatest Players—Better than All The Rest." *The Sporting News* 223 (November 8, 1999): 58-59, 62.

Barber, Phil. "NFL: Football's One Hundred Greatest Players—The Hit Men." *The Sporting News* 223 (November 1, 1999): 12-16.

Pro Football Hall of Fame. http://www.profootballhof.com.

NASHUA PUBLIC LIBRARY

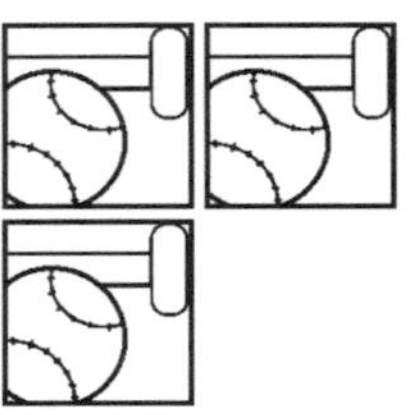

FERNANDO VALENZUELA

Sport: Baseball

Born: November 1, 1960
Etchohuaquila, Mexico

Early Life

Fernando Anguamea Valenzuela was born on November 1, 1960, in the village of Etchohuaquila, Mexico, near the southern tip of the state of Sonora, not far inland from the Gulf of California. Nearby is the larger town of Navojoa, which some sources list as Fernando's birthplace.

Life in Etchohuaquila was not easy. The house where Fernando was born was made of adobe, with windows that were simply openings cut into the walls: no glass. Not until the 1970's did the village receive electricity, and when Fernando reached the major leagues in 1980 the houses in Etchohuaquila were still without running water.

Fernando was the youngest of the twelve children of Avelino and Maria Valenzuela. Like most of the families in the village, his family farmed a small plot of land. Fernando, however, did not have to work as much as his brothers and sisters. He spent a lot of time playing baseball. Sometimes he even skipped school in order to play.

AP/Wide World Photos

St. Louis Cardinal Fernando Valenzuela pitching in June, 1997.

The Road to Excellence

The first team Fernando played on was the Etchohuaquila town team, which also featured his six older brothers. Even as a boy, the left-handed Fernando was clearly an exceptional athlete—what baseball people call a "natural," gifted at all phases of the game. His oldest brother, Rafael, who had played professional baseball in Mexico, was the first to encourage Fernando to think of baseball as a career.

In 1976, at the age of fifteen, Fernando signed his first professional contract. By 1979 he had progressed to the big league level in the Mexican League, pitching for the Yucatán Leones and winning Rookie of the Year honors. That same year, Mike Brito, a scout for the Los Angeles Dodgers, signed Fernando, who was sent to the Dodgers' Class A team in Lodi, California.

STATISTICS												
Season	*GP*	*GS*	*CG*	*IP*	*HA*	*BB*	*SO*	*W*	*L*	*S*	*ShO*	*ERA*
1980	10	0	0	17.2	8	5	16	2	0	1	0	0.00
1981	25	25	11	192.1	140	61	**180**	13	7	0	**8**	2.48
1982	37	37	18	285.0	247	83	199	19	13	0	4	2.87
1983	35	35	9	257.0	245	99	189	15	10	0	4	3.75
1984	34	34	12	261.0	218	106	240	12	17	0	2	3.03
1985	35	35	14	272.1	211	101	208	17	10	0	5	2.45
1986	34	34	20	269.1	226	85	242	**21**	11	0	3	3.14
1987	34	34	12	251.0	254	124	190	14	14	0	1	3.98
1988	23	22	3	142.1	142	76	64	5	8	1	0	4.24
1989	31	31	3	196.2	185	98	116	10	13	0	0	3.43
1990	33	33	5	204.0	223	77	115	13	13	0	2	4.59
1991	2	2	0	6.2	14	3	5	0	2	0	0	12.15
1993	32	31	5	178.2	179	79	78	8	10	0	2	4.94
1994	8	7	0	45.0	42	7	19	1	2	0	0	3.00
1995	29	15	0	90.1	101	34	57	8	3	0	0	4.98
1996	33	31	0	171.2	177	67	95	13	8	0	0	3.62
1997	18	18	1	89.0	106	46	61	2	12	0	0	4.96
Totals	453	424	113	2,930.0	2,718	1,151	2,074	173	153	2	31	3.54

Notes: Boldface indicates statistical leader. GP = games played; GS = games started; CG = complete games; IP = innings pitched; HA = hits allowed; BB = bases on balls (walks); SO = strikeouts; W = wins; L = losses; S = saves; ShO = shutouts; ERA = earned run average

After the 1979 season was over, the Dodgers asked Fernando to report to the Instructional League in Scottsdale, Arizona. It was there that he learned the screwball, the pitch that completed his repertoire. The screwball has been described as a "reverse curveball." When throwing a curve, a pitcher turns his wrist so the back of his hand faces outward. A screwball, in contrast, is thrown with an inward twist. The motion is difficult for most pitchers to master, but Fernando was soon throwing the "scroogie" with ease.

Fernando began the 1980 season with the Dodgers' Double A team in San Antonio, Texas. Late in the season he was called up to the big club. Although he pitched nearly 18 innings for the Dodgers after his September 10 promotion, he was very impressive, not allowing a single earned run.

The Emerging Champion

When the Dodgers began the 1981 season they had high hopes for Fernando, but no one could have guessed what was ahead. Jerry Reuss, the scheduled Opening Day starter for the Dodgers, suffered an injury, and Fernando got the call. The twenty-year-old rookie proceeded to shut out the Houston Astros (champions of the National League West in 1980), 1-0. In his second start, against the San Francisco Giants, Fernando pitched the Dodgers to a 7-1 victory. In his third start, he shut out the San Diego Padres, 2-0. The Astros fell again, 1-0, in his fourth start.

By this time, the unknown kid from Mexico had become a sensation. Fernandomania, the media called it. Huge crowds came to see him wherever he pitched, in Los Angeles or on the road. A host of reporters followed him everywhere, documenting one of the most remarkable beginnings in the history of major league baseball.

By the end of his first full season, Fernando had led his team to the National League pennant and the World Series championship, as the Dodgers defeated the Montreal Expos in the league playoffs and the New York Yankees in the World Series, avenging Series losses to the Yankees in 1977 and 1978. Fernando was named Rookie of the Year, and he received the Cy Young Award—becoming the first player ever to win both of these coveted awards in the same year. He completed the year by getting married, on December 19, 1981; he and his wife Linda (a schoolteacher whom he had met while pitching for Yucatán) have four children.

Continuing the Story

The only trouble with such a storybook beginning is that it is impossible to sustain—the magic

MAJOR LEAGUE RECORDS

Most shutouts by a rookie pitcher, 8 (1981) (record shared)
Did not allow an earned run for 41.1 innings from the start of the 1985 season
Most consecutive strikeouts in an All-Star Game, 5 (1986) (record shared)

HONORS AND AWARDS

1981	National League Cy Young Award *Sporting News* Major League Baseball Player of the Year National League Rookie of the Year
1981-86	National League All-Star Team
1986	National League Gold Glove Award

does not last forever. Many athletes, unable to cope with the letdowns that inevitably follow golden moments, have seen their careers disintegrate. Fernando, however, was uniquely equipped to deal with such pressures.

Teammates and opponents, broadcasters, journalists, and fans—all who watched Fernando in his rookie year marveled at his maturity and poise. Whether faced with a bases-loaded jam or a media onslaught, he always remained calm.

Some observers thought that this quality reflected Fernando's Indian heritage. Others said that he was much older than he claimed to be. (To put an end to such charges, the Dodgers produced a copy of his birth certificate.)

Whatever its source, Fernando's unflappable cool helped him throughout his career. When he came to the United States, he did not speak English at all. For several years he gave interviews only in Spanish; an interpreter translated his responses into English. Later he gave interviews in both languages. His success inspired many people, and particularly Hispanic youths.

In addition to barriers of language and culture, Fernando had to contend with physical problems. An athlete's greatest fear is a prematurely disabling injury. In July, 1988, Fernando was placed on the disabled list for the first time in his career as a result of severe damage to his left shoulder. At the time he was only twenty-seven years old. Since his Opening Day appearance in 1981, he had made 255 starts without missing a turn.

Rather than undergo surgery, Fernando chose the option of rest and a demanding rehabilitation program. While his teammates were winning the Dodgers' first World Series since the year of Fernando-mania, upsetting the Oakland Athletics, he had to watch from the sidelines. In 1989, he returned to the rotation. On June 29, 1990, against the St. Louis Cardinals, he pitched his first no-hitter since his return. Despite that brilliant performance, Fernando's overall record for the 1990 season was poor; the injury had taken its toll. In March, 1991, following several subpar outings in spring training, Fernando was released by the Dodgers.

Fernando signed with the Angels in 1991 but started only two games, both losing efforts. His injured left shoulder was not improving. In 1992, he joined the Mexican League's Jalisco team. In 1993 Fernando was invited to spring training by the Baltimore Orioles. In his first 15 innings, he did not allow an earned run and eventually made the Orioles roster. A favorite with the Baltimore fans, much as he was in Los Angeles, Fernando shut out the defending world champion Blue Jays on September 30.

After a short season with Philadelphia in 1994, Fernando signed with the San Diego Padres in 1995 and pitched two solid seasons. Following a 2-8 start in 1997, however, he was waived by the Padres. He finished the season in St. Louis, where he went 0-4 in five starts and finished with an earned run average of 5.56.

In early 1999, having spent the previous year out of baseball, Fernando was offered a chance to compete for a spot in the Dodgers' bullpen. The thirty-eight-year-old former Dodger star and local hero declined and returned to pitch in the Mexican League.

Summary

For many fans, dismayed by the strike that shortened the 1981 season, Fernando Valenzuela's wonderful, improbable rookie year was a saving grace, a reminder of what baseball is supposed to be all about. At first glance the portly Fernando did not look like a professional athlete, let alone a superstar, yet pitching for more than ten years for the Los Angeles Dodgers, he was one of the most popular players ever to perform for one of the sport's most successful franchises. He brought his enthusiasm for the game to each team with which he played, generating support with hometown fans and inspiring respect from his teammates.

John Wilson

Additional Sources:

Burchard, S. H. *Sports Star, Fernando Valenzuela.* San Diego, Calif.: Harcourt Brace Jovanovich, 1982.

Kirkjian, T. "Fernandomania II." *Sports Illustrated* 74, no. 23 (1991).

Littwin, Mike. *Fernando Valenzuela, the Screwball Artist.* Chicago: Children's Press, 1983.

MARCO VAN BASTEN

Sport: Soccer

Born: October 31, 1964
Utrecht, Netherlands

Early Life

Marco van Basten was born on October 31, 1964, in the historic city of Utrecht in the Netherlands. As a boy, Marco excelled in most sports and wanted to become a famous gymnast. He never even dreamed of being a professional soccer player. Even as a youngster, he revealed the confidence and ambition that would later put him ahead of the competition. He once wrote on his school desk, "There's nobody better than me, apart from me."

The Road to Excellence

Marco's enjoyment of soccer led him to join the Dutch amateur soccer club Elinwijk. He still had little thought of making a living from the game, but this was to change when his soccer skills, which were startlingly mature for a sixteen-year-old, came to the attention of the Dutch club Ajax. Ajax, the foremost club in Holland, at the time boasted the great Johann Cruyff as its star

Hulton Getty/Archive Photos

Marco van Basten (center) in action against England during the 1988 European Championships.

HONORS AND AWARDS

1986	Golden Boot Award
1988	Italian Super Cup champion
1988-89,1992-94	European Player of the Year
1989-90, 1994	European Super Cup champion
1989-90, 1994	European Cup champion
1989,1992-93	Italian League champion
1990	World Club Cup champion
1992	World Player of the Year

player. Marco joined Ajax in 1981 and made his First Team debut that same year at age seventeen, when he came on late in a game as a substitute for Cruyff. In light of later events, the moment would come to seem highly symbolic, for Marco was soon known as the "second Cruyff."

From the beginning of his career, Marco showed an almost uncanny ability to score goals from his position of center forward. Cruyff, though, saw in the young Marco more than merely a powerful and graceful goal scorer. He noticed that Marco had the same leadership qualities that he himself had possessed at a young age, and he took Ajax's new star under his wing. Marco was always to remain grateful to Cruyff, his first mentor, whom he regards as one of the finest soccer coaches in the world. Under Cruyff's guidance, Marco's ambitions came to be concentrated entirely on soccer. All thoughts of becoming a gymnast vanished.

The Emerging Champion

In 1983, Marco came to the attention of soccer fans throughout the world with his fine performances for his country in the World Youth Cup Finals in Mexico. For his club team, Ajax, he was scoring goals at a prolific rate, almost one a game. It was Marco's all-around skill that impressed people most; his game seemed to have no weak spots. He was fast, equally effective with left or right foot, good in the air, strong, and exciting to watch. Marco thrilled the fans; in addition to his all-around skills, he was a daring player, prepared to take risks and attempt the unexpected. "You mustn't be afraid to fall on your face," he once said. "If you don't dare to make mistakes, you'll never shine."

In 1986, Marco's fifth year with Ajax, he became team captain at the age of twenty-two. In that year, he also won the prestigious Golden Boot Award for his feat of scoring 37 goals in twenty-six games during the 1985-86 season. He followed this up with 31 goals the next season, when he led his team to victory in the European Cup Winners' Cup competition, scoring the winning goal against Locomotive Leipzig in the final.

The soccer world now lay at Marco's feet. Many of Europe's top clubs competed to tempt him away from Ajax. In 1987, he was transferred to the crack Italian team Milan for a fee of $2.2 million. Milan beat out competition from Italy's Roma, Spain's Barcelona, and Germany's Werder Bremen to win Marco's services. At Milan, Marco joined up with another Dutchman, Ruud Gullit, who was also one of the finest players in Europe. The two were to form a brilliantly effective partnership.

Continuing the Story

Marco was now ready for his greatest achievements for both his club and his country, but one of his finest moments was preceded by a setback. During the European Championships finals in 1988, he was named only as a substitute in Holland's opening game against the Soviet Union. He was disappointed, but Johann Cruyff told him to be patient. In the next game, Marco was included in the team from the outset, and he scored all three goals in Holland's 3-0 defeat of England. He scored again in the semifinal against West Germany. In the final, Marco scored a brilliant goal from a seemingly impossible angle, and this helped Holland to a 2-0 win over the Soviet Union. Marco said later he could hardly believe that he had scored such an extraordinary goal and would never be able to repeat it.

Marco was also helping Milan to become what many experts regarded as the best club in the world. In the 1988-89 season, he was Milan's top scorer. The following season, he was top scorer in the Italian League with 19 goals. He also scored twice in Milan's 4-0 win over Steaua Bucharest in the final of the European Champions Cup, and he won another winner's medal in that competition the following year after Milan's 1-0 win over Portugal's Benfica. Marco was top scorer in the Italian League again in 1991-1992 with 25 goals, and he would have repeated the feat in 1992-1993 had it not been for an ankle injury that kept

MILESTONES

58 international appearances for Holland
24 international goals
Inducted into International Football Hall of Fame

him out of action for several months.

Marco's career has had its disappointments. He did not reach his true form during the World Cup Finals in Italy in 1990, and Holland was quickly eliminated. Nor did he excel during the 1992 European Championships, missing a penalty kick in the semifinals against Denmark. Yet Marco's limitless ambition and determination always enabled him to recover from setbacks. During the early 1990's, soccer fans throughout the world were increasingly of the opinion that Marco had overtaken Argentina's Diego Maradona as the greatest soccer player in the world.

In 1993 Marco suffered severe ankle injuries that required surgery. After two years of rehabilitation in an effort to regain his form, he announced his retirement in 1995.

Summary

Marco van Basten's stature in the soccer world can perhaps best be understood from the fact that he has consistently been one of the best players on the best team in the best league in the world. According to no less an authority than Johann Cruyff, Marco's talent, skill, and unforgettable goals made him the world's greatest striker.

Bryan Aubrey

Additional Sources:

Gardner, Paul. "The Sport 1990 World Cup Preview." *Sport* 81, no. 7 (July, 1990): 60.

Goff, Steven. "Euro 2000 Title Is up for Grabs, Dutch Are Favorites, but France Is Strong." *The Washington Post,* June 9, 2000, p. D4.

Shulman, Ken. "A 'Classic Attacker' Leads the Dutch." *The New York Times Current Events Edition,* May 11, 1990, p. A29.

NORM VAN BROCKLIN

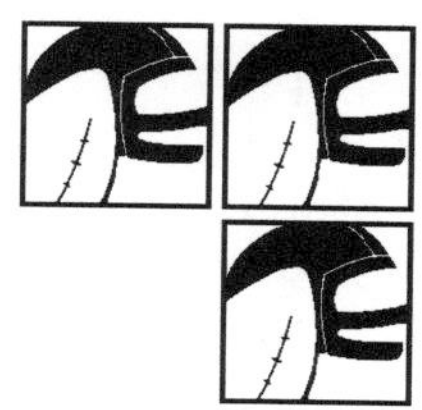

Sport: Football

Born: March 15, 1926
Eagle Butte, South Dakota
Died: May 2, 1983
Atlanta, Georgia

Early Life

Norman Van Brocklin was born on March 15, 1926, in the town of Eagle Butte, South Dakota. Norm was the eighth of nine children born into a middle-class farming family. Ethel and Mac Van Brocklin instilled a hard-driving, determined attitude into their son. Norm applied this ethic to his schooling, his work, and most significantly, his football ability. Though lacking natural athletic talent, Norm possessed an inner drive that would help him to succeed later on in life.

Football was just one of the sports that caught Norm's attention. As he grew older, it became apparent that the love for this particular game would fire up that inner drive. Norm put his mind to the task, and nothing was going to deter him. Succeeding in football was a way to prove himself, which in the ensuing years he did to a great extent. He played high school football and looked forward to college football. World War II, however, was under way, and serving in the military seemed to be the best thing to do.

The Road to Excellence

After graduating from high school in 1943, Norm entered the United States Navy and completed a tour of duty before entering the University of Oregon in 1946. At 6 feet 1 inch and 199 pounds, he showed real promise during his second year as quarterback for the Oregon Ducks.

After graduating from college in only three years with a degree in physical education, "The Dutchman" was taken in the third round of the National Footbal League (NFL) draft by the Los Angeles Rams. In fact, Norm had approached the Rams before the draft and told them that he was interested in playing for them. This information gave the Rams a tremendous advantage since the rest of the league did not realize that Van Brocklin was ready to turn professional. He actually had a year of college eligibility left. The Rams knew that Norm's lack of speed would be a big disadvantage, but they were also very aware of his abilities. He knew how to throw the ball extremely well. Norm was considered a

Courtesy of Amateur Athletic Foundation of Los Angeles

soft passer, or one who could get the ball into the receiver's hands without having to drill it. He showed a remarkable ability for judging the speed of a man running downfield and being able to drop the pass right on the mark, with the receiver never having to break stride.

The Emerging Champion

Two years later, Norm led the Rams to their only National Football League (NFL) title, with a 24-17 victory over the Cleveland Browns following the 1951 season. He was not only a winning quarterback but an awesome punter. The times, however, were not always pleasant for Norm, and many times the problem lay within himself. He had a short temper, both with teammates and with the press. He had no patience with writers, especially with those who in his opinion did not do their jobs properly. Former coaches used to say that with his talent, Van Brocklin could break all of football's passing records—assuming someone did not kill him first. He did, eventually, break every passing record in the books.

Norm enjoyed some of his greatest years after being traded to the Philadelphia Eagles. The situation in Los Angeles was such that the quarterback position was being shared by two players. Norm was uneasy in this situation and in 1958, after nine years with the Rams, was sent to the Eagles. While conceding a lot in the trade, Philadelphia still reaped the benefits from Norm's great arm and leadership qualities. Eight times during the 1960 season the team came back to win football games in the fourth quarter. That year the Eagles won the NFL Championship Game against the Green Bay Packers. Norm was voted the NFL Player of the Year and the Championship Game most valuable player.

Continuing the Story

At the age of thirty-four, and at the height of his playing career, Norm abruptly retired. He was the league's outstanding passer three times and was also the best punter in football twice during his career. At the peak of his career, Norm was one of the two highest-paid players in the game. He could have retired quietly and awaited Hall of Fame induction. Instead of going out quietly, Norm became the Minnesota Vikings' head coach in 1961. Of all the great quarterbacks to have played in the NFL, only three (Van Brocklin, Sammy Baugh, and Otto Graham) went on to become head coaches. It was in the coaching profession that Norm added to his successful, yet controversial, reputation. His ongoing feuds with then-Minnesota quarterback Fran Tarkenton, other team players, and the press kept Norm's name in the newspapers. To fans and players, it seemed amazing that a person with such a turbulent personality could last this long in a team-oriented sport. His coaching career came to an end in the middle of the 1974 season. His great record as a player far overshadowed his poor coaching mark of sixty-six wins, one

STATISTICS

Season	*GP*	*PA*	*PC*	*Pct.*	*Yds.*	*Avg.*	*TD*	*Int.*
1949	8	58	32	.552	601	10.4	6	2
1950	12	233	127	.545	2,061	**8.9**	18	14
1951	12	194	100	.515	1,725	8.9	13	11
1952	12	205	113	.551	1,736	**8.5**	14	17
1953	12	286	156	.545	2,393	8.3	19	14
1954	12	260	139	.535	2,637	**10.1**	13	21
1955	12	272	144	.529	1,890	7.0	8	15
1956	12	124	68	.548	966	7.8	7	12
1957	12	265	132	.498	2,105	7.9	20	21
1958	12	374	198	.529	2,409	6.4	15	20
1959	12	340	191	.562	2,617	7.7	16	14
1960	12	284	153	.539	2,471	8.7	24	17
Totals	140	2,895	1,553	.536	23,611	8.2	173	178

Notes: Boldface indicates statistical leader. GP = games played; PA = passes attempted; PC = passes completed; Pct. = percent completed; Yds. = yards; Avg. = average yards per attempt; TD = touchdowns; Int. = interceptions

hundred losses, and seven ties. This time the departure from professional football was final. In the next few years Norm did some football broadcasting and coached a college team in Georgia. In 1971, he was elected to the Pro Football Hall of Fame. He died on May 2, 1983, in Atlanta, Georgia.

HONORS, AWARDS, AND RECORDS

1951	NFL record for the most passing yards in a game (554)
1951-56, 1959-61	NFL Pro Bowl Team
1954-55	*Sporting News* NFL All-Star Team
1960	Associated Press NFL Co-Player of the Year United Press International NFL Player of the Year Bell Trophy Newspaper Enterprise Association NFL Player of the Year *Sporting News* NFL Player of the Year Thorpe Trophy National Football Association Championship Game most valuable player *Sporting News* NFL Eastern Division All-Star Team
1963	NFL All-Pro Team of the 1950's
1966	Inducted into College Football Hall of Fame
1971	Inducted into Pro Football Hall of Fame

Summary

As one of the greatest talents ever to play the game, Norm Van Brocklin brought many things to professional football. His tremendous arm and throwing ability set new standards for quarterbacks to follow. He was temperamental yet had the courage to overlook disagreements and to push forward with the job of the day. By concentrating on the task at hand, Norm was able to focus on the team's welfare and to produce the kind of results expected from an athlete with his extraordinary abilities.

Carmi Brandis

Additional Sources:

Hickok, Ralph. *A Who's Who of Sports Champions.* Boston: Houghton Mifflin, 1995.

LaBlanc, Michael L., and Mary K. Ruby, eds. *Professional Sports Team Histories: Football.* Detroit: Gale, 1994.

Porter, David L., ed. *Biographical Dictionary of American Sports: Football.* Westport, Conn.: Greenwood Press, 1987.

STEVE VAN BUREN

Sport: Football

Born: December 28, 1920
LaCeiba, Honduras

Early Life

Steve Van Buren was born in LaCeiba, Honduras, on December 28, 1920. His father was a busy fruit inspector while Steve was a small child. Unfortunately, his parents both died when he was very young, and Steve went to live in New Orleans with his grandparents. While growing up in Louisiana, Steve became interested in football. When he was old enough to play, however, he realized he was too tall and thin, a mere stripling. In fact, he weighed only 125 pounds. At first, his size discouraged him from trying out for his high school football team. The skinny orphan very nearly missed becoming a football player.

The Road to Excellence

Steve dropped out of Warren Eastern High School during his sophomore year and got a job in a steel foundry. For the next two years, he worked long and hard at the job. As a result, he built his body into that of a broad-shouldered, muscular athlete. By then Steve weighed 155 pounds.

Steve went back to finish high school, and he played high school football so successfully that he won an athletic scholarship to Louisiana State University (LSU). As a college halfback, Steve began to make headlines. He was now 6 feet tall and weighed 200 pounds. He was an over-powering runner, who would rush his way past all enemy tacklers. There was nothing glamorous about the way he rushed, but he had enough power to race right past opposing players without trying to dodge them.

At LSU, Steve played blocking back until his senior year. Then his coach, Bernie Moore, tried him as a ball carrier. As a result, Steve broke the Southeastern Conference (SEC) rushing record and went on to score two touchdowns in LSU's 1944 Orange Bowl win over Texas A&M.

Courtesy of the Philadelphia Eagles Football Club, Inc.

That kind of playing could not fail to attract the attention of major league professional football scouts. After graduating with a bachelor's degree in mechanical engineering from LSU, Van Buren was invited by the Philadelphia Eagles to join them in National Football League (NFL) competition. At last the "boy from the bayous" would be able to play professionally.

The Emerging Champion

During his first season as a professional, Steve had to overcome first a bout with influenza and then an attack of appendicitis. Nevertheless, Steve managed to lead the league in both scoring and rushing. He burst through his opponents' defenses year after year. He proved himself to be a mighty blocker and an excellent punter. He was also extremely reliable at receiving forward passes.

In 1947, Steve set a new NFL record by rushing for 1,008 yards. That year the Eagles lost the NFL Championship Game to the Chicago Cardinals. The following year, during a treacherous blizzard, the Eagles played the Cardinals again, and this time the Eagles' 7-0 win resulted from Steve's touchdown plunge. That touchdown brought the Eagles their first championship ever.

It was soon to be followed by another in 1949. With Steve's raw power rushing at enemy lines to maximize yardage, the Eagles' offense was described by one simple play: Just give the ball to Steve and let him run.

In the 1949 championship playoff for the NFL title, Steve had to slosh through a fierce rainstorm with inches of mud sucking at his heels. He cut through the Los Angeles Rams' defense for a remarkable 196 yards on 31 carries. His performance led the Eagles to a 14-0 victory and enhanced Steve's reputation as one of the greatest rushing halfbacks in football history.

Continuing the Story

In 1952, his career ended when Steve tore a ligament in his left knee. As a result of the injury, Steve had to retire after having played only eight years of professional football.

In his short career, Steve managed to set several all-time NFL records: most career rushes, most career yards rushing, most rushes in one year, most yards gained rushing in one season, most touchdowns in one year, and most touchdowns rushing in one year. He also held the Eagles' all-time record for punt return average (13.9 yards), career touchdowns (77), and kickoff return average (26.7 yards). Steve's lifetime record included 1,320 carries for 5,860 yards. As the second runner in NFL history to gain 1,000 yards in a season, he was the first to rush for over 1,000 yards in each of two seasons. Though most of his records have since been broken, the fact that he held so many at one time is evidence of his enormous talent.

In 1965, Steve was inducted into the Pro Football Hall of Fame at Canton, Ohio. He and his wife and three children resided in the Philadelphia area.

STATISTICS

		Rushing				*Receiving*			
Season	*GP*	*Car.*	*Yds.*	*Avg.*	*TD*	*Rec.*	*Yds.*	*Avg.*	*TD*
1944	9	80	444	5.5	5	—	—	—	—
1945	10	143	**832**	5.8	**15**	10	123	12.3	2
1946	9	116	529	4.6	5	6	55	9.1	0
1947	12	217	**1,008**	4.6	**13**	9	79	8.7	0
1948	11	201	**945**	4.7	**10**	10	96	9.6	0
1949	12	**263**	**1,146**	4.4	**11**	4	88	22.0	1
1950	10	188	629	3.3	4	2	34	17.0	0
1951	10	112	327	2.9	6	4	28	7.0	0
Totals	83	1,320	5,860	4.4	69	45	503	11.2	3

Notes: Boldface indicates statistical leader. GP = games played; Car. = carries; Yds. = yards; Avg. = average yards per carry *or* average yards per reception; TD = touchdowns; Rec. = receptions

HONORS AND AWARDS

1948	*Sporting News* NFL All-Star Team
1963	NFL All-Pro Team of the 1940's
1965	Inducted into Pro Football Hall of Fame Uniform number 15 retired by Philadelphia Eagles

Summary

Steve Van Buren started out as an underweight orphan boy and built himself up into a terrific athlete. He led the NFL in rushing during four of his eight years as a professional football player. He became the equal of the finest rushing halfbacks in the history of football. At a time when runners of his size were uncommon, Steve demonstrated that men of his size and speed could prove valuable on football teams.

Nan White

Additional Sources:

Hickok, Ralph. *A Who's Who of Sports Champions.* Boston: Houghton Mifflin, 1995.

LaBlanc, Michael L., and Mary K. Ruby, eds. *Professional Sports Team Histories: Football.* Detroit: Gale, 1994.

Porter, David L., ed. *Biographical Dictionary of American Sports: Football.* Westport, Conn.: Greenwood Press, 1987.

DAZZY VANCE

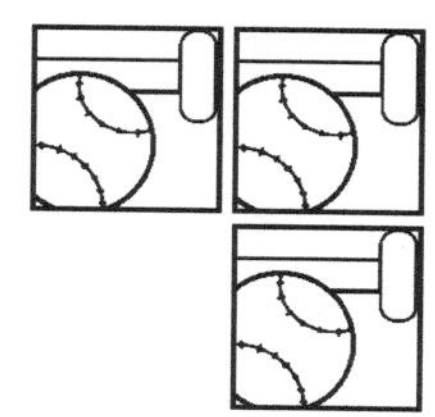

Sport: Baseball

Born: March 4, 1891
Orient, Iowa
Died: February 16, 1961
Homosassa Springs, Florida

Early Life

Arthur Charles "Dazzy" Vance was born on March 4, 1891, in Orient, Iowa, a small town in the southwestern part of the state. According to a family bible, he was named Clarence Arthur Vance, but he claimed Arthur Charles as his name.

Dazzy's Scots-Irish parents, A. T. and Sarah (Ritchie) Vance, were farmers. They moved from Orient to a farm near Hastings, Nebraska, when Dazzy was five. The young farm boy grew to a strapping 6 feet 2 inches tall, and, in addition to his farm chores, he played baseball for his Hastings High School team and a town team in nearby Cowles, Nebraska.

As a youth, Arthur would visit an old cowboy near Cowles who had a marvelous collection of chaps, spurs, saddles, and weapons. "Ain't that a dazzy?" mispronouncing "daisy," he would say to the young boy. Arthur picked up the phrase and soon he was being called "Dazzy."

The Road to Excellence

Dazzy graduated from Hastings High School in 1911 and continued to farm and play town-team ball. A tall, redheaded kid with an overpowering fastball, Dazzy drew the attention of the professionals, and in 1912, at the age of twenty-one, he signed his first professional contract, with Superior in the Nebraska State League. He earned $100 a month. After three years in the league, he was promoted to the Western League team at St. Joseph, Missouri, for the 1915 season.

His exaggerated high leg kick made it difficult for him to control his pitches and, although Dazzy showed great potential at times, there was little indication of his later greatness. He pitched

National Baseball Library, Cooperstown, New York

well for St. Joseph, and twice in 1915 the Pittsburgh Pirates and New York Yankees gave him a try. He was 0-4 as a major leaguer, however, and arm trouble began to plague him.

To cure his ailing arm, his doctor prescribed rest; it did not look like Dazzy would ever make it back to the majors. He persevered, however, worked on his control, developed a curveball, and rested his arm as much as he could. For five long years he bounced from team to team with minimal success. His travels read like a lesson on the geography of the United States: Columbus, Toledo, Memphis, Rochester, and Sacramento.

In 1921, Dazzy's career took a positive turn. Pitching for New Orleans, he compiled a 21-10 record with no sign of a sore arm. At season's end, he was signed by Charles Ebbets, the owner of the Brooklyn Dodgers, or "Robins," as they were then called, and in 1922 he entered the majors as a thirty-one-year-old rookie.

The Emerging Champion

Dazzy's patience, hard work, and sense of humor finally paid off. Unlike his disasters with the Pirates and Yankees in 1915, his first year as a Dodger was excellent. He won eighteen games and led the league in strikeouts. In fact, he led the league in strikeouts for a record-setting seven straight years.

Not only had Dazzy emerged as a premier pitcher, he was also one of the funniest and most colorful men in baseball. He was witty and a great storyteller. One of his favorite stories was when three hapless Dodgers wound up on third base. With Dazzy on second and Chick Fewster on first, Babe Herman hit a ball to right field. Dazzy waited to see if it would be caught, and when it hit the wall, he could only make it halfway to home. He retreated and slid back into third base, where Fewster already stood and where Herman came sliding in from the direction of second base. The third baseman tagged all three and a great argument ensued. Lying with his feet on third and his head toward home, Dazzy is reported to have said: "Mr. Umpire, Fellow Teammates, and Members of the Opposition, if you carefully peruse the rules of our National Pastime you will find that there is one and only one protagonist in rightful occupancy of this hassock—namely yours truly, Arthur C. Vance." He was right.

His roommate, Rube Bressler, claimed he was impossible to hit on Mondays. Dazzy would cut the sleeve of his white undershirt up to the elbow; then, when he pitched, his sleeve flapped and the batter would lose the ball completely against the laundry waving in the breeze in the background of Ebbets Field.

STATISTICS

Season	*GP*	*GS*	*CG*	*IP*	*HA*	*BB*	*SO*	*W*	*L*	*S*	*ShO*	*ERA*
1915	9	4	1	30.2	26	21	18	0	4	0	0	4.11
1918	2	0	0	2.1	9	2	0	0	0	0	0	15.43
1922	36	30	16	245.2	259	94	**134**	18	12	0	5	3.70
1923	37	35	21	280.1	263	100	**197**	18	15	0	3	3.50
1924	35	34	30	308.2	238	77	**262**	28	6	0	3	**2.16**
1925	31	31	26	265.1	247	66	**221**	22	9	0	**4**	3.53
1926	24	22	12	169.0	172	58	**140**	9	10	1	1	3.89
1927	34	32	25	273.1	242	69	**184**	16	15	1	2	2.70
1928	38	32	24	280.1	226	72	**200**	22	10	2	**4**	**2.09**
1929	31	26	17	231.1	244	47	126	14	13	0	1	3.89
1930	35	31	20	258.2	241	55	173	17	15	0	**4**	**2.61**
1931	30	29	12	218.2	221	53	150	11	13	0	2	3.38
1932	27	24	9	175.2	171	57	103	12	11	1	1	4.20
1933	28	11	2	99.0	105	28	67	6	2	3	0	3.55
1934	25	6	1	77.0	90	25	42	1	3	1	0	4.56
1935	20	0	0	51.0	55	16	28	3	2	2	0	4.41
Totals	442	347	216	2,967.0	2,809	840	2,045	197	140	11	30	3.24

Notes: Boldface indicates statistical leader. GP = games played; GS = games started; CG = complete games; IP = innings pitched; HA = hits allowed; BB = bases on balls (walks); SO = strikeouts; W = wins; L = losses; S = saves; ShO = shutouts; ERA = earned run average

Continuing the Story

A sense of humor was essential for a Dodger in the 1920's. They finished in sixth place seven of the eleven years Dazzy was with them. His and the Dodgers' best year during his tenure was 1924, when he won twenty-eight games and led the league in strikeouts and earned run average; he was also voted the league's most valuable player. Still, the Dodgers finished second to the New York Giants. On September 13, 1925, Dazzy threw a no-hitter against the Philadelphia Phillies.

Dazzy was traded to the St. Louis Cardinals in 1933. In 1934, he went to the Cincinnati Reds but was back with the Cardinals by the end of the season. His only appearance in a World Series was with the Cardinals in 1934. He finished his career in 1935, appropriately back with the Dodgers. Even though he did not win his first major league game until he was thirty-one, he finished with 197 wins and recorded more than 2,000 strikeouts.

Dazzy retired from baseball after the 1935 season and settled with his wife Edyth in Homosassa Springs, Florida. There he managed his real estate holdings and operated a hunting-fishing lodge, where he also sold his own driftwood carvings. He helped organize the Homosassa Springs Chamber of Commerce and served as its chair. He stayed active by hunting, fishing, and playing golf. Dazzy also kept his hand in baseball, managing a local amateur team. On February 16, 1961, just two weeks before his seventieth birthday, Arthur Charles "Dazzy" Vance died in his sleep.

MAJOR LEAGUE RECORDS
Most consecutive strikeouts in a game, 7 (1924)

NATIONAL LEAGUE RECORDS
Most consecutive seasons leading the league in strikeouts, 7

HONORS AND AWARDS	
1924	National League most valuable player
1955	Inducted into National Baseball Hall of Fame
1957	Inducted into Nebraska Sports Hall of Fame

Summary

The fun-loving Dazzy Vance earned the respect of his fellow players. He overcame control problems and a sore arm and paid his dues with ten years in the minor leagues before becoming one of baseball's greatest pitchers. In 1955, he was elected to the National Baseball Hall of Fame in Cooperstown, New York, along with Joe DiMaggio, Ted Lyons, and Gabby Hartnett.

Jerry E. Clark

Additional Sources:

Appel, Martin, and Burt Goldblatt. *Baseball's Best: The Hall of Fame Gallery.* New York: McGraw-Hill, 1977.

Newcombe, Jack. *The Fireballers.* New York: G. P. Putnam's Sons, 1964.

Shatzkin, Mike, et al., eds. *The Ballplayers: Baseball's Ultimate Biographical Reference.* New York: William Morrow, 1990.

PIETER VAN DEN HOOGENBAND

Sport: Swimming

Born: March 14, 1978
Geldrop, Netherlands

AP/Wide World Photos

Pieter van den Hoogenband after winning the semifinal heat of the 100-meter freestyle in the 2000 Olympics. He went on to win the gold in the event final.

Early Life

Pieter van den Hoogenband was born on March 14, 1978, in Geldrop, Netherlands. He grew up in Geldrop, outside of Eindhoven, in the southern part of the Netherlands. His mother, Astrid Verver, was a former 800-meter freestyle silver medal winner at the European Championships. His father, Dr. Cees-Rein van den Hoogenband, was a trauma surgeon and former water polo player who served as the team doctor for the well-known Dutch soccer team PSV Eindhoven.

As a youngster, Pieter enjoyed soccer, judo, and field hockey. Although he learned to swim at age four, he had only a recreational interest in the sport at first, preferring team sports. His potential as a swimmer was obvious, however, and by age nine he was frequenting the pool, finding the swim club an enjoyable social group as well as a competitive challenge.

Pieter's mother was frustrated by the lack of a quality swimming program. The Dutch team, in fact, had never produced many Olympic finalists, and the sport was not highly popular. With her husband's soccer contacts, the couple raised several tens of thousands of dollars from soccer-related businesspeople who served as sponsors, and started a small foundation to train swimmers. They hired Jacco Verhaeren as a coach and for the first year had just a handful of swimmers. Pieter's father also negotiated deals with major sportswear labels and put together televised swimming competitions, which helped fund the swim program.

The Road to Excellence

Pieter grew in speed and technical skills in his teens. In 1993, at age fifteen, he won a gold medal in the 100-meter freestyle and one silver in the 200-meter freestyle at the European Young Olympic Days meet in Eindhoven. At the Junior European Championships the following year, he picked up three gold medals in the 100-, 200-, and 400-meter freestyles. His times averaged about 2 seconds better per 100 meters than the year before, a remarkable drop.

In 1995, Pieter moved to higher competition at the European Championships. He placed sixth overall in the 100-meter freestyle, seventh in the 200-meter freestyle, and fifth in the 4×100-meter freestyle relay. He trailed Aleksandr Popov by just 1.22 seconds in the 100, closing in more and more on a swimmer Pieter had always seen as a "superman."

The Emerging Champion

Pieter trained hard under Jacco Verhaeren for the 1996 Atlanta Olympic Games, and expectations were high for the eighteen-year-old. His top finishes were fourth in the 100- and 200-meter freestyle events; he also placed fifth in the 4×100-meter freestyle relay, seventh in the 4×200-meter freestyle relay, ninth in the 50-meter freestyle, and tenth in the 4×100-meter individual medley relay. After the outcome of the Atlanta Olympics, which was worse than he had expected, Pieter decided to take a break from swimming. Already enrolled in medical school, he concentrated on his studies and on enjoying a fuller social life than that previously afforded by his training schedule.

Pieter took up training again just eight weeks before the 1997 European Championships in Seville, Spain. Two months was a very short time to regain the strength needed to equal his previous times, and his times and rankings at the Championships fell to fifth in the 100-meter freestyle and much lower in the 50 and 200. Of some encouragement, however, was the fact that his 200-meter freestyle was relatively fast at 1:48.59, actually a faster time than various swimmers in the winning heat. Unfortunately, his performance did not count for a medal as he had not swum in the top final heat.

Pieter knew that if he could train just eight weeks and perform at this level, strenuous training and a positive attitude could bring further gains. His next competition was the 1998 World Championships in Perth, Australia, where he won the bronze medal in the 200-meter freestyle, with a time of 1:48.65. Though just a hair over the time he had clocked in Seville, Pieter had finally won a medal at an international competition, and he set his sights on continuing to do so.

Continuing the Story

In 1999, Pieter put his medical studies on hold and attended a training camp in Sydney, Australia. The change of culture, weather, and attitude and an intense, focused training regimen proved successful. At the 1999 European Championships in Istanbul, Pieter had a remarkable showing, winning six golds in the 50-meter butterfly, 50-meter freestyle, 100-meter freestyle, 200-meter freestyle, 4×100-meter freestyle relay, and the 4×200-meter freestyle relay. His victory in the 100 broke Aleksandr Popov's eight-year winning streak in that event in all major competitions.

Pieter competed at two more international competitions that year; at the Short Course World Championships he took the bronze in the 200-meter freestyle, fifth in the 100-meter freestyle, 1st in the 4×200-meter freestyle relay,

STATISTICS

Year	Competition	Event	Place
1996	Olympic Games	100-meter freestyle	4th
		200-meter freestyle	4th
1998	World Championships	200-meter freestyle	3d
		100-meter freestyle	4th
		4×200-meter freestyle	2d
	European Championships	200-meter freestyle	1st
		100-meter freestyle	2d
		50-meter freestyle	3d
		4×50-meter freestyle relay	1st
1999	European Championships (Long Course)	50-meter butterfly	1st
		50-meter freestyle	1st
		100-meter freestyle	1st
		200-meter freestyle	1st
		4×100-meter freestyle relay	1st
		4×200-meter freestyle relay	1st
	World Championships (Short Course)	200-meter freestyle	3d
		4×200-meter freestyle relay	1st
		4×200-meter freestyle	2d
	European Championships (Short Course)	100-meter freestyle	1st
		200-meter freestyle	1st
		50-meter freestyle	2d
2000	Olympic Games	100-meter freestyle	Gold
		200-meter freestyle	Gold
		50-meter freestyle	Bronze
		4×200-meter freestyle relay	Bronze
	European Championships (Long Course)	200-meter freestyle	2d
		4×200-meter freestyle relay	3d

and second in the 4×100-meter freestyle relay. At the Short Course European Championships he scored two golds, in the 100- and 200-meter freestyles, and a silver in the 50-meter freestyle.

At the September, 2000, Olympic Games in Sydney, Pieter was poised to score big. The competition was aware of his prowess, but they were not prepared for total domination by the "Flying Dutchman," as Pieter is known. His first gold came in the 200-meter freestyle, in which he beat Australian favorite Ian Thorpe and set a world record of 1:45.35. The television cameras captured the look of complete shock and joy on Pieter's face, which became one of the memorable moments of the Games' swimming events.

The next day, Pieter competed against heavyweights Aleksandr Popov and Gary Hall in the preliminary heat of the 100-meter freestyle, racing to a world record first-place time of 47.84 seconds and becoming the first swimmer to break the 48-second mark in the event. He took the gold medal in the final heat of the 100, clocking in at 48.30. Pieter also won bronzes in the 50-meter freestyle and 4×200-meter freestyle relay and finished fourth in the 4×100-meter individual medley relay.

A natural characteristic of Pieter's from birth is a concave chest, which reduces drag and allows him to ride high in the water. He is slender and tall, 6 feet 3 inches, and weighs considerably less than the majority of his competitors. He has an ideal power-to-weight ratio; his lightness allows him a high stroke rate, and he has sufficient strength to power this stroke rate.

Summary

Pieter van den Hoogenband's career began to reach new heights at the end of the millennium and continued to improve. Aside from his winning times, Pieter has become known as a winning personality; he has shown confidence, lack of arrogance, openness, and friendliness to the press and spectators. He is the first Dutch male to win an Olympic medal, and one of only a few swimmers to win six titles at one European Championships. He was also the first swimmer to break 48 seconds in the 100-meter freestyle. In 1999 Pieter was named Athlete of the Year in the Netherlands, the number-two Athlete of the Year in Europe, and Best Swimmer of Europe.

Michelle C. K. McKowen

Additional Sources:

Dillman, Lisa. "Nice Guy Finishes First." *Los Angeles Times*, December 5, 1999, p. 16.

Longman, Jere. "Hyman, in Surprise, Joins #1 van den Hoogenband." *The New York Times*, September 21, 2000, p. Sports 1.

Lord, Craig. "The Flying Dutchman." *Swimming World and Junior Swimmer*, November 1, 1999, 20.

AMY VAN DYKEN

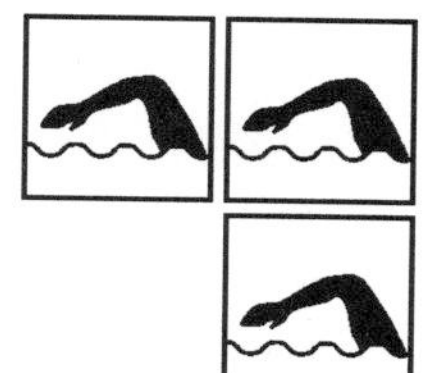

Sport: Swimming

Born: February 15, 1973
Denver, Colorado

Early Life

Amy Van Dyken was born on February 15, 1973, in Denver, Colorado, to Don and Becky Van Dyken. Amy's younger siblings, Katie and David, also became swimmers. Another sibling, Donnie, died from a brain tumor at age three when Amy was just five years old.

When Amy was eighteen months old, she suffered her first asthma attack. Doctors called it one of the most severe cases they had ever seen. Growing up, simple activities such as climbing stairs or laughing were painful for Amy, who developed three kinds of asthma: exercise-induced, allergy-induced, and infection-induced. This means that nearly any sort of exercise or sports, exposure to allergens, or simple colds could trigger her asthma. Amy was thus prevented from taking part in many activities, such as school recess, sleepovers at friends' houses, and sports.

Asthma was a stigma that was difficult for a child to overcome, and Amy's peers picked on her

AP/Wide World Photos

Amy Van Dyken after winning a heat in the 1996 Olympics. She won four gold medals at the Games.

throughout her grade school and teenage years. At age six, Amy's doctor suggested swimming as a way of improving her lung capacity within a beneficial humid atmosphere. She enjoyed the sport, although she was a slow swimmer and until age twelve could not swim a full lap without stopping on the wall or lane line to catch her breath.

The Road to Excellence

Amy joined the high school swim team at Cherry Creek High. She was not popular: Teammates ridiculed her for her height (she reached her full height of 6 feet as a teen) and slowness, often refusing to be on relay teams with her. Through this all, Amy kept swimming patiently and trying to improve. As a high school junior, she had advanced to the point of setting several high school records, and during her senior year she was recruited by various colleges.

Amy chose to attend Arizona State University. While there she competed successfully at the 1993 NCAA Championships, winning a silver medal in the 50-yard (45.7-meter) freestyle. Later that year she fell ill with mononucleosis and dropped out of swimming during the summer of 1993. As her health improved, she realized how much she missed the sport. In 1994 she transferred from Arizona to Colorado State University, where her performance improved and she was named NCAA Female Swimmer of the Year.

The Emerging Champion

Amy then decided to leave college temporarily and join the United States resident team in Colorado Springs, Colorado, to train with ex-Olympian Jonty Skinner. Skinner pushed Amy to drive herself to the end of every race and encouraged her mental toughness and stubbornness. The results were spectacular: In 1995 she won a 50-meter freestyle gold in the Pan-Pacific Championships and broke her own record, as well as taking a gold in the 100-meter butterfly and a silver in the 100-meter freestyle at the Pan-American Games.

Her eyes set on the 1996 Olympic Games in Atlanta, Amy qualified for the team in five events: the 50-meter freestyle, the 100-meter freestyle, the 100-meter butterfly, and the 4×100 freestyle and medley relays. Although she was prepared physically and mentally, she had not been part of the international spotlight for very long and was not favored to be a big winner.

She surprised the world by racing to four gold medals, in the 50-meter freestyle, 100-meter butterfly, and both relays, becoming the first American woman to carry away that many medals from a single Olympics. Her time of 24.87 in the 50-meter freestyle was a personal best as well as an Olympic record. In the 4×100-meter freestyle relay, her split of 53.13 was the second-fastest split by a woman. Both relay times were new American records; five of her times were career bests. Amy also placed fourth in the 100-meter freestyle.

Continuing the Story

After the Atlanta Olympics, Amy took a break from media-related activities and swam when she was able. Feeling out of shape and wanting to get back into the water, she began training again. During a strenuous weight-training practice one day, her shoulder popped. Amy ignored the injury, painful as it was. At the 1998 World Champi-

MAJOR CHAMPIONSHIPS

Year	*Competition*	*Event*	*Place*
1994	World Trials	50-meter freestyle	1st
	World Championships	4×100-meter freestyle relay	2d
		4×100-meter medley relay	2d
		50-meter freestyle	3d
1995	Pan-American Games	100-meter freestyle	2d
		100-meter butterfly	1st
1995	Pan-Pacific Championships	50-meter freestyle	1st
		4×100-meter freestyle relay	1st
		4×100-meter medley relay	2d
1996	Olympic Games	50-meter freestyle	Gold
		100-meter butterfly	Gold
		400-meter freestyle relay	Gold
		400-meter medley relay	Gold
1998	World Championships	50-meter freestyle	1st
		100-meter freestyle	1st
		4×100-meter freestyle relay	1st
1999	National Championships	50-meter freestyle	1st
2000	Olympic Games	4×100-meter freestyle relay	Gold
		50-meter freestyle	4th

onships she won both the 50- and the 100-meter freestyle, as well as the 4×100-meter freestyle relay. Still plagued by the shoulder, however, she saw a doctor, who discovered she had torn cartilage. In June, 1998, Amy underwent surgery to repair the cartilage, a surgery which might well have ended the careers of many athletes. Amy soon began an intensive program of rehabilitation, setting her sights on competition.

Her first meet back was in June, 1999, where she won the 50-meter freestyle. Swimming continued to be prohibitively painful, and in early January, 2000, Amy had follow-up surgery. She decided the butterfly event would be too damaging to the shoulder, but with rehabilitation and acupuncture decided to focus on preparing for the freestyle events at the Sydney Olympics, only months away.

Amy resumed training with the U.S. resident team, switching to coach John Mattos at Colorado State University in February, 2000. She trained six days a week, for about six hours a day. She was realistic about her dreams; she knew she was limited with her shoulder but wanted to win at least one medal.

Amy swam the 50-meter freestyle at Sydney and came in fourth with a time of 25.04. Her dream of winning one more medal came true, however: She helped the 4×100-meter freestyle relay to a qualifying place in the preliminaries; although she did not swim in the final heat, this previous performance earned her the gold.

The Sydney Olympics were Amy's last races. She expressed satisfaction with her accomplishments. All totaled, Amy won five Olympic golds during her career. She holds many distinctions, including the United States Swimming 1996 Athlete of the Year award, the 1996 National Athletic Awards Female Athlete of the Year award, and the 1996 Associated Press Worldwide Female Athlete of the Year award.

Amy wed Denver Broncos punter Tom Rouen in February, 2001, her second marriage. She continued her work as a spokesperson for athletes with asthma and Paws with a Cause (a group that prepares dogs for work with the hearing impaired) and remained involved with swimming in various capacities.

HONORS, AWARDS, AND MILESTONES

1994	Female NCAA Swimmer of the Year
	Colorado Sportswoman of the Year
1995	*Swimming World* American Female Swimmer of the Year
1996	First American woman to earn four Gold Medals in one Olympic Games
	Set American record for 400-meter medley relay
	Set American record for 400-meter freestyle relay
	U.S. Olympic Committee Female Athlete of the Year
	Associated Press Worldwide Female Athlete of the Year
	U.S. Swimming Athlete of the Year
	Colorado Athlete of the Year
	Inducted into Colorado State University Hall of Fame
	Phillips 66 Performance of the Year (50-meter freestyle at Olympic Games)
	Women's Sports Foundation Individual Athlete of the Year
	National Athletic Awards Female Athlete of the Year
	ARETE Performance of the Year Award
	Glamour Women of the Year Award
1999	Netherlands Athlete of the Year
	Best Swimmer of Europe
	Number-two European Athlete of the Year

Summary

Amy Van Dyken has the distinction of winning four medals at one Olympic Games, and five as a career total. Amy's spectacular Olympic performance, coupled with her friendly, down-to-earth personality, made her a favorite with the public. Her story is one of patience and determination; she found a way to overcome the challenges of severe asthma to become a top swimmer and an example to others.

Michelle C. K. McKowen

Additional Sources:

Dyer, Nicole. "Swimming for the Gold." *Science World* 56 (May 8, 2000): 8-11.

Gosman, Mike. "Swimmers with an Attitude." *Swimming World and Junior Swimmer,* August 1, 1996, 35.

Kramer, Sydelle, and James Campbell. *Wonder Women of Sports.* New York: Grosset & Dunlap, 1997.

Kravitz, Bob. "Pool Shark." *ESPN Magazine* Online. http://espn.go.comlpremiumlespninc/magazine/columns/vol3no11amy/S35204.html. July 14, 2000.

HARRY VARDON

Sport: Golf

Born: May 9, 1870
Grouville, Jersey, Channel Islands
Died: March 20, 1937
Totteridge, Herefordshire, England

Early Life

Harry Vardon was born May 9, 1870, in Grouville, Jersey, one of the Channel Islands in the English Channel. He was one of seven sons born to a professional gardener. He attended the village school along with his brothers. The Royal Jersey Golf Club was laid out over the Grouville Common area, and at age seven Harry had his introduction to golf as a caddy.

Childhood in the Channel Islands gave Harry limited opportunities to play golf. Brother Tom was influential in continuing Harry's involvement with the game. They made their own clubs from materials that were readily available; blackthorn was popular for the shafts and bent oak roots served as the club heads. The two materials were crudely united with nails and string. Later on, the brothers acquired real heads from broken clubs and attached them to the blackthorn shafts. The grip was smaller than common for the times. The grip had no felt or leather, so the boys modified the traditional ten-finger grip with thumbs wrapped around by placing their thumbs on top of the shaft. Thus, they established a new technique to avoid getting sore hands.

Courtesy of the PGA of America

The Road to Excellence

By age twenty, Harry had played only two or three dozen times, usually on public holidays. Following the lead of his brother, who was making money at golf, Harry himself appointed professional and greenskeeper at a new course named the Studby Royal Club at Ripon, Yorkshire.

Harry moved to Bury Club, Lancashire, where he played the first professional match of his life against

MAJOR CHAMPIONSHIP VICTORIES

1896, 1898-99, 1903, 1911, 1914	British Open
1900	U.S. Open

OTHER NOTABLE VICTORIES

1911	German Open
1912	British Professional Match Play

Sandy Herd, who was then at Herders-field Club. Herd won easily. From Bury Club, Harry became the professional at Ganton. He played his first British Open Championship in 1893 at Prestwich, to no great effect. J. H. Taylor made his first appearance that year and went on to win the next two Opens in 1894 and 1895. Harry's second year at the Open found him finishing fifth. In 1895, he led after the first round but finished ninth.

The Emerging Champion

J. H. Taylor was the biggest name of the time. In 1896, about a month before the Open, the Ganton members raised the money for a challenge match between Harry Vardon and Taylor. Harry won by 8 and 6 strokes. The two next went to play the Open. There Vardon began with an 83 to trail Taylor by 6 strokes. He was still behind by 3 with a round to go. The final day, they finished in a tie. After a thirty-six-hole playoff, Harry had won his first British Open by a 4-stroke margin.

Harry Vardon was one of the game's greatest innovators in terms of technique. The grip he used, with forefinger and little finger interlocking and thumbs on top of the shaft, was called the "Vardon Grip" at the time and later the "interlocking grip." Although the grip probably originated with a gifted amateur player named Johnny Laidlay, and was used by J. H. Taylor, it was Harry Vardon who was imitated.

When Harry came to prominence, the ideal swing was long with a tendency toward flatness. The idea was to hit the ball low. Harry showed that an upright swing with a high-ball trajectory worked well. As his reputation grew, other players began to copy his style. Many commented that he had the most graceful and easy swing that golf had yet seen. On the "take away," he had a full shoulder and hip turn around a straightened right leg, which ended with his back turned toward the hole.

Harry's play was most noted for accuracy. It was said that he could not play the same golf course twice because his ball would land in his own divots. This statement was incorrect, however, because Harry seldom took divots, preferring to shave the top of the turf.

By the end of the century, Harry Vardon was considered the greatest of the "Great Triumvirate," which included Harry Vardon, J. H. Taylor, and James Braid. He was playing at the peak of his game.

From his first British Open win in 1896, Harry went on to win a record six British Open Championships, in 1896, 1898, 1899, 1903, 1911, and 1914. He was runner-up in 1900, 1902, and 1912. During a nearly year-long tour of the United States in 1900, he won the United States Open as well. Another astonishing feat is that he lost only one exhibition game during the time that he was touring the United States. Challenge and exhibition matches were played by golf professionals of the day, rather than the tournament format that became prevalent in the 1900's.

Continuing the Story

Harry Vardon placed second to Sandy Herd in the British Open of 1901. Herd used a wound rubber ball for the first time while Harry used the gutta-percha ball, said to be the only one available at the time. During the 1903 Open win, Harry felt so ill he believed he would not be able to finish. Shortly after the event, he entered a sanatorium, suffering from tuberculosis. Thereafter, he suffered from the disease, and some

RECORDS AND MILESTONES

Won a record six victories in the British Open
British Open runner-up (1900, 1902, 1912), third (1906, 1913), second (1920)
French Open runner-up (1912, 1914), third (1909-10)
Trophies for low-scoring average on the PGA and European tours were named in his memory

HONORS AND AWARDS

1974	Inducted into PGA/World Golf Hall of Fame

have traced his decline in putting to that cause. Harry's putting became so poor as a result of his affliction that it was difficult for people to believe that he had been a major golfer. Gene Sarazan in the 1920's thought Harry was the worst putter he had ever seen. He remarked that Harry did not three putt, he four putt.

Harry may have been as a good a putter as anyone, but, because of illness and age, he began to have more and more difficulty with short putts. Even during his early playing days, however, it was noted that putting had seemed to be his weakness. Harry died on March 20, 1937, in Totteridge, Herefordshire, England.

Summary

At the peak of his career from 1896 to 1914, Harry Vardon was one of the dominant players in golf. He was considered the best of the "Great Triumvirate" players. He was also a catalyst for change not only in style and technique but also in popularizing the game of golf. A game that had begun as a strictly Scottish pursuit had gained worldwide popularity, much of which can be attributed to Harry's admirable style and travel throughout the United States.

Judy C. Peel

Additional Sources:

Howell, Audrey. *Harry Vardon.* London: Stanley Paul, 1991.

Vardon, Harry. *The Complete Golfer.* Rev. ed. New York: Doubleday, 1919.

_______. *The Gist of Golf.* New York: Doran, 1922.

_______. *How to Play Golf.* Philadelphia: G. W. Jacobs, 1916.

GLENNA COLLETT VARE

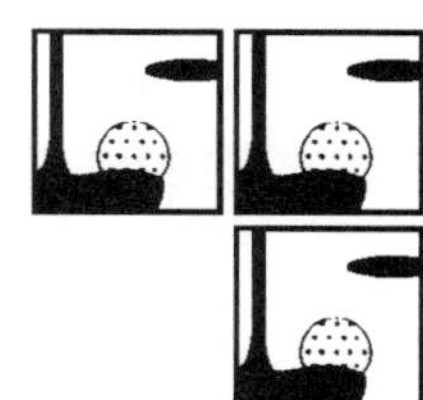

Sport: Golf

Born: June 20, 1903
New Haven, Connecticut
Died: February 3, 1989
Gulf Stream, Florida

Early Life

Glenna Collett was born on June 20, 1903, in New Haven, Connecticut. Growing up in the neighboring state of Rhode Island, she spent her earliest years enjoying the competitiveness of all athletics. Although she excelled at swimming and diving, her favorite sport was baseball. In fact, she played baseball so well that she became an important member of her brother's team.

The social attitudes of pre-World War I New England did not include athletics as a recommended endeavor for the daughters of wealthy parents. Glenna's natural athletic ability and desire to participate in sports caused her parents to worry about their "tomboy" daughter, so Mrs. Collett took her daughter to the tennis courts, a socially acceptable game for women at the time. Glenna learned to play tennis very well, but when her father took her to the golf course, she was captivated by the game and its challenge. Early success at hitting a golf ball inspired Glenna to study and practice the game at every opportunity.

The Road to Excellence

Glenna played her first round of golf at the age of fourteen. It would take several years of play and practice before she would become a competitive force. Even when her skill level had reached its peak, she had to overcome the mental difficulties of performing in pressure situations.

During the 1921 Berthellyn Cup competition in Philadelphia, Glenna was matched against the English golfing star Cecil Leitch. Major golf tournaments during that era used the common match play scoring system. A match pits one player against another over a scheduled number

Ralph W. Miller Golf Library

of holes, usually eighteen. Holes are won by the player scoring fewer strokes than the opponent. In her role of underdog, Glenna decided to match her opponent stroke for stroke rather than attempt superdifficult shots to win outright. To her credit, the new strategy carried the match to the final hole, where she sank a 10-foot putt for a one-hole victory.

Glenna had known the competitive pressure of golf but had never been able to handle it until now. Learning how to win the difficult matches was the last piece of the puzzle. Armed with mental confidence and physical skill, she was poised to challenge the best golfers in the world.

The Emerging Champion

In her nineteenth year, Glenna Collett won the North and South and the Eastern Amateur Championships. Her performance caught the public's attention. An excellent golf swing, combined with the good looks of the All-American girl, made Glenna popular with the sporting world. Her manner and etiquette on or off the golf course were pleasant, gracious, and all business. She enjoyed playing competitive golf and doing it well. Reports state that she once drove the golf ball a distance of 307 yards, proof that she indeed had a sweet golf swing as well as a winning way.

Glenna won fifty-nine out of sixty matches in 1924. The one defeat was administered by Mary Kimball Browne on the nineteenth hole of the semifinals at the Women's National Golf Championship. So many victories by one person should be hailed as a brilliant athletic achievement, and rightly so, but the single defeat should be noted for the reason that Browne was better known for her tennis play. She ranks as the only person in history to reach the final round of competition in both the National Tennis and Golf Championships in the same year.

Glenna devastated the best women golfers in America, winning the National Women's Amateur Championship six times and finishing as runner-up on three separate occasions during the period from 1922 to 1935. This accomplishment has no equal in amateur golf. Yet even her eloquent swing and admirable distance were not enough to conquer the world of golf.

Glenna's nemesis proved to be the celebrated English golfer, Joyce Wethered, later to become the Lady Heathcoat-Armory. They matched scores for the first time in the summer of 1925 at the British Women's Championship. Although Glenna played well enough to beat most opponents, Wethered played fifteen of the holes in an average 4 shots, a rare standard for the time. A second match four years later at St. Andrews, Scotland, has been reported by witnesses to be the best women's match ever played. Glenna played the first nine holes of the morning round in 34 shots, magnificent for the time. She seemed to be an easy winner after moving to a lead of five holes up in the match, but the Englishwoman answered with a blistering 73 strokes over the next eighteen holes. By the time the players reached the seventeenth hole of the afternoon round, Wethered was ready to close Glenna out. Gracious in defeat, Glenna acknowledged the other's brilliant play. These worthy opponents met once more in the first Curtis Cup Match of 1932. Again, the English golfer prevailed in repelling the American's challenge.

Continuing the Story

Considered the greatest American woman golfer of the 1920's and 1930's, Glenna Collett is given credit for changing country club tradition. She proved women capable of playing a quality game of golf when she became the first to break 80 strokes (shot 79) in qualifying for the 1924 U.S. Women's Amateur Championship.

In 1931, Glenna became the wife of Edwin H. Vare, Jr., of Philadelphia. By 1935, the mother of

MAJOR CHAMPIONSHIP VICTORIES	
1922, 1925, 1928-30, 1935	U.S. Women's Amateur Championship

OTHER NOTABLE VICTORIES	
1922-24, 1927, 1929-30	North and South Amateur Championship
1922-24, 1927, 1932, 1935	Eastern Amateur Championship
1923-24	Canadian Amateur Championship
1925-27	French Amateur Championship
1932, 1934, 1936, 1938, 1948	Curtis Cup Team
1950	Curtis Cup nonplaying captain

MILESTONES

LPGA prize for low-scoring average named after her (Vare Trophy)
British Open Amateur Championship runner-up (1929-30)

HONORS AND AWARDS

1965	USGA Bobby Jones Award
1975	Inducted into PGA/World Golf Hall of Fame
1981	Inducted into Sudafed International Women's Sports Hall of Fame

a daughter, Glenna, and a son, Edwin III, was back on the competitive circuit. That year at Interlachen Country Club in Minnesota, Glenna won her sixth U.S. Women's Amateur Championship. Her opponent and runner-up was the young, but soon to be famous, Patty Berg.

Curtis Cup competition did not become a prestigious event until 1932. The biannual tournament, between the best amateurs of the United Kingdom and the United States, consists of single matches and foursomes played over a two-day period. Glenna Collett Vare had the honor of playing or serving as team captain on six separate occasions. The American team won all but the 1936 competition, which finished in a tie, while Glenna was a participant.

As the years passed, there were fewer competitive days but more work days. Glenna did not play as much, but she showed her "giving" personality by working to develop the game. As a member of the United States Golf Association (USGA), she served on various committees for fifty years, all for the purpose of advancing the quality of women's golf. To crown her achievements and sportsmanship in the game, the USGA presented Glenna with the Bobby Jones Award in 1965.

The Vare Trophy, named in her honor, is awarded once a year to the woman professional golfer averaging the lowest strokes-per-round figure. Because Glenna Vare is credited with opening golf to women, recognition by the professional tour was most appropriate. She died in Gulf Stream, Florida, on February 3, 1989.

Summary

Glenna Collett Vare always remained close to her roots. She kept her membership current at the Point Judith Country Club in Narragansett, Rhode Island, throughout her playing career. The club championship was a scheduled event on her calendar for sixty-two consecutive years.

Golf became a universal sport for women when she first strolled down the fairway. Her quality play and etiquette forced skeptical male players to accept women as very capable golfers. Always an amateur who earned international admiration, Glenna had many golf authorities labeling her as the "female Bobby Jones" of golf.

Thomas S. Cross

Additional Sources:

Grimsley, Will. *Golf: Its History, People, and Events.* Englewood Cliffs, N.J.: Prentice-Hall, 1966.

Jacobs, Helen H. *Famous American Women Athletes.* New York: Dodd, Mead, 1964.

Layden, Joe. *Women in Sports.* Santa Monica, Calif.: General Publishing, 1997.

Markel, Robert, Susan Waggoner, and Marcella Smith, eds. *The Women's Sports Encyclopedia.* New York: Henry Holt, 1997.

GREG VAUGHN

Sport: Baseball

Born: July 3, 1965
Sacramento, California

Early Life

Gregory Lamont Vaughn was born on July 3, 1965, in Sacramento, California. His father began to teach him to play baseball at the age of six, the same year his older cousin, Jerry Royster, also Sacramento-born, began a long professional baseball career at Bakersfield of the California League. Young Greg admired Royster, but his all-time favorite baseball player, as with so many other African American youths, was the great Jackie Robinson. Greg had another cousin on the east coast, Maurice Vaughn, who would also become an outstanding major league baseball player.

Greg played Little League and Babe Ruth League baseball and starred at John F. Kennedy High School in Sacramento, where his favorite subjects were mathematics and black history. Although major league scouts were already interested in him, he decided on a college education, first at a local junior college, Sacramento City College.

The Road to Excellence

Later, pursuing his bachelor's degree in finance at the University of Miami, Greg had the opportunity to test his baseball skills against talented opposition. Having already turned down an offer from the St. Louis Cardinals, he played so well at Miami that the Milwaukee Brewers, the Pittsburgh Pirates, and the California Angels all tried to recruit him. When in his final season of college baseall, the Milwaukee Brewers again selected him in the secondary phase of the 1986 draft, he signed with them and was assigned to Helena, Montana, in the Pioneer League for the rest of that season. In sixty-six games as an outfielder with Helena, he batted .291 and showed power, blasting 16 home runs.

AP/Wide World Photos

Greg Vaughn shortly after joining the Tampa Bay Devil Rays in 2000.

The next season at Beloit, Wisconsin, in the Midwest League, he hit a solid .305 and led the league in both home runs and runs scored. In 1988 he repeated that feat at El Paso in the Texas League, also leading the league in two-base hits and runs batted in. In 1989 at Denver, facing Class AAA pitching, his batting average dropped off a bit, but he was leading the American Association in home runs and runs batted in when, early in August, the parent Brewers called him up with a month of the season to go. Even at the end of the season no American Association batter had managed to catch up with his league-leading totals. Meanwhile, as an outfielder and designated hitter for Milwaukee, he batted .265 and looked good enough to manager Tom Trebelhorn to be depended on as a regular the next season.

The Emerging Champion

So far Greg Vaughn's story had been replete with successes, but few players advance that far without eventually finding rough going. Greg played in 120 games for the Brewers in 1990 and continued to hit home runs, 17 of them, but his batting average at season's end stood at a low .220. Major league pitchers had quickly learned that while Greg was an outstanding fast ball hitter, he could be held in check by a diet of curves and change-ups. In addition, although Greg made few errors in the outfield, his fielding range was considered below average. Despite the fact that he seemed destined to be a low-average hitter, he continued to demonstrate extra-base power and clutch hitting ability in the seasons that followed, with 27 home runs in 1991, 23 in 1992, and 30 in 1993, the year his younger cousin Mo Vaughn was establishing himself with 29 homers for the Boston Red Sox. Even more impressive than Greg's long-distance slugging was his attitude. In an era when spiraling salaries made some players lackadaisical, Greg Vaughn impressed all onlookers as an all-out player, determined to make the best of his talent.

In the years that followed, Greg continued to spark the Milwaukee offense, though he was playing for a team that never seemed good enough for post-season play. In 1992 the team finished second in the Eastern Divison of the American League but fell off badly to seventh the next year. In 1994 when realignment sent the Brewers into the American League Central Division, injuries and a player strike limited Greg to only ninety-five games and 19 home runs. The following year his average and home runs dipped further. However, 1996 proved to be a very good year. As of the end of July he was batting .280, his highest major league average yet, and with 31 home runs and 95 runs batted in, he was battling Mark McGwire for the lead in both categories. On July 31, though, the Brewers traded him to the San Diego Padres for three young, unestablished players.

Continuing the Story

In the next five seasons Greg Vaughn would perform for three major league teams. He hit 10 home runs for the Padres the last two months of

STATISTICS

Season	GP	AB	Hits	2B	3B	HR	Runs	RBI	BA	SA
1989	38	113	30	3	0	5	18	23	.265	.425
1990	120	382	84	26	2	17	51	61	.220	.432
1991	145	542	132	24	5	27	81	98	.244	.456
1992	141	501	114	18	2	23	77	78	.228	.409
1993	154	569	152	28	2	30	97	97	.267	.482
1994	95	370	94	24	1	19	59	55	.254	.478
1995	108	392	88	19	1	17	67	59	.224	.408
1996	145	516	134	19	1	41	98	117	.260	.539
1997	120	361	78	10	0	18	60	57	.216	.393
1998	158	573	156	28	4	50	112	119	.272	.597
1999	153	550	135	20	2	45	104	118	.245	.535
2000	127	461	117	27	1	28	83	74	.254	.499
Totals	1,504	5,330	1,314	246	21	320	907	956	.247	.481

Notes: GP = games played; AB = at bats; 2B = doubles; 3B = triples; HR = home runs; RBI = runs batted in; BA = batting average; SA = slugging average

1996 for a grand total of 41 that year. In 1998 and 1999, with San Diego and Cincinnati he blasted a total of 95 home runs. Ordinarily that feat would capture headlines, but in those years the home run rampages of Mark McGwire and Sammy Sosa dwarfed Greg's performance. Nevertheless the Padres, a team in financial straits, traded Greg to the New York Yankees in mid-1997, although the deal was voided two days later. Then, after a 1998 season in which Greg became only the twelfth player in major league history to hit 50 home runs in one year, they traded him to the Cincinnati Reds. One year later, he declared for free agency and found himself back in the American League with the Tampa Bay Devil Rays.

Summary

Wherever Greg Vaughn has played, he has proven himself an outstanding power hitter, and despite a quiet demeanor has been recognized as a leader. Yet, as of the 2000 season, he had been traded three times and had played for four major league teams. Through it all, however, he remained one of the most feared sluggers in the game and was always labeled a team player, no matter which team it was.

Robert P. Ellis

Additional Sources:

Blum, Ronald. "Devil Rays Sign Greg Vaughn to Four-Year Deal." TotalSports.net. http://www.totalsports.net/news/19991213/bbo/991213.0448.html. December 14, 1999.

"Greg Vaughn." ESPN.com. http://espn.go.com/mlb/profiles/profile/4378.html.

Shatzkin, Mike, et al., eds. *The Ballplayers: Baseball's Ultimate Biographical Reference.* New York: William Morrow, 1999.

"You Asked for Greg Vaughn." *Teen* 40 (September, 1996): 32.

MO VAUGHN

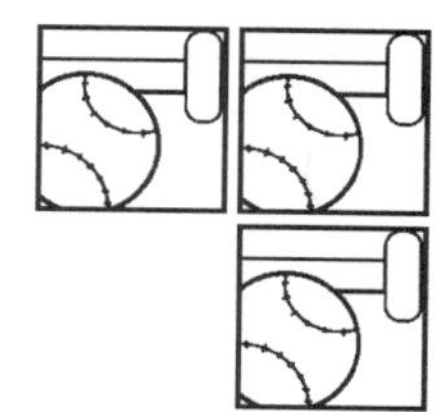

Sport: Baseball

Born: December 15, 1967
Norwalk, Connecticut

Early Life

Maurice Samuel Vaughn, the youngest of Leroy and Shirley Vaughn's three children, was born in Norwalk, Connecticut, on December 15, 1967. Both his parents were schoolteachers. Leroy also coached baseball and later became a school principal, but it was Shirley who taught her naturally right-handed son to bat left-handed. Like many young boys, Maurice loved sports, and chose George Gervin as his favorite basketball player and Jackie Robinson as his favorite baseball player. When his grades dropped in junior high school, however, his father made him withdraw from the basketball team. Having learned his lesson, Maurice performed well academically thereafter.

At Trinity-Pawling Preparatory School in Pawling, New York, he played shortstop and earned letters in each of his four years, as he also did in football and basketball. At Seton Hall University, where he earned many athletic honors, baseball coach Mike Sheppard took to calling him Mo, and a fraternity brother conferred on him his other well-known nickname, "Hit Dog."

AP/Wide World Photos

Anaheim Angel Mo Vaughn watches his two-run homer clear the right field wall during a game against the Toronto Blue Jays in 1999.

The Road to Excellence

The Boston Red Sox drafted Mo in the first round of the June, 1989, baseball draft, and Red Sox scout Matt Sczesny signed him to his first contract. On the strength of his brilliant college achievements, he was sent upon graduation to the Red Sox AA farm team in New Britain, Connecticut—a challenging level for a young man just turning twenty-two. He had only an average year, batting .278 with just 8 home runs, and he was also prone to committing errors at his new position, first

STATISTICS

Season	GP	AB	Hits	2B	3B	HR	Runs	RBI	BA	SA
1991	74	219	57	12	0	4	21	32	.260	.370
1992	113	355	83	16	2	13	42	57	.234	.400
1993	152	539	160	34	1	29	86	101	.297	.525
1994	111	394	122	25	1	26	65	82	.310	.576
1995	140	550	165	28	3	39	98	**126**	.300	.575
1996	161	635	207	29	1	44	118	143	.326	.583
1997	141	527	166	24	0	35	91	96	.315	.560
1998	154	609	205	31	2	40	107	115	.337	.591
1999	139	524	147	20	0	33	63	108	.281	.508
2000	161	614	167	31	0	36	93	117	.272	.498
Totals	1,346	4,966	1,479	250	10	299	784	977	.298	.533

Notes: Boldface indicates statistical leader. GP = games played; AB = at bats; 2B = doubles; 3B = triples; HR = home runs; RBI = runs batted in; BA = batting average; SA = slugging average

base. Nevertheless the Red Sox assigned him in 1990 to the their top minor league affiliate, Pawtucket of the International League. As a member of the Pawsox his numbers improved: a .295 batting average and 22 home runs. In both of the next two seasons he divided his time between Pawtucket and the parent Boston club, where he displayed hitting power but inconsistency at the plate.

The Emerging Champion

It was in 1993 that Mo Vaughn earned the respect of pitchers throughout the American League. He barely missed batting .300 and clubbed 64 extra-base hits, including 29 home runs in a ball park with dimensions that favor right-handed hitters more than left-handed swingers like Vaughn. His 6-foot 1-inch, 240-pound frame was an imposing sight for pitchers, who walked him 130 times in that first full season in Boston. He continued to have troubles defensively, however, leading the league's first basemen in errors for the second consecutive year and forcing manager Butch Hobson to use him part of the time as a designated hitter.

After a good but not spectacular 1994 season, he blossomed in 1995, when he hit 39 home runs and drove in a league-leading 126 runs to lead the Red Sox to a first-place finish in the American League's Eastern Division. For his feats that year he was named the league's most valuable player. His only 1995 disappointment came when the Red Sox were eliminated in the divisional playoffs in three games as Mo went hitless.

Continuing the Story

Mo Vaughn's 1996 season proved even more spectacular. Although he did not repeat as most valuable player, he increased his home runs from 39 to 44, his runs batted in from 126 to 143, and his batting average from .300 to .326. Despite these awe-inspiring numbers the Red Sox, under manager Kevin Kennedy, could do no better than third in the American League East. On September 24, however, Mo hit 3 home runs in one game for the first time in his career. The following year he repeated this feat on May 30 but then spent over three weeks on the disabled list in June and July and fell short of 100 runs batted in for only the second time in his five full seasons with the Red Sox, although he still finished with a respectable 96. The team slipped another notch to fourth place under new manager Jimy Williams.

Red Sox hopes soared in 1998 when the team acquired pitcher Pedro Martinez from the Montreal Expos to anchor their pitching staff, and Mo Vaughn ravaged American League pitchers for a .337 average with 40 homers and 115 runs batted in. But although the team finished second, they were never in the race against the New York Yankees, who finished 22 games ahead of the Red Sox. Mo's teammates considered him their clubhouse leader, the man any player not performing up to standard had to answer to. The Red Sox qualified for the playoffs but again lost in the first round despite Mo Vaughn's .412 average and 2 home runs in four games.

These were the last games he would play for

the Sox. Months of negotiations with the team's front office had failed to produce an agreement on a new contract, and at the end of the 1998 season he filed for free agency. Signed in December, 1998, by the Anaheim Angels, Mo moved his operations from the East to the West Coast. With the Angels he put together two more seasons of 30-plus home runs and 100-plus RBIs in 1999 and 2000.

Mo was looking forward to an even better year in 2001, but a ruptured tendon in his left bicep ended his season before it even started.

Summary

Mo Vaughn averaged 30 home runs and just under 100 runs batted in for ten years, even though he divided time between Boston and Pawtucket in both 1991 and 1992. He made himself into an adequate first baseman, and his value as a designated hitter was well documented. A true team player, he established himself as one of the game's great modern sluggers as well as one of the game's most respected men.

Robert P. Ellis

Additional Sources:

Leavy, Walter. "Baseball's Two of a Kind." *Ebony* 51 (July, 1996): 100-102.

Montville, Leigh. "Guardian Angel." *Sports Illustrated* 90 (April 14, 1999): 92-96.

Santella, Andrew. *Mo Vaughn: Big Mo.* New York: Children's Press, 1996.

Vaughn, Mo, with Greg Brown. *Follow Your Dreams.* Dallas: Taylor, 1999.

HONORS	
1995	American League most valuable player

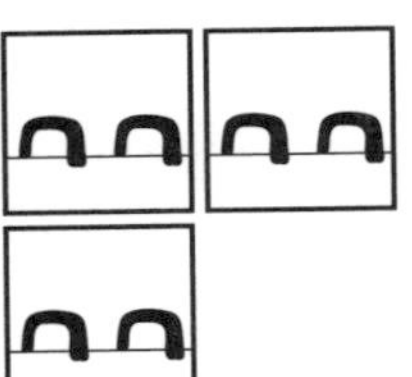

PETER VIDMAR

Sport: Gymnastics

Born: June 3, 1961
Los Angeles, California

Early Life

Peter Vidmar was born June 3, 1961, in Los Angeles, California. In his early life, Peter loved television sports and would often try to imitate the athletes he watched. If he saw high jumpers, he would take every cushion he could find and pile them in the living room and jump over a bar. He loved sports, but he was often frustrated about his small size. When he played Little League baseball he was considered a liability. At one game he was playing outfield when he missed a fly ball. His coach became angry at him, which lessened Peter's self-esteem and added pressure on him to do well the next time.

In 1971, though, Peter discovered gymnastics and began to channel all his energy into that one sport. (His initial interest in gymnastics came from his father, John Vidmar, who was a gymnast in high school.) Later that year, Peter's parents enrolled him in the nearby Culver City Gym Club under coaches Makoto and Isamu Sakamoto. In 1972, Peter watched Olga Korbut on television during the Munich Olympics, and he decided then to be an Olympic gymnast.

Peter began training at the gym six days a week for three to four hours a day with ten hours of workouts on Saturdays. When he was fifteen, his coaches were pleased with his efforts and insisted he work out on Sundays. Peter was deeply committed to his Mormon faith and told his coaches he could not train on Sunday for religious reasons. They kicked him out of the club. After Peter had continued to

LAOCC Collection, Department of Special Collections, University Research Library, UCLA

Peter Vidmar at four positions in the horizontal bar.

STATISTICS

Year	Competition	Event	Place	Event	Place
1979	World Championships	Team	3d		
1981	U.S. National Championships	All-Around	1st		
	World Championships	All-Around	13th	Team	5th
1982	NCAA Championships	All-Around	1st		
	U.S. National Championships	All-Around	1st	Pommel horse	6th
		Horizontal bar	2d	Rings	1st
		Parallel bars	1st	Vault	9th
	World Cup	All-Around	14th	Pommel horse	6th
		Horizontal bar	3d		
1983	NCAA Championships	All-Around	1st		
	U.S. National Championships	All-Around	2d	Rings	5th
		Parallel bars	2d		
	World Championships	All-Around	9th	Team	4th
		Horizontal bar	8th		
1984	U.S. National Championships	All-Around	2d	Parallel bars	1st
		Floor exercise	1st	Pommel horse	2d
		Horizontal bar	1st	Rings	2d
	Olympic Games	All-Around	Silver	Pommel horse	Gold
		Floor exercise	7th	Team	Gold
		Horizontal bar	4th		

train alone for four weeks, the Sakamotos realized Peter was honoring his religious convictions, and they reinstated him into the club.

The Road to Excellence

After graduating from high school, Peter enrolled in the nearby University of California at Los Angeles (UCLA), since Makoto Sakamoto would be his coach there as well. Peter would also be able to continue training with his best friends, Tim Daggett and Mitch Gaylord; all three would eventually be on the U.S. Olympic gymnastics team. For six hours and fifteen minutes each day, six days a week, Peter would train. That constant training and his determination to perfect his skills made the difference in his performances. When he became frustrated or discouraged he would look to his friends, Daggett and Gaylord, and they would offer one another encouragement.

Peter continued to receive invaluable support from his family at home. His parents would often go to his competitions, no matter how far away. His engineer father would keep careful statistics and scores at the meets. Peter credits the majority of his success to his family's support. His parents did not necessarily place significant emphasis on Peter's performances; they just wanted to show their commitment to Peter's ambitions. They showed the same support to each of their six children.

The Emerging Champion

Because of Peter's excellence, he became the youngest member of the 1980 U.S. Olympic team, but he was not able to compete because of the United States boycott of the Moscow Olympics. In 1982, Peter won the all-around title in the United States Gymnastics Championship. This victory entitled him to compete in 1982 at the World Championships in Germany. The gymnasts arrived in Germany the night before the championships and had to compete the following two days. Although the team was tired, Peter motivated them to do their best. Because of Peter's enthusiastic spirit and determination to succeed, he won a gold medal for the floor exercise. He was named the 1982 Male Gymnast of the Year. Peter also won the all-around titles in the National Collegiate Athletic Association (NCAA) championships for the four years from 1981 to 1984, the Los Angeles Pre-Olympics in 1983, and the American Cup in 1983 and 1984.

The highlight of Peter's gymnastic career was the 1984 Los Angeles Olympics. Peter Vidmar was the premier male gymnast for the United States in the 1984 Olympics. As the U.S. team captain, he led his teammates to the United States' first-ever gold medal, with an upset victory over the People's Republic of China. Peter went on to win the silver medal in the individual all-around competition (missing the gold by just

HONORS AND AWARDS

1982, 1984	Male Gymnast of the Year
1984	Inducted into U.S. Gymnastics Hall of Fame—along with entire 1984 U.S. Men's Gymnastics Team
1991	Inducted into U.S. Olympic Hall of Fame
1998	Inducted into International Gymnastics Hall of Fame

.025 point), becoming America's only male ever to have won an Olympic all-around medal. He then captured the gold medal on the pommel horse. Peter was the highest-scoring gymnast (an incredible 9.89 average), male or female, in the history of U.S. gymnastics. In 1984, he was again named the United States Male Gymnast of the Year.

Continuing the Story

After the Olympics, Peter and his wife, Donna, a former UCLA gymnast, graduated from UCLA, Peter with a degree in economics. He became a television announcer covering gymnastic events for major television networks. As a journalist, he wrote articles for national newspapers and magazines and appeared on numerous national television talk shows.

When not spending time with his wife and their five children, Peter has spoken often on the corporate lecture circuit with the 1984 Olympic steeplechaser Henry Marsh, introducing a comprehensive stress management program to America's top corporations. President George H. W. Bush appointed Peter to serve on the President's Council on Physical Fitness and Sport, and he testified before Congress on behalf of the United States Olympic Committee. He has served on the executive board of the U.S. Olympic Committee and the executive committee of the U.S. Gymnastics Federation. The Peter Vidmar Invitational is an annual gymnastics meet in California that Peter sponsors. He has also served as an analyst for NBC sports and was involved in the coverage of the 2000 Olympic Games. Peter also has been involved with charities such as the American Lung Association, American Cancer Society, and Special Olympics.

Summary

Peter Vidmar, at 5 feet 5 inches and 135 pounds, was a powerhouse in men's gymnastics. He led the 1984 U.S. Men's Olympic gymnastic team to a gold medal victory not only with his abilities but also with his spirit. He continued to motivate himself, his family, and others to achieve excellence.

Rodney D. Keller

Additional Sources:

Long, Annerin. "Whatever Happened to Peter Vidmar?" *Whatever Happened to . . . Former Gymnasts.* http://watarts.uwaterloo.ca/~jkisbist/mag/vidmar.htm. January 1, 2000.

"Meet Peter Vidmar." *Peter Vidmar.* http://www.vidmar.com/meetpete.html.

Vidmar, Peter, and Karen Cogan. *Gymnastics.* Morgantown, W.V.: Fitness Information Technology, 2000.

"Where Are They Now: Peter Vidmar." *International Gymnast* Online. http://www.intlgymnast.com/paststars/psdec99/psdec99.html. December, 1999.

"Going for the Gold." *Child Life,* April/May, 2000, 27.

GUILLERMO VILAS

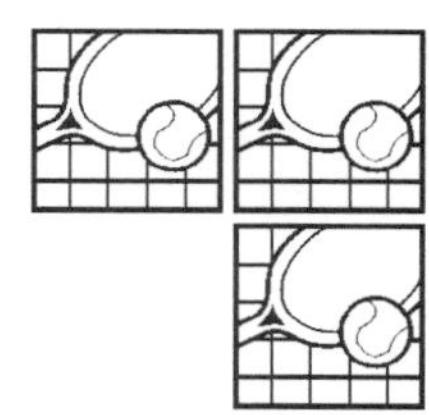

Sport: Tennis

Born: August 17, 1952
Mar del Plata, Argentina

Early Life

Guillermo Vilas was born on August 17, 1952, in Mar del Plata, a seaside resort 250 miles south of Buenos Aires, Argentina. Guillermo's father, José Roque Vilas, was a wealthy lawyer and president of a local tennis club. He encouraged his son to take up the game, and the young man began to practice seriously when he was not yet ten years old.

At age ten, Guillermo started to take lessons from a local professional, Felipe Locicero. Like many outstanding athletes, Guillermo manifested remarkable early talent. Within one year of commencing his lessons, he was already winning local tournaments, and he soon became the best junior player in Argentina.

Guillermo did not fully commit himself to tennis as a career until the beginning of the 1970's. By the late 1970's, however, he had become a fixture on Argentina's Davis Cup team.

The Road to Excellence

Several factors helped place Guillermo among those with championship potential. He was known as "The Bull" because of his solid physique and power. He had a fast and effective serve and also possessed sharp and accurate ground strokes. Although his power was an asset, he was matched in this regard by several of his contemporaries, such as the American player Jimmy Connors.

What made Guillermo stand out was the topspin he put on his strokes, particularly on his backhand. This spin is difficult to control, but Guillermo was able to manage the feat, at the same time striking the ball with devastating efficiency. A topspin drive under such conditions is difficult to return; mastery of this type of hitting probably was the most essential factor elevating Guillermo to the first rank.

He developed his skill at topspin by modeling himself on Rod Laver, one of the greatest players

Impress/Archive Photos

Guillermo Vilas during a match in 1980.

of all time. The court conditions of Guillermo's native Argentina also contributed to his stress on the topspin. Most Argentine courts are clay, the comparative slowness of which encourages the development of clever shotmaking and discourages reliance on power alone.

The Emerging Champion

Guillermo seemed to be in an excellent position to do well internationally. When he turned to a full-time professional career at the start of the 1970's, he immediately compiled a fine record. He proved unable to win any major tournaments, however, and was frequently criticized for lacking a killer instinct.

Guillermo also had bad luck in that his road to excellence coincided with the peak period of the great Swedish player Björn Borg, the dominant force of the 1970's. Guillermo played many matches against Borg, usually marked by extremely long rallies, as both possessed unusually accurate strokes and were otherwise similar in their style of play. Although Guillermo gave stiff competition to his great rival, the phlegmatic Swede almost always defeated the mercurial Argentine.

Guillermo refused to be discouraged and continued to perfect his game. His dedication and hard work paid off in 1974, when, in a three-month period, he won fifty-four out of sixty matches. In that year, he was also one of the leading money-winners on the tour.

Although Guillermo seemed destined for the top, he still had not won any of the game's premier tournaments. These are the Grand Slam events: the United States Open, the French Open, the Australian Open, and Wimbledon.

Continuing the Story

Guillermo's battle to reach the top was far from over. After his outstanding 1974 year, his game went into a slump. He was once again equal to the challenge and resolved to do whatever was necessary to perfect his game.

He sought help, turning to Ion Tiriac, an outstanding Romanian player and coach. Tiriac as a player had never reached the commanding heights and was best known as the doubles partner of Ilie Nastase. As a coach, however, Tiriac was supreme. He advised Guillermo to become more aggressive and instructed him to follow his ground strokes with a move to the net. He put Guillermo through a rigorous exercise program, the result of which was to make him the best-conditioned player on the tour.

Guillermo's work with Tiriac paid off in spectacular fashion. In 1977, he ran up a streak of fifty-five straight wins. He achieved his first Grand Slam victories the same year, winning both the French Open and the United States title at Forest Hills. These victories placed him at last among the world's best. Of this there was no room for doubt, as he had won the United States title by a thorough demolition of Jimmy Connors in the finals.

Guillermo added to his Grand Slam victories two Australian Opens, won in 1978 and 1979. Although he continued to be an outstanding player, never finishing below sixth among the top money-winners in the years from 1974 to 1982, he never matched the position of supremacy he reached during 1977 and early 1978.

Guillermo's struggles with the game's top players, combined with his romantic personality, made him a hero in Latin America. His achievements helped to popularize tennis in that part of the world.

In 1983, Guillermo became embroiled in a controversy about accepting appearance money

MAJOR CHAMPIONSHIP VICTORIES AND FINALS	
1975, 1978, 1982	French Open finalist
1977	French Open U.S. Open Australian Open finalist
1978-79	Australian Open

OTHER NOTABLE VICTORIES	
1974	Swiss Championships The Masters Canadian Open doubles (with Manuel Orantes)
1974, 1976	Canadian Open
1977	South African Open
1978	Swiss Open
1978	German Open
1980	Italian Open
1982	Monte Carlo Open

to play in tournaments. (Appearance money is a fee paid to a player to participate in a tournament, whether or not he wins a prize.) The criticism deeply affected the temperamental Argentine, and his game steadily declined after 1983. He continued an active role on the circuit throughout the 1980's. In 1993, Guillermo began competing on the Worldwide Senior Tennis Circuit.

Summary

Guillermo Vilas rose to prominence from a region that had not previously produced many topflight international players. His mastery of the topspin stroke, learned on the slow clay courts of his native country, gave him a great advantage over his less dexterous rivals. In spite of his talent, he did not attain supreme excellence except for the short period of 1977 and 1978. Nevertheless, he ranks as one of the outstanding players of the 1970's and early 1980's.

Bill Delaney

HONORS, AWARDS, AND MILESTONES

1970-84	Argentinian Davis Cup team
1974-75, 1977	First in Grand Prix standings
1977	55 consecutive Grand Prix match wins 57 consecutive match wins on clay
1982	Nationally ranked number one
1991	Inducted into International Tennis Hall of Fame

Additional Sources:

Bodo, Peter. "Viva Vilas." *Tennis* 32 (November, 1996): 68-72.

"Guillermo Vilas." In *International Who's Who in Tennis*, edited by Jane Cooke. Dallas, Tex.: World Championship Tennis, 1983.

Nirschl, Robert. "They're the Greatest!" *World Tennis* 28 (January, 1981): 37-41.

Stevenson, Samantha. "The Road Less Traveled." *World Tennis* 36 (August, 1988): 36-41.

JACQUES VILLENEUVE

Sport: Auto racing

Born: April 9, 1971
St-Jean-sur-Richlieu, Quebec, Canada

Early Life

Jacques Villeneuve was born on April 9, 1971, in St-Jean-sur-Richlieu, Quebec, Canada. His father was Gilles Villeneuve, a man obsessed with racing both snowmobiles and cars. Jacques grew up in a world of speed, following his father to races around Canada and, later, Europe. When Gilles was hired to drive for Ferrari in Formula One races he began to build a reputation as a daredevil, and his over-the-edge style of driving thrilled racing fans and impressed his fellow competitors.

In 1983, Gilles Villeneuve was killed in a crash while qualifying for the Belgian Grand Prix. Jacques was eleven years old. Though he had won few races and never won a championship, Gilles had become one of the most famous drivers in racing history. His reputation would both help and hinder Jacques throughout his own driving career.

Through Gilles's racing success, the family was financially well-off, and at age twelve Jacques was sent from his home in France to a private boarding school in Switzerland. He excelled in his classes when he applied himself, but overall he was less interested in school than in skiing. On snow he was fast, daring, and competitive, and it is said that he could have been a ski champion had his interest not changed to cars. Here he made fast friends with his ski instructor, Craig Pollock, who would later become Jacques's manager and play an important role in his life and career.

Racer Jacques Villeneuve poses with his team's new car in 2001.

The Road to Excellence

In the summers, Jacques and his family returned to Canada. There his uncle Jacques, also a successful racing driver, encouraged young

Jacques's interest in motor racing, first in go-karts, then with sessions at racing schools. His instructors praised his natural speed and declared that he had the family talent.

Back in Europe in 1988, Jacques entered three races in the Italian Touring Car Championship, a move made easier by the fame of his father in Italy. He finished tenth in his first race, a respectable result for a seventeen-year-old beginner with little driving experience. The next year he quit school before graduating in order to compete in the Italian Formula Three series. Here too he found sponsorship and patient instruction because of his name. He proved to be a quick learner and dedicated himself to racing, finishing tenth in the championship in 1990 and sixth the following year.

Jacques was uncomfortable in Italy, being constantly compared to his famous father, so he jumped at the chance to move to Japan to race in the Formula Three series there. At the age of twenty, the experience of living on his own far from home helped him mature and grow into the life of a professional racer. His driving continued to improve as well, and he finished second in the Formula Three championship.

In 1992 Jacques made a "guest appearance" at a Formula Atlantic race in Montreal, Canada, racing against his uncle Jacques. The younger Jacques finished third amid much media attention. This experience convinced him to return to Canada for the 1993 season, driving in the Formula Atlantic series for the Players-Forsythe team.

FORMULA ONE AND OTHER VICTORIES

Year	*Series*	*Place*
1988	Italian Touring Car Championship	10th
1989	Italian Formula Three	
1990	Italian Formula Three	10th
1991	Italian Formula Three	6th
1992	Japanese Formula Three Formula Atlantic	2d 3d
1993	Formula Atlantic	3d
1994	PPG IndyCar Indianapolis 500	6th 2d
1995	PPG IndyCar	1st
1996	World Formula One	2d
1997	World Formula One	1st
1998	World Formula One	5th
1999	World Formula One	22d
2000	World Formula One	7th

The Emerging Champion

The Formula Atlantic series took Jacques all over the United States and Canada and introduced him to oval tracks as well as to road and street courses. He had five first-place finishes in fifteen races and placed third in the overall championship. These results convinced team owner Jerry Forsythe to enter him in the PPG Indy car World Series for 1994.

Jacques was immediately comfortable in these faster and more powerful machines and started the year with impressive qualifying times. Two accidents early in the season though, revived comparisons with the reckless style of his father. Jacques's race engineer, Tony Cicale, defended him, saying that he drove carefully and intelligently, never exceeding the limits of the car or his driving skill. Good results followed, including a second-place finish at the Indianapolis 500, and he finished the year in sixth place overall. He also won Rookie of the Year honors for 1994.

In 1995 Jacques conquered the world of Indy cars, with an impressive win at Indianapolis after being 2 laps down early in the race. Four first-place finishes, along with consistent results in the rest of the seventeen races, brought Jacques the Indy car championship.

Jacques's impressive success in Indy cars brought him a job offer from the top-ranked Williams Formula One team. Adapting quickly to the differences in Formula One cars, Jacques nearly won his first race in Australia. Winning four races in the 1996 season, he finished a close second to his teammate, Damon Hill, for the championship. In 1997, Jacques drove again for Williams; this time seven wins were enough to bring him the world championship at the age of twenty-six.

Continuing the Story

In 1998 the tide turned against the Williams team, and Jacques finished fifth in the champi-

HONORS AND AWARDS

1993	Rookie of the Year
1994	IndyCar Rookie of the Year
1995	IndyCar Champion
1997	Formula One World Champion

onship behind the cars of the McLaren and Ferrari teams. In 1999 the former world champion took on the difficult job of helping to bring a new team to success, driving for British American Racing. This team, formed by his old friend and manager Craig Pollock, had a dismal first year, finishing few races and earning no points. Jacques finished twenty-second in the series, and his teammate Ricardo Zonta was last at twenty-fourth. The 2000 season started with better results, but Jacques admitted in magazine interviews that he might be interested in driving for another team in 2001 if his fortunes with British American Racing did not improve.

Summary

In only eight years Jacques Villeneuve went from a beginning racer to the world champion. Along the way he proved that he was an intelligent and calculating driver, a man who knew his limits and those of his car. He used that knowledge, along with courage and determination, to emerge from the shadow of his famous father to become a champion in his own right.

Joseph W. Hinton

Additional Sources:

Collings, Timothy. *The New Villeneuve: The Life of Jacques Villeneuve.* Osceola, Wis.: Motorbooks International, 1997.

Hilton, Christopher. *Jacques Villeneuve: In His Own Right.* Osceola, Wis.: Motorbooks International, 1996.

Sparling, Ken. *Jacques Villeneuve: Born to Race.* Willowdale, Ont.: Firefly Books, 1999.

Voeglin, Rick. "The Son Also Races." *Sport*, September, 1998, 38.

DAVE VILLWOCK

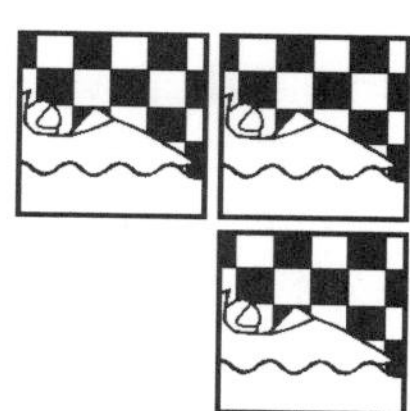

Sport: Hydroplane racing

Born: February 10, 1954
Bremerton, Washington

Early Life

The son of Gerald and Doris Villwock, David Villwock was born on February 10, 1954, in Bremerton, Washington. When he was five years old, Dave moved with his family to a farm in nearby Port Orchard, Washington. During Dave's childhood, his family participated in weekend boat races throughout the Pacific Northwest. In his uncle's shop, Dave helped his father and uncle, Al, build boats for racing, including stock outboards and hydroplanes. Al encouraged Dave to race for recreational benefits as well as to develop his competitive nature.

The Road to Excellence

In his early races, Dave learned to drive various boat types. Recognizing his potential, retired racers, including Steve Jones, served as mentors, teaching Dave driving and other techniques based on their experiences. Jones's philosophy of refusing to lose strengthened Dave's resolve to win despite any personal or financial obstacles as well as rough waters, wet engines, or poor starts.

Sometimes lacking sufficient equipment and money, Dave relied on his willpower for motiva-

AP/Wide World Photos

Hydroplane racer Dave Villwock (right) with his boat's owner, Bernie Little, after winning a race in 2000.

tion and attributed his early victories to this positive attitude. He began his professional racing career driving 20-inch boats known as crackerboxes. Using these powerboats, he won several American Power Boat Association (APBA) national championships. Dave next piloted E racing runabouts and began setting world records. He accomplished similar feats in the Superstock runabout, Ski racing runabout, and Pro Competition runabout classes and won national championships in all three categories in 1984. That year, he was inducted into the APBA Hall of Champions.

The Emerging Champion

With Jerry Yoder, Dave built a hydroplane that he competed with in the 6-liter class. Known as the *Sunset Chevrolet Special*, this hydroplane enabled Dave to win every heat and race he entered with it in 1988, earning yet another national championship and setting world records. Fran Muncey, representative of the *Circus Circus* Unlimited Hydroplane team, saw Dave race the 6-liter hydroplane in San Diego. She contacted him, and he began working as *Circus Circus* team manager in November, 1988. Unlimited Hydroplanes were considered the world's fastest race boats.

In his new position, Dave worked with driver Chip Hanauer, who set a world speed record with the *Circus Circus* hydroplane, traveling 158.87 miles per hour on a 2.5-mile qualifying lap in 1989. This Unlimited Hydroplane was the first to surpass 150 mph on a 2-mile lap. The following year, Dave's team earned a national championship.

MAJOR CHAMPIONSHIPS

1974-1975	APBA National Championship, High Point Championship Western Division Championship in crackerbox class
1984	APBA National Superstock Runabout Championship APBA Ski Runabout National Championship Pro Competition Runabout National Championship
1987	National High Point Championship in the 6-liter hydroplane class Ten Grand Prix Championship in the 7-liter class
1988	Western Division Championship for the 6-liter hydroplane class Western Division championship in the Superstock Runabout Class
1990	National Championship in the Unlimited Hydroplane Class as team manager of *Circus Circus* team with driver Chip Hanauer
1996	UHRA National Driver Championship APBA Gold Cup
1997	APBA Gold Cup
1998	UHRA National Driver Championship APBA Gold Cup
1999	UHRA National Driver Championship

RECORDS AND MILESTONES

1979-1982	Set four world speed records in E Racing Runabout class
1984	Set fifth world speed record
1986	Set world speed record in the Superstock Runabout Class
1988	Set seventh and eighth world speed records Set record for winning eight seasonal races
1999	Set ninth world speed record Repeated record of eight seasonal victories

Ron Jones, Jr., invited Dave to test-drive a powerboat with unique design features. Dave suggested ways to increase the boat's speed; he also designed and created a propeller. Piloting this craft, known as the *Coors Dry*, he won his first Unlimited Hydroplane race, in 1992 at San Diego. The next year, he agreed to drive for a reorganized *Circus Circus* team. His technical expertise benefited the team because of his innovations in hull structure.

In 1994, he won two straight races in Seattle and San Diego. He continued to place first or second in qualifying heats and races throughout 1996. Also that year, he drove the *PICO American Dream* to victory at the Unlimited Hydroplane Racing Association (UHRA) National Driver Championships and won the APBA Gold Cup championship, which has been compared to the Indianapolis 500 car race.

Continuing the Story

Dave next agreed to drive the *Miss Budweiser* when Bernie Little, the boat's owner, asked him to replace Chip Hanauer in 1996. After winning the first four races of the 1997 season and secur-

HONORS AND AWARDS

1984	First induction into the APBA Hall of Champions Dickie Webb Memorial Award for outstanding driver
1987	Boren Memorial Award for outstanding driver
1998	Second induction into the APBA Hall of Champions

ing another APBA Gold Cup, Dave crashed the *Miss Budweiser* on the Columbia River near Pasco, Washington, in July and was hospitalized. His right arm was broken; his hand almost severed. Physicians amputated two infected fingers and told Dave that his professional hydroplane racing career was over. He refused to accept that prognosis and underwent approximately twenty-one surgeries and eight months of physical therapy.

During his recovery, he and his racing team prepared for his return to racing. They reinforced the *Miss Budweiser* with a sturdier hull and redesigned the steering wheel. Dave returned to UHRA racing by winning the Pontiac Grand Am Thunder race on the Ohio River near Evansville, Indiana. It was his third consecutive victory in that race. He attained an average speed of 137.01 miles per hour, proving that he was physically able to race hydroplanes. He finished ten races in one season and won eight of them, an unrivaled achievement in that sport. He won his third consecutive Gold Cup at a Detroit River race in Michigan, earned his second UHRA National Driver Championship, and was inducted again into the APBA Hall of Champions in recognition of his accomplishments.

In 1999, Dave repeated his record of securing eight seasonal victories. He won his third UHRA National Driver Championship and set a world speed record when he attained a speed of 173.38 mph in a San Diego race on Mission Bay. Each win meant that Dave would be handicapped by being moved to a lane farther from the course's center, adding extra mileage to his course.

He won the first UHRA race in 2000 at Lake Havasu, Nevada, giving boat owner Little a record 125 career wins. Dave's domination of the sport led to the UHRA practice of penalizing winning drivers with fuel decreases. The association's new policy meant that drivers started with 4.3 gallons of fuel per minute to power the engine, but lost one-tenth of a gallon per victory, effective at their next race.

Summary

Dave Villwock has won or placed in a record-setting percentage of races on the Unlimited Hydroplane circuit. As driver or team manager of Unlimited Hydroplanes, he has collected numerous victories in addition to his earlier racing titles earned while driving other types of boats. His technical knowledge has contributed to the advancement of hydroplane technology.

Elizabeth D. Schafer

Additional Sources:

Armijo, Mark. "Can Anything Stop Villwock?: Hydro Officials Plan New Rules." *The Arizona Republic*, May 19, 2000, p. C-5.

Boeck, Scott. "'Miss Bud' Driver Undeterred: Villwock Back from Horrific Crash in '97." *USA Today*, May 22, 1998, p. F-15.

CHUCK VINCI

Sport: Weightlifting

Born: February 28, 1933
Cleveland, Ohio

Early Life

Charles T. (Chuck) Vinci was born on February 28, 1933, in Cleveland, Ohio, to Italian American parents. He grew up in a predominantly lower-class quarter of the city, a rough-and-tumble environment where formal education took second place to making a living. Chuck attended school off and on, but sought independence early by taking a job shining shoes in the downtown Cleveland stores.

Although mentally tough, Chuck was known to his friends as the "little, bowlegged runt" since in his teens he had already reached his full adult height of 4 feet 10 inches and weighed a scant 85 pounds.

To survive amid the rough, gang-style life of shoe shine boys, Chuck fortified himself first by learning to wrestle and box. Then, to increase his size, he took up weightlifting. The choice was a good one, for in a few short years, he would develop into one of the strongest small men of all time.

The Road to Excellence

In the early 1950's, Chuck joined John Shubert's Olympic Health Club in Cleveland. Under Shubert's guidance, his life took a positive turn. At age nineteen, he competed in the National Golden Gloves Championships and the Junior National Weightlifting Championships in the 123-pound division.

Training with weights usually reserved for much larger lifters, Chuck progressed swiftly. In 1954, he won the first of his seven Senior National Weightlifting titles. In 1955, he won the Pan-American Games bantamweight division. Powerfully built, he weighed 130 pounds with biceps measuring 16 inches.

Despite his enormous strength, Chuck would

AP/Wide World Photos

Weight lifter Chuck Vinci displays his gold medal from the 1956 Games.

often lose early matches because he was unable to control the weight at critical stages of the lift. To improve his technique, he moved to the famous York Gym in York, Pennsylvania. There, owner/coach Bob Hoffmann discovered that an inner-ear problem affected Chuck's balance. With Hoffman's help, Chuck overcame this impediment.

Chuck trained under the motto "Think Big, Lift Big." Such positive thinking reaped big rewards. In the 1956 Olympics in Melbourne, Australia, Chuck won the bantamweight gold medal. At the weigh-in, he was 1½ pounds overweight, so he ran for an hour trying to sweat off the extra weight. Still 7 ounces over the limit with only minutes to go, he submitted to a radical shearing of his thick, black hair, made the cutoff, and set a new world record (754 pounds total).

A very religious man, Chuck carried his Bible in his hands when he accepted the gold medal.

The Emerging Champion

Nicknamed "Mighty Mouse," Chuck trained using a combined program of body building, Olympic lifting, and power-lifting routines. His early victories seemed to announce a long career ahead. After his victory in the 1956 Olympics, however, Chuck's life changed.

Family responsibilities led him to accept a job as a crane operator in a Cleveland steel mill. He married, had three children, and elected not to go on several international tours, preferring to remain with his family. Yet his competitive spirit continued to call. One challenge remained, to win a second gold medal, at the 1960 Olympics in Rome.

Responding to the encouragment of fans and friends, he began to train hard again—too hard, apparently, because he injured his back. The spirit of survival acquired in the rough quarters of Cleveland never deserted him, though. Recovering from his injuries, he trained with heavier weights than he had ever used before. When he left for Rome, he was fortified physically and spiritually, carrying his Bible with him.

When the bantamweight event began in Rome, Chuck was surprised to learn that, as a result of training injuries, his toughest competitor, the Russian Vladimir Stogov, would not compete. Chuck won the gold medal, but not by default. He equaled the world record of 761 pounds and was the only American gold-medal winner in weightlifting in the 1960 Olympics.

Continuing the Story

To understand Chuck's enormous strength, one has to remember that he competed at a body weight of 123 pounds while he trained using 335 pounds in the bench press and 480 pounds in the dead lift. He was capable of curling as much as 170 pounds, nearly 50 pounds over his body weight.

Such power can be partially attributed to natural ability. Chuck's greatest attribute was not his heredity, though, but his perseverance and will to win. In addition, he had the unique ability to relax so that his body could recover from exhausting workouts. He could sleep any place, any time, sometimes up to twenty hours per day. He also paid close attention to his diet, which was carefully monitored by his coaches.

The 1960 Olympics marked Chuck's final international victory. In 1961, he entered the World Weightlifting Championships in Vienna, Austria, where he placed fourth behind Stogov (Russia), Foldi (Hungary), and Miyake (Japan).

Chuck's enthusiasm for his sport gradually led to overtraining. By 1962, he had gained too much muscle from using isotonic-isometric routines. He also let his weight rise as high as 151 pounds. In general, weightlifters are discouraged from doing certain types of exercises, such as curls or weighted pushups, that Chuck persisted in doing. While building strength in the biceps and pectoral muscles, such exercises interfere with the flexibility needed for overhead lifts. Ultimately, Chuck eliminated himself from competitive weightlifting by becoming too muscular.

Retiring from competition in 1962, Chuck

MAJOR CHAMPIONSHIP TITLES

1954-56, 1958-61	U.S. bantamweight champion
1956, 1960	Olympic gold medalist (bantamweight division)
1955, 1958	World Championship silver medalist (bantamweight division)
1955, 1959	Pan-American Games gold medalist (bantamweight division)

continued to work as a crane operator with LTV Steel Mills, in Cleveland, Ohio. He again focused his attention on his family.

Summary

Chuck Vinci's early life toughened him to the rigors of weightlifting training and competition. Through his "hard knocks" street education, he learned to deal with disappointment, and never to admit defeat.

His sport brought him international recognition as a champion. In 1954, he traveled worldwide as part of a good-will tour, giving exhibitions before the crowned heads of Iran, Iraq, and Afghanistan, the leaders of India, and the vice president of the United States. He had come a long way from shining shoes on the streets of Cleveland.

William C. Griffin

Additional Sources:

Hickok, Ralph. *A Who's Who of Sports Champions.* Boston: Houghton Mifflin, 1995.

Levinson, David, and Karen Christenson, eds. *Encyclopedia of World Sport: From Ancient Times to Present.* Santa Barbara, Calif.: ABC-CLIO, 1996.

Schapp, Dick. *An Illustrated History of the Olympics.* New York: Alfred A. Knopf, 1975.

Wallechinsky, David. *The Complete Book of the Olympics.* Boston: Little, Brown and Company, 1991.

LASSE VIREN

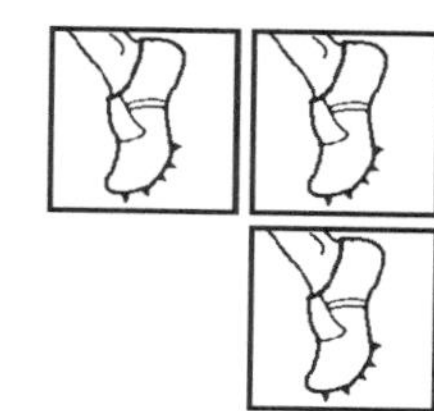

Sport: Track and field (long-distance runs)

Born: July 22, 1949
Myrskyla, Finland

Early Life

Lasse Artturi Viren was born on July 22, 1949, in Myrskyla, Finland. Myrskyla means "stormy village." His parents, Elvi and Illmarie Viren, had three other sons, Erkki, Nisse, and Heikki.

Lasse grew up in Myrskyla on the family farm. He went to elementary school for eight years and worked on the farm and helped his father drive and repair trucks.

Lasse began running as a teenager and had initial success by winning the Finnish Junior Championships in the 3,000-meter run. He ran regularly even when he worked late with his father. Lasse ran for the local running club, named Myrskylan Myrsky, which means "the storm of the stormy village."

The Road to Excellence

At eighteen, Lasse was attending mechanical trade school but quit to train more. He began serious long-distance training in 1969, when he was nineteen.

Lasse was coached by Rolf Haikkola from Myrskyla. Haikkola was a former world-class 5,000-meter runner. Haikkola's training philosophy was influenced by the great New Zealand coach, Arthur Lydiard.

Generally, under Haikkola's direction, Lasse ran long distances mixed with speed work conducted on forest trails or dirt roads. Haikkola was very interested in Lasse's development as a runner and focused primarily on peaking him for only a few key races each year. Lasse trained hard during the long Finnish winter months and used the short summer season for peaking.

Lasse worked to support himself early in his career as a country police officer. This job allowed him valuable time off for travel and training.

By 1971, Lasse had improved substantially in his training and racing. He excelled at the 5,000- and 10,000-meter distances.

AP/Wide World Photos

Lasse Viren of Finland (number 301) won the 5,000 meters in the 1976 Olympics.

STATISTICS

Year	Competition	Event	Place	Time
1971	European Championships	5,000 meters	7th	13:38.6
		10,000 meters	17th	28:33.2
1972	Olympic Games	5,000 meters	Gold	13:26.4 OR
		10,000 meters	Gold	27:38.35 OR, WR
1976	Olympic Games	5,000 meters	Gold	13:24.76
		10,000 meters	Gold	27:40.38
		Marathon	5th	2:13:10.8
1980	Olympic Games	10,000 meters	5th	27:50.5

Notes: OR = Olympic Record; WR = World Record

He was not known well at the international level of competition because Coach Haikkola limited his exposure to racing.

Prior to the 1972 Munich Olympics, Lasse set a world record in the 2-mile run. He qualified in both the 5,000 and 10,000 meters to represent Finland at Munich.

The Emerging Champion

At the Munich Olympics, Lasse first qualified for the finals of the 10,000 meters. The final field was one of the fastest groups of distance runners ever assembled.

Midway into the final, Lasse was involved in some jostling back in the pack of runners and fell to the track. He had lost 10 meters to the pack by the time he recovered. Appearing unfazed by his fall, Lasse gained the lead by the last lap of the race and sprinted away to victory in world record time.

Lasse's win was the first Olympic victory for Finnish distance runners since 1936. His win made him a national hero and marked the resurgence of distance running enthusiasm in Finland.

By the time of the Olympic 5,000-meter race, Lasse had become the clear favorite to win based on his 10,000-meter performance. That placed tremendous pressure on Lasse to live up to the world's expectations.

Lasse won his preliminary round of the 5,000 meters. In the final, the pace was slow until the last mile of the race. At that point, the pace rapidly increased, and it was a five-man race going into the last lap. Once again, Lasse displayed a powerful kick and won in Olympic record time. He covered his last mile in 4 minutes and 1 second, an outstanding feat.

Continuing the Story

Following the Munich Olympics, Lasse was besieged with business opportunities and speaking engagements. His schedule became quite hectic and he got very little rest. The disruptions in his personal life had a negative influence on his training. Coach Haikkola encouraged Lasse to commit himself to preparation of the defense of his Olympic titles at Montreal in 1976.

Lasse struggled in the off years between the Olympics because of illness and injuries. There were also rumors that he had used "blood doping" (a method of increasing the oxygen-carrying capacity of the blood) to improve his performance. Some track experts thought this might explain how Lasse had improved at the elite level so quickly. The rumors were unsettling because blood doping was illegal, and an athlete could be banned from competition if the charges were substantiated.

Lasse and Coach Haikkola denied the doping charges. They pointed out that their well-planned training program was responsible for the remarkable peaking ability that Lasse had displayed.

In 1976, Lasse again qualified for the 5,000- and 10,000-meter runs at the Montreal Olympics. He had trained as much as 150 miles per week in preparation.

Once again, Lasse beat all of his rivals to claim the gold medals in both races. His accomplishments were unprecedented in Olympic history.

HONORS, AWARDS, AND RECORDS

1970	Set national records at 3,000, 5,000, and 10,000 meters, and 2, 3, and 6 miles
1972	World Trophy Set a world record at 3,000 meters (8:14.0) Set a world record at 5,000 meters (13:16.4) Set a world record at 10,000 meters (27:38.35) *Track and Field News* World Athlete of the Year
1972, 1976	*Athletics Weekly* World Athlete of the Year

If that was not remarkable enough, he entered the marathon following the 5,000-meter race and finished in fifth place.

Summary

Following the Montreal Olympics, Lasse Viren returned to his privacy in Myrskyla. Rumors continued to fly concerning his possible involvement with blood doping. Lasse and his coach blamed the rumors on misunderstandings with the media and jealous rivals.

In 1980 at the Moscow Olympics, Lasse participated in his third Olympics and finished fifth in the 10,000-meter run. He also started the marathon but had to drop out before finishing.

Based on his Olympic performances, Lasse Viren ranks as one of the best (if not the best) 5,000- and 10,000-meter runners ever. He was a legend in the world of Finnish distance running.

Tinker D. Murray

Additional Sources:

Wallechinsky, David. *The Complete Book of the Olympics.* Boston: Little, Brown and Company, 1991.

Watman, Mel. *Encyclopedia of Track and Field Athletics.* New York: St. Martin's Press, 1981.

RUBE WADDELL

Sport: Baseball

Born: October 13, 1876
Bradford, Pennsylvania
Died: April 1, 1914
San Antonio, Texas

Courtesy of Amateur Athletic Foundation of Los Angeles

Early Life

George Edward "Rube" Waddell was born October 13, 1876, in the Pennsylvania town of Bradford. He grew up in several industrial and mining towns of Western Pennsylvania. As a teenager, Eddie, as he preferred to be called, played on various town teams, including those of Butler, Oil City, and Homestead. He attended Volant College in Pennsylvania long enough to star for the baseball team. Scouts for the National League team in Louisville signed him to a contract in 1897. The big left-hander was about to be propelled from obscure small-town baseball into the big leagues.

The Road to Excellence

Eddie came to professional baseball at a time when there was only one major league, the National League. Louisville was one of the weaker franchises in a financial sense.

Eddie pitched in only two games his first season, 1897, before being sold to a minor league team in Detroit. He bounced around several minor league teams in 1898 and 1899 before returning to Louisville for part of the 1899 season.

When the Louisville club folded before the 1900 season, Eddie was shipped off to play for Pittsburgh. He did not distinguish himself until the 1902 season, when he jumped to the new rival American League and the Philadelphia Athletics (A's), owned and managed by Connie Mack.

Connie Mack was a practitioner of the type of baseball that relied on good pitching and good defense. Mack's teams won games without scoring many runs, often by preventing opponents from scoring any runs. Mack also looked for pitchers who had the stamina to hurl complete games. Eddie was a big man with a big, strong left arm. He could pitch all season long without fatigue or injury.

The Emerging Champion

Eddie was nicknamed "Rube" to signify his country origins. He immediately put his talent to work for the A's, winning twenty-four games in 1902. He made his reputation as a strikeout pitcher. In 1903, he again surpassed the twenty wins mark, and also struck out 302 batters. Rube's peak year for victories was 1905, when he won twenty-six games and led the Athletics to the American League pennant.

Baseball fans across the country eagerly awaited the World Series between Mack's A's and the National League champion New York Giants. Newspapers of the time looked forward to Game One, when it was expected that New York's star, Christy Mathewson, would take the mound against Rube Waddell. Instead, Rube took himself out of the Philadelphia lineup and did not appear in the Series. He claimed that he had hurt himself tripping over his suitcase. Unsubstantiated rumors circulated that he had been paid by gamblers not to appear.

Until surpassed by Washington's Walter Johnson, Rube Waddell was the premier strikeout pitcher of his day. He had the finest curveball in the American League, and his fastball had such movement that he made hitters look foolish as they flailed away at the ball.

In exhibition games after the regular season, he often played a trick in the ninth inning that delighted the crowd. He would beckon to his three outfielders to come to the dugout. He would then proceed to strike out the other side to prove that he did not need an outfield.

Continuing the Story

Rube Waddell has sometimes been described as an antihero. He often made the newspapers for unbecoming behavior off the field. Managers and teammates recognized that he had a problem with alcohol. Rube also made headlines with numerous marriages and divorces and with a failure to pay child support.

Children may not have looked to Rube as a role model of adult behavior, but they responded positively to his love for them and for the game of baseball. Rube enjoyed simple pleasures such as riding fire engines, fishing, or simply playing marbles with neighborhood children.

Connie Mack traded Rube to St. Louis after the 1907 season and publicly called the lefty an inef-

HONORS AND AWARDS

1946	Inducted into National Baseball Hall of Fame

STATISTICS

Season	*GP*	*GS*	*CG*	*IP*	*HA*	*BB*	*SO*	*W*	*L*	*S*	*ShO*	*ERA*
1897	2	1	1	14.0	17	6	5	0	1	0	0	3.21
1899	10	9	9	79.0	69	14	44	7	2	1	1	3.08
1900	29	22	16	208.2	176	55	**130**	8	13	0	2	2.37
1901	31	30	26	251.1	249	75	172	13	17	0	0	3.01
1902	33	27	26	276.1	224	64	**210**	24	7	0	3	2.05
1903	39	38	34	324.0	274	85	**302**	21	16	0	4	2.44
1904	46	46	39	383.0	307	91	**349**	25	19	0	8	1.62
1905	46	34	27	328.2	231	90	**287**	**26**	11	0	7	**1.48**
1906	43	34	22	272.2	221	92	**196**	15	17	0	8	2.21
1907	44	33	20	284.2	234	73	**232**	19	13	0	7	2.15
1908	43	36	25	285.2	223	90	**232**	19	14	3	5	1.89
1909	31	28	16	220.1	204	57	141	11	14	0	5	2.37
1910	10	2	0	33.0	31	11	16	3	1	1	0	3.55
Totals	407	340	261	2,961.1	2,460	803	2,316	191	145	5	50	2.16

Notes: Boldface indicates statistical leader. GP = games played; GS = games started; CG = complete games; IP = innings pitched; HA = hits allowed; BB = bases on balls (walks); SO = strikeouts; W = wins; L = losses; S = saves; ShO = shutouts; ERA = earned run average

fective pitcher. Rube got his revenge when Mack brought the A's to St. Louis. Mack watched sixteen Philadelphia batters strike out against Rube, a record that lasted for more than half a century.

Rube played in the minor leagues after being released by St. Louis. While playing in Kentucky in 1914, he volunteered to help combat a flood by piling sandbags. After standing many hours in cold, swirling water, he contracted lung disease and died in a San Antonio, Texas, hospital at only thirty-seven years of age.

Summary

Rube Waddell belonged to a simpler age of baseball. He played for the love of the game. He might have had a longer career had he taken better care of himself, but that was not his goal. He was an original, a country boy who liked to have fun in the big city.

James W. Oberly

Additional Sources:

Levy, Alan H. *Rube Waddell: The Zany, Brilliant Life of a Strikeout Artist.* Jefferson, N.C.: McFarland, 2000.

Newcombe, Jack. *The Fireballers.* New York: G. P. Putnam's Sons, 1964.

Shatzkin, Mike, et al, eds. *The Ballplayers: Baseball's Ultimate Biographical Reference.* New York: William Morrow, 1990.

VIRGINIA WADE

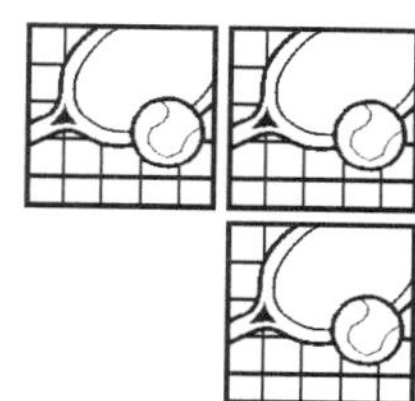

Sport: Tennis

Born: July 10, 1945
Bournemouth, England

Early Life

Sarah Virginia Wade was born on July 10, 1945, at Bournemouth, on England's southern coast. Her parents were Eustace Holland Wade and Joan Barbara Wade. She was the youngest child in the family, with two older brothers and an older sister.

Virginia grew up in Durban, South Africa, where her father served as archdeacon of Durban. She attended the Gordon Road Girls' School and Durban High School. She excelled at her schoolwork, particularly mathematics. She also studied piano and became an accomplished pianist.

When she was nine years old, she began playing tennis with a racket that she had found while cleaning a closet. She loved the game immediately and showed a natural talent for the sport. She played as often as possible at the Durban Lawn Tennis club, which was next to her home. Although she received help from her brothers

AP/Wide World Photos

Virginia Wade won the 1977 Wimbledon title after sixteen years of trying.

MAJOR CHAMPIONSHIP VICTORIES AND FINALS

1968	U.S. Open
1969	U.S. National Championship doubles (with Margaret Court)
1970	Wimbledon doubles finalist (with Françoise Durr)
1970, 1972, 1976	U.S. Open doubles finalist (with Rosie Casals; with Court; with Olga Morozova)
1972	Australian Open
1973	Australian Open doubles (with Court) French Open doubles (with Court)
1973, 1975	U.S. Open doubles (with Court)
1977	Wimbledon
1979	French Open doubles finalist (with Durr)

OTHER NOTABLE VICTORIES

1967	British Hard Court Championship doubles (with Ann Jones)
1967-68, 1973-74	British Hard Court Championship
1968, 1971, 1973, 1983	Italian Open doubles (with Court; with Helga Niessen Masthoff; with Morozova; with Virginia Ruzici)
1968, 1974-75, 1978	On winning British Wightman Cup team
1971	Italian Open
1976	U.S. Indoor Championship
1977	Colgate Championships doubles (with Durr)
1978	Virginia Slims of Los Angeles doubles (with Betty Stove)

and sister, along with some additional instruction, her tennis skills were mainly self-taught.

The Road to Excellence

In 1961, when Virginia was fifteen years old, her family returned to England. Although she was disappointed to leave her friends and tennis teammates in South Africa, the move advanced her development as a tennis player. She played in many junior tournaments, participated in a training program in London for promising junior players, and qualified for Wimbledon at age sixteen.

Upon graduation from secondary school, Virginia entered the University of Sussex to pursue a degree in mathematics and physics. From 1964 through 1966, Virginia continued to play tennis while attending college. The difficulty of balancing tennis and studies reached a climax in June, 1966, when she took her final exams at the same time that she competed on Great Britain's Wightman Cup team in its annual match against the United States. Great Britain lost the Wightman Cup, but Virginia earned her B.S. degree.

Once Virginia had completed her formal education, she began playing tennis full-time. For two years, in 1966 and 1967, she competed as an amateur on the international tennis circuit. Her record was uneven. She had some important victories in Wightman Cup competition and as British Hard Court champion in 1967 and 1968. At the same time she did not do as well in some of the Grand Slam tournaments, especially Wimbledon, where British crowds hoped that she might become the champion that her country had not had for many years. Overall, she gained important experience that benefited her game.

The Emerging Champion

The late 1960's were significant for the sport of tennis and for women's tennis in particular. In 1968 the major events became open to both professional and amateur players. Also, a group of women's tennis players joined together to promote greater equality in prize money for the female professionals.

Virginia was part of this movement and turned professional in 1968. In September, 1968, she won her first Grand Slam tournament, the U.S. Open. It was the first time that this tournament had been played as an event open to professionals. By the end of 1968 Virginia Wade was the second-ranked woman tennis player in the world.

Virginia's active career as a professional tennis player extended from the late 1960's through the early 1980's. During this time she was always highly ranked. She won several major tournaments, including the Italian Open in 1971, the Australian Open in 1972, and the British Hard Court Championship in 1973 and 1974. She was the captain of the British Wightman Cup team from 1973 to 1986. She also played World Team Tennis for the New York Sets.

Virginia brought a great intensity and perfectionism to the game of tennis. She had an excellent serve and volley game, well suited for grass courts and hard courts. At times, her performance in tennis matches was uneven because of her mental frustration when the technical execution of her strokes did not meet the high standard of excellence that she set for herself.

The greatest triumph of Virginia Wade's tennis career came when she won the Wimbledon title in 1977. As a British citizen, becoming a Wimbledon champion held special meaning for Virginia. After sixteen years of playing in the tournament she became the ladies champion at Wimbledon. Her win in the finals over Betty Stove was even more exciting because it was the one hundredth anniversary of the Wimbledon tournament. It was also the year of Queen Elizabeth's Silver Jubilee, celebrating her twenty-five years as British monarch. When Virginia won Wimbledon, Queen Elizabeth II presented her the championship trophy.

Continuing the Story

By the time Virginia won Wimbledon, she had already achieved a full career as a professional tennis player. She continued as an active professional for several more years into the early 1980's. She did not, however, have any more victories as notable as her Wimbledon triumph.

Virginia remained involved with tennis in several ways: playing in ladies' senior competitions, presenting commentaries on tennis for television, and writing two books on tennis: her autobiography, *Courting Triumph* (1978), and *Ladies of the Court* (1984), on women players at Wimbledon.

Virginia Wade has received numerous awards and honors for her accomplishments both on and off the tennis court. In 1973, she was made a Member of the British Empire by Queen Elizabeth II. The University of Sussex awarded her an honorary LL.D. in 1985. She was inducted into the International Tennis Hall of Fame in 1989. She continued to pursue a wide variety of interests, including reading and the arts. Beginning in the early 1980's, Virginia worked as a tennis commentator for the BBC and the USA Network.

Summary

Virginia Wade's most memorable win was the 1977 Ladies Championship in Wimbledon's centenary year. Virginia's passion for tennis and her graceful style of play throughout her long professional career contributed much to this sport during an exciting period of growth for women's tennis.

Karen Gould

Additional Sources:

Kalyn, Wayne. "A Tale of Two Champions." *World Tennis* 28 (May, 1981): 74-78.

"Virginia Wade." In *International Who's Who in Tennis*, edited by Jane Cooke. Dallas, Tex.: World Championship Tennis, 1983.

Wade, Virginia, with Mary Lou Mellace. *Courting Triumph*. New York: Mayflower Books, 1978.

HONORS, AWARDS, AND MILESTONES

1965-85	British Wightman Cup team
1967-83	British Federation Cup team
1973-86	British Wightman Cup team captain
1973	Member of the British Empire
1977	WTA Player of the Year
1982	First woman elected to Wimbledon Committee
1989	Inducted into International Tennis Hall of Fame

HONUS WAGNER

Sport: Baseball

Born: February 24, 1874
Mansfield, Pennsylvania
Died: December 6, 1955
Carnegie, Pennsylvania

Early Life

John Peter "Honus" Wagner was born on February 24, 1874, in the town of Mansfield, Pennsylvania. Called first Johannes, then Hans, and finally Honus by his family, he was one of nine children. His father worked eighteen hours a day in the coal mines, and at the age of twelve, Honus too began loading two tons a day onto a boy's car for the wage of seventy-nine cents a ton. During the winter, Honus never saw the sun, for he reported to work in the early morning darkness and returned home at night. On the job, he learned to admire and respect rats, for he realized that they could sense an approaching cave-in. When they ran for safety, Honus ran too.

During the spring, his brothers would bring a ball and glove to the mines and during lunch hour the Wagner boys would play catch. Thus encouraged by his older brothers, young Honus came to love baseball, and he occasionally walked the seven miles to Pittsburgh to watch the Pirates play. He dreamed of his future as a big-leaguer and began to play sandlot and semiprofessional baseball. Honus soon attracted attention and was offered a minor league contract. Now, able to earn $35 a month playing ball, he bade farewell to the coal mines.

The Road to Excellence

When Honus reported to Steubenville, Ohio, of the Tri-State League, he was prepared to play any position. In the course of a month, he played them all, for his remarkable hitting kept him in the lineup every day. Later in the season, he jumped to Warren of the Iron-Oil League for a raise to $75 a month. The rapidly developing Honus was spotted one day by Edward Grant Barrow, a future Hall of Famer who in 1895 was the very young owner of the Paterson, New Jersey, team. With a shrewd eye for baseball talent, Barrow recognized the potential of the long-armed, bow-legged, versatile Honus and bought his contract for $300.

Pittsburgh Baseball Club

STATISTICS

Season	GP	AB	Hits	2B	3B	HR	Runs	RBI	BA	SA
1897	61	237	80	17	4	2	37	39	.338	.468
1898	151	588	176	29	3	10	80	105	.299	.410
1899	147	571	192	43	13	7	98	113	.336	.494
1900	135	527	201	**45**	**22**	4	107	100	**.381**	**.573**
1901	141	556	196	**37**	11	6	100	**126**	.353	.491
1902	137	538	177	**33**	16	3	**105**	**91**	.329	**.467**
1903	129	512	182	30	**19**	5	97	101	**.355**	.518
1904	132	490	171	**44**	14	4	97	75	**.349**	**.520**
1905	147	548	199	32	14	6	114	101	.363	.505
1906	142	516	175	**38**	9	2	**103**	71	**.339**	.459
1907	142	515	180	**38**	14	6	98	82	**.350**	**.513**
1908	151	568	**201**	**39**	**19**	10	100	**109**	**.354**	**.542**
1909	137	495	168	**39**	10	5	92	**100**	**.339**	**.489**
1910	150	556	**178**	34	8	4	90	81	.320	.432
1911	130	473	158	23	16	9	87	89	**.334**	.507
1912	145	558	181	35	20	7	91	102	.324	.496
1913	114	413	124	18	4	3	51	56	.300	.385
1914	150	552	139	15	9	1	60	50	.252	.317
1915	151	566	155	32	17	6	68	78	.274	.422
1916	123	432	124	15	9	1	45	39	.287	.370
1917	74	230	61	7	1	0	15	24	.265	.304
Totals	2,789	10,441	3,418	643	252	101	1,735	1,732	.327	.466

Notes: Boldface indicates statistical leader. GP = games played; AB = at bats; 2B = doubles; 3B = triples; HR = home runs; RBI = runs batted in; BA = batting average; SA = slugging average

As a star with the Paterson team, Honus in 1896 batted .349 during this era of the notorious "dead ball." His skilled fielding began to dominate the diamond, for his huge hands easily compensated for the tiny fielders' gloves of the time. In 1897, Barrow sold Honus's contract to Louisville, then a member of the National League. Here Honus began to play for Fred Clarke, the man who was to be his big-league manager for twenty years.

Louisville was not a strong ball club, floundering in the second division; nevertheless, in 1899, Honus Wagner hit .336 and began to intimidate opponents with his power, skill, and speed. While he continued to develop, however, the Louisville franchise did not prosper, and in 1900, with the withdrawal of the team from organized baseball, fifteen players—among them Honus Wagner—were transferred to Pittsburgh. Honus's boyhood dream, to play for the Pirates, had come true.

The Emerging Champion

The career of the new Pirate shortstop, the baseball legend who quickly began to be referred to as "The Flying Dutchman," now ascended to full orbit. He began to dominate the league. In 1900, Honus won the first of his eight National League batting titles, hitting .381. He led the league in doubles and triples. The following year, hitting .353 and winning the stolen base title, Honus led Pittsburgh to a pennant. He was recognized as the premier shortstop playing the game, an athlete with no weaknesses. His often acrobatic fielding prowess was complemented by powerful hitting and dedicated team play. He led the league in batting in 1903 and 1904 and from 1906 through 1909. In the World Series of 1909, Honus hit .333 as the Pirates defeated the Detroit Tigers and Ty Cobb in seven games. Along the way, Honus stole 6 bases, a record that stood until 1967. When the aggressive Cobb called the genial Honus "Krauthead" and came sliding hard into second base with spikes flying high, he found the "Dutchman" waiting to tag him in the mouth.

Alongside Honus's acclaimed athletic ability was his outstanding spirit of sportsmanship on and off the field. A model of clean living, Honus withdrew his baseball card from circulation because it was distributed by a cigarette company. Although he was fiercely competitive, he never

HONORS AND AWARDS

1936	Inducted into National Baseball Hall of Fame
	Uniform number 33 retired by Pittsburgh Pirates

disputed the decision of an umpire. His life and career reflected the highest values of a gentleman-athlete. Throughout America, The Flying Dutchman was regarded as a hero.

Continuing the Story

For seventeen years with the Pirates, Honus Wagner continued his outstanding, productive career. He led the league in hitting eight times, in slugging percentage six times, and in stolen bases five times. By 1914, however, the arthritis in his legs, a condition that had been aggravated by his early years in the dank coal mines, began to pain him greatly. He could no longer speed along the basepaths with the skill and artistry of the past. Yet each time he talked about his inevitable retirement, Pirate management always persuaded him to come back one more time. Although he could no longer generate league-leading statistics, Honus's intangible contributions were important to the club, especially his inspirational value to the young players. Honus played his last major league game September 17, 1917. He managed the team very briefly, then left professional baseball altogether.

Turning down many lucrative business offers, Honus became the baseball and basketball coach at Carnegie Tech (now Carnegie-Mellon University) in Pittsburgh. He organized a semiprofessional baseball team called the Honus Wagner All-Stars. In 1933, however, when he was fifty-nine, Honus Wagner was called back by his Pittsburgh Pirates; he was, simply, coach, teacher, dugout presence, and hero/role model.

In 1936, Honus was in the first group of players elected into the National Baseball Hall of Fame in Cooperstown, New York. At the time of his death in Carnegie, Pennsylvania, on December 6, 1955, he was still the National League all-time leader in games played, times at bat, hits, singles, doubles, and triples.

Summary

By acclamation, Honus Wagner is regarded as the greatest shortstop ever to have played. Some experts will even assert that he was the greatest player at any position. Revered for his awesome talent, acclaimed for his athletic accomplishments, and beloved for his sterling character, Honus was simultaneously a Hall of Fame ball player and a Hall of Fame human being. Overcoming the hardships of his youth, he came to symbolize the real possibilities in the American Dream for those children of immigrants who aspired to success and who worked hard to achieve their goals.

Abe C. Ravitz

Additional Sources:

DeValeria, Dennis, and Jean B. DeValeria. *Honus Wagner: A Biography.* New York: Henry Holt, 1996.

Hageman, William. *Honus: The Life and Times of a Baseball Hero.* Champaign, Ill.: Sagamore, 1996.

Hittner, Arthur D. *Honus Wagner: The Life of Baseball's "Flying Dutchman."* Jefferson, N.C.: McFarland, 1996.

Kavanagh, Jack. *Honus Wagner.* New York: Chelsea House, 1994.

LISA WAGNER

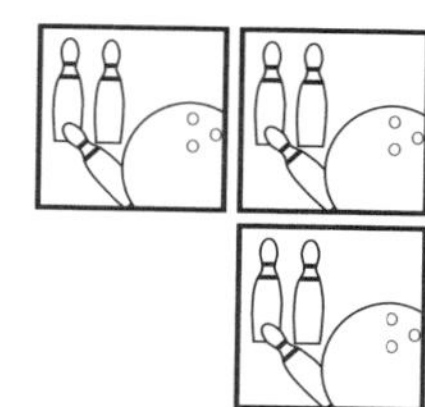

Sport: Bowling

Born: May 19, 1961
Hillsboro, Illinois

Early Life

Lisa Wagner was born on May 19, 1961, in Hillsboro, Illinois. By the age of six, bolstered by her parents' involvement in a local junior bowling league, Lisa began to bowl regularly. After her parents had finished with their own games, she would throw practice balls. With tips and practical advice from her parents, the young bowler soon began to compete in local tournaments.

When Lisa was fifteen, professional bowler Tommy Evans began coaching the future champion. The lessons that she learned from her parents and from Evans have remained with her throughout her career. After competing in and winning amateur tournaments, Lisa began a career as a professional bowler in 1980.

The Road to Excellence

Although Lisa had been bowling from the time she was six years old, had the support of her family, and had been coached by a professional bowler, she still had to struggle for her first break in professional bowling. Even so, Lisa was able to amass enough money and experience in amateur tournaments to consider a career as a professional bowler. Because women bowlers' earnings have traditionally been lower than the winnings collected on the men's tour, when she turned professional Lisa had to use the prize money she had won in amateur tournaments to fund trips to her first several professional tournaments.

Early in her professional career, at a tournament in Las Vegas, Nevada, Lisa and her doubles partner, Carolyn Dorin, were so surprised to qualify to compete in the tournament that they were unprepared when they did. Because the women did not expect to qualify, they had not purchased team uniforms and had to make a spur-of-the-moment shopping trip to find matching clothes for the tournament. Despite their surprise qualification and hastily chosen outfits, the pair managed to win the tournament in the last frame of the final game.

The Emerging Champion

Lisa began to prove herself early in her career by winning the Ladies Professional Bowlers Tour Rookie of the Year title in 1980. In her first ten

International Bowling Museum

years of professional competition, Lisa netted twenty titles and earned more than $360,000. In 1988 she reached the impressive milestone of becoming the first woman bowler to reach $100,000 in earnings in one year.

By the end of the 1980's, Lisa, in addition to her twenty titles, had been named Bowler of the Decade by *Bowling Magazine*. She had become firmly established as a top bowler by the beginning of the 1990's. However, because of a hectic slate of personal appearances, the fatigue of tournaments, and her work as a member of Brunswick's advisory staff, Lisa began to compete in fewer tournaments. In addition to her hectic schedule, she was still recovering from an ankle injury she had received in an automobile accident in 1988. While Lisa had fully recuperated from a sprained left ankle, she discovered that she was developing arthritis in the injured ankle. The champion bowler did not let the injury affect her game. Instead, her list of titles and achievements continued to grow.

Continuing the Story

Lisa's success continued into the next decade, and, by 1996, Lisa was inducted into the Ladies Pro Bowlers Tour Hall of Fame and had won the Tour's Bowler of the Year Award three times, in 1983, 1988, and 1993. Then, the following year, she added to her busy schedule when she landed an endorsement contract with bowling-product manufacturer AMF. Along with fellow professional bowlers Wendy Macpherson, Marianne Dirupo, Dana Miller-Mackie, and Kim Adler, Lisa signed a $750,000, three-year sponsorship contract with AMF to represent the company and their products. As a professional bowler, Lisa has had endorsements with AMF and Mongoose Gloves.

Early in 1999, Lisa became the leading titleholder by winning her thirty-first title. She further secured her hold on the record by winning her thirty-second title in August of 1999. In 2000 Lisa led all other women's professional bowlers in the number of titles won. Having earned more than $900,000 in her career, Lisa entered the new century as one of the top money earners in women's bowling.

Further adding to her achievements, she was inducted into the Women's International Bowling Congress Hall of Fame in October of 1999. After two decades on the professional bowling tour, Lisa has added a new dimension to her career as competitor by also becoming a broadcaster for her sport. Lisa's first love is caring for her pets, an assortment of dogs and ferrets. Lisa's love of animals is so strong that she hoped to run a pet resort after retiring from bowling.

Summary

Lisa Wagner, who began bowling early in life, has proven that she has both the determination and stamina it takes to become a champion woman bowler. Although she has had to struggle, she has shown that hard work and determination are effective tools to reach goals. Having won many of bowling's highest honors, Lisa demonstrates exactly what it takes to become a champion.

Kimberley H. Kidd

Additional Sources:

Cary, Stan. "AMF Is Aiding Five Female Pros." *The Richmond Times Dispatch*, April 21, 1997, p. C4.

Cosgrove, Bob. "Wagner Planning Strong Finish." *The Washington Times*, September 27, 1989, p. D7.

Lisa Wagner Home Page. http://www.lisawagner.com.

Patterson, Don. "Not Rolling in Dough; You Won't Find a Lot of Millionaires on the Ladies Pro Bowlers Tour." *Los Angeles Times*, February 22, 1989, p. 5A.

HONORS AND AWARDS

1980	Ladies Pro Bowlers Tour Rookie of the Year
1983, 1988, 1993	Ladies Pro Bowlers Tour Bowler of the Year
1989	Bowler of the Decade
1999	Inducted into Women's International Bowling Congress Hall of Fame Inducted into Ladies Pro Bowlers Tour Hall of Fame

GRETA WAITZ

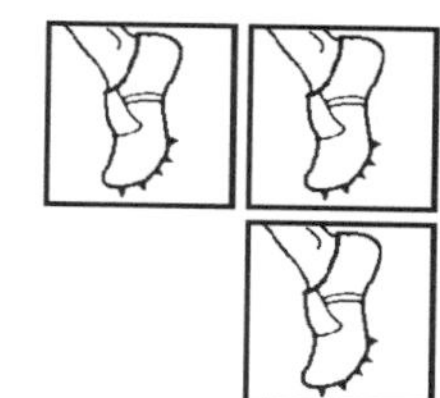

Sport: Track and field (marathon)

Born: October 1, 1953
Oslo, Norway

Early Life

Greta Waitz was born Greta Andersen on October 1, 1953, in Oslo, the capital city of Norway. She was the youngest of three children in a working-class family. The family was heavily involved in athletics, and Greta took up sports, especially handball, at an early age. Later she moved on to gymnastics and track. She first started running when she was twelve, putting on a pair of old running shoes and racing back and forth on a stretch of grass near her home.

Greta's next-door neighbor was Olympic javelin champion Terje Pedersen. He was impressed by Greta's abilities and recruited her for his track team. Greta idolized him and did everything she could to please him.

The Road to Excellence

As a teenager, Greta joined the athletic club Vidar, where she met her future husband, Jack Waitz, a distance runner. At first Greta ran as a sprinter, but then she moved on to the 400 meters. She began to get serious about running. At this early stage in her career, she owed a great deal to Jan Gulbrandsen, her high school gym teacher. Gulbrandsen realized that, although Greta was not yet an outstanding runner, she had the ability and determination to work hard and systematically improve her performance. When she was faced with a challenge, her ambition knew no bounds, Gulbrandsen has said.

When Greta was sixteen, she became the Norwegian junior champion in the 400 and 800 meters. By 1972, she was competing in the 1,500 meters. She realized in her training that it was easier for her to develop strength and endurance than speed, and this made her better suited to racing over longer distances. At that time, however, there were few opportunities for women to run competitively in distances of more than 1,500 meters.

AP/Wide World Photos

Greta Waitz as she crossed the finish line for the silver medal in marathon at the 1984 Olympics.

In 1972, when she was only eighteen, Greta competed in her first Olympic Games, in Mu-

STATISTICS

Year	Competition	Event	Place	Time
1974	European Championships	1,500 meters	3d	4:05.2
1977	World Cup	3,000 meters	Gold	8:43.5
1978	European Championships	1,500 meters	5th	—
		3,000 meters	3d	8:34.30
	New York Marathon	Marathon	1st	2:32.30
1979	New York Marathon	Marathon	1st	2:27.33
1980	New York Marathon	Marathon	1st	2:25.42
1982	New York Marathon	Marathon	1st	2:27.14
1983	London Marathon	Marathon	1st	2:25.29
	World Championships	Marathon	1st	2:28.09
	New York Marathon	Marathon	1st	2:27.00
1984	Olympic Games	Marathon	Silver	2:26.18
	New York Marathon	Marathon	1st	2:29.30
1985	New York Marathon	Marathon	1st	2:28.34
1986	London Marathon	Marathon	1st	2:24.54
	New York Marathon	Marathon	1st	2:28.06
1988	Stockholm Marathon	Marathon	1st	2:28.24
	New York Marathon	Marathon	1st	2:28.07

nich, West Germany, running for Norway in the 1,500 meters. She did not reach the finals, but the experience of competing at such an important venue made her ambitious for the success she was shortly to achieve.

The Emerging Champion

In 1974, Greta placed third in the 1,500 meters in the European Championships. The following year, she set a world record for the women's 3,000 meters. She reached the semifinals of the Olympic 1,500 meters in 1976 in Montreal, Canada, and in 1977 she won the World Cup 3,000 meters. With these successes, she felt she had reached her limit. She even thought of retiring from running, although she was only twenty-five.

Then her husband encouraged her to tackle the marathon, and from that moment on she discovered her true distance. In her very first attempt, in the New York City Marathon in 1978, she cut 2 minutes off the women's world record, finishing the 26-mile 385-yard course in a time of 2 hours, 32 minutes, and 30 seconds (2:32.30). She decided to quit her job as a school-teacher in Norway and concentrate full-time on running.

Her decision was followed by a string of almost unbroken successes. In 1978, 1979, and 1980, she won the world cross-country championships. In New York City in 1979, she created a new record of 31 minutes 14.4 seconds for the 10,000-meter L'eggs Mini-Marathon. Later that year, she again won the New York City Marathon, in a time of 2:27.33. That made her the first woman to run a marathon in less than 2½ hours.

One of the secrets of Greta's success was her consistent training. She rarely skipped a day, even training the day after she ran a marathon. She built her whole life around her training schedule. A typical day would begin at 5:15 A.M. with a brisk run. She would run again in the afternoon. In two or three sessions a week she would concentrate on speed work; one session would be devoted to a fifteen to eighteen mile run; and in the remainder she would run moderate distances at a steady pace of 6 minutes a mile.

Greta's achievements won her worldwide recognition, and she was honored in her own country. Norwegians voted her "The Name in the Decade of the Seventies," and she received the Saint Olav medal, the only athlete ever to do so. The medal is awarded to outstanding citizens who have "put Norway on the map."

Continuing the Story

In 1980, Greta set new world records for 5 miles, 10 miles, 15,000 meters, and 20,000 meters. She again won the New York City Marathon, in 2:25.42, breaking her own record time of the previous year. She went on to win this event a record nine times.

In 1983, she won the London Marathon and the first World Championship Marathon. She won the L'eggs Mini-Marathon in New York five times; she also had five wins in the world cross-country championships.

Greta had such an impact on women's distance running that the Olympic Committee decided to add the 3,000 meters and the marathon to the women's Olympic competition. In the first women's Olympic marathon ever in Los Angeles in 1984, Greta won the silver medal.

For many young female athletes, Greta became a role model. Her cool, confident manner, her modesty, and her humble attitude toward her increasing fame won her universal admiration. "I'm just a very, very normal person and I just happen to run fast," she said.

Toward the end of her career, Greta was troubled by injuries. A stress fracture kept her out of the World Championship Marathon in Rome in 1987. She underwent knee surgery before the Olympic Games in Seoul in 1988, and this weakened her performance. She was forced to drop out of the marathon after 18 miles.

Reducing her running schedule allowed her to devote more time to the Greta Waitz Foundation, which she and her husband had started in 1984 to assist young women athletes in Norway.

Summary

Greta Waitz set world records for distances ranging from 5 miles to the marathon. As the most celebrated women's distance runner in the 1970's and 1980's, she opened many doors for female athletes. In 1991 *Runner's World* magazine named Greta the "Best Female Distance Runner" in the past quarter century. She was also honored by her country in 1997 when Norway issued a stamp featuring her picture. A model of calm concentration, endurance, and excellence, Greta was instrumental in promoting a more positive image of women's athletics.

Bryan Aubrey

Additional Sources:

The Lincoln Library of Sports Champions. 16 vols. Columbus, Ohio: Frontier Press, 1993.

Waitz, Grete, and Gloria Averbuch. *World Class: A Champion Runner Reveals What Makes Her Run, with Advice and Inspiration for All Athletes.* New York: Warner Books, 1986.

Wallechinsky, David. *The Complete Book of the Olympics.* Boston: Little, Brown and Company, 1991.

Watman, Mel. *Encyclopedia of Track and Field Athletics.* New York: St. Martin's Press, 1981.

RECORDS AND MILESTONES

Three world records at 3,000 meters: 1975 (8:46.6), 1976 (8:45.4), 1980 (8:50.8)
World record at 10,000 meters: 1979 (31:14.4)
World records at 5 miles, 10 miles, 15,000 meters, and 20,000 meters in 1980
Won five world cross-country championships
Won a record nine New York City Marathons
Won the L'eggs Mini-Marathon five times
First woman to run a marathon in less than 2 hrs 30 mins
Won the Saint Olav Medal

DOAK WALKER

Sport: Football

Born: January 1, 1927
Dallas, Texas
Died: September 27, 1998
Steamboat Springs, Colorado

Early Life

Ewell Doak Walker, Jr., was born on New Year's Day, 1927, in Dallas, Texas. Doak grew up in a middle-class family, neither rich nor poor. His father was a teacher. Doak had one sister. The Walker family lived in the Dallas suburb of Highland Park. An all-around athlete, Doak played many sports as a young boy.

The Road to Excellence

Doak continued to play many sports at Highland Park High School. He swam the breast stroke on the swim team, played guard on the basketball team, played catcher on the baseball team, and ran sprints on the track team. Altogether he won 16 athletic letters in high school sports.

Football was by far Doak's best sport. At Highland Park he teamed with future National Football League (NFL) Hall of Famer Bobby Layne to lead the team to two semifinal finishes in the Texas high school playoffs. Highland Park did even better in Doak's senior season, when it advanced to the state championship game, where it lost.

Doak and Bobby both joined the Merchant Marine following that season. World War II was in progress and they did not know when or if they would ever get to college. Yet they vowed to play together on the same team at the University of Texas.

When the war ended in 1945, Bobby, true to his word, enrolled at Texas, but at the last minute Doak changed his mind and decided to stay in his hometown and attend Southern Methodist University. He and Bobby were destined to become friendly rivals in the Southwest Conference.

AP/Wide World Photos

Detroit Lion Doak Walker in 1950.

STATISTICS

Season	GP	Rushing Car.	Rushing Yds.	Rushing Avg.	Rushing TD	Receiving Rec.	Receiving Yds.	Receiving Avg.	Receiving TD
1950	12	83	386	4.7	5	35	534	15.3	6
1951	12	79	356	4.5	2	22	421	19.1	4
1952	7	26	106	4.1	0	11	90	8.2	0
1953	12	65	337	5.1	2	30	502	16.7	3
1954	12	32	240	7.5	1	32	564	17.6	3
1955	12	23	95	4.1	2	22	428	19.5	5
Totals	67	308	1,520	4.9	12	152	2,539	16.7	21

Notes: GP = games played; Car. = carries; Yds. = yards; Avg. = average yards per carry *or* average yards per reception; TD = touchdowns; Rec. = receptions

At 5 feet 11 inches and 168 pounds, Doak was small for a major college back, but he made up for his lack of size by being able to do a lot of different things on the field.

Southern Methodist University used a combination single- and double-wing offense, which is similar to the modern-day shotgun formation. Doak often received the snap from center and could both run and pass well. He was also an excellent receiver. He could also punt and placekick. On defense Doak was a sure tackler and excelled at pass defense. In addition, he led the team in punt returns and kickoff runbacks.

He played only the last half of his freshman season because he did not get out of the Merchant Marine until late in the year. Yet he was outstanding, gaining 289 yards rushing and completing 38 of 65 passes for 387 yards. In 1946, Doak was drafted into the United States Army and missed his second season.

The Emerging Champion

When Doak returned to Southern Methodist following his Army discharge, he led the Mustangs to national prominence in 1947 and 1948. They rolled through the 1947 season undefeated. They beat his old friend Bobby Layne and the University of Texas Longhorns 14-13, but were tied in the last game of the season, 13-13, by Texas Christian University. Nine wins and one tie gave the Mustangs the Southwest Conference championship and a number-three national ranking. Southern Methodist was invited to play in the Cotton Bowl against Pennsylvania State University.

Doak played a great game in the Cotton Bowl. He threw a 53-yard touchdown pass, ran for a touchdown, and kicked an extra point in a 13-13 tie. Doak was named to most All-American teams that season, an unusual honor for a sophomore.

The Mustangs did almost as well in 1948. They again beat the University of Texas, and won the Southwest Conference championship. An early season loss to the University of Missouri and another late season tie with Texas Christian gave Southern Methodist a final season record of 8-1-1. They did beat the University of Oregon 21-13 in the Cotton Bowl, where Doak scored a touchdown and kicked two extra points. The Mustangs were ranked tenth in the nation that season.

Doak had had an excellent 1948 season. He had gained 537 yards rushing, 318 yards passing, and 264 yards receiving, and had intercepted 3 passes. He scored 11 touchdowns and kicked 22 extra points. Doak had been named to every All-American team and in only his junior year had won the Heisman Trophy as the nation's outstanding college football player.

Continuing the Story

In his senior season at Southern Methodist, Doak was not as good because of injuries. Still, he was selected by many all-American teams for a third straight time. While at Southern Methodist he also earned 3 varsity letters in baseball as an outfielder, and 1 varsity letter in basketball.

Although most experts believed that at 5 feet 11 inches and 173 pounds Doak was too small to do well as a professional football player, he was signed to a National Football League (NFL) contract by the Detroit Lions, where he rejoined his old high school teammate, Bobby Layne.

The duo led the Lions to a break-even season

HONORS AND AWARDS

1947	Maxwell Award
1947-49	Consensus All-American
1948	Heisman Trophy
1950	NFL Rookie of the Year
1950-51, 1953-54	All-NFL Team
1950-52, 1954-56	NFL Pro Bowl Team
1951, 1954-55	*Sporting News* NFL All-Star Team
1959	Inducted into College Football Hall of Fame
1986	Inducted into Pro Football Hall of Fame Uniform number 37 retired by Detroit Lions

in 1950. Doak showed that his versatility would work as well in professional football as it had in college. He was second on the team in running, pass receiving, and place kicking and punting. He led the league in scoring with 128 points. He was the league's Rookie of the Year and was named to the All-NFL and the Pro Bowl teams.

What could Doak do to top his rookie season? He led the Lions to Western Division Championships in 1952, 1953, and 1954. The Lions went on to win the NFL Championship Game when they beat the Cleveland Browns 17-7 in 1952, and again in 1953 when they beat the Browns 17-16.

After only six seasons Doak retired from football. During his short career he twice led the league in scoring and was four times an All-Pro.

Doak was very successful in the construction business in Dallas. He was honored by being inducted into both the College and the Pro Football Halls of Fame.

Summary

Doak Walker was small in size, but he had the ability to make the big play that changed the course of games and even seasons. He was respected by teammates and opponents not only for his ability on the field but also for his modesty off the field.

C. Robert Barnett

Additional Sources:

Canning, Whit. *Doak Walker: More than a Hero.* Indianapolis, Ind.: Master Press, 1997.

Grimsley, Will. *Football: The Greatest Moments in the Southwest Conference.* Boston: Little, Brown, 1968.

LaBlanc, Michael L., and Mary K. Ruby, eds. *Professional Sports Team Histories: Football.* Detroit: Gale, 1994.

HERSCHEL WALKER

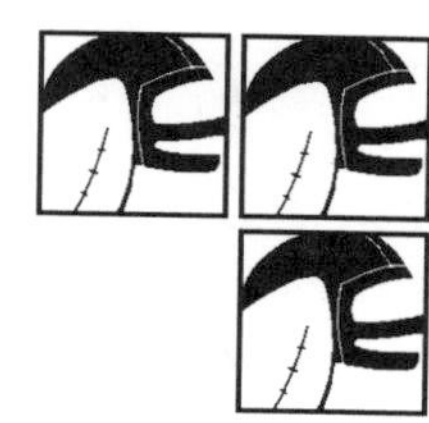

Sport: Football

Born: March 3, 1962
Wrightsville, Georgia

Early Life

Herschel Junior Walker was born on March 3, 1962, in Wrightsville, Georgia, to Willis Walker and Christine Taylor Walker. He was the fifth of seven children of the Walkers, who believed in the virtues of persistence, pride, and honesty.

Growing up in the countryside outside Wrightsville, Georgia, the Walker children watched their parents work first as tenant farmers and later as factory workers. The whole family attended a local Baptist church, where Herschel sang in the youth choir. True to the principles of hard work they taught their children, the Walkers moved their family from a shanty to a modest wood frame house on a dirt road when Herschel was eight years old.

Surprisingly, Herschel was the least athletic of his brothers and sisters. His mother called him the runt of the family. Probably because of a temporary speech impediment, he was a shy boy who withdrew into reading and writing poetry.

When he was in the fifth grade, Herschel's classmates urged him to play football with them at recess. Out of admiration for his older brothers Willis and Renneth, who were then on the local high school's varsity football team, he finally decided to get involved with sports. He was also upset because his older sister Veronica could beat him in foot races.

The Road to Excellence

When Herschel was twelve years old, he went to the local track-and-field coach, Tom Jordan, and asked him how to go about building muscles. He followed the coach's advice and developed an intense daily workout of sit-ups, push-ups, and wind sprints, a program he would continue throughout his career.

AP/Wide World Photos

Running back for the Dallas Cowboys Herschel Walker in a 1987 game.

The exercises worked, and by the time Herschel was in the ninth grade he stood 5 feet 10 inches, weighed a solid 185 pounds, and could run the 100-yard dash in 9.9 seconds. No longer could Veronica outrun him.

He started his football career at Johnson County High School as a fullback, but he eventually moved to the tailback position. At 200 pounds and close to 6 feet tall, he bowled over linesmen and earned the nickname "Hurt." He developed his characteristic "float and glide" style of running. "Floating" around the blockers, he would "glide" past, find an opening, and race to the end zone.

Herschel's favorite sport in high school, however, was track, and he helped his team win the 1979 state class-A track-and-field championship by winning the shot put, the 100-yard dash, and the 200-yard dash. He also played basketball as the starting varsity forward. His teammates dubbed him "Skywalker" because of his ability to leap so high when rebounding.

The Johnson County Trojans won the state class-A football championship in Herschel's senior year. He had rushed for 3,167 yards and scored 45 touchdowns in the effort, and was named a consensus prep All-American and *Parade* magazine's national high school back of the year.

Herschel had not neglected the classroom. With an A average, he was named valedictorian of his class and president of the Beta Club, a scholastic honor society.

The Emerging Champion

Such achievements in the classroom and on the playing field brought Herschel national attention. He was the most sought-after schoolboy prospect in the country in 1980. Over one hundred colleges offered him scholarships. Herschel's parents wanted him to go to the University of Georgia in Athens, a small college town only ninety-eight miles from home. His sister Veronica was already on the Bulldogs track team, and after flipping a coin, Herschel decided to join her.

Before the end of his first game for the University of Georgia, the whole state knew his name because he had scored 2 touchdowns to beat the University of Tennessee. Herschel would become the main character in a storybook season for the university.

He became the regular starting tailback for the rest of the season and set a new freshman National Collegiate Athletic Association (NCAA) rushing record with 1,616 yards, eclipsing Tony Dorsett's mark of 1,568. He finished third in the balloting for the Heisman Trophy, college football's highest honor—the highest finish ever by a freshman. He was named First Team All-American in six polls, and in two of them, by the Football Writers Association of America and by Kodak, he was the first freshman ever to be so honored.

Most importantly, Herschel rushed for 150 yards and 2 touchdowns in earning most valuable player honors in the 1981 Sugar Bowl victory over the University of Notre Dame. His performance helped secure Georgia's first national championship ever and made him that state's favorite native son for many years to come.

STATISTICS

		Rushing				Receiving			
Season	GP	Car.	Yds.	Avg.	TD	Rec.	Yds.	Avg.	TD
1983	18	412	**1,812**	4.4	**17**	53	489	9.2	1
1984	17	293	1,339	4.6	16	40	528	13.2	5
1985	18	438	**2,411**	5.5	**21**	37	467	12.6	1
USFL Totals	53	1,143	5,562	4.9	54	130	1,484	11.4	7
1986	16	151	737	4.9	12	76	837	11.0	2
1987	12	209	891	4.3	7	60	715	11.9	1
1988	16	361	**1,514**	4.2	5	53	505	9.5	2
1989	16	250	915	3.7	7	40	423	10.6	2
1990	16	184	770	4.2	5	35	315	9.0	4
1991	15	198	825	4.2	10	33	204	6.2	0
1992	16	267	1,070	4.0	8	38	278	7.3	2
1993	16	174	746	4.3	1	75	610	8.1	3
1994	16	113	528	4.7	5	50	500	10.0	2
1995	16	31	126	4.1	0	31	234	7.5	1
1996	16	10	83	8.3	1	7	89	12.7	0
NFL Totals	171	1,948	8,205	4.2	61	498	4,710	9.5	19

Notes: Boldface indicates statistical leader. GP = games played; Car. = carries; Yds. = yards; Avg. = average yards per carry *or* average yards per reception; TD = touchdowns; Rec. = receptions

Continuing the Story

With Herschel in the backfield, Georgia's football team contended for the national championship for the next two seasons. In 1981, he rushed for 1,891 yards, the most ever by a sophomore, and finished second in the Heisman vote. In his junior year he scored 17 touchdowns, was a consensus All-American for the third year, and won the Heisman Trophy by a landslide vote.

In three years of collegiate football, Herschel set eleven NCAA records, sixteen Southeastern Conference records, and forty-two University of Georgia records. Yet Herschel always claimed to enjoy track more than football and there, too, he was a stand-out competitor. In the classroom, as a pre-law major with a specialty in criminal justice, he maintained a B average. He told of his desire to work with the Federal Bureau of Investigation once his sports career was over.

Shortly after winning the Heisman Trophy, Herschel was jogging on campus when he ran across a burning car. He ripped open the door and rescued the sixty-seven-year-old woman trapped inside. Not waiting for thanks, he finished his solitary run. No wonder the citizens of Athens remember him fondly.

Because he had negotiated with a professional team, the New Jersey Generals of the new United States Football League (USFL), in February, 1983, he lost his senior season of collegiate eligibility. After signing with the club, he went on to lead the first-year league in rushing with 1,812 yards.

That same year he married Cynthia De Angelis. The two met on the track team at the University of Georgia.

In 1985, the Dallas Cowboys gambled on the failure of the USFL and drafted Herschel. He eventually found himself on the same team with the man whose record he had broken in college, Tony Dorsett. In 1989, the Minnesota Vikings, anxious to acquire Herschel for their backfield, negotiated with Dallas for his services. His two seasons with the Vikings were disappointing ones, but Herschel continued to be a triple threat as a kickoff return man, a receiver, and a running back. When the Vikings went five games in 1990 without a loss, most analysts attributed it to Herschel's "having turned it up a notch."

In 1991 Herschel was still with the Vikings and rushed for 825 yards and 10 touchdowns on 198 carries. He spent the next three seasons, 1992-1994, with the Philadelphia Eagles. He had his best year with the Eagles in 1992, when he ran for 1,070 yards on 267 carries. Herschel spent 1995 with the New York Giants and 1996 with the Dallas Cowboys, retiring from professional football at the end of the 1996 season. In August, 2000, he was inducted into the College Football Hall of Fame.

HONORS AND AWARDS

1980	Camp Award
1980-82	Consensus All-American Consensus All-Southeastern Conference Team
1981	Sugar Bowl Game most valuable player
1982	Heisman Trophy Maxwell Award *Sporting News* College Football Player of the Year United Press International Southeastern Conference Offensive Player of the Year
1983, 1985	*Sporting News* USFL All-Star Team
1985	*Sporting News* USFL Player of the Year
1988-89	NFL Pro Bowl Team
2000	Inducted into College Football Hall of Fame

Summary

Herschel Walker captured the attention of the sports world with his dazzling career as a collegiate tailback. Ever modest, Herschel was one of the most popular sports figures in the nation, and many a young player dreams of someday exploding down the football field just as he did.

William V. Eiland

Additional Sources:

Bayless, Skip. "Pro Football." *Sports Illustrated* 85, no. 9 (August 26, 1996): 24-31.

Benagh, Jim. *Sports Great Herschel Walker.* Hillside, N.J.: Enslow, 1990.

Burchard, S. H. *Herschel Walker.* San Diego, Calif.: Harcourt Brace Jovanovich, 1984.

Lieber, Jill. "Throughout His Nine Seasons." *Sports Illustrated* 76, no. 26 (June 29, 1992): 26-29.

Prugh, Jeff. *Herschel Walker: From the Georgia Backwoods and the Heisman Trophy to the Pros.* New York: Random House, 1983.

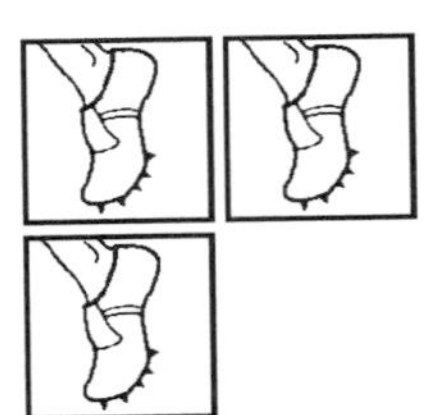

JOHN WALKER

Sport: Track and field (middle-distance runs)

Born: January 12, 1952
Papukura, North Island, New Zealand

Early Life

John Walker was born on January 12, 1952, in the village of Papukura, on the North Island of New Zealand.

As a teenager, John had the heavy build of a rugby player. At school, John loved to play tennis, participated in several other sports, and ran a bit of track, but despite the legion of New Zealand running heroes who had won Olympic gold medals, such as John Lovelock in 1936, Murray Halberg in 1960, and Peter Snell in 1960 and 1964, John's first love was tennis.

The Road to Excellence

One of the major reasons for John's successful career in track and field (nearly twenty years of running sub-4-minute miles) was that, as a teenager playing many sports, he did not experience physical exhaustion. His athletic versatility won over the intensive and demanding training required of athletes who specialize in a specific athletic activity.

Although New Zealand has a highly regarded university system, there is no such thing as intercollegiate athletic scholarships. Gifted athletes study at home or abroad and somehow balance academics and athletics in order to reach their athletic goals. They often find a job that can afford them some flexibility in time scheduling, or they manage to find another source of financial support to assist them.

In John's case, he worked as a salesman in radio advertising, and in the early 1970's, he gradually began increasing the intensity and the quality of his training. Although John was influenced by the exploits of triple-Olympic gold medalist Peter Snell and by the distance mileage philosophy of Snell's coach, Arthur Lydiard, John was primarily self-coached. He did not, however, ignore the advice and training ideas of coaches and athletes, including the advice of Herb Elliot's coach, Percy Cerutty. (Elliot was the Australian Olympic champion at 1,500 meters in 1960.) With John, however, a retrospective overview of his career charts an athlete who, while he sought much advice, essentially directed his own athletic fortunes.

Agence France Presse/Archive Photos

John Walker wins the 3,000-meter event during a meet in Paris in 1976.

John burst to prominence at the relatively advanced age of twenty-two at the 1974 Commonwealth Games, where he competed in the 1,500-meter event. Filbert Bayi of Tanzania stormed his way around the four laps of the race to set a new world record of 3 minutes 32.2 seconds. John, however, challenged Bayi all the way, and, at the finishing line, was only a couple of yards behind in second place. His time of 3 minutes 32.5 seconds also broke the former 1,500-meter world record, held by Jim Ryun of the United States.

The Emerging Champion

In many respects, 1975 was when John firmly established himself in the front ranks of distance runners. He came close to besting Bayi's 1,500-meter record of 3 minutes 32.2 seconds. His greatest moment may have been when he became the first man to run under 3 minutes 50 seconds for the 1 mile, with a time of 3 minutes 49.4 seconds. British track writer Mel Watman, in his *Encyclopedia of Track and Field Athletics* (1981), observed that this time was "exactly ten seconds faster than Roger Bannister's historic run [the first sub-4-minute mile] of 21 years earlier."

Not surprisingly, this performance garnered John much international acclaim, highlighted by the World Athlete of the Year awards of *Track and Field News* and *Athletics Weekly*.

By early 1976, the world track and field press was previewing what was felt would be the race of the century at the 1976 Montreal Olympics between Bayi of Tanzania and Walker of New Zealand.

John was in tremendous form prior to the Olympics. He set a world record for the 2,000 meters of 4 minutes 51.4 seconds. It should be stressed that world records are normally broken by a fraction of a second. In this case, John reduced the old world record by a whopping 4.8 seconds.

Sadly, the 1976 Olympics were plunged into disarray by a boycott of more than twenty African countries. The problem began when the New Zealand Rugby Football Union went ahead with a planned rugby tour to South Africa, which, at that time, was enforcing strict rules on apartheid. Many African countries, including Tanzania, protested this by boycotting the Montreal Olympics.

John was therefore unable to run against his great African rival. Nevertheless, his victory in the 1,500 meters with a time of 3 minutes 39.17 seconds should not be seen as a hollow one.

John's Olympic gold medal was a hard-earned victory that came after two years of high expectations buffeted by intense pressure. The time was the slowest since the 1956 Olympics, but that was just an indication of the tactics required to win such a race. Don Cameron in his *Memorable Moments in New Zealand Sport* commented that John "strode magnificently to the victory which so many people had waited for, and even demanded."

Continuing the Story

In 1980, John almost had a marvelous opportunity to take on Steve Ovett and Sebastian Coe of Great Britain in the final of the 1,500 meters, but another boycott impasse plagued the Olympics. On this occasion, because of the Soviet invasion of Afghanistan, the United States, supported by allies like New Zealand, refused to participate in the Olympics.

Following John's 1976 Olympic success, a career threatening leg injury in 1977 reduced the amount of training that John was able to carry out. By the 1980's, John had recovered remarkably well from this injury, but he was never able to subject his legs to the sort of demanding regimens that make the difference between competitive competence and sustained excellence.

What became amazing in the 1980's was that

STATISTICS

Year	Competition	Event	Place	Time
1974	Commonwealth Games	1,500 meters	Silver	3:32.5
	National AAU Indoor Championships	1 mile	Gold	4:01.6
1976	Olympic Games	1,500 meters	Gold	3:39.17
1983	World Championships	1,500 meters	9th	3:44.24
1984	Olympic Games	5,000 meters	8th	13:24.46
1986	Commonwealth Games	5,000 meters	5th	13:35.34
1990	Commonwealth Games	1,500 meters	12th	3:53.77

John still continued to run with the world's best. Although world records for 1 mile and 1,500 meters were denied him on many occasions, it was his presence in the field that added status and prestige to the race.

John made breaking the 4-minute mile seem almost as easy as a training run. John was a tough competitor who constantly challenged himself to give the rising new stars a "good run for their money."

As the 1980's waned, John and his rival Steve Scott, the fine American middle-distance runner, became the focus of attention, as the track and field world waited to see which one of them would become the first to complete one hundred 1-mile races at an average of under 4 minutes per mile. With each successive race, the media and the fans alike celebrated the performances of both athletes. John won that series handsomely, and although he struggled to run well in the 5,000 meters at the 1984 Los Angeles Olympics, he will always be remembered for his 1976 Olympic gold and for a track career in which he ran more top-quality 1-mile and 1,500-meter races than any other athlete in the history of track and field.

HONORS, AWARDS, AND RECORDS

1975	*Track and Field News* World Athlete of the Year
	Athletics Weekly World Athlete of the Year
	World Trophy
	First athlete in history to run a sub-3:50 miles (3:49.4) (the new world record)
1976	Set a world outdoor record at 2,000 meters (4:51.4)
1979	Set a U.S. indoor record at 1,500 meters (3:37.4)

Summary

John Walker's Olympic success in 1976 electrified the whole country and filled New Zealanders with a wonderful mixture of euphoria and national pride.

John, with his black running garb and bold silver fern on the tunic, promoted New Zealand and stood as a tough competitor to whom running was not simply a job or a way of life but an avocation.

John is now retired from full-time athletic competition and lives with his family in New Zealand. Intriguingly enough, the competitive fires still burn, and his sporting passion is breeding horses, training them, and driving a number of promising ones in harness racing.

Scott A. G. M. Crawford

Additional Sources:

Wallechinsky, David. *The Complete Book of the Olympics*. Boston: Little, Brown and Company, 1991.

Watman, Mel. *Encyclopedia of Track and Field Athletics*. New York: St. Martin's Press, 1981.

RUSTY WALLACE

Sport: Auto racing

Born: August 14, 1956
St. Louis, Missouri

Early Life

Russell William "Rusty" Wallace, Jr., was born on August 14, 1956, in St. Louis, into a family of stock car racers. Russ Wallace, Rusty's father, raced as a hobby into the late 1970's and won three St. Louis track championships. His mother, Judy Buckles Wallace, also occasionally raced and had a winning record. All three of the Wallace sons—Rusty, Mike, and Kenny—would participate in the top divisions of the National Association for Stock Car Auto Racing (NASCAR).

AP/Wide World Photos

Driver Rusty Wallace displays his trophy from a NASCAR exhibition race in 1996.

The Road to Excellence

On August 12, 1972, Rusty and his mother went to court to obtain an order to allow Rusty to begin racing cars. He was sixteen years old and therefore legally entitled to drive, but the local track required that competing drivers under eighteen years of age have a court order and release from their parents. Although Rusty had already been competing in go-kart racing and in motocross events for motorcycles, he was eager to race cars. Six days later, Rusty debuted at Lake Hills by winning his heat but, in his excitement, he forgot to fill the tank for the actual race and ran out of gas.

In their never-ending struggle to provide funds for their racing, Rusty and his brothers delivered newspapers and worked at the family's vacuum-cleaner shop. They then joined with Charlie Chase and Don Miller, who was a local representative for Penske Racing Products, and other friends to found the Poor Boy Chassis Company, which produced and sold race car chassis. The company's staff, deemed the "Evil Gang" by famed racer Bobby Allison, was made

MAJOR RACES AND CHAMPIONSHIPS

1972	First amateur stock car race and win
1980	First Winston Cup race
1983	American Speed Association Championship
1986	First Winston Cup wins
1989	Winston Cup Championship
2000	Fiftieth Winston Cup win

up of volunteers whose compensation was going to races and working on race cars.

The Emerging Champion

Rusty was racing full-time by his twenty-first birthday. In 1979 he chose to compete on the United States Auto Club (USAC) circuit because of its larger markets and the publicity generated by its renowned star, A. J. Foyt. That season Rusty was selected as Rookie of the Year.

On two levels, 1980 was a memorable and significant year for Rusty. First, he married his girlfriend, Patti Hall, on January 16. Second, at the urging of Don Miller, Rusty drove Roger Penske's car in the 1980 Winston Cup spring race at Atlanta. Though Rusty finished second, Penske opted to concentrate on his Indy car program the next year rather than run in NASCAR. Rusty returned to competing on other circuits and won the American Speed Association championship in 1983 with three first-place and fourteen top-ten finishes.

Cliff Stewart, a longtime Winston Cup car owner, hired Rusty to drive his car in 1984. The rookie received a salary of $40,000 and 40 percent of his winnings—his first salary since his days in the vacuum-cleaner shop. Though it was not a wholly successful year, Rusty finished fourteenth in the Winston Cup championship points standing and earned Rookie of the Year honors. However, the relationship between Stewart and Rusty deteriorated as the team struggled the next year.

As a result, Rusty moved to Raymond Beadle's Blue Max racing operation for the 1986 season. The fifth race of the season was at Bristol, Tennessee, and it was there that Rusty recorded his first Winston Cup victory. The win solidified his racing reputation and caused his popularity with fans—and sponsors—to surge. He followed this with another win at Martinsville, Virginia, sixteen top-ten finishes, and more than $500,000 in prize money to end the year in sixth position in the points standings.

He won twice in 1987 and led the points race briefly in the 1988 season; however, at a practice run at Bristol Motor Speedway, the right front tire on the car blew, causing the car to flip five times. Rusty, unconscious and not breathing, was resuscitated. Though the crash cost him the championship, he was left with only severe bruises and a major headache.

In 1989 Rusty achieved the pinnacle of stock-car racing success, the Winston Cup Championship. He said, "In 1989, we made the decision to win," and the team did so despite its precarious financial situation, which led to bounced payroll checks, difficulty in obtaining needed supplies, and constant duns from creditors. Rusty filed a lawsuit against Beadle to obtain back pay and release from his contract. The suit was eventually settled, with Rusty agreeing to race for Blue Max the next year. Despite the continuing turmoil, Rusty was able to win five times during the season to clinch the championship.

Continuing the Story

At Blue Max, 1990 was not a good year for Rusty; two wins were offset by six incomplete races and continuing financial problems, even though the Miller Brewing Company sponsored the team. Rusty, his old friend Don Miller, and Penske formed a new partnership, Penske Racing South, for the 1991 season. Momentum for success began to build over the next few years despite spectacular and frightening crashes in 1993 at Daytona and Talledega. Crashes notwithstanding, Rusty won ten races in 1993, eight in 1994, two in 1995, five in 1996, one in 1997, one in 1998, and one in 1999, leading to his fiftieth Winston Cup win in 2000 at Bristol, the site of his first Winston Cup victory.

HONORS AND AWARDS

1973	Central Auto Racing Association Rookie of the Year
1979	U.S. Auto Club Rookie of the Year Award
1984	Winston Cup Rookie of the Year
1988, 1993	NMPA Driver of the Year
1998	Inducted into Missouri Sports Hall of Fame

Summary

In the interim between his first and fiftieth wins, Rusty Wallace posted victories each year, establishing one of the longest winning streaks among NASCAR drivers, and earned over $21 million in prize money in twenty-one years of Winston Cup racing. His unquenchable desire to compete and tenacious pursuit of speed guided him to victory in various types and levels of auto racing, contributed to the growth of his sport, and led him to the zenith of his profession.

Susan Coleman

Additional Sources:

Mello, Tara Baukus. *Rusty Wallace.* Philadelphia, Pa.: Chelsea House, 2000.

White, Ben. *Rusty Wallace: Stats and Standings.* Phoenix, Ariz.: Futech Interactive Products, 1999.

Zeller, Bob, and Rusty Wallace. *Rusty Wallace: The Decision to Win.* Phoenix, Ariz.: David Bull Publishing, 1999.

BOBBY WALTHOUR

Sport: Cycling

Born: January 1, 1878
Walthourville, Georgia
Died: September 2, 1949
Boston, Massachusetts

Early Life

Robert (Bobby) Walthour was born on the first day of January, 1878, in Walthourville, Georgia. His birthplace was named after his grandfather, William L. Walthour, a famous general in the Civil War. Bobby's family heritage was clearly of the Southern aristocracy, but following the Civil War his grandfather's vast landholdings were confiscated for tax reasons. Consequently, the family's wealth did not transfer into his grandson's hands.

Bobby was one of nine children. His childhood was not much different from that of youngsters in other rural families then: plenty of religion, homegrown food, daily chores, and a good deal of neighborhood play.

What did somewhat separate Bobby from his playmates was his attraction to the newest sporting sensation of the nineteenth century: the bicycle. Even though it was cumbersome and hard to ride, Bobby mastered riding solo on this new-

Library of Congress

fangled contraption by the time he was three years old. From the very beginning, he was destined to ride.

The Road to Excellence

Before he was fifteen, Bobby was drawn to the world of bicycle racing. He set out for Atlanta, Georgia, the southern center of cycling competition. There he landed a job as a bicycle messenger to support himself while he began his self-coached competitive training.

At the first opportunity he entered a local race. He competed in the boys' event and the five men's events, and won them all. For the next two years Bobby raced throughout the South, winning the Georgia and the southern sprint titles in the same year. His fame began to spread.

While racing in Birmingham, Alabama, Bobby met a young girl named Daisy Blanche Bailey. As the story goes, Bobby and Daisy, both underaged, were determined to tie the knot. One night they eloped, pedaling their way on a two-seater bicycle into a rural community, where they convinced the village parson to perform the ceremony. The press picked up the romantic story, as did the poets. In turn, the poets inspired the song-writers, and the world was given the famous song, "On a Bicycle Built for Two."

By the turn of the century, Bobby had begun to scrape out a meager living as a professional bicycle racer. To become really successful in the sport, Bobby had to prove himself up north in places like Newark, New Jersey, and New York City, where racers from all over the world competed against each other.

The Emerging Champion

Up north, Bobby was successful enough at the short sprints, but what caught his attention were two other forms of racing: the six-day indoor endurance races and the newest of the racing events, motor-paced racing.

In Boston he won a ten-hour individual event that helped him qualify for the six-day race at New York's Madison Square Garden. In these races, the riders competed in teams of two. One of the two riders had to be on the track every minute of the twenty-four-hour-day, six-day week. With his teammate Archie McEachern, Bobby won his first six-day race.

HONORS, AWARDS, AND MILESTONES

1901, 1903	New York Six-Day Indoor Cycling Co-Champion
1902-03	Professional Motor-Paced Cycling U.S. Champion
1904-05	Professional Motor-Paced Cycling World Champion
1932	Named one of Georgia's three greatest athletes
1989	Inducted into U.S. Bicycling Hall of Fame

What especially attracted Bobby was motor-paced racing, in which the cyclist rode a few inches behind a huge, powerful motorcycle. The motors, as they were called, gave the riders windshields and a constant pace. Rider and motor, almost touching, whizzed around small, banked, oval tracks at speeds from thirty to fifty miles per hour.

Bobby's physical and mental toughness combined to make him the top U.S. motor-paced racer by the time he was twenty-four years old. He was invited to Europe to compete for the world championship title. He won sixteen of seventeen starts in 1904 and won the world championship, a 62.5-mile event, in London that year. He repeated as world champion in 1905. Bobby, the Dixie Flyer, without question was becoming the premier motor-paced racer of his day.

Continuing the Story

Motor-paced racing was extremely dangerous. If the motor broke a chain or blew a tire, the bicycle racer crashed directly into the back of the motor. If the cyclist went down on the track because of a collision or a flat tire on his own bike, there was the danger of being run over by the other motors or cyclists.

During his some twenty years of racing, Bobby had broken almost every bone in his body at one time or another. He broke his collarbone twenty-nine times. He was twice pronounced "dead" by doctors after track smashups. A number of his racing friends were killed during these races. Bobby's broken bones, stitches, and scars never proved fatal.

Bobby was a captain in the Army during World War I, serving as the secretary to the Young Men's Christian Association division in France. He raced for a few years after the war, mainly in Europe, eventually giving up competition after a nasty track accident in the late 1920's. The Germans had confiscated his racing winnings and personal savings during the war. When he finally returned to the United States in the 1930's, he took up work with a New York sporting goods company, and, later, he worked in Boston for an automobile magazine publisher. Bobby contracted cancer in 1949 and died of pneumonia later that year at the age of seventy-one.

Summary

For the first two decades of the twentieth century, Bobby Walthour was the world's most famous motor-paced cyclist. At a celebration given in his honor in Atlanta in 1932, Bobby was ranked with baseball star Ty Cobb and golfer Bobby Jones as one of the three greatest athletes to come out of Georgia. His world championships and his inspirational, record- and bone-breaking rides, made him one of the greatest and hardiest racing cyclists the sport has ever had. It is generally agreed that Bobby Walthour was to cycling what Babe Ruth was to baseball.

William Harper

Additional Sources:

Hickok, Ralph. *A Who's Who of Sports Champions.* Boston: Houghton Mifflin, 1995.

Nye, Peter. *Hearts of Lions: The History of American Bicycle Racing.* New York: W. W. Norton, 1988.

BILL WALTON

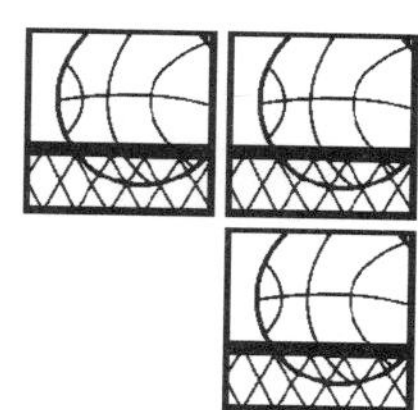

Sport: Basketball

Born: November 5, 1952
La Mesa, California

Early Life

William Theodore Walton III was born on November 5, 1952, in La Mesa, California, a suburb of San Diego. He was the second child of William Theodore II and Gloria Walton. The Walton children were encouraged to be active in a variety of interests, including sports and music. Bill played baritone horn at the family musicales.

Bill was sent to Blessed Sacrament School in San Diego, as were the rest of the Walton children. He played both basketball and football at the parochial school and excelled as a ball handler on the basketball team. Bill was the team's center when it was on defense and its guard when it switched to offense.

The Road to Excellence

Bill went to Helix High School in San Diego. His older brother, Bruce, also attended and was a member of the basketball team. Bruce was 6 feet 5 inches tall and weighed 285 pounds, and took it upon himself to protect his younger brother. By his junior year at Helix, Bill had grown to 6 feet 7 inches in height but weighed only 185 pounds. Because he was so slender, Bill tended to tire easily and was bullied by opposing players. His bulkier brother made sure that opposing players did not push his brother around; he did this by elbowing anyone who tried to take advantage of Bill.

During his senior year, Bill was heavier and learned how to pace himself. He led Helix to a 33-0 record by averaging 29 points and 24 rebounds a game. Many colleges wanted Bill to attend, but he finally chose the University of California at Los Angeles (UCLA).

Bill Walton in 1973, when he played for UCLA.

A remarkable basketball tradition had already been established at UCLA under the legendary coach John Wooden, and Bill wanted to be a part of the winning tradition. He was also going to be filling the void left by the departure of Lew Alcindor (Kareem Abdul-Jabbar). Because freshmen were not allowed to play on the varsity squad, Bill had to wait until his sophomore year before he could compete for the national championship with the UCLA Bruins. The Bruins, with Bill at center and standing 6 feet 11 inches tall, went undefeated for the entire year and won the National Collegiate Athletic Association (NCAA) championship. Coach Wooden was proud of Bill's determination and willingness to put the team first. Even with being a team player, he averaged 21.1 points and 15 rebounds per game.

The Bruins were no less powerful during Bill's junior year, as they compiled another 30-0 record and another NCAA championship. UCLA won an amazing eighty-eight games in a row before losing in January, 1974, to the University of Notre Dame. The only year that Bill did not lead the Bruins to the national championship was his senior year, when they were upset in the semifinals by the eventual champions, North Carolina State. During his three seasons at UCLA, Bill was named an All-American and Player of the Year. Among his many awards was the 1973 James E. Sullivan Memorial Award as the nation's premier amateur athlete.

The Emerging Champion

Bill was drafted by the Portland Trail Blazers in 1974. He signed a five-year contract that was worth close to $3,000,000. Expectations ran high in Portland for their new center from UCLA.

Coach Wooden knew how to bring out the best in Bill, but the situation in the professional ranks was considerably different. At UCLA, Bill had been active in antiwar activities and was part of what has been termed the "counter-culture." He was able to fit in at the collegiate level, but Bill found resistance to his radical politics in Portland. Bill was a determined individual and willing to stand on his principles, and the first couple of seasons with the Trail Blazers were rocky at best. He had a number of health problems that also made the situation in Portland difficult. During his first season, Bill lost fifteen pounds, suffered a dislocated finger, had a bone spur on his left ankle, and was hobbled by tendinitis in his knees. All these factors forced Bill to miss more than half of his first season.

The Trail Blazers finished in third place in the Pacific Division of the NBA's Western Conference in Bill's first year, but dropped to fifth place in his second. He was criticized as not being able to play through his injuries. His third season, however, was a complete reversal of the previous two. Bill had been a vegetarian since his college days and was no less a radical, but he was healthier than he had been in some time.

Bill was elected team captain, and a bond was created between himself and his teammates. The Trail Blazers were now a unit. A major factor was

NCAA DIVISION I RECORDS

Highest field goal percentage in NCAA Tournament play, .686
Highest field goal percentage in one NCAA Tournament, .763 (1973)

NBA RECORDS

Most blocked shots in an NBA Finals game, 8 (1977)

HONORS AND AWARDS

1972-73	NCAA Tournament Most Outstanding Player Rupp Trophy
1972-74	United Press International Division I Player of the Year U.S. Basketball Writers Association Division I Player of the Year Naismith Award *Sporting News* College Player of the Year Citizens Savings College Basketball Player of the Year (1974 co-recipient) NCAA All-Tournament Team Consensus All-American
1973	Sullivan Award
1974	Lapchick Award Overall first choice in the NBA draft
1977	NBA Finals most valuable player
1977-78	NBA All-Star Team All-NBA Team NBA All-Defensive Team
1978	NBA most valuable player
1986	NBA Sixth Man Award
1993	Inducted into Naismith Memorial Basketball Hall of Fame
1996	NBA 50 Greatest Players of All Time Team
1997	Inducted into National High School Sports Hall of Fame
1999	Silver Anniversary Award Uniform number 32 retired by Portland Trail Blazers

STATISTICS

Season	GP	FGM	FG%	FTM	FT%	Reb.	Ast.	TP	PPG
1974-75	35	177	.513	94	.686	441	167	448	12.8
1975-76	51	345	.471	133	.583	681	220	823	16.1
1976-77	65	491	.528	228	.697	934	245	1,210	18.6
1977-78	58	460	.522	177	.720	766	291	1,097	18.9
1979-80	14	81	.503	32	.593	126	34	194	13.9
1982-83	33	200	.528	65	.556	323	120	465	14.1
1983-84	55	288	.556	92	.597	477	183	668	12.1
1984-85	67	269	.521	138	.680	600	156	676	10.1
1985-86	80	231	.562	144	.713	544	165	606	7.6
1986-87	10	10	.385	8	.533	31	9	28	2.8
Totals	468	2,552	.521	1,111	.660	4,923	1,590	6,215	13.3

Notes: GP = games played; FGM = field goals made; FG% = field goal percentage; FTM = free throws made; FT% = free throw percentage; Reb. = rebounds; Ast. = assists; TP = total points; PPG = points per game

the addition of Jack Ramsay as Portland's new coach. Ramsay was convinced that Bill was an asset and not a liability, and Ramsay believed in the team concept, where unselfish play was rewarded. The 1976-1977 season became the Trail Blazers' dream season. With a speeded-up form of play that looked for fast breaks at every opportunity. Portland finished the year by defeating the Philadelphia 76ers for the NBA championship.

Continuing the Story

Besides winning the championship in the 1976-1977 season, Bill was named most valuable player for the playoffs. During the regular season, he averaged 14.4 rebounds, 18.6 points, and 3.2 blocked shots per game. Bill increased these statistics in the playoffs to 15.2 rebounds, 18.2 points, and 3.4 blocked shots average per game for the nineteen games.

Injuries once again hampered Bill's contribution to the team for the next season. Even worse, he was forced to miss the entire 1978-1979 season because of chronic injuries. Bill was traded to the San Diego Clippers in the spring of 1979. Once again, he was criticized for not living up to his potential. He occasionally showed glimpses of outstanding play, but for the most part the spark seemed to be gone. Bill was so frustrated by his nagging injuries that he brought suit against the Trail Blazers, claiming that their insistence that he play, even with a serious injury, led to his being permanently injured.

During the 1979-1980 season, Bill cut his hair, trimmed his beard, began eating meat again, and tried to mend fences with the media. In 1981, he underwent radical surgery to restructure his badly injured left foot. During his time off, he attended Stanford Law School. The operation worked, allowing Bill to play again and to help the Clippers improve in the 1983-1984 and 1984-1985 campaigns.

The Clippers finally traded Bill in 1985 to the Boston Celtics. This move was his chance to make a contribution to a team that had a proven winning tradition. Bill helped the Celtics win the NBA title for 1985-1986 in the role of a reserve. He had found new life coming off the bench as the crafty veteran and was immensely happy to win the NBA Sixth Man Award. It was to be his last opportunity to be an NBA champion.

During the next two seasons, Bill was crippled by a painful foot injury, missing the entire 1987-1988 season. During his thirteen years in the NBA, Bill had managed to play in only 44 percent of the games during the regular season and ended his career with a modest 13.3 scoring average. In 1990, he had major surgery on his ankles for the third time. This time his ankle bones were fused and, therefore, the ankles could no longer flex. For the first time in many years, Bill no longer suffered from chronic pain.

Bill continued to stay close to basketball by working as a broadcaster. In 1990, he was an NBA analyst for the Prime Ticket Network. He served as a color commentator for the National Broadcasting Corporation (NBC) on NBA television games during the 1990's. Bill has also been a commentator and color analyst for the Turner Sports Network, the Fox Sports Network, and MSNBC. In 1992, 1993, 1995, 1996, 1998, 1999, and 2000, Bill received the Best Television Analyst/Commentator award from the Southern California Sports Broadcasters Association.

In 1991, Bill received the NBA Players Association Oscar Robertson Leadership Award. He received the prestigious honor of being inducted into the Naismith Basketball Hall of Fame in 1993. As part of the celebration of the golden anniversary of the NBA during the 1996-1997 season, he was selected as a member of the NBA's 50 Greatest Players of All Time Team. In 1997, Bill was inducted into the National High School Sports Hall of Fame. The National Collegiate Athletic Association honored Bill in 1999 with the Silver Anniversary Award for having made significant professional and civic contributions since completing his collegiate eligibility twenty-five years earlier.

Bill received an Emmy Award in 1979 for his work on an environmental documentary filmed in the Philippines. In 1995 and 1996, he was nominated for an Emmy Award for his television broadcasting work. Bill has had roles in such movies as *He Got Game* (1998), *Forget Paris* (1995), *Celtic Pride* (1996), and *Ghostbusters* (1984). He has also appeared on numerous television programs and has done a number of television commercials. He continued to stay active as a commentator and analyst on NBC professional and collegiate basketball games, as well as on broadcasts for the Los Angeles Clippers.

Summary

Bill Walton was one of the most intelligent and flexible "Big Men" basketball has ever known. Always a rebel who rubbed the establishment the wrong way, he could change the course of a game by his all-around play and unselfishness. Under the proper coaching of John Wooden and Jack Ramsay, Bill blossomed into a basketball player with a major impact. It is sad that injuries and circumstances cut short his professional career.

Michael Jeffrys

Additional Sources:

Mallozzi, Vincent M. *Basketball: The Legends and the Game.* Willowdale, Ont.: Firefly Books, 1998.

Sachare, Alex. *One Hundred Greatest Basketball Players of All Time.* New York: Simon and Schuster, 1997.

Scott, Jack. *Bill Walton: On the Road with the Portland Trail Blazers.* New York: Crowell, 1978.

CHARLIE WARD

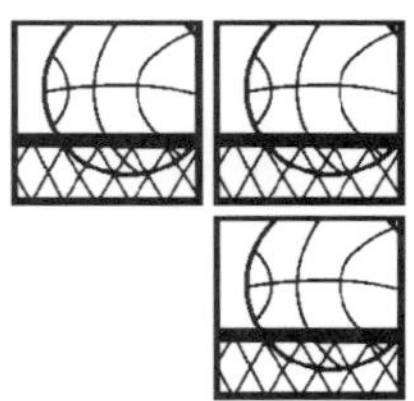

Sport: Basketball

Born: October 12, 1970
Thomasville, Georgia

Early Life

Charlie Ward was born October 12, 1970, in Thomasville, Georgia. Both of Charlie's parents were teachers. They brought him up with a strong commitment to Christianity and the desire to excel at all sports. He attended community college in Tallahassee, Florida, then Florida State University, where he won the Heisman Trophy in 1993, with 91 percent of the first-place votes, a record. He was the first African American quarterback to win the Heisman.

The Road to Excellence

In 1993 he was also named to the College All-America First Team by the *Sporting News*, while leading the Florida State Seminoles to a national championship. As a senior, Charlie threw for 3,032 yards and 27 touchdowns, completing 69.5 percent of his passes, as opposed to only 4 interceptions.

He earned a degree in Therapeutic Recreation from Florida State University, graduating with a 3.3 grade point average. Charlie was also part of the Arthur Ashe AIDS Tennis Challenge prior to the outset of the 1994 U.S. Open tournament. Despite his never having played college baseball, both the Milwaukee Brewers and the New York Yankees selected him in the baseball draft.

When Charlie was not picked in the first round of the National Football League (NFL) draft, he knew he could command a much higher salary going into the National Basketball Association (NBA). After Bill emerged as the most valuable player (MVP) of the New York summer basketball league, the New York Knicks

AP/Wide World Photos

New York Knick Charlie Ward dribbles in a 2001 game against the Washington Wizards.

drafted him the next year, as their first-round pick.

The Emerging Champion

In 1994-1995, his rookie season, Charlie appeared in only ten games for the Knicks, averaging 1.6 points in 4.4 minutes per game. He missed the first half of December with a sprained right wrist, and a sore left shoulder caused him to miss a month. Charlie was not on the Knicks' postseason roster as they advanced to the conference semifinals before losing to the Indiana Pacers in seven games.

The next season Charlie raised his playing time to 62 games, playing point guard, backing up teammate Derek Harper. He averaged 12.7 minutes per game, but the arrival of veteran Gary Grant in November, 1995, cut into his playing time. Charlie played in seven of eight postseason games with the Knicks, averaging 4.6 points and 2.4 assists in 13.1 minutes per game. The Knicks would eventually lose to the Chicago Bulls in the Eastern Conference finals.

Continuing the Story

At the start of the 1996-1997 season, his third in the NBA, Charlie continued to be the Knicks' backup point guard, this time playing behind Chris Childs. Charlie started in twenty-one games, seventeen of which the Knicks won. Charlie averaged 6 assists, ranking second on the team, but did not play as many minutes as in his first two seasons combined. He played in nine playoff games but the Knicks once again lost, this time to the Miami Heat in seven games in the second round.

FOOTBALL HONORS

1993 Heisman Trophy
Sullivan Award
Maxwell Award

Charlie really came into his own as one of the top basketball players in the NBA during the 1997-1998 season. He started in all eighty-two regular-season games. He led the Knicks in assists, at 5.7 per game—ranking seventeenth in the NBA—and steals, at 1.7 per game. He also reached his personal best scoring average of 7.8 points per game. His 466 total assists set a team record for the Knicks. Charlie participated in the AT&T Shootout during the All-Star weekend that took place in New York City and finished fourth; the Utah Jazz's Jeff Hornacek took first place. The Knicks lost to the Indiana Pacers in the semifinal round of the playoffs.

Charlie and teammate Allan Houston were the only players to start all fifty games for the Knicks in the strike-shortened 1998-1999 season. Charlie led the team in assists at 5.4 per game, which was tied for twenty-first rank in the NBA, and in steals at 2.1 per game, tied for tenth place in the NBA. He played an average of 31.1 minutes per game, a career high for Charlie, and was a major part of the Knicks' surprise run to the NBA finals.

Charlie started at point guard again in the 1999-2000 season and came through for the Knicks in the playoffs. Against the Miami Heat, Charlie averaged 12.7 points in the first four games. He scored a career playoff-high 20 points

PRO BASKETBALL STATISTICS

Season	*GP*	*FGA*	*FGM*	*FG%*	*FTA*	*FTM*	*FT%*	*Reb.*	*Ast.*	*TP*	*PPG*
1994-95	10	19	4	.211	10	7	.700	6	4	16	1.6
1995-96	62	218	87	.399	54	37	.685	102	132	244	3.9
1996-97	79	337	133	.395	125	95	.760	220	326	409	5.2
1997-98	82	516	235	.455	113	91	.805	274	466	642	7.8
1998-99	50	334	135	.404	78	55	.705	172	271	378	7.6
1999-00	72	447	189	.423	58	48	.828	228	300	528	7.3
2000-01	61	373	155	.416	70	56	.800	159	273	433	7.1
Totals	416	2,244	938	.418	508	389	.766	1,161	1,772	2,650	6.4

Notes: GP = games played; FGA = field goals attempted; FGM = field goals made; FG% = field goal percentage; FTA = free throws attempted; FTM = free throws made; FT% = free throw percentage; Reb. = rebounds; Ast. = assists; TP = total points; PPG = points per game

in a game 4 win that evened the series at two games apiece. The Knicks would later win the series in seven games. The Knicks' coach, Jeff Van Gundy, considered Charlie the team MVP in the playoffs.

Summary

Charlie Ward is one of the best college football players ever to play in the NBA. As a quarterback at Florida State, he led the Florida State Seminoles to a national title in 1993 and won numerous awards, including the Heisman Trophy, the Sullivan Award, and the Maxwell Award. Charlie is well known for spending time in the off-season with such community services as youth basketball camps.

Richard Slapsys

Additional Sources:

Lupica, Mike. "Eyes On The Prize." *Esquire* 121, no. 3 (March, 1994): 61-62.

Murphy, A. "Twice Blessed." *Sports Illustrated* 77 (October 5, 1992): 32-35.

Ward, Charlie, and Joe Cooney. *Charlie Ward: Winning by His Grace.* Laguna Hills, Calif.: Sports Publishing, 1998.

PAUL WARFIELD

Sport: Football

Born: November 28, 1942
Warren, Ohio

Early Life

Paul Warfield was born on November 28, 1942, in Warren, Ohio. His football playing days started in grammar school. It was there, while playing in the touch football league for youngsters, that Paul started to refine a craft that would carry him all the way to the Pro Football Hall of Fame.

The Road to Excellence

Many obstacles lay in the road for Paul, with one of the bigger ones being his weight. In junior high school, Paul weighted only 95 pounds, and his mother, worried about injuries, refused to let him play football. He had to wait until he was a freshman in high school before he got his first opportunity to let people see what he could do. His abilities won him a place on the team as a starter, and he became a star as a swift running back. The door to further success was opening wider as his talents were honed. Colleges from all across the land were offering scholarships to Paul. In all, more than seventy schools tried to lure him to their campuses. Finally, after talking to two older, local kids, Paul decided to attend Ohio State University.

Courtesy of Amateur Athletic Foundation of Los Angeles

Nothing would come easily to Paul. His football coach at Ohio State, the legendary Woody Hayes, liked to play power football and was not ready to change his offense to a breakaway game that suited Warfield. Paul did, however, make the All-Big Ten Conference team on two separate occasions, mainly due to his fine blocking ability. More often than not, Paul was a decoy. Opposing teams knew of his speed and running ability, so they spent manpower and effort trying to cover him.

This coverage led to many scoring opportunities for the rest of the squad.

At Ohio State Paul was also part of the track team. He ran hurdles and competed in the long jump. Paul's jumping ability was so strong that he had to choose between a professional football contract or remaining an amateur and trying out for the Olympic Games. Neither the Cleveland Browns of the National Football League (NFL) nor the Buffalo Bills of the American Football League (AFL) would guarantee their contract offers, so young Warfield, concerned about his long-term future, signed with the Browns.

The Emerging Champion

Cleveland drafted Paul with the hope of making him a defensive back but quickly gave up that idea when it became evident that Paul could run and catch as few had before him. The team was short-staffed in the area of talented flankers. Paul turned out to be just the right pick. He made the Pro Bowl team in his very first season by catching 52 passes and scoring 9 touchdowns. He would go on to make the All-Pro team in two of six seasons with Cleveland. He also participated in four NFL Championships. The Browns won in 1964 against the Baltimore Colts but lost the Championship game in 1965 and the Championship Playoffs in 1968 and 1969.

After the 1969 season, Paul was traded by the Browns to the then-lowly Miami Dolphins. He had to convince himself that the trade was not an indication of his talents. He decided to view the transaction as a positive move in his career. Paul was more concerned about the move his family would have to make but, like a truly dedicated professional, Paul moved with his family from Cleveland to Miami, where greater glory awaited.

STATISTICS

Season	GP	Rec.	Yds.	Avg.	TD
1964	14	52	920	17.7	9
1965	1	3	30	10.0	0
1966	14	36	741	20.6	5
1967	14	32	702	21.9	8
1968	14	50	1,067	21.3	**12**
1969	14	42	886	21.1	10
1970	11	28	703	25.1	6
1971	14	43	996	23.2	**11**
1972	12	29	606	20.9	3
1973	14	29	514	17.7	11
1974	9	27	536	19.9	2
1976	14	38	613	16.1	6
1977	12	18	251	13.9	2
Totals	167	452	8,987	19.9	88

Notes: Boldface indicates statistical leader. GP = games played; Rec. = receptions; Yds. = yards; Avg. = average yards per reception; TD = touchdowns

HONORS AND AWARDS

1962-63	All-Big Ten Conference Team
1963	College All-American
1964	*Sporting News* NFL Eastern Division All-Star Team
1965, 1969-75	NFL Pro Bowl Team
1968-69, 1971-73	NFL All-Pro Team
1970-73	*Sporting News* AFC All-Star Team
1980	NFL All-Pro Team of the 1970's
1983	Inducted into Pro Football Hall of Fame
1985	AFL-NFL 1960-1984 All-Star Team

Continuing the Story

In his five years with Miami, the team appeared in the playoffs five times. Paul made All-Pro three times and played on two Super Bowl Championship teams. When his contract expired following the 1974 season, Paul signed on with the Memphis Southmen of the new World Football League (WFL). He played there for only one injury-filled season before returning to Cleveland and the NFL. Finally, after the 1977 season, Paul retired. He was ready for a new life after his playing days were over. He had university degrees from Ohio State University and Kent State University to help prepare him for a career in radio and television. The call of football, however, was still strong and Paul decided to accept a job with the Cleveland Browns as assistant to the president. In 1981, he became director of player relations. In 1983, his first year of eligibility, Paul was elected to the Pro Football Hall of Fame. He has worked as a football consultant with teams such as the Dallas Cowboys. In 1999 he was given the title of independent wide receiver consultant. He has spent his time helping the Cowboys scout free agents and has had weekly conversations with the Cowboy's owner about the state of the Dallas passing game.

Summary

Paul Warfield's career was filled with stellar performances. His records for passes caught, yards per catch, and total yards gained are near the top of the list of all receivers who have ever played the game. While Paul seemed to be a quiet, unemotional player, his actions on the field spoke loudly. He had the respect of his teammates. Whether he caught 10 passes in a game or was a decoy so that others could do their jobs better did not really matter to Paul. He was a team player who wanted to win, whatever the cost. His ability to perform at such a high level significantly helped every team for which he played. His championship seasons attest to that fact.

Carmi Brandis

Additional Sources:

Devaney, John. *Star Pass Receivers of the NFL*. New York: Random House, 1972.

Fleming, David. "Inside the NFL." *Sports Illustrated* 91, no. 18 (November 8, 1999): 100-101.

King, Peter. "Inside the NFL: 1925-1975." *Sports Illustrated* 83, no. 14 (October 2, 1995): 63-65.

CORNELIUS WARMERDAM

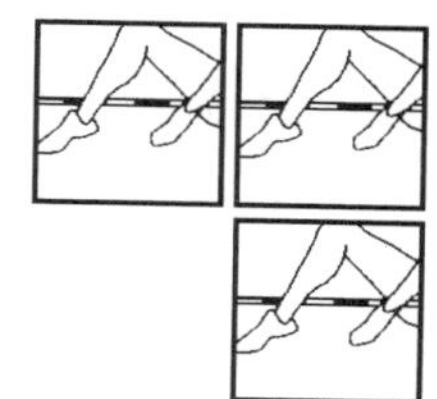

Sport: Track and field (pole vault)

Born: June 22, 1915
Long Beach, California

Early Life

The son of Dutch immigrants, Cornelius Warmerdam was born in Long Beach, California, on June 22, 1915. While still a young child, Cornelius, with his family, moved to a farm near Hanford in California's San Joaquin Valley. As a senior at Hanford High School, Cornelius pole vaulted 12 feet 3 inches, placing third in the state. In 1933 a traveling salesman observed him vaulting 13 feet in a spinach field and recommended him to the track coach at nearby Fresno State College, later known as the California State University, Fresno. The coach there convinced Cornelius to enroll at Fresno State, where, after he graduated in 1938, he became a teacher.

The Road to Excellence

While a student at Fresno State, Cornelius vaulted an impressive 14 feet 1¾ inches. He first won the United States vaulting championship in 1937. That year, William Sefton and Earl Meadows, known as the "Heavenly Twins," had both achieved a world record height of 14 feet 10¾ inches, but no vaulter had broken the long-sought 15-foot barrier.

The Emerging Champion

Standing about 6 feet tall and weighing approximately 170 pounds, Cornelius established his first world record in the pole vault in a track and field meet in Berkeley, California, on April 13, 1940, when he vaulted 14 feet 11⅞ inches. Several months later, in Fresno, he became the first to break the 15-foot mark with a vault of 15 feet 1⅛ inches. In 1941 he set a new world record—three times. He vaulted 15 feet 2⅝ inches and followed that with a vault of 15 feet 4¼ inches. In Compton, California, on June 26, 1941, he leaped over the bar at 15 feet 5¾ inches.

The following year, 1942, he raised the world record twice, first to 15 feet 6⅛ inches and then on May 23, 1942, in Modesto, California, Cornelius vaulted 15 feet 7¾ inches. It was not until 1951 that another pole vaulter, the Reverend

AP/Wide World Photos

WORLD POLE VAULT RECORDS SET

Date	Location	Height
Apr. 13, 1940	Berkeley, Calif.	15′
June 29, 1940	Fresno, Calif.	15′ 1⅛″
Apr. 12, 1941	Stanford, Calif.	15′ 2⅝″
June 6, 1941	Compton, Calif.	15′ 4¼″
June 26, 1941	Compton, Calif.	15′ 5¾″
May 2, 1942	Berkeley, Calif.	15′ 6⅛″
May 23, 1942	Modesto, Calif.	15′ 7¾″

Bob Richards, was even able to negotiate 15 feet. The world mark Cornelius established at Modesto stood for almost fifteen years before it was broken by Occidental College's Robert Gutowski.

Indoor competition was equally rewarding for Cornelius. He broke the indoor record for the pole vault on February 7, 1942, before a crowd of seventeen thousand at the Millrose Games in New York's Madison Square Garden. His favorite vaulting pole had been delayed in transit from the West Coast, and he was forced to resort to a borrowed pole, shorter than he generally used, but he still vaulted 15 feet ⅜ inch. In 1943, in Chicago, he established an indoor record with a vault of 15 feet 8½ inches. All in all, he made forty-three successful vaults over 15 feet during his athletic career.

Cornelius became widely known by his nickname, "the Flying Dutchman." In 1942 he was the recipient of the Amateur Athletic Union's prestigious Sullivan Award, given to the athlete "who by his or her performance, example and influence as an amateur, has done the most during the year to advance the cause of sportsmanship."

Continuing the Story

In addition to winning the Sullivan award, Cornelius was elected to the National Track and Field Hall of Fame when it was established in 1974. One honor he did not achieve was an Olympic gold medal. Like many athletess, he was not able to compete in 1940 or 1944, as no Olympics Games were held during World War II.

Cornelius served in the United States Navy during the war. He retired from vaulting competition in 1946 at the age of thirty-one, becoming an assistant track coach at Stanford University, where he earned a master's degree. He thus did not compete in the 1948 Olympic Games in London, where American Guinn Smith's winning pole vault measured 14 feet 1¼ inches, a height Cornelius probably could have surpassed.

He returned to Fresno State College as the head track coach, a position he held for many years, and led the Fresno State Bulldogs to the National Collegiate Athletic Association Division II track and field championship in 1964. Cornelius retired as professor of physical education in 1980 after thirty-three years of coaching and teaching at his alma mater. He and his wife had five children, four sons and a daughter, but none of them followed his path to athletic greatness.

Summary

In time, Cornelius Warmerdam's numerous 15-foot vaults seemed to pale when compared to the 20-foot vaults of Russia's Sergei Bubka, and by the end of the twentieth century women vaulters had broken the once-formidable 15-foot barrier. Whereas Cornelius and his contemporaries used bamboo poles in their vaulting efforts, Bob Gutowski broke Cornelius's outdoor record in 1957 using an aluminum pole, which was soon to be superceded by the fiberglass pole. The latter provides much more flexibility, or "whip," for the vaulter, which explains the significant advance in vaulting records since Cornelius's era.

In 1943, at the height of his fame and prowess, "the Flying Dutchman" became the subject of a popular comic book published by True Comics: *Cornelius Warmerdam, Human Sky Scraper.* In 1975 Cornelius was still vaulting, if not as high as in his youth. In that year, at the age of sixty, Cornelius vaulted 11 feet 4 inches to win the national decathlon championship for competitors sixty years of age and older.

Eugene Larson

Additional Sources:

Crane, O. "No Looking Back for Fresno's Flying Dutchman." *Biography News* (March, 1974): 363.

Fimbrite, R. A. "A Call to Arms." *Sports Illustrated* 75 (Fall, 1991): 98-107.

"Where Are They Now?" *Newsweek* 79, no. 11 (March 20, 1972): 11.

KURT WARNER

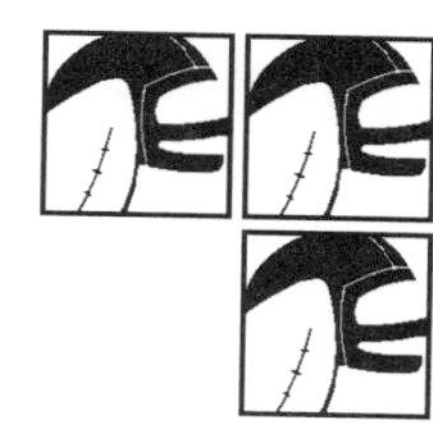

Sport: Football

Born: June 22, 1971
Burlington, Iowa

Early Life

Kurtis Eugene Warner was born on June 22, 1971, in Burlington, Iowa, on the Mississippi River. His parents, Sue and Gene Warner, divorced when Kurt was eight. Sue raised him and his older brother in Cedar Rapids, Iowa. Gene lived nearby in the small town of Solon. Kurt grew up Roman Catholic and attended All Saints Catholic Grade School in Cedar Rapids. He first played organized sports as a fourth-grader on a Cedar Rapids YMCA flag football team. In grade school he loved playing all sports, particularly basketball.

The Road to Excellence

Kurt went to Cedar Rapids Regis, a Catholic high school of about four hundred students. He lettered in baseball and basketball, in addition to football. He wanted to be a receiver or defensive

AP/Wide World Photos

St. Louis Rams quarterback Kurt Warner, the 1999 NFL most valuable player.

end, but as a freshman he was forced to play quarterback because there was no one else to play the position. By graduation he was a recognized team leader in football and basketball. He was a good passer in football, and his senior year he led Regis to the state playoffs, finishing 7-2. He participated in the Iowa Shrine football game and was named First Team All-Conference and *Des Moines Register* All-State.

Although he hoped for a scholarship in basketball or football to a National Collegiate Athletic Association Division I team, he was recruited by the University of Northern Iowa (UNI), a Division IAA team an hour's drive from his home, to play football.

The Emerging Champion

The UNI Panthers played in the UNI-Dome, and coach Terry Allen had a reputation for developing good quarterbacks. Kurt had to be patient, however. He red-shirted in 1989, and then was backup quarterback for three years. In 1993 he finally got his chance to lead the Panthers, and he took them to the Division IAA Playoffs. He was named Gateway Conference most valuable player (MVP).

When Kurt was not drafted by the National Football League (NFL) in 1994, he signed as a free agent with the Green Bay Packers organization, which already had three young quarterbacks. The timing was not right, and Kurt was cut. Once again he had to be patient and wait for the right chance. He returned to Cedar Rapids and worked as a night stockman at HyVee supermarket. Within six months, Kurt was recruited by the Iowa Barnstormers, a new arena football franchise starting up in Des Moines. There Warner was nicknamed "Houdini" because he could usually sidestep pass rushes and he had a fast release. He was named All-League arena quarterback in 1996 and 1997.

While in Des Moines, Kurt worked off-season for the YMCA Barnstormer Youth Sports Alliance. Sponsored by the Greater Des Moines YMCA, pairs of Barnstormers went to elementary schools to serve as role models, directing structured playground activities and tutoring kids in academic basics.

In the summer of 1997 Kurt was recruited by the Amsterdam Admirals of the NFL World League. He was signed by the St. Louis Rams for the regular season, then sent immediately to Amsterdam.

Continuing the Story

After Kurt finished his season in Amsterdam, he returned to the Rams training camp in mid-June, 1998. There he played quarterback for the Rams' scout team. Once again he had to wait for his chance to be a starter.

The 1999 season began with Kurt remaining the Rams' backup quarterback behind their new aquisition, Trent Green. During the third preseason game, Green suffered a season-ending injury, and Kurt suddenly and unexpectedly got his long-awaited chance to lead the Rams. Fans, management, and media were all concerned about Kurt's lack of NFL playing time. The only person with confidence in his abilities was Kurt himself. True to his expectations, he led the Rams to a series of upset victories, and it became apparent that the 1999 St. Louis Rams were a team to be respected. The team had a tremendous season of 16-3. Passing for 41 touchdowns and more than 4,000 yards during the season, Kurt earned the NFL MVP award. Then he led the Rams to the Super Bowl. As St. Louis embraced Kurt, he did not let success go to his head. He spoke with faith and conviction, was direct and articulate with the media, and was a positive role model.

Kurt led the Rams to a 23-16 victory over the Tennessee Titans in the 2000 Super Bowl. He set a Super Bowl record of 414 yards of completed passing. His 73-yard

STATISTICS

Season	*GP*	*PA*	*PC*	*Pct.*	*Yds.*	*Avg.*	*TD*	*Int.*
1998	1	11	4	.364	39	3.55	0	0
1999	16	499	325	.651	**4,353**	8.72	**41**	13
2000	11	347	235	.677	3,429	9.88	21	18
Totals	28	857	564	.658	7,821	9.13	62	31

Notes: Boldface indicates statistical leader. GP = games played; PA = passes attempted; PC = passes completed; Pct. = percent completed; Yds. = yards; Avg. = average yards per attempt; TD = touchdowns; Int. = interceptions

HONORS AND AWARDS	
1999	NFL most valuable player
2000	Super Bowl most valuable player
	Sporting News Sportsman of the Year (shared with Marshall Faulk)

touchdown pass to Isaac Bruce with less than two minutes left to play was the highlight of the game. Kurt was Super Bowl MVP and his sensational season continued at the Pro Bowl.

Off-season, Kurt contracted with PLB Sports, a Pittsburgh, Pennsylvania, food company, to make Warner's Crunch Time, a breakfast cereal. All proceeds were donated to Camp Barnabas, a Missouri Christian camp for youth with special needs. Kurt's son, Zachary, who as an infant was left with impaired vision and other special needs after an illness, had attended the camp during the summer.

Summary

Kurt Warner exemplifies the belief that those who keep trying will ultimately succeed. Even with his skill, he was often disregarded but was patient and did whatever was needed to continue toward his dream. Overlooked in the NFL draft, then cut during training camp as a free agent at Green Bay, Kurt returned home and worked as a supermarket stock clerk for minimum wage. He made the best of his opportunity with arena ball but jumped at the chance to play NFL ball in Europe. In 1998 he got his second chance in the NFL, only to play backup quarterback for the season. His real chance came in the third preseason game in the fall of 1999. Kurt rose to the occasion and took full advantage of all opportunities, leading the St. Louis Rams to the Super Bowl championship and being selected MVP. Kurt believed in himself, his faith, hard work, and patience, making him a tremendous role model.

Carol Cooper

Additional Sources:

Balzer, Howard. *Kurt Warner: The Quarterback.* St. Charles, Mo.: GHB Publishers, 2000.

Clark, Peter J. *101 Fun Facts About Kurt Warner.* Champaign, Ill.: Sport Publishing, Inc., 2000.

Wolfe, Rich, and Bob Margeas. *Kurt Warner: And the Last Shall Be First.* Springfield, Mo.: Rich Wolfe, 2000.

BOB WATERFIELD

Sport: Football

Born: July 26, 1920
Elmira, New York
Died: March 25, 1983
Burbank, California

Early Life

Robert Waterfield was born on July 26, 1920, in Elmira, New York. Bob spent his early boyhood playing ball in the vacant lots of his upstate New York hometown. Later on, his family moved to Van Nuys, California. When he entered high school, he weighed less than 150 pounds. For an aspiring football player, he was considered underweight.

Bob was determined to go to college following his high school graduation. His parents did not have enough money to pay his tuition, so Bob decided to take a job in an aircraft factory in order to earn enough money to attend the University of California at Los Angeles (UCLA). His factory job was a tedious one, but it paid well enough to make him keep it. Bob worked diligently at this job, in addition to keeping up with his school work. Somehow, he still found the time and energy to play high school football in his off-hours.

AP/Wide World Photos

Bob Waterfield in 1946.

The Road to Excellence

In time, all that football practice paid off. His talent for the sport became obvious to everyone who watched him play. When he finally graduated from high school, UCLA made him its first-string quarterback. Bob played so well that year that his team won the conference title and went on to play in the Rose Bowl. By then, Bob had turned himself into a gifted athlete.

In 1943, Bob decided to leave college and become an officer in the United States Army. He enlisted in the Army's Officer Candidate School at Fort Benning, Georgia. He did not stay long with the Army, though, as he suffered an injury to his knee. When he was given a medical discharge, he went back to finish his degree at UCLA. Before long, the Cleveland Rams heard that Bob Waterfield was back in the quarterback business. They quickly signed him in 1945 to play for them.

The Emerging Champion

Bob's first year with the Rams turned out to be sensational. In his first professional season, he led his team to a National Football League (NFL) Championship. The highlight of that season was Cleveland's defeat of the Washington Redskins. Bob's contribution to that victory was immeasurable. He threw 2 touchdown passes and completed 14 of 17 aerials. As a result, he made All-Pro in his first year as a professional football player. In addition, another remarkable award was presented to him. For the first time ever, the coveted most valuable player award, the Carr Trophy, was presented to a first-year player, Bob Waterfield.

In 1945, after the football season was over, the Cleveland Rams were moved to Los Angeles. There, Bob continued to demonstrate his remarkable versatility on the playing field. By 1946, he was the highest-paid NFL player at the time, with a yearly salary of $20,000. From 1949 through 1951, Bob led the Rams to the Western Conference title. His abilities as a field general, as well as a talented runner, passer, and kicker, were crucial to these victories. In 1946, Bob demonstrated his exceptional abilities as a passer, leading the league in completions. He was one of the first quarterbacks to throw the long pass consistently on third down.

Bob's NFL career spanned eight years. In that time, he scored 98 touchdowns and kicked 60 field goals. He threw 1,617 passes and completed 813 of them, for a total of 11,849 yards. His remarkable ability to boot 88-yard punts gave him a career record of 315 punts, for a total of 13,382 yards. On defense, he made 127 interceptions. As a result of these achievements, Bob was recognized with All-Pro honors for two years during his eight seasons.

Punting was definitely a specialty of Waterfield, whose lifetime punting average was 42.4 yards. In 1951, during the Western Conference championship, Bob performed his greatest punts and field goal kicks ever. Eighty thousand fans watched the Rams play the Detroit Lions. During that game Bob did not let the fans down. From positions all over the field, Waterfield kicked 5 field goals—an NFL record at the time.

Continuing the Story

It was Bob's versatility that made him so successful on the field. Early on, he quickly proved himself to be an exceptional passer and an adept runner. He was superb at punting, at kicking field goals, and at leading his team. Because of this, he has been described as the most versatile quarterback ever. He is generally credited with introducing the "bomb," a long pass that results in a touchdown. The bomb is now a standard NFL play. In Bob's day, most teams were reluctant to use this home-run pass, as it was called. When Bob came on the scene, however, he used it often, lofting 40- and 50-yard passes that caught the defense off guard.

STATISTICS

Season	*GP*	*PA*	*PC*	*Pct.*	*Yds.*	*Avg.*	*TD*	*Int.*
1945	10	171	88	.514	1,609	**9.4**	**14**	16
1946	11	251	127	.506	1,747	7.0	**18**	17
1947	12	221	96	.434	1,210	5.5	8	18
1948	11	180	87	.483	1,354	7.5	14	18
1949	12	296	154	.520	2,168	7.3	17	24
1950	12	213	122	.573	1,540	7.2	11	13
1951	11	176	88	.500	1,566	**8.9**	13	10
1952	12	109	51	.468	655	6.0	3	11
Totals	91	1,617	813	.503	11,849	7.3	98	127

Notes: Boldface indicates statistical leader. GP = games played; PA = passes attempted; PC = passes completed; Pct. = percent completed; Yds. = yards; Avg. = average yards per attempt; TD = touchdowns; Int. = interceptions

Bob retired from professional football in 1952. In 1965, he was inducted into the Pro Football Hall of Fame in Canton, Ohio. He died on March 25, 1983, in Burbank, California.

Summary

Bob Waterfield was the first football player ever to receive most valuable player recognition in his first year as a professional. Remembered as the most versatile of quarterbacks, Bob was superb at punting, at kicking field goals, and at leading his team. He was an exceptional passer, and one of the first quarterbacks to throw the long pass consistently on the third down. Bob was able to do more things better than most any other football player—and it was this versatility that made him so successful on the field.

Nan White

HONORS AND AWARDS	
1945	Carr Trophy
1946, 1949	NFL All-Pro Team
1951-52	NFL Pro Bowl Team
1963	NFL All-Pro Team of the 1940's
1965	Inducted into Pro Football Hall of Fame Uniform number 7 retired by Los Angeles Rams

Additional Sources:

Hickok, Ralph. *A Who's Who of Sports Champions.* Boston: Houghton Mifflin, 1995.

LaBlanc, Michael L., and Mary K. Ruby, eds. *Professional Sports Team Histories: Football.* Detroit: Gale, 1994.

Porter, David L., ed. *Biographical Dictionary of American Sports: Football.* Westport, Conn.: Greenwood Press, 1987.

TOM WATSON

Sport: Golf

Born: September 4, 1949
Kansas City, Missouri

Ralph W. Miller Golf Library

Early Life

Thomas Sturges Watson was born on September 4, 1949, in Kansas City, Missouri. His father, an insurance executive, was an avid amateur golfer, and Tom became a caddy for his father at the Kansas City Country Club at age six.

Tom soon displayed both talent and enthusiasm for golf and by his teen years had won several amateur tournaments. He came under the influence of Stan Thirsk, the professional at the Kansas City club, who taught Tom the basic swing he has used throughout his career.

The pattern of early interest and talent is standard among topflight golfers, but in one aspect Tom's development was unusual. He attended Stanford University and graduated with a degree in psychology in 1971. His university career was not a mere sideline to his pursuit of athletic excellence; quite the contrary, Tom manifested high intelligence as well as physical skill. In golf, he became known as a thinking person's player.

The Road to Excellence

Because of his talent, intelligence, and keen desire to win, Tom soon attracted attention after he turned professional in 1972. He put in countless hours of practice and became known for his extraordinary seriousness about his game.

In 1973, he seemed destined for early triumph. Playing in the United States Open at Winged Foot in that year, Tom led the tournament for three rounds. He collapsed in the final round with a disastrous 79 and won no tournaments during the entire year.

At this point, Tom came under the influence of Byron Nelson, an outstanding player of the 1930's and 1940's, who is regarded as one of the foremost golfers of all time. Nelson advised Tom that there were technical faults in his swing. Principally, Tom was failing to shift his weight properly from right-to-left during the downswing. His quick swing tempted him to avoid the necessary weight shift.

MAJOR CHAMPIONSHIP VICTORIES	
1975, 1977, 1980, 1982-83	British Open
1977, 1981	The Masters
1982	U.S. Open

OTHER NOTABLE VICTORIES	
1974, 1977, 1984	Western Open
1975, 1978-80	Byron Nelson Golf Classic
1977	Wickes-Andy Williams San Diego Open
1977, 1978	Bing Crosby National Pro-Am
1977, 1981, 1983, 1989	Ryder Cup Team
1979, 1996	Memorial Tournament Tournament of Champions
1979, 1982	Sea Pines Heritage Classic
1980	Andy Williams-San Diego Open
1980, 1982	Glen Campbell-Los Angeles Open
1980, 1984	MONY Tournament of Champions
1981	Atlanta Classic
1987	Nabisco Championship of Golf
1992	Hong Kong Open
1997	Dunlop Phoenix (Japan)
1998	MasterCard Colonial
1999	Bank One Championship
2000	IR Senior Tour Championship

Nelson also gave Tom advice about the psychological side of golf. He urged him not to despair over his collapse during the 1973 Open. Such things happen to nearly every golfer, but the true test of a champion is how he or she copes with them.

The Emerging Champion

Tom quickly showed he had taken Nelson's lessons to heart. He made the necessary changes in his swing and soon established himself as one of the outstanding golfers of the 1970's. In 1977, he won both the British Open and the Masters, two of the four tournaments that constitute golf's major championships.

Even more significant than his victories were the circumstances under which he achieved them. In both events, he found himself locked in rivalry with Jack Nicklaus, generally considered the greatest golfer of all time. In the 1977 Masters, Tom held a 3-stroke lead over Nicklaus after the first thirty-six holes of play. Nicklaus proceeded to shoot the next two rounds in 70 and 66. The last round is astonishingly low, because in major championships the courses are exceptionally difficult and sub-par scores are rare.

Tom could not equal Nicklaus's last two rounds. He scored a 70 and 67, however, and thus lost only 1 stroke of his lead, even after Nicklaus's surge. Tom had conclusively shown that he could withstand pressure.

Tom repeated his triumph over Nicklaus at the 1977 British Open. The two were paired for the last two rounds. Nicklaus shot a 65, only to be matched by Watson. Not to be outdone, Nicklaus returned the next day to shoot a 66. Watson responded with a 65, winning the tournament by a stroke.

During the 1970's and early 1980's, Tom became the tour's leading money-winner, supplanting Nicklaus. He won two Masters championships and five British Opens.

Continuing the Story

One essential for a great golfer had so far eluded Tom: victory in the U.S. Open, the most important American tournament. Every great American player except Sam Snead had won this event. Tom's turn came in 1982. In that year, the Open was played at the difficult Pebble Beach course in California, a site Tom knew well. At the end of three rounds, Tom seemed in good position to win the event. Once more, the great Nicklaus proved to be the major obstacle. Nicklaus had a characteristically excellent final round. Finishing before Tom, Nicklaus could watch from the clubhouse to see whether Tom held on to his lead.

Once more Tom proved equal to the pressure. At the seventeenth hole, he sank a long second shot to give him a birdie. This shot proved enough, and he won the Open by 2 strokes.

In the early 1980's, Tom seemed established as the foremost golfer in the world. Not only had he won a number of major titles, he had also bested Nicklaus in several head-to-head confrontations. Although he by no means always defeated Nicklaus, he seemed to hold the edge in their rivalry.

Unfortunately for Tom, his play in the late 1980's did not equal the supreme achievements of his struggles with Nicklaus. Although he continued to do well throughout the 1980's, he was not able to establish a long-standing dominance over the game in the style of Nicklaus. Nevertheless, he remained a threat in any tournament he entered.

Tom had limited success on the PGA tour during the early 1990's. He won the Memorial Tournament in 1996 and the MasterCard Colonial in 1998. In 1999, Tom joined the Senior Tour. Playing in only two official events in his first year, he won one and finished in the top twenty-five in the second. Tom also played in thirteen PGA tournaments.

In 2000, Tom had greater success in both PGA and Senior PGA tournaments. He shot a final round 66 to win the IR Senior Tour Championship. He had two second-place finishes and lost two playoffs for second place. On the PGA tour, Tom's best finish was a tie for ninth at the PGA Championship. Tom got off to a good start in 2001, finishing in a tie for eighth place at the MasterCard Championship.

Summary

Tom Watson showed unusual talent and enthusiasm for golf from his early youth. His ability was combined with high intelligence and the determination to devote unlimited time toward perfecting his game. In his early years as a professional, he became a protégé of Byron Nelson, who advised him on his swing. Tom became the golfer of the 1970's, doing so in dramatic fashion. He defeated Jack Nicklaus by close scores in several major championships.

Bill Delaney

Additional Sources:

Allis, Peter. *The Who's Who of Golf.* Englewood Cliffs, N.J.: Prentice-Hall, 1983.

Editors of *Golf Magazine. Golf Magazine's Encyclopedia of Golf: The Complete Reference.* New York: HarperCollins, 1993.

Kindred, Dave. "Watson's World Is Turning." *Golf Digest* 50, no. 8 (1999).

Verdi, Bob. "Twilight of a Superstar." *Golf World* 52, no. 19 (1998).

Wilner, Barry. *Golf Stars of Today.* Philadelphia, Pa.: Chelsea House, 1998.

RECORDS AND MILESTONES

Won thirty-four times on the PGA Tour

PGA Tour money leader five times (1977-80, 1984)

Became the only player to lead the money list (1977-80) and be named PGA Player of the Year (1977-80, 1982, 1984) four consecutive years

Biggest year was 1980,when he won six times on the tour in addition to winning the British Open, and won a record $530,808. He was the first player to break the $500,000 mark in earnings

HONORS AND AWARDS

1974	*Golf Digest* Most Improved Player
1977-81, 1984	*Golf Digest* Byron Nelson Award for Tournament Victories
1977-80	GWAA Player of the Year
1977-79	PGA Vardon Trophy
1977-80, 1982, 1984	PGA Player of the Year
1978-79	Seagram's Seven Crowns of Sports Award
1987	USGA Bobby Jones Award
1988	Inducted into PGA/World Golf Hall of Fame
1991	GWAA Richardson Award

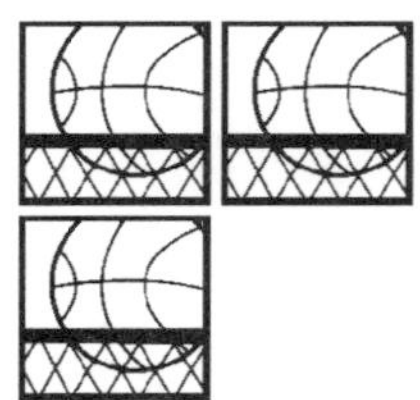

CHRIS WEBBER

Sport: Basketball

Born: March 1, 1973
Detroit, Michigan

Early Life

Mayce Christopher Webber III was born in Detroit on March 1, 1973. His father was originally from the South and had moved to Michigan to work in the automobile industry. His mother was a teacher. Although Chris's parents both worked, he grew up in a rough neighborhood. Chris discovered basketball early in life and from the age of twelve often competed successfully against players bigger and stronger than he.

In 1987 Chris received an academic scholarship to the prestigious Country Day High School. Chris's talents shone on the basketball court, as he made the All-State team as a freshman. Country Day had not traditionally been a basketball powerhouse, but with Chris on the team this soon changed. By the 1989-1990 season, when Chris was a junior, Country Day was one of the strongest teams in Michigan. Not only did they win their own Division B title in a dramatic 68-57 win over Albion, but they also beat the Division A champion, Battle Creek.

The Road to Excellence

For college, Chris chose the University of Michigan in Ann Arbor because of its academic reputation. Although Michigan had won the na-

AP/Wide World Photos

Chris Webber of the Sacramento Kings in a 2000 game.

STATISTICS

Season	*GP*	*FGA*	*FGM*	*FG%*	*FTA*	*FTM*	*FT%*	*Reb.*	*Ast.*	*TP*	*PPG*
1993-94	76	1,037	572	.552	355	189	.532	694	272	1,333	17.5
1994-95	54	938	464	.495	233	117	.502	518	256	1,085	20.1
1995-96	15	276	150	.543	69	41	.594	114	75	356	23.7
1996-97	72	1,167	604	.518	313	177	.565	743	331	1,445	20.1
1997-98	71	1,341	647	.482	333	196	.589	674	273	1,555	21.9
1998-99	42	778	378	.486	174	79	.454	**545**	173	839	20.0
1999-00	75	1,548	748	.483	414	311	.751	788	345	1,834	24.5
2000-01	70	1,635	786	.481	461	324	.703	777	294	1,898	27.1
Totals	475	8,720	4,349	.499	2,352	1,434	.610	4,852	2,019	10,345	21.8

Notes: Boldface indicates statistical leader. GP = games played; FGA = field goals attempted; FGM = field goals made; FG% = field goal percentage; FTA = free throws attempted; FTM = free throws made; FT% = free throw percentage; Reb. = rebounds; Ast. = assists; TP = total points; PPG = points per game

tional basketball championship in 1989, most of the players from that team were gone. Chris's entering class included Jimmy King, Ray Jackson, Juwan Howard, and Chris's friend Jalen Rose. Freshmen rarely make an impact in major college programs, but by midseason coach Steve Fisher had the confidence to put all five of these players in the starting lineup. The unit quickly became known as the "Fab Five." Though they achieved a good regular-season record, the Michigan Wolverines were not expected to be a factor in the National Collegiate Athletic Association (NCAA) tournament. They surprised observers by leapfrogging over several teams to face the much more experienced Duke team in the finals.

The following year Michigan had a superb season, as the youth and energy the Fab Five had shown in their first season were supplemented by a growing knowledge of the game. With their distinctive fashion sense, baggy shorts and black socks, the Fab Five represented a new wave of Generation X basketball players who were not afraid to show off their own style. Michigan coasted through the 1993 NCAA tournament and faced North Carolina in the finals. The last game was hard-fought. With 20 seconds left, Michigan was down by 2 points. Chris got the ball in time to make a game-tying shot. However, misunderstanding what his teammates were saying from the bench, Chris mistakenly called for a time-out when the team, in fact, had none left. A technical foul was called agains Chris, and North Carolina sealed its victory.

The entire nation had seen his foolish mistake. Chris himself came to have a sense of humor about the incident, eventually putting "TIMEOUT" on his car license plate and naming the foundation he established to help inner-city children Time Out. The sad ending to Michigan's season helped convince Chris it was time to turn professional.

The Emerging Champion

In the 1993 NBA draft, Orlando had first pick and, seeing that Chris was the best player available, chose him. They already had a big man in Shaquille O'Neal, however, and the Magic traded Chris to the Golden State Warriors for a number of draft picks including Anfernee "Penny" Hardaway. Golden State looked to Chris to provide badly needed muscle and inside rebounding presence. Chris responded by winning the Rookie of the Year award. This was especially impressive, as for most of the season Chris played center, not his usual position of power forward.

Though the Warriors did not get far in the playoffs in the 1993-1994 season, they had a good regular-season record. The next season, though, everything collapsed for Chris and Golden State. He and coach Don Nelson did not get along, and Chris demanded a trade. When Nelson did not budge, Chris voided his contract, effectively forcing the Warriors to trade him. Chris was finally traded, for far less than he was worth, to the Washington Bullets. There, he rejoined his old Fab Five teammate Juwan Howard. Things seemed to be looking up for Chris.

The situation in Washington never quite jelled. Chris was injured in 1995. In 1997-1998, though, the Bullets, for many years an under-

HONORS AND AWARDS

1994	Schick NBA Rookie of the Year Unanimously named to the NBA All-Rookie First Team
1997	NBA Player of the Week for the week ending April 20
1997	NBA All-Star
1998-1999	All-NBA Second Team
1999	NBA Player of the Week for the week ending April 25
1999-2000	All-NBA Third Team NBA All-Interview Second Team
2000	Player of the Week for the weeks ending January 2, January 16
2001	All-NBA First Team

achieving team, almost made the playoffs. The next year, they did make the playoffs and challenged the Chicago Bulls before succumbing. However, the Bullets felt they could not win with a team centered around two big men, Chris and Howard. Off-field controversies had given Chris a bad reputation, and few in Washington were surprised when the Bullets traded Chris to the Sacramento Kings for two older and less talented players, Mitch Richmond and Otis Thorpe.

Continuing the Story

In Sacramento, Chris was the key element in one of the NBA's freshest and most exciting teams. "C-Webb" was having fun playing basketball again, and the old excitement he had felt in college with the Fab Five returned. The Kings posted their highest winning percentage in seventeen years and made an appearance in the playoffs. Chris became popular with Sacramento fans; his articulate comments on his team's play and on basketball as a whole combined with his accessibility to the media to make him a good interviewee. People saw past his earlier bad-boy image and began to understand other sides of his character.

In 1999-2000, things got even better in Sacramento as Chris came into his own as a leader and motivator. The Kings again made the playoffs and took the vastly favored Los Angeles Lakers to the final game of a best-of-five series. Though his team lost, Chris could look back on a successful season.

In the 2000-2001 season, Chris was named All-NBA First Team and led the Kings to their best-ever record and a tie for the Pacific Division championship. However, after they beat Phoenix in the first round of the playoffs, they were swept by the Lakers. As an unrestricted free agent, Chris entertained offers from many teams but eventually signed a long-term contract with the Kings.

Summary

Chris Webber's story has been that of a person vastly talented in many areas, not just basketball, who made public mistakes and had to overcome them. From the timeout error to the contract haggling with Don Nelson, the face Chris showed to the public was not always his best. Yet he was never discouraged, and he eventually turned his fortunes around.

Additional Sources:

Albom, Mitch. *Fab Five: Basketball, Trash Talk, the American Dream.* New York: Warner Books, 1993.

Knapp, Ron. *Chris Webber, Star Forward.* Springfield, N.J.: Enslow, 1997.

McMullen, Jackie. "Webb Feat." *Sports Illustrated,* January 31, 2000.

MILESTONES

1993-94	Became the first NBA rookie to total more than 1,000 points, 500 rebounds, 250 assists, 150 blocks, and 75 steals

DICK WEBER

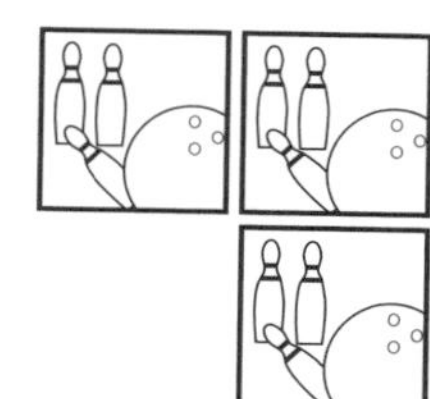

Sport: Bowling

Born: December 23, 1929
Indianapolis, Indiana

Early Life

Richard Anthony (Dick) Weber was born on December 23, 1929, in Indianapolis, Indiana. He was the son of Carl John Weber, a gas station attendant and bowling alley manager, and Marjorie Wheeler Weber, a schoolteacher.

Bowling was a popular sport during the Depression, and, as a young boy, Dick often went to the bowling alley with his father, who bowled in a weekly league. When Dick was ten, his family joined a family league so that he could bowl with them.

Dick attended Indianapolis Technical High School, where he played basketball and shortstop on the baseball team. He also spent a considerable amount of time at the local bowling alley. He took a job as a pinsetter, and when he was not setting pins, he was bowling. He graduated from high school in 1948, earning letters in both basketball and baseball.

After graduation, Dick married Juanita "Neet" Dirk and took a job in a post office sorting mail. To supplement his salary from the post office, he began to work at night as a professional bowling shop operator.

The Road to Excellence

Dick gained experience bowling in local leagues in Indianapolis for several years while he continued to work in the post office during the day and the bowling alley at night. He was small, weighing about 125 pounds, but he soon grew to 5 feet 9 inches and 140 pounds. His increased size enabled him to establish an average of 200 pins per game.

His appearance in professional bowling came rather suddenly, even though he had worked to

Archive Photos

Dick Weber in 1962.

improve his game for many years. In 1954, he was competing in Chicago in an All-Star tournament. On the lane next to him was the famous professional team known as the "Budweiser Five." The captain of the team, Don Carter, was impressed with Dick's bowling and invited him to join the team. Dick immediately accepted the offer.

To compete with the famous team, Dick had to travel from Indianapolis to St. Louis, and he had no money for the trip. A longtime friend and local bowling lane owner, Carl Hindel, came to his rescue. He lent him a loud, pin-striped suit with wide lapels and gave him money to make the trip.

With his wife and small baby, Richard, Dick drove to St. Louis to join Don Carter, Ray Bluth, Whitey Harris, Pat Patterson, and Tom Hennessey for his first professional competition.

The Emerging Champion

Dick replaced Don McLaren and had a wonderful first year with the "Buds." He teamed with Ray Bluth to win the first of four national doubles titles and helped his team capture the Bowling Proprietors Association of America (BPAA) national title in 1955.

His brilliant first year began a career that extended over thirty years. The Budweiser team won the BPAA national title in 1956, 1958, 1959, 1961, and 1965 and the BPAA All-Star championship in 1962, 1963, 1965, and 1966. With Bluth, he won the national doubles title in 1960, 1961, and 1964.

In 1961 and 1962, Dick accomplished an amazing feat—he had a string of seven Professional Bowlers Association (PBA) victories out of nine competitions that included the nation's best bowlers. He was the American Bowling Congress (ABC) tournament average leader and was chosen Bowler of the Year by the Bowling Writers Association of America (BWAA) in 1961. During the same year, he was also the year's top money-winner, earning nearly $100,000. By the age of thirty-one, he had won eighteen major tournaments and had earned a major reputation.

Dick had his best year in 1965, however. He averaged 211 pins per game for 960 games and was the ABC tournament average leader for the second consecutive year. During the Houston Open, he became the first professional bowler to roll three perfect games in one tournament. For his accomplishments in the first half of the 1960's, Dick was three times named the Bowler of the Year by the BWAA (1961, 1963, and 1965).

Continuing the Story

In 1970, Dick became the youngest man ever to be elected into the ABC Hall of Fame. In 1975, he became one of the eight charter members of the PBA Hall of Fame.

Beginning in the 1970's, Dick competed in only half of the major tournaments on the tour. In 1976, however, his earnings passed the $500,000 mark, and he ranked first in all-time winnings. In 1977, he won his 26th professional tournament to place second on the all-time PBA list.

In addition to touring as a professional, Dick became part-owner of a St. Louis bowling establishment and served as an adviser for American Machine and Foundry (AMF). His interest in bowling also led him to give exhibitions, clinics, and television series dealing with bowling techniques, and he wrote articles and books on bowling. He became

PBA TOUR VICTORIES

1959	Paramus; Dayton
1960	Albany
1961	Dallas; Shreveport; Houston; Redondo Beach; San Jose
1962	Chicago; Puerto Rico
1963	New Brunswick; Las Vegas
1964	Dallas
1965	Wichita; Houston
1966	Denver; Fresno
1969	New Orleans; Altoona
1970	Hawaii
1971	Denver; Toledo; Hawaii
1973	Toledo
1976	Garden City
1977	Kansas City
1983	Senior Championship at Canton
1986	Senior Invitational at Las Vegas
1989	Senior/Touring Pro Doubles at Buffalo

OTHER MAJOR VICTORIES

1962, 1963, 1965-66	U.S. Open

PBA RECORDS
Most 300 scores in a tournament, 3 (1965)
Most consecutive top-five finishes, 7 (1961)
Most consecutive top-twenty-four finishes, 23 (1963)

HONORS AND AWARDS	
1960-67, 1969, 1971	*Bowler's Journal* All-American Team
1961, 1963, 1965	BWAA Bowler of the Year
1965	PBA Player of the Year
1969-70	President of PBA
1970	Inducted into ABC Hall of Fame
1975	Inducted into PBA Hall of Fame

the president of the PBA in 1969-1970 and was elected to the Indiana and St. Louis Halls of Fame.

Dick was a popular star, and his career extended over an unusually long period of time. His long career has been attributed to his ability to change his game to meet the changing conditions of the game. When he first began his career, lacquer was used on the lanes, and the big hook was the most successful delivery. Years later, lacquer was replaced with harder finishes, which required a different style of delivery. Dick adopted a straighter, softer pitch, which allowed him to continue to be a champion. Dick continued to win tournaments well into the 1980's. He won the Showboat Invitational tournament for three consecutive years from 1986 to 1988. In 1987, he was named professional bowling host at the Showboat Center in Atlantic City, New Jersey.

Dick and his wife, Juanita, have four children, Richard Jr., Paula, John, and Peter. Dick would continue an active lifestyle by playing golf.

Summary

Dick Weber's first year as a professional bowler in 1955 was a successful one; he helped the Budweisers to the first of six national team titles and four All-Star championships. With Ray Bluth, he won the first of four national doubles titles in the same year. He was named Bowler of the Year three times by the Bowling Writers Association of America. *Bowler's Journal* chose him a record ten times to the All-America First Team and five times to the Second Team. He was selected to the ABC Hall of Fame in 1970, and, in 1975, became a charter member of the PBA Hall of Fame. He was voted the Second Greatest Bowler of All Time by sportswriters in a 1970 poll. He established a 202-pin lifetime average, rolled eighteen sanctioned 300-pin games, and rolled high pin series scores of 815, 814, 804, and 800 during his long and distinguished career.

Susan J. Bandy

Additional Sources:

McCallum, Jack. "The Perils of Life in the Fast Lane." *Sports Illustrated* 63 (July 15, 1985): 37-41.

Porter, David L., ed. *Biographical Dictionary of American Sports: Basketball and Other Indoor Sports.* Westport, Conn.: Greenwood Press, 1989.

Weber, Dick, and Roland Alexander. *Weber on Bowling.* Englewood Cliffs, N.J.: Prentice-Hall, 1981.

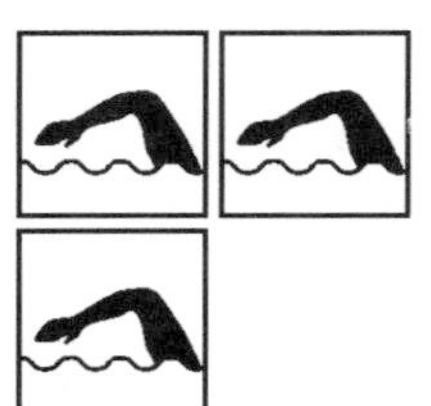

JOHNNY WEISSMULLER

Sport: Swimming

Born: June 2, 1904
Windber, Pennsylvania
Died: January 20, 1984
Acapulco, Mexico

Early Life

Peter John Weissmuller was born on June 2, 1904, in Windber, a small coal-mining town in Pennsylvania. His father, a coal miner, developed tuberculosis and was unable to support his family. Johnny's mother, an excellent cook, maintained the family through sales of her pies, cakes, and other bakery products. The father, unable to cope with his situation, took to drink and died when Johnny was sixteen.

Johnny began to swim at the age of eight. His mother hoped that swimming would be a good corrective for a mild physical weakness from which the boy suffered. The cure proved a spectacular success, and Johnny immediately demonstrated his inborn talent for swimming and love of the water.

The Road to Excellence

By age twelve, Johnny had taken up swimming on a serious basis. He joined the local YMCA, along with his friends "Hooks" and "Hank" Miller, who later became noted competition swimmers. Johnny practiced for several hours a day and won local competitions. By age sixteen,

U.S. Swimming

he was ready to pursue swimming as the major area of his life. To do so, he required the assistance of a first-rate coach.

Johnny found the person he was looking for at the Illinois Athletic Club. William Bachrach was the trainer of the United States Olympic team and coach of more national champions than anyone else. When Bachrach saw Johnny swim, he sensed that a future world champion was at hand. A serious obstacle, however, stood in the way of Johnny's immediate rise to the top. Johnny was almost entirely self-taught and had a poor technique. He needed to remake his strokes from the beginning, and the blunt Bachrach did not conceal from the young swimmer the immense difficulty involved.

In addition to talent, Johnny always possessed the determination necessary for a true champion. Under Bachrach's guidance, he embarked on an arduous training program. Bachrach reduced swimming almost to an exact science and instructed Johnny in the proper manner of making each movement. Until Johnny was able to meet Bachrach's rigorous standards, the coach kept him out of competition racing. Although Johnny was anxious to compete, he showed another trait of a true champion—he followed the advice of his coach exactly.

The Emerging Champion

Finally, Bachrach allowed Johnny to compete in a junior 100-yard tryout race in 1921. Although Johnny finished second, he lost only because his swim cap fell in front of his face, temporarily blinding him. Even with this obstacle, he came within 1 second of the world's record. Because the race was only a tryout, it is not usually counted in Johnny's record. Thus, he was still able to claim at the close of his career that he won every competitive race he entered. After this tryout, Johnny's rise to success proceeded smoothly. Bachrach recognized that every swimmer needed to specialize, and he trained Johnny as a sprinter rather than as a long-distance swimmer.

In order to increase the attention paid to Johnny, Bachrach devised an unusual training stunt. He invited local businesspeople to watch Johnny train on the terms that they would have to buy the young man lunch or dinner if he broke a world's record. The publicity was invaluable, not to mention the meals for the impoverished young athlete. Even more important was that Johnny had to break a world's record every day. That was a task of surpassing difficulty; if Johnny achieved it, nothing could stand against his march to excellence.

Only one American swimmer was in a position to pose an effective challenge to Johnny Weissmuller. He was Duke Kahanamoku, busily preparing himself for a third Olympic triumph. Johnny went on an exhibition tour to Hawaii in 1922, where a match was scheduled between him and the great Hawaiian star. The ever-cautious Bachrach skillfully maneuvered Kahanamoku into canceling the race by first arranging for him to watch Johnny swim. When the Duke timed Johnny and saw that his young rival had broken his world's record, he pulled out of the race.

Continuing the Story

Bachrach was not afraid of Kahanamoku; he simply preferred to wait. The two rivals eventually clashed at the 1924 Paris Olympics, and the result was a complete triumph for Johnny. He won three gold medals and defeated Kahanamoku in the 100-meter race. After his triumph at the Olympics, Johnny went on a successful European tour and engaged in a number of exhibition races.

The stories of champions after their rise to the top often take disappointing turns. It is easy for someone who has defeated all comers to assume that he is invincible and can dispense with further training. Johnny did not make this mistake.

MAJOR CHAMPIONSHIPS

Year	Competition	Event	Place	Time
1924	Olympic Games	100-meter freestyle	Gold	59.0 WR, OR
		400-meter freestyle	Gold	5:04.2 OR
		4×200-meter freestyle relay	Gold	9:53.4
1928	Olympic Games	100-meter freestyle	Gold	58.6 OR
		4×200-meter freestyle relay	Gold	9:36.2

Notes: OR = Olympic Record; WR = World Record

He continued his training just as rigorously as when he was an unknown teenager.

Johnny's unbending persistence once more paid off at the 1928 Olympics in the Netherlands, in which he won an individual gold medal and a relay team gold. In the 100-meter freestyle, he broke his own Olympic record. After this, Johnny had no more worlds to conquer. He once more made a number of exhibition tours, including one to Japan in which he refused an offer to become coach of the Japanese Olympic team.

Johnny could have decided to remain a competitive swimmer until the 1932 Olympic Games, held in Los Angeles, but he elected not to do so. His swimming had all been done as an amateur, and Johnny needed to earn a living. After his retirement from athletics in 1930, he achieved fame once more, this time as a film actor, especially for his portrayal of Tarzan in a series of films. After a long and financially successful life, he died in 1984.

RECORDS AND MILESTONES

- Won a combined 52 national championships and gold medals
- Won 36 individual national titles
- Set 51 world records
- Set 107 national records
- His record in the 100-yard freestyle of 51 seconds, set in 1927, stood for seventeen years
- Played on two U.S. Olympic water polo teams
- Played the role of Tarzan nineteen times in almost twenty years

HONORS AND AWARDS

1922	American Swimmer of the Year
1923	World Trophy
1950	Named the greatest swimmer of the first half-century
1965	Inducted into International Swimming Hall of Fame
1983	Inducted into U.S. Olympic Hall of Fame

Summary

Johnny Weissmuller perfectly illustrates the recipe for athletic excellence. Blessed with outstanding talent, he early showed his willingness to endure years of grueling effort in order to reach the heights of success. Under the instruction of William Bachrach, he practiced every detail of the proper swimming stroke for years. His efforts made him the world's foremost swimmer during the 1920's.

Bill Delaney

Additional Sources:

Behlmer, Rudy. "Johnny Weissmuller: Olympics to Tarzan." *Films in Review* 47, no. 7-8 (July-August, 1996): 20-33.

Dawson, Buck. *Weissmuller to Spitz: An Era to Remember.* Fort Lauderdale, Fla.: International Swimming Hall of Fame, 1988.

Mueller, Arlene. "Johnny Weismuller Made Olympian Efforts to Conceal His Birthplace." *Sports Illustrated* 61 (August 6, 1984): 12-14.

Onyx, Narda. *Water, World, and Weissmuller: A Biography.* La Jolla, Calif.: Vion, 1964.

Weissmuller, Johnny, and Clarence A. Bush. *Swimming the American Crawl.* Boston: Houghton Mifflin, 1930.

BUDDY WERNER

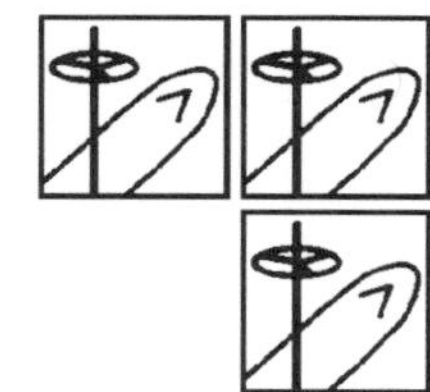

Sport: Skiing

Born: February 26, 1936
Steamboat Springs, Colorado
Died: April 12, 1964
Samedan, Switzerland

Early Life

Wallace Jerold "Buddy" Werner was born on February 26, 1936, in Steamboat Springs, located in northwestern Colorado at the western edge of the mountains. In the heart of ranching country, Steamboat Springs was also near Howelson Hill, where Buddy learned to ski. Buddy was second of three children born to Ed and Hazel Werner. Buddy, his sister Skeeter, and their brother Loris were all to become Olympic skiers. The Werners lived on a ranch until 1942, when they moved to town to be close to school.

Family activities were important and included skiing in the winter and fishing and picnicking in the summer. Buddy's first skiing experience was on a family outing before he was two years old. Buddy's father was his first ski instructor and the most important influence in Buddy's life. Buddy's ski competition began at age six during the Steamboat Winter Carnival.

Buddy Werner at the 1964 Winter Olympics in Innsbruck, Austria.

The Road to Excellence

Love of skiing and instruction in a junior program started Buddy's skiing career. Junior skiing was a program sponsored by the local ski club to provide instruction and competition for school children from first to twelfth grades. At age nine, Buddy soared 72 feet in the air off the Howelson Hill jump, at ten won his first regional championship in ski jumping, and at eleven earned first place in the alpine events, downhill, slalom, and giant slalom at the Junior Championship Meet in Steamboat.

When Gordon Wren became the juniors' coach, he recognized several qualities in Buddy that help make champions. Buddy had perseverance; when he broke his arm, he skied in a cast. Buddy was never satisfied with himself; he always worked to improve his performance. In a race he studied the course and planned his strategy. Gordon influenced Buddy by teaching that success comes with hard work, discipline, and mastery of fundamentals.

As a member of the Colorado junior team, Buddy won the Junior National Alpine Championship in 1952. In 1953 he earned the distinction of being the greatest junior jumper in the United States, jumping 160 feet.

MAJOR CHAMPIONSHIPS

Year	Competition	Event	Place
1954	Holmenkollen, Norway	Slalom	6th
		Downhill	1st
		Combined	3d
1955	Kandahar, Andes	Slalom	1st
		Downhill	1st
		Combined	1st
1956	Hahnenkamm, Austria	Downhill	2d
	Olympic Games	Giant slalom	21st
		Downhill	11th
	Chamonix, France	Downhill	1st
	St. Moritz, Switzerland	Downhill	1st
	Holmenkollen, Norway	Giant slalom	7th
		Slalom	9th
		Downhill	1st
		Combined	1st
	Zermatt, Switzerland	Downhill	1st
1958	Lauberhorn, Switzerland	Slalom	3d
		Downhill	2d
		Combined	1st
1959	Lauberhorn, Switzerland	Downhill	4th
	Hahnenkamm, Austria	Downhill	1st
	Lenzerheide, Switzerland	Downhill	1st
	North American Championships	Giant slalom	2d
		Slalom	1st
		Downhill	1st
		Combined	1st
1962	Holmenkollen, Norway	Giant slalom	1st
		Slalom	3d
		Combined	1st
1963	National Collegiate Championship, USA	Slalom	2d
	North American Championship	Giant slalom	2d
		Slalom	2d
		Combined	2d
1964	U.S. National Championships	Giant slalom	1st
	Olympic Games	Slalom	8th
		Downhill	17th

There were other important activities in Buddy's life too, and the drive and desire to be best was distinct in all of them. He played first chair coronet in the high school band, was a sprinter in track, and lettered three years in football.

The Emerging Champion

Buddy joined Skeeter in representing the United States in international ski competition—at the age of seventeen—the youngest man on the team. Buddy's fearless love of speed and his determination to be the best contributed to his excellent performance in the 1954 competitions. Racing against the best skiers in the world challenged Buddy's fierce competitiveness, and within the next six years, he was called the "best American skier ever."

Winning the "Nose-Dive Race" in Vermont earned Buddy a place on the 1956 Olympic team, but taking nose-dives was his downfall during the Olympics. Buddy fell in all three events, yet finished 11th in the downhill on one ski. Crouching into an "egg position" in the downhill was Buddy's technique to increase speed, but the wooden skis of the time made stability over the bumps difficult.

The years 1958 and 1959 were the height of Buddy's skiing career. The first American to win the Lauberhorn Trophy of Switzerland, he went on to set several course records in the downhill event throughout Europe and the United States. In U.S. competition, Buddy dominated all alpine events. He seemed to be in a class by himself and was surely on the path toward an Olympic medal in 1960.

However, Olympic hopes plummeted with Buddy when he fell in practice and broke his leg. Many competitors would have gotten discouraged and given up, but not Buddy. In a toboggan with his leg in a cast, he coached, encouraged, and cheered his friends.

Continuing the Story

Breaking his leg made Buddy realize there were other things in life besides skiing. College, marriage, and business, added to skiing, made Buddy's life very busy. In 1960, he enrolled at Colorado University, and in June, 1961, he married Vanda Norgren, a teacher who also loved the outdoors. Vanda helped Buddy become more understanding toward others, which made him a good team leader. A family ski shop in Steamboat Springs put him into business.

By 1962, Buddy was in peak condition. His

best event changed from the downhill to the slalom, through Bob Beattie's skillful coaching. At the Olympic training camp Buddy emerged as top man; he would have another chance at an Olympic gold medal.

Success in pre-Olympic events was encouraging, and fans again believed Buddy was a top contender. Once again, however, bad luck struck during the Olympic events. That bad luck was falling. Disappointed by his eighth-place finish in the slalom, seventeenth place in downhill, and disqualification in the giant slalom, Buddy nevertheless maintained his smile and self-discipline to cheer on his teammates to silver and bronze medals. Buddy announced his retirement from racing in March following a superb demonstration of skill in the National Championships.

International fame and skiing expertise took Buddy to Switzerland in April, 1964, to film a ski movie. A last, courageous race with an avalanche abruptly ended Buddy's life when he fell again, just 20 feet from safety, and was buried under 10 feet of wet snow.

Summary

Some people think being great means always winning the championship. Buddy Werner was great because he was an example to fellow skiers and others who knew him. What mattered most was the quality of effort he gave in skiing and in his life. Buddy went all-out in his effort to win, but when he fell and failed to achieve the World Championship or Olympic gold medal, he lived by his own words: "I never look back. If I crash this week ... there's another race coming up next week. If I ski as hard as I can maybe I'll win it."

Wanda Green

Additional Sources:

Burroughs, John R. *"I Never Look Back": The Story of Buddy Werner.* Boulder, Colo.: Johnson, 1967.

Needham, Richard, et al., eds. *Ski Magazine's Encyclopedia of Skiing.* Rev. ed. New York: Harper & Row, 1979.

Porter, David L., ed. *Biographical Dictionary of American Sports: Outdoor Sports.* Westport, Conn.: Greenwood Press, 1988.

HONORS, AWARDS, AND RECORDS

1956, 1960, 1964	Men's U.S. Olympic Alpine Ski Team
1958	First American to win the Swiss Lauberhorn Trophy
1959	National Ski Association Skier of the Year
1964	Inducted into National Ski Hall of Fame
1965	Storm Mountain Ski Area renamed Mt. Werner in his honor Buddy Werner Memorial Library dedicated
1967	Inducted into Colorado Sports Hall of Fame
1977	Inducted into Colorado Ski Hall of Fame
1991	Legends of Skiing Award

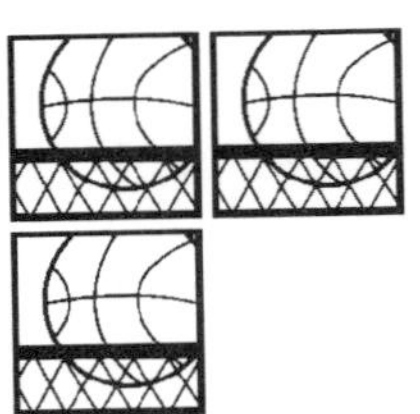

JERRY WEST

Sport: Basketball

Born: May 28, 1938
Cheylan, West Virginia

Early Life

Jerry Alan West was born on May 28, 1938, in Cheylan, West Virginia, near the state capital of Charleston. Cheylan was a small town of approximately five hundred people. The West family mailing address was listed as Cabin Creek, West Virginia.

AP/Wide World Photos

Los Angeles Laker Jerry West dribbles down the court in a 1970 game.

Life in the coal mining community of Cheylan was quiet and conservative. Jerry's father, Howard, worked as a machine operator, gas station owner/operator, and electrician. The family lived in a six-bedroom house. Jerry, one of six children, had three brothers and two sisters.

Jerry had experience in several junior high school and high school sports; basketball, however, became his most successful sport.

The Road to Excellence

Jerry first played basketball on the Cheylan Junior High School team and went on to play at East Bank High School. He set basketball records for East Bank High School in field goals scored, free throws scored, and total points.

Jerry's high school coach, Roy Williams, instilled in Jerry the desire to learn all aspects of the game (shooting, defense, passing, and playmaking). During his sophomore year in high school, Jerry suffered a broken ankle. This was to be the first of a series of major injuries in his career. After much hard work and practice, Jerry was able to continue his brilliant high school basketball career.

Jerry led East Bank High School to the West Virginia State Championship in 1956. His senior year, Jerry averaged 34.2 points per game and became the first player in West Virginia to score more than 900 points in a single season. He was selected to the All-State and All-Tournament teams.

Fred Schaus, West Virginia University basketball coach and, later, general manager of the Los Angeles Lakers, recruited Jerry to attend West Virginia University. As a sophomore, Jerry played on the West Virginia team, which was ranked number one in the country in 1958.

During his three-year varsity career at West Virginia University, Jerry averaged 24.8 points and 13.3 rebounds per game, while shooting 50.6 percent. He was voted most valuable player each

STATISTICS

Season	GP	FGM	FG%	FTM	FT%	Reb.	Ast.	TP	PPG
1960-61	79	529	.419	331	.666	611	333	1,389	17.6
1961-62	75	799	.445	712	.769	591	402	2,310	30.8
1962-63	55	559	.461	371	.778	384	307	1,489	27.1
1963-64	72	740	.484	584	.832	443	403	2,064	28.7
1964-65	74	822	.497	648	.821	447	364	2,292	31.0
1965-66	79	818	.473	840	.860	562	480	2,476	31.3
1966-67	66	645	.464	602	.878	392	447	1,892	28.7
1967-68	51	476	.514	391	.811	294	310	1,343	26.3
1968-69	61	545	.471	490	.821	262	423	1,580	25.9
1969-70	74	831	.497	647	.824	338	554	2,309	**31.2**
1970-71	69	667	.494	525	.832	320	655	1,859	26.9
1971-72	77	735	.477	515	.814	327	747	1,985	25.8
1972-73	69	618	.479	339	.805	289	607	1,575	22.8
1973-74	31	232	.447	165	.833	116	206	629	20.3
Totals	932	9,016	.474	7,160	.814	5,376	6,238	25,192	27.0

Notes: Boldface indicates statistical leader. GP = games played; FGM = field goals made; FG% = field goal percentage; FTM = free throws made; FT% = free throw percentage; Reb. = rebounds; Ast. = assists; TP = total points; PPG = points per game

of his three years on varsity. He also went on to play for the 1958 Pan-American Games team and the 1960 gold medal Olympic team in Rome. Finally, Jerry was named most valuable player in the 1959 National Collegiate Athletic Association Final Four.

The Emerging Champion

Jerry West entered the National Basketball Association (NBA) in 1961, playing for the Los Angeles Lakers. His first year as a professional was disappointing, as he averaged only 17.6 points per game. With much dedication and perseverance, he finished his second year with an average of 30.8 points per game. One of the highlights of his second season (January 17, 1962) was a 63-point effort against the New York Knickerbockers, a single-game scoring record for guards. Jerry averaged a career high of 31.3 points per game during the 1965-1966 playing season.

By this time in Jerry's career, he was beginning to be recognized as "Mr. Clutch." He earned this nickname because of his ability to win numerous college and professional games in highly pressurized situations. One of his most memorable clutch shots was a 60-foot shot he made in game 3 of the 1970 NBA Championship against New York to send the game into overtime.

Jerry became the fifth player in NBA history to score 20,000 points and the third player to score 25,000 points.. He was also recognized for his defensive skills by being selected to the NBA All-Defensive team from 1969 to 1973. Jerry led the Lakers to the NBA finals nine times. In the 1969 finals against the Boston Celtics, Jerry became the only player on a losing team to win the finals most valuable player (MVP) award.

In 1972, Jerry led the Lakers to their first NBA championship in Los Angeles. Including the playoff games, the Lakers record for the 1971-1972 season was an incredible eighty-one wins and only sixteen losses. Jerry continues to hold many of the Los Angeles Lakers team records. He was named to the NBA Thirty-fifth Anniversary All-Time team in 1980 and to the Naismith Memorial Basketball Hall of Fame in 1979.

Jerry met his wife, Jane, while they were students at West Virginia University. They have three sons, David, Michael, and Mark.

Continuing the Story

Jerry had a distinguished fourteen-year career in the NBA. Former opponents, teammates, coaches, fans, and officials respected Jerry's talent and referred to him as the complete ballplayer. His speed, quickness, shooting ability, leadership, consistency, and perfectionist attitude made him one of college basketball's and the NBA's best players. It is perhaps his dedication and hard work that characterize Jerry's basketball career.

The fame and recognition that Jerry received

HONORS, AWARDS, AND RECORDS

1958	U.S. Pan-American Games Gold Medalist
1959	NCAA Tournament Most Outstanding Player NCAA All-Tournament Team
1959-60	Consensus All-American
1960	U.S. Olympic Gold Medalist Inducted into U.S. Olympic Hall of Fame
1962-74	NBA All-Star Team
1962-73	All-NBA Team
1965-66	NBA record for the most free throws made in a season (840)
1969	NBA Finals most valuable player
1969-73	NBA All-Defensive Team
1972	NBA All-Star Game most valuable player
1979	Inducted into Naismith Memorial Basketball Hall of Fame
1980	NBA 35th Anniversary All Time Team Uniform number 44 retired by Los Angeles Lakers
1995	NBA Executive of the Year
1996	NBA 50 Greatest Players of All Time Team
1999	Named one of the twenty best players of all time

did not change his personality. He remained modest, respectful, and courteous. He suffered numerous injuries throughout his high school, college, and professional careers. He overcame these injuries to become a thirteen-time NBA All-Star. Jerry was named to the All-NBA First Team twelve times. This success has inspired many youths, particularly West Virginia youths, to participate in basketball. His career path from the coal mines of West Virginia to the NBA All-Stars represents the American Dream. Jerry was appointed as the Lakers' head coach in 1976. In three seasons, he guided the Lakers to a 145-101 record. From 1979 to 1982, he served as a scout and special consultant for the Lakers. He was hired as general manager in 1982 and appointed president of the Los Angeles Lakers in the summer of 1988, helping build the Lakers' dynasty of the 1980's.

In 1995 he was promoted to executive vice president of basketball operations for the Lakers. After the Lakers posted their best record in four campaigns, Jerry was named the NBA Executive of the Year for 1995. As part of the celebration of the golden anniversary of the NBA during the 1996-1997 season, Jerry was selected as a member of the NBA's 50 Greatest Players of All Time Team. In 1999, he was named as one of the twenty best NBA players of all time. After the Lakers won the NBA championship in 2000, Jerry announced his retirement from basketball. When the Lakers repeated in 2001, he had the satisfaction of knowing they had done it with a team that he built.

Summary

For many fans, the names "Mr. Clutch" or "Mr. Consistency" are synonymous with Jerry West. His cool, calm, and collected personality and leadership ability on the court were a coach's dream. Jerry remains one of the NBA's most popular players.

Dana D. Brooks

Additional Sources:

Lace, William W. *The Los Angeles Lakers Basketball Team.* Berkeley Heights, N.J.: Enslow, 1998.

Lazenby, Roland. *The Lakers: A Basketball Journey.* New York: St. Martin's Press, 1993.

Thornley, Stew. *Basketball's Original Dynasty: The History of the Lakers.* Minneapolis, Minn.: Nodin Press, 1989.

PETER WESTBROOK

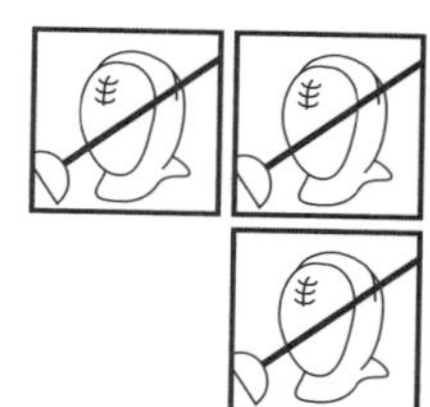

Sport: Fencing

Born: April 16, 1952
St. Louis, Missouri

Early Life

Peter Westbrook was born on April 16, 1952, in St. Louis, Missouri. He was born of Japanese and African American parents. Peter's family moved from St. Louis to Newark, New Jersey, where they lived in the projects in a poor neighborhood for fifteen years. At an early age, Peter realized that he could use sports as a means of getting out of this poor environment and achieving personal success. As a young child, Peter demonstrated a love for fencing. He often spent time watching and imitating the television hero Zorro.

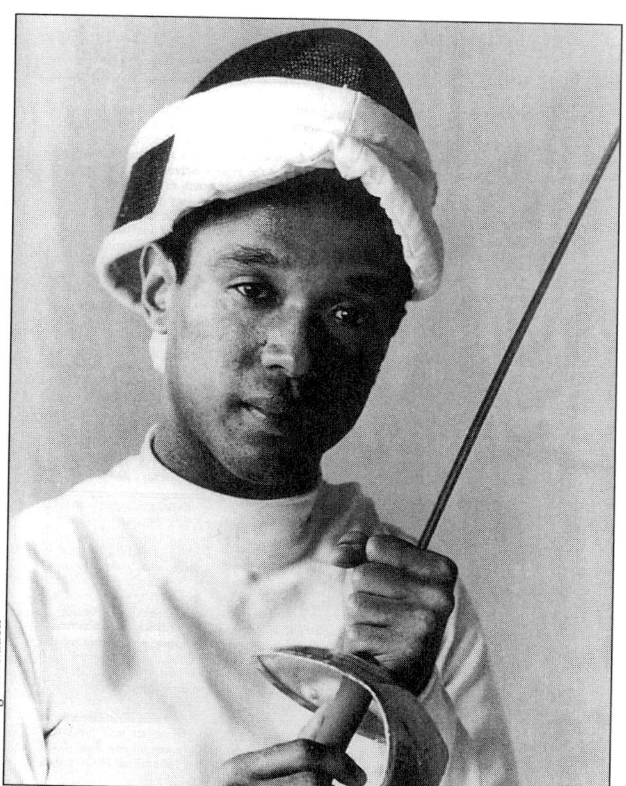

U.S. Fencing Association

The Road to Excellence

Peter's early athletic participation was in the sports of boxing and track and field. His mother, however, recognized Peter's desire to fence and encouraged him to take fencing lessons at Essex Catholic High School in Newark. Peter began taking fencing lessons at the age of fifteen, and by age twenty-one, he was a national and international champion. Dr. Sam D'Ambola was Peter's high school coach; he provided him with encouragement and taught him the basics of fencing.

Fencing is one of the oldest modern sports, dating back to 1896. Today, the foil, épée, and sabre are the three weapons used in the sport of fencing. The foil and épée are thrusting weapons, while the sabre is a thrusting and cutting weapon. The sabre target is larger than that of the foil because the arms and head are also valid targets. Peter concentrated his skills on mastery in sabre fencing.

In 1972, Peter was awarded a fencing scholarship to New York University. At the university, Csaba Elthes (a native Hungarian and 1939 World University Champion) became his fencing coach. Csaba strongly influenced Peter's fencing career development and encouraged him to pursue sabre fencing. Csaba would be Peter's coach for more than seventeen years, and Peter would credit much of his success to Csaba.

Peter was recognized by his teammates and coach for his fencing skills and became team captain. Peter graduated from New York University with a B.S. degree in marketing. In 1985, he was inducted into the New York University Sports Hall of Fame.

The Emerging Champion

Under Csaba's leadership, Peter was exposed to intense and demanding fencing practice sessions, which would often last three hours. This hard work and concentration paid off. In 1974,

MAJOR CHAMPIONSHIPS

Year	Competition	Event	Place
1974-75, 1979-86, 1988-89	U.S. National Championship	Men's sabre	1st
1975	Pan-American Games	Men's sabre	Bronze
1978, 1981, 1983, 1985-86, 1989	U.S. Olympic Festival	Men's sabre	Gold
1979	U.S. Olympic Festival	Men's sabre	Silver
1979, 1987	Pan-American Games	Men's sabre	Silver
1983	Pan-American Games	Men's sabre	Gold
1984	Olympic Games	Men's sabre	Bronze

Peter was selected to the United States World Championship Fencing team and went on to win national sabre titles in 1974 and 1975. His fencing success continued, and he became a member of the 1976 United States Olympic team. Peter sustained an injury during this Olympic competition and finished tied for thirteenth. He also was a member of the 1980, 1984, and 1988 Olympic fencing teams.

During the 1984 Olympics, Peter became the first American to win an Olympic fencing medal (bronze). One of his early significant athletic achievements was winning a gold medal in the 1983 Pan-American Games. He also won silver medals in the 1979 and the 1987 Pan-American Games.

As a further testimony to his fencing prowess, he set an American fencing record when he won the United States Sabre Championships in 1989 for the twelfth time. Never before in the history of American fencing has anyone reached this sustained level of performance. Peter has been blessed with speed, agility, quickness, analytical skill, technical knowledge, and overall athletic ability.

Continuing the Story

At age thirty-seven, Peter was recognized as one of the best sabre fencers in the world. In 1990, he was ranked eighth in sabre fencing. One of the most significant highlights of his fencing career occurred during the 1989 World Championships. During this competition, he defeated world champion Jean François and Fernando Meglis to advance to the finals of the World Fencing Championship. That was a significant event because it marked the first time since 1958 that an American had advanced to the finals in this competition.

Peter would compete in two more Olympic Games after Seoul, but he never equaled his bronze-medal triumph in 1988. Though he did not compete in the 2000 Olympic Games in Sydney, Australia, three of his students from the Peter Westbrook Foundation did. Peter created the foundation in 1991 to enrich the lives of New York's inner-city youth through the sport of fencing. Since 1991, the Peter Westbrook Foundation has become one of the most successful organizations of its kind, receiving national media attention and producing numerous world-class fencers, including Keeth Smart, the top-ranked U.S. fencer in 1999 and two-time National Collegiate Athletic Association (NCAA) champion from St. John's University.

Summary

The name Peter Westbrook means excellence in sabre fencing. He is recognized as America's greatest fencer. His longevity and world ranking in the sport of fencing are testimony to his greatness. He has gained the respect and admiration of his friends and opponents alike.

Dana D. Brooks

Additional Sources:

Mallon, Bill, and Ian Buchanan. *Quest for Gold: The Encyclopedia of American Olympians*. New York: Leisure Press, 1984.

Wallechinsky, David. *The Complete Book of the Olympics*. Boston: Little, Brown and Company, 1991.

Westbrook, Peter. *Blood and Steel: The Memoirs of an American Fencer.* Brooklyn, N.Y.: Cool Grove Press, 1996.

HONORS, AWARDS, AND RECORDS

1980, 1983-84, 1989	USFA Athlete of the Year
1984	First American to win an Olympic fencing medal
1985	Inducted into New York University Sports Hall of Fame

BYRON "WHIZZER" WHITE

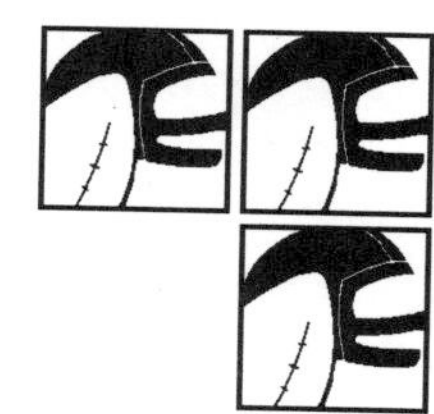

Sport: Football

Born: June 8, 1917
Fort Collins, Colorado

Early Life

Byron "Whizzer" White was born on June 8, 1917, in Fort Collins, Colorado, the son of Alpha Albert White, and Maude (Burger) White. He was raised in the nearby town of Wellington, where his father worked as a lumber dealer and also served as mayor. As a child, Byron worked in the local sugar beet fields and for the railroad as a section hand. The heavy manual labor helped transform the 103-pound youngster into a powerful 175-pound man. The physical work also instilled in him a stamina and determination that he would carry with him throughout his life.

At Wellington High School he compiled a straight-A average and graduated as valedictorian of his class. In addition to his achievements in the classroom, Byron excelled on the football field. However, it was not his athletic skills but his exceptional academic record that led to his enrollment at the University of Colorado in Boulder, where he was awarded a scholarship.

The Road to Excellence

Byron's record of achievement on and off the field continued at the University of Colorado. He received A's in all but two courses and was elected to Phi Beta Kappa. He also served as student body president during his senior year and at his graduation was again the class valedictorian.

Byron was a multitalented athlete. He not only lettered in football but also was an All-Conference guard in basketball and a three-year starter on the baseball team. The athletic editor of the university's yearbook, the *Coloradoan*, noted that "Byron is the ideal athlete. He is a born leader.

New York Times Co./Archive Photos

Byron "Whizzer" White in 1938.

He plays his best game under stiff competition and never fails to come through at the critical moments. A more modest and unassuming young man there never was. But above all these achievements stands Byron himself, a man of strong character."

STATISTICS

For 1938, 1940, and 1941

	Rushing				Receiving			
	Car.	Yds.	Avg.	TD	Rec.	Yds.	Avg.	TD
Total	387	1,319	3.4	11	16	301	18.8	1

Notes: GP = games played; Car. = carries; Yds. = yards; Avg. = average yards per carry *or* average yards per reception; TD = touchdowns; Rec. = receptions

The Emerging Champion

As a swift, elusive halfback, Byron's spectacular runs as a sophomore led a sportswriter for the *Denver Post* to dub him "Whizzer." In his junior year, he began to attract the attention of the nation's sports fans with kickoff returns of 90 and 102 yards, while leading the Mountain State Conference in scoring.

Byron's best season came during his senior year in 1937. The 6-foot 2-inch, 180-pound halfback led the nation in rushing with 1,121 yards in 181 attempts, an average of 6.2 yards per carry, and scoring with 122 points. He scored 16 touchdowns, passed for 475 yards and 2 touchdowns, kicked 23 extra points, and 1 field goal. He led Colorado through an unbeaten season and into the 1938 Cotton Bowl against Rice University.

Byron led the Buffaloes to an early 14 to 0 lead by returning an interception for a touchdown, passing for another, and kicking both extra points. However, Rice came back to win the game by a score of 28 to 14. As a result of his exploits, Byron was named to the 1937 Grantland Rice All-America Team. At the time, he was considered the most popular football player in the United States.

Continuing the Story

Though he earned a Rhodes scholarship to study law at Oxford University following graduation, Byron delayed his graduate schooling to play for the Pittsburgh Pirates (now the Steelers) for $15,800, at the time the highest single-season salary in the National Football League (NFL). In his rookie season, he led the NFL in rushing with 567 yards and was named the league's Rookie of the Year.

Byron began his study of law at Oxford in January, 1939, but his stay there was a brief one. World War II had broken out in September of that year, prompting his return to the United States. Following his arrival, he enrolled in the Yale University Law School but again interrupted his education to play two seasons for the Detroit Lions. In 1940 he repeated as the league's leading rusher with 514 yards, while earning All-NFL honors. After the 1941 season, he retired from football to concentrate on his law studies.

During his professional career, Byron rushed for 1,319 yards in 387 attempts and scored 11 touchdowns. He caught 16 passes for 301 yards and 1 touchdown. In 1954 he was selected for the NFL Hall of Fame. In 1962 he was awarded a gold medal from the National Football Foundation and Hall of Fame in honor of his distinguished service and devotion to the game of intercollegiate football.

From 1942 to 1946, Byron served as an intelligence officer in the U.S. Navy and won two Bronze Stars and a Presidential Unit Citation. It was during this period that he renewed an acquaintance with future U.S. President John F. Kennedy. Following his discharge, Byron returned to Yale to complete his law degree, graduating magna cum laude. In 1962 he was appointed to the U.S. Supreme Court by President Kennedy, where he served until his retirement in 1993.

Summary

Byron "Whizzer" White was the epitome of the scholar-athlete. He was a star athlete at both the professional and collegiate levels, a Rhodes scholar, a wartime naval intelligence officer, a top graduate at Yale Law School, a corporate lawyer, deputy attorney general, and at age forty-four a Supreme Court justice.

Byron's early years of success shaped not only his convictions but also his attitude toward the public spotlight. He was an unpretentious person who avoided publicity, particularly during his role as Supreme Court justice. Later in life, at age eighty-two, he received the Citizen of the West award, which is given annually to the person who exemplifies "the spirit and determination of the western pioneer." For a man who was born in near poverty and rose to the pinnacle of athletic and academic achievement, it was an appropriate honor.

William H. Hoffman

Additional Sources:

"All-Around Nominee: Byron Raymond White." *The New York Times*, March 31, 1962, p. 10.

Hutchinson, Dennis J. *The Man Who Was Whizzer White.* New York: Free Press, 1988.

McAllister, Bill. "Justice Byron 'Whizzer' White Preferred to Stay out of the Limelight." *Denver Post*, January 9, 2000, p. E-01.

RANDY WHITE

Sport: Football

Born: January 15, 1953
Pittsburgh, Pennsylvania

Early Life

Randy Lee White was born on January 15, 1953, in Pittsburgh, Pennsylvania, a city rich in football tradition. He grew up in Wilmington, Delaware, not far from the University of Maryland, where he would become one of the finest defensive tackles ever to play the game. His father, Guy White, had played college football at West Chester State College (now West Chester University of Pennsylvania), the most successful Division II football program in National Collegiate Athletic Association (NCAA) history. He had also served in World War II as a paratrooper.

Dallas Cowboys

The Road to Excellence

Randy's ultimately being named an All-American came as no surprise to his father. Guy White had always expected his son to outwork the competition, to be tough, and to win. Young Randy had been All-State as a fullback and football team captain at Thomas McKean High School in Wilmington, Delaware. He was captain of the basketball and baseball teams his senior year at McKean and was a tri-captain in the 1970 Delaware Blue-Gold All-State football game.

In Randy's senior year, he was seriously recruited only by the University of Delaware, and the University of Maryland in the Atlantic Coast Conference (ACC). He eventually chose to attend Maryland. That choice was to be as good for Randy as it was for new coach Jerry Claiborne. Randy would later credit Claiborne with helping him to organize his life priorities and to focus on football.

The Emerging Champion

Randy showed considerable promise as a freshman at Maryland, playing both fullback and defensive tackle. Against the University of Virginia in 1971, Randy scored on a 17-yard touchdown run by running over six different defenders en route to the end zone. Claiborne arrived in December of 1971 to revive the 1-10 team. An advocate of strong defense and weight training, Claiborne developed Randy into the prototype defensive tackle in Claiborne's innovative defensive scheme. Randy would lead his team not only on defense but in the weight room as well, in off-season training.

White served his mentor well, growing from a 212-pound youth who could run a 4.9-second forty-yard dash to a 262-pound Atlas with a 4.6-second forty-yard dash who could run down halfbacks from behind. Randy set a team bench press record of 460 pounds. In 1974, his senior year, he made 147 tackles, with 68 first hits, and had 12 quarterback sacks on a defense that shut out five opponents and outscored the ACC opposition 198-35.

Randy's senior year at Maryland saw him earn more honors than a defensive tackle could ever imagine. He was a two-time All-American, the Outland Trophy winner, the Lombardi Trophy winner, the ACC Player of the Year, the United Press International Lineman of the Year, the most valuable player in the Liberty Bowl, a two-time All-ACC team nominee, and the New York Downtown Athletic Club's University Player of the Year. Randy led his team to the ACC title, a Liberty Bowl berth against the University of Tennessee, a top twenty national ranking, and national acclaim.

HONORS AND AWARDS

1974-75	College All-American All-Atlantic Coast Conference Team
1975	Rockne Award Outland Trophy Lombardi Award United Press International Lineman of the Year Atlantic Coast Conference Player of the Year Liberty Bowl most valuable player East-West Shrine All-Star Team Chicago College All-Star Team University Player of the Year Amateur Athlete of the Year
1978	Seagram's Seven Crowns of Sports Award NFL Super Bowl co-most valuable player
1978-86	NFL Pro Bowl Team
1994	Inducted into Pro Football Hall of Fame

Continuing the Story

Randy White was selected in the first round of the 1975 National Football League (NFL) draft. He subsequently played fourteen seasons, a long career at any position, for the great Dallas Cowboy teams of Coach Tom Landry. Due to his tremendous athletic ability, the Cowboys initially used him at several positions: linebacker, defensive end, and defensive tackle. They planned for Randy to replace the great Lee Roy Jordan at middle linebacker.

The Dallas organization had hoped Randy could make this positional change, but eventually realized that for Randy defensive tackle was the better choice. As a tackle, he played with ferocity and dominance. The press nicknamed him "Manster," half man, half monster.

Randy had a fantastic NFL career. He accumulated a career total of 111 quarterback sacks; his 701 solo tackles and 403 assisted tackles gave him a total of 1,104 tackles. With the Cowboys, as at the University of Maryland, he was greatly assisted by a fine middle linebacker, Lee Roy Jordan, a player in a much better position to chase the ball. Randy was also named to the Dallas Cowboys' Twenty-Five-Year Silver Season Team as a defensive tackle, made the Pro Bowl team nine times, and was named an All-Pro eight times. His crowning achievement was being named the co-most valuable player following the Super Bowl XII victory over the Denver Broncos in 1978. In 1994 Randy received the final and highest honor when he was inducted into the Pro Football Hall of Fame.

Summary

The uniqueness that made Randy White such a great player went far beyond his physical talents of tremendous speed, strength, agility, and toughness. What took his talents to their ultimate potential were his intense concentration and his focus on excellence. Randy had an indomitable drive to be the best, an indifference toward individual awards, and a competitive ferocity that was frightening. Yet he was also a pleasant, respectful, and humble person. Randy commonly gave levels of effort not seen in the NFL, and his work ethic was legendary.

Thomas R. Park

Additional Sources:

Aseng, Nathan. *Football's Punishing Pass Rushers.* Minneapolis, Minn.: Lerner Publishing, 1984.

Barber, Phil. "NFL: Football's One Hundred Greatest Players—The Hit Men." *Sporting News* 223 (November 1, 1999): 12-16.

Reilly, Rick. "Point After: The Heavenly Hundred." *Sports Illustrated* 70, no. 20 (May 22, 1989): 104-106.

Zimmerman, Paul. "Gangs of Four, the Four-Man Defensive Lines Born in the 50's, Ruled the NFL Until Changes in the Game Spelled Their Doom." *Sports Illustrated* 83, no. 14 (October 2, 1995): 66-73.

REGGIE WHITE

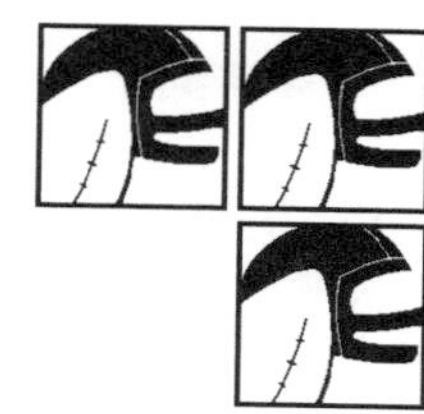

Sport: Football

Born: December 19, 1961
Chattanooga, Tennessee

Early Life

Reginald Howard White was born on December 19, 1961. His mother, Thelma, married Leonard Collier when Reggie was seven years old. Reggie had an older brother, Julius, and a younger half sister, Christie.

At Howard High School in Chattanooga, Tennesee, Reggie played basketball, track, and football. He lettered in football three years as a nose tackle and a tight end. Robert Pulliam, his high school football coach, was an important influence on Reggie, teaching him the fundamentals of football as well as discipline and toughness. While in high school, Reggie was an All-State selection in basketball and an All-American in football. When he was seventeen years old, he became a licensed minister.

The Road to Excellence

Reggie attended the University of Tennessee and became one of the nation's best defensive ends, earning the nickname "Minister of Defense." As a senior, he was named the Southeastern Conference Player of the Year and a consensus All-American. Although Reggie left college before graduating to begin his professional football career, he later returned to earn a bachelor's degree in human services in 1990.

Although Reggie was chosen by the Philadelphia Eagles in the 1984 National Football League (NFL) draft, he began his pro career with the Memphis Showboats of the United States Football League. He played for the Showboats in 1984 and the first part of 1985, and during this time he tackled the quarterback 23 times—the talent for which he would become best known. Early in the 1985 season, Reggie joined the NFL Philadelphia Eagles. As a defensive end, he was named the Rookie of the Year for the National Football Conference (NFC) and recorded 13 sacks and 62 tackles.

AP/Wide World Photos

Reggie White in October, 2000.

The Emerging Champion

After his rookie season in the NFL, Reggie quickly became one of the defensive stars of the league. At 6 feet 5 inches and weighing 300 pounds, he was physically powerful and remarkably quick. In 1986 he was an All-NFL First Team pick after having accumulated 18 sacks during the season. In 1987, Reggie improved his performance with 21 sacks, an NFC record, and was named the NFL Defensive Player of the Year. He also scored a touchdown in 1987, after he took the ball from Washington quarterback Doug Williams and ran 70 yards for a score. He was one of the most durable NFL players, never missing a regular-season game while with the Eagles.

Reggie was also active off the field during this period. In 1991 he published a book titled *The Reggie White Touch Football Playbook* and donated much of his earnings to a maternity home. From 1989 to 1992, he spent many Friday afternoons after practice talking to young people in Philadelphia about the dangers of drugs and alcohol, urging them to stay in school.

In 1993, Reggie was signed by the Green Bay Packers as a free agent. By this time he had married, and he and his wife, Sara, had a son in 1986, Jeremy, and a daughter in 1988, Jecolia. At Green Bay, Reggie was widely recognized as the best defensive lineman in the NFL and the leader of the Packers defense. Green Bay defensive coordinator Fritz Shurmer called Reggie the best defensive end ever to play in the NFL.

Continuing the Story

Reggie made a big difference in the performance of the Packers. Beginning in 1993, Green Bay went to the playoffs six years in a row, winning the Super Bowl after the 1996 season. The Packers improved dramatically on defense after Reggie's arrival, going from twenty-third to second in the league in one year. Although Reggie was thirty-one when he moved to Green Bay and was beyond the prime years of his career, he averaged 11 sacks per year, compared to 15 sacks per year while an Eagle. He became an inspirational team leader. In 1996, the Packers' defense was ranked first in the NFL and allowed only 19 touchdowns throughout the sixteen-game season. Reggie was voted to the NFL All-Pro team year after year.

Reggie announced his retirement from pro football after the 1998 season, his fourteenth in the NFL. At that time, he was recognized as one of the greatest defensive linemen in NFL history. He held the NFL career record of 192½ regular-season sacks (a figure he later raised) and had made twelve Pro Bowl appearances. From 1985 to 1994 he had started 117 consecutive regular-season games and was feared by many quarterbacks—in fact, he sacked 62 different quarterbacks during his career.

In July, 2000, he came out of retirement and signed a new contract with the Carolina Panthers. He hoped to make another trip to the Super Bowl, but the season was a disappointment, and he again considered retirement

Summary

In 1992 Reggie's leadership off the field was recognized, as he was awarded the Byron "Whizzer" White Humanitarian Award by the NFL Players Association. In 1996 he received the Tolerance Award from the Simon Wiesenthal Center. Reggie was also active in helping inner-city

STATISTICS

Season	*GP*	*Tac.*	*Sac.*	*FF*	*FR*	*Int.*
1985	13	100	13.0	0	2	0
1986	16	98	18.0	1	0	0
1987	12	76	**21.0**	4	1	0
1988	16	133	**18.0**	1	2	0
1989	16	123	11.0	3	1	0
1990	16	83	14.0	4	1	1
1991	16	100	15.0	2	3	1
1992	16	81	14.0	3	1	0
1993	16	79	13.0	3	2	0
1994	16	49	8.0	2	1	0
1995	15	42	12.0	2	0	0
1996	16	39	8.5	3	3	1
1997	16	46	11.0	0	2	0
1998	16	47	16.0	4	0	0
2000	16	16	5.5	1	0	0
Totals	232	1,112	198.0	33	19	3

Notes: Boldface indicates statistical leader. GP = games played; Tac. = total tackles; Sac. = sacks; FF = forced fumbles; FR = fumble recoveries; Int. = interceptions

residents of both Knoxville, Tennessee, and Green Bay. He continued to preach in many different churches and was ordained as a nondenominational minister in 1992. However, Reggie also became somewhat controversial because he was outspoken about his Christian faith and his opposition to homosexuality. Despite his controversial views, his achievements in football were never questioned.

Additional Sources:

Gutman, Bill. *Reggie White: Star Defensive Lineman.* Brookfield, Conn.: Millbrook, 1994.

White, Reggie, and Jim Denney. *In the Trenches: The Autobiography.* Nashville, Tenn.: Thomas Nelson Publishers, 1997.

White, Reggie, and Andrew Thomas. *Fighting the Good Fight.* Nashville, Tenn.: Thomas Nelson Publishers, 1999.

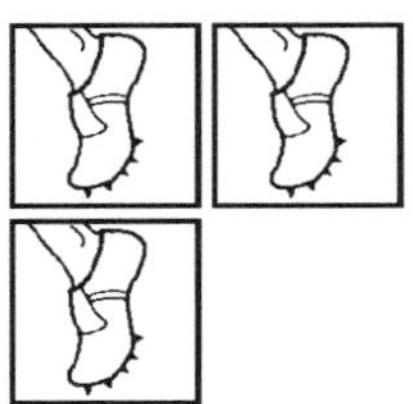

MAL WHITFIELD

Sport: Track and field (middle-distance runs)

Born: October 11, 1924
Bay City, Texas

Early Life

Malvin Greston "Marvelous Mal" Whitfield was born in Texas on October 11, 1924. For African Americans in the segregated South, life offered few avenues for advancement. One was the military. Mal enlisted in the United States Air Force and was stationed in Columbus, Ohio. While there, one of his officers was impressed by Mal's running ability and recommended him to Ohio State University track coach Larry Snyder. Snyder agreed that Whitfield had great potential, and Mal enrolled as a twenty-two-year-old freshman at Ohio State. He would soon prove to be one of the school's greatest athletes.

The Road to Excellence

In 1948 Mal won the national collegiate title in the 880-yard (about 800 meter) race and qualified for the Olympic team. He did so in the most incredible single-day performance of his life, by winning both the 800-meter and the 400-meter dash at the Olympic trials. In his first Olympics he captured gold medals in the 800 meters and in the 400-meter relay and took a bronze in the 400 meters. In 1949 he won another national collegiate title in the 880-yard race and then in 1950 set a world record in that event. Mal was still on active duty as an Air Force sergeant, and he flew twenty-seven bomber missions in the Korean War as a tailgunner.

The Emerging Champion

While in Korea, Mal stayed in shape by training on the icy runways with a pistol at his side. He also worked to keep in good form by running in place in front of a mirror, rapidly pumping his arms. When he returned to competition in 1952, he was ready to defend his titles. In the Olympics that year he again won a gold medal in the 800 meters and also picked up a silver medal in the 4×400-meter relay. He broke his own world record for the 880-yard race that year and finished first in the national Amateur Athletic Union championship in the 400-meter event.

In 1953, in New York's Madison Square Garden, he set a world record in the 600 meters, only an hour after winning the 880 yards in a Garden record. That year also saw Mal establish the world mark in the 1000 meters. For these achievements he received the Sullivan Award in 1954, which recognized him as the top amateur athlete in the United States. He was the first African American to win that distinction.

AWARDS, HONORS, AND VICTORIES

1948	Gold Medal, Olympic 4×400-meter relay Bronze Medal, Olympic 400 meters
1948, 1949	NCAA 880 title
1948, 1952	Gold Medal, Olympic 800 meters
1949, 1950, 1951, 1953, 1954	AAU 880 title
1952	AAU 440 title Silver Medal, Olympic 4×400-meter relay
1954	Sullivan Award
1988	Inducted into U.S. Olympic Hall of Fame

Continuing the Story

Mal finished his college education at Los Angeles State College, graduating in 1956. While completing his studies he tried out for a third U.S. Olympics but narrowly missed making the team. Luckily, he had already found another way to utilize his talents and channel his energies. In 1955 the

AP/Wide World Photos

Mal Whitfield (right) won the 800 meters at the 1948 Olympics.

U.S. government sent Mal on a tour of Africa as part of an effort to generate goodwill among peoples of color around the world. This President's Fund Program featured successful African American athletes and entertainers; other notable participants included Louis Armstrong. Mal had a particularly successful visit to Northern Rhodesia (now Zambia), where he taught secondary school runners some of the secrets of his success and also ran a demonstration race. His visit to the Belgian Congo was much less enjoyable because he found the conditions in which the Africans lived under Belgian rule atrocious.

The trip made quite an impression on Mal, and he continued to work on improving relations between the United States and African nations. One of his main efforts involved training African athletes. Another was working for the International Communication Agency during the Jimmy Carter administration during the late 1970s, serving as a Regional Youth and Sports Officer. One of his accomplishments in that position was to help organize a 1980 tour of Africa by boxer Muhammad Ali.

Summary

Because of his dominant consistency in the 800-meter and 880-yard races in the late 1940's and early 1950's, Mal Whitfield was known as the "Carbon-Copy Two Lap Master." During his career he won a total of five Olympic medals and eight national Amateur Athletic Union titles and set six world records. A fierce competitor who truly cared more about winning than setting records, Mal always shook his opponents' hands after races to see how much strength they had left.

Between 1948 and 1954, Mal won sixty out of the sixty-three races he competed in that were over 400 meters long. Of the sixteen best times

WORLD RECORDS SET

Year	*Event*	*Time*
1952	880 yards	1:48.6
	1,000 meters	2:20.8
1953	880 yards, indoors	1:50.9
	600 meters, indoors	1:09.5

recorded for the 800-meter or 880-yard events up to 1954, Mal was responsible for nine of them. In 1974 he was inducted into the National Track and Field Hall of Fame, and in 1988 he was chosen to be a member of the United States Olympic Hall of Fame. "Marvelous Mal" ranks as one of the greatest middle-distance runners in U.S. history. Moreover, Mal bravely served his country in the Korean War and also made great contributions to international relations as a longtime cultural ambassador to Africa.

Andy DeRoche

Additional Sources:

Guttmann, Allen. *The Olympics: A History of the Modern Games.* Urbana: University of Illinois Press, 1992.

Hickok, Ralph. *A Who's Who of Sports Champions.* New York: Houghton Mifflin, 1995.

Page, James. *Black Olympian Medalists.* Englewood, Colo.: Libraries Unlimited, 1991.

Whitfield, Mal. *Learning to Run.* Nairobi, Kenya: East African Publishing House, 1967.

SIMON WHITFIELD

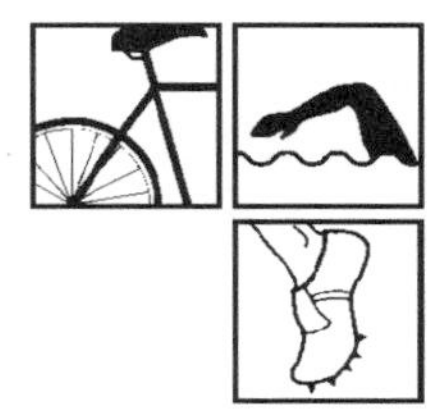

Sport: Triathlon

Born: May 16, 1975
Kingston, Ontario, Canada

Early Life

Simon Whitfield was born in Kingston, Ontario, Canada, on May 16, 1975. In 1987, when he was just twelve, he competed in his first triathlon. He did not have any special equipment and later recalled that he raced in a pair of boxer shorts with little cows on them. And instead of a fancy racing bicycle, he used his mountain bike. Even without the specialized equipment Simon was an instant fan. At that moment, in his own words, he became a "triathlon groupie."

The Road to Excellence

In the fall of 1992 he left Canada to attend Knox Grammar School in Sydney, Australia. His father, Geoff, was raised in Sydney and also attended Knox. Geoff had accepted a scholarship to the University of Alberta, eventually settling in Kingston, Ontario. Simon was now heading in the opposite direction and returning to his father's birthplace. He finished high school at Knox, continuing to train in the triathlon before returning to his native Canada. In 1995 he became a member of Canada's junior national triathlon team and was named the Canadian junior triathlon champion that year. The following year he became a member of Canada's national team.

In 1997 Simon established himself as an international champion when he placed ninth at the World Championships in Perth, Australia. In addition to racing in Australia, he also returned to his second home to train during the difficult Canadian winters. Australia would always hold a place in his heart.

The Emerging Champion

After his world championship showing Simon continued moving steadily up the ranks at national and international competitions. Still a member of the national team, he competed around the world. In 1998 he found himself racing in places as diverse as Hungary and Mexico, eventually becoming the Canadian triathlon champion.

By this time he also began thinking of the 2000 Olympics, in which the men's triathlon event would debut. He started putting all his efforts not only into the sport but also into earning the right to race in his adopted country.

The year preceding the Olympics, 1999, was a successful one for Simon. He made strong showings in the World Championships in Montreal and the ITU World Cup.

AP/Wide World Photos

The 2000 Olympic triathlon was won by Simon Whitfield.

He was becoming known for performing spectacularly under pressure. He added to his previous performances by winning a bronze medal at the Pan-American Games, a win he said was one of the highlights of his career. In 1999 he was again Canadian triathlon champion, as well as being named Triathlon Canada Athlete of the Year.

Prior to the Olympics in September, 2000, Simon had a number of other races to occupy his attention. Although the preparation and training would culminate in the Olympics, races earlier in the year would establish his reputation and standing when he arrived in Sydney.

He placed second in the Rio World Cup and in the Corner Brook World Cup event in Canada and was named Rookie of the Year at the 2000 Aussie Grand Prix. Although he placed only fourth in the 2000 Toronto World Cup, he also found himself in a much more competitive field, good practice to take him into the Olympics. By the time he arrived in Sydney he was ranked the top North American triathlete and twenty-first in the world.

Continuing the Story

After the first leg of the Olympic triathlon, a 1,500-meter swim, Simon emerged from the sixty-one degree waters in Sydney Harbor in twenty-eighth place. The swim was followed by the 40-kilometer (25-mile) bike ride. During this leg of the race tragedy almost struck when he was forced to jump off his bike in order to avoid a pileup, which had already spilled riders across the course. The riders in front of him had lost their concentration, nearly leading to disastrous results for Simon. He jumped off the bike, yelled at the other riders, and then remounted. By the end of this leg he was still more than one minute behind the leaders, with the 10-kilometer (6.2-mile) run left to go.

The race was between Olivier Marceau of France and Stephan Vuckovic of Germany. Vuckovic pulled ahead of Marceau and seemed assured of the win. Simon, however, was an incredible runner, moving steadily up the pack one runner at a time. He surged ahead, nearly catching Vuckovic. The German was not ready to concede the race, however, and poured on additional speed. With only 200 meters (656 feet) left Simon sprinted ahead of Vuckovic, who no longer had the reserves to retake the lead. Simon won the race in 1 hour, 48 minutes, and 24.02 seconds, with a 13.56 second lead over Vuckovic. Simon's family, including his ninety-two-year-old grandmother, were at the finish to cheer him on. In addition to winning the gold in the triathlon's debut, Simon received another honor when that evening he received a call from Canadian prime minister Jean Chrétien congratulating him. Simon won the first gold medal for the Canadians in the 2000 Olympics.

Summary

Simon Whitfield raced because he loved it. Whether in his adopted Australia or in his native Canada he continued to train, slowly inching up the ranks. When he had the opportunity to leave the Olympic village on the eve of his race, he decided to stay because he was inspired by the other athletes. Simon is an example of an athlete who succeeded at his sport not only because he was

MAJOR CHAMPIONSHIPS

Year	Competition	Place
1996	Canadian Duathlon Championships	1st
1997	Triathlon World Championships	9th
	Stage 4 French IronTour	1st
1998	Canadian Triathlon Championships	1st
	Canadian Duathlon Championships	1st
	Ontario Provincial Championships	1st
	sea2summit Adventure Race	1st
1999	Pan-American Games	3d
	Triathlon World Championships	7th
	International Points Race Zundert, Holland (Olympic qualifying race)	1st
	Canadian Triathlon Championships (Olympic qualifying race)	1st
	Nike/Tag Heuer Eliminator	1st
	Stage 5 French IronTour	1st
	World Cup, Noosa, Australia	9th
2000	World Cup, Rio	2d
	World Cup, Corner Brook, Canada	2d
	World Cup, Toronto	4th
	Olympic Games: Triathlon	Gold

driven to win but also because he loved what he was doing. He will be remembered as the first winner of the Olympic gold medal in triathlon.

Deborah Service

Additional Sources:

Allen, Karen. "Teamwork Earns Olympic Triathlon Slot." *USA Today*, July 26, 1999, p. C8.

Fish, Mike. "Men's Triathlon: Whitfield Gets First Gold for Canada." *The Atlanta Journal-Constitution*, September 17, 2000, p. F6.

Layden, Tim. "Testing the Waters." *Sports Illustrated*, September 25, 2000, 52-54.

Pennington, Bill. "A Canadian Hits His Best Stride When It Matters the Most." *The New York Times*, September 17, 2000, p. 8.

Weir, Tom. "Canadian Winner Feels Right at Home." *USA Today*, September 18, 2000, p. E7.

KATHY WHITWORTH

Sport: Golf

Ralph W. Miller Golf Library

Born: September 27, 1939
Monahans, Texas

Early Life

Kathrynne Ann Whitworth was born on September 27, 1939, in Monahans, Texas. The daughter of Dama Ann and Morris Clark Whitworth, Kathy was one of two girls. Her family did not stay long in Texas, but moved to Jal, New Mexico, where her father became the proprietor of a hardware store.

Kathy grew into an overweight teenager. Nevertheless, sports came naturally to her. When she was fifteen, her tennis partners introduced her to the game of golf. She felt herself challenged as never before because it was a game in which one was on one's own—in which one depended only on one's self and accepted responsibility for whatever happened.

An additional bonus also made golf immeasurably appealing to the adolescent Kathy: It proved to be the one sport that helped her to lose weight.

The Road to Excellence

At the Jal Country Club, Kathy studied with golf teacher Harry Loudermilk until he taught her all he knew. When she was ready for more advanced teaching, Loudermilk sent her to Harvey Penick in Austin, Texas. Kathy's supportive mother drove her faithfully the four hundred miles to Austin at regular intervals until she graduated from high school and could move there herself.

By the time Kathy enrolled in a junior college in Odessa, Texas, she had lost fifty pounds. She was still sensitive about her weight, and it cost her the self-confidence necessary to win at golf. Consequently, when she withdrew from college to turn professional, she failed miserably. She then took a year off from professional competition to lose weight and practice her game.

Back on the tour in 1959, Kathy still kept losing during her first three months. Again she thought she would quit. Fortunately, her family supported her. They encouraged her, gave moral support, and arranged for financial backing as well because she was not yet earning any winnings.

She continued on the tour, in spite of a discouraging start. It proved to be a good thing that she did.

The Emerging Champion

By the end of Kathy's first season on tour, she had recorded a scoring average of 80.30 strokes per round, and she had earned some winnings, although only $1,217. It took another two years before she was good enough to pay her own bills and a total of four years on tour before she made a name for herself.

In 1962, Kathy at last won her first two events and came in second in eight others; for this she was named Most Improved Professional of the Year. In 1963, Kathy won eight tournaments and netted $27,000 dollars in winnings. She was thrilled.

The next year, she won $40,000. By 1965 and 1966, she ranked number one among women golf professionals in terms of highest cash winnings and lowest scoring average. She averaged 72.61 and 72.81 strokes per round in the Ladies Professional Golf Association. As a result, during both years, the Associated Press poll voted her Female Athlete of the Year.

Kathy Whitworth had made it, except for one cherished goal—the United States Women's Open, the one championship title she coveted. It was said that Kathy was the best under pressure of anyone who ever played on the tour. Whenever she had the chance to play for the United States Open title, however, she became tense and made too many mistakes.

When she lost the Open in 1972, she decided to change her swing to a more traditional motion rather than the upright one she was used to. This cost her. Then she called on her old golf teacher, Harvey Penick, whose instruction pulled her out of her slump. That season, Kathy went on to play superb golf and to win $85,000. She continued winning for a career total of more than eighty-eight tournaments.

Continuing the Story

Kathy was always fascinated by golf because she felt it impossible to master. She certainly mastered many of its shots, however. Although she was primarily recognized as a long-ball hitter, her forte was the putt. She never seemed to make mistakes on the green or to have to three-putt. She sank her ball every time. On the fairways, she was so focused on scoring that she never cared about style, or relating to onlook-

RECORDS AND MILESTONES

Leading money winner eight times (1965-68, 1970-73)

Recorded lowest scoring average seven times (1965-67, 1969-72)

U.S. Women's Open runner-up (1971), third (1981)

First player to cross the $1 million barrier in career earnings (with a third-place paycheck at the 1981 U.S. Women's Open)

In 2001, her eighty-eight career tournament victories ranked her number one among all golfers, men and women.

HONORS AND AWARDS

1960, 1962	*Golf Digest* Most Improved Player
1965-66	Associated Press Female Athlete of the Year
1965-68, 1971-73	*Golf Digest* Mickey Wright Award for Tournament Victories
1965-67, 1969-72	LPGA Vare Trophy
1966-69, 1971-73	LPGA Player of the Year Rolex Player of the Year
1968-77	*Golf* magazine Golfer of the Decade
1972-73	GWAA Player of the Year
1975	Inducted into LPGA Hall of Fame
1982	Inducted into PGA/World Golf Hall of Fame
1984	Metropolitan Golfwriters and Golfcasters Golf Tee Award Inducted into Sudafed International Women's Sports Hall of Fame
1986	GWAA Richardson Award William and Mousie Powell Award

ers. She no longer worried about her appearance, and she turned out to be a trim, 5-foot 9-inch golfer, weighing 145 pounds.

Kathy served as president of the Ladies Professional Golf Association (LPGA) for many years. She worked to persuade major companies to sponsor the organization's tournaments and to enhance its prizes. Later, as a role model for younger golfers, she became a golf teacher, living in Richardson, Texas.

After 1985, Kathy was no longer able to finish in the top ten. Much of her $1.7 million in winnings was lost when she became the victim of an investment scam. She still had her wealth of knowledge, however, and students who idolized her for her concentration, consistency, and coolness under pressure.

Kathy continued to appear in selected tournaments throughout the 1990's. She competed in the Sprint Senior Challenge from 1991 to 1995 and again in 1997. In each event, she finished in the top five, including two second-place finishes. She was also selected as the team captain in the inaugural Solheim Cup Tournament in 1990 and in 1992. Kathy did not compete in any events in 2000.

Summary

Kathy Whitworth overcame her weight problem to become the leading money-winner of the women's professional golf tour, winning nearly every major LPGA title. She was chosen as the Associated Press Female Athlete of the Year twice and the LPGA's Player of the Year seven times. For her lowest scoring average, she earned the Vare Trophy seven times. Her eighty-eight tournament titles are more than any other golfer, male or female, in history.

Nan White

Additional Sources:

Allis, Peter. *The Who's Who of Golf.* Englewood Cliffs, N.J.: Prentice-Hall, 1983.

Editors of *Golf Magazine. Golf Magazine's Encyclopedia of Golf: The Complete Reference.* New York: HarperCollins, 1993.

Whitworth, Kathy, with Rhonda Glenn. *Golf for Women.* New York: St. Martin's Press, 1992.

MAJOR CHAMPIONSHIP VICTORIES

1965-66	Titleholders Championship
1967, 1971, 1975	LPGA Championship
1967	Western Open Colgate Dinah Shore

OTHER NOTABLE VICTORIES

1963	Carvel Open
1965	Lady Carling Midwest Open
1966	Sutton Lady Carling
1966, 1968	Baltimore Lady Carling
1967	Columbus Lady Carling Los Angeles Open
1968-70, 1974	Orange Blossom Classic
1969	Atlanta Lady Carling Wendell West Open
1971	Lady Carling
1976	Bent Tree Classic
1977	American Defender Classic
1981	Kemper Open

DEENA WIGGER

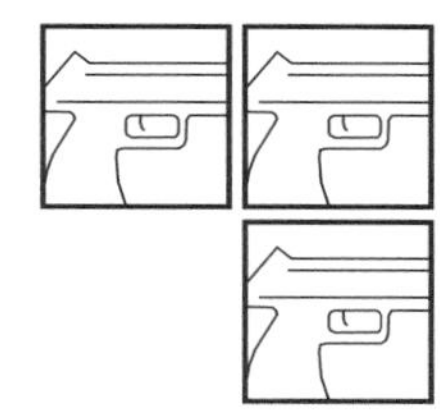

Sport: Shooting

Born: August 27, 1966
Great Falls, Montana

Tim DeFrisco/Allsport

Early Life

Deena Lynn Wigger was born on August 27, 1966, in Great Falls, Montana. Although her childhood was much like that of any other little girl's, she grew up in a family of shooters. Her father, Lones Wigger, was a champion marksman and her two older brothers were competitive rifle shooters as well.

Deena claims she was a "tomboy," preferring rough-and-tumble activities with her brothers and their friends rather than indoor activities. She loved softball and quickly developed the skills and coordination to play alongside the boys. It was no surprise, then, when she asked her father to take her to the shooting range. She was twelve years old and the only girl at the range.

The Road to Excellence

Her shooting career began at the Ft. Benning Rifle Club in Columbus, Georgia, where her father and brothers were active shooters. With the help of her family and the club members, Deena quickly mastered the fundamentals of rifle shooting. She started by shooting an air rifle. Then, as her skills developed, she shot the small-bore .22-caliber rifle.

Progressing rapidly, Deena began to win local competitions within a year. She surprised many experts as she continued to improve in each of the three different rifle events—10-meter air rifle, 50-meter standard rifle, and three-position rifle. Most shooters specialize in only one event.

Shooting is typically dominated by adults. The technical equipment, meticulous routine, and extreme precision of the sport often frustrate youngsters. Deena, however, seemed to thrive on the challenges of the exacting sport. In 10-meter air rifle, the bull's-eye seems no larger than the period at the end of this sentence. Yet Deena often found her mark.

At the age of thirteen, she was the Sub-Junior National Indoor Champion. By the time she was sixteen, she had competed at national level competitions and had won more events and titles in four years than many competitors win in a lifetime.

She continued to compete as she entered high school, and as the competition toughened, so did Deena. As she gained experience, Deena realized that her dreams of becoming a world-

MAJOR CHAMPIONSHIPS

Year	Competition	Event	Place
1983	Pan-American Games	50-meter standard rifle, prone	1st
1985	Championship of the Americas	Air rifle	1st
		50-meter standard rifle, three positions	2d
	World Air Gun Championships	Air rifle	2d
1986	World Shooting Championships	10-meter air rifle	2d
1987	Pan-American Games	50-meter standard rifle, prone	1st
		10-meter air rifle	3d
1989	Championship of the Americas	Air rifle	1st
		50-meter standard rifle, three positions	1st
		50-meter standard rifle, prone	1st
	World Air Gun Championships	Air rifle	1st
1990	World Shooting Championships	Small-bore standard rifle	2d
	World Cup	Air rifle	1st
		Small-bore standard rifle	2d
		Air rifle	3d
	World Cup Finals	Air rifle	2d
	U.S. Olympic Festival	Small-bore standard rifle	Bronze
		Air rifle	Bronze
		Air rifle	Bronze
	U.S. Nationals	Small-bore standard rifle	1st
		Small-bore standard rifle, prone	1st
	NCAA Championships	Air rifle	2d
1991	World Cup USA	Air rifle	2d
1995	Pan-American Games	Standard rifle 3-by-20	1st
1999	Oceania 99	50-meter standard, three positions	1st
2000	Rocky Mountain Rifle Championships	Air rifle, prone	1st

class competitor could become a reality. Analyzing her father's success, the young athlete charted a course to her own great accomplishments. She intensified her training, often practicing six days a week. Her scores soared.

The Emerging Champion

In 1983, her training paid off. Deena made the Pan-American Games team in the women's standard rifle event. She was sixteen years old and a freshman in high school. She was the youngest competitor among all the shooters, yet she was performing at the level of a much more experienced shooter.

In fact, she performed like a champion and won the gold medal. It was her first major victory and certainly a victory for the entire Wigger family. Deena's father also made the Pan-American team, and the father-daughter combination attracted attention worldwide.

Featured on television talk shows, in newspaper and magazine articles, and on radio, Deena and her father made headlines. Deena lived up to the media's expectations, winning competition after competition. She eventually earned a full athletic scholarship at Murray State University, Kentucky. America had high hopes for this young star.

Deena failed to make the 1984 United States Olympic team, falling short by only a few points. Nevertheless, she turned disappointment into an intense desire to succeed. She set a series of goals for herself, including a world shooting title.

In 1986, she came within 3 points of her goal. At the World Shooting Championships in Suhl, East Germany, Deena won a silver medal. Her dominance at the national level was no fluke; she had established herself as a world-class shooter at the age of twenty.

Continuing the Story

In 1988, Deena earned a spot on the United States Olympic team but was again denied a medal by only a few points. Still, her performance in Seoul, South Korea, provided the valuable experience she needed to prepare for the 1989 World Championships in Munich, Germany.

After the semifinal round of the competition for the Women's Air Rifle title in Munich, Deena was in seventh place. She was the last competitor to qualify for the final shoot-off round. Fighting off tremendous pressure, Deena scored ten straight bull's-eyes to take the lead and the gold medal.

Deena also won a medal in the 1990 World Shooting Championships in Moscow. In fact, she has won more than thirty medals in nearly twenty world-level competitions. She consistently dominates her competition and continues to improve her scores. At the Zurich World Cup Competition, in May, 1990, she set a world record in the women's air rifle event, scoring 398 points out of a possible 400.

She became a resident of the Olympic Training Center in Colorado Springs, Colorado, so that she could train year-round. Although her competitive lifestyle might seem ideal to some people, the demands of competition are many. Deena says her life "revolves around shooting," and she has had to make many sacrifices.

Deena does not see the years spent in competitive shooting as wasted time. She applies the skills learned in shooting to other areas in her life. Because of her great concentration and dedication, she earned a 3.5 grade-point average in college. In addition, the self-confidence Deena gained over the years helped her to become a fashion model during the off-season.

In the 1991 World Cup USA in Chino, California, Deena finished second in the women's standard rifle three-position behind Valentina Chertasoua of the Soviet Union, who broke Deena's world record with 399 out of 400 points.

Deena's Olympic disappointments continued in 1992, when she failed to qualify for the U.S. team. In 1994 she enlisted in the Wyoming Air National Guard and began active duty in 1995. She served as assistant coach to the Air Force Academy's rifle team. She also finished first in the standard rifle 3×20 event at the 1995 Pan-American Games and was named Air Force Female Athlete of the Year in 1996.

Deena did not make the 1996 or 2000 U.S. Olympic teams, though she continued to finish well in other competitions. She took first place in the prone air rifle event at the Rocky Mountain Rifle Championship, a tune-up event that opens the shooting season. She also finished fourth in the 50-meter sport rifle competition at the 2000 World Military Shooting Championship in Ankara, Turkey.

Summary

Though Deena Wigger's goal of winning Olympic gold has remained unfulfilled, she has distinguished herself in national and international events, winning gold medals in the 1983, 1987, and 1995 Pan-American Games. She, and other top female competitors, have done much to help popularize a sport that boasts seventeen Olympic events.

William B. Roy

Additional Sources:

Beeman Home Page. http://www.beeman.com/more/.htm.

Jones, Robert F. "Triggers for Wiggers." *Sports Illustrated* 66 (March 30, 1987): 79.

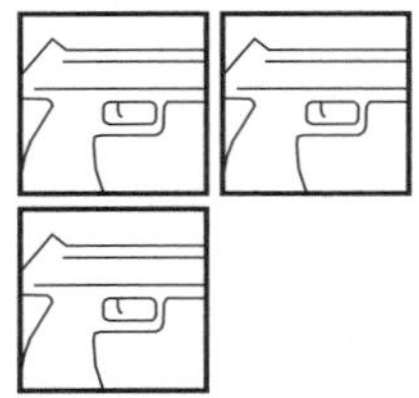

LONES WIGGER

Sport: Shooting

Born: August 25, 1937
Great Falls, Montana

Early Life

Lones Wesley Wigger, Jr., was born on August 25, 1937, in Great Falls, Montana. As a child, Lones developed a love for sports, especially basketball and baseball. Unfortunately, Lones was neither big nor fast as a child. Nevertheless, he wanted to compete.

The Wigger family lived in Carter, Montana, a rural community without many organized activities for young boys. So when his father offered to take him shooting at the local range, eleven-year-old Lones jumped at the chance.

As his father watched Lones shoot, he could not have known what was in store for his son. After all, no one could guess that this small but determined young man would become the most successful shooter in the history of the sport.

The Road to Excellence

Usually the first person to arrive and the last to leave, Lones soon became a fixture at the shoot-

Tim DeFrisco/Allsport

Lones Wigger, left, with daughter Deena.

ing range. First, he learned to fire the small-bore .22-caliber rifle, then the larger, .30-caliber rifle. He loved to shoot, and his skills grew along with his love for the sport. Lones Wigger had finally found his niche.

With his father as a coach, Lones became proficient enough to compete with the senior members of the Carter Gun Club. Lones won his first medal at the age of twelve, shooting against older competitors. In fact, Lones was the only youngster among the club members.

Very often, the young man beat more experienced adults. Competing against better shooters forced Lones to set high goals, a situation that prepared him for a lifetime of stiff competition.

As he entered high school, Lones's scores were the ones to beat. In 1955, as a seventeen-year-old, Lones competed at the National Matches at Camp Perry, Ohio, and won his state's championship. A year later, he became the top shooter at Montana State University, where he joined the Army Reserve Officer's Training Corps (ROTC) marksmanship team.

While competing for his ROTC team, he caught the eye of Bill Krilling and Gary Anderson, champion shooters with the United States Army Marksmanship Unit (USAMU). They could hardly wait for the young Wigger to receive his Army commission; once on active duty, Lones would be eligible to shoot for the USAMU.

The Emerging Champion

In 1961, Lieutenant Lones Wigger was assigned to the USAMU, and his illustrious career took off. Within two years, he was on the Pan-American Games team, and in 1964, he made the United States Olympic team. At the 1964 Olympiad, in Tokyo, Japan, he won a gold medal in the small-bore three-position event. He established a world record of

MAJOR CHAMPIONSHIPS

Year	Competition	Event	Place
1963	Pan-American Games	Small-bore rifle, individual	2d
		Small-bore rifle, team	1st
1964	Olympic Games	Small-bore rifle, three-position individual	Gold
		Small-bore rifle, English match individual	Silver
1966	World Championships	Small-bore rifle, various team events	1st (3)
		Small-bore rifle, team	3d
		Free rifle, team	1st
1970	World Championships	Small-bore rifle, individual	3d
		Free rifle, individual	2d
		Air rifle, team	2d
		Army rifle, team	2d
		Small-bore rifle, team	1st
		Small-bore rifle, various team events	2d (3)
		Free rifle, team	2d
		Free rifle, various team events	1st (2)
1971	Pan-American Games	Small-bore rifle, individual	2d
		Small-bore rifle, team	1st
1972	Olympic Games	Free rifle, individual	Gold
1973	Championship of the Americas	Small-bore rifle, various individual events	1st (3)
		Free rifle, individual	1st
		Free rifle, individual	2d
		Small-bore rifle, team	1st
		Free rifle, team	1st
1974	World Championships	Small-bore rifle, individual	1st
		Small-bore rifle, individual	2d
		Free rifle, individual	3d
		Army rifle, individual	2d
		Small-bore rifle, various team events	1st (2)
		Small-bore rifle, team	2d
		Free rifle, various team events	1st (3)
		Free rifle, team	2d
		English match, team	2d
		Army rifle, team	1st
1975	Pan-American Games	Small-bore rifle, individual	2d
		Small-bore rifle, team	1st
1977	Championship of the Americas	Small-bore rifle, various individual events	2d (2)
		Free rifle, individual	1st
		Air rifle, individual	3d
		Small-bore rifle, various team events	1st (2)
		Free rifle, team	1st
		Air rifle, team	2d
1978	World Championships	Small-bore rifle, individual	2d
		Free rifle, individual	1st
		Free rifle, individual	2d
		Free rifle, individual	3d
		Small-bore rifle, various team events	1st (3)
		Free rifle, various team events	1st (3)
		Free rifle, team	2d
1979	Pan-American Games	Small-bore rifle, various individual events	1st (2)
		Small-bore rifle, various team events	1st (2)

1,164 in that event, shattering the old record by 7 points.

Most athletes could only hope to compete in an Olympiad, and for the majority, winning a medal remains only a lifelong dream. For Lones, the 1964 Olympiad was only the first of four in which he competed. He also made the 1968, 1972, and 1980 Olympic teams. He won a total of three Olympic medals, two golds and a silver.

For Lones, success was measured in both excellence and longevity. Throughout a career that spanned nearly four decades, he set more national and world records than any Olympic competitor in history. He has held twenty-eight world records, several hundred national records, and untold match records.

For more than twenty years, Lones Wigger was the dominant competitor in the shooting sports. His most enduring accomplishment is his winning twenty-two World Championship gold medals, a feat that may never be equaled. Other accomplishments are also legendary. He competed in six Pan-American Games and won eighty national championships in various shooting events. At the World Championships in 1974, he set four world records in one day.

Continuing the Story

The enduring significance of this great career is easy to appreciate. He won 145 medals in international competition and set the standard for the world of shooting—he was clearly the one to beat. Even after thirty-seven years as a competitor, however, he was not through with shooting. Lones decided to contribute to his sport in a different way.

Retiring in 1987 from the Army as a lieutenant colonel, Lones became the director of the United States shooting team at the Olympic Training Center in Colorado Springs, Colorado. In his new position, he found himself in a familiar role as coach. For many years during his own competitive life, he had nurtured young men and women on their way to successful careers as competitors.

For example, his three children, Ronald, Danny, and daughter Deena, each developed a passion for competitive shooting. Following closely in his father's footsteps, Ronald shot on the USAMU. Deena became one of America's most successful women shooters. In addition, more than a dozen of his students have gone on to compete for United States teams, and his Ft. Benning Junior Rifle Club was virtually unbeatable for ten years.

While many young competitors would love to know the formula for his success, Lones claims his only secret was an appreciation of hard work. Vowing never to be outworked by his opponents, Lones spent many thousands of hours shooting on the firing line, meticulously placing bullets through the same hole on a target.

In addition to preaching hard work as the main ingredient for training, Lones encouraged his shooters to increase their intensity whenever they represent a

MAJOR CHAMPIONSHIPS

Year	Competition	Event	Place
1981	Championship of the Americas	Small-bore rifle, individual	1st
		Small-bore rifle, individual	2d
		Free rifle, individual	1st
		English match, individual	2d
		Standard rifle, individual	1st
		Small-bore rifle, various team events	1st (2)
		Free rifle, team	1st
		Standard rifle, team	1st
		English match, team	1st
1982	World Championships	Free rifle, individual	3d
		Standard rifle, individual	2d
		Free rifle, various team events	2d (2)
		Free rifle, various team events	3d (2)
1983	Pan-American Games	Small-bore rifle, individual	1st
		Small-bore rifle, individual	2d
		Free rifle, individual	1st
		English match, individual	2d
		Small-bore rifle, various team events	1st (2)
		Free rifle, team	1st
		English match, team	1st
1985	Championship of the Americas	Small-bore rifle, various individual events	1st (2)
		Small-bore rifle, individual	2d
		Free rifle, various individual events	2d (3)
		Small-bore rifle, various team events	1st (4)
		Free rifle, various team events	1st (4)
1986	World Championships	Free rifle, various team events	2d (3)
		Standard rifle, team	2d

HONORS, AWARDS, AND MILESTONES

Won 145 medals overall in international competition
Inducted into U.S. Army Marksmanship Unit Hall of Fame
Inducted into Montana State University Sports Hall of Fame

team, whether their team is a local gun club or the United States team. Lones always viewed his membership on United States shooting teams as added incentive to perform well.

Summary

There can be little doubt that Lones Wigger is the greatest shooter ever. Many people believe he is the greatest competitor ever, in any sport. His longevity, unequaled victory tally, and series of national and world records seem to support that claim. Yet this personable man is most proud of his work with young shooters, starting them in a sport they can enjoy for years. He transformed his intense, competitive nature into a desire to mold young men and women into better shooters as well as better citizens.

William B. Roy

Additional Sources:

Hickok, Ralph. "Wigger, Lones W., Jr." In *A Who's Who of Sports Champions.* Boston: Houghton Mifflin, 1995.

Irwin, Michael R. "Wigger, Chesser Win National Titles." *American Rifleman* 140 (October, 1992): 38-42.

Jones, Robert F. "Triggers for Wiggers." *Sports Illustrated* 66 (March 30, 1987): 79.

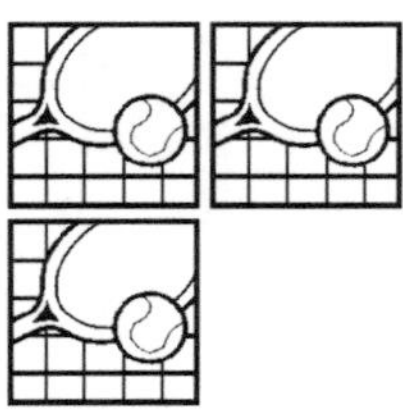

HAZEL WIGHTMAN

Sport: Tennis

Born: December 20, 1886
Healdsburg, California
Died: December 5, 1974
Chestnut Hill, Massachusetts

Early Life

Hazel Virginia Hotchkiss, one of the most durable women's tennis champions in the United States, was born in Healdsburg, California, on December 20, 1886. Her father, William Hotchkiss, had come to California from Kentucky in a covered wagon train when he was two years old. Her mother, Emma Groves, met William when her family settled on a ranch right next to the Hotchkiss family's land in the Sonoma Valley. After their marriage, William and Emma had five children. Their fourth child, their only daughter, was Hazel.

Hazel was considered a rather delicate child, so her family provided her with many opportunities to develop her strength. She enjoyed the sports her brothers played, and they encouraged her participation. It is said that the vigor Hazel grew to possess reflected that of her mother. Mrs. Hotchkiss showed her indomitable strength even in her sixties, when a car she thought she had parked rolled over her foot. The clear-thinking woman, realizing that the brake had slipped, managed to reach the brake handle and stop the car before she collapsed. A Christian Science practitioner treated her that evening, and by the next morning she was up and about, showing no signs of injury.

The Road to Excellence

By the time Hazel was fourteen, her family had moved to Berkeley, California, and there Hazel was introduced to tennis. Her brothers also played the game, so she nearly always had someone to hit with her. When they were not available, Hazel hit against the wall of the house. Hazel and her brothers played on a gravel area in their backyard. Their net was a rope, and in an effort to defend themselves from flying gravel and the erratic bounces of the ball, they became excellent volleyers. (To volley a tennis ball is to hit it before it bounces.) This skill later became the earmark of Hazel's success and helped her to revolutionize women's tennis.

Courtesy of Amateur Athletic Foundation of Los Angeles

Soon after Hazel began to play tennis, she had the opportunity to see the Sutton sisters, Ethel, Violet, Florence, and May, in action. These sisters were renowned as the finest women players in California. Hazel was excited by their performance and eager to compete at their level, but she found their style of play, which relied almost completely on a backcourt game with only ground strokes (forehands and backhands), a bit too tame. She preferred to play the more aggressive game that the boys played, which was characterized by volleys as well as ground strokes.

Her primary goal, however, was to beat the Suttons. She soon defeated Violet, Ethel, and Florence, but she was twenty-three before she defeated May. The intense rivalry between these two players, both before and after that conquest, provided some of the most exciting tennis in California and is credited with making the game popular for women there.

The Emerging Champion

While Hazel was developing her tennis skills, she was also sewing, playing the piano, and graduating from high school and entering the University of California. In 1909, when she had completed her sophomore year there, her father took her to Philadelphia to play in her first U.S. National Championship. She had a very successful time, winning the women's singles, women's doubles, and the mixed doubles events. She won the women's doubles with Edith E. Rotch of Boston, with whom she had never played before. She won the mixed doubles with Wallace F. Johnson, a top California player. Hazel matched this feat in both 1910 and 1911. In 1911, the weather was so bad that she had to play all three finals matches on the same day.

In 1912, Hazel married George Wightman and settled in the Boston area. During the following seven years, she retired somewhat from tennis to raise three children. She did compete in the 1915 U.S. National Championship, and lost to Molla Bjurstedt of Norway, in the finals. In 1919, however, she returned to win her last U.S. National Championship singles title; that year marked the real beginning of her doubles successes.

Continuing the Story

Hazel was a cheerful, tireless, and gracious player, and her skill at the net made her very popular as a doubles partner. Over the years, she played doubles with the finest players, men and women, in the game, including such players as Helen Wills and Bill Tilden. In 1923, she donated a cup that was to be awarded to the winner of a team match between women of the United States and Great Britain. The cup, known as the Wightman Cup, was originally meant to parallel

MAJOR CHAMPIONSHIP VICTORIES AND FINALS

1909-11, 1919	U.S. National Championship
1909-11, 1915	U.S. National Championship doubles (with Edith E. Rotch; with Eleanora Sears)
1909-11, 1915, 1918, 1920	U.S. National Championship mixed doubles (with Wallace F. Johnson; with Joseph R. Carpenter, Jr.; with Harry C. Johnson; with Irving C. Wright)
1915	U.S. National Championship finals

OTHER NOTABLE VICTORIES

1919, 1927	U.S. Indoor Championship
1919, 1921-22, 1924, 1927, 1928-31, 1933	U.S. Indoor Championship doubles (with Marion Zinderstein Jessup; with Sarah Palfrey)
1923-24, 1926-28	U.S. Indoor Championship mixed doubles (with Burnham N. Dell; with Bill Tilden; with G. P. Gardner, Jr.; with Henry L. Johnson, Jr.)
1924	Olympic Gold Medal doubles (with Helen Wills) Olympic Gold Medal mixed doubles (with Richard Norris Williams)
1940-42, 1944, 1946-50, 1952, 1954	U.S. Grass Court Championship-Women's 40 doubles (with Edith Sigourney; with Molly T. Fremont-Smith; with Jessup; with Marjorie G. Buck; with Nell Hopman)

the Men's Davis Cup and include many nations, but the idea was not carried through. The Wightman Cup matches, however, have continued with few interruptions since 1923.

MILESTONES

U.S. Wightman Cup team captain (1923-24, 1927, 1929, 1931, 1933, 1935, 1937-39, 1946-48)

Presented the USLTA with a sterling vase for international women's team competition (known as the Wightman Cup)

HONORS AND AWARDS

1940, 1946	Service Bowl Award
1957	Inducted into National Lawn Tennis Hall of Fame
1960	Marlboro Award
1973	Order of Honorary Commander of the British Empire

Hazel continued to play tennis for the rest of her life, winning forty-five national titles in the sport. She won her last national title in 1954, at the age of sixty-eight. She also won the national squash championship, and was runner-up for the national badminton doubles title when she was in her fifties.

Hazel gave as much as she received in tennis. For years she spent hours teaching eager young players all the important aspects of the game. One day she spent an impromptu seven straight hours working with young students, without leaving the court even to eat. She was also a tireless hostess to legions of top tennis players who had come to play in the Boston area. She was deeply respected and appreciated by all in the tennis world and was elected to the International Tennis Hall of Fame at Newport, Rhode Island, in 1957. Hazel died at the age of eighty-seven in Chestnut Hill, Massachusetts, in 1974.

Summary

Hazel Wightman was one of the most respected and durable tennis players in the game's history. She played the game for more than seventy years and won forty-five National Championships in the process. Her game was characterized by power and accuracy at the net and by brilliant strategy. A small woman, Hazel brought vigor and determination to the game, but she balanced these qualities with grace and never allowed her opponents to be humiliated regardless of their competitive level. She gave back to tennis years of teaching that helped to foster some of the game's top women players. She also opened her home to needy players and was known for her capabilities as a hostess. In addition to her accomplishments in tennis, she was also a national champion in squash and badminton. With her passing, tennis and all racquet sports lost a true friend and champion.

Rebecca J. Sankner

Additional Sources:

Collins, Bud, and Zander Hollander, eds. *Bud Collins' Modern Encyclopedia of Tennis.* 3d ed. Detroit: Gale, 1997.

Grimsley, Will. *Tennis: Its History, People, and Events.* Englewood Cliffs, N.J.: Prentice-Hall, 1971.

Sherrow, Victoria, ed. *Encyclopedia of Women and Sports.* Santa Barbara, Calif.: ABC-CLIO, 1996.

Wightman, Hazel H. *Better Tennis.* Boston: Houghton Mifflin, 1933.

MATS WILANDER

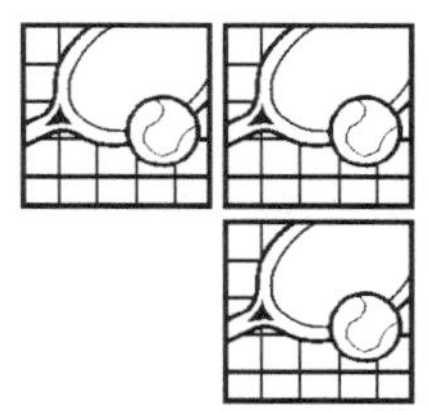

Sport: Tennis

Born: August 22, 1964
Växjö, Sweden

Early Life

Mats Arne Wilander was born on August 22, 1964, in Växjö, a small industrial city in southern Sweden, to Einar Wilander, a factory foreman, and Karin Wilander, an assembly-line worker. Mats was the youngest of three brothers. At the age of six, he began playing tennis on a makeshift court that his father had fashioned in a factory parking lot. When Mats was not playing against his father, he would challenge anyone who passed by, and sometimes his father would have to return late at night to force Mats to come home.

AP/Wide World Photos

Mats Willander goes for the ball in a 1996 match.

In addition to tennis, he also enjoyed playing ice hockey. Mats won his first national tennis tournament as an eleven-year-old playing in the under-twelve division. He would go on to also win the under-fourteen and under-sixteen division titles. Mats soon decided to stop playing ice hockey and concentrate all of his efforts toward improving his tennis game.

The Road to Excellence

Encouraged by his coaches and family but never pressured, Mats continued to make strides as a tennis player. Because of the success of tennis great Björn Borg, an organized tennis program had sprouted in Sweden. After turning professional in 1980, in 1981 Mats joined Team SIAB, which was named for and sponsored by a Swedish construction company. Mats and his teammates traveled together on the professional tennis circuit, and he remained on the team until 1983.

Borg had won his final French Open in 1981. With his retirement from competitive tennis, Sweden did not know from where its next tennis champion would come. Mats entered the 1982 French Open—one of tennis' four Grand Slam tournaments—as an unseeded player. He had foot speed, a solid forehand, and a good two-handed backhand, and he was an unrelenting competitor. He was only seventeen, though, and no one gave him much chance to advance very far in the tournament.

Mats proved the experts wrong by beating four top players—Ivan Lendl, Vitas Gerulaitis, Jose-Luis Clerc, and Guillermo Vilas—to win the title. In the final, Mats defeated the powerful former champion Vilas in four grueling sets (1-6, 7-6, 6-0, 6-4). With the victory, he became the youngest player to become the French Open champion (a record he held until Michael Chang's victory in 1989). In Sweden, Mats was hailed as the next Borg. Mats, though, did not want to compete with the memory of Borg. He resented the comparison and wanted to be recognized for his own talents.

The Emerging Champion

Because of his fine play in 1982, Mats became the seventh-ranked player in the world. He also was named *Tennis* magazine's Rolex Rookie of the Year. Mats had made an auspicious entrance into the world of professional tennis.

At 6 feet tall, the right-handed Mats had the potential of becoming more than a tenacious baseline competitor, and he worked hard to add power to his serve and to become comfortable volleying at the net. In 1983, he won his second Grand Slam title, capturing the Australian Open on the grass courts of Kooyong, near Melbourne. That year, he also reached the final of the French Open, where he lost to Yannick Noah. Mats finished 1983 ranked fourth in the world.

MAJOR CHAMPIONSHIP VICTORIES AND FINALS	
1982, 1985, 1988	French Open
1983, 1987	French Open finalist
1983-84, 1988	Australian Open
1985	Australian Open finalist
1987	U.S. Open finalist
1988	U.S. Open
OTHER NOTABLE VICTORIES	
1984-85, 1987	On victorious Swedish Davis Cup team
1988	Lipton International Players' Championship

Mats won the Australian Open title again in 1984. He also helped Sweden to win the 1984 and 1985 Davis Cup team competitions. He had become a complete tennis player, and he was a threat to win on all court surfaces.

One of the most stabilizing events of Mats's life was when he met his future wife, Sonya Mulholland, at the 1985 U.S. Open. Sonya was a Manhattan-based model who was born in Zambia but reared in South Africa. Mats had become weary of the constant traveling on the tennis tour, but Sonya helped him to become a more focused and much happier person. On January 3, 1987, Mats and Sonya were married in South Africa.

In 1985, Mats won his second French Open, defeating Lendl in the final. His 1985 world ranking rose one spot to number three, where it remained for 1986 and 1987. In 1987, Mats was runner-up to Lendl at both the French Open and the U.S. Open, but he did help Sweden to once again capture the Davis Cup. Mats had continued to improve his game; with the help of his coach, John-Anders Sjogren, he had added new strokes, including a one-handed slice backhand. Mats and Joakim Nystrom won the 1986 Wimbledon doubles title, an indication of how much he had improved his play around the net.

In 1988, Mats would have his best year. He won three of the four Grand Slam titles, including the Australian, French, and U.S. Opens. At the U.S. Open, Mats outlasted Lendl in a final that was more than four hours long (6-4, 4-6, 6-3, 5-7, 6-4). Mats became the first tennis player to win three Grand Slam titles in a single year since Jimmy Connors in 1974. Lendl had been the number-one ranked player in the world for the previous three years, but with Mats's wonderful string of victories, he became the number-one player.

Continuing the Story

Mats had proven that he was a tough competitor in the Grand Slam tournaments. He had fought very hard to become the world's top-ranked player, but once he had attained the summit, his motivation began to wane. Always a low-key individual, Mats was content that he had reached number one; he was not as worried

HONORS, AWARDS, AND MILESTONES

1982	Rolex Rookie of the Year
1988	Ranked number one in the world

about maintaining the ranking. He liked to relax at his home in Greenwich, Connecticut, and he preferred savoring what he had accomplished to fighting hard on the tennis court. Nagging injuries, his father's death, and the birth of a daughter led Mats to look at tennis as something that he enjoys but did not crave, and he retired from competitive tennis in 1991. Mats had earned more than $7 million in prize money and had won thirty-three career titles, including eight Grand Slam titles.

Mats came out of retirement in 1993, saying that he expected to play tennis for as long as he found competing to be fun. In addition to his family and tennis, Mats loved playing the electric guitar, and he toured Sweden with his group, Wilander. He began playing on the Worldwide Senior Tennis Circuit in 1997. On October 10, 2000, the second annual Mats Wilander Celebrity Tennis and Golf Challenge was held.

Summary

Mats Wilander was one of the fiercest competitors in the history of tennis. Although his tennis game was more suited to playing on clay courts, he adapted his style of play to become a threat on all court surfaces. During his prime years, Mats was always in contention to win a major title.

Jeffry Jensen

Additional Sources:

Bodo, Peter. "Mats Wilander: A Classic Champion from an Unclassical Mold." *Tennis* 20 (September, 1984): 50-57.

Evans, Richard. *Open Tennis: 1968-1988.* Lexington, Mass.: Stephen Greene Press, 1989.

Shmerler, Cindy. "Mats Wilander: The Former World No. 1 Now Spends Most of His Time Playing Mom to His Four Children, and Loving It." *Tennis* 36 (March, 2000): 18.

Wind, Herbert Warren. "Wilander's Open." *The New Yorker* 64 (October 17, 1988): 84-94.

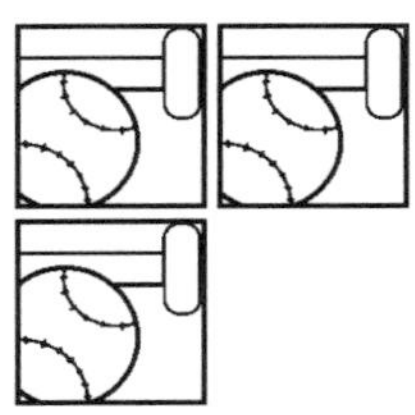

HOYT WILHELM

Sport: Baseball

Born: July 26, 1923
Huntersville, North Carolina

Early Life

Hoyt Wilhelm grew up as one of eleven children in a poor tenant farm family in the rural South during the era of the Great Depression. Born in Huntersville, a small town outside Charlotte, North Carolina, in 1923, Hoyt moved as a child with his family to a farm five miles away in the countryside. He developed an early interest in baseball and, encouraged by his father, often played the game with older boys. He began to throw the knuckleball at age twelve, after reading about this unusual pitch in a Charlotte newspaper's feature article on the Washington Senators. Since few pitchers master the knuckleball, Wilhelm's early success with it for his Cornelius High School team in the late 1930's and early 1940's gained much local attention.

The Road to Excellence

Hoyt played his first season of professional baseball in 1942 with the Mooresville team of the North Carolina State League. He won ten games and lost only three but had a less-than-stellar earned run average of 4.25. His main pitch, the knuckleball, was also a problem. For a knuckleball pitch, the ball is grasped by the fingertips, not the knuckles, and is thrown with an easy motion so as to release the pitch with virtually no spin. The absence of spin combines with the stitching on the surface of the ball to make it move in an irregular, unpredictable path from the mound to home plate. A properly thrown knuckleball is difficult to hit, but it is also difficult to catch. The absence of experienced catchers in the minor leagues meant that knuckleball pitchers had difficulty moving up through the very competitive system in professional baseball to earn a chance to play in the major leagues.

AP/Wide World Photos

Atlanta Brave Hoyt Wilhelm demonstrates his knuckleball in 1970.

After three years in the Army during World War II, including combat service in the Battle of the Bulge, Hoyt returned to baseball but moved up slowly in the farm system of the New York Giants. He reached the highest level of the minor leagues at Minneapolis of the American Association in 1951. By this time, however, he was twenty-eight years old, an age when most major league players have established themselves.

The Emerging Champion

Leo Durocher, manager of the New York Giants, gave Hoyt a chance to pitch in the big leagues, and the knuckleball specialist responded with an unexpected and resounding success. Working as a relief pitcher, Hoyt won fifteen games, lost only three, and had the best winning percentage—83.3 percent—and the lowest earned run average—2.43—in the National League. For the next two years, he was a remarkably effective relief pitcher for Durocher's teams, including the 1954 Giants squad that won the National League pennant and then defeated the Cleveland Indians in the World Series. In establishing himself as the most respected knuckleball pitcher in baseball, Hoyt had the benefit of relying on Wes Westrum, one of the most capable defensive catchers of that era.

Continuing the Story

Hoyt's work with the New York Giants from 1952 to 1954 made him a respected performer, but it was his twenty-one-year record of success with a total of nine different major league teams that earned him entry into the National Baseball Hall of Fame in 1985. His mastery of the knuckleball was unusual, and many managers and most catchers did not want to use that pitch in close ball games when a wild pitch or a passed ball—a pitch in or near the strike zone that the catcher fails to catch or block—can lose the contest. Hoyt found that he was most successful on teams with managers who were willing to take a chance on the knuckleball and catchers who had the reflexes and patience to handle it.

After playing for three different teams in the 1957-1958 season, Hoyt found a new home on the Baltimore Orioles under manager Paul Richards. A former major league catcher, Richards not only purchased Hoyt's contract from the Cleveland Indians but also converted him into a starting pitcher—with impressive results. Hoyt

STATISTICS

Season	*GP*	*GS*	*CG*	*IP*	*HA*	*BB*	*SO*	*W*	*L*	*S*	*ShO*	*ERA*
1952	**71**	0	0	159.1	127	57	108	15	3	11	0	**2.43**
1953	**68**	0	0	145.0	127	77	71	7	8	15	0	3.04
1954	57	0	0	111.1	77	52	64	12	4	7	0	2.10
1955	59	0	0	103.0	104	40	71	4	1	0	0	3.93
1956	64	0	0	89.1	97	43	71	4	9	8	0	3.83
1957	42	0	0	58.2	54	22	29	2	4	12	0	4.14
1958	39	10	4	131.0	95	45	92	3	10	5	1	2.34
1959	32	27	13	226.0	178	77	139	15	11	0	3	**2.19**
1960	41	11	3	147.0	125	39	107	11	8	7	1	3.31
1961	51	1	0	109.2	89	41	87	9	7	18	0	2.30
1962	52	0	0	93.0	64	34	90	7	10	15	0	1.94
1963	55	3	0	136.1	106	30	111	5	8	21	0	2.64
1964	73	0	0	131.1	94	30	95	12	9	27	0	1.99
1965	66	0	0	144.0	88	32	106	7	7	20	0	1.81
1966	46	0	0	81.1	50	17	61	5	2	6	0	1.66
1967	49	0	0	89.0	58	34	76	8	3	12	0	1.31
1968	72	0	0	93.2	69	24	72	4	4	12	0	1.73
1969	52	0	0	78.0	50	22	67	7	7	14	0	2.19
1970	53	0	0	82.0	73	42	68	6	5	13	0	3.40
1971	12	0	0	20.0	12	5	16	0	1	3	0	2.70
1972	16	0	0	25.1	20	15	9	0	1	1	0	4.62
Totals	1,070	52	20	2,254.1	1,757	778	1,610	143	122	227	5	2.52

Notes: Boldface indicates statistical leader. GP = games played; GS = games started; CG = complete games; IP = innings pitched; HA = hits allowed; BB = bases on balls (walks); SO = strikeouts; W = wins; L = losses; S = saves; ShO = shutouts; ERA = earned run average

responded on September 20, 1958, with a no-hitter against the New York Yankees, the team that won the World Series that fall. The next year the thirty-six-year-old pitched more than 200 innings for the first and only time in his major league career, won fifteen games, and had the American League's lowest earned run average: 2.19. Richards instructed his catcher, Gus Triandos, to use a specially made, oversized catcher's mit when working with Hoyt, which made it easier to block or knock down the unpredictable knuckleball. Hoyt gave much of the credit for his comeback to Richards and Triandos.

Hoyt solidified his reputation as one of baseball's all-time greats in his years with the Chicago White Sox, from 1963 to 1968. In that span, he appeared extensively in relief with remarkably low earned run averages that ranged from 1.99 to 1.31. He began this impressive stretch at the age of forty, when most players have retired. He ended his career in 1972, after two seasons of limited play with the Atlanta Braves and the Los Angeles Dodgers.

Summary

Hoyt Wilhelm reached the major leagues at age twenty-nine, several years later than most players, but then set out on a twenty-one-year career that was exceptional not only for its length but also for the quality of his work. A quiet county boy, Hoyt claimed that much of his success came from his capacity to stay calm in close games and from his willingness to use the knuckleball in difficult situations.

John A. Britton

Additional Sources:

Hollenberg, Joel W. "Knuckleballs." *Scientific American* 257, no. 1 (July, 1987): 22.

Kurkjian, Tim. "The End of an Era?" *Sports Illustrated* 74, no. 19 (May 20, 1991): 68-69.

Libby, Bill. *Star Pitchers of the Major Leagues.* New York: Random House, 1971.

Trader, Hugh. "Prize Fingernails." *Baseball Digest* 18, no. 7 (August, 1959): 5-8.

LENNY WILKENS

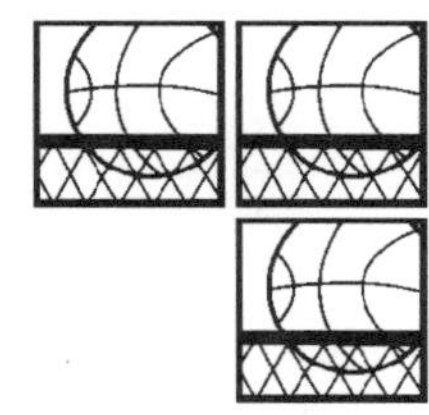

Sport: Basketball

Born: October 28, 1937
Brooklyn, New York

Early Life

Leonard Randolph Wilkens was born on October 28, 1937, in Brooklyn, New York. Lenny grew up in a tough neighborhood in the area of the city known as Bedford-Stuyvesant. This area has produced many fine athletes, but it has also produced many youngsters who were unable to escape the ghetto.

Lenny's mother made sure her son avoided the traps of such a life, stressing the importance of staying in school so he could make something of himself.

The young left-hander became well-known throughout the neighborhood, starring in local youth leagues and in Catholic Youth Organization (CYO) leagues in Brooklyn during his early teens.

The Road to Excellence

Lenny did not begin to play varsity basketball in high school until his junior year because he did not like the coach, viewing him as too aggressive and hard on his players.

His boyhood friend Tommy Davis—who later went on to win a batting title for the Los Angeles Dodgers—finally convinced him to join the team. Davis was the star, and Lenny's job was to pass the ball to Davis. Lenny averaged 11 points per game in his senior year and received enough notice to earn a scholarship to Providence College.

In college, Lenny played essentially the same role—that of the playmaker. He scored almost 15 points per game in his career at Providence, and impressed basketball scouts with his ability to pass and create shots for his teammates.

Providence was not known for being a basketball school in those days, but Lenny put the Friars on the map. The basketball team had never won

Seattle Supersonics

more than nineteen games in a season before Lenny arrived, but won eighteen, twenty, and twenty-four games in his three varsity seasons. In each of his last two seasons, Providence played in the National Invitational Tournament (NIT), which was nearly as important in those days as the NCAA Tournament is today.

The two twenty-win seasons that Lenny helped to produce brought so much prestige and so many good players to the school's basketball pro-

STATISTICS

Season	GP	FGM	FG%	FTM	FT%	Reb.	Ast.	TP	PPG
1960-61	75	333	.425	214	.713	335	212	880	11.7
1961-62	20	140	.385	84	.764	131	116	364	18.2
1962-63	75	333	.399	222	.696	403	381	888	11.8
1963-64	78	334	.413	270	.740	335	359	938	12.0
1964-65	78	434	.414	416	.746	365	431	1,284	16.5
1965-66	69	411	.431	422	.793	322	429	1,244	18.0
1966-67	78	448	.432	459	.787	412	442	1,355	17.4
1967-68	82	546	.438	546	.768	438	679	1,638	20.0
1968-69	82	644	.440	547	.770	511	674	1,835	22.4
1969-70	75	448	.420	438	.788	378	683	1,334	17.8
1970-71	71	471	.419	461	.803	319	654	1,403	19.8
1971-72	80	479	.466	480	.774	338	766	1,438	18.0
1972-73	75	572	.449	394	.828	346	628	1,538	20.5
1973-74	74	462	.465	289	.801	277	522	1,213	16.4
1974-75	65	134	.439	152	.768	120	235	420	6.5
Totals	1,077	6,189	.432	5,394	.774	5,030	7,211	17,772	16.5

Notes: GP = games played; FGM = field goals made; FG% = field goal percentage; FTM = free throws made; FT% = free throw percentage; Reb. = rebounds; Ast. = assists; TP = total points; PPG = points per game

gram that Providence won twenty games for the next seven years after Lenny left.

Lenny was picked by the St. Louis (now Atlanta) Hawks of the National Basketball Association (NBA). Although some thought him too small to make an impact in professional basketball, all the quiet Wilkens wanted was a chance.

The Emerging Champion

Lenny continued to shine as a point guard with St. Louis. The Hawks had a team of established stars, such as Cliff Hagan and Bob Pettit, so once again Lenny was asked to pass instead of shoot.

Lenny was satisfied with that role for, although he could score, he realized the importance of distributing the ball and playing unselfishly. As good a player as he was, Lenny's greatest talent might have been for making the players around him better. Many times, Lenny would drive to the basket, drawing an extra defender, and slip the ball to a teammate for an easy lay-up and two points for his team. Known as one of the great playmakers in the history of basketball, Lenny led the NBA in total assists for the 1969-1970 and the 1971-1972 seasons. He was selected as the most valuable player (MVP) of the 1971 NBA All-Star game.

Most players equate ability with scoring points. Lenny did not feel that way. He was happy to do his job with the same cool, quiet precision that he displayed from his rookie season. He was content to let someone else receive the honors and accolades.

After eight years in St. Louis, Lenny was traded to Seattle, which had just entered the league. The Seattle management thought that, with a player like Lenny, the team might improve quickly. The Supersonics even gave Lenny the chance to be player-coach of the team. In his third year as player-coach, he guided the Sonics to a 47-35 record. Lenny played for the Cleveland Cavaliers for two seasons, representing the Cavs in the 1973 NBA All-Star game. He finished his playing career in 1975 as the player-coach for the Portland Trail Blazers. In fifteen seasons in the NBA, Lenny scored 17,772 points, made 7,211 assists, and was selected as a member of the NBA All-Star team nine times.

Continuing the Story

Lenny decided that he liked coaching and continued in the game after his retirement as an active player. He coached in Portland for two years, laying the foundation for the Trail Blazer team that won the NBA title in 1976-1977.

Lenny returned to the Supersonics as the director of player personnel in May, 1977. In 1977-1978, Lenny took over a struggling Seattle team that had won only five of its first twenty-two games. He took a collection of young, unknown players to the finals that season, where they lost in a hard-fought seven-game series to Washington. The next season, Lenny and the Sonics finally took the championship.

Lenny took over the losing Cleveland Cavaliers in the late 1980's and helped turn that team around as well. During the 1988-1989 and the 1991-1992 seasons, Lenny led the Cavaliers to fifty-seven wins, the most victories in the history of the franchise. After the playoffs in 1993, he left the Cavs and signed on as head coach of the Atlanta Hawks. For the first time in his coaching career, Lenny was selected as the NBA Coach of the Year in 1994. On January 6, 1995, Lenny became the all-time winningest coach in NBA history with 939 victories, surpassing the 938 wins of the Boston Celtics' great coach Red Auerbach.

As of 2000, Lenny had won more than twelve hundred games in his NBA coaching career. After serving as an assistant coach under Chuck Daly on the United States "Dream Team I" that won the Olympic gold medal in Barcelona, Spain, in 1992, Lenny coached the United States Dream Team II to the gold medal in the Summer Olympics in Atlanta in 1996.

Through it all, Lenny remained the same shy person he was as a player. Even when his team won the championship, he gave all the credit to the players. He seldom raised his voice at his players or at the referees, and he never tried to draw attention to himself. When dealing with players, Lenny was known as tough but fair. He remembered all too well what it was like to be a player and treated his team members the way he would have wanted to be treated while he was still in uniform.

In 1996, Lenny was selected as a member of the NBA Top Ten Coaches list. As part of the celebration of the golden anniversary of the NBA during the 1996-1997 season, he was chosen as a member of the NBA's 50 Greatest Players of All Time Team. In June, 2000, Lenny took a job as head coach of the Toronto Raptors.

Summary

Lenny Wilkens was never interested in who got the credit for winning games or championships. He left it to others to score the points and get the headlines. Still, those who know basketball always knew how much Lenny contributed to his teams. Lenny and John Wooden are the only two individuals enshrined in the Basketball Hall of Fame as both a player and a coach.

John McNamara

Additional Sources:

Dolin, Nick, Chris Dolin, and David Check. *Basketball Stars: The Greatest Players in the History of the Game.* New York: Black Dog and Leventhal, 1997.

Pluto, Terry. *Tall Stories: The Glory Years of the NBA, in the Words of the Men Who Played, Coached, and Built Pro Basketball.* New York: Simon & Schuster, 1992.

Triche, Arthur, ed. *From Sweet Lou to 'Nique: Twenty-Five Years with the Atlanta Hawks.* Atlanta, Ga.: Longstreet Press, 1992.

HONORS AND AWARDS

1960	NIT most valuable player Consensus All-American
1963-65, 1967-71, 1973	NBA All-Star Team
1971	NBA All-Star Game most valuable player
1989	Inducted into Naismith Memorial Basketball Hall of Fame as player
1994	NBA Coach of the Year
1996	One of NBA Top Ten coaches in history NBA 50 Greatest Players of All Time Team
1998	Inducted into Naismith Memorial Basketball Hall of Fame as coach Uniform number 19 retired by Seattle Supersonics

DAVID WILKIE

Sport: Swimming

Born: March 8, 1954
Scotland

Early Life

David Andrew Wilkie, born in Scotland on March 8, 1954, grew up in Colombo, Ceylon, in the Indian Ocean. After graduating from boarding school in Edinburgh, Scotland, David came to the United States for college and swimming. He went to the University of Miami, Florida, and was a world-record breaststroker and Olympic champion, knighted by the Queen of England. His only trouble in swimming was beating the United States' John Hencken. They took turns breaking the world record and winning United States nationals and Olympic championships for four years.

The Road to Excellence

David's first victory was at the 1970 British Commonwealth Games in Edinburgh. There, as a newcomer, he managed to win a bronze medal in the 200-meter breaststroke. Coached by David Haller in Britain, David liked his first taste of success, although it was small compared to what he would earn just two short years later.

David "found" himself at the Olympics of 1972, when he was the surprise silver medalist in the 200-meter breaststroke behind America's John Hencken. That success changed David's whole way of life. He left boarding school in Edinburgh to take up a scholarship at the University of Miami, Florida, where, as well as studying, he learned what big-time swimming was all about.

The Emerging Champion

David loved the warm weather in Miami, which reminded him of Ceylon. He learned well from his coaches Bill Diaz and Charlie Hodgson—well enough to win the world 200-meter breaststroke title from Hencken in world record time (2 minutes 19.28 seconds) at Belgrade in 1973 at the World Championships. This big meet, second only to the Olympics, brings the world's best aquatic athletes together every four years, falling halfway between the Olympic Games. In Belgrade, David took the bronze in the 200-meter individual medley in addition to his gold. At the 1974 European Championships in Vienna, Austria, he won the 200-meter breaststroke and individual medley titles (the latter in a world record 2 minutes 6.32 seconds) and also led Britain to a silver medal in the medley relay. For his great performance, David Wilkie was honored with a Member of the Order of the British Empire on the Queen's Birthday Honor's List.

Courtesy of the International Swimming Hall of Fame

In the next year, 1975, in Cali,

STATISTICS

Year	Competition	Event	Place	Time
1972	Olympic Games	200-meter breaststroke	Silver	—
1973	World Championships	200-meter breaststroke	1st	2:19.28 WR
		200-meter individual medley	3d	2:08.84
	NCAA Championships	200-yard breaststroke	1st	2:03.407
1974	European Championships	100-meter breaststroke	1st	1:09.13
		200-meter individual medley	1st	2:06.32 WR
	Commonwealth Games	100-meter breaststroke	2d	1:07.37
		200-meter breaststroke	1st	2:24.42 CGR
		200-meter individual medley	1st	2:10.11
	NCAA Championships	100-yard breaststroke	1st	56.727
1975	World Championships	100-meter breaststroke	1st	1:04.26
		200-meter breaststroke	1st	2:18.23
		4×100-meter medley relay	3d	3:52.80
1976	Olympic Games	100-meter breaststroke	Silver	1:03.43
		200-meter breaststroke	Gold	2:15.11 WR, OR
	NCAA Championships	200-yard breaststroke	1st	2:00.74
	AAU Indoor Championships	100-meter breaststroke	1st	1:04.46
		200-meter breaststroke	1st	2:18.48
		200-meter individual medley	1st	2:06.25

Notes: OR = Olympic Record; WR = World Record; CGR = Commonwealth Games Record

Colombia, David won both world breaststroke championships in majestic style at the World Championships. He retained his 200-meter crown by 5.5 meters in 2 minutes 18.23 seconds, only two-hundredths outside Hencken's world record; won the 100 meters by 1.5 meters, in 1 minute 4.26 seconds, from Olympic champion Nobutaka Taguchi of Japan; and took a bronze for Britain in the medley relay.

These times were European and Commonwealth records and the fastest by any man in 1975. For all this, and his three victories in the Europa Cup, David was voted Sportsman of the Year by members of the Sports Writer's Association of Great Britain.

David Wilkie was Great Britain's first male swimming Olympic gold medalist in sixty-eight years (since Hall of Famer Henry Taylor in 1908). This versatile swimmer won Scottish national titles in the 400-meter freestyle and the 100-meter backstroke. He won Commonwealth, European, and American titles in the four-stroke, 200-meter individual medley, in which he also held the world record briefly, but he was at his best, with his trademark bathing cap and goggles, bobbing through Scottish, British, United States, American Athletic Union, National Collegiate Athletic Association, European, Commonwealth, and Olympic breaststroke championships.

In 1976, at the Montreal Olympics, David won his coveted gold in the 200-meter breaststroke along with a silver in the 100-meter breaststroke, reversing his finish with rival John Hencken, whom he had beaten in the 200. David's 200 breaststroke gold medal was the only men's race at the Montreal Olympic Games not won by the Americans, most of whom knew David well enough to know there was no way the personable swimmer could be psyched out. Winning at Montreal against the Americans was quite an achievement, as the United States coach "Doc" Counsilman, among others, considered the swimming at these Games the greatest United States team performance ever by a men's Olympic team. David's record achievement during the years earned the Scotsman European Swimmer of the Year three times and British Sportsman of the Year once.

Continuing the Story

Although David's medal collection was huge, his medal tally could have been greater but for some strange mental lapses which cost him dearly. In Belgrade, he could have won the 200-meter medley, but a careless turn, which sent him crashing head-on into the pool, dropped him to third place. In Christchurch, New Zealand, he had to bow to England's David Leigh in the 100-meter breaststroke because he had not taken the meet seriously enough.

In Vienna, he threw away an almost certain gold in the 100 meters. During the heats, David stopped swimming after the dive-in, having mistaken the sound of a horn in the crowd for a false start recall signal. He did not qualify for the final. "Not excuses," says the tall Scotsman, "but explanations to be remembered next time out."

In Cali, as joint world-record holder, he was expected to win a third gold in the 200-meter medley but did not qualify for the finals. Exhaus-

RECORDS AND MILESTONES

Set three world records

European Swimmer of the Year (3 times)

British Sportsman of the Year

Great Britain's first male Olympic gold medalist in swimming in sixty-eight years

HONORS AND AWARDS

1982	Inducted into International Swimming Hall of Fame

tion from a needless journey from Miami to Majorca (for an unimportant Scottish international before returning across the Atlantic) finally overtook him and he was 6 seconds outside his best in his heat.

David retired after the 1976 Olympics to a successful new hobby in Masters Swimming, where he trained at his own pace and went right on winning. Over the years, he has worked in London for the Sports Aide Foundation, written books, and kept his hand in on the business side of swimming as the British representative for Team Arena.

Summary

Whenever the media call the International Swimming Hall of Fame for information, David Wilkie's name frequently comes up. This Scot is remembered for his impact on swimming as the only male swimmer from the United Kingdom to win an Olympic gold medal between 1908 and 1976 and is also remembered in the record books as the first swimmer to wear goggles. When he came to the Hall of Fame for his official induction in 1982, David donated a pair of his famous goggles, which were placed on display in Fort Lauderdale.

Buck Dawson

Additional Sources:

Besford, Pat. *Encyclopedia of Swimming*. New York: St. Martin's Press, 1976.

Levinson, David, and Karen Christenson, eds. *Encyclopedia of World Sport: From Ancient Times to Present*. Santa Barbara, Calif.: ABC-CLIO, 1996.

Schapp, Dick. *An Illustrated History of the Olympics*. New York: Alfred A. Knopf, 1975.

Wallechinsky, David. *The Complete Book of the Olympics*. Boston: Little, Brown and Company, 1991.

DOMINIQUE WILKINS

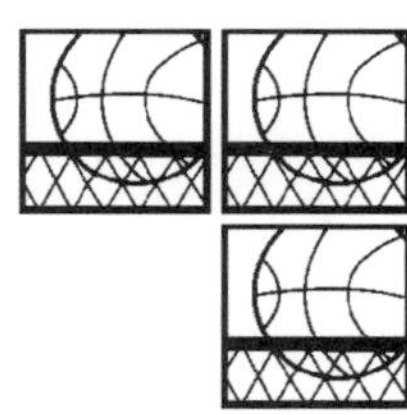

Sport: Basketball

Born: January 12, 1960
Paris, France

Early Life

Jacques Dominique Wilkins was born in Paris, France, on January 12, 1960, the son of a United States Army sergeant stationed near there. He was the second of eight children produced by Gertrude and John Wilkins.

John Wilkins left the family when Dominique was just thirteen. The family later moved to Washington, North Carolina, where Dominique lived under his mother's watchful eye. Gertrude felt her son was a target for all kinds of criminal types. He trusted just about everyone he met.

The young Dominique was quite enterprising. At fifteen he would challenge men in their twenties to games of one-on-one basketball; the winner of each game would collect one dollar. Dominique would beat them regularly and would give the money to his mother to buy food for the family. "I always thought he was doing odd jobs, raking grass," Gertrude said in *People Weekly*. Dominique was more exacting: "She thought I was stealing it. She was always second-guessing me."

The Road to Excellence

Playing for a dollar a game against men of the street was not to be Dominique's full-time occupation, however. As a high school senior, he established himself as a basketball phenomenon and attracted the attention of many large universities with his free-wheeling, run-and-dunk-the-ball play.

The University of Georgia was the school that finally lured Dominique onto campus. In his freshman season (1979-1980), he played in sixteen games, scoring a total of 297 points for an average of 18.6 points per game. This kind of performance while on the second team prompted the coaches to make Dominique a starter the next season.

In the 1980-1981 season, Dominique saw twice as much playing time as he had as a freshman. Playing in thirty-one games, he scored 732 points for a 23.6-points-per-game average and grabbed more than 200 rebounds. Dominique was named to *The Sporting News* All-America Second Team for his season performance.

Courtesy of the Atlanta Hawks

Dominique Wilkins (right) of the Atlanta Hawks.

The next season was nearly as good. Again playing in thirty-one games, Dominique scored a total of 659 points and had a 21.3 points-per-game average. Again his rebounds exceeded 200, and again he received All-American honors. Although he was still an undergraduate, the National Basketball Association (NBA) was seriously interested in his talents.

The Emerging Champion

Drafted by the Utah Jazz of the NBA in the first round in 1982, Dominique dropped out of college to become a professional basketball player. Before the 1982-1983 NBA season could begin, however, Dominique was traded to the Atlanta Hawks for two players and an undisclosed amount of cash.

The trade worked out well for Atlanta. In the first two seasons with Dominique on the team, the Hawks made the playoffs. Although Dominique was making a contribution to his team's wins, he fell under the criticism of the press for not being a true team leader.

Dominique was viewed by some as a mere curiosity whose talents were best used in jumping high and winning slam-dunk competitions. He was not considered a "real" player. Atlanta teammate Scott Hastings said in a *Sports Illustrated* article by Jack McCallum, " 'Nique used to do slam dunk championships in the warmups, and it tired him out. He had a second-quarter sweat going before the game started."

Dominique took such criticism to heart and changed his style of play. "I wanted to prove I was a total player," Dominique said in *Sports Illustrated*. "I wanted to change people's opinion of me. It bothered me that I had never made the All-Star team, that people thought all I could do was dunk." No longer would he be known solely as the player who runs up the floor to make the spectacular slam-dunk. Dominique developed a smooth jump shot and assumed a leadership role on the team.

When Atlanta coach Mike Fratello installed Dominique at the "big-guard" spot on the team, observers were amazed at the results. In the 1985-1986 season, Dominique was the NBA's scoring champion with an average of 30.3 points per game. In the playoffs that same season, Dominique had a game high of 50 points against the Detroit Pistons, whom the Hawks beat 140-122. None of those points were scored by slam-dunks, and it was the first 50-point performance in the playoffs since 1975, when Bob McAdoo scored as many for Buffalo.

In the 1985-1986 season, Dominique was named to the Eastern Conference All-Star team for the first time. This honor was the result of dedicated play for the Hawks. His Atlanta teammates remarked that Dominique had accepted

STATISTICS

Season	*GP*	*FGM*	*FG%*	*FTM*	*FT%*	*Reb.*	*Ast.*	*TP*	*PPG*
1982-83	82	601	.493	230	.682	478	129	1,434	17.5
1983-84	81	684	.479	382	.770	582	126	1,750	21.6
1984-85	81	853	.451	486	.806	557	200	2,217	27.4
1985-86	78	888	.468	577	.818	618	206	2,366	**30.3**
1986-87	79	828	.463	607	.818	494	261	2,294	29.0
1987-88	78	909	.464	541	.826	502	224	2,397	30.7
1988-89	80	814	.464	442	.844	553	211	2,099	26.2
1989-90	80	810	.484	459	.807	521	200	2,138	26.7
1990-91	81	770	.470	476	.829	732	265	2,101	25.9
1991-92	42	424	.464	294	.835	295	158	1,179	28.1
1992-93	71	741	.468	519	.828	482	227	2,121	29.9
1993-94	74	698	.440	442	.847	481	169	1,923	26.0
1994-95	77	496	.424	266	.782	401	166	1,370	17.8
1996-97	63	397	.417	281	.803	402	119	1,145	18.2
1998-99	27	50	.379	29	.690	71	16	134	5.0
Totals	1,074	9,963	.461	6,031	.811	7,169	2,677	26,668	24.8

Notes: Boldface indicates statistical leader. GP = games played; FGM = field goals made; FG% = field goal percentage; FTM = free throws made; FT% = free throw percentage; Reb. = rebounds; Ast. = assists; TP = total points; PPG = points per game

the responsibility of being their leader, the man who got them going. From the 1985-1986 season through the 1988-1989 season, Dominique led the Hawks to fifty or more wins each campaign.

Continuing the Story

With a $6.5 million contract that his mother negotiated for him ("I think he should be paid more," she said in *People Weekly*), Dominique was able to support his mother, three sisters (they are his housekeepers), two brothers, and his daughter, Aisha. A trusting, slow-to-anger person, Dominique is still managed by his mother, for whom he bought a $250,000 house in Atlanta. "He's the target for crooks and leeches because he trusts everyone," his mother said. Dominique himself settled in a four-bedroom house outside of Atlanta and bought two cars, a Ferrari and a Mercedes.

In addition, Dominique continued to anchor the Atlanta team and lead the NBA in scoring statistics. No longer accused of being an undisciplined player on the court, he earned the respect of the league. "I don't see any part of his game that hasn't improved," said Mike Fratello, Atlanta Hawks coach, in *People Weekly*.

In the early 1990's, Dominique became an all-around contributor to the Hawks. During the 1990-1991 season, he averaged 25.9 points, 9.0 rebounds, and 3.3 assists per game. Midway through the 1991-1992 season, Dominique ruptured his Achilles tendon, but he came back strong the next season to post a 29.9 scoring average for the Hawks. After finishing the 1994 season with the Los Angeles Clippers, he played for the Boston Celtics during the 1994-1995 campaign, averaging 17.8 points per game.

In August, 1995, Dominique played in the Greek League for Panathinaikos Athens. He averaged 20.7 points and 7.7 rebounds in leading the team to the European Championship for Men's Clubs in 1996. He was named a member of the United States Olympic "Dream Team II," which captured the gold medal in Atlanta in 1996.

Dominique returned to the NBA for the 1996-1997 campaign, playing for the San Antonio Spurs. Dominique was a pleasant surprise as he led the Spurs in scoring with 18.2 points per game and also contributed 6.4 rebounds per game. During the 1997-1998 season, he played in Europe for Teamsystem Bolognia in Italy. He then made another NBA comeback during the 1998-1999 season with the Orlando Magic. He saw limited action and only averaged 5.0 points per game. Dominique ended his NBA career in 1999. He had been selected to the All-NBA First Team in 1986; to the All-NBA Second Team in 1987, 1988, 1991, and 1993; and to the All-NBA Third Team in 1989 and 1994. He finished with 26,668 career points, an average of 24.8 points per game.

HONORS AND AWARDS

1981-82	*Sporting News* All-American
1983	NBA All-Rookie Team
1983-84, 1986-91	NBA All-Star Team
1986	All-NBA First Team
1987-88, 1991, 1993	All-NBA Second Team
1989, 1994	All-NBA Third Team
1996	Gold Medal, Olympic basketball

Summary

Known as the "Human Highlight Film," Dominique Wilkins emerged from the University of Georgia to become one of the greatest players to wear an Atlanta Hawks uniform. A member of the All-NBA team four times and NBA scoring champion in 1986, Dominique became a master of the game and a true team leader.

Rustin Larson

Additional Sources:

Bjarkman, Peter C. *The Biographical History of Basketball.* Chicago: Masters Press, 1998.

_______. *Sports Great Dominique Wilkins.* Springfield, N.J.: Enslow, 1996.

Dolin, Nick, Chris Dolin, and David Check. *Basketball Stars: The Greatest Players in the History of the Game.* New York: Black Dog and Leventhal, 1997.

Shouler, Kenneth A. *The Experts Pick Basketball's Best Fifty Players in the Last Fifty Years.* Lenexa, Kans.: Addax, 1998.

Triche, Arthur, ed. *From Sweet Lou to 'Nique: Twenty-Five Years with the Atlanta Hawks.* Atlanta: Longstreet Press, 1992.

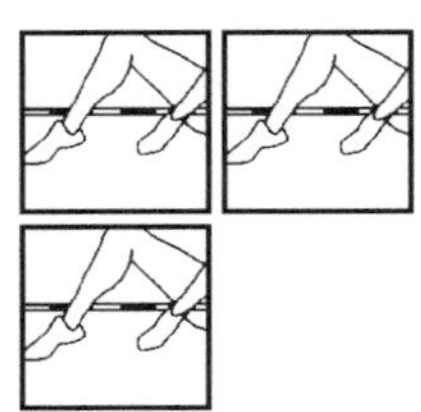

MAC WILKINS

Sport: Track and field (discus throw)

Born: November 15, 1950
Eugene, Oregon

Early Life

Mac Maurice Wilkins was born on November 15, 1950, in Eugene, Oregon. His father, Dick Wilkins, had been a star basketball player in the 1940's at the University of Oregon. Mac grew up in Beaverton, Oregon, near Portland. He was a natural athlete, and by the time Mac reached Beaverton High School, he excelled in track, basketball, and football. By his senior year, it became clear that Mac's greatest triumphs were to be in track and field. He won the Oregon state championship in the discus and placed a respectable fifth in the shot put during his last year at Beaverton.

The Road to Excellence

In 1970, Mac entered the University of Oregon in Eugene. It seemed only natural that he would end up at Oregon, where his father had been an outstanding basketball player and where a topnotch track program was offered. During his college years, Mac competed in the hammer throw, the shot put, the javelin, and the discus. He worked hard to be good in all of these events. Mac set an Oregon freshman record in the javelin by throwing it 257 feet 4 inches. Unfortunately, an injury to his elbow curtailed the training necessary for him to make much progress with the javelin, so Mac began concentrating on the discus. He remained an all-around thrower at Oregon, but the discus was to be where Mac really excelled.

Mac tried out for the 1972 United States Olympic team, but was disappointed when he did not make it. His best discus throw was only 195 feet 11 inches, not good enough for Olympic competition. This setback only made Mac more determined. He knew that if he wanted to add distance to his discus throw, he would have to gain weight and increase his strength. With the help of his roommate, decathlete Craig Brigham, Mac designed a special diet that would add the necessary pounds. His training program,

AP/Wide World Photos

Discus thrower Mac Wilkins in a 1976 event.

combined with the new diet, helped him to add muscle, which was a prerequisite to adding distance to his discus throws. Mac wanted to do more than merely set Oregon discus records. He wanted to be the best in the world.

The Emerging Champion

Mac was an All-American in his junior year at the University of Oregon, but he was still disappointed by his failure to make the Olympic team. In his senior year, with the added bulk to his body, Mac began to see the results for which he had hoped. He increased his distance to 212 feet 6 inches. He was also becoming more consistent. For his efforts in 1973, Mac won the National Collegiate Athletic Association (NCAA) discus championship and moved up in the world rankings to number eight. In his senior year, Mac was able to increase his distance by another foot and also earned All-American honors for the second year in a row. Mac received a bachelor's degree in business administration from the University of Oregon in 1974.

After graduation, Mac set his sights on the 1976 Olympics in Montreal, Canada. By 1975, Mac was sixth in the world and had thrown the discus a career best of 219 feet 2 inches. He went into 1976 strong physically and mentally. He now stood 6 feet 4 inches and weighed 255 pounds. All the ingredients were falling into place for him to reach his goals. In April, at his second meet of 1976, Mac set a world record with a throw of 226 feet 11 inches. He amazed even himself with what he had accomplished. One week later, at the San Jose Invitational track meet in California, Mac broke his world record three more times. No one had ever before broken a world record three times at the same meet.

Before the Montreal Olympics, Mac won the discus at the Amateur Athletic Union (AAU) national championships, which made him the favorite to win the gold medal. Mac did not disappoint anyone with his effort at Montreal. He won the gold medal, throwing the discus more than 4 feet beyond the distance of his nearest competitor.

STATISTICS

Year	Competition	Event	Place	Distance
1973	NCAA Championships	Discus	1st	204′11″
	National AAU Championships	Discus	1st	211′ 11″
1974	National AAU Championships	Discus	2d	205′ 9″
1975	National AAU Championships	Discus	2d	208′ 0″
1976	Olympic Games	Discus	Gold	221′ 5″
	National AAU Championships	Discus	1st	230′ 0″
1977	National AAU Championships	Shot put	1st	69′ 1¼″
	National AAU Championships	Discus	1st	227′ 0″
1978	National AAU Championships	Discus	1st	219′ 9″
1979	National AAU Championships	Discus	1st	231′ 10″
	Pan-American Games	Discus	1st	207′ 8″
1980	National AAU Championships	Discus	1st	224′ 3″
1982	National AAU Championships	Discus	2d	223′ 9″
1983	National AAU Championships	Discus	3d	217′ 6″
1984	Olympic Games	Discus	2d	217′ 6″
	National AAU Championships	Discus	2d	231′ 1″

Continuing the Story

Mac was a controversial figure at the 1976 Olympics. He irritated United States Olympic officials with his outspoken criticism of the way the United States develops its athletes. He never lost sight of what he was there to do, though, and Mac performed to the best of his ability and came away with the Olympic gold medal.

The discus was Mac's specialty, but he was also more than proficient with the shot put. In 1976, he was the fifteenth world-ranked shot-putter. He won the 1977 Sunkist Invitational meet in Los Angeles with a distance of 67 feet 9 inches. With that victory, he defeated Alexander Barishnikov from the Soviet Union, who held the world record in the event at the time.

By the time of the Olympic trials in 1980, Mac had won every major discus competition. He was more than ready for his second Olympics when the United States decided to boycott the 1980 Moscow Olympics. Mac retired from competition for a brief period until he regained his motivation and began training for the 1984 Olympics in Los Angeles. Unfortunately, Mac could not recapture the form that had made him the best in the past.

At the 1984 games, Mac could do no better than the silver medal with a throw of 217 feet 6 inches. His dominance in the discus during the late 1970's was over. Still, Mac has continued to train and compete and to be an articulate spokesperson on behalf of athletes everywhere.

RECORDS AND MILESTONES

Set 4 world records in discus in 1976: 226′ 11″, 229′ 0″, 230′ 5″, 232′ 6″ (last three set in same day)
Twice ranked top discus thrower in the world

HONORS AND AWARDS

1976	Dieges Award

In the 1988 Olympic Games in Seoul, Mac finished fifth in the discus event and once again decided to retire. After his retirement, he remained an active advocate of sports education as a member of the Sport and Entertainment Advisory Board, seeking to involve athletes and entertainers in the support of public schools.

Summary

Mac Wilkins is considered by many experts to be the greatest all-around thrower that the United States has ever produced. He was good in the javelin, the shot put, and the hammer throw, but he was great at the discus. He won not only the Olympic gold medal but also the gold medal in the 1979 Pan-American Games, and he won the NCAA title and six AAU titles. Probably the most amazing feat was his bettering of the discus world record four times in 1976. When speaking of remarkable track and field performers, Mac Wilkins must be respectfully mentioned. He has earned his place in track and field history and was inducted into the National Track and Field Hall of Fame in 1993.

Michael Jeffrys

Additional Sources:

Bateman, Hal. *United States Track and Field Olympians, 1896-1980.* Indianapolis, Ind.: The Athletics Congress of the United States, 1984.

Hickok, Ralph. *A Who's Who of Sports Champions.* Boston: Houghton Mifflin, 1995.

Wallechinsky, David. *The Complete Book of the Olympics.* Boston: Little, Brown and Company, 1991.

Watman, Mel. *Encyclopedia of Track and Field Athletics.* New York: St. Martin's Press, 1981.

LAURA WILKINSON

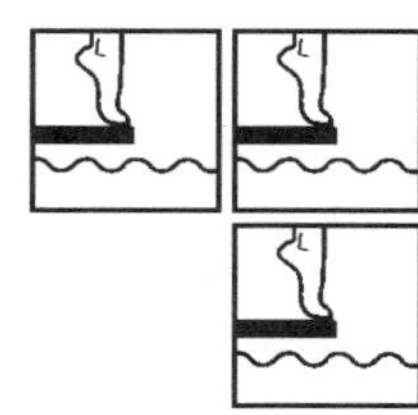

Sport: Diving

Born: November 17, 1977
Houston, Texas

Early Life

Laura Wilkinson was born in Houston, Texas, on November 17, 1977. She is the only daughter of Edward and Linda Wilkinson and has one elder brother, Robert. At elementary school she enjoyed a variety of sports but eventually focused on gymnastics. At the age of fifteen she tried diving for the first time and immediately liked it. It seemed much more natural to fly through the air and enter water rather than to twist and land on a gymnastics mat, although she saw great similarities between diving and gymnastics. Moreover, Laura found that she had an aptitude for diving and never tired of the challenges and discipline that the sport demanded of her.

In high school Laura improved her diving. Rather than attend college immediately after graduating, she participated in international competitions and was noticed by college coaches. She chose to attend the University of Texas because of its skilled swimming team. Laura later gave up her last year of swim eligibility at the University of Texas so that she could train full-time, under the tutelage of coach Ken Armstrong.

The Road to Excellence

In her first major competition, the 1994 Speedo National Junior Diving Championship, the 5-foot 6-inch, 115-pound Laura placed twenty-ninth in the 10-meter platform event with 259.65 points. A year later at the Diving World Cup Laura teamed up with Patty Armstrong in the synchronized diving event. They took third place in the synchronized diving platform competition with 232.23 points.

At the 1995 Phillips 66 National Outdoor Diving Championships she placed tenth in the 3-meter springboard event and second in the platform competition for single divers. In the synchronized diving events, again teamed with Patty Armstrong, she took first place in both the 3-meter and platform competitions.

The Emerging Champion

In every sense of the word, 1998 was Laura's breakthrough year. She won the platform event at the Cinergy/PSI National Diving Championships with a score of 490.35 points. At the U.S. Summer National Diving Championships she was runner-up in the platform event. In the international arena at the FINA World Aquatic Championships she placed fifth in the platform event.

AP/Wide World Photos

Diver Laura Wilkinson won the 10-meter platform event at the 2000 Olympics.

At the 1998 FINA/USA Diving Grand Prix she finished fourth in the 3-meter diving competition.

It was at the Goodwill Games that Laura achieved real excellence with her gold-medal performance in the platform. The Games challenged Laura on a number of levels. Her coach was not able to attend, so she felt vulnerable, isolated, and alone. As the competition went on Laura found herself searching, being sustained by her religious faith. She desperately wanted to be successful but suddenly came to the realization that she could not do it by herself. The competition became, for her, an epiphany. She said, "I got up there to dive still not seeing my spots, but believing in God. I felt taller, tighter, and stronger than ever before. I knew I was no longer alone."

In 1999, an especially critical year for athletes hoping to be selected to the 2000 U.S. Olympic team, Laura continued to be a key player in American platform diving. At the U.S. Spring National Diving Championships, she placed fifth in the platform event. Several months later, at the U.S. Summer National Diving Championships, she took first place in the platform.

Continuing the Story

In 2000 Laura won the platform event at the U.S. Olympic team trials and was the victor at the U.S. Outdoor National Diving Championships. At the 2000 Communidad de Madrid Competition in Spain she won both the synchronized platform event and the individual competition. Nevertheless, a March 8, 2000, training injury very nearly put an end to Laura's dreams of Olympic participation. She broke her foot in three places and was told that she needed surgery. She declined to have the injury operated on, as it would have prevented her from taking part in the Olympic trials. She had trained for the Olympics five to seven hours a day, thirty-five hours a week, and she was determined to participate.

She recalled the first time that she made her way up the 10-meter platform following her foot injury: "It took me ten minutes to get up there. I had to pull on the rails with my arms." She used a kayaker's boot to protect her damaged foot, then removed it when she reached the platform.

Going into the later stages of the 10-meter platform event at the Sydney Olympics Laura was off medal pace and held the fifth position at the end of the semifinals. However, Laura edged out Li Na to win an upset gold medal by the narrow margin of 1.74 points, and the diver from Texas became "the most implausible American heroine" of the Sydney Olympics.

Summary

Laura Wilkinson was a 1999 National Collegiate Athletic Association (NCAA) platform champion and 3-meter silver medalist and an eight-time NCAA All-American. As a relatively young diver, she won an Olympic gold medal in 2000. Her unexpected Olympics success and her wholesome personality made her a favorite in Sydney.

Scott A. G. M. Crawford

Additional Sources:

Farber, Michael. "Bent on Winning." *Sports Illustrated* 93, no. 13 (October 2, 2000): 76-77.

"High Marks." *Sports Illustrated* 93, no. 16 (October 18, 2000): 64.

Schaller, Bob, comp. *The Olympic Dream and Spirit.* Vol. 1. Grand Island, Nebr.: Ex-Husker Press, 2000.

STATISTICS

Year	Competition	Event	Place
1995	IX World Cup	Synchronized diving	3d
	Phillips 66 National Outdoor Championship	Platform diving	2d
1998	Cinergy/PSI Championship	Platform diving	1st
	U.S. Summer Championship	Platform diving	2d
	Goodwill Games	Platform diving	1st
1999	U.S. Summer Championship	Platform diving	1st
2000	U.S. Olympic Trials	Platform diving	1st
	U.S. Outdoor National Championship	Platform diving	1st
	Olympic Games	Platform diving	Gold

BILLY WILLIAMS

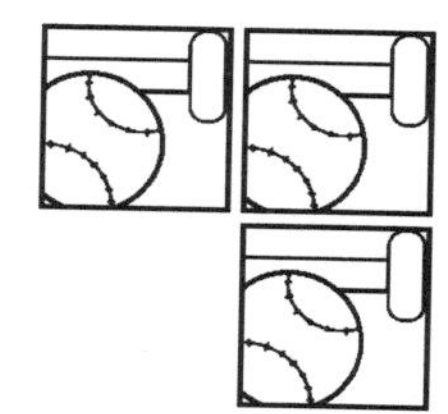

Sport: Baseball

Born: June 15, 1938
Whistler, Alabama

Archive Photos

Early Life

Billy Leo Williams was born on June 15, 1938, in Whistler, Alabama, to Frank Williams and Jesse Mary Williams. He and his four brothers and sisters grew up in a poor African American neighborhood, and Billy attended public schools in Whistler. Possessed of raw baseball talent, he played third base on his high school baseball team. Billy batted from the left side, but he threw right-handed. Chicago Cubs scout Ivy Griffin was so impressed with Billy's play that he signed him out of high school in 1956, and the Cubs sent Billy to play for their minor league team at Ponca City, Oklahoma. While playing at Ponca City, he was switched from third base to the outfield.

The Road to Excellence

During Billy's first season in the minors, he hit .310 and drove in 95 runs. He worked hard to learn how to play in the outfield, but he struggled somewhat, committing 25 errors in the 1957 season. In 1958, he played for the Cubs' minor league teams in Pueblo, Colorado, and Burlington, Iowa. He was sent to their Texas League team at San Antonio in 1959. Frustrated by his slow progress, Billy became discouraged and almost decided that it was time to give up baseball. He even went so far as to return to Whistler to think about his future. Eventually, Billy decided to give a baseball career another chance. He reported back to San Antonio, and within two months was called up to the Cubs. He played in eighteen games for the Cubs during 1959 and in twelve during 1960, spending most of the 1960 season with the Cubs' minor league team in Houston. In 1960, he also married Shirley Ann Williams, with whom he would have four children.

STATISTICS

Season	GP	AB	Hits	2B	3B	HR	Runs	RBI	BA	SA
1959	18	33	5	0	1	0	0	2	.152	.212
1960	12	47	13	0	2	2	4	7	.277	.489
1961	146	529	147	20	7	25	75	86	.278	.484
1962	159	618	184	22	8	22	94	92	.298	.466
1963	161	612	175	36	9	25	87	95	.286	.497
1964	162	645	201	39	2	33	100	98	.312	.532
1965	164	645	203	39	6	34	115	106	.315	.552
1966	162	648	179	23	5	29	100	91	.276	.461
1967	162	634	176	21	12	28	92	84	.278	.481
1968	163	642	185	30	8	30	91	98	.288	.500
1969	163	642	188	33	10	21	103	95	.293	.474
1970	161	636	**205**	34	4	42	**137**	129	.322	.586
1971	157	594	179	27	5	28	86	93	.301	.505
1972	150	574	191	34	6	37	95	122	.333	**.606**
1973	156	576	166	22	2	20	72	86	.288	.438
1974	117	404	113	22	0	16	55	68	.280	.453
1975	155	520	127	20	1	23	68	81	.244	.419
1976	120	351	74	12	0	11	36	41	.211	0.339
Totals	2,488	9,350	2,711	434	88	426	1,410	1,474	.290	0.490

Notes: Boldface indicates statistical leader. GP = games played; AB = at bats; 2B = doubles; 3B = triples; HR = home runs; RBI = runs batted in; BA = batting average; SA = slugging average

Billy had a very good season at Houston, hitting .323 and slugging 26 home runs, and the Cubs finally decided that Billy was ready for the major leagues. For the 1961 season, he was in the Cubs' starting lineup. Billy took advantage of the chance he was given. Always an unassuming man, he proved by his performance on the field that he was a quality ballplayer. At 6 feet 1 inch and 175 pounds, Billy became one of the Cubs' star players. He was named National League (NL) Rookie of the Year for 1961 after batting a respectable .278, hitting 25 home runs, and collecting 86 runs batted in (RBIs).

The Emerging Champion

Billy won the respect of his fellow ballplayers by quietly doing his job. Along with other Cubs stars Ernie Banks and Ron Santo, Billy could always be counted on to give the fans a solid performance, although the Cubs did not usually fare well in the standings.

Billy did not allow the team's disappointing performances to affect his output. Early in his development, he received hitting tips from all-time greats Henry Aaron and Rogers Hornsby; later, his hitting stroke was described as "poetry in motion" by Pittsburgh Pirates slugger Willie Stargell. Natural talent, a quiet ambition, and proper instruction all contributed to make Billy a dangerous offensive weapon.

Always willing to play whether he was hurt or not, Billy did his job without fanfare. From 1964 to 1970, he played in 1,117 consecutive games, a National League record. Billy had his first year batting more than .300 in 1964, when he hit .312. During that season, he also slugged 33 home runs and drove in 98 runs. Billy had another .300-plus season in 1965. To go with a .315 average, Billy hit 34 home runs and had 106 RBIs. In 1965, he led the Cubs in every major offensive category.

Billy continued to excel throughout the rest of the 1960's. In 1969, Chicago came close to winning the NL Eastern Division title, raising Cubs fans' hopes of seeing their stars in postseason play at last. Billy batted .293 for the season, but the Cubs stumbled toward the end of the year and were overtaken by the New York Mets.

From 1970 to 1972, Billy had three consecutive .300 or better years, hitting .322 in 1970, .301 in 1971, and .333 in 1972. Billy led the NL in both batting and slugging percentage in 1972. For that year, *The Sporting News* named him Major League Player of the Year, but Billy finished second in the voting for the Baseball Writers' Association most valuable player award to Cincinnati

Reds catcher Johnny Bench; Billy also had finished behind Bench in the MVP voting in 1970.

Billy remained with the Cubs through the 1974 season. That year, he batted a respectable .280 with 16 homers, but his best years were clearly behind him. That fall, the Cubs traded him to the Oakland A's of the American League (AL).

Continuing the Story

Billy played with Oakland for two seasons, primarily as a designated hitter. Although he batted merely .244 in 1975, he still hit 23 home runs and collected 81 RBIs. He got his first and only chance to participate in postseason play in 1975 in the American League Championship Series, but he was denied a chance to play in the World Series when the A's lost to the Boston Red Sox.

After the 1976 season, Billy decided that it was time to retire. During his eighteen-year career, he had collected 2,711 hits, 426 home runs, and 1,474 RBIs, and had compiled a .290 lifetime batting average. After his retirement, Billy remained in major league baseball as a coach and hitting instructor for the Cubs, the A's, and the Cleveland Indians. In 1982, Billy was inducted into the Chicago Sports Hall of Fame, and in 1987, he was inducted into the National Baseball Hall of Fame.

MAJOR LEAGUE RECORDS

First to play in 1,117 consecutive National League games

HONORS AND AWARDS

1961	National League Rookie of the Year
1962,1964-65,1968,1972-73	National League All-Star Team
1972	*Sporting News* Major League Player of the Year

Summary

Billy Williams was one of baseball's most durable performers. Always willing to play regardless of injury, Billy was a modest superstar who quietly produced more runs, more doubles, and more total bases than any other player during his prime years of 1967 to 1973. Even though he never got the chance to play in a World Series, Billy was a consummate professional who always gave his best.

Jeffry Jensen

Additional Sources:

Berke, Art. *Unsung Heroes of the Major Leagues.* New York: Random House, 1976.

Kuenster, John. "Billy Williams Talks About the Fine Art of Good Hitting." *Baseball Digest* 56, no. 7 (1997).

Williams, Billy, and Irv Haag. *Billy: The Classic Hitter.* Chicago: Rand McNally, 1974.

ESTHER WILLIAMS

Sport: Swimming

Born: August 8, 1923
Inglewood, California

Early Life

Esther Jane Williams was born August 8, 1923, in Inglewood, a Los Angeles suburb. Her father, Lou Williams, was a commercial artist and master sign painter. Her mother, Bula Williams, was a teacher and specialist in family relationships. The family had little money, but Mrs. Williams was intensely supportive of her daughter. Mrs. Williams also was concerned that the city provide a swimming pool for their area, which was considered deprived. Working with the Parent Teacher Association, she was successful.

Esther had earlier been taught to swim by a sister. Now, at the pool, she took a job counting locker room towels to pay for swimming time. At noon, when the pool was not much used, lifeguards taught her the techniques that were to make her famous, including the butterfly stroke, which was not usually taught to girls at that time.

The Road to Excellence

At age fifteen, Esther was asked to join the Los Angeles Athletic Club swimming team. If she would swim for the club, she would not be required to pay dues, which her family could not afford. Aileen Allen, swimming coach and athletic director for the club, assured her that, if she worked hard, she could become a champion.

While training, she attended Los Angeles public schools. She later was to graduate from Los Angeles City College and to attend the University of Southern California (USC).

In 1938, her discipline was rewarded when she placed third in the 200-yard freestyle at the Women's Senior Indoor Championships in Los Angeles and, in the same year, placed third in the 100-yard freestyle of the Women's Senior Outdoor Swimming Championships. In May, 1939,

Courtesy of Amateur Athletic Foundation of Los Angeles

in Los Angeles, Esther won a 50-yard breaststroke competition with a time of 33.1 seconds. Her most important swimming victories were to occur in that year. She was to remain in competitive amateur swimming for only two years.

In an article for *Parents' Magazine,* her mother wrote that Esther won because she enjoyed it. Her mother also observed that Esther's even temper and lack of moodiness were important to her success. These same qualities helped her in the rigorous training in speech, drama, singing, and dancing, in part responsible for her worldwide success in films. A disciplined athlete, she was comfortable with the regimented life that major studios then imposed upon their stars.

STATISTICS

Year	Competition	Event	Place	Time
1938	AAU Outdoor Championships	100-yard freestyle	3d	—
	AAU Indoor Championships	200-yard freestyle	3d	—
1939	AAU Championships	100-meter freestyle	1st	1:09
		300-meter medley relay	1st	3:52.8
		400-meter medley relay	1st	4:46
	Short Course Competition	50-yard breaststroke	—	33.1

The Emerging Champion

In 1939, at the National Senior Outdoor Championship competition in Des Moines, Iowa, Esther won the 100-meter freestyle and was on the winning 300-meter medley and 400-meter medley relay teams. In the relay, she helped her team to victory by introducing the butterfly stroke. Officials found that a woman could not be disqualified for using the stroke, although women had never done so.

She would normally have gone on from these victories to the 1940 Olympic Games, but the Olympics were canceled because of World War II. Although disappointed, Esther was later to advise young athletes not to be overwhelmed by such disappointments, because something good may be around the corner.

Esther was invited to join Billy Rose's Aquacade for the 1940 San Francisco World's Fair. She hesitated, not wanting to lose amateur status at a time when a swimmer could not even take a job as a lifeguard without doing so. Rose, whose show had been a New York success, convinced her that there would be no more Olympics for many years. Her Aquacade appearance led to a film offer, but again she hesitated. At this time, she was planning to be a department store sportswear buyer.

Louis B. Mayer, then head of MGM Studios, offered her a chance to invent a swimming musical. Just as Sonja Henie had popularized ice skating in films of the 1930's, so Esther was to do the same thing for swimming. In addition, the synchronized swimming of her most famous films introduced dance routines so that swimming became a matter of grace and style as well as speed.

Esther appeared in *Andy Hardy's Double Life* (1942) and, briefly, in *A Guy Named Joe* (1943) before her first starring swimming role in *Bathing Beauty* (1944), which turned her into an international star. Called "Hollywood's Mermaid" and "The Queen of the Surf," Esther became one of the top ten box office attractions. By the end of her film career in 1961, she had appeared in twenty-four films.

Continuing the Story

Knowing in advance that a film star or athlete will peak early and must plan for years ahead, Esther invested her film earnings wisely in a variety of business enterprises. In 1958, she began a swimming pool company that popularized the backyard pool. When flying across the country, she says, she can recognize the distinctive styles of her pools across the landscape below.

After making her last film in 1961, she produced and starred in four television specials and appeared as special guest on other shows. She retired completely from public life during her marriage to actor Fernando Lamas. Until his death in 1982, she did not even give interviews. In 1988, she went back to work, designing swimsuits. Her collection first appeared in the spring and summer fashion lines for 1989.

Summary

Esther Williams's many successes illustrate what she sees to be the primary benefit of athletic success: The athlete learns to think like a cham-

MILESTONES

Esther Williams was preparing for the 1940 Olympic Games when it was canceled because of World War II

She won the female lead in the San Francisco World's Fair Aquacade opposite Johnny Weissmuller (1940)

She began her professional career as an Aquacade and movie star in 1940

Her movies made swimming and synchronized swimming attractive to competitive-minded youngsters and made her an outstanding contributor to swimming

HONORS AND AWARDS

1939 National Champion
1966 Inducted into International Swimming Hall of Fame

pion. Once a person has become a champion, she says, that person can become a champion at everything. Champions know, all their lives, that they are champions. When a problem or obstacle comes along, champions can look inside themselves and find the resources to carry on, and then can go on to succeed in completely new fields. There can be no better example of this than her own life.

Betty Richardson

Additional Sources:

Perry, Pat. "Esther Williams: Still in the Swim." *Saturday Evening Post* 270, no. 1 (January-February, 1998): 36-38.

Sherrow, Victoria, ed. *Encyclopedia of Women and Sports.* Santa Barbara, Calif.: ABC-CLIO, 1996.

Williams, Esther, and Digby Diehl. *The Million Dollar Mermaid: An Autobiography.* New York: Simon & Schuster, 1999.

NATALIE WILLIAMS

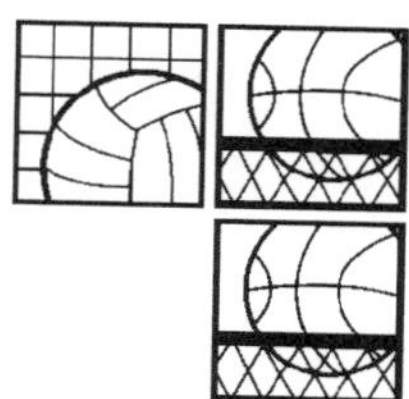

Sports: Basketball and Volleyball

Born: November 30, 1970
Taylorsville, Utah

Early Life

Natalie Williams was born to Nate Williams and Robyn Barker in Taylorsville, Utah, near Salt Lake City, in 1970. She has one sister and one brother. Her father played nine seasons in the National Basketball Association (NBA) for the Cincinnati Royals, Kansas City Kings, New Orleans Jazz, and Golden State Warriors.

While in high school, Natalie excelled in basketball, volleyball, and track and field, winning the Utah state long jump championship. During her senior year, she led the Taylorsville volleyball and basketball teams to state championships. Animals were her next love, and while growing up, she had thoughts of becoming a veterinarian.

The Road to Excellence

Natalie attended the University of California at Los Angeles (UCLA), where she led the volleyball team to the Final Four each of her four years. With her tremendous spiking ability, the UCLA Bruins won the national volleyball championship in 1990 and 1991. Natalie was twice named National Player of the Year and was a four-year All-American in volleyball at UCLA. She represented the United States in volleyball at the 1991 and 1993 World University Games. During the 1993 World University Games in Buffalo, New York, Natalie carried the torch in the opening ceremonies.

During her four seasons on the Bruin basketball team (1991-1994), Natalie averaged 20.4 points and 12.8 rebounds per game. She led

AP/Wide World Photos

Utah Starzz forward Natalie Williams (right), with Monarch Yolanda Griffith, reaches for the ball in 2000.

UCLA to the Sweet Sixteen in the NCAA tournament in 1992. She was named to the All-American First Team in 1993 and 1994 by the United States Basketball Writers Association and was a Naismith Player of the Year finalist both years. She was also a 1993 Kodak All-American. In addition, Natalie was named to the Pacific-10 Conference All-Decade Team, which encompassed all sports for the 1990's.

The Emerging Champion

After graduating from UCLA with a degree in sociology, Natalie played professional volleyball for two years with the Utah Predators. In 1996, she was named an alternate to the 1996 United States Olympic volleyball team and also received the prestigious honor of being selected as Utah's Female Athlete of the Century.

During the 1996-1997 season, Natalie played for the Portland Power in the newly formed American Basketball League (ABL) and was a unanimous All-ABL selection. The following season, she was the league's leading scorer and rebounder and was named the most valuable player in the ABL. Led by her play, the Power went from sitting in last place to being the Western Conference champions of the ABL in just one year. During her three seasons with the Power, Natalie averaged 20.0 points per game and 11.7 rebounds per game.

In 1998, Natalie led the United States national team to a gold medal in the World Championships. With 86 rebounds, she set an American women's record for a single World Championship series. In the 1999 draft of the Women's National Basketball Association (WNBA), she was selected by the Utah Starzz as the third overall pick. Throughout the 1999 campaign, Natalie was a dominant scorer and rebounder, with an average of 18 points per game and 9.2 rebounds per game. She played in the first WNBA All-Star game on July 14, 1999, and was the leading scorer for the victorious Western Conference. Natalie then led the Starzz into the WNBA playoffs.

Natalie and Utah Jazz star guard Jeff Hornacek won the two-ball contest during the 1999 National Basketball Association events associated with the All-Star game. As a member of the United States senior women's national team, Natalie represented the United States in the 1999 Hall of Fame enshrinement game in October. Playing against the WNBA select team composed of WNBA stars, Natalie was the leading scorer and rebounder in the game.

Continuing the Story

Showing tremendous dedication, athleticism, footwork, and ability to outplay opponents under the basket, Natalie developed a well-balanced offensive game. Like her father Nate during his NBA days, Natalie became adept at scoring bank shots off the glass. She also developed a consistent midrange jump shot and developed into a good free-throw shooter. Natalie patterned her game after Utah Jazz power forward Karl Malone, being strong and powerful yet having a soft touch on her shot. In seventeen of the twenty-nine games she played for the Starzz in the 2000 season, she scored and rebounded in double figures. During 2000, she averaged 18.7 points per game and 11.6 rebounds per game and was again selected to play in the WNBA All-Star game. She was also selected to the 2000 All-WNBA First Team.

Natalie won an Olympic gold medal in 2000 as the United States women's national team defeated Australia in the gold-medal game in Sydney, Australia. Natalie scored 15 points and col-

STATISTICS

Season	*GP*	*FGM*	*FGA*	*FG%*	*FTM*	*FTA*	*FT%*	*Reb.*	*Ast.*	*TP*	*PPG*
1999	28	180	347	.519	144	191	.754	257	25	504	18.0
2000	29	179	365	.490	182	228	.798	336	51	543	18.7
Totals	57	359	712	.504	326	419	.778	593	76	1,047	18.4

Notes: GP = games played; FGA = field goals attempted; FGM = field goals made; FG% = field goal percentage; FTA = free throws attempted; FTM = free throws made; FT% = free throw percentage; Reb. = rebounds; Ast. = assists; TP = total points; PPG = points per game

HONORS AND AWARDS

1993-1994	All-American First Team Kodak All-American at UCLA
1994	Pac-10 Athlete of the Decade
1996	Utah's Woman Athlete of the Century
1996-1997	All-ABL First Team
1998	ABL most valuable player
1999, 2000	WNBA All-Star Team
2000	Gold Medal with U.S. Women's Olympic Basketball Team All-WNBA First Team

lected 9 rebounds in the deciding game. Her primary goal then became winning a WNBA championship. During her spare time, Natalie has participated in basketball clinics for various boys and girls clubs.

Summary

A two-sport athlete, Natalie Williams earned All-America honors in both basketball and volleyball at UCLA. She was a key member of the United States women's basketball teams that won gold medals in the 1998 World Championships and the 2000 Summer Olympics. An athletic player around the basket, Natalie was a dominant force in the ABL and then began to make a major impact in the WNBA.

Alvin K. Benson

Additional Sources:

Braun, Eric. *The History of the Utah Starzz.* New York: Creative Education, 2000.

Gutman, Bill. *Shooting Stars: The Women of Pro Basketball.* New York: Random House, 1998.

Layden, Joseph. *Superstars of U.S.A. Women's Basketball.* New York: Aladdin, 2000.

Owens, Tom, and Diana Star Helmer. *Teamwork: The Utah Starzz in Action.* New York: Rosen Publishing Group, 1999.

Tang, Jeanne, Tracey Reavis, and Rita Sullivan. *Official WNBA Guide and Register 2000.* St. Louis, Mo.: The Sporting News, 2000.

RICKY WILLIAMS

Sport: Football

Born: May 21, 1977
San Diego, California

Ricky Williams of the New Orleans Saints in 1998.

Early Life

Errick Lynne "Ricky" Williams was born in San Diego, where he grew up with his mother, Sandy; his twin sister, Cassie; and younger sister, Nisey. Ricky's mother would not let him play football until he was thirteen years old because she was worried he would get hurt. By the time he attended high school at Patrick Henry High School in San Diego, he excelled not only at football, but also at baseball, track, and wrestling.

Ricky was named Offensive Player of the Year in football by the *San Diego Union-Tribune* as a senior when he rushed for 2,099 yards and scored 25 touchdowns. He earned All-State football honors playing defense as a linebacker. Ricky also earned All-State and All-League honors as an outfielder in baseball, where he batted .340 with 26 stolen bases as a senior. He was picked in the eighth round of the 1995 major league baseball draft by the Philadelphia Phillies Class A Batavia Muckdogs.

Ricky was also recruited by more than fifty universities when he graduated from Patrick Henry. He passed up the opportunity to stay on the West Coast, and chose to become a Longhorn at the University of Texas in Austin.

The Road to Excellence

As a freshman at Texas in 1995, Ricky rushed for 990 yards to break former Heisman Trophy winner Earl Campbell's 1978 freshman rushing record of 928 yards. He was an All-Southwest Conference second-team pick and shared 1995 Newcomer of the Year honors with teammate Shon Mitchell.

In 1996, Ricky started every game at fullback and rushed for 1,272 yards while catching 25 passes for 291 yards. Based on his performances he was named an All-Southwest Conference First Team pick. He also earned ABC Player of the Game honors in the Texas-Notre Dame game as well as Fox Sports Player of the Game honors against Missouri, Oklahoma State, and Kansas.

As a junior, Ricky broke Earl Campbell's 1977 single-season record for rushing by gaining 1,893 yards. He finished first in the country in rushing and averaged 172.1 yards per game. His 1997 awards included being named a consensus Associated Press All-American, winning the Doak Walker Award as the Best Running Back in the

National Collegiate Athletic Association (NCAA), and being First Team All-Big Twelve Conference choice, Big Twelve Offensive Player of the Year, and most valuable player for the Longhorns. He finished fifth in the 1997 Heisman Trophy balloting.

The Emerging Champion

As a senior, his goal was to attempt to break the 22-year-old National Collegiate Athletic Association (NCAA) Division I-A rushing record of 6,082 yards held by Tony Dorsett. Ricky also was the pre-season Heisman Trophy favorite, and he eventually won the award. During the 1998 season he gained 2,124 yards and scored 27 touchdowns. He set or tied twenty NCAA rushing records, including two consecutive 300-yard rushing games and eleven 200-yard games in his career. His 6,279 yards of total rushing set a record that year.

Continuing the Story

The New Orleans Saints traded eight National Football League (NFL) draft choices to sign Ricky in 1999. Mike Ditka, the famous NFL former player and coach of the Saints, felt that Ricky was the type of player who could improve the Saints' team hopes immediately.

Unfortunately, Ricky suffered several injuries during the 1999 season and did not regain the form that made him famous as a college player. He gained only 884 yards rushing and 172 yards receiving for the Saints that year.

Ricky's struggles were also personal during the season because he had signed a controversial incentive-based contract, which some experts thought that his agent should have negotiated differently. Ricky also found that he had difficulties adjusting from life in college to that of a professional football player, partly because he enjoyed living in Austin more than New Orleans.

Some sportswriters felt that Ricky had too much pressure on him in his first year to singlehandedly improve the Saints' record. Ricky also struggled with the New Orleans media because of negative press he got as a result of his lower-than-expected 1999 performance. At the end of 1999, the Saints hired Jim Haslett as their new head coach in hopes of turning the team's win/loss record around.

Ricky broke his fibula in early November, 2000, and was forced to miss months of play. However, the 93 yards he gained during that game put him at 1,000 yards for the season. The last New Orleans back to reach the 1,000-yard mark was Dalton Hilliard in 1989.

Summary

Ricky Williams is one of the most decorated athletes in college history. His tremendous power and strength were evident in college, as 3,889 of his 6,279 total yards came after initial contact by opponents.

Tinker D. Murray

Additional Sources:

Richardson, Steve. *Ricky Williams: Dreadlocks to Ditka.* Champaign, Ill.: Sports Publishing, 1999.

"Ricky Williams." *New Orleans Magazine,* July, 1999, 57-59.

"Ricky Williams." *People,* November 15, 1999, 98-99.

STATISTICS

		Rushing				Receiving			
Season	GP	Car.	Yds.	Avg.	TD	Rec.	Yds.	Avg.	TD
1999	12	253	884	3.5	2	28	172	6.1	0
2000	10	248	1,000	4.0	8	44	409	9.3	1
Totals	22	501	1,884	3.8	10	72	581	8.1	1

Notes: GP = games played; Car. = carries; Yds. = yards; Avg. = average yards per carry *or* average yards per reception; TD = touchdowns; Rec. = receptions

SERENA WILLIAMS

Sport: Tennis

Born: September 26, 1981
Saginaw, Michigan

Early Life

The youngest of the five daughters of Richard and Oracene Williams, Serena Williams was born in Saginaw, Michigan, on September 26, 1981. When Serena was just a preschooler her family moved from Michigan to California, where, in Compton, her father worked as a neighborhood tennis coach.

Although Richard Williams had access only to run-down, dilapidated courts, he was enthusiastic about tennis. The son of a Louisiana sharecropper, he was an ambitious man who wanted a good, full life for his family and himself. When Serena and her sister Venus were quite young, he began teaching them how to play tennis. He was certain that his daughters, whom he called Cinderellas from the ghetto, had the potential to become tennis champions.

Tennis had traditionally been the sport of middle- and upper-class white Americans. No African Americans had managed to dominate the game since 1975, when Arthur Ashe won Wimbledon. The record for black women in tennis was even less impressive. No black woman had won a Grand Slam event since Althea Gibson won both the U.S. Open and Wimbledon in 1957 and again in 1958.

The Road to Excellence

Breaking into competitive tennis was not easy for Serena. Her father recalled that at one Southern California tournament he had heard some people questioning his daughters' presence at the competition. He also noted misunderstandings between black and white competitors. Richard Williams had some reservations about allowing the girls to become involved in what he consid-

AP/Wide World Photos

Serena Williams serves during a tournament in October, 2000.

MAJOR CHAMPIONSHIPS

Year	Event
1998	U.S. Open, mixed doubles Wimbledon, mixed doubles
1999	U.S. Open, singles U.S. Open, doubles French Open, doubles Paris Indoors, singles Grand Slam Cup, singles
1999, 2001	Indian Wells, singles
2000	Wimbledon, doubles

ered a sometimes hostile world. However, he decided to keep his daughters on the tennis circuit, believing that their talent and skill would triumph over discrimination. In order to enhance their chances of mastering the game, the Williams family moved to Florida, where Venus and Serena trained with Rick Macci at the Macci Tennis Academy near Fort Lauderdale.

Serena spent most of her young life working to become a tennis champion. Her winning technique grew out of talent, discipline, dedication and good coaching as well as much time in the gym and on the practice court.

In 1991 Serena's family made the difficult decision to withdraw her and Venus from the junior competition circuit. In addition to relieving some of the enormous pressure on the sisters, this move allowed them to focus on schoolwork—and practice.

The Emerging Champion

Serena caught the attention of tennis fans in 1997 when she was able to defeat five top-ten players faster than any other professional tennis player in history. The Women's Tennis Association (WTA) identified her as their most impressive newcomer in 1998. Serena, under her father's coaching and management, had earned $348,378 by December of 1998. She was seventeen years old.

In 1999 the young woman who had been known as the younger and less-talented sister of Venus Williams won a Grand Slam title. It was not her first victory that year. In February, at the Open Gaz de France in Paris, Serena defeated Amellie Mauesmo 6-2, 3-6, 7-6 (7-4). In March Serena overwhelmed Steffi Graf 6-3, 3-6, 7-5 at the Evert Cup in Indian Wells, California.

Serena suffered a minor but unusual setback at the Lipton Championships in Key Biscayne, Florida, later that month. She and her sister Venus became the first sisters to meet in the finals of a professional tournament in 115 years. Venus defeated Serena 6-1, 4-6, 6-4. For the remainder of the 1999 tour, the sisters planned their schedules so that they would be playing in different tournaments.

However, on September 10, 1999, Venus and Serena played back-to-back semifinal matches at the U.S. Open in New York City. Determined that one of them would win a Grand Slam event, Serena allegedly retreated to the practice courts for some last-minute reinforcement after she saw Venus lose to Sweden's Martina Hingis. The next day Serena triumphed over Hingis 6-3, 7-6 (7-4). Serena's victory made her the first African American woman to win a Grand Slam singles title since Althea Gibson's 1958 Grand Slam win.

Competing in several major tournaments during any given tour takes a toll on the most talented of athletes. Serena was no exception. In 1999 she pulled out of the Hilton Head Tournament, citing a knee problem, and she skipped Wimbledon on account of the flu. Tendinitis in her right shoulder made her unable to compete at Toronto. She also missed the Seat Open in Luxembourg, citing exhaustion as the cause.

In spite of her injuries, 1999 was a good year for Serena. *Forbes* magazine listed both her and her sister among the highest paid black athletes in the United States. Additionally, Serena earned a considerable amount in endorsements, her clothing contracts totaling about $2.5 million.

Continuing the Story

The year 2000 began on a high note for Serena, who was ranked number four in the tennis world. She defeated Czech Denisa Chlad-

HONORS AND AWARDS

1998	WTA Most Impressive Newcomer *Tennis* magazine/Rolex Rookie of the Year
2000	Gold Medal, Olympic women's tennis doubles (with Venus Williams)

kova to win the Faber Grand Prix. However, she lost to Mary Pierce in the Tennis Master Series—Indian Wells Tournament in California. In April Serena withdrew from the Family Circle Tournament in Hilton Head, South Carolina, out of respect for the National Association for the Advancement of Colored People's boycott of South Carolina for its use of the Confederate flag. A few weeks later she decided against playing in the French Open on account of a knee injury. Though she competed at Wimbledon in July, it was her sister Venus who won. Serena won the Estyle.com Classic, beating Lindsay Davenport, but Davenport stopped Serena at the U.S. Open, which would ultimately be Venus's victory. Serena won the Princess Cup in Tokyo in October. In the 2000 Sydney Olympics, Serena won the gold medal in the doubles competition with her sister Venus.

Summary

Serena Williams is a tennis champion who has made an impact on the game. Both she and her sister made beaded braids their trademark—a symbol of their ethnic identity.

Cliff Drysdale, a tennis analyst for ESPN, noted Serena's cannonball serve and a high-voltage ground stroke, superb volleys, terrific overhead, and astonishing speed. Drysdale said her success on the court is, in large part, due to her penetrating volley. Calling Serena a complete package, he went on to say her athleticism and aggressive, in-your-face attitude worked together to make her a world-class tennis champion.

Betty L. Plummer

Additional Sources:

Aronson, Virginia. *Venus and Serena Williams.* Philadelphia: Chelsea House, 2001.

Blackistone, Kevin B. "Serena Williams Slams into History." *Emerge*, November, 1999, 74.

Sparling, Ken. *Venus and Serena Williams.* Chicago: Warwick Publishing, 2000.

Stewart, Mark. *Venus and Serena Williams: Sisters in Arms.* Brookfield, Conn.: Millbrook Press, 2000.

TED WILLIAMS

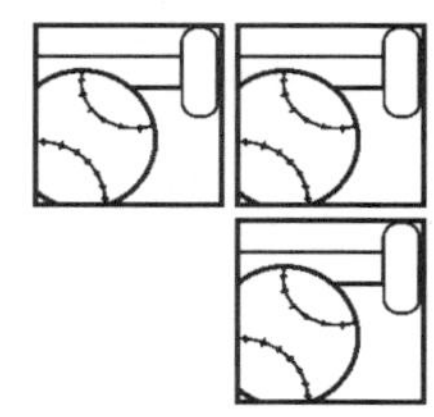

Sport: Baseball

Born: August 30, 1918
San Diego, California

Early Life

Theodore Samuel Williams was born on August 30, 1918, in San Diego, California. Ted was the firstborn of Samuel Steward and May (Venzer) Williams. Samuel was a veteran of the Spanish-American War, and, unfortunately, he had a tough time providing for his family. Ted's mother became the major influence of the household, though she spent much time away working for the Salvation Army. Ted learned how to fend for himself. At times, he would have the responsibility of buying and cooking his own meals.

Ted began spending much of his time at the local playground. The game of baseball became his one passionate interest. He would play whenever he could and for as long as there was daylight. A San Diego playground director by the name of Rod Luscomb was impressed by Ted's love for the game and talked him into starting a strength program to build up some muscle in his skinny arms. By the time he was ready for high school, Ted had developed into an all-around tough competitor who could pitch as well as hit. He threw right-handed, but he batted from the left side.

The Road to Excellence

At Herbert Hoover High School in San Diego, Ted excelled on the baseball field, but he was not a strong student. He played varsity baseball at Herbert Hoover for three years, earning an overall batting average of .430. The San Diego Padres of the Pacific Coast League wanted to sign Ted to a contract. Because he was only seventeen years old, his parents had to give their consent. They finally agreed, and Ted signed in 1936.

Ted's first season with the Padres was respectable, but it was recognized that he could be more than merely respectable. During his second season, he raised his batting average to .291, and he added more power to his game, which was reflected in the 23 home runs and 98 runs batted in (RBIs) he collected for the season.

After Ted's two seasons with San Diego, the major league teams began to take notice of him.

Courtesy of Amateur Athletic Foundation of Los Angeles

The first major league team to express a desire to sign Ted was the New York Yankees. His parents did not think that the bonus offered by the Yankees was large enough, so they made a counter offer that the Yankees felt was too steep. With the Yankees now out of the picture, the Boston Red Sox came forward and agreed to Ted's parents' terms. The Red Sox signed Ted to a two-year contract in which Ted would make $3,000 the first year and $4,500 dollars the second. The bonus he received totaled $1,000.

The Emerging Champion

In the spring of 1938, Ted reported to the Red Sox training camp. Still only nineteen years old, he carried himself with a certain amount of arrogance. Ted knew that he was good and that he only needed a chance to prove it. The Boston organization recognized his potential but did not believe he was quite ready to play on the Red Sox. Ted was sent to their AA minor league team in Minneapolis, Minnesota. The 1938 season with Minneapolis was better than even Ted could have imagined. He led the league in batting average (.366), home runs (42), and RBIs (142).

The only problem Ted had during the season was with his lack of maturity. He was prone to lose his temper when something bothered him, and he had a bad habit of joking around on the field. The manager of the Minneapolis team, Donie Bush, was not sure if Ted was ready for the Red Sox, but he could not argue with what Ted had done offensively for the year.

Ted was promoted to the Boston team for the 1939 season. He soon proved to everyone that he was going to be a force to reckon with in the major leagues. During his first season, Ted batted .327, hit 31 home runs, and drove in a league-leading 145 runs. Ted was a tough competitor and always a perfectionist, rarely satisfied with his performance. After batting .344 the following season, Ted was determined to be even more successful in 1941. He became the first player to bat over .400 for a season since 1930. On the final day of the season, Ted collected 6 hits in 8 times at bat during a doubleheader and finished with a .406 batting average. This was an amazing accomplishment, and, as of 1991, no one else had been able to finish an entire season with a batting average of .400 or better.

Continuing the Story

Because of World War II, Ted left baseball from 1943 to 1945 and became a Marine pilot.

STATISTICS

Season	*GP*	*AB*	*Hits*	*2B*	*3B*	*HR*	*Runs*	*RBI*	*BA*	*SA*
1939	149	565	185	44	11	31	131	**145**	.327	.609
1940	144	561	193	43	14	23	**134**	113	.344	.594
1941	143	456	185	33	3	**37**	**135**	120	**.406**	.735
1942	150	522	186	34	5	**36**	**141**	**137**	**.356**	**.648**
1946	150	514	176	37	8	38	**142**	123	.342	**.667**
1947	156	528	181	40	9	**32**	**125**	**114**	**.343**	**.634**
1948	137	509	188	**44**	3	25	124	127	**.369**	**.615**
1949	155	566	194	**39**	3	**43**	**150**	**159**	.343	**.650**
1950	89	334	106	24	1	28	82	97	.317	.647
1951	148	531	169	28	4	30	109	126	.318	**.556**
1952	6	10	4	0	1	1	2	3	.400	.900
1953	37	91	37	6	0	13	17	34	.407	.901
1954	117	386	133	23	1	29	93	89	.345	**.635**
1955	98	320	114	21	3	28	77	83	.356	.703
1956	136	400	138	28	2	24	71	82	.345	.605
1957	132	420	163	28	1	38	96	87	.388	**.731**
1958	129	411	135	23	2	26	81	85	.328	.584
1959	103	272	69	15	0	10	32	43	.254	.419
1960	113	310	98	15	0	29	56	72	.316	.645
Totals	2,292	7,706	2,654	525	71	521	1,798	1,839	.344	.634

Notes: Boldface indicates statistical leader. GP = games played; AB = at bats; 2B = doubles; 3B = triples; HR = home runs; RBI = runs batted in; BA = batting average; SA = slugging average

HONORS AND AWARDS

1940-42, 1946-51, 1953-60	American League All-Star Team
1941-42, 1947, 1949, 1957	*Sporting News* Major League Player of the Year
1946, 1949	American League most valuable player
1957	Associated Press Male Athlete of the Year
1966	Inducted into National Baseball Hall of Fame
1999	MLB All-Century Team Uniform number 9 retired by Boston Red Sox

He therefore lost some of his prime baseball years to service in the United States military. Ted did not come back to baseball until 1946. In that year, he won the American League most valuable player award and helped the Red Sox make it to the World Series, where they lost to the St. Louis Cardinals. Ted continued in the following years to prove that he was one of the great hitters of all time. He won his second Triple Crown in 1947, after previously winning it in 1942. He was awarded his second most valuable player award in 1949.

Ted suffered his most serious injury in 1950, when he cracked his elbow as he made a catch against the left field wall. It was necessary for him to have surgery. In Ted's mind, he would never be the same hitter again. He was never satisfied with less than perfection in himself. When the Korean War broke out, his Marine reserve unit was called up, and so once again he had to leave baseball to serve his country. Ted came back in 1954 and played until he retired in 1960. He even won batting titles in 1957 and 1958, when he was thirty-eight and thirty-nine years old.

Throughout his career, Ted was always an intelligent hitter, and he had exceptional eyesight and very quick wrists. For his career, he ranks second in slugging average (.634) and sixth in batting average (.344). Even though he lost some years that could have been his most productive, he still ranks high in most of his career statistics.

After retiring as a player, Ted stayed out of baseball for a number of years but eventually tried his hand at managing. It was a frustrating experience for a perfectionist like Ted, so he only spent four years at this endeavor. He also gained acclaim as a master fisherman and has also kept his hand in baseball by being a hitting instructor for the Boston Red Sox. Ted has been married and divorced three times and has two children.

Summary

Ted Williams was voted into the National Baseball Hall of Fame in 1966. He was always a determined competitor and a perfectionist who rubbed a number of fans and sportswriters the wrong way, but it is safe to say that Ted ranks as one of baseball's greatest hitters. Over his nineteen-year career, he won the American League batting title six times and led the league in home runs and RBIs four times each. His one accomplishment that will not be easily equaled or surpassed is his batting a remarkable .406 for an entire season. Many experts would agree that this left-handed hitter is the greatest baseball has ever seen.

Michael Jeffrys

Additional Sources:

Linn, Edward. *Ted Williams, the Eternal Kid.* New York: Bartholomew House, 1961.

Pope, Edwin. *Ted Williams.* Englewood Cliffs, N.J.: Prentice-Hall, 1970.

Seidel, Michael. *Ted Williams: A Baseball Life.* Lincoln: University of Nebraska Press, 2000.

Williams, Ted. *My Turn at Bat: The Story of My Life.* New York: Simon & Schuster, 1988.

VENUS WILLIAMS

Sport: Tennis

Born: June 17, 1980
Lynwood, California

AP/Wide World Photos

Venus Williams celebrates after winning the 2000 Wimbledon singles title. She also won in doubles with her sister, Serena.

Early Life

Venus Ebone Starr Williams was born on June 17, 1980, in Lynwood, California. She was the fourth of five daughters born to Richard Williams, co-owner of a security services business, and Oracene ("Brandi") Williams, a nurse. Education was important to the Williams family, but Richard recognized that there was money to be made in tennis. He first taught himself, then his entire family, how to play tennis by reading books and watching videos. Venus began to play at the age of four on public courts in Compton, California, a suburb of Los Angeles. Venus and her younger sister, Serena, showed talent very early on. Their sisters Yetunde, Isha, and Lyndrea went on to excel in other professions.

The Road to Excellence

By the age of ten, Venus had won numerous junior tennis competitions, including the Southern California girls' title in the under-twelve division. The family relocated to Florida, where she was enrolled in Rick Macci's Tennis Academy. By the age of twelve she had won sixty-three consecutive tournaments and had been featured in *Sports Illustrated*, *Tennis,* and the *New York Times*. In 1991 Richard Williams surprised the tennis world when he withdrew Venus and Serena from the junior competition circuit to protect them from undue pressure and to allow them to concentrate on practicing and schoolwork. Critics felt that this was an unwise decision and that Venus would not be prepared for professional competition. Ignoring these complaints, Venus and her family believed that they knew what was best for her.

The Emerging Champion

In 1994, at the age of fourteen, Venus entered the professional tennis circuit at the Bank of the West Classic in Oakland, California. She amazed the tennis world by defeating the Women's Tennis Association's (WTA) fifty-ninth-ranked player and by nearly upsetting the number-two-ranked Arantxa Sanchez-Vicario. Over the next three years, the 6-foot-1½ inch prodigy proved to be a powerful player and clocked a 108-miles per hour serve, the ninth-fastest serve recorded on the WTA tour in 1996. In 1997 Venus showed a meteoric rise when she started the season ranked number 211 and jumped to number 64. She had her first win over a top-ten player in the Evert Cup championships and made her first appearance at Wimbledon, one of the most prestigious tennis tournaments in the world.

The world was watching the rapid rise of this new star, but Richard, who remained Venus's coach and manager, restricted the number of tournaments she entered. He did not want her to burn out or neglect her education. An outspoken and candid person, he was the subject of criticism for stating in an interview that racial epithets were directed at Venus during the U.S. Open tournament. It was not the first time that an African American player or coach had suggested that the predominantly white tennis community was not accepting of them. However, Richard has also been called a racist for remarks that he reportedly made regarding white players when defending his daughters. Venus and Serena have not escaped controversy and have been criticized by fellow players for being distant during and after matches. Venus once responded by saying that she comes to the courts to play and win.

MAJOR CHAMPIONSHIPS

Year	Event
1998	Grand Slam Cup, singles Australian Open, mixed doubles French Open, mixed doubles Lipton, singles
1999	French Open, doubles U.S. Open, doubles Lipton, singles Italian Open, singles
2000	Wimbledon, singles Wimbledon, doubles U.S. Open, singles
2001	Ericsson Open, singles Wimbledon, singles

Continuing the Story

In 1998 Venus won her first WTA singles title at the IGA Classic, upgrading her WTA ranking to number twelve. She captured two other tournament titles that year, the Lipton championship and the Grand Slam Cup. During the Swisscom Challenge she set a WTA record by clocking an unprecedented 127-mph serve during the quarter final.

Along with her partner, sister Serena, Venus captured two doubles titles at the IGA Classic and the European championship. At the Australian championships and the French Open she walked away with mixed doubles titles, having won the French Open against Serena and her partner. The Williams sisters met in two singles matches that year, with Venus defeating Serena in the second round of the Australian and the quarter final round of the Italian tournaments.

Venus continued her victories in 1999 by securing six singles and three more doubles titles. She won her second Lipton title by defeating Serena in the final round. She won the IGA Classic again, as well as titles at the Betty Barclay Cup Italian Open, Pilot Pen, and the Swisscom Challenge.

The Williams sisters made tennis history in 1999 in several categories: Their meeting at the Lipton tournament marked the first time that sisters played each other in a WTA title match; when Venus won the IGA Classic and Serena won the Paris Open, they became the first sisters to win title matches in the same week; the French Open doubles title made them the first sisters in the 20th century to win a Grand Slam title crown together; and in April, 1999, they became the first sisters to be ranked at the same time in the WTA top ten since April, 1991. The sisters, with their beaded, cornrow-braided hairstyles, have

HONORS AND AWARDS	
1997	WTA Most Impressive Newcomer U.S. Olympic Committee Female Athlete of the Month: September *Tennis* magazine Most Improved Female Pro
1998	*Tennis* magazine Most Improved Player
2000	Gold Medal, Olympic women's singles tennis Gold Medal, Olympic women's doubles tennis (with Serena Williams)

been called the "beaded wonders." In June, 2000, Venus was ranked number five and Serena was ranked number eight in the WTA. In 2001, Venus repeated her 2000 Wimbledon singles championship win.

Summary

Venus Williams is listed in *Who's Who Among African Americans* and is a role model for youngsters, including those who believe that tennis is not a black person's sport. She is articulate and radiates confidence; her serves broke speed records. The Williams sisters won prestigious tennis titles, made tennis history, and earned millions of dollars in winnings and endorsements. However, the family kept these successes in perspective and Richard stated in a *Jet* magazine interview that he believed his talented daughters were capable of excelling at anything they chose to do. Venus adopted this attitude.

Felicia Friendly Thomas

Additional Sources:

Edwards, Tamala. "At the Top of Their Game." *Essence*, August, 1998, 78-80.

Peyser, Marc, and Allison Samuels. "Venus and Serena Against the World." *Newsweek*, August 24, 1998, 44-48.

Sherman, Josepha. *Venus Williams*. Chicago: Heinemann, 2001.

Sparling, Ken. *Venus and Serena Williams*. Chicago: Warwick Publishing, 2000.

Stewart, Mark. *Venus and Serena Williams: Sisters in Arms*. Brookfield, Conn.: Millbrook Press, 2000.

WALTER RAY WILLIAMS, JR.

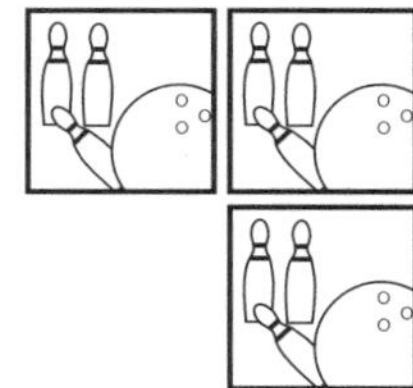

Sport: Bowling and Horseshoe pitching

Born: October 6, 1959
San Jose, California

AP/Wide World Photos

Bowler Walter Ray Williams, Jr., celebrates after a strike in the PBA National Championships in 2001, which he won.

Early Life

Walter Ray Williams, Jr., was born on October 6, 1959, in San Jose, California. His interest in bowling began when he was eleven years old, when a fellow competitor at a horseshoe pitching tournament took Walter Ray and his younger brother bowling. He enjoyed bowling and connected with the game immediately. As a result of this early bowling experience, the brothers joined a bowling league later that year. Because his family did not have the financial means for the novice bowler to practice as much as he would have liked, Walter Ray was only able to bowl sporadically.

It was not until his senior year in high school, when he was able to take bowling as a physical education credit, that he was able to bowl seriously. Skipping the usual Junior Bowling League route, Walter Ray began to compete in adult men's bowling leagues when he was seventeen. In addition to a busy schedule competing in both bowling and horseshoe pitching, Walter Ray also found time to earn a bachelor of science degree in physics from California State Polytechnic University.

The Road to Excellence

Walter Ray maintained a busy schedule, entering both bowling tournaments and horseshoe-pitching tournaments, putting him in the unusual position of competing in and winning titles in two different sports. The young bowler joined the Professional Bowlers Association (PBA) in 1980 and began a string of steadily increasing earnings on the tour.

In 1993 Walter Ray was still known as much for his horseshoe-pitching championships as for his bowling. He continued to compete in tournaments, and, in 1993, his perseverance paid off. By the end of 1993, Walter Ray had bowled four 300 games; had bowled 1,300 games in one year, the most ever in a year; and had bowled sixty-one successive 200 games: All three achievements were PBA records. In addition to these achievements, he won seven titles and had total earnings of over $290,000, winning the George Young High Average Award for the first time. Then, in 1994, Walter Ray won two titles, stayed at the top of the points battle, and finished in second place for the season with winnings topping $195,000.

HONORS AND AWARDS

1986, 1993, 1996, 1997, 1998	Professional Bowlers Association Player of the Year
1993, 1994, 1996, 1997	Harry Smith Point Leader Award
1993, 1996, 1997	George Young High Average Award
1995, 1996	President, Professional Bowlers Association
1995	Inducted into Professional Bowlers Association Hall of Fame
1999	Victor Award

The Emerging Champion

Walter Ray continued his impressive streak into 1995, when he won one title and took home more than $153,000 in earnings. He was also inducted into the PBA Hall of Fame in 1995. Statistically, the best years for Walter Ray were from 1996 through 1998, during which he won thirteen titles and emerged as points leader and high-average award winner. In addition, he claimed the PBA's Bowler of the Year award for those three years.

By 1998 he had won the PBA Bowler of the Year award five times, in 1986, 1993, 1996, 1997, and 1998; the George Young High Average Award again in 1996 and 1997; and the Harry Smith Point Leader Award in 1993, 1994, 1996, and 1997. A high point in his career came for Walter Ray when he was named the PBA Player of the Decade for the 1990's. Walter Ray was then elected president of the PBA for the 1995-1997 term. He ended the 1997 season as the Professional Bowlers Association's top-ranked player.

Continuing the Story

By early 1998, Walter Ray had become the first bowler to garner career earnings over $2 million. He was named one of the twenty greatest players of the twentieth century by *Bowling Magazine*, and, with total winnings over $2.4 million, Walter Ray holds the record as the Professional Bowlers Association's top money winner.

However, in 1999, knee problems kept Walter Ray from repeating his victories from the first eight years of the 1990's, and he began to fall in the rankings. Though Walter Ray had suffered no injury to his knee, he began wearing a knee brace to help correct the effects of his knee problems. Characteristically, Walter Ray made no excuses for his faltering game and persevered through the next few years. Though he continued to bowl and to win during the 1999-2000 season, he did not perform up to his previous standards, falling from first to seventh in the rankings.

Although 1999 was not his best year, the five-time Bowler of the Year did become one of only three players to win thirty titles. Walter Ray, who only won one title in 1999, seemed to have lost his momentum, and he fared little better at the beginning of the 2000 season. However, by the end of 2000, Walter Ray was once again racking up impressive victories in PBA tournaments. In addition to his bowling titles, he had won a total of six world horseshoe pitching titles by the end of 2000.

Even though Walter Ray is a successful and top-ranked bowler, he has set difficult goals for himself. One such goal has been to score more first-place than second-place finishes, a goal that he had achieved and maintained at the end of the 2000 season. Another goal was to win both the World Horseshoe Pitching Championship and the PBA Player of the Year award in the same year.

Summary

Throughout his career, Walter Ray Williams, Jr., has shown what hard work and dedication to a sport can produce. Though he did not follow the typical route to his victories, he has nonetheless achieved his goals in both bowling and horseshoe pitching. By winning championships in both sports, Walter Ray serves as an inspiration to aspiring bowlers and horseshoe pitchers alike.

Kimberley H. Kidd

Additional Sources:

Brewington, Peter. "Williams Trying to Pin Down a Major Victory." *USA Today*, April 18, 1998, p. 15C.

Graves, Gary. "Williams Goal: Unique Double." *USA Today*, July 11, 2000, p. 3C.

Pezzano, Chuck. "Williams Back Among the Elite." *The (New Jersey) Record*, October 22, 2000, p. S13.

MAURY WILLS

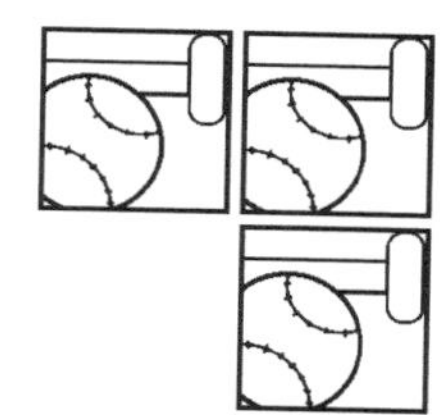

Sport: Baseball

Born: October 2, 1932
Washington, D.C.

Early Life

Maurice Morning Wills was born on October 2, 1932, in Washington, D.C., one of eight sons and five daughters born to the Reverend and Mrs. Guy O. Wills.

The large Wills family scraped by with the basics, thanks to the parents' hard work and sacrifices. Maury's father worked full time as a machinist at the Washington Navy Yard while also serving as the preacher of a small Baptist parish. His mother operated an elevator at the Navy Yard.

With little money for real equipment, six-year-old Maury and his young friends first learned baseball on the paved city playground using tennis balls and broomsticks. They shaped paper bags into gloves.

The Road to Excellence

Maury's love for baseball developed late because there was no Little League program for youngsters where he grew up. When Jackie Robinson became the first black player to make the major leagues in 1947, fourteen-year-old Maury took greater notice. Although small—when he entered Cardozo High School, he was 5 feet 8 inches tall and only 150 pounds—Maury was gifted with a pitching arm strong enough to strike out much bigger men in a local semiprofessional baseball league.

A three-sport All-Star in high school, Maury performed brilliantly at a local baseball "talent hunt" and at later tryouts. The New York Giants dismissed Maury as too small for a big league pitcher, but his speed impressed the Brooklyn Dodgers, who signed the high school senior to his first professional contract in 1951. By then, Maury had married Gertrude Elliott and the young couple was expecting their first child.

At minor league training camp in Vero Beach, Florida, Maury's size led him from the pitching mound to the infield. His minor league career started at the bottom, in Class D, and was a long and discouraging eight years. His play was inconsistent and he faced the chill of racism in places that had never had African American players.

Courtesy of Amateur Athletic Foundation of Los Angeles

At each step up the ladder, Maury made the most of his great baserunning speed and his teachers. They taught him how to hit both left-handed and right-handed and do it well.

During the 1959 pennant race, the Dodgers called up the hot-hitting speedster. He had a shaky start, but his running won over local fans. When the Dodgers beat the Chicago White Sox in the World Series, Maury started all six games at shortstop and played well.

The Emerging Champion

Maury's first full season with the club in 1960 was a test of his faith in himself. In the first half, he hit horribly and was ready to quit when he got help from coach Pete Reiser, who told Maury never to give up. They worked and worked, trying new bats and new batting stances until Maury found the winning combination.

He ended the season with a .295 batting average, and, with more chances on base, Maury finished with 50 stolen bases, tops in the league. He later called Pete Reiser "my guiding light."

Maury would go on to lead the National League in stolen bases in each of the next five seasons, but 1962 was the year everyone would remember.

That season, Maury seemed unstoppable. As he closed in on Ty Cobb's record of 96 stolen bases, even opposing fans cheered him on. The whole world seemed to be keeping count. Besides the pressure, Maury had to fight off pain from a pulled leg muscle that was sore from stopping and starting.

He stole his 97th base in the 156th game of the season, the same number Cobb had played when he set the record. Maury stole 7 more, for 104, a record that stood until 1974. With a .299 batting average, he was named the league's most valuable player and Associated Press Athlete of the Year and won a Gold Glove award.

Continuing the Story

Maury's exploits on the base paths trailed off some in the years after; he stole 40 and 53 in the next two seasons. Yet even age did not slow him down. His 94 stolen bases in 1965, at age thirty-two, were a big reason the Dodgers won the National League crown. More important, Maury carved out his place as one of the most exciting players of his time. The competitiveness that had shone in even the darkest days of his minor league career kept him on the move. Some opposing players accused him of overdoing it—stealing just to rub it in—but Maury's base-running helped bring in a new era in baseball, one where speed again became as important as power hitting.

Suffering a sore leg in 1966, Maury was traded to the Pittsburgh Pirates, where he had his best year at the plate the following year with a .302 average, 3 home runs, and 45 runs batted in.

STATISTICS

Season	*GP*	*AB*	*Hits*	*2B*	*3B*	*HR*	*Runs*	*RBI*	*BA*	*SA*
1959	83	242	63	5	2	0	27	7	.260	.298
1960	148	516	152	15	2	0	75	27	.295	.331
1961	148	613	173	12	**10**	1	105	31	.282	.339
1962	165	695	208	13	10	6	130	48	.299	.373
1963	134	527	159	19	3	0	83	34	.302	.349
1964	158	630	173	15	5	2	81	34	.275	.324
1965	158	650	186	14	7	0	92	33	.286	.329
1966	143	594	162	14	2	1	60	39	.273	.308
1967	149	616	186	12	9	3	92	45	.302	.365
1968	153	627	174	12	6	0	76	31	.278	.316
1969	151	623	171	10	8	4	80	47	.274	.335
1970	132	522	141	19	3	0	77	34	.270	.318
1971	149	601	169	14	3	3	73	44	.281	.329
1972	71	132	17	3	1	0	16	4	.129	.167
Totals	1,942	7,588	2,134	177	71	20	1,067	458	.281	.331

Notes: Boldface indicates statistical leader. GP = games played; AB = at bats; 2B = doubles; 3B = triples; HR = home runs; RBI = runs batted in; BA = batting average; SA = slugging average

After a stopover at the Montreal Expos, he returned to the Dodgers and retired in 1972 with a lifetime .281 average, 20 home runs, 458 runs batted in, and 586 stolen bases. Along the way, he was named to the National League All-Star team five times and played in four World Series.

Maury coached in the Mexican Winter League one season. He later became a sports announcer for NBC. He was criticized for controversial remarks made in 1974 as Lou Brock closed in on his stolen base record. In 1980, Maury was named the manager of the Seattle Mariners but was fired in 1981 after a 6-18 start. After several turbulent years involving drug and alcohol abuse, Maury returned to baseball in 1998 as the running coach for the Toronto Blue Jays.

NATIONAL LEAGUE RECORDS

Most consecutive seasons leading the league in stolen bases, 6

HONORS AND AWARDS

1961-62	National League Gold Glove Award
1961-62, 1965	*Sporting News* Outstanding National League Shortstop
1961-63, 1965-66	National League All-Star Team
1962	National League most valuable player *Sporting News* Major League Co-Player of the Year National League All-Star Game most valuable player Associated Press Male Athlete of the Year Hickok Belt

Summary

One example of what made Maury Wills a special ballplayer is, of all things, the banjo. As a minor leaguer, he taught himself to play it by constant practice, never quitting even when teammates told him it sounded awful. Years later, he became accomplished enough to play professionally in big-city clubs. Small but determined, Maury put his head down and ran—always full speed ahead.

Kenneth Ellingwood

Additional Sources:

Gelman, Steve. *The Greatest Dodgers of Them All.* New York: Putnam, 1968.

Wills, Maury. *How to Steal a Pennant.* New York: Putnam, 1976.

_______. *On the Run: The Never Dull and Often Shocking Life of Maury Wills.* New York: Carroll & Graf, 1991.

HACK WILSON

Sport: Baseball

Born: April 26, 1900
Elwood City, Pennsylvania
Died: November 23, 1948
Baltimore, Maryland

Courtesy of Amateur Athletic Foundation of Los Angeles

Early Life

Lewis Robert Wilson was born an illegitimate child on April 26, 1900, in the bleak mining town of Elwood City, Pennsylvania. Unhappy in his squalid home and with a poor record at school, he dropped out of the sixth grade to go to work in a print shop for four dollars a week. Seeking better wages, he found employment in a locomotive factory, a steel mill, and a shipyard, but what he enjoyed most was playing semiprofessional baseball whenever he could find a team that would let him be its catcher.

The Road to Excellence

It was dirty, painful work to crouch for several hours in the summer sun wearing heavy pads over a "wool flannel" uniform and being bruised by foul tips, hurtling baserunners, and fastballs banging into the thin leather of his borrowed catcher's mitt, yet the young Wilson thrived on it. Despite thin ankles and small feet (he wore a size 5½ shoe), he was developing a barrel chest and heavily muscled arms, and he could already hit the ball farther than most of the older men with whom he played.

In 1921, "Hack," as he had already been nicknamed, after a burly wrestler some of his pals thought he resembled, signed his first professional contract with a team in Martinsburg, West Virginia. A broken leg suffered while sliding home in his first game did not keep him sidelined for long, but, unable to bend the stiff limb so as to squat behind home plate, he began playing the outfield. Soon he realized it was his natural position. Batting .356 and .366 during his two years at Martinsburg, he was promoted for the 1923 season to Portsmouth, Virginia, where he hit a spectacular .388.

Near the end of the 1923 season, he was signed by the World Champion New York Giants. In 1924, he became their regular center fielder, replacing the notorious Casey Stengel and playing all seven World Series games that fall against Washington. New York manager John McGraw called Hack the greatest judge of fly balls he had seen since the fabulous Tris Speaker, who set the standard for center fielders in his prime. Nevertheless, when Hack, who had begun to spend much of his off the field time drinking whiskey with admiring fans, got off to a poor start in 1925, McGraw sent him to the American Association Toledo Mud Hens. There Hack's all-around ability impressed the astute Joe McCarthy, the manager of the rival Louisville Cardinals.

The Emerging Champion

Hired to manage the Chicago Cubs for the 1926 season, McCarthy persuaded the team's owners to purchase Hack's contract. The "li'l round man" did not disappoint his benefactor. Despite a continuing love affair with the bottle, Hack led the National League in home runs and walks, finished second in runs batted in, and was third in doubles. Largely because of his inspiring play, the Cubs, who had finished last the previous year, ended the 1926 season in second place, only two games behind the Cardinals.

A right-handed hitter, Hack swung from his heels with one of the heaviest bats ever used by a major leaguer. He tied for the league lead in home runs in both 1927 and 1928 and ranked second and third in runs batted in, as McCarthy struggled to build a pennant winner around his stumpy star. In 1929 he did so.

The Cubs of 1929 were one of the most awesome teams in baseball history. With Hack leading the league with a spectacular 159 runs batted in, the Chicagoans finished ten games ahead of their nearest rivals. Hack, said his admiring manager, was the best outfielder in baseball. Despite drinking whiskey at all hours and once having to be sobered up in the clubhouse before a game by being plunged into a tub of ice water, the center fielder, according to his mentor, could hit, field, run, and throw with any player.

Continuing the Story

In the fourth game of the 1929 World Series, however, Hack lost a fly ball in the sun, enabling the Philadelphia Athletics to score three times en route to a 10-run rally that was the Series turning point. Sportswriters derisively dubbed him "Sunny boy" and blamed the Cub defeat on him, despite his .471 batting average for the five games.

Stung by the epithets of his critics, the "sawed-off" man had one of the finest seasons in 1930 that any ballplayer ever experienced. Batting an impressive .356, he hammered out 56 home runs, the most ever in National League history, and knocked in an almost unbelievable 190 runs, still a record for both major leagues.

STATISTICS

Season	*GP*	*AB*	*Hits*	*2B*	*3B*	*HR*	*Runs*	*RBI*	*BA*	*SA*
1923	3	10	2	0	0	0	0	0	.200	.200
1924	107	383	113	19	12	10	62	57	.295	.486
1925	62	180	43	7	4	6	28	30	.239	.422
1926	142	529	170	36	8	**21**	97	109	.321	.539
1927	146	551	175	30	12	**30**	119	129	.318	.579
1928	145	520	163	32	9	**31**	89	120	.313	.588
1929	150	574	198	30	5	39	135	**159**	.345	.618
1930	155	585	208	35	6	**56**	146	**190**	.356	**.723**
1931	112	395	103	22	4	13	66	61	.261	.435
1932	135	481	143	37	5	23	77	123	.297	.538
1933	117	360	96	13	2	9	41	54	.267	.389
1934	74	192	47	5	0	6	24	30	.245	.365
Totals	1,348	4,760	1,461	266	67	244	884	1,062	.307	.545

Notes: Boldface indicates statistical leader. GP = games played; AB = at bats; 2B = doubles; 3B = triples; HR = home runs; RBI = runs batted in; BA = batting average; SA = slugging average

Yet fate had a cruel awakening in store for the exuberant Wilson. Near the end of the 1930 season, the tolerant McCarthy was replaced as the Cubs' manager by the puritanical, nononsense Rogers Hornsby, whose aversion to Hack's dissipations led him to play the "little giant" in only 112 games in 1931. Dispirited and unwilling to abandon his dissolute habits in order to placate Hornsby, Hack hit only .261 with but 13 homers. At the end of the season, he was traded to Brooklyn.

Temporarily sobered and trimmed down for the 1932 season, Hack hit 23 home runs and had 123 runs batted in, to go with a respectable .297 batting average. It was his last significant season, however. In 1933, he was in and out of the Brooklyn lineup. Late in the following season, the Dodgers traded him to Philadelphia, where he hit only .100 in seven games and was released. He never played another big league game.

Hack's few remaining years were spent in menial jobs. He was a bartender in a saloon, a bouncer in a dance hall, and a maintenance man in a public park. He died, alone and almost penniless, at age forty-eight on November 23, 1948.

HONORS AND AWARDS

1930	National League most valuable player Major league record for the most runs batted in a season (190)
1979	Inducted into National Baseball Hall of Fame

Summary

Despite a weakness for alcohol that limited his career to only six good years and eventually killed him, genial, uncomplicated Hack Wilson was one of the greatest players of baseball's "golden age." It seems unlikely that either one of his two records will soon be broken.

Norman B. Ferris

Additional Sources:

Boone, Robert. *Hack: The Meteoric Life of One of Baseball's First Superstars, Hack Wilson.* Highland Park, Ill.: Highland Press, 1978.

Parker, Clifton Blue. *Fouled Away: The Baseball Tragedy of Hack Wilson.* Jefferson, N.C.: McFarland, 2000.

Shatzkin, Mike, et al., eds. *The Ballplayers: Baseball's Ultimate Biographical Reference.* New York: William Morrow, 1990.

LARRY WILSON

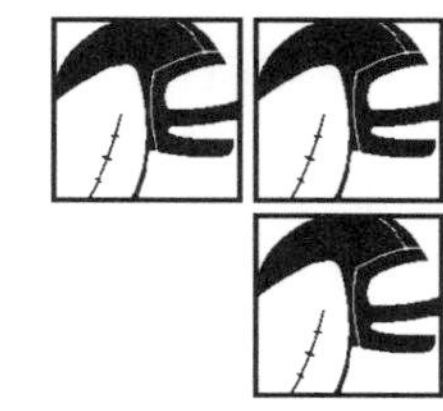

Sport: Football

Born: March 24, 1938
Rigby, Idaho

Courtesy of Amateur Athletic Foundation of Los Angeles

Early Life

Lawrence Frank Wilson was born in Rigby, Idaho, on March 24, 1938. His father was a truck driver for the Utah Power and Light Company. When Larry was ten, his mother died. Larry's dad never remarried. Larry has said he owes much of his success to his father, who, alone, reared him and his brother John. At Rigby High School, Larry was a small but aggressive athlete. He won sixteen varsity letters and led Rigby to the state football championship. He excelled in track, setting state records in the high jump and high hurdles. The high school athletic field at Rigby has been named Larry Wilson Field.

The Road to Excellence

Larry enrolled at the University of Utah in 1956, at the request of his father. He continued to be successful as a high jumper in track as well as a two-way player on the football field. He learned to be aggressive and to have fun under two football coaches. Jack Curtice taught Larry the fun of the game, and Ray Nagel taught Larry the importance of outhitting one's opponent. Larry was used mostly as an offensive player. As a fullback he held many scoring records at Utah by the time he graduated in 1960. He earned third team All-American honors his senior year.

He was selected in the seventh round of the National Football League (NFL) draft by the St. Louis Cardinals with little fanfare. The Cardinals agreed to try Larry on defense when it seemed that he had little chance of making the team on offense.

The Emerging Champion

Larry thought he was going to be cut by the Cardinals after their final pre-season game in San Francisco. He even asked his wife Dee Ann to meet him in San Francisco so they could drive to Idaho together once the cut was official. To their surprise, he made the team and started at defensive safety in the opening regular season game. He continued to start at that position for the next thirteen years.

Wilson became famous for the safety blitz, designed especially for him by Cardinals defensive coach Chuck Drulis. Larry was also known as a fierce competitor. He wore only a single bar on his helmet for a face mask. His clearly visible crooked nose (from multiple fractures) and his missing front teeth conveyed to fans and opponents just how determined and aggressive he was. His familiar number 8 was seemingly everywhere on the field making plays. The deadly tackler and pass defender demonstrated great courage by playing against the Pittsburgh Steelers in 1965 with both hands in casts; he made a key interception that led to a Cardinals victory. In 169 games Wilson intercepted 52 passes for 800 yards and 5 touchdowns. He intercepted 3 passes in one game twice, led the NFL with 10 interceptions in 1966, and tied an NFL mark by making interceptions in seven straight games.

Continuing the Story

Larry was a five-time All-NFL selection. He played in eight Pro Bowl games. Considered the best NFL safety ever, Larry twice was named Cardinals most valuable player between 1966 and 1968, and in 1966 finished second for the NFL Player of the Year award. It was somehow fitting that in Larry's final game in 1972, he played with a painful cracked rib that required special wrapping. It would have been easy to quit, but that was just not Larry's style. He played in pain right to the very end of his career.

Wilson served as director of scouting for the Cardinals from 1973 to 1976 before being promoted to assistant director of operations. In 1980 he was named the club's director of professional personnel. Besides being selected to the NFL All-Pro Team of the 1960's and to the AFL-NFL 1960-1984 All-Star team, Wilson in 1978 was elected to the Pro Football Hall of Fame. He and his first wife, Dee Ann, had two sons and one daughter. In 1980 Wilson married radio personality Nancy Drew. He also accepted a job as the general manager of the Cardinals in 1988, the year they moved to Phoenix. In 1994 Larry was honored as a champion by being named to the NFL's 75th Anniversary All Time Team.

HONORS AND AWARDS	
1960	College All-American
1963-64, 1966-71	NFL Pro Bowl Team
1963, 1966-69	All-NFL Team
1966	Halas Trophy
1970	NFL All-Pro Team of the 1960's
1978	Inducted into Pro Football Hall of Fame
1985	AFL-NFL 1960-1984 All-Star Team Uniform number 8 retired by Phoenix Cardinals
1994	NFL 75th Anniversary All Time Team

Wilson's courage served to inspire his teammates, and even his retirement provided a lasting benefit for the city of St. Louis. In the team's hometown, a dinner in his honor raised some $30,000 for the St. Louis Children's Hospital. Roughly $20,000 of the money was used to start the Larry Wilson Fund for children with special medical needs. The plight of disabled children has always been of concern to Larry. He has long been close to the problem. Jed Wilson, Larry and Dee Ann's oldest son, was born with a spinal defect that left him permanently paralyzed from the waist down.

Summary

Larry Wilson was a courageous and determined professional football player who overcame many obstacles to become one of the best players ever at his position. He was an inspirational player who became a fixture in the St. Louis community, working to raise money for handicapped children. In both his career and his retirement, Larry has exemplified the marks of a true champion.

Kevin R. Lasley

Additional Sources:

Anderson, Dave. *Great Defensive Players of the NFL.* New York: Random House, 1967.

Attner, Paul. "NFL: Football's One Hundred Greatest Players—Better than All the Rest." *The Sporting News* 223 (November 8, 1999): 58-59, 62.

Barber, Phil. "NFL: Football's One Hundred Greatest Players—The Hit Men." *The Sporting News* 223 (November 1, 1999): 12-16.

DAVE WINFIELD

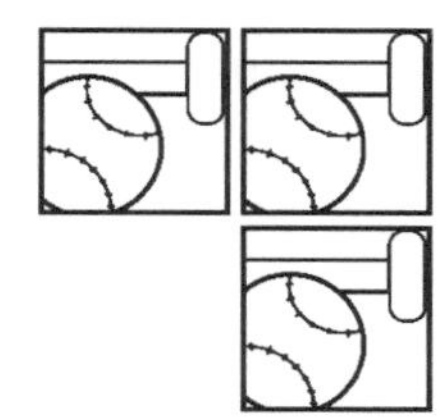

Sport: Baseball

Born: October 3, 1951
St. Paul, Minnesota

Early Life

David Mark Winfield was born on October 3, 1951, in St. Paul, Minnesota. His parents, Frank and Arline Winfield, were Minnesota natives. Dave was the younger of their two sons. By the time Dave was three, his parents separated. His father moved to the West Coast, while the rest of the family remained in St. Paul.

AP/Wide World Photos

Minnesota Twin Dave Winfield after getting his three thousandth hit, in 1993.

When Dave was about ten, he and his brother, Steve, became interested in baseball. They were not only fans but also avid players, participating in local youth leagues. Dave played third base and shortstop. Mrs. Winfield and her mother took a great interest in the boys' activities. They encouraged Dave and Steve not only to excel in sports but also to value hard work and education.

The Road to Excellence

By the time Dave entered high school in 1965, he was more than 6 feet tall. As a member of the school's baseball team, he pitched and played shortstop. American Legion baseball provided him with the opportunity to play during the summer.

At the end of his senior year of high school, in 1969, Dave's skill as a player provided him with choices. The Baltimore Orioles of the American League drafted him and assigned him to a minor league team. The University of Minnesota, Minneapolis, offered Dave a partial baseball scholarship, which provided a chance for a college education and the opportunity to play ball. He chose the scholarship.

Dave entered the University of Minnesota in 1969. He described himself as an unenthusiastic student, but in his second year, he began to take his class work seriously and declared a double major in black studies and political science. He studied hard and received good grades.

During his four years in college, Dave pitched for the baseball team and, during his freshman, junior, and senior years, he also played basketball. He received a full scholarship for basketball. In his senior year, the basketball team won the Big Ten Conference Championship and played in the National Invitational Tournament. The baseball team participated in the College World Series. Dave was named the tournament's most valuable player. For the season, he batted .385 and pitched for thirteen wins and one loss.

The Emerging Champion

Dave's athletic ability had made him prominent by the end of his college career. In the spring of 1973, four professional sports teams selected him in their drafts. He was chosen as an outfielder by the San Diego Padres of the baseball National League, the Atlanta Hawks of the National Basketball Association, the Utah Stars of the American Basketball Association, and the Minnesota Vikings of the National Football League. The last selection was unusual because Dave had not played football in high school or in college.

Dave signed a contract with San Diego. He became a member of the Padres in 1973, bypassing the minor leagues. To develop his skills, he played winter baseball in Mexico after his first major league season.

Between 1974 and 1977, Dave became an excellent professional baseball player. His talent was recognized in 1977 when he was named to the National League All-Star team for the first time.

In the 1970's, major league baseball's management adopted the policy of free agency. This allowed players with seven or more years of major league service who had fulfilled their contracts to sign contracts with other teams. Dave became a free agent after the 1980 season. He signed a ten-year agreement with the New York Yankees. As an outfielder for the Yankees from 1981 through 1988, Dave was named to the American League All-Star team each year. He won seven Gold Glove awards for excellence in fielding and four Silver Bat awards for his hitting.

An injury forced Dave to undergo back surgery after the 1988 season. He was unable to play baseball in 1989, but he was able to return to play the 1990 season as a newly signed member of the California Angels of the American League. After a slow start, Dave enjoyed a successful year. He batted 475 times and finished with a .267 batting average and 21 home runs. During the 1991 season, he accomplished the rare feat of hitting for the cycle—hitting a single, double, triple, and

STATISTICS

Season	*GP*	*AB*	*Hits*	*2B*	*3B*	*HR*	*Runs*	*RBI*	*BA*	*SA*
1973	56	141	39	4	1	3	9	12	.277	.383
1974	145	498	132	18	4	20	57	75	.265	.438
1975	143	509	136	20	2	15	74	76	.267	.403
1976	137	492	139	26	4	13	81	69	.283	.431
1977	157	615	169	29	7	25	104	92	.275	.467
1978	158	587	181	30	5	24	88	97	.308	.499
1979	159	597	184	27	10	34	97	**118**	.308	.558
1980	162	558	154	25	6	20	89	87	.276	.450
1981	105	388	114	25	1	13	52	68	.294	.464
1982	140	539	151	24	8	37	84	106	.280	.560
1983	152	598	169	26	8	32	99	116	.283	.513
1984	141	567	193	34	4	19	106	100	.340	.515
1985	155	633	174	34	6	26	105	114	.275	.471
1986	154	565	148	31	5	24	90	104	.262	.462
1987	156	575	158	22	1	27	83	97	.275	.457
1988	149	559	180	37	2	25	96	107	.322	.530
1990	132	475	127	21	2	21	70	78	.267	.453
1991	150	568	149	27	4	28	75	86	.262	.472
1992	156	583	169	33	3	26	92	108	.290	.491
1993	143	547	148	27	2	21	72	76	.271	.442
1994	77	294	74	15	3	10	35	43	.252	.425
1995	46	115	22	5	0	2	11	4	.191	.287
Totals	2,973	11,003	3,110	540	88	465	1,669	1,833	.283	.475

Notes: Boldface indicates statistical leader. GP = games played; AB = at bats; 2B = doubles; 3B = triples; HR = home runs; RBI = runs batted in; BA = batting average; SA = slugging average

HONORS AND AWARDS

1973	College World Series Most Outstanding Player *Sporting News* College Baseball All-American
1977-80	National League All-Star Team
1979-80	National League Gold Glove
1981-84	American League Silver Bat Award
1981-88	American League All-Star Team
1982-85, 1987	American League Gold Glove
1987	Honorary Doctor of Laws, Syracuse University
2001	Inducted in the National Baseball Hall of Fame

home run in the same game—in a 9-4 victory over the Kansas City Royals on June 24.

Continuing the Story

Dave never fit the image of the selfish professional athlete. Although he left the University of Minnesota without completing his bachelor's degree, he remained interested in education. In 1974, he established a scholarship and awards dinner for minority students in St. Paul.

Also in 1974, he began to buy blocks of tickets to Padres games, which were given to disadvantaged children. In 1977, after signing a new contract with San Diego, he created the David M. Winfield Foundation. At first, the Foundation purchased tickets to the annual All-Star games and gave them to children. In 1980, he committed the Foundation to spending money to provide physical examinations, health education, and health care for thousands of disadvantaged children.

After he had joined the Yankees in 1981, Dave moved the Foundation's offices to Fort Lee, New Jersey. His contract with the New York team required the Yankees to contribute $300,000 each year to the Winfield Foundation. Although there were some disagreements over the payments, Dave persisted, and the money was paid by the team.

In the middle of the 1980's, Dave and the Winfield Foundation's directors changed the focus of the organization. They were very concerned about the problem of drug abuse among young people. Dave appeared in a short film on drug abuse prevention, and the Foundation sponsored a program called the Drug Awareness Program, which made educational presentations in schools.

Dave signed with the Toronto Blue Jays in 1992. In addition to the 2 home runs that he hit in the American League Championship Series against Oakland that year, Dave also drove in the winning run in the eleventh inning of game 6 of the World Series against the Braves, making Toronto the first foreign team to win the world championship.

In 1993, Dave returned to his hometown team, the Twins. He became only the third player in baseball history to record 3,000 hits and 400 or more home runs on September 16 when he singled off of Dennis Eckersley.

Dave played one more season with the Twins in 1994 and signed with the Indians in 1995. After surgery to repair a torn rotator cuff, he decided to retire, finishing his career as baseball's active leader in hits and runs batted in. Dave continued to stay close to baseball in his retirement. He joined the staff of Fox television's Saturday pregame show *Baseball on Fox* in 1996. In 2001 he was inducted into the Hall of Fame.

Summary

Dave Winfield's contributions to sports and to American society have been extensive. He took advantage of the opportunities his athletic talents provided to win college scholarships, obtain an education, and pursue a successful career in professional baseball. His success enabled him to assist many young people through his charitable foundation.

Ann M. Scanlon

Additional Sources:

Cameron, Layne. "Batting a Thousand." *Child Life*, 74, no. 3 (1995).

Kirkjian, Tim. "Mr. Longevity." *Sports Illustrated* 79, no. 13 (1993).

Verducci, Tom. "He's a Hall of Famer, George." *Sports Illustrated* 84, no. 7 (1996).

Winfield, Dave, with Tom Parker. *Winfield: A Player's Life.* New York: Norton, 1988.

HANS WINKLER

Sport: Equestrian

Born: July 24, 1926
Barmen, Germany

Early Life

Hans Günter Winkler was born July 24, 1926, in Barmen, a small town near Dortmund, Germany. His father, Paul Winkler, was an equerry and riding instructor, but he wanted his son to follow another career, such as business.

From earliest childhood, however, Hans Winkler was interested in horses and horsemanship, and, by the time he was thirteen, he had managed to participate in several competitions and horse shows.

When World War II broke out in 1939, the Winkler family moved to Frankfurt, where the father managed a small riding academy and Hans managed to spend time every day with horses. He decided he would make show jumping his specialty. He had hoped to continue his early training since, because of his age, no one believed he would have to serve in the military. In 1944, however, at the age of eighteen, he was drafted and immediately sent to the Eastern Front, which was already collapsing under the Soviet advance. His father, who had been drafted earlier, was killed on the Western Front a week before the war ended.

Captured and imprisoned in eastern Germany, Hans managed to escape and made his way back to Frankfurt, where he finally found his mother in the almost completely destroyed city. Ill from the hardships of the prison camp, suffering from hepatitis, with no money, hardly any food, and with a mother to support, Hans Winkler was still determined to pursue a career as an equestrian.

The Road to Excellence

Although pursuing such a career seemed impossible in impoverished, bombed-out postwar

AP/Wide World Photos

Hans Winkler in 1964.

Germany, Hans Winkler was fortunate in meeting the stable master for the Landgrave of Hesse, who invited Winkler to work for him at Friedrichshof Castle near Frankfurt. There Hans stayed for two years, gaining valuable experience. He met a young woman from Frankfurt, the daughter of a successful textile merchant, who suggested to Hans that they set up a stable of horses for performing in competitions and horse shows.

Hans Winkler always felt his success was to a large extent the result of his ability to understand horses. Through kindness and patient training, he could coax a performance out of horses with severe nervous problems and other handicaps. Because of this ability, he felt he could buy with his limited funds three horses that were considered to be ruined because of misuse or nervous problems. He participated in a number of competitions and horse shows so successfully that he managed to pay off his debts.

More important, Hans and his horses attracted the attention of Dr. Gustav Rau, the director of DOKR, the German Olympic Committee for horsemanship. In 1951, Dr. Rau invited Hans to come to Warendorf in northwest Germany, near the Dutch border, where the committee had its stables. At first, the situation at Warendorf was difficult. Hans faced considerable competition and even jealousy. Yet that first year, he won twenty-four first prizes and twenty-three second and third prizes in local competitions and shows. In spite of these successes, Hans knew that without a first-rate horse, he would never achieve his goal of becoming a champion show jumper.

The Emerging Champion

In 1950, Hans had ridden a young mare named Halla. Because she was temperamental, nervous, and inclined to buck, her owner wanted to get rid of her. The year that Hans came to Warendorf, Halla's owner offered her to the German Olympic Committee, but after several performances, they declared the horse unfit to train for the Olympics. The owner again approached Hans, who, firmly believing she had championship qualities, decided to try to train her. The work was difficult, but gradually he developed an understanding with the nervous but intelligent animal. Halla, said Hans, was the greatest thing that ever happened to him. It was she who enabled him to become a champion.

The months of patient training paid off. Hans, riding Halla, became World Riding Champion in 1954 and 1955. The following year at the Olympics in Stockholm, Hans and Halla won the gold medal in the individual show jumping event and in the team event. Involving as it does enlarged obstacles and a close working relationship with two other team members, winning a team event is as difficult and as important as winning an individual event.

Winning both the individual and team event was a great psychological boost not only for Hans but also for the Germans. Because of the war, they had only recently been allowed to take part in the Olympics.

Continuing the Story

In 1957, Hans, riding Halla, became the European Riding Champion. Because of an injury, he could not defend his show jumping title at the 1960 Olympics, although he was a participant in the team event, again winning the gold medal. That same year, Halla made her last winning jump, having completed 125 show jumps, a record for a German horse. In gratitude, Winkler wrote a book, *Halla: Die Geschichte ihrer Laufbahn* (1960; Halla: the history of her career).

By 1964, Hans Winkler had been a winner in nearly one thousand events, including five hundred international events. He participated in the Olympic Games until 1976, when his team won a silver medal in the team event. Hans Winkler is considered the world's most successful Olympic show jumping rider and is the only rider in Olympic history to win five gold medals. Although he retired from competition jumping, he remained active in the equestrian area both through teaching and business activities. His leisure activities included skiing and hunting. Hans Winkler made his home in Warendorf and was married twice.

MAJOR CHAMPIONSHIPS

Year	Competition	Event	Place
1954-55	World Riding Championship	—	1st
1956	Olympic Games	Individual jumping Team event	Gold Gold
1957	European Riding Championship	—	1st
1960, 1964, 1976	Olympic Games	Team event	Gold
1965, 1968	King George V Cup	—	1st
1968	Olympic Games	Team event	Bronze
1976	Olympic Games	Team event	Silver

HONORS AND AWARDS

1954	Needle of Honor, Senate of West Berlin
1956	Gold Band, German Sports Press Association
1960	Named Best Sportsman of the Decade
1964	Needle of Honor, International Riding Association
1974	Grand Cross of Honor, Federal Republic of Germany
1976	German Riding Association Award

Summary

Hans Winkler's brilliant career as an equestrian and show jumper is proof not only that hard work and perseverance can achieve success despite great obstacles but also that kindness to and understanding of the horses can be a major factor in bringing about the success.

Nis Petersen

Additional Sources:

Brown, Gene, ed. *The New York Times Encyclopedia of Sports.* 15 vols. New York: Arno Press, 1979-1980.

Wathen, Guy. *Great Horsemen of the World.* North Pomfret, Vt.: Trafalgar Square, 1991.

Wise, Michael T., Christina Bankes, and Jane Laing, eds. *Chronicle of the Olympics, 1896-1996.* New York: DK Publishing, 1996.

KATARINA WITT

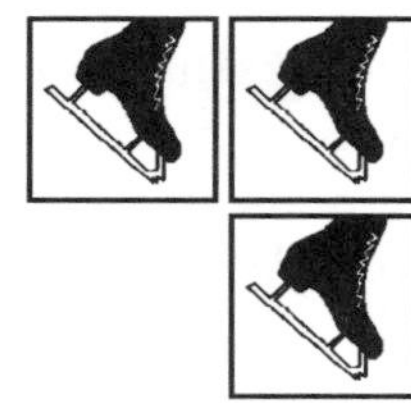

Sport: Figure skating

Born: December 3, 1965
Karl-Marx-Stadt, East Germany (now Chemnitz, Germany)

Early Life

Katarina Witt was born on December 3, 1965, in Karl-Marx-Stadt, now Chemnitz, in the German Federal Republic, which was then the German Democratic Republic, or East Germany. Katarina's father was the manager of an agriculture cooperative; her mother was a physical therapist. Her sister-in-law, Anett Pötzsch, was a figure skater who won the Olympic gold medal in 1980.

Katarina was fascinated by figure skating while still in kindergarten. At the age of five, she persuaded her parents to let her try the sport. In her own words, the first time on ice she said, "This is for me" and decided to make figure skating her life's work.

The Road to Excellence

Bernd Egert, the head coach of the Karl-Marx-Stadt Sports Club and School, one of the best in East Germany, by chance saw Katarina skating and was so impressed by her performance that he enrolled her in the school's intensive training program.

The training was strict and demanded the complete attention of the trainee, but Katarina was an excellent pupil. She trained every day from seven in the morning until eight in the evening and spent more time with her coaches then she did with her family. She had no time for anything other than her training and no friends outside of those with whom she worked.

The work paid off. By the age of nine, Katarina had become so skillful that her talents were recognized by Jutta Müller, East Germany's most fa-

AP/Wide World Photos

Two-time Olympic gold medalist Katarina Witt at the World Professional Championships in 1998.

mous skating coach, who now took over the young girl's training and made her into a world-famous sports figure. Many criticized East Germany's training system as too rigid and severe, but Katarina Witt maintains she could not have achieved her success in any other way.

The Emerging Champion

Under Jutta Müller's coaching, Katarina soon demonstrated her extraordinary skill, when, at the age of eleven, she made her first triple jump, a salchow, involving rotating the body in mid-air. At the age of fourteen, she finished tenth in the world championship competition, and two years later, at the age of sixteen, she captured the European championship and placed second in the World Championships.

In 1984, now nineteen, she achieved the world championship, defeating Rosalynn Sumners of the United States, a two-time national champion. Katarina's greatest triumph, however, which made her a world star, was her amazing performance that same year at the Winter Olympics held in Sarajevo, Yugoslavia, where she again defeated Rosalynn Sumners to capture the gold medal. What impressed the judges was not only Katarina's skating but also her artistic ability combined with a radiant personality and natural beauty. An observer commented that her performance was a perfect blend of athleticism and art. It so impressed the viewers that Katarina received more than thirty-five thousand love letters.

After Sarajevo, Katarina Witt's triumphs continued; she now was first in the field of women's figure skating. In the World Championships held in March, 1985, in Tokyo, she defeated Kira Ivanova of the Soviet Union, thereby preventing Soviet skaters from capturing all the top titles. Katarina skated to the music of George Gershwin, landing each of her triples smoothly in perfect time with the music.

In 1986, Katarina lost the world championship title to the American contender, Debi Thomas, the first African American woman to gain the title. The following year, Katarina regained her title after a fierce contest with Thomas, perfectly completing five triple jumps and two double axels and receiving top ratings from seven of the nine judges. To win that contest, Katarina claimed she had trained harder than she ever had before. Even Debi Thomas had to admit that her rival was amazing: "She's tough; she just goes out there and does what she has to."

MAJOR CHAMPIONSHIPS

Year	Competition	Place
1980	European Championships	13th
	World Championships	10th
1981	European Championships	5th
	World Championships	5th
1982	European Championships	2d
	World Championships	2d
1983	European Championships	1st
	World Championships	4th
1984	European Championships	1st
	Olympic Games	Gold
	World Championships	1st
1985	European Championships	1st
	World Championships	1st
1986	European Championships	1st
	World Championships	2d
1987	European Championships	1st
	World Championships	1st
1988	European Championships	1st
	Olympic Games	Gold
	World Championships	1st
1994	Olympic Games	7th

The two superstars competed again in February, 1988, at the Winter Olympics in Calgary, Canada, in what was known as "The Battle of the Carmens." Both skated to the music of *Carmen,* an opera by the French composer Georges Bizet. The contest was close, but what won the gold medal for Katarina was her artistic interpretation of the opera's heroine. For two years, Katarina had studied acting, and, as a critic noted, Thomas skated brilliantly to the music but Katarina became Carmen. Some skating fans were irritated because they thought Katarina relied too much on her radiant good looks, her acting ability, and her beautiful costumes, thereby unfairly influencing the judges. Katarina defended her performance, saying one should stress what one has and what is attractive.

Katarina Witt again won the world title at the competition held less than a month after Calgary in Budapest, Hungary. She retired from amateur competition after the World Championships and returned to Germany. She was very grateful for the excellent training she had received free of charge from the state.

Continuing the Story

After her 1988 triumphs in Calgary and Budapest, Katarina became a highly sought after and successful professional skater. Her grace, sensuality, theatricality, and poise were perfectly suited to the professional arena. She also became a savvy businesswoman in marketing and public relations, carefully selecting her engagements, endorsements, and exhibitions. In addition, she pursued television and film work. In 1990, she starred in the television special *Carmen on Ice.* She earned an Emmy Award for her performance—the first female figure skater to do so. In addition to television ice skating specials, she has had many guest appearances on television shows and in film. She has also done figure skating commentary and analysis for Germany's ZDF and CBS Sports.

On the ice, shortly after retirement, Katarina joined Brian Boitano, the men's gold medal winner in Calgary, for several years on a very successful and popular tour. A special rule made her eligible for the 1994 Olympics in Lillehammer, Norway. She knew that she would not be a medal contender and was very pleased with her seventh-place finish. She was, however, a crowd favorite, a spectacular performer, a poised, gracious, calming, and mature presence in the midst of the media frenzy surrounding America's top skaters, Tonya Harding and Nancy Kerrigan.

In 2001, Katarina was still a hard-working professional. She was still skating, still working in front of and behind the cameras, and still juggling appearances, exhibitions, and charity work.

Summary

In her brilliant career, Katarina Witt won the European Championships in figure skating six times, the World Championships four times, the Olympic gold medal twice, and professional titles numerous times. She is proof of what talent, inspiration, excellent training, and hard work can do. Possibly Katarina's greatest contribution to figure skating is that, through her acting ability, the use of music, and the careful selection of costumes, she helped raise an athletic event to an art form.

Nis Petersen

Additional Sources:

Brennan, Christine. *Inside Edge: A Revealing Journey into the Secret World of Figure Skating.* New York: Simon and Schuster, 1996.

Coffey, Wayne R. *Katarina Witt.* Woodbridge, Conn.: Blackbirch Press, 1992.

Heimo, Bernard. *Katarina Witt.* Altstätten, Germany: Panorama, 1988.

Kelly, Evelyn B. *Katarina Witt.* Philadelphia: Chelsea House, 1999.

Smith, Pohla, and Joel H. Cohen. *Superstars of Women's Figure Skating.* Philadelphia: Chelsea House, 1999.

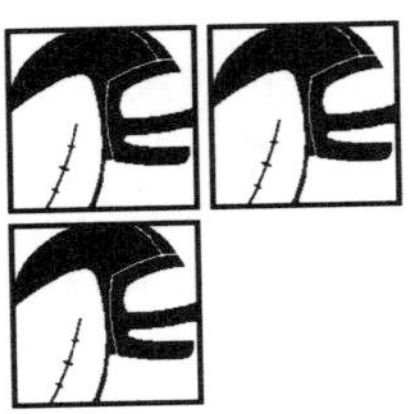

WILLIE WOOD

Sport: Football

Born: December 23, 1936
Washington, D.C.

Early Life

William Vernell Wood was born in Washington, D.C., on December 23, 1936. Both of his parents worked for the federal government. Willie was not interested in a career, in sports, or in school as a youngster. Instead, he joined a gang and spent most of his time hanging around on street corners in Washington. His gang sometimes got into fights with groups of boys from other neighborhoods.

Willie's amazing story does not end here. Fortunately, his situation began to improve. A boy's club opened up just a block from his house, and one of the counselors there took a special liking to him. Suddenly, sports became a new way of life for Willie.

Courtesy of Amateur Athletic Foundation of Los Angeles

The Road to Excellence

Willie became a good athlete at Armstrong High School in Washington, but his grades were not good enough for him to attend college, and he was forced to turn down scholarships. He attended Coalinga Junior College in Southern California, and moved on to the University of Southern California (USC). He played both quarterback and defensive back for the USC Trojans, although he sat out part of his junior and senior seasons because of a shoulder separation. He was used primarily on defense in his last year and drew little attention from professional football teams.

Willie was not offered a job by any National Football League (NFL) team. Yet he knew he wanted to try to play professionally, and he did not give up on his dream. He sat down and wrote letters to all the teams in the league. Only the Green Bay Packers wrote back, offering him the chance to try out.

The Emerging Champion

Willie was only 5 feet 10 inches and about 170 pounds, so when he came in for his physical he hid weights in his socks so that no one would find out how light he really was.

Despite the odds against him, Willie

HONORS AND AWARDS	
1962, 1965, 1967-69	*Sporting News* Western Conference All-Star Team
1963, 1965-71	NFL Pro Bowl Team
1963-68	NFL All-Pro Team
1970-71	*Sporting News* NFC All-Star Team
1970	NFL All-Pro Team of the 1960's
1989	Inducted into Pro Football Hall of Fame

made the team. Just making the team, however, was not enough for him. He wanted to be a starter. The only way an unknown rookie could prove himself to the coaches was by making the most of whatever opportunities arose. Wood became a standout player on the special teams. He became known as a fierce tackler, and his speed helped him to become an excellent punt returner. By the time he began his second season with the team, the coaches were convinced, and Willie had become a starter in the defensive backfield.

In his second season, he led the league in punt returns. A year later, he led the league in interceptions, with 9, and was on his way to stardom. In each of his first three seasons, he helped the Packers reach the NFL championship game. Because he was small and had no special college reputation to speak of, Willie had to use every means at his disposal to succeed. His devotion was such that he did anything necessary to help the team.

Continuing the Story

Willie was a gifted athlete, with great speed and jumping ability. He was also a smart player. Because he had played quarterback in high school and in college, on defense he tried to outthink the other team's quarterback, anticipating the next play. His ability to guess what might happen next helped him get many of his 48 career interceptions.

One of Willie's most important interceptions helped the Packers win the first Super Bowl. Green Bay was the champion of the more established NFL, while their opponents, the Kansas City Chiefs, were from the newer American Football League (AFL). Many fans felt that it would be embarrassing for the Packers if they lost, or even if the game was close. Early in the second half, with his team ahead only 14-10, Willie intercepted a pass. He scooted down the sidelines and set up a touchdown that gave the Packers a 21-10 lead. Green Bay won the game, 35-10.

He was not famous only for his speed on interceptions and punt returns. He worked out with weights to build himself up, eventually getting his playing weight up to 190 pounds. In time, he became a punishing tackler.

Willie had a very successful career, helping the Packers win the first two Super Bowls. After his playing days were over, he remained in demand as a coach. He joined the San Diego Chargers as an assistant coach the year after he retired as a player. Eventually, he became a head coach with a team in the World Football League, a rival organization. After that league folded, Wood worked his way up through the ranks of assistant coaches to become the first African American head coach in the history of the Canadian Football League.

Willie eventually retired from coaching. He continued to visit Green Bay during the football season and even bought a business there. Willie settled in his hometown, Washington, D.C., and became involved in social issues there, such as voting rights.

Summary

Few observers gave Willie Wood any chance of making it in professional football. Once he did, they said he had no chance to become a star. Willie fooled them all. He had to overcome many obstacles: a bad start as a youth, an injury that hurt his professional chances, and a lack of great size. Yet he never gave up, and he kept working hard even after he had become a star in the NFL.

John McNamara

Additional Sources:

Pro Football Hall of Fame. http://www.profootballhof.com.

Staff. http://cbs.sportsline.com/u/football/nfl/legends/hof/wood.htm. (NFL Legends and Lore, Hall of Fame—CBS Sportsline).

"WCL Professor Makes Case for DC Voting Rights." *WCL* Online. http://www.wcl.american.edu/pub/journals/jurist/9.98/voting.html.

LYNETTE WOODARD

Sport: Basketball

Born: August 12, 1959
Wichita, Kansas

Early Life

Lynette Woodard was born on August 12, 1959, in Wichita, Kansas, the youngest in a family that included three sisters and one brother.

Lynette became excited about basketball at an early age as she watched her cousin, Geese Ausbie, perform his Harlem Globetrotter ballhandling tricks. At age five she began to practice what she saw him do and spent a lot of time playing basketball.

The Road to Excellence

While in high school, Lynette led her Wichita North High basketball team to two state championships. Having grown to a height of 6 feet by the end of her high school career, she was highly recruited by college coaches. Coach Marian Washington convinced her to attend the University of Kansas in 1977.

Though only a freshman, Lynette quickly established herself as one of the country's top players. She led the nation in rebounding her first year and was named Freshman of the Year by two nationwide publications. In 1979, she followed her nation-leading rebound feat by leading the nation in scoring with a 31.7-points-per-game average. On January 6, 1981, Lynette Woodard broke the women's career scoring record of 3,199 points when she scored the first basket in a home contest against Stephen F. Austin College. Lynette also led the nation in steals for three years.

The Emerging Champion

Her Kansas career was filled with accomplishment after accomplishment. By the time she graduated with a speech communications degree in 1981, Lynette held eight University of Kansas career records, seven single-season records, and five single-game records. Four times she was named a Kodak All-American and twice an Academic All-American, matching her hardwood performances with dedication in the classroom. Lynette was recognized as the nation's best collegiate female basketball player when she won the Wade Trophy in 1981. During her career, the Kansas Jayhawks compiled a 108-32 record. Her accomplishments were recognized by her alma mater when she became the first woman to be inducted into the university's Athletic Hall of Fame. She also received the National Collegiate

Tony Duffy/Allsport

Athletic Association (NCAA) Today's Top Five Award in 1982.

Before her collegiate career ended, Lynette was also becoming an international basketball sensation. Her scoring and rebounding abilities made her an asset for the United States teams. She played on three United States teams in 1978 and 1979, including the gold-medal-winning 1979 World University Games team. She was also selected for the 1980 Olympic team that did not play when the United States chose to boycott the Moscow Olympics. The boycott was a disappointment for Lynette and for all the players who had trained so hard for the Games.

Following graduation, Lynette continued her career in a women's professional basketball league in Skio, Italy. After a year overseas, she returned to the United States and played on the 1983 Pan-American gold-medal-winning U.S. team and World University Games silver-medal-winning team. Lynette again became an Olympian in 1984, and this time she captained the U.S. squad that won the gold medal at the Olympics in Los Angeles.

Continuing the Story

Where to play after the Olympics was the question facing Lynette. She became an assistant coach at the University of Kansas. But in 1983, Lynette saw a newspaper ad saying the Harlem Globetrotters would be holding tryouts to select one woman to sign as a Globetrotter. Two tryout camps were held in late summer and early fall of 1985. Eighteen women, the nation's best, were selected for the tryouts. When the tryouts were finished and the player was chosen, Lynette's lifelong dream had come true: She would become a Globetrotter.

Lynette's cousin Geese Ausbie was no longer a member of the team, and the other members were a bit unsure of Lynette at first. They figured her selection might be just a publicity stunt. Geese encouraged her from afar, though, and Lynette's talent and outgoing personality helped to win the quick approval of her male teammates. Lynette had little time to adjust herself, as she played her first game with the Globetrotters in Brisbane, Australia, just ten days after joining the team. Thus began a schedule that would include almost two hundred games a year and a series of "firsts" for her and for the Globetrotters: her first game as a Globetrotter in the United States; her first live television appearance with the team; her first game in her hometown of Wichita as a Globetrotter. Lynette enjoyed playing for fun and making people laugh. The fans also seemed to enjoy seeing her perform with the team.

In October, 1987, Lynette announced that her lifelong dream of being a Globetrotter had been fulfilled and, after two years, it was time to move on. Lynette's two-year contract expired before the season, and terms of a new contract could not be worked out to her satisfaction. The major road-block in the contract negotiations was the

COLLEGE STATISTICS

Season	*GP*	*FGM*	*FG%*	*FTM*	*FT%*	*Reb.*	*Ast.*	*TP*	*PPG*
1977-78	33	366	.497	101	.664	490	47	833	25.2
1978-79	38	519	.562	139	.656	545	97	1,177	31.7
1979-80	37	372	.504	137	.714	389	165	881	23.8
1980-81	30	305	.533	122	.693	281	196	732	24.5
Totals	138	1,562	.526	499	.682	1,705	505	3,623	26.3

WNBA STATISTICS

Season	*GP*	*FGM*	*FG%*	*FTM*	*FT%*	*Reb.*	*Ast.*	*TP*	*PPG*
1997	28	87	.399	43	.672	116	67	217	7.8
1998	27	36	.387	23	.575	66	22	95	3.5
Totals	55	123	.395	66	.635	182	89	312	5.7

Notes: GP = games played; FGM = field goals made; FG% = field goal percentage; FTM = free throws made; FT% = free throw percentage; Reb. = rebounds; Ast. = assists; TP = total points; PPG = points per game

Globetrotters policy limiting the players' outside projects, particularly promotions. Lynette felt her contract was too binding and that it was in her best interest to leave the Globetrotter organization. Lynette's upcoming projects would include an instructional basketball video, speaking engagements, camps, and clinics. She would again serve as a Kansas assistant coach in the 1989-1990 season.

Lynette played professional basketball for four seasons in Italy (1980-1981, 1987-1990) and led the Priolo team to the 1989 Italian National Championship. From 1990 to 1993, she played in Japan for Daiwa Securities, guiding the 1992 team to the divisional championship. She won a bronze medal with the United States team in the 1991 Pan-American Games. From 1993 to 1995, Lynette served as the athletic director for the Kansas City school district.

While playing in Japan, Lynette became interested in the stock market. She joined the Magna Securities Corporation in New York in 1995, serving as vice president of the first brokerage firm to be owned by African American women. In her spare time, Lynette continued to organize basketball training clinics for aspiring young athletes and also served on the 1996 Olympic Committee Board of Directors.

At the age of thirty-seven, Lynette took the opportunity to play for the Phoenix Mercury in 1997 in the Women's National Basketball Association (WNBA). She averaged 7.8 points and 2.4 assists per game. Lynette spent the 1998 season with the Detroit Shock, averaging 3.5 points per game. Retiring from the WNBA at the age of thirty-nine, she again joined the coaching staff at Kansas University in 1999.

Summary

Lynette Woodard's career has demonstrated that dreams can come true. From the age of five, she dreamed of becoming a Harlem Globetrotter. As a collegian, she became one of the all-time greats in the women's game, propelling herself into a tryout and eventual selection as the first female player for the Globetrotters. Lynette was the most prolific scorer in the history of women's college basketball, having scored a career total of 3,649 points.

Rita S. Wiggs

Additional Sources:

Brill, Marlene Targ. *Winning Women in Basketball.* Haupauge, New York: Barrons Educational Series, 2000.

Frisch, Aaron. *The History of the Detroit Shock.* New York: Creative Education, 1999.

Layden, Joseph, and James Preller. *Inside the WNBA.* New York: Scholastic Trade, 1999.

Nichols, John. *The History of the Cleveland Rockers.* New York: Creative Education, 1999.

Smith, Michelle. *She's Got Game.* New York: Scholastic Trade, 1999.

MILESTONES

First female athlete to win the NCAA Today's Top Five Award

HONORS AND AWARDS

1978	*Street and Smith's* College Freshman of the Year Inducted into University of Kansas Athletic Hall of Fame
1978-81	All-Big Eight Conference Team Kodak All-American
1979	U.S. World University Games Gold Medalist
1979-81	Big Eight Conference Tournament most valuable player
1980	Women's U.S. Olympic basketball team
1980-81	Academic All-American
1981	*Street and Smith's* College Basketball Co-Player of the Year Broderick Award Wade Trophy
1982	NCAA Today's Top Five Award National Association for the Advancement of Colored People Woman of the Year
1983	U.S. World University Games Silver Medalist U.S. Pan-American Games Gold Medalist
1984	U.S. Olympic Gold Medalist
1985	NCAA Salute to the 1984 U.S. Olympians
1986	Women's Sports Foundation Professional Sportswoman of the Year
1989	Big Eight Conference Player of the Decade Inducted into National High School Sports Hall of Fame
1991	Bronze Medal, Pan-American Games

JOHN WOODEN

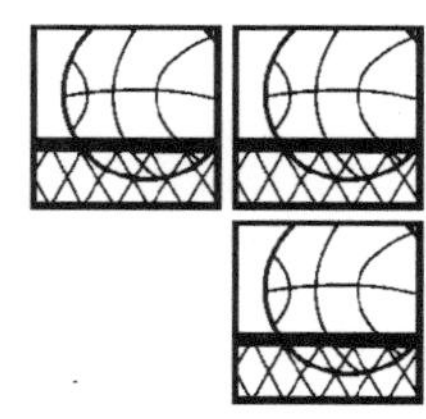

Sport: Basketball

Born: October 14, 1910
Hall, Indiana

Early Life

John Robert Wooden was born on October 14, 1910, in Hall, Indiana. He lived his early days on farms in the local rural area. There was no running water or electricity in the Wooden home. John was the third of six children in a close, hardworking family. John's father was a strong and steady influence in his life. He was a stern but caring man who instilled discipline and honesty in John. John and his brothers were fond of playing a form of basketball with a rag ball and a tomato basket nailed to the hay loft in the barn.

AP/Wide World Photos

Basketball legend John Wooden during his playing days at Purdue.

The Road to Excellence

During the depression of the 1930's, John's father lost the family farm, and the family moved to Martinsville, Indiana, where John attended high school. At Martinsville he met Nellie, his wife to be. His high school basketball coach was Glenn Curtis (a man he would later succeed as Indiana State University's basketball coach). As a sophomore, John once quit the team over Curtis's treatment of certain favorite players. John later said that incident taught him to listen to players who disagreed with him as a coach. John went on to win All-State honors in basketball three straight years while excelling in baseball as well. He led the basketball team to a state championship in 1927.

After high school, John enrolled at Purdue University in West Lafayette, Indiana. There, he captained the 1932 National Collegiate Athletic Association (NCAA) championship team. John, a scrappy 5-foot 10-inch guard, was named All-American three times; he is one of the few people named to the Naismith Memorial Basketball Hall of Fame as both a player and a coach.

After graduating from Purdue in 1932, John

began teaching at Dayton High School in Kentucky, where he was the coach for all sports. At Dayton, he experienced his only losing season as a coach, an experience from which he later said he learned much. From Dayton, John returned to his native Indiana to coach at Central High School in South Bend. In eleven years of high school basketball coaching, he compiled an overall won-lost record of 218-42.

During that time his coaching career was interrupted by three years with the Navy in World War II. Wooden went on to serve as athletic director at Indiana State University in Terre Haute. For two years, John coached basketball and baseball. Then he headed west for the University of California at Los Angeles (UCLA) in 1948.

The Emerging Champion

In his first two years at UCLA, John built and trained a fine team. That group of basketball players won the Pacific Coast Conference (PCC) championship in 1950 for Wooden. The UCLA Bruins marched to the PCC title again in 1952 and 1956, but Wooden's success within his own conference was only part of the story.

John's first really great team emerged in 1963-1964. The heart of the team was a pair of scrappy, sharpshooting guards named Walt Hazzard and Gail Goodrich. The team was unranked in the pre-season polls, but the Bruins swept to a 30-0 season and the National Collegiate Athletic Association (NCAA) championship.

Goodrich was back the following season, but the Bruins lost their first game. The team then rallied to sweep its second national crown in a row. In the NCAA final, Goodrich scored 42 of the Bruins' 91 points, and UCLA knocked out the University of Michigan 91-80.

The UCLA team had an off-year in 1965-1966, but as coach, John had a banner season in recruiting. He landed the greatest collection of new basketball talent ever assembled at one school. His prize player was 7-foot 2-inch Lew Alcindor (who later became Kareem Abdul-Jabbar) of New York, the most sought-after high school player in the nation. John also landed a sharpshooting guard named Lucius Allen. For forwards, he recruited a pair of 6-foot 8-inch players, Lynn Shackleford and Mike Lynn.

From 1966 to 1968, Wooden's Bruins had a

STATISTICS

Season	GP	FGM	FTM	FT%	TP	PPG
1929-30	13	45	26	—	116	8.9
1930-31	17	53	54	.693	140	8.2
1931-32	18	79	61	.709	219	12.2
Totals	48	177	141	—	475	9.9

Notes: GP = games played; FGM = field goals made; FTM = free throws made; FT% = free throw percentage; TP = total points; PPG = points per game

forty-seven-game winning streak. The streak was finally snapped by the University of Houston, sparked by Elvin Hayes, in a game at Houston's Astrodome. Alcindor was injured and did not play well in the game, which was the team's only loss; the Bruins finished the season with a 29-1 record. UCLA enjoyed revenge against Houston in the NCAA Tournament, defeating the Cougars 101-69. The Bruins' victory over the University of North Carolina gave them another NCAA championship.

In 1969, the Alcindor-led Bruins became the first team to win three straight NCAA titles. They beat John's alma mater, Purdue, in the championship game.

Continuing the Story

John seemed long overdue to come off his winning streak. With the graduation of the awesome Alcindor, many thought UCLA's reign was finished, yet the coach had a few more tricks for his rivals. The next season, Alcindor's understudy, Steve Patterson, had the help of sophomore forwards Sidney Wicks and Curtis Rowe, and the Bruins captured their fourth straight NCAA crown in 1970. The trio of Patterson, Rowe, and Wicks came back in 1971 to win a fifth straight title.

The next year, Wooden built his team around another outstanding center, Bill Walton. UCLA went undefeated in 1971-1972 and 1972-1973, and captured two more NCAA championships. UCLA's win streak was finally stopped by Notre Dame in January, 1974, at a record 88. That year, the Bruins were at last defeated in NCAA Tournament play. They dropped a double-overtime thriller to North Carolina State in the national semifinals.

In 1975, UCLA captured its tenth national crown under John. He announced his retirement to the team before the final game against Kentucky, and the Bruins gave their coach a going-away present. They defeated the Wildcats 92-85.

There is little doubt about Wooden's coaching genius. Whatever kind of team he had, he managed to produce a winner.

In his career at UCLA, Wooden won 80 percent of his games. He coached more than a dozen players who went on to play professional basketball.

Summary

John Wooden has spoken to many people since he retired about how he achieved so much success. He states that "Success is peace of mind, which is a direct result of self-satisfaction in knowing you did your best to become the best that you are capable of becoming." John believes that attaining success is like the process of building a pyramid, only each block is a character trait such as discipline, faith, or patience. John continues to be an inspiration to his former athletes and to those who admire him as a successful leader.

Kevin R. Lasley

Additional Sources:

Chapin, Dwight, and Jeff Prugh. *The Wizard of Westwood: Coach John Wooden and His UCLA Bruins.* Boston: Houghton Mifflin, 1973.

Heisler, Mark. *They Shoot Coaches, Don't They?: UCLA and the NCAA Since John Wooden.* New York: Macmillan, 1996.

Kirkpatrick, Curry. "Same as He Ever Was." *Sport* 89, no. 1 (January, 1998): 70-75.

Wooden, John R., and Steve Jamison. *Wooden: A Lifetime of Observations and Reflections on and off the Court.* Chicago: Contemporary Books, 1997.

Wooden, John R., and Jack Tobin. *They Call Me Coach: The Fascinating First-Person Story of a Legendary Basketball Coach.* Rev. ed. Waco, Tex.: Word Books, 1985.

MILESTONES

Coaching record in NCAA Tournament play includes sixteen appearances, twelve Final Four appearances, and ten championship titles, for an overall won-lost record of 47-10

Overall NCAA coaching record (including tournament games) is 664-162, for an .804 winning percentage

Only member of the Naismith Memorial Basketball Hall of Fame inducted both as a player and as a coach

HONORS AND AWARDS

1930-32	Helms Athletic Foundation All-American
1932	Citizens Savings College Basketball Player of the Year Big Ten Conference medal for outstanding achievement in scholarship and athletics
1960	Inducted into Naismith Memorial Basketball Hall of Fame (as a player)
1964, 1967, 1969-70, 1972-73	United Press International Division I Coach of the Year
1964, 1967, 1970, 1972-73	U.S. Basketball Writers Association Division I Coach of the Year
1967, 1969-70, 1972-73	Associated Press Division I Coach of the Year
1969-70, 1972	National Association of Basketball Coaches Division I Coach of the Year
1970	*Sporting News* Sportsman of the Year
1972	*Sports Illustrated* Co-Sportsman of the Year Inducted into Naismith Memorial Basketball Hall of Fame (as a coach)
1974	John W. Bunn Award Awarded honorary doctorate in physical education by the Purdue University Board of Trustees for his outstanding contribution to coaching

CYNTHIA WOODHEAD

Sport: Swimming

Born: February 7, 1964
Riverside, California

Early Life

Cynthia Woodhead was born on February 7, 1964, in Riverside, California. Life in Riverside was happy for Cynthia as she grew up. She went to school with the other children her age, but, from an early age, a difference could be seen when she began to swim. Coaches noticed her special talent, and she got better and better. Her family and friends were supportive of her swimming. As Cynthia got older, she would have to go to practice before and after school in order to get in enough training for her grueling sport. She did not mind; she loved giving one hundred percent, as she had learned from her family from an early age. She believed that, in order to give anything an honest try, one must always try one's best.

U.S. Swimming

The Road to Excellence

Cynthia emerged as a star swimmer in 1977, when she was thirteen. At the Amateur Athletic Union (AAU) short-course nationals, Cynthia finished third in both the 200- and 500-meter freestyle. Then, only three months later at the AAU long-course championships, she tied for second in the 200-meter freestyle and finished eighth in the 400 meters. She made the United States national team and placed fourth in the 200-meter freestyle at a meet with the German Democratic Republic team.

Almost overnight, Cynthia became a champion. When the United States swam against the Soviet Union, she placed first in the 200-meter freestyle. Although she was swimming against girls who were older and more experienced than she was, her natural talent and determination carried her through. She had always felt that she was this good, and now she was getting a chance to prove it.

Cynthia did very well in her thirteenth year in 1978, winning races from as short as 100 yards to as long as 1,650 yards at many world-caliber meets. She swam at many international meets, including the AAU Championships and the World Championships.

The Emerging Champion

In 1978, Cynthia set her first world record in the 200-meter freestyle at the

STATISTICS

Year	Competition	Event	Place	Time
1977	AAU Long Course	200-meter freestyle	2d	—
	AAU Short Course	200-meter freestyle	3d	—
		500-meter freestyle	3d	—
1978	World Championships	200-meter freestyle	1st	1:58.53 WR
		400-meter freestyle	2d	4:07.15
		800-meter freestyle	2d	8:29.35
		4×100-meter freestyle relay	1st	3:43.43
		4×100-meter medley relay	1st	4:08.21
1979	Pan-American Games	100-meter freestyle	1st	52.22 PAR
		200-meter freestyle	1st	1:58.43 WR, PAR
		400-meter freestyle	1st	4:10.56 PAR
		4×100-meter freestyle relay	—	3:45.82
		4×100-meter medley relay	—	4:13.24
1983	Pan-American Games	200-meter freestyle	1st	2:01.33
		400-meter freestyle	1st	4:14.07
1984	Olympic Games	200-meter freestyle	Silver	—

Notes: WR = World Record; PAR = Pan-American Record

World Championships at the age of fourteen. When the swimming world began the 1979 season, no one had any idea that Cynthia was going to take the world by storm. Her first major meet was the Women's International, where she earned a first in the 500-yard freestyle, a second in the 200-yard freestyle, third in the 1,650 yards, and fourth in the 100-meter freestyle. During this year, she set the world and American records in the 200-meter freestyle and the American record in the 200-yard freestyle, and dominated the middle-distance events. For the next two years, Cynthia seemed almost unstoppable in the middle-distance events. Watching her swim in races was an incredible sight; she was always at least a second or two ahead of the field.

In 1979, she won five national titles and took three gold medals in the Pan-American Games. During those games, she was also named most valuable player. She broke her existing world record in the 200-meter freestyle with a time of 1 minute 58.43 seconds. She then went on to win three more gold medals in middle-distance events in the FINA Cup International Swim Meet. Only a few weeks later, the young swimmer picked up five more gold medals at the World Cup in Tokyo, once again lowering her mark in the 200-meter freestyle, to 1 minute 58.23 seconds. Coach Riggs, her coach at the time, could not believe how hard she worked, but the hard work paid off.

In January, 1980, Cynthia helped the United States team to victory at the United States Women's National Meet with a first, second, and fourth place. In June of 1980 at Mission Viejo, California, she again won the 200-meter freestyle. The next month she won the 400-meter freestyle at the Santa Clara International Invitational Swimming Meet.

Continuing the Story

Just as it seemed that Cynthia could only win races, she began to lose, and the more she lost, the harder she trained; as she trained harder, she swam even worse.

It is difficult for an athlete to lose and not know why. Cynthia spent much time switching coaches and finally settled down with coach Mark Schubert.

She was known as a hard worker and worked harder than most male swimmers who had trained with Coach Schubert. She lowered her body fat percentage to a dangerously low 8 percent, believing that the more fit she was, the faster she would go. Only after she and Schubert figured out that Cynthia was training too hard did they ease off training. Once they eased off, her times began to come down and she began to win again. This development culminated with her win at the 1983 Pan-American Games and a silver medal at the Olympic Games in 1984. Even though she was viewed as over the hill by the public, she came back and showed them she could still swim as fast as she did before.

Cynthia had a difficult time believing that she was training too hard because she was brought up with a strong work ethic. If she had not had success herself with a lighter training load, she probably never would have believed it. There is a fine line in athletics between giving too little and giving too much, and champions seem to always discover it sooner or later.

Summary

Retirement seems to be inevitable when a swimmer goes into a slump for as long as Cynthia

Woodhead did in 1980. Yet, Cynthia proved that, with the proper training and determination, it is possible to come back better than before.

In 1994 Cynthia was inducted into the International Swimming Hall of Fame.

Brooke K. Zibel

Additional Sources:

Levinson, David, and Karen Christenson, eds. *Encyclopedia of World Sport: From Ancient Times to Present.* Santa Barbara, Calif.: ABC-CLIO, 1996.

Mallon, Bill, and Ian Buchanan. *Quest for Gold: The Encyclopedia of American Olympians.* New York: Leisure Press, 1984.

Wallechinsky, David. *The Complete Book of the Olympics.* Boston: Little, Brown and Company, 1991.

TIGER WOODS

Sport: Golf

Born: December 30, 1975
Cypress, California

Early Life

Eldrick "Tiger" Woods grew up in Cypress, California, thirty-five miles southeast of Los Angeles. His mother, Kultida, came from Thailand; his father, Earl, was a retired lieutenant colonel in the U.S. Army. Earl called his son "Tiger" after the nickname he had given to Vuong Dang Phong, a friend who had saved him from sniper fire during the Vietnam War.

AP/Wide World Photos

Tiger Woods celebrates his birdie putt on the 18th hole at Augusta National on April 8, 2001, where he won his second Masters title and became the only player in golf history to hold all four major titles concurrently.

At the age of six months, Tiger watched from his highchair as his father practiced hitting golf balls. Earl gave ten-month-old Tiger a sawed-off putter, which the boy took everywhere with him. When Tiger swung that club, it was a perfect imitation of his father's swing. It was apparent that he was in love with the game of golf, and his parents did everything they could to encourage him. At age two, Tiger played on a real course for the first time. A few months later he appeared on the *Mike Douglas Show*, putting with Bob Hope. At age three Tiger shot a 48 for nine holes; at age five he was featured in *Golf Digest*. At the age of six he sank his first hole in one.

With Earl's urging, Tiger signed up for, then quit, other sports, including baseball and cross-country. Games and practice interfered with his golf tournaments. By the age of eleven, Tiger had entered more than thirty junior golf tournaments and won them all.

The Road to Excellence

When he was twelve, he won his third Junior World Tournament. Wally Goodwin, golf coach at Stanford University, heard of

Tiger's accomplishment and wrote him a letter. Though he was not yet in high school, Tiger had decided he would one day attend Stanford. Meanwhile, he worked toward his goal of beating Jack Nicklaus's accomplishments—Tiger had a list of them tacked on his bedroom wall. Another goal was to be the youngest player ever to enter a Professional Golf Association (PGA) tournament.

With junior tournament titles under his belt, Tiger was ready—and old enough—to play at national tournaments. Earl retired in order to travel to these events with his son. By age fourteen, Tiger had three coaches. Though he had been working on the physical and mental aspects of golf for more than half his life, he struggled in dealing with the racism he encountered in the sport. Tiger considers himself "just American" and counts Thai, Chinese, American Indian, white, and black ancestry among his heritage.

At the age of fifteen, while holding the number one spot on his high school golf team, Tiger tried to qualify for the 1991 Nissan Los Angeles Open, a PGA tournament. He started out badly—hitting golf paths, slicing through trees—but managed to par on each hole. In what would become typical for Tiger, as his nerves calmed and he got a feel for the course, he would "burn up" remaining holes for a comeback. On the eighteenth hole, Tiger needed a birdie (1 under par) to finish the event 7 under par. He ended with a bogey (1 over par) and did not qualify.

The following year, when Tiger was sixteen, the Los Angeles Open was held at the Riviera Country Club. The Riviera committee invited him to play—he did not have to qualify, though he was still an amateur. Tiger had realized his goal of being the youngest player ever to compete in a PGA tournament, where he would be playing against the pros.

On day 1 of the Open, he shot a 72. On the second day he shot 75. This score did not allow him to qualify for the weekend tournament, but he learned a lot to help him on the road to championship.

The Emerging Champion

By the middle of Tiger's freshman year at Stanford University, he had already won his first college event and was ranked the number one collegiate player in the country. He competed in the 1995 Masters Tournament in Augusta, Georgia, shooting a 72 the first two days and making the cut to continue competing in the tournament. The third day his score sagged to 77, but he rallied for a 72 the final day. He finished his first Masters tournament only 5 over par. More important than his score was that the pros had noted his cool temperament.

During his second and final year at Stanford, he worked at putting on weight and muscle. As he added bulk, he shattered course records and won nearly every collegiate tournament he entered. More important, he continued to play against the pros, managing to keep up with them. At the U.S. Open in June, 1996, he was leader until the sixteenth hole—he nearly won the event as an amateur. In July, 1996, at the British Open, he finished in the middle of the pack, an amateur

PGA TOUR VICTORIES

1996	Las Vegas Invitational
	Walt Disney World/Oldsmobile Classic
1997	Mercedes Championships
	Masters Tournament
	GTE Byron Nelson Golf Classic
	Motorola Western Open
1998	BellSouth Classic
1999	Buick Invitational
	Memorial Tournament
	Motorola Western Open
	PGA Championship
	WGC NEC Invitational
	National Car Rental Golf Classic/Disney
	THE TOUR Championship
	WGC American Express Championship
2000	Mercedes Championships
	AT&T Pebble Beach National Pro-Am
	Bay Hill Invitational Memorial Tournament
	U.S. Open Championship
	British Open Championship
	PGA Championship
	WGC NEC Invitational
	Bell Canadian Open
2001	Masters Tournament

INTERNATIONAL VICTORIES

1997	Asian Honda Classic (Asia)
1998	Johnnie Walker Classic (Asia)
1999	Deutsche Bank Open - TPC of Europe (Europe)
2000	Johnnie Walker Classic (Asia)

ranked second in the tournament. However, he made history at the U.S. Amateur tournament in August: He won, a record-breaking third time in a row. Tiger knew it was time to turn pro.

Continuing the Story

At a press conference on Wednesday, August 28, 1996, he made the announcement that he was turning professional. He had signed $60 million in deals to endorse Nike and Titleist products. The next day, at the Greater Milwaukee Open in Wisconsin, he teed up his first professional shot. As a slew of teenage fans followed a new role model across the country, Tiger improved his game with each week he played as a pro. At his second PGA tournament he placed eleventh. At the Canadian Open, in Ontario, he placed sixth. At the Quad City Classic in Coal Valley, Illinois, he placed third. His first professional win was the Las Vegas Invitational in 1996. In 1997 he won the Masters Tournament in Augusta, Georgia—the first nonwhite golfer to do so. He was twenty-one years old.

At the age of twenty-three he claimed twenty-one professional victories, surpassing the record of Horton Smith, who, in 1931, had fifteen career victories by that age. Tiger, at twenty-three, had five major championship victories: two professional and three U.S. amateur titles. He tied Jack Nicklaus, who had three professional and two amateur titles at that age.

In January, 2000, Tiger won his fifth consecutive PGA victory. He continued on to win the U.S. Open by a record margin, the British Open, and the PGA Championship. In 2000 he also won his second straight Vardon Trophy and was named the Associated Press Male Athlete of the Year.

In 2001, Tiger won four of the first ten tourna-

AWARDS AND HONORS

1992	*Golf Digest, Golfweek,* and *Golf World* Top Amateur Player
1993	*Golf World* Top Amateur Player
1994	*Golf World* Man of the Year U.S. World Amateur team
1995	Walker Cup team
1996	Collegiate Player of the Year PGA Rookie of the Year *Sports Illustrated* Sportsman of the Year
1997	PGA of America and Golf Writers Association of America Player of the Year First golfer selected Associated Press Male Athlete of the Year in 26 years Sports Star of the Year Award, given to athletes who combine excellence in their sport with significant charitable endeavors
1997, 1999, 2000	PGA Player of the Year
1997, 1999	Ryder Cup team
1998	Dunhill Cup team The Presidents Cup team PGA Grand Slam of Golf winner
1999	World Cup team
1999, 2000	Vardon Trophy AP Athlete of the Year
2000	CNN-*Sports Illustrated* Sportsman of the Year

RECORDS AND MILESTONES

1993	First golfer to have won three U.S. Junior Amateur Championships
1994	Became youngest winner of U.S. Amateur
1996	Became first player to win three consecutive U.S. Amateur titles (1994, 1995, 1996) Joined Jack Nicklaus and Phil Mickelson as the only players to win NCAA and U.S. Amateur in same year Set U.S. Amateur records for consecutive match-play victories (18) and winning percentage (.909)
1997	Associated Press named Tiger's Masters win the top sports story of 1997 Masters Tournament rounds of 70-66-65-69-270 set 72-hole record Masters Tournament 12-stroke margin of victory set a Masters record
1998	Eighth athlete to be named a permanent Wheaties representative, after Bob Richards (1958), Bruce Jenner (1977), Mary Lou Retton (1984), Pete Rose (1985), Walter Payton (1986), Chris Evert (1987), and Michael Jordan (1988)
2000	Becomes the first player at the U.S. Open to finish 72 holes at double digits, under par

ments in which he played and finished in the top ten in eight of them. His second Masters Victory gave him his fourth consecutive major title. Once again, he appeared headed for a record-breaking year.

Summary

Tiger Woods racked up one of the most impressive amateur records in golf history before turning pro. He was the youngest person to win the Masters Tournament, at the age of twenty-one. He then became the youngest person to win all the Grand Slam events. Tiger's victories along the way set numerous records as well, as he mastered a sport previously dominated by whites.

Lisa A. Wroble

Additional Sources:

Boyd, Aaron. *Great Athletes: Tiger Woods.* Greensboro, N.C.: Morgan Reynolds, 1997.

Durbin, William C. *Black Americans of Achievement: Tiger Woods.* Philadelphia, Pa.: Chelsea House, 1998.

Rosaforte, Tim. *Tiger Woods: The Making of a Champion.* New York: Fireside, 1997.

Savage, Jeff. *Tiger Woods: King of the Course.* Minneapolis, Minn.: Lerner Publishing, 1998.

Woods, Earl, and Pete McDaniel. *Training a Tiger.* New York: HarperCollins, 1997.

CHARLES WOODSON

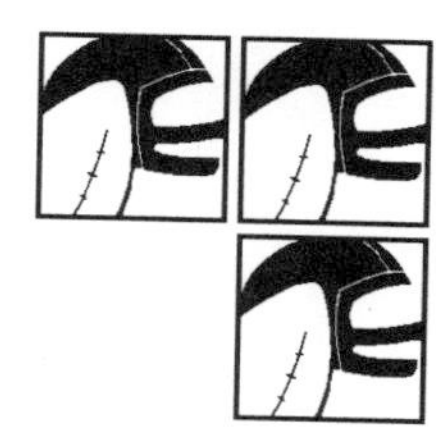

Sport: Football

Born: October 7, 1976
Fremont, Ohio

AP/Wide World Photos

Oakland Raiders cornerback Charles Woodson celebrates a victory over the Buffalo Bills in 1999.

Early Life

Charles Woodson was born in the blue-collar town of Fremont, Ohio, on October 7, 1976. His mother, Georgia, raised Charles and his brother and sister on her own. She often worked twelve-hour shifts as a forklift driver for a canning company to keep the family going. Though times could be tough, Georgia never let obstacles stand in her way. Her strength and perseverance would deeply influence Charles in his later athletic career.

Until he was four years old, Charles had to wear corrective braces on his feet. When they finally came off, he and his older brother, Terry, would play football in the living room, using a rolled up sock for a ball. As a teenager, Charles helped the family by making burgers and carrying shingles on roofing jobs. It was hard work, inspiring Charles to seek a way out of Fremont through sports.

The Road to Excellence

Charles quickly established himself as a star athlete upon entering Ross High School in Fremont. Though he played basketball and ran track, it was on the football field that his natural talent and instincts shone most brightly. He was so good, he not only played defensive back but also ran the ball on offense. Charles completed his high school career holding school all-time records in rushing with 3,861 yards and in scoring with 466 points. During his prep years, he amassed 5,996 all-purpose yards through running, catching, and returning punts. Incredibly, he rushed for 2,028 yards and scored 230 points his senior year. Charles was named Mr. Football for the state of Ohio in 1994 and selected as the Midwest Region co-most valuable player.

As one of the top high school prospects in the Midwest, Charles had college scouts from across the country trying to sign him. He chose to enroll at the nearby University of Michigan. Charles made an immediate impact, soon working his way into the starting lineup as cornerback.

Though only a freshman, he developed a rep-

STATISTICS

Season	GP	Tac.	Sac.	FF	FR	Int.
1998	16	64	0.0	2	0	5
1999	16	61	0.0	0	0	1
2000	16	79	0.0	3	0	4
Totals	48	204	0.0	5	0	10

Notes: GP = games played; Tac. = total tackles; Sac. = sacks; FF = forced fumbles; FR = fumble recoveries; Int. = interceptions

utation for never letting anything get to him. Minutes before the big game against arch-rival Ohio State, Charles was found sleeping in the locker room. The older players could not believe he could be so calm. When he woke up, Charles had what his coach, Lloyd Carr, called "the greatest performance by a Michigan freshman in the history of that series." He shut down an All-American wide receiver and intercepted two balls, the last one clinching the game for his team. At the end of the season, Charles was voted the Big Ten Freshman of the Year while also picking up Conference First Team honors.

The Emerging Champion

After a standout freshman year, the coaches at Michigan started using Charles more creatively in his sophomore season. He began running the ball on a few plays in addition to catching passes and returning kicks. Meanwhile, he was developing into one of the best defensive backs in the country. He had speed, great footwork, and a penchant for hard hitting but also an uncanny ability to read plays. He set a Michigan record with 15 broken-up passes that season and was named an AP First Team All-American. In recognition of his outstanding year as cornerback, he was chosen the Chevrolet Defensive Player of the Year.

Charles entered the 1997 season as a candidate for the Heisman Trophy, the award given annually to the best player in college football. He kicked off the campaign by setting up the first 10 points in the season opener with an interception and a 29-yard pass reception. Michigan racked up win after win as Charles made spectacular plays on both defense and offense. Against Michigan State, he made a dazzling one-handed sideline interception that earned him ESPN Player of the Game honors. In the regular season finale against Ohio State, Charles returned a punt 78 yards for a key touchdown.

Michigan finished the 1997 regular season with a perfect 11-0 record and went on to play Washington State in the Rose Bowl game. Charles contributed by intercepting a pass in the end zone late in the game. The interception sealed the victory, and Michigan became co-national champions with Nebraska, the first time the Wolverines had reigned since 1948.

Shortly afterward, Charles received nearly every major national award, including being named a unanimous First Team All-American. The biggest honor of all came when he won the Heisman Trophy, beating out future pro stars Peyton Manning and Randy Moss. In doing so, Charles became the first predominantly defensive player ever to take home the prestigious prize.

Continuing the Story

After accomplishing everything he possibly could at Michigan, Charles decided to forego his senior year and make himself available for the 1998 National Football League (NFL) draft. He was chosen by the Oakland Raiders with the fourth pick overall. Understandably, Charles became an instant standout, starting all sixteen regular season games at cornerback. In his professional debut against Kansas City, he recorded a season-high 7 tackles, in addition to forcing a fumble.

HONORS AND AWARDS

1994	Ohio Mr. Football
1995	Big Ten Freshman of the Year All-Big Ten Conference First Team
1996	Chevrolet Defensive Player of the Year AP, Football Writers Association First Team All-American
1997	Heismann Trophy winner (First predominantly defensive player to win award) Unanimous First Team All-American Chevrolet, Bronko Nagurski, Harley-Griffin National Player of the Year
1998	NFL Rookie of the Year
1998, 1999	Pro Bowl selection

Though only a rookie, Charles maintained a cool demeanor and obvious self-assuredness on the field. Quarterbacks around the league began to take notice and stopped throwing the ball in his direction. Charles ended his first season with 5 interceptions and 2 forced fumbles and was selected to the Pro Bowl team. He added another award to his already bulging trophy case when he was named the Rookie of the Year.

The Raiders had suffered through several disappointing seasons before Charles's arrival. Now, he was fueling a comeback of Oakland's proud football history. The defensive unit jelled into one of the most efficient and rugged in the NFL. Charles made the Pro Bowl again in 1999. In 2000, the Raiders had their best start in years and made it to the conference championship game. Having won at every level of his career, it was no more than Charles expected.

Summary

Multitalented and versatile, Charles Woodson presented many threats to the teams against which he played. His gift for reading plays and appearing to know exactly what the offense was going to do made him one of the great defensive players. He was part of winning teams at every level of his career while still achieving great personal success. Remarkably confident, Charles maintained a cool, detached attitude, which could unnerve his opponents.

John Slocum

Additional Sources:

Georgatos, Dennis. "The Dominator." *Football Digest* 29, no. 5 (January, 2000): 16.

Roessing, Walter. "Born to Win." *Boys' Life* 89, no. 10 (October, 1999): 32.

Silver, Michael. "Joy Ride." *Sports Illustrated* 91, no. 8 (August 30, 1999): 74.

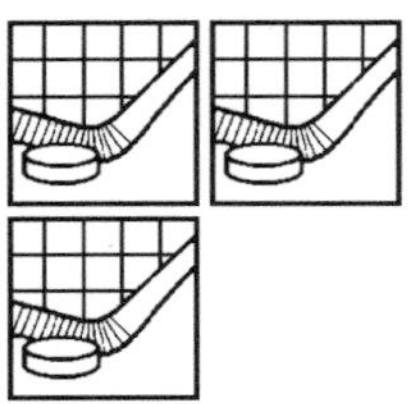

GUMP WORSLEY

Sport: Ice hockey

Born: May 14, 1929
Montreal, Quebec, Canada

Early Life

Lorne John "Gump" Worsley was born on May 14, 1929, in Montreal, Quebec, Canada. Just as the Great Depression affected so many lives in the United States, it had a similar effect in Canada. Lorne's father, an ironworker by trade, found work hard to find for four years. Of Scottish descent, Lorne was one of three children who grew up in a Montreal suburb of working-class families.

His childhood buddies thought that Lorne resembled a comic book character of that time, Andy Gump, and thus the nickname. As Gump grew up, he no longer resembled the comic character, but the name stuck with him throughout his hockey career. Playing all sports as a youngster, Gump found himself leaning more and more toward goaltending. At first, he was in nets during playground games and later played goalie for the Verdun Cyclones, a Junior League team. It was here that the New York scouts first noticed him and put Lorne on their negotiations list.

The Road to Excellence

For two years, the young Gump played goal for the New York Rovers of the Eastern Amateur League and was also the practice netkeeper for

Gump Worsley in 1956.

STATISTICS

Season	GP	W	L	T	GAA	PIM
1952-53	50	13	29	8	3.06	2
1954-55	65	15	33	17	3.03	2
1955-56	70	32	28	10	2.90	2
1956-57	68	26	28	13	3.24	19
1957-58	37	21	10	6	2.32	10
1958-59	67	26	29	12	3.07	10
1959-60	41	8	25	8	3.57	12
1960-61	58	19	**28**	9	3.33	10
1961-62	60	22	**27**	9	2.97	12
1962-63	67	22	**34**	9	3.30	14
1963-64	8	3	2	2	2.97	0
1964-65	19	10	7	1	2.78	0
1965-66	51	29	14	6	2.36	4
1966-67	18	9	6	2	3.18	4
1967-68	40	19	9	8	**1.98**	10
1968-69	30	19	6	4	2.25	0
1969-70	14	8	2	3	2.51	0
1970-71	24	4	10	8	2.50	10
1971-72	34	16	10	7	2.12	2
1972-73	12	6	2	3	2.88	22
1973-74	29	8	14	5	3.22	0
Totals	862	335	353	150	2.90	145

Notes: Boldface indicates statistical leader. GP = games played; W = wins; L = losses; T = ties; GAA = goals against average; PIM = penalties in minutes

the parent club, the New York Rangers. In 1950, he signed his first professional contract with the St. Paul Saints, where he was the leading goalie in the United States Hockey League. A promotion followed, and Gump played the next season with the Saskatoon Quakers. Finally, during the 1952-1953 season, he broke into the big leagues with the New York Rangers and promptly went on to win the Calder Memorial Trophy as the league's outstanding rookie performer. Nothing is assured in the game of professional sports, and Gump was about to learn that. The very next season saw him demoted to the minor leagues. He had a good season there, and the next year he was brought back to the parent club, where he toiled between the pipes for the next ten years.

The New York Rangers was not a good club. In the ten years that Gump played with them, they missed the playoffs six times. When a reporter once asked the always humorous Gump which team gave him the most trouble, he responded that it was the Rangers, his own squad.

The Emerging Champion

At the age of thirty-four, when most athletes are winding down their careers, Gump got a big break. He was traded from the lowly Rangers to the Montreal Canadiens, perennial contenders for the championship. Luck, however, would take time to develop for Gump. After only eight games, an injury forced him to miss several weeks. When he returned, another hot goalie, Charlie Hodge, had taken his place. He went back to the minors to regain his form. During the next season, Gump was called up when Hodge needed a rest. It was obvious by the second half of the year that the promotion was permanent. In fact, during this season (1964-1965) Gump was to play a vital part in Montreal's successful bid for another Stanley Cup.

The following year would be even better, with Gump and Hodge sharing the honor of winning the Vezina Trophy for the best goaltenders in the game. Also, the Canadiens won the championship again, and Gump was selected to the All-Star team.

Except for his fear of flying, there was very little that could make Gump lose his cool. On the ice, he had a coolness about him that helped him surmount the tensions of every season, even in Montreal, where the pressure to win was great and constant. Even with these growing pressures, Gump's play continued to improve. During the 1967-1968 season, he once again made the All-Star team and repeated as Vezina Trophy winner while his team was clinching yet another league championship. The following year, the Montreal team, with Gump as their main goalie, won the Stanley Cup again.

Continuing the Story

It was during the 1969-1970 season, after a particularly bumpy airplane ride, that Gump had enough. He got off the airplane in Toronto and took a train home to Montreal. He announced his retirement the next day. Three months later, after resting and distancing himself from hockey and airplanes, Gump announced his fitness and

HONORS AND AWARDS	
1953	Calder Memorial Trophy
1966, 1968	Vezina Trophy
1980	Inducted into Hockey Hall of Fame

willingness to return to hockey, this time with the Minnesota North Stars.

He played eight games with this team before the season came to a close, but that was enough of a late surge so that the underdog North Stars made the playoffs. The situation proved so good for Gump that he signed on with Minnesota for the following year. The 1971-1972 season was a great one for Gump. He was forty-three years old and playing some of the best hockey of his life. In 1973, age and injuries were catching up with him. Finally, a leg injury slowed him down so much that Gump felt he would be cheating his teammates if he played when he was not completely fit. He retired from active play in January, 1973.

Summary

People who did not know Gump Worsley would see him clowning around or hear him making jokes and would conclude that he was not very serious. They would be mistaken. With a rotund appearance that belied his quickness and a competitive nature that few other players could match, Gump became one of the outstanding goalies ever to play in the National Hockey League.

Carmi Brandis

Additional Sources:

Hollander, Zander, and Hal Bock, eds. *The Complete Encyclopedia of Ice Hockey.* Rev. ed. Englewood Cliffs, N.J.: Prentice-Hall, 1974.

Hunter, Douglas. *A Breed Apart: An Illustrated History of Goaltending.* New York: Viking, 1995.

Irvin, Dick. *In the Crease: Goaltenders Look at Life in the NHL.* Toronto: HarperCollins, 1990.

Worsley, Lorne, and Tim Moriarty. *They Call Me Gump.* New York: Dodd, Mead, 1975.

JAMES WORTHY

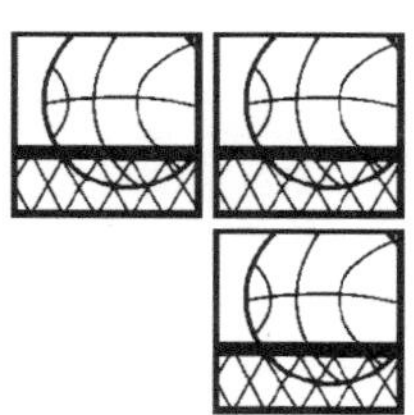

Sport: Basketball

Born: February 27, 1961
Gastonia, North Carolina

Early Life

James Ager Worthy was born to a minister and registered nurse on February 27, 1961, in Gastonia, North Carolina. A natural athlete, James won headlines with his basketball exploits even before he entered high school. The tall—he would eventually grow to the height of 6 feet 9 inches—and lanky James led his Ashbrook High School to three state championships. His average of 21.5 points per game and 12.5 rebounds per game in his senior year at Ashbrook attracted the attention of college programs from around the country, and James was recognized as one of the best high school basketball players in America.

AP/Wide World Photos

James Worthy in 1993.

The Road to Excellence

James chose to attend college in his home state, at the University of North Carolina. He arrived with high expectations and became one of the school's first freshmen to start his first game. Midway through his freshman year, however, James slipped and broke his ankle. He missed the season's final fourteen games, and many people doubted that he could return to his previous form.

James proved his doubters wrong, as he returned to Carolina and won All-Atlantic Coast Conference honors. That team advanced to the National Collegiate Athletic Association (NCAA) championship game but lost to Indiana University. As a junior James led one of the most talented college teams ever assembled to a 32-2 record and the 1981-1982 NCAA national championship. James was named a First Team consensus All-American.

The Emerging Champion

An unheralded freshman on that team named Michael Jordan stole some of James's thunder by sinking a decisive jump shot against Georgetown University in the NCAA finals, but James was the team's undisputed leader and greatest player. James's 28 points on 13-for-17 shooting and a key defensive steal won him the tournament's most outstanding player award, and he shared national Player of the Year honors with the University of Virginia's Ralph Sampson.

James left college and was the first pick in the 1982 National Basketball Association (NBA) draft. He joined the defending NBA champion Los Angeles Lakers. With Magic Johnson and Kareem Abdul-Jabbar he would go on to win three championship rings, in 1985, 1987, and 1988.

Continuing the Story

In 1982 the Los Angeles Lakers had an All-Star small forward in Jamaal "Silk" Wilkes. James would have started—and starred—immediately for almost any team in the NBA, but in Los Angeles he could not even crack the starting lineup. Instead of sulking, James resolved to study the game and learn as much as he could from the veteran Wilkes. He made the best of the situation and put up very respectable statistics before fracturing his tibia late in the season. James missed the 1983 playoffs, in which the Lakers were swept in the NBA finals by the Philadelphia 76ers, but was named to the NBA's All-Rookie team.

While recuperating, James returned to the University of North Carolina to work on finishing his degree. The Lakers traded starting forward Norm Nixon in the 1983 off-season, and the following season James joined Wilkes, Kareem Abdul-Jabbar, Magic Johnson, and Michael Cooper in the Lakers' starting lineup. They would win three championships in the next five years after epic battles with the Boston Celtics, the Philadelphia 76ers, and the Detroit Pistons.

James's accomplishments in the 1988 NBA finals against the Detroit Pistons cemented his reputation as one of the game's top performers at the highest levels of competition. He posted the first and only triple-double of his professional career in the decisive game 7 of the 1988 finals, with 36 points, 16 rebounds, and 10 assists, and was named the series' most valuable player (MVP). Magic Johnson later called him one of the "top five players in playoff history," and few who saw James play would argue with Johnson's statement.

James did not revolutionize the small forward position in the way that his contemporaries Julius "Dr. J" Erving and Larry Bird did, but his peers did consider him one of the greatest forwards of his generation. For basketball fans who came of age during the peak of the NBA's popularity in the 1980's and 1990's, the sight of James finishing a Magic Johnson-led fast break for the Lakers is an enduring memory. For these fans, James epitomized the word "clutch": He performed at his highest possible level when the games were most important.

Instantly recognizable for his trademark goggles (a pair of which now rests in the Smithsonian Institution), after his retirement in 1994, James was an ardent advocate of protective eyewear. Shortly after retiring, James launched Big Game James, a sports marketing firm that links sports celebrities with major corporations for endorsement purposes. James then put his basketball expertise to work as a commentator for the Fox Sports Network and CBS Sports.

STATISTICS

Season	*GP*	*FG%*	*FT%*	*Reb.*	*Ast.*	*TP*	*PPG*
1982-83	77	.579	.624	399	132	1,033	13.4
1983-84	82	.556	.759	515	207	1,185	14.5
1984-85	80	.572	.776	511	201	1,410	17.6
1985-86	75	.579	.771	387	201	1,500	20.0
1986-87	82	.539	.751	466	226	1,594	19.4
1987-88	75	.531	.796	374	289	1,478	19.7
1988-89	81	.548	.782	489	288	1,657	20.5
1989-90	80	.548	.782	478	288	1,685	21.1
1990-91	78	.492	.797	356	275	1,670	21.4
1991-92	54	.447	.814	305	252	1,075	19.9
1992-93	82	.447	.810	247	278	1,221	14.9
1993-94	80	.406	.741	181	154	812	10.2
Totals	926	.521	.769	4,708	2,791	16,320	17.6

Notes: GP = games played; FG% = field goal percentage; FT% = free throw percentage; Reb. = rebounds; Ast. = assists; TP = total points; PPG = points per game

Summary

A champion at every level of organized basketball, James Worthy earned the nickname "Big Game James" for his performances in the 1982 NCAA Final Four and in three NBA Championship Series. A seven-time NBA All-Star with 16,320 career points, James was selected to the NBA's 50 Greatest Players of All Time Team in 1996.

Todd Moye

Additional Sources:

Carpenter, Jerry, and Steve DiMeglio. *James Worthy.* Bloomington, Minn.: Adbo & Daughters, 1988.

Rapoport, Ron. "One on One with James Worthy." *Sport* 82 (May, 1991): 15-16.

Welch, James E. "Worthy, James Ager." In *Biographical Dictionary of Sports: 1989-1992 Supplement for Baseball, Football, Basketball, and Other Sports*, edited by David L. Porter. Westport, Conn.: Greenwood Press, 1992.

BILLY WRIGHT

Sport: Soccer

Born: February 6, 1924
Ironbridge, England

Early Life

Billy Wright was born on February 6, 1924, in Ironbridge in the English Midlands, 20 miles from Wolverhampton. As a schoolboy he was a fan of the London soccer team Arsenal, who in the 1930's were the leading English team.

Billy always wanted to become a professional soccer player, even though at school he was slightly built and did not excel at the game. However, Norman Simpson, his sports master at Madely Senior School, took note of his potential. In 1937, when Billy was fourteen, Simpson wrote to the famous Wolverhampton Wanderers Football Club (nicknamed the "Wolves") to ask if Wright could be given a job on the ground staff. Billy's father, a worker at the local iron foundry, would have preferred Billy to have joined Aston Villa, another famous Midlands club. Billy's mother, however, was happy with the choice of the Wolves, and as soon as Billy had completed his schooling, he set off for Wolverhampton.

Express Newspapers/Archive Photos

Billy Wright in 1959.

The Road to Excellence

At Wolverhampton, Billy came under the influence of the team manager, Major Frank Buckley, a stern disciplinarian who put him to work doing routine chores. Billy respected Buckley and was bitterly disappointed the next year when Buckley told him he was too small to make the grade as a player and that Buckley was sending him home. Nevertheless, Buckley reversed his decision when the groundsman told him how hardworking and useful Billy was.

By 1939, Billy had played center-forward for the Wolves' "B" team and had made his first-team debut at outside-right. He signed as a professional at the age of seventeen in 1941. After this he settled down as a halfback, the position he was to occupy for the rest of his career.

In the early stages of Billy's career he was indebted to Frank Broome, one of his colleagues on the Wolves team. Broome was a seasoned international forward who taught Billy how to place passes and take up the correct position.

In May, 1942, Billy suffered the worst setback of his career when he broke his ankle during the semifinal of the League War Cup. It was a bad injury, and Buckley and the medical specialists feared it would finish Billy's career—almost before it had begun. Billy remained determined during his recovery, however, and several months later he returned to the Wolves as fit as ever.

The Emerging Champion

In 1947 Billy made his first appearance for England's national team against Belgium at Wembley Stadium in London. Soon he was captaining the Wolves team, and in 1949 he led them to victory in the Football Association Cup final against Leicester City. In the same year he became captain of England.

Billy's game was outstanding for its consistency. He rarely had a bad match. He was fast and had strong tackling ability. Former England manager Ron Greenwood has said that Billy was one of the best ball winners of his era. However, if Billy was beaten in a tackle, he was extremely quick to recover. He was also formidable in the air, since he was usually able to outjump opposing forwards (most of whom were several inches taller than Billy, who stood 5 feet 8 inches).

Billy was a steady and determined player rather than a flamboyant one. He was not an individualist but rather a team player whose style could be integrated easily into that of the rest of the team. He was not known for his forays upfield to support the attack but for solid defensive work. Reluctant to take risks, he put safety first.

As Billy's skills and reputation grew, he learned a great deal from Stan Cullis, who took over from Frank Buckley as the Wolves' manager in 1949. Cullis was a former center-half for the Wolves and for England, and he gave Billy the benefit of his knowledge about tactics and captaincy.

Continuing the Story

In 1952, Billy won the English Footballer of the Year award, and this was a prelude to seven years of almost unbroken success. The Wolves became one of the glamour teams of the 1950's, and Billy captained them to three League championships, in 1954, 1958, and 1959. He also helped the Wolves to some famous victories over some of the best European teams, including Moscow Spartak, Honved of Hungary, and Spain's Real Madrid.

From 1951 to 1959, Billy played 70 consecutive matches for England, a record. He was also the first man to play 100 times for England, most of them as captain. Billy represented England in three World Cup competitions: in Brazil in 1950, Switzerland in 1954, and Sweden in 1958. During the World Cup in 1954, he switched positions from wing-half to center-half, and it is generally thought that this move extended his playing career. Playing in the center of the field meant that he did not have to cover as much ground as he had done at wing-half.

Billy was renowned for his sportsmanship and sense of fair play. He rarely showed anger, and he never argued with a referee over a decision. His loyalty to his club and his country won for him the respect and admiration of the British public. Even when he was well into his thirties, he retained his boyish enthusiasm for the game. Many younger players were thankful to him for his kindness in helping them through their first big matches.

Wright retired from the game in 1959 and was made a Commander of the British Empire (C.B.E.) by Queen Elizabeth II. The award honored his outstanding contribution to English soccer.

For a brief period in the mid-1960's, Wright served as the manager of the Arsenal Football Club in London. He did not achieve the same success as a manager that he had as a player. Some years later, Wright became a successful television executive.

RECORDS AND MILESTONES

90 times national team captain (world record)
105 international appearances for England

HONORS AND AWARDS

1949	English Football Association Cup champion
1952	English Footballer of the Year
1954, 1958-59	English League champion
1959	Commander of the British Empire

Summary

Billy Wright was one of the finest and most popular players England has produced. An honest and straightforward man, both on the field and off, he was dedicated to his craft. His skill and reliability made him the defensive rock around which the Wolves and England built their teams in the 1950's.

Bryan Aubrey

Additional Sources:

Henshaw, Richard. *The Encyclopedia of World Soccer.* Washington, D.C.: New Republic Books, 1979.

Wright, Billy. *Captain of England.* London: Stanley Paul, 1950

_______. *Football Is My Passport.* London: Stanley Paul, 1957.

MICKEY WRIGHT

Sport: Golf

Born: February 14, 1935
San Diego, California

Early Life

Mary Kathryn Wright was born in San Diego, California, to attorney Arthur Wright and Mary Kathryn Wright on February 14, 1935. With the same legal name as her mother, she soon became known as "Mickey." Mickey grew into an adolescent with a larger-than-ordinary body. Her friends at school sometimes teased her, calling her "Moose." This teasing gave her an inferiority complex and motivated her to outshine everyone at some skill in order to feel good about herself.

Golf proved to be Mickey's niche. Luckily for her, she was already good at it. Her father was an amateur golfer, and he had encouraged her to practice on a driving range since she was nine years old. By the age of eleven, she played her first round and scored 145. At twelve, she broke 100; at thirteen, she was already down to 80
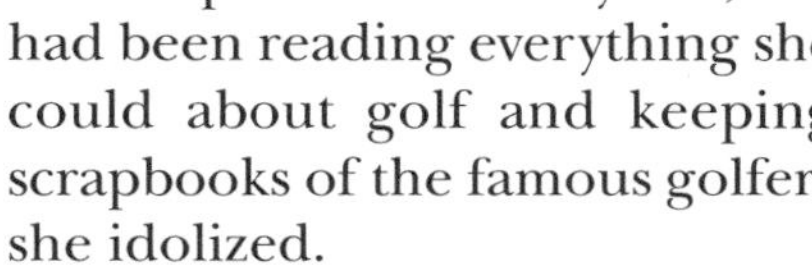
strokes per round. For years, she had been reading everything she could about golf and keeping scrapbooks of the famous golfers she idolized.

Ralph W. Miller Golf Library

The Road to Excellence

Mickey played in her first tournament in San Diego when she was fifteen. There, she shot a 70. By the next year, she was beating the male professionals at her local course. At one point, her elbow kept flying out too much on the backswing. Professional Paul Runyan showed her how to weaken her grip to fix that. Mickey's mother made her an elastic band that let her arms swing freely but would not allow her elbows to separate. Mickey practiced by the hour, wearing the contraption. By 1952, she had progressed so well and quickly that she was able to claim victory at the United States Golf Association's Junior Girls' Championship.

Mickey then enrolled in college at Stanford University. When summer came, she was back on the links, proving herself as the best-scoring amateur in the United States Open, as well as the St. Petersburg Open and the Tam O'Shanter tournaments. She was also the runner-up in the United States Amateur. After only one year in college, she convinced her father to let her take a leave of absence from school in order to play as an amateur on the professional tour that coming winter.

Mickey did so well on the tour that, when she calculated what she would have earned had she played as a professional instead of as an amateur, she saw that it made sense for her to immediately switch to professional status.

The Emerging Champion

As a professional, Mickey earned an excellent income right from the start. When she was twenty years old, she earned $7,000, and then in the next two years, $8,500 and $12,000, respectively. By then, 1958, she was winning major tournaments like the Ladies Professional Golf Association (LPGA) Championship and the United States Open.

Later in that year, though, she went into a slump during the St. Petersburg Open. Her roommate, Betsy Rawls, recognized Mickey's self-pity for what it was and snapped her out of it. Betsy made Mickey see that she could blame her performance on no one but herself.

In 1960, an important year for Mickey, she began to work with her new golf teacher, Earl Stewart, the professional at the Oak Cliff Country Club in Dallas, Texas. She moved to Dallas to be near him. As a first and essential lesson, Stewart taught Mickey how to relax her perfectionistic attitude toward work. He wanted her to play one shot at a time without getting emotionally involved in the shots to come or those behind her. Stewart's primary assistance was psychological, but he also worked on Mickey's swing.

As a result, that same year Mickey won the Vare Trophy for lowest average strokes per round. For the next three years, no one surpassed her average. That was still only the beginning for Mickey. The following year, she achieved a remarkable Grand Slam: She was the winner of the United States Women's Open, the LPGA Championship, and the Titleholders Championship.

It was 1963 that proved to be Mickey's greatest year ever. It was also the greatest year ever achieved by a woman golfer. She won thirteen major tournaments that year, for a lifetime total of fifty-three tournament victories, including her fourth LPGA title. In addition, her average score that year was 72.81, the lowest among all her competitors, for the fourth time. The Associated Press polled sports editors nationwide for their annual selection of Female Athlete of the Year. The choice was easy that year: Mickey Wright.

Continuing the Story

Between 1961 and 1964, Mickey's income surpassed that of all other women golfers. It rose from $18,000 to $31,269. As the finest player in the history of women's golf, she more than deserved it.

In addition to being the best paid, Mickey was also the best long-ball hitter. She surprised many male professionals, who never thought they would see a woman hit the ball 300 yards, by outhitting them on the fairways. Mickey consistently hit drives averaging 225 to 270 yards. Once, aided by a strong wind, she overshot the green of a 385-yard hole. Mickey was a strong, 5-foot 9-inch golfer; she was no longer self-conscious about her size, a trim figure at 150 pounds. Her weaknesses in golf changed, she found. When a weakness was evident in her swing, she practiced and analyzed her swing in front of a mirror. At other times, she was considered weak on the greens in

MAJOR CHAMPIONSHIP VICTORIES	
1958-59, 1961, 1964	U.S. Women's Open
1958, 1960-61, 1963	LPGA Championship
1961-62	Titleholders Championship
1962-63, 1966	Western Open
1973	Colgate Dinah Shore
OTHER NOTABLE VICTORIES	
1960	Eastern Open Memphis Open
1961, 1963, 1966	Mickey Wright Invitational
1961, 1963	St. Petersburg Open
1963	Babe Zaharias Open
1966-67, 1969	Bluegrass Invitational
1967	Baltimore Lady Carling Pensacola Invitational

RECORDS AND MILESTONES

Eighty-two career victories

Won a record thirteen victories in 1963

Tour's leading money winner four times (1961-64)

Had at least one tournament victory a year (1956-70)

Only woman golfer to win the U.S. Women's Open and the LPGA Championship in the same year twice (1958, 1961)

Her collection of four U.S. Women's Open titles is a record shared with Betsy Rawls

HONORS AND AWARDS

1957	*Golf Digest* Most Improved Golfer
1958, 1960-64	*Golf Digest* Mickey Wright Award for Tournament Victories
1958-67	*Golf* magazine Golfer of the Decade
1960-64	LPGA Vare Trophy
1963-64	Associated Press Female Athlete of the Year
1964	Inducted into LPGA Hall of Fame
1976	Inducted into PGA/World Golf Hall of Fame
1981	Inducted into Sudafed International Women's Sports Hall of Fame
1999	Associated Press Female Golfer of the Century

the short game—shots from 130 to 140 yards onto the green.

Her swing was considered the best of all time. Golfers everywhere marveled at her grace and balance and at how well her swing was synchronized. She never appeared to be swinging hard, yet she could hit as far as the men professionals. She was the Jack Nicklaus of women's driving, with the best combination of distance and distance on the fly.

Later on, Mickey went into the brokerage business, while living in Port St. Lucie, Florida. When she injured her back, she stopped playing golf regularly.

Though she made her last official LPGA Tournament appearance in 1980, Mickey competed in the Senior Sprint Challenge from 1993 to 1995. She finished in the top five each year, including a second-place finish in 1994. Her paycheck from that event was $30,000, the largest of her career.

Summary

Mickey Wright was the greatest long-ball hitter in the history of women's golf. She is often considered the finest woman golfer ever. She won both the LPGA title and the United States Women's Open four times and the Vare Trophy four years in a row. For two years in succession, she was named Female Athlete of the Year by the Associated Press. She was the first woman ever to win as many as thirteen major tournaments in a single year. Mickey has the second-highest number of tournament titles (82) behind Kathy Whitworth, and in 1999 the Associated Press named her Golfer of the Century. For these achievements, she was inducted to the LPGA Hall of Fame.

Nan White

Additional Sources:

Editors of *Golf Magazine. Golf Magazine's Encyclopedia of Golf: The Complete Reference.* New York: HarperCollins, 1993.

Emory, Pam. "Mickey Wright." *Golf Digest* 44, no. 7 (1993).

Glenn, Rhonda. *The Illustrated History of Women's Golf.* Dallas, Tex.: Taylor, 1991.

Wright, Mickey. *Play Golf the Wright Way.* Dallas, Tex.: Taylor, 1990.

EARLY WYNN

Sport: Baseball

Born: January 6, 1920
Hartford, Alabama
Died: April 4, 1999
Venice, Florida

Courtesy of Amateur Athletic Foundation of Los Angeles

Early Life

Early Wynn was born on January 6, 1920, in Hartford, Alabama, a village in southeastern Alabama where his father, a semiprofessional baseball player, worked as an auto mechanic. A fine athlete as a young boy, Early always could throw hard and seemed destined to pitch, as he did for the Hartford baseball team. He was also an excellent halfback for the high school football team, but this ended soon because, midway through high school, he broke his leg just before football season. As a result, in the following spring, baseball became his only sport. He quit school during that spring, attended a baseball training camp in Sanford, Florida, and was offered a one-hundred-dollar-a-month contract by a scout from the Washington Senators. Even though he had intended to return to high school, this was too tempting an offer for a boy who had spent the previous summer working on a cotton gin.

The Road to Excellence

Early's first season was spent on the Sanford team in the Florida State League, where he earned sixteen victories in 235 innings. The next years brought tragedy, however. While playing for the Charlotte, North Carolina, team in 1939, Early married Mabel Allman. Two years later, after the birth of a son, Joe Early, he lost her in an automobile accident as she drove a baby-sitter home.

The pain of this event and the responsibility of a baby son caused Early to work at his career with more earnestness. As a result, he was called up to the Washington Senators in 1940. In 1943, he earned eighteen wins, but the following year brought only an 8-17 season. With World War II still raging, Early enlisted in the Army. During the same year, he married Lorraine Follin. By 1946, he had returned to pitching for the Senators, but the failing Senators team, combined with Early's one-pitch repertoire (fastball), brought three lacklustre seasons. Early was traded to Bill Veeck's Cleveland Indians along with Micky Vernon at the end of 1948 for Joe Haynes, Ed Klieman, and Eddie Robinson. This stands as one of the most beneficial trades in the history of the Cleveland Indians.

The Emerging Champion

The trade was beneficial to Early Wynn's career also. He began to work under the tutelage of coach Mel Harder, who helped Early to control a curveball, a knuckleball, a slider, and a change-up. With such variety and skill, Early was able to achieve 163 wins and four 20-game seasons during his nine-year stay with the Indians. Besides this, he served in one of the greatest rotations in baseball history: Early, Bob Lemon, Mike Garcia, and Bob Feller, replaced by Herb Score. They brought the team to second place in 1952 and 1953 when Garcia, Lemon, and Wynn were named Cleveland Men of the Year. They guided the team to the pennant in 1954, one of only two seasons when the New York Yankees did not take it during their stellar 1950's decade.

Nearing the age of thirty-eight, Early Wynn, along with Al Smith, was traded to the fast-moving, weak-hitting Chicago White Sox for Minnie Minoso and Fred Hatfield. They were intended to help the Chicago team's chances for an American League pennant, and help they did. In the 1959 season, Early pitched a twenty-two-win season, which helped to cinch the American League pennant. He won the Cy Young Award and continued to a thirteen-win season at the age of forty in 1960.

Continuing the Story

With 284 career wins, Early was only sixteen games from the magic 300-win career, but at the end of a 7-15 season in 1962, the gout-plagued Wynn was released by the White Sox with 299 wins.

His old team, the Cleveland Indians, offered him a year's contract, which gave him an opportunity to earn that one final victory. On July 13, after three failed attempts, Wynn pitched 5 in-

STATISTICS

Season	GP	GS	CG	IP	HA	BB	SO	W	L	S	ShO	ERA
1939	3	3	1	20.1	26	10	1	0	2	0	0	5.75
1941	5	5	4	40.0	35	10	15	3	1	0	0	1.58
1942	30	28	10	190.0	246	73	58	10	16	0	1	5.12
1943	37	**33**	12	256.2	232	83	89	18	12	0	3	2.91
1944	33	25	19	207.2	221	67	65	8	17	2	2	3.38
1946	17	12	9	107.0	112	33	36	8	5	0	0	3.11
1947	33	31	22	247.0	251	90	73	17	15	0	2	3.64
1948	33	31	15	198.0	236	94	49	8	19	0	1	5.82
1949	26	23	6	164.2	186	57	62	11	7	0	0	4.15
1950	32	28	14	213.2	166	101	143	18	8	0	2	**3.20**
1951	37	**34**	21	**274.1**	227	107	133	20	13	1	3	3.02
1952	42	33	19	285.2	239	**132**	153	23	12	3	4	2.90
1953	36	34	16	251.2	234	107	138	17	12	0	1	3.93
1954	40	**36**	20	**270.2**	225	83	155	**23**	11	2	3	2.73
1955	32	31	16	230.0	207	80	122	17	11	0	6	2.82
1956	38	35	18	277.2	233	91	158	20	9	2	4	2.72
1957	40	**37**	13	263.0	**270**	104	**184**	14	17	1	1	4.31
1958	40	34	11	239.2	214	104	**179**	14	16	2	4	4.13
1959	37	**37**	14	**255.2**	202	**119**	179	**22**	10	0	5	3.17
1960	36	35	13	237.1	220	112	158	13	12	1	**4**	3.49
1961	17	16	5	110.1	88	47	64	8	2	0	0	3.51
1962	27	26	11	167.2	171	56	91	7	15	0	3	4.46
1963	20	5	1	55.1	50	15	29	1	2	1	0	2.28
Totals	691	612	290	4,564.0	4,291	1,775	2,334	300	244	15	49	3.54

Notes: Boldface indicates statistical leader. GP = games played; GS = games started; CG = complete games; IP = innings pitched; HA = hits allowed; BB = bases on balls (walks); SO = strikeouts; W = wins; L = losses; S = saves; ShO = shutouts; ERA = earned run average

HONORS AND AWARDS

1955-60	American League All-Star Team
1959	Cy Young Award *Sporting News* Major League Player of the Year
1972	Inducted into National Baseball Hall of Fame

nings against Kansas City, leaving the mound with a score of 5-4, and the Indians enforced the win 7-4. Early became the fourteenth pitcher in history to win three hundred games.

While continuing to pitch for the remainder of the season, Early never earned another victory. He coached for the Indians for three years and then for the Minnesota Twins for three years, where, in 1969, he was named a super scout. He was inducted into the National Baseball Hall of Fame in 1972.

Summary

A hard loser, known for his toughness, Early Wynn joked that he would knock down his grandmother if she dug in against him. He enjoyed three hundred wins in a twenty-three-year career, the longest in the major leagues to that time. Such longevity and enormous success are indeed rare among pitchers.

Vicki K. Robinson

Additional Sources:

Appel, Martin, and Burt Goldblatt. *Baseball's Best: The Hall of Fame Gallery.* New York: McGraw-Hill, 1977.

Hickok, Ralph. *A Who's Who of Sports Champions.* Boston: Houghton Mifflin, 1995.

Shatzkin, Mike, et al., eds. *The Ballplayers: Baseball's Ultimate Biographical Reference.* New York: William Morrow, 1990.

KRISTI YAMAGUCHI

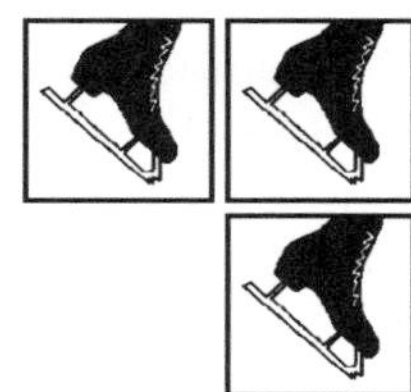

Sport: Figure skating

Born: June 12, 1971
Hayward, California

Early Life

The second of three children, Kristi Tsuya Yamaguchi was born on June 12, 1971, in Hayward, California. She was a tiny, club-footed baby; to correct the inward turn of her feet, she was fitted with casts for the first nine months of her life.

AP/Wide World Photos

Kristi Yamaguchi performing at the 1992 Olympics. She won the gold medal.

As a child, Kristi wore special shoes and took dance lessons as therapy. She saw an ice skating show at a mall one day with her mother, Carol Yamaguchi, and was so entranced that she started taking skating lessons as soon as her mother would let her.

Kristi's grace on the ice developed with much hard work and great support from her family. She practiced her skating early in the mornings, worked hard in school in the afternoons, and went to bed very early. She also spent many hours with her mother driving to and from training and competitions. Meanwhile, Kristi's father, a dentist, was helping her younger brother Brett and older sister Lori pursue their own goals. The family also made financial sacrifices to pay for Kristi's training. Training a competitive figure skater is very expensive, but the Yamaguchis believed that it was worth it to help Kristi continue to skate.

The Road to Excellence

Incredibly disciplined and hardworking, Kristi pursued both single and pairs competition. She started working with singles coach Christy Kjarsgaard in 1981, and when she was eleven years old, she started training for pairs with Jim Hulick. Jim found Kristi a partner in Rudy Galindo, who was a stronger and more advanced skater than Kristi. Kristi fought to keep up, and the extra effort paid off for her. In 1986 she and Rudy won a bronze medal in the pairs competition at her first Olympic Festival. At the 1987 World Junior Championships in Brisbane, Australia, Kristi took first place both in her singles competition and in her doubles performance with Rudy.

In 1988 Kristi competed at the U.S. Championships, moving to the senior level in singles competition. She finished in tenth place and was on her way to national prominence. The stress of competing in two events, however, was tremendous; moreover, in the late summer of 1988, her trainer, Jim Hulick, was diagnosed with colon cancer. He needed to give up coaching for his health, but Jim continued to work with Kristi and Rudy, coaching their breathtaking side-by-side triple jumps, which they could perform again and again in routines.

At the U.S. Championships in February, 1989, Kristi qualified for both pairs and singles; she was the first woman to do this since Margaret Graham in 1954. In the pairs competition, with Jim Hulick watching his star students, Kristi and Rudy performed beautifully together. The crowd sat spellbound watching their triple jumps and artistry, set to "Prologue and Fanfare for the Prince" from Peter Ilich Tchaikovsky's *Romeo and Juliet,* and Kristi and Rudy won first place. The next day, Kristi took second place in her singles competition, skating as a high-kicking cancan dancer to "Gaieté Parisienne."

The Emerging Champion

In March of 1989, Kristi debuted in Paris at her first World Championships. The world of figure skating was eagerly awaiting her performance, and Kristi took sixth place in the singles division and fifth place with Rudy in the pairs. After two more years of increasing her strength and speed, she would be capturing first place in world competitions. In the spring of 1989, her singles coach, Christy Kjarsgaard, married Andrew Ness, a doctor in Edmonton, Alberta, Canada. Kristi's hard work continued; she simply commuted to Edmonton to train.

The tremendous stress of competing in both pairs and singles, however, was wearing hard on Kristi, and in December of 1989, Jim Hulick died. Kristi and Rudy skated together only one more year. In 1990, they won first and fifth place in the U.S. and World Championships, respectively. Kristi's singles performances brought her second place in the U.S. Championships and fourth place in the subsequent World Championships.

Skating in the U.S. Championships in 1991, Kristi came in second to a very strong performance by Tonya Harding. Determined to improve, Kristi studied videotape of her most recent competitive performances and saw what she needed to do. In the World Championships in Munich later that year, Kristi skated faster and more aggressively. She was not favored to win, but with a performance that included six triple jumps, she received a perfect artistic scoring from the judges and captured first place. That year the Americans swept the women's medals: Kristi in first, Tonya Harding in second, and Nancy Kerrigan in third. A few months later, at the beginning of 1992, Kristi earned her U.S. national championship title.

At the 1992 Winter Olympic Games in Albertville, France, Kristi faced strong competition. Although she was the reigning world and U.S. champion, thus certainly considered a favorite, she was confronted with the athleticism and jumping power of Tonya Harding and Japan's Midori Ito, the first woman to land a triple axel in world competition. Kristi proved that she possessed all the necessary qualities to be the best with her short program. She skated a flawless routine in which her speed, artistry, and musicality seem to effortlessly wrap the required technical elements and difficult jumps into a seamless whole. Even with a fall

MAJOR CHAMPIONSHIP

Year	Competition	Place
1986	U.S. National Junior Ladies Championships	4th
1987	U.S. National Junior Ladies Championships	2d
1988	World Junior Championships	1st
	U.S. National Senior Ladies Championships	10th
1989	U.S. National Senior Ladies Championships	2d
	World Championships	6th
1990	U.S. National Senior Ladies Championships	2d
	Goodwill Games	1st
	Nations Cup	1st
	World Championships	4th
1991	U.S. National Senior Ladies Championships	2d
	World Championships	1st
1992	Olympic Games	Gold
	U.S. National Senior Ladies Championships	1st
	World Championships	1st

HONORS AND AWARDS

1989	Women's Sports Foundation Up and Coming Athlete of the Year *Skating* magazine Readers' Choice Awards
1998	Inducted into U.S. Figure Skating Hall of Fame

in her long program, no skater could overcome her lead, and she took home the gold medal.

A month later she won her second consecutive world title, a feat not accomplished by an American woman since Peggy Fleming in 1967 and 1968. Kristi had the triple crown in 1992; she held the U.S., Olympic, and world titles.

Continuing the Story

Kristi turned professional in 1993, which was a dream come true for her. She toured with Stars on Ice, enjoying the travel, the creative opportunities, and the chance to grow artistically. All the time, however, she maintained her training schedules to keep the technical aspects of her skating in top form. As a result, through the 1990's, she dominated the World Professional Figure Skating Championships and other professional competitions. She was also involved in television specials, exhibitions, and endorsement contracts. In 1996 she established the Always Dream foundation to help foster the dreams of children. Kristi married professional hockey player Bret Hedican in July, 2000.

Summary

Kristi Yamaguchi is proof of the success hard work, determination, and a supportive family can bring. Her shy but fiercely determined good nature shines as an example to all in the intense world of figure skating. Kristi's devotion to and love of the sport is unsurpassed. Her every performance highlights her beautiful combination of grace, artistry, speed, and athleticism.

Alicia Neumann

Additional Sources:

Burby, Liza N. *Kristi Yamaguchi: World-Class Ice Skater.* New York: Rosen Publishing Group, 1997.

Donohue, Shiobhan. *Kristi Yamaguchi: Artist on Ice.* Minneapolis, Minn.: Lerner Publishing, 1994.

Rambeck, Richard. *Kristi Yamaguchi.* Chanhassen, Minn.: Child's World, 1997.

Savage, Jeff. *Kristi Yamaguchi: Pure Gold.* New York: Maxwell Macmillan International, 1993.

Wellman, Sam. *Kristi Yamaguchi.* Philadelphia: Chelsea House, 1999.

Yamaguchi, Kristi, with Greg Brown. *Always Dream.* Dallas: Taylor Publishing, 1998.

YASUHIRO YAMASHITA

Sport: Judo

Born: 1958
Yabe, Kyushu, Japan

Early Life

Yasuhiro Yamashita was born in 1958 in a farming village of sixteen thousand people in the Miharashi-Dai hills of Yabe, Kyushu, Japan. Yasuhiro's grandfather had previously lost two of his own children, and he did not want to lose his grandson Yasuhiro, so he made sure that Yasuhiro was properly taken care of and well fed.

The Sports Nippon Newspapers, Tokyo

Yasuhiro Yamashita (left) grapples with rival Hitoshi Saito.

Therefore, at the age of one, Yasuhiro won a local contest as the healthiest baby. When Yasuhiro was in elementary school, he was full of energy and determination; he was not satisfied until he became the best at everything he tried, and he was not afraid to fight older and even bigger boys to protect his smaller and weaker friends. He was very strong but kind and fair.

He first became interested in judo at age ten, when his mother took him to a local dojo (martial arts school) because she wanted him to gain control over his aggression. Yasuhiro loved judo. He could now trip and fling other children and get smiles from his teachers instead of angry looks. One day, Reisuke Shiraishi, who was a sensei (martial arts master) at a distant Kumamoto junior high school, saw Yasuhiro compete in a judo tournament. Shiraishi asked Yasuhiro to move to Kumamoto and vowed to make him a champion. Yasuhiro felt the Japanese traditional loyalty to his family, friends, and school, and he said no. One night, however, his father and younger brother took Yasuhiro to Kumamoto while he was asleep. The sensei gave Yasuhiro a white uniform and asked him to practice with the other students. The well-trained students tossed Yasuhiro left and right because he had not been trained as well. That day, Yasuhiro discovered that he hated losing more than moving to Kumamoto, so he moved to Kumamoto to study judo.

The Road to Excellence

On school days, Yasuhiro practiced from 4:30 to 8:00 P.M. When there was no school, he practiced ten hours a day.

MAJOR CHAMPIONSHIPS

Year	Competition	Weight Class	Place
1977-79	All-Japan Weight-Class Championships	Openweights	1st
1977-85	All-Japan Judo Championships	—	1st
1978	Jigoro Kano Cup International Championships	Heavyweight	1st
1978, 1982	Jigoro Kano Cup International Championships	Openweights	1st
1979	Paris International	+95 kilograms	1st
1979, 1981, 1983	World Judo Championships	+95 kilograms	Gold
1980, 1982-83	All-Japan Weight-Class Championships	+95 kilograms	1st
1981	World Judo Championships	Openweights	Gold
1984	Olympic Games	Openweights	Gold

The first thing the sensei did was change Yasuhiro from being right-handed to being left-handed, which made him a more difficult opponent. During a single year, he gained 55 pounds and began to progress toward the heavyweight division at judo competitions. Yasuhiro was taught to see each opponent as a man who had just slain his parents, to bow to him with respect, and then to attack without mercy.

One day, a sensei from Tokai University, an institution famous for martial arts, asked Yasuhiro to finish his last two years at their feeder school (a school universities use to prepare future students), because the competition would be more fierce than at Yasuhiro's traditional school. At first, Yasuhiro declined, but when he lost in the semifinals of the national high school championships, defeat made him once more remember that he hated losing more than moving, and he left right away.

When Yasuhiro went to Tokai University, he began training with Radomir Kovacevic, a young martial arts student from Yugoslavia. They would train with Kovacevic riding piggyback up hills on Yasuhiro's back to build Yasuhiro's strength. Because he was working with someone stronger and heavier, Yasuhiro soon turned his body fat to muscle, and his stamina improved. As a result of his training, at the age of nineteen, Yasuhiro became the youngest man to win the All-Japan Judo Championships (the Japanese equivalent to football's Heisman Trophy).

The Emerging Champion

Because Yasuhiro was so good, Dr. Shigeyoshi Matsumae, President of the International Judo Federation, used him as a judo leader and coach. Matsumae sent Yasuhiro to many countries to encourage foreigners to come and train under him at Tokai University and to promote friendship and world peace. No one else had ever had such a significant judo position in Japan's recent history.

In October, 1977, Yasuhiro was jolted. In the final of the Japan Student Championships, he hesitated, believing the match was over. Because of his hesitation, the judges awarded the decision to his rival. This setback helped Yasuhiro to remain consistently aggressive throughout his matches. He then became an undefeated champion and began to prepare himself for the 1980 Olympics.

In 1980, however, before a national television audience and members of the Japan Amateur Sports Federation, Yasuhiro stood weeping and pleading that the Sports Federation not devastate his dream of going to the 1980 Moscow Olympics because of the international boycott. A week later, he walked onto the mat to face another judo champion, Sumio Endo. Because of his disappointment about the Olympics, Yasuhiro was not able to concentrate and, during the match, Endo used a questionable throw that broke Yasuhiro's ankle. Yasuhiro's long recovery heightened his desire to win.

Not long after, the promoters of Japanese Professional Wrestling (sumo wrestling) paid Yasuhiro's grandfather the equivalent of $45,000 to help them recruit his grandson as a professional athlete. If Yasuhiro agreed, the grandfather would receive another $250,000. Yasuhiro, however, wanted to maintain his amateur standing in judo. He told his grandfather to return the money and never to talk to the professional wrestling committee again or his relationship with his grandfather was over.

Yasuhiro lived a simple life in a small home crammed with gifts and trinkets given to him by friends. He continued to compete, earning 203 consecutive wins. Finally, in 1984, Yasuhiro captured the Olympic gold medal in judo by winning the open-weights event (no weight restrictions on his 5-foot 10-inch, 280-pound body) during the Summer Olympics in Los Angeles. He finally had won the medal of his dreams. The twenty-six-year-old Tokai University judo coach had now won all the major judo awards possible. His Olympic victory confirmed his reputation as the undisputed world judo champion.

He retired from competition in 1985, at the age of twenty-seven and at the top of the judo world.

Continuing the Story

Yasuhiro became a Japanese hero, a great example of true sportsmanship because he did not sell out to money. Many Japanese children long to be like him. Yasuhiro gained strength day by day and year by year through hard training, but he never forgot his spirit. He could make significant amounts of money because of his fame, but he says, "Of course I need money, but even more, I want to push my chest out and lift my head and work proudly." He would maintain a simple life, spending his time training future judo athletes and endorsing various products.

Yasuhiro continued to help Dr. Matsumae's dream come true to use judo to promote world peace. His personality as well as his fame helped to accomplish this dream.

Summary

No one has been able to equal Yasuhiro Yamashita's accomplishments in judo. He has won more awards and titles than anyone else in the sport, including three World Judo Championships, nine All-Japan Judo Championships, and a judo gold medal in the 1984 Olympics. He became an influential master sensei of martial arts at Tokai University and would maintain his gentle personality despite his formidable size.

Rodney D. Keller

Additional Sources:

Mason, Gary. "The Master Sensei—Yasuhiro Yamashita." *Vancouver Sun* Online. http://www.ijf.org/whatnew/latenews/wn-bb-092.html. May 7, 1998.

"Olympic Stars." http://www.t3.rim.or.jp/~sports/stars/os.html.

"Yasuhiro Yamashita." http://www.kyoto-su.ac.jp/information/famous/yamashitay.html.

CALE YARBOROUGH

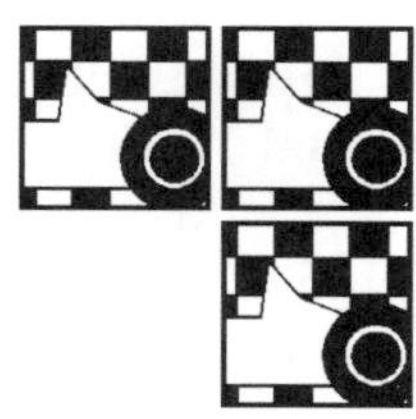

Sport: Auto racing

Born: March 27, 1939
Timmonsville, South Carolina

Early Life

William Caleb Yarborough was born on March 27, 1939, in Timmonsville, South Carolina. He grew up on his parent's tobacco farm in Sardis, South Carolina, a small rural community of little more than 150 people. Cale had a happy home life and loved to play and explore on the family farm. Even as a very young boy, Cale was used to being at the wheel of a car or truck. He would often sit on the lap of one of his father's farm workers as they drove errands in the pickup. By the age of eight, he was driving around the farm on his own.

Cale's first taste of driving competition came in 1950, when he entered a local soapbox race. Cale spent hours preparing his racer and looked forward to competing against other children. In the end, Cale did not win the race. Losing was a terrible feeling, and from this moment on, Cale decided that he wanted to be a winner. This competitive edge, which Cale acquired so young, was ultimately to enable him to become one of the greatest stock car racers of all time.

The Road to Excellence

From an early age, Cale loved anything having to do with cars and driving, but he was also an outstanding all-around athlete while attending Timmonsville High School. Cale won the South Carolina Golden Gloves welterweight boxing title and he was also an All-State running back. Clearly, Cale had many athletic talents and it was by no means certain that he would end up in auto racing.

At one stage, it appeared that Cale was headed for a career in professional football. After attending Clemson University on a football scholarship for a short while, Cale played semiprofessional football for the Sumter, South Carolina, Generals. He was even offered a tryout with the Washington Redskins. Cale declined the offer and once and for all decided that he was going to make a career in his first love—auto racing.

By the age of seventeen, Cale was an accomplished stock car driver, having won the South Carolina Stock Car Sportsman Championship. This level of racing allowed Cale to make enough money to support himself and his new bride, but he had a burning ambition to get to the top of the sport.

To make it big in stock car racing, Cale knew he would have to be successful on the highly

AP/Wide World Photos

Driver Cale Yarborough won the Motor State 400 stock car race in 1970.

competitive Grand National Circuit of the National Association for Stock Car Auto Racing (NASCAR). For a long time, NASCAR success eluded Cale; he went seven years on the circuit without a win. Finally, in 1965, Cale secured his first victory, and in that season, he went on to finish in the top ten in thirty-four races. He also amassed $25,140 in prize money. After years of patient learning, Cale had arrived on the NASCAR circuit.

The Emerging Champion

Between 1965 and 1970, Cale won fourteen NASCAR championship races. His big year came in 1968, however, when he won six NASCAR races and $136,786 in prize money. Probably his most satisfying victory of the 1968 season came in the Southern 500, held in Darlington, South Carolina, near his home. In a grueling race, Cale eventually outlasted David Pearson to record an emotional victory on the track he had frequented as a child.

Having come to dominate the NASCAR circuit, Cale became restless and looked for a new challenge. To this end, in the early 1970's, Cale tried his hand at single-seater racing on the USAC circuit. Although not a total failure, Cale found it difficult to adjust to this form of competition. After two frustrating seasons, he returned to stock car racing.

In 1973, Cale returned to the NASCAR circuit with great enthusiasm, and in the following two years he won a total of seventeen NASCAR races. The aggressive driving and fierce will to win, which hampered his performances in single-seater racing, once again made him a dominating force in stock car competition.

Cale was reaching his peak as an auto racer and was about to embark upon the most successful phase of his career. Between 1976 and 1978, Cale dominated the stock car scene like no one else before him. In these three seasons, Cale won twenty-eight NASCAR

NASCAR AND OTHER VICTORIES

1957	South Carolina Stock Car Sportsman Championship
1967-69, 1974, 1981, 1983	Coca-Cola 500
1967-68, 1976, 1981	Pepsi 400
1968, 1973-74, 1978, 1982	Southern 500
1968, 1974, 1977	Virginia 500
1968, 1977, 1983-84	Daytona 500
1969	Miller Genuine Draft 500
1970, 1974, 1977, 1982, 1984-85	Daytona 500 Twin 125 Qualifying Race
1970, 1975, 1978, 1980	Nationwide 500
1970, 1977	Miller Genuine Draft 400
1973-74, 1976-77	Valleydale Meats 500
1973, 1979	National 500
1973, 1976, 1978-79	Music City 420
1974	Riverside 400
1974, 1976-78, 1980	Busch 500
1974, 1977	Mason-Dixon 500
1974, 1975	Nashville 420
1974, 1976, 1978	Wilkes 400
1975, 1980, 1982	Carolina 500
1976	Delaware 500 Capital City 400
1976, 1977	Staley 400
1976, 1978	Old Dominion 500 NASCAR Winston Cup Champion
1977, 1979	Richmond 400
1978, 1984	Winston 500
1978, 1982-83	Gabriel 400
1979	Mountain Dew 500
1980	Texas 400 Atlanta Journal 500
1980, 1983	Champion Spark Plug 400
1984	International Race of Champions Van Scoy Diamond Mines 500
1985	Miller High Life 500 Talladega 500
1986	Budweiser International Race of Champions, third-round winner

HONORS, AWARDS, AND RECORDS	
1967	NASCAR Winston Cup Most Popular Driver
1968	Ford Motor Company Man of the Year
1968-69, 1978-79	Union 76-Darlington Record Club
1977	Olsonite Driver of the Year
1978	Only driver to win three consecutive NASCAR Winston Cup Championships
1982	Only driver to win the Southern 500 five times
1991	Inducted into American Auto Racing Writers and Broadcasters Association Hall of Fame

races and won the Winston Cup (the NASCAR circuit driving title) three times. These triumphs earned him nearly $1.5 million in prize money.

Continuing the Story

Following his three-year domination of the stock car world, Cale gradually concentrated less and less on racing. Between 1979 and his retirement in 1986, he competed in an average of only sixteen races a year.

Despite his relative inactivity, Cale was still successful, winning twenty-four more races, to bring his career total to eighty-eight NASCAR victories. As of 1991, this figure ranks him fourth on the all-time list behind Richard Petty, David Pearson, and Bobby Allison. Cale's victory at the Southern 500 in 1982 gave him an unprecedented fifth triumph in that race. It is perhaps fitting that Cale should so dominate the race held in his own "backyard."

Throughout his racing career, Cale displayed a single-minded confidence in his own ability and a fierce competitive spirit. These attributes enabled him to amass $5,003,616 in prize money by the time of his retirement in 1986. Cale invested his earnings wisely and would manage his numerous thriving business interests with the same drive and determination that characterized his racing career.

Summary

Cale Yarborough always believed in his ability to make it to the top as a stock car driver. He kept this self-confidence even through the long, unsuccessful learning phase of his career. As a result of his patience and perseverance, Cale ultimately realized his dream, becoming one of the best stock car racers the sport has ever seen.

David L. Andrews

Additional Sources:

Cutter, Robert, and Bob Fendell. *The Encyclopedia of Auto Racing Greats.* Englewood Cliffs, N.J.: Prentice-Hall, 1973.

Hickok, Ralph. *A Who's Who of Sports Champions: Their Stories and Records.* Boston: Houghton Mifflin, 1995.

Huff, Richard M. *Stock Car Racing: Running with NASCAR's Best.* Chicago: Bonus Books, 2000.

Sowers, Richard. *Stock Car Racing Lives.* Phoenix, Ariz.: David Bull, 2000.

Yarborough, Cale with William Neeley. *Cale: The Hazardous Life and Times of America's Greatest Stock Car Driver.* New York: Times Books, 1986.

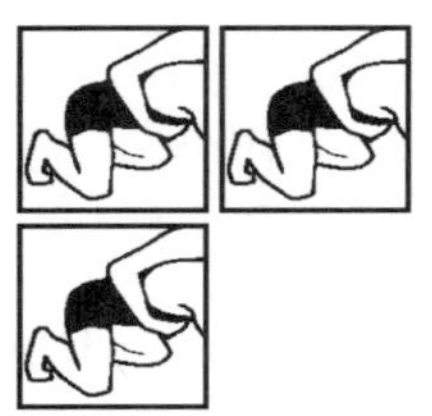

IVAN YARYGIN

Sport: Wrestling

Born: November 7, 1948
Vst'-Kamzas, Siberia, U.S.S.R. (now Russia)

Early Life

Ivan Yarygin was born on November 7, 1948, in Vst'-Kamzas, Siberia, the Soviet Union. He was the seventh child in a family where children were expected to help with chores such as cutting grass for the cattle, chopping wood, and working in the blacksmith's shop. His family eventually settled in Sizaya, Siberia.

Ivan attended a school three kilometers from his home. In the summer, he covered the distance by running or biking, and in the winter, on cross-country skis. By the age of fifteen, he was of exceptional size and strength. He stayed late after school to play his favorite sport, soccer. He played goalie, and it seemed to be impossible to score a goal against him.

After completing school, Ivan went to Abakan to attend a training school for truck drivers. He also played on the school's soccer team. It was at one of these games that the coach of the local wrestling school, Vladimir Charkov, saw him and thought that this big strapping man would be a natural on the wrestling mat. He would eventually grow to 6 feet 4 inches and 220 pounds.

The Road to Excellence

It took a while for Charkov to overcome Ivan's great love for soccer. Through his persistence, he finally induced Ivan to attend a wrestling school. At an early meet, Ivan took last place because of a lack of technical skills, became discouraged, and returned to his hometown without saying goodbye.

Charkov tracked him down, going first to his home, and then driving a motorboat 170 kilometers up a river to a remote point in the Russian taiga, where Ivan and his father had gone for logging. Ivan's father, despite some misgivings, did not stand in the way, and Ivan agreed to return to Abakan. After three months of intensive training, Ivan went to Krasnoyarsk for a meet. It was there that coach Dmitry G. Mindiashvili of the Krasnoyarsk wrestling school saw him for the first time and immediately thought that he would go far.

After a few more wrestling meets, Ivan moved to Krasnoyarsk to be coached by Mindiashvili at Charkov's suggestion. He lived at the coach's

AP/Wide World Photos

Russia's Ivan Yarygin tries to pin Canada's Harry Gerris during the 1972 Olympic Games.

MAJOR CHAMPIONSHIPS

Year	Competition	Weight Class	Place
1972	Olympic Games	100 kilograms	Gold
1973	World Championships	100 kilograms	1st
	World Cup	100 kilograms	1st
1976	Olympic Games	100 kilograms	Gold
	World Cup	100 kilograms	1st

house and held down a job as a metal worker at a tire factory. Ivan's training was interrupted by the required term of military service in which, based on his athletic promise, he was assigned to a company for athletes. He also married Natasha, and a daughter, Annuska, was born in 1971, and a son, Sergei, in 1973.

The Emerging Champion

As the 1972 Munich Olympics approached, Ivan was selected for the freestyle team and began to achieve great success at major national and international meets. Ivan won the gold medal (100 kg weight division) at the 1972 Olympics held in Munich, Germany. The Mongolian Hollogin Baianmunh, finished second and Josef Csatari of Hungary finished third. At the 1973 World Cup in Toledo, Ohio, Ivan again won the gold medal, with Josef Csatari finishing second and Demitar Nekov of Bulgaria, third.

A slump, beginning in 1974 and continuing through 1975, cast doubts on Ivan's wrestling career as well as his possibility of making the 1976 Olympic team. He fell ill at the 1974 European Championships in Madrid, losing to the East German Harold Buttner in the final. He could not shake his sickness and finished fifth in the Nationals at Uf. After recovering but still only taking third at the Spartacade of Soviet People in Kiev in 1975, he thought of retiring, but renewed his mind and body as he had done at other critical parts of his life by spending time in the wilderness. This time he spent a whole month hunting in the dense forests of the Russian taiga.

Ivan regained his form for the 1976 World Cup in Toledo, winning all his matches. He then emerged from the European Championships in Leningrad with a ferocious new vigor. At the Montreal, Canada, Olympics, in 1976, he ironically drew Harold Buttner, the rival to whom he had lost not just once, but twice, for his first match. He defeated Buttner and went on to win the gold medal. Russ Hellickson of the United States finished second and Demo Kostov of Bulgaria, third.

Continuing the Story

Ivan became a champion in spite of the fact that he started wrestling at the rather advanced age of seventeen. Ivan continued training for the 1980 Moscow Olympics. He made a final massive personal effort in 1979, but to his great disappointment, failed to make the team. The next generation of gold medal winners was already beginning to take over.

In 1980, Ivan became the Soviet national team coach at thirty-three years old. In the course of the 1980's, his wrestlers achieved great success despite the ever-increasing quality of the international competition. It was not unusual for every one of Ivan's wrestlers to win a medal at the various World Championships. The majority would usually win gold medals.

Ivan has made Krasnoyarsk his hometown. A new wrestling tournament is now held annually in Krasnoyarsk in Ivan's honor, called the Yarygin International.

Summary

Ivan Yarygin was a great two-time Olympic wrestling champion and an outstanding Soviet

INTERNATIONAL COACHING RECORD

Year	Competition	Team Place
1982	World Championships	1st
1983	World Championships	1st
1985	World Championships	1st
1986	Goodwill Games	1st
	World Championships	1st
1987	World Championships	1st
1988	Olympic Games	1st
1989	World Championships	1st
1990	Goodwill Games	2d
	World Championships	1st
1991	World Championships	1st

national wrestling team coach. Twice during his wrestling career, Ivan conquered a loss of self-confidence resulting from wrestling defeats to become a champion. During the 1980's, his wrestlers dominated the various World Wrestling Championships.

Carl F. Rothfuss
Walter R. Schneider

Additional Sources:

Levinson, David, and Karen Christenson, eds. *Encyclopedia of World Sport: From Ancient Times to Present.* Santa Barbara, Calif.: ABC-CLIO, 1996.

Schapp, Dick. *An Illustrated History of the Olympics.* New York: Alfred A. Knopf, 1975.

Wallechinsky, David. *The Complete Book of the Olympics.* Boston: Little, Brown and Company, 1991.

LEV YASHIN

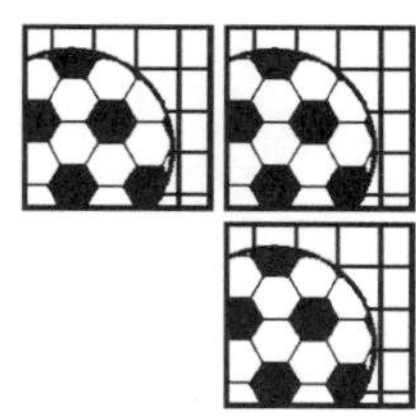

Sport: Soccer

Born: October 22, 1929
Moscow, U.S.S.R. (now Russia)
Died: March 21, 1990
Moscow, U.S.S.R. (now Russia)

Early Life

Lev Ivanovich Yashin was born in Moscow, the capital of Russia and of the Soviet Union, on October 22, 1929. His parents were factory workers, and the family lived in an older-style wooden communal apartment building on the outskirts of the city.

Archive Photos

Lev Yashin tends goal for the Moscow Dynamo.

When Lev was a boy during the 1930's, life in Moscow was difficult. Most people were poor, and many were persecuted by the Soviet government. One of the few pleasant distractions from such concerns was participation in sports. As a boy, Lev began his sports career by playing hockey with friends on a frozen pond near his home. From an early age, he earned a reputation as an uncanny keeper of the goal. Working with very limited equipment—often no mask, no body padding, and no glove—Lev would do whatever he had to do to stop the puck from getting past him. He was of ordinary size, but with long legs and arms, and he was extremely wiry and quick. Because it seemed that he could always get an arm out to intercept any shot at the goal, his friends began to call him "Octopus."

The Road to Excellence

The distractive powers of sport proved even more important in Lev's life during World War II. In late 1941, Nazi armies had almost reached Moscow. They were repelled only by the most concerted effort, involving not only the military, in which Lev was still too young to serve, but the civilian population of the city as well. Lev's parents were heroically engaged in the effort. Lev himself spent all his nonschool time playing on hockey teams sponsored by the Communist Youth Organization in order to entertain the struggling populace. In the summer, Lev and his friends would turn their athletic skills to soccer, the sport in which he was to achieve lasting renown. By the time the war ended, Lev had become one of the most highly regarded goalkeepers in the Moscow youth leagues.

HONORS AND AWARDS

1954-55, 1957, 1959, 1963	Soviet League champion
1956	Olympic Gold Medal
1960	European Championship champion
1960, 1965-66	Soviet Goalkeeper of the Year
1963	European Player of the Year (Ballon d'Or)

MILESTONES

78 international appearances for the Soviet Union

When Lev finished high school in 1946, he went to work in the factories, as his parents had before him. He stayed active in soccer, however, by playing with a number of Moscow soccer clubs. He then played on a Soviet army team while completing his two-year military service obligation. Returning to civilian life in 1950, Lev was accepted as a backup goalkeeper for one of Moscow's most popular world-class soccer teams, Dynamo. The remainder of Lev's career was associated with this great team.

In 1954, Dynamo's regular goalkeeper became ill, and Lev was called upon to play in important games. His performance assured his permanence in the position. His athletic dives to stop opposing kicks thrilled the huge crowds that attended Dynamo's games with teams from other cities and with Moscow rivals Torpedo and Spartak. In the next two years, no team scored more than two goals against Lev's defense, and Dynamo was the national champion in 1954 and again in 1955. Lev's popularity soared as did his standard of living in Soviet society. He was chosen to represent his country in the 1956 Olympic Games in Melbourne, Australia, and thanks largely to his sparkling defense, his team was victorious.

The Emerging Champion

In 1956, Soviet Premier Nikita Khrushchev initiated a thaw in the restrictions on art, dance, music, and literature, a development that occasioned much hope among the Soviet people. With such a spirit of hope, Lev Yashin became a member of the Communist Party in 1957. It is also possible that Party membership played a part in his selection for the Soviet Union's World Cup team in 1958 and for the Soviet team that won the first European Championship in 1960. Lev's play in these tournaments was extraordinary, establishing him internationally as soccer's leading goalkeeper.

In the remaining years of the 1960's, Lev was active on two more Soviet Olympic teams (1960 in Rome and 1964 in Tokyo) and on two more World Cup teams. With the exception of a disconcertingly mediocre series of games in South America during the 1962 World Cup competition, Lev was continually remarkable in defense of the goal. Soccer analysts attributed his success to his amazingly quick reactions and his fine sense of anticipation of the action, but Lev himself often said he was simply willing to sacrifice more of himself physically than others were in order to stop the ball.

Yet despite such apparent sacrifice, Lev was rarely injured. Perhaps his luck can be attributed to his schedule of almost constant play: daily practice, weekly games with Dynamo, and a record seventy-eight games with the Soviet national team. In 1963, he was the first goalkeeper named European Player of the Year and received soccer's coveted Ballon d'Or Award.

Continuing the Story

As he approached forty years of age, Lev gradually began to take more of a coaching rather than a playing role with Dynamo. He also served as adviser to the Soviet national team. In 1972, he announced his official retirement as a soccer player. In that year also he was graduated from the prestigious Moscow Higher Party School, a leadership training institution of the Communist Party's Central Committee. He then became an administrator of the Dynamo team and a member of the Soviet Union's State Council on Physical Culture and Sports. In his eighteen years in this capacity, he was central in the Soviet Union's eventual formal recognition of the professional status of its athletes. Before his death of stomach cancer on March 21, 1990, he approved a measure to give state pensions to world-class athletes whose competitive youth deprived them of other life skills in a society that gave them little reward except renown.

In June of 1990, two months after Lev's death in Moscow, the yearly Lev Yashin Invitational Soccer Tournament was instituted in his honor in Anchorage, Alaska.

Summary

Lev Yashin's remarkable saves as a soccer goalie helped change the popular view of that position from that of a peripheral function to one of central importance to a team's success. Fans of soccer all over the world still recognize a "Yashin style" of play for goalkeepers. After his days as a player were over, Lev continued to devote his life to the advancement of sport.

Lee B. Croft

Additional Sources:

Brown, Gene, ed. *The New York Times Encyclopedia of Sports.* 15 vols. New York: Arno Press, 1979-1980.

Cantor, Andrés, and Daniel Arcucci. *Goooal!: A Celebration of Soccer.* New York: Simon & Schuster, 1996.

Henshaw, Richard. *The Encyclopedia of World Soccer.* Washington, D.C.: New Republic Books, 1979.

CARL YASTRZEMSKI

Sport: Baseball

Born: August 22, 1939
Southampton, New York

Early Life

Carl Michael Yastrzemski was born on August 22, 1939, in Southampton, New York, the son of Hedwig and Carl Yastrzemski. He grew up in the small Long Island town of Bridgehampton, a Polish community of potato farmers. His parents' families, the Skoniecznys and the Yastrzemskis, worked the potato fields together.

Although his parents expected him to contribute to the family farm, Carl practiced his hitting and pitching almost every day from the age of six. His family encouraged his early interest in the sport; indeed, his father was a talented player who had to pass up an opportunity to sign minor league contracts with the Brooklyn Dodgers and the St. Louis Cardinals because they offered so little money. Instead, Carl's father managed and played on a local team, the Bridgehampton White Eagles. Carl got his first taste of organized baseball when he became the team's batboy.

The Road to Excellence

Carl was the best player at all the levels of baseball he attempted, in Little League, Babe Ruth baseball, and high school and semiprofessional teams. At fifteen, he joined his father on the White Eagles. While his father played second base and batted fourth, Carl played shortstop and batted third. Throughout his early playing days, Carl's father remained the major influence in his life as a teacher and an inspiration to do his best.

AP/Wide World Photos

Carl Yastrzemski in 1967.

Carl was not only an outstanding hitter and pitcher but also a talented basketball player. After considering several offers, Carl accepted a scholarship to play baseball and basketball at the University of Notre Dame in 1957.

Following a disappointing year when he was not permitted to train with the varsity teams, Carl signed a professional contract with the Boston Red Sox. He had tryouts and offers from many teams, including the Detroit Tigers, the Los Angeles Dodgers, the Philadelphia Phillies, and his childhood favorite, the New York Yankees. His father, however, believed Carl would have greater success hitting at Boston's Fenway Park, so the nineteen-year-old became a member of the Red Sox in 1958.

Carl enjoyed two spectacular years in the minor leagues. In 1959 at Raleigh, North Carolina, he batted a Carolina League-leading .377. The following sea-

STATISTICS

Season	GP	AB	Hits	2B	3B	HR	Runs	RBI	BA	SA
1961	148	583	155	31	6	11	71	80	.266	.396
1962	160	646	191	43	6	19	99	94	.296	.469
1963	151	570	**183**	**40**	3	14	91	68	**.321**	.475
1964	151	567	164	29	9	15	77	67	.289	.451
1965	133	494	154	**45**	3	20	78	72	.312	**.536**
1966	160	594	165	**39**	2	16	81	80	.278	.431
1967	161	579	**189**	31	4	**44**	**112**	**121**	**.326**	**.622**
1968	157	539	162	32	2	23	90	74	**.301**	.495
1969	162	603	154	28	2	40	96	111	.255	.507
1970	161	566	186	29	0	40	**125**	102	.329	**.592**
1971	148	508	129	21	2	15	75	70	.254	.392
1972	125	455	120	18	2	12	70	68	.264	.391
1973	152	540	160	25	4	19	82	95	.296	.463
1974	148	515	155	25	2	15	**93**	79	.301	.445
1975	149	543	146	30	1	14	91	60	.269	.405
1976	155	546	146	23	2	21	71	102	.267	.432
1977	150	558	165	27	3	28	99	102	.296	.505
1978	144	523	145	21	2	17	70	81	.277	.423
1979	147	518	140	28	1	21	69	87	.270	.450
1980	105	364	100	21	1	15	49	50	.275	.462
1981	91	338	83	14	1	7	36	53	.246	.355
1982	131	459	126	22	1	16	53	72	.275	.431
1983	119	380	101	24	0	10	38	56	.266	.408
Totals	3,308	11,988	3,419	646	59	452	1,816	1,844	.285	.462

Notes: Boldface indicates statistical leader. GP = games played; AB = at bats; 2B = doubles; 3B = triples; HR = home runs; RBI = runs batted in; BA = batting average; SA = slugging average

son, Carl barely missed winning the International League batting title with Minneapolis, hitting .339.

The Emerging Champion

In 1960, Boston all-time great Ted Williams retired, and the Red Sox decided that Carl was ready to replace him in left field. His rookie season in 1961, however, was difficult. Fans and reporters expected him to replace a baseball legend, and he felt pressured to succeed immediately. Despite the difficulties, Carl batted a strong .266 and established himself as a master in handling balls hit off the famous "Green Monster" left field fence in Fenway Park.

Although he continued to improve as a hitter and won the American League batting title in 1963, Carl and Boston fans remained disappointed with the team's repeated failures. During his first six seasons, the team never finished higher than sixth in the standings. Determined to improve himself and the team, Carl spent the winter after the 1966 season working with Hungarian Olympic coach Gene Berde.

Joining the trimmer, stronger Yastrzemski on the 1967 Red Sox were emerging stars Jim Lonborg, George Scott, Reggie Smith, and Tony Conigliaro. They became the "Impossible Dream" team for Boston fans. Baseball experts picked them to finish ninth, but the Red Sox won the American League pennant on the last day of the season. Carl, as he would do throughout his career in tough situations, was almost perfect at the plate in the last two games. He had base hits in his last six at bats.

The Red Sox could not complete the "Dream." They lost the World Series to the St. Louis Cardinals in seven games. The loss did nothing to diminish the significance of Carl's year. He became the last player in either league to win the Triple Crown. Carl led the league in batting with a .326 average, in home runs with 44, and in runs batted in with 121. The baseball writers named him the league's most valuable player, *Sports Illustrated* named him Sportsman of the Year, and the Associated Press chose him as Male Athlete of the Year.

Continuing the Story

Carl would have other great seasons. In 1970, he hit .329 with 40 home runs and 102 runs bat-

MAJOR LEAGUE RECORDS

Most intentional walks, 190
Highest fielding percentage, season, 1.000 (1977) (record shared)

AMERICAN LEAGUE RECORDS

Most consecutive seasons playing 100 games, 20

HONORS AND AWARDS

Year(s)	Honor
1963, 1965-79, 1982-83	American League All-Star Team
1963, 1965, 1967	*Sporting News* American League All-Star Team
1963, 1965, 1967-69, 1971, 1977	American League Gold Glove Award
1963, 1965, 1967-69, 1971, 1977	*Sporting News* American League All-Star Fielding Team
1967	American League most valuable player *Sporting News* Major League Player of the Year *Sporting News* American League Player of the Year Associated Press Male Athlete of the Year *Sports Illustrated* Sportsman of the Year Hickok Belt
1970	All-Star Game most valuable player
1989	Inducted into National Baseball Hall of Fame Uniform number 8 retired by Boston Red Sox

ted in. He also played in another World Series in 1975, against the Cincinnati Reds. Again, the Red Sox came up a game short, losing four games to three.

In 1978, the Red Sox tied the New York Yankees for first place in the American League Eastern Division and played them in a one-game playoff. Although Carl hit a first-inning home run, the Red Sox lost 5 to 4.

In big games, Carl always hit well. His regular season career batting average was a respectable .285, but in playoffs, the World Series, and All-Star contests, he hit over .340. His achievements were all the more remarkable because he was not a gifted, all-around athlete. Carl made up for his lack of speed and strength by his almost obsessive determination to improve every facet of his game.

Carl's commitment attracted widespread attention after the first game of the 1967 World Series. Having gone hitless against St. Louis Cardinal ace pitcher Bob Gibson, Carl took extra batting practice. Sports reporters thought it remarkable, but Carl had taken extra hitting after games on several occasions.

Always intense, Carl constantly worked on his batting stance and swing. He wanted to be perfect and was willing to work many hours a day to adjust his approach to hitting.

Carl played his last major league season in 1983.

Summary

Carl Yastrzemski considered himself to be a craftsman. He endured because he always sought to improve his skills. He led by example, playing with injuries and sacrificing his personal statistics for the good of the team. Fans respected him as much for his drive to excel as for his achievements.

Larry Gragg

Additional Sources:

Ryan, Bob. "1967—Carl Yastrzemski Wins A.L. Triple Crown." *Baseball Digest* 59, no. 11 (2000).

Yastrzemski, Carl, and Gerald Eskenazi. *Yaz: Baseball, the Wall, and Me.* New York: Doubleday, 1990.

Yastrzemski, Carl, with Al Hirschberg. *Yaz.* New York: Viking, 1968.

CY YOUNG

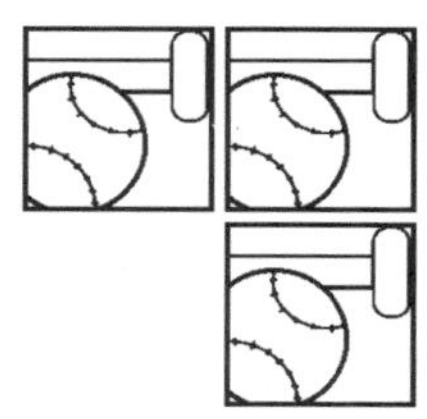

Sport: Baseball

Born: March 29, 1867
Gilmore, Ohio
Died: November 4, 1955
Peoli, Ohio

Early Life

Cy Young was born Denton True Young on March 29, 1867, in Gilmore, Ohio. His middle name was said to be the last name of a soldier who had saved his father's life in the Civil War.

When "Dent," as he was called in his youth, was growing up, much of America was agricultural. In fact, it was on these wide open fields that the game of baseball began to be played. When Dent was old enough, he began working as a farmer and a rail-splitter in Gilmore, which was rich Ohio farmland. It was also in these fields that he first played baseball with the other farmhands.

The Road to Excellence

By 1890, Dent was a strapping 6-foot 2-inch, 210-pound twenty-three-year-old. His fast pitch was the talk of the county, and Dent wanted to use it in organized competition. At first, his parents felt he should remain a farmer, but reluctantly, they gave in, and Dent got a tryout with the Canton, Ohio, team in the Tri-State League.

It was at that tryout that Denton Young was first called "Cy," although there are at least two different stories behind the nickname. According to one story, Dent reported to the Canton team in clothes so ill-fitting that he was at once branded as a hick fresh off the farm and given the name "Cyrus." According to another story, Young's warm-up pitches were so powerful that they left the fence of the ballpark looking like a cyclone had hit it, and a sportswriter began calling the new pitcher "Cyclone" Young.

In midseason, Cy pitched a no-hitter against McKeesport, striking out 18 batters. News of the game spread to the Cleveland Spiders of the National League, which paid Canton $250 for the big right-hander.

National Baseball Library, Cooperstown, New York

The Emerging Champion

In his first major league game, Cy pitched a 3-hitter for Cleveland against Chicago. It was a promise of things to come.

Cy Young blossomed in 1892, winning thirty-six games while losing just twelve. He also led the league in earned run average (ERA), allowing only 1.93 earned runs per game. Over the next eight seasons, Cy won an incredible 237 games, winning better than 30 games a season three times—astronomical numbers for a pitcher in any era.

Baseball was a different game in the late 1800's from what it is today, and Cy had to adapt to a number of rule changes in the middle of those amazing eight years. For instance, in 1892, pitchers threw off a flat dirt surface 50 feet from the catcher; the following season, the distance was increased to the modern-day 60 feet, 6 inches, and a pitchers "mound" was allowed.

Another change that came to baseball during this time was the start of a new major league, the American League, in 1901. In 1899, the Spiders had moved from Cleveland to St. Louis. The Boston team, soon to become known as the Red Sox, lured Cy, now thirty-four years old, to the new league by offering more money and a cooler climate. In 1901, Cy led the league in victories, strikeouts, and ERA.

In 1903, Boston finished first in the American League and Pittsburgh was the top team in the National League. At the end of the season, the two teams agreed to play each other to see which was better, and the World Series was born. Cy, who had won the most games of any American League pitcher in each of the last three years, started three games in that best-of-nine Series, losing the first game but winning the fifth and seventh to help Boston win the Series, 5-3.

The following year, some believed Cy, at age thirty-seven, was washed up. Rube Waddell, the twenty-eight-year-old pitching star for the Philadelphia Athletics, promised he would win when the two pitched against each other. The matchup occurred on May 5, 1904, and Cy pitched a perfect game, retiring all 27 batters who faced him, as Boston won, 3-0. Cy pitched three no-hitters during his major league career, the last on June 8, 1908, at age forty-one.

STATISTICS

Season	*GP*	*GS*	*CG*	*IP*	*HA*	*BB*	*SO*	*W*	*L*	*S*	*ShO*	*ERA*
1890	17	16	16	147.2	145	30	39	9	6	0	0	3.47
1891	55	46	43	423.2	431	140	147	27	22	2	0	2.85
1892	53	49	48	453.0	363	118	168	36	12	0	**9**	1.93
1893	53	46	42	422.2	442	103	102	34	16	1	1	3.36
1894	52	47	44	408.2	488	106	101	26	21	1	2	3.94
1895	47	40	36	369.2	363	75	121	**35**	10	0	**4**	3.24
1896	51	46	42	414.1	477	62	**140**	28	15	**3**	**5**	3.24
1897	46	38	35	335.0	391	49	88	21	19	0	2	3.79
1898	46	41	40	377.2	387	41	101	25	13	0	1	2.53
1899	44	42	40	369.1	368	44	111	26	16	1	4	2.58
1900	41	35	32	321.1	337	36	115	19	19	0	4	3.00
1901	43	41	38	371.1	324	37	**158**	**33**	10	0	5	**1.62**
1902	45	43	41	384.2	350	53	160	**32**	11	0	3	2.15
1903	40	35	34	341.2	294	37	176	**28**	9	2	**7**	2.08
1904	43	41	40	380.0	327	29	200	26	16	1	**10**	1.97
1905	38	33	32	320.2	248	30	210	18	19	0	4	1.82
1906	39	34	28	287.2	288	25	140	13	21	2	0	3.19
1907	43	37	33	343.1	286	51	147	21	15	1	6	1.99
1908	36	33	30	299.0	230	37	150	21	11	2	3	1.26
1909	35	34	30	295.0	267	59	109	19	15	0	3	2.26
1910	21	20	14	163.1	149	27	58	7	10	0	1	2.53
1911	18	18	12	126.1	137	28	55	7	9	0	2	3.78
Totals	906	815	**750**	**7,356.0**	7,092	1,217	2,796	**511**	**315**	16	76	2.63

Notes: Boldface indicates statistical leader. GP = games played; GS = games started; CG = complete games; IP = innings pitched; HA = hits allowed; BB = bases on balls (walks); SO = strikeouts; W = wins; L = losses; S = saves; ShO = shutouts; ERA = earned run average

Cy credited his longevity to farming. He continued to swing an ax as a rail-splitter in the off-season and said his farm chores strengthened his back and legs.

In 1909, Cy was sold to Cleveland of the American League, where he played two seasons, winning nineteen games his first year there. In 1911, he went to Boston of the National League and retired at the end of the season after twenty-two years in the major leagues.

MAJOR LEAGUE RECORDS

Most victories, 511
Most losses, 315
Most innings pitched, 7,356
Most complete games, 750

HONORS AND AWARDS

1937 Inducted into National Baseball Hall of Fame
After each season, and in honor of Cy Young, the Baseball Writers Association of America presents the Cy Young Award to the best pitcher from each league. This award was originated in 1956.

Continuing the Story

During Cy Young's career, relief pitchers were not commonly used; the pitcher who started the game usually finished it. Thus, many of Cy's records will most likely never be broken. He finished his career with more wins (511) and more losses (315) than any pitcher in baseball. He also completed more games (750) and pitched more innings (7,356) than any pitcher ever has and probably ever will. He won at least twenty games in each of sixteen seasons, and won thirty or more in five of those years.

After he retired, Cy went back to Ohio and to farming. When his wife died in 1933, he sold his land and went to live with friends who were also farmers. In 1937, Cy was elected to the National Baseball Hall of Fame.

Cy still loved baseball and was a frequent visitor to the ballpark at Cleveland Indians games until his death on November 4, 1955, in Peoli, Ohio, at the age of eighty-eight. The next year, baseball began giving out the Cy Young Award for pitching excellence at the end of every season.

Summary

Cy Young grew up with baseball and became one of its legends. He came to the sport when both baseball and he were fresh off the farm and became one of its star players who helped make the game popular with fans.

Cy was baseball's most indestructible pitcher; he threw more innings and won more games than anyone else. His records are so secure that the name baseball chose for the prize given annually to the best pitchers in both leagues is the Cy Young Award.

W. P. Edelstein

Additional Sources:

Browning, Reed. *Cy Young: A Baseball Life.* Amherst: University of Massachusetts Press, 2000.

Macht, Norman L. *Cy Young.* New York: Chelsea House, 1992.

Porter, David L., ed. *Biographical Dictionary of American Sports: Baseball.* Westport, Conn.: Greenwood Press, 1987.

Veccione, Joseph J., ed. *The New York Times Book of Sports Legends.* New York: Times Books, 1991.

SHEILA YOUNG

Sport: Speed skating and Cycling

Born: October 14, 1950
Birmingham, Michigan

Early Life

Sheila Young was born on October 14, 1950, in Birmingham, Michigan, not far from the city of Detroit, where the Young family eventually moved. Her parents were both sports-minded; they were champion cyclists and outstanding skaters.

Sheila's father, Clair, founded the Wolverine Sports Club, devoted to developing talent in skating and cycling. Sports, he said, "kept my family together [and were] a terrific influence in bringing up my kids." Sheila got her early training at the Sports Club.

Tony Duffy/Allsport

She was given her first pair of skates when she was two. She waited till she was nine, though, before she started skating. "I wasn't that interested in skating when I was little," Sheila remembered. "The family would take off; I didn't want to go."

Once Sheila decided to try skating, the speed fascinated her. "I love the feeling of going fast," she explained.

The Road to Excellence

Sheila was soon winning junior skating championships. A top-notch coach, Peter Schotting, was impressed with Sheila's stamina and style. He sparked her competitive spirit when he told her, "Train with me for a year, and you'll be a world champion."

Schotting's training plan included four hours of skating a day, as well as cycling, jogging, sprinting, and dry-land exercises such as the duckwalk, an exercise performed with the upper body parallel to the ground and the legs bent at the knees.

While training, Sheila had little time for the activities that normally absorb teenagers. Her best friends became the girls she competed with on weekends, who lived in other towns.

While still in high school, Sheila finished second in the U.S. National Outdoor Speed Skating Championships. She placed first in 1970 and again in 1971, and won membership on the 1972 U.S. Olympic team.

The Emerging Champion

At the 1972 Winter Olympic Games in Japan, Sheila missed winning the bronze medal in the 500-meter race by a mere .08 of a second. The very next year, however, was a triumphant one for her. She captured the world championship in speed skating and set a world record for the 500-meter sprint at 41.8 seconds. Skating was not her only claim to fame, though; six months later, Sheila became the first American woman in fifty years to win the world track cycling championship. To everyone's surprise, she overcame the titleholder, as well as injury; with startling determination, she raced the final match with cuts on her arms and legs, along with a deep gash in her scalp. With that victory, Sheila had become the first woman to achieve world-class titles in two different sports in the same year.

In 1974, a fall in the sprint races deprived Sheila of a second world championship in speed skating. Demonstrating her never-say-die spirit, she rallied and regained her title the following year.

The 1976 Olympics in Austria brought Sheila the distinction of being the first U.S. athlete to take home three medals from the Winter Games. Capturing the gold in the 500-meter race, she also won the silver in the 1,500-meter course and the bronze in the 1,000-meter. After her third medal, she was surprised by a congratulatory call from President Gerald Ford.

Sheila's sleek outfit for the Olympic meet also won her a nickname: "The American Frogman." Wearing tight clothes helped her to cut down wind resistance and thus increase speed. "I never wear socks," Sheila explained. "With my bare toes, I have a better rapport with my skates. I can really feel them."

As a bonus, Sheila broke Anne Henning's Olympic record with a time of 42.76 seconds in the 500-meter race. Later that year, she set a world record in the 500-meter course at 40.68 seconds.

MAJOR CHAMPIONSHIPS

Year	Competition	Event	Place
1972	Olympic Games	500 meters	4th
1973, 1975-76	World Speed Skating Championships	—	1st
1973, 1976	World Track Cycling Championships	—	1st
1976	Olympic Games	500 meters 1,000 meters 1,500 meters	Gold Bronze Silver

HONORS, AWARDS, AND RECORDS

1973	Set a world record in the 500-meter sprint (41.8 seconds)
1976	Set a world record in the 500-meter sprint, 42.76 seconds, then lowered that mark to 40.68 seconds the same year
1991	Inducted into Amateur Skating Union Speedskating Hall of Fame

A month after Sheila's big Olympic win, she captured her third world sprint speed skating title. That year, 1976, she also won the world title in track cycling, as she beat the favorite in the finals. For the second time, Sheila's daring and determination had made her a double world champion.

Continuing the Story

After her Olympic and world championships in 1976, Sheila announced her retirement from amateur sports competition. That summer, she married Jim Ochowicz, an Olympic cyclist.

In 1978, Sheila and Jim moved to Lake Placid, New York, where Sheila went to work for the U.S. Olympic Organizing Committee. She kept in shape cycling and jogging, and in the fall of 1980 she began training seriously again for a chance to compete in the 1984 Winter Olympics in Yugoslavia.

Sheila had set herself a daunting challenge. "You have to have a certain explosiveness in competition," she acknowledged. "It's hard to get that back."

At the age of thirty and the mother of a two-year-old, Sheila placed first in the U.S. sprint championships for a spot on the national team. Sheila's comeback, however, provoked controversy. Her amateur status was in question: Since her Olympic victory, she had been paid $12,500 to appear in ads for Kellogg's Corn Flakes, as well as in the television programs *Superstars* and *Challenge of the Sexes*.

Determined to compete again, Sheila agreed to turn over her earnings in commercial sports to the International Speedskating Association. She was willing to make the sacrifice for the chance to strive again athletically. "My sports have been terrific to me," she explained.

Although Sheila failed to make the 1984 Olympic team, her place in skating history was secure. In May, 1991, she was inducted into the Amateur Skating Union's Speedskating Hall of Fame.

Summary

Every athlete needs to stay in shape. Sheila Young turned this necessity into an opportunity. She translated her cycling practice into a shot at achievement and acclaim. Twice capturing world championships in more than one sport in the same year, breaking records as she blazed trails, Sheila illuminated the peaks the human body and spirit, working in exquisite harmony, can reach.

Amy Adelstein

Additional Sources:

Hickok, Ralph. "Young, Sheila G." In *A Who's Who of Sports Champions.* Boston: Houghton Mifflin, 1995.

Soucheray, Joe. *Sheila Young.* Mankato, Minn.: Creative Education, 1977.

Woolum, Janet. "Sheila Young." In *Outstanding Women Athletes: Who They Are and How They Influenced Sports in America.* Phoenix, Ariz.: Oryx Press, 1998.

STEVE YOUNG

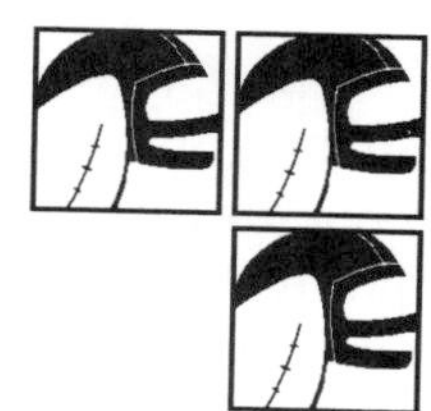

Sport: Football

Born: October 11, 1961
Salt Lake City, Utah

Early Life

Steve Young was born on October 11, 1961, in Salt Lake City, Utah, to the family of LeGrande Young, a corporate lawyer. When Steve, the oldest of five children, was eight years old, the Young family moved to Greenwich, Connecticut.

Though his family never pushed him toward sports, Steve was a naturally gifted athlete who quarterbacked his Greenwich High football team with an attack that relied on his prowess as a runner rather than a passer.

AP/Wide World Photos

Quarterback Steve Young assists coaches in a 1995 game.

The Road to Excellence

In selecting a college, Steve decided on Brigham Young University (BYU) because of his family's Mormon background. Steve is the great-great-great grandson of Brigham Young, the Mormon leader for whom the school is named.

Steve's football fortunes at first seemed bleak, given BYU's reliance on a wide-open, professional-style passing offense. When he first arrived at BYU in 1979, Steve was the school's eighth-rated quarterback, far behind starter Jim McMahon, who was also destined for an outstanding professional career. Discouraged at the prospect of being switched to defense, the raw left-hander was on the verge of quitting football until BYU quarterback coach Ted Tollner, sensing Steve's intensity and capacity to learn, convinced BYU head coach LaVell Edwards to stick with the youngster as a possible successor to McMahon.

Tollner's hunch paid off. In 1983, the quarterback's senior year at BYU, Steve completed 71.3 percent of his passes, a National Collegiate Athletic Association (NCAA) single-season record, and threw for 3,902 yards and 33 touchdowns. For his efforts, Steve was selected a consensus All-American and was runner-up for the Heisman Trophy, behind Nebraska's Mike Rozier.

The Emerging Champion

Steve's outstanding career at BYU made him a top professional prospect. After his graduation from BYU in 1984, Steve's talents were sought by both the established National Football League (NFL) and its upstart rival, the United States Football League (USFL). In a heated bidding war, the USFL's Los Angeles Express offered Steve the then-richest deal in football history, a deferred contract worth $37.2 million through the year 2027. The Express also offered Steve an opportunity to start immediately and to work with veteran head coach Sid Gillman.

With Gillman's wide-open offense, Steve put up big numbers for the Express, including a game in which he became the first professional quarterback to run for 100 yards and pass for 300 yards in the same game. The USFL soon collapsed, however, and Steve became the first selection of the NFL's 1985 supplemental draft. His new team was the Tampa Bay Buccaneers, a floundering NFL expansion team. During the 1985 and 1986 seasons, the beleaguered young quarterback ran for his life with a dreary team that managed only four wins. In 1987, though, Steve's prospects soared with his trade to the San Francisco 49ers, the Super Bowl champions of 1981 and 1984. Here was a chance to work under Bill Walsh, the 49er's brilliant head coach, while understudying Joe Montana, arguably the game's greatest quarterback.

Continuing the Story

Steve's trade was viewed as part of a master plan to continue San Francisco's dominance by ensuring a smooth transition in quarterbacking chores. Though a logical plot, it did not take account of Montana's durability and almost mythic status among 49ers fans. Steve performed well as Joe's backup, rescuing the 49ers whenever the brittle and oft-injured Montana was knocked out by injuries. In the late 1980's, however, it was the miraculous Montana, the battered but dazzling veteran, who kept returning from the sick bay for yet one more charge.

In 1988, Montana was out for much of the season, and Steve, who was still learning Walsh's complex offensive system, managed only a 6-5 start. When Montana returned to the lineup, the classy veteran reeled off a string of victories culminating in yet another Super Bowl triumph. San Francisco won yet another Super Bowl after the 1989 season. Although Steve again made mighty contributions as Montana's fireman, it was Montana who captained the 49ers to the winner's circle.

With Montana's injuries becoming more frequent and severe, a Montana-Young quarterback controversy heated up, fanned by the Bay Area media. When Montana missed most of the 1991 and 1992 seasons with injuries, San Franciscans joked that "Young isn't Montana, and, unfortunately, Montana isn't young."

In 1991, when the 10-6 49ers failed to make the playoffs, disconsolate fans failed to appreciate the fact that Young was the NFL leader in passing efficiency. In 1992, Young led the 49ers to the National Football Conference (NFC) championship game, but the team lost to the Dallas Cowboys, 30-20. Young, though, had an outstanding season, rushing for 537 yards and passing for 3,465; his quarterback efficiency rating was the fifth-best in NFL history. For his superlative ac-

STATISTICS

Season	GP	PA	PC	Pct.	Yds.	Avg.	TD	Int.
1985	5	138	72	52.2	935	6.78	3	8
1986	14	363	195	53.7	2,282	6.29	8	13
1987	8	69	37	53.6	570	8.26	10	0
1988	11	101	54	53.5	680	6.73	3	3
1989	10	92	64	69.6	1,001	10.88	8	3
1990	6	62	38	61.3	427	6.89	2	0
1991	11	279	180	64.5	2,517	**9.02**	17	8
1992	16	402	268	**66.7**	3,465	**8.62**	**25**	7
1993	16	**462**	314	68.0	4,023	**8.71**	**29**	16
1994	16	461	324	**70.3**	3,969	8.61	**35**	10
1995	11	447	299	66.9	3,200	7.16	20	11
1996	12	316	214	67.7	2,410	7.63	14	6
1997	15	356	241	67.7	3,029	8.51	19	6
1998	15	**517**	**322**	62.3	**4,170**	8.07	**36**	12
1999	3	84	45	53.6	446	5.31	3	4
Totals	169	4,149	2,667	64.2	33,124	8.00	232	107

Notes: Boldface indicates statistical leader. GP = games played; PA = passes attempted; PC = passes completed; Pct. = percent completed; Yds. = yards; Avg. = average yards per attempt; TD = touchdowns; Int. = interceptions

HONORS AND AWARDS	
1983	College All-American O'Brien National Quarterback Award
1992-98	NFL Pro Bowl Team
1992	Associated Press NFL Player of the Year Bert Bell Trophy Professional Football Writers Association NFL Player of the Year *Pro Football Weekly* NFL Offensive Player of the Year *Sporting News* NFL Player of the Year United Press International NFC Offensive Player of the Year
1994	Super Bowl most valuable player NFL Player of the Year

complishments, Steve was named the NFL's most valuable player.

In the spring of 1993, the 49ers' ongoing quarterback controversy was solved when Montana signed with the Kansas City Chiefs. In turn, the 49ers signed Steve to a five-year agreement worth $26.5 million, at the time the richest contract in NFL history. Finally out from under Montana's long shadow, Steve again led San Francisco to the NFC championship game. Though the 49ers fell one game short of the Super Bowl when they lost again to the Cowboys, Steve had clearly emerged as one of the NFL's top quarterbacks—and, perhaps more important, had firmly established himself as number one on his own team.

In 1994 Steve was named NFL Player of the Year, was again selected for the Pro Bowl, set an NFL single-season record with his 112.8 quarterback rating, and was named Super Bowl most valuable player when he led the 49ers to victory over the San Diego Chargers. In 1995, 1996, and 1997 Steve was again selected to the Pro Bowl. In 1998 he tied the NFL record with his sixth league passer ratio title, reached the 3,000-yard mark in passing for the fifth time in his career, and was selected to the Pro Bowl for the seventh consecutive year. At the end of the 1999 season, Steve announced his retirement from professional football.

Even before his retirement Steve was involved in a number of different activities. He has served as an international spokesperson for the Children's Miracle Network, which has raised more than $1 billion worldwide for children's hospitals. He also became a member of the board of directors of American Indian Services. In 1996 he published a children's book, *Forever Young*, geared toward fourth-graders.

Summary

Steve Young had to endure a long wait before he got the chance to show his talent as the undisputed leader of a top NFL team. When he did, he made it clear that he needed to take a back seat to no one in the game.

Chuck Berg

Additional Sources:

Boch, Hall. *Steve Young*. New York: Chelsea House, 1996.

Christopher, Matt. *In the Huddle with . . . Steve Young*. Boston: Little, Brown, 1996.

Knapp, Ron. *Steve Young: Star Quarterback*. Springfield, N.J.: Enslow Publishers, 1996.

Morgan, Terri, and Shmuel Thaler. *Steve Young: Complete Quarterback*. Minneapolis: Lerner Publishing, 1996.

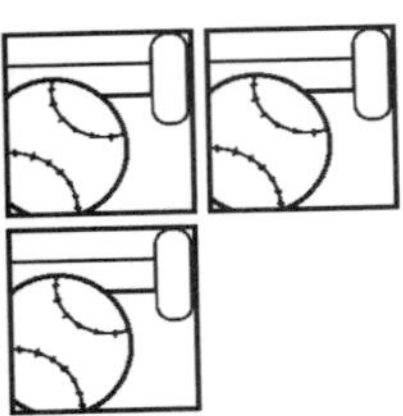

ROBIN YOUNT

Sport: Baseball

Born: September 16, 1955
Danville, Illinois

Early Life

Robin R. Yount was born on September 16, 1955, in Danville, Illinois. When he was a year old, his family moved to Los Angeles, California, where his father, Phil, took a job as an aerospace engineer. Robin grew up in an affluent community in the San Fernando Valley.

Courtesy of the Milwaukee Brewers Baseball Club

Even though neither of Robin's parents was athletic, Robin and his two older brothers played sports constantly. The Younts' huge back yard served as a baseball diamond, football field, and golf course. Robin exhibited a natural athletic ability almost from the beginning. He started playing golf at the age of nine and began hitting holes-in-one four years later, even though he had had no formal training. At age eleven, he advanced to the more dangerous sport of motorcycle racing and began winning trophies in motocross events at age thirteen. Phil Yount explained Robin's success by pointing out that Robin first made up his mind to do something and then he did it.

The Road to Excellence

Robin could have become a professional golfer if baseball had not captured his interest. When he was in junior high school, he completely demolished (through overuse) a batting cage that his father had built for him. In high school, he was named the outstanding baseball player in Los Angeles. His role model during these years was his older brother, Larry, who had a brief career as a pitcher for the Houston Astros.

Robin began playing baseball professionally in his senior year, when he was picked in the first round of the 1973 draft by the Milwaukee Brewers. He spent only one year in the Class A New York-Pennsylvania League before the Brewers chose him as their starting shortstop. The manager, Del Crandall, was so impressed with Robin's fielding and hitting ability that he completely disregarded the fact that Robin was only eighteen years old.

STATISTICS

Season	GP	AB	Hits	2B	3B	HR	Runs	RBI	BA	SA
1974	107	344	86	14	5	3	48	26	.250	.346
1975	147	558	149	28	2	8	67	52	.267	.367
1976	161	638	161	19	3	2	59	54	.252	.301
1977	154	605	174	34	4	4	66	49	.288	.377
1978	127	502	147	23	9	9	66	71	.293	.428
1979	149	577	154	26	5	8	72	51	.267	.371
1980	143	611	179	**49**	10	23	121	87	.293	.519
1981	96	377	103	15	5	10	50	49	.273	.419
1982	156	635	210	**46**	12	29	129	114	.331	**.578**
1983	149	578	178	42	**10**	17	102	80	.308	.503
1984	160	624	186	27	7	16	105	80	.298	.441
1985	122	466	129	26	3	15	76	68	.277	.442
1986	140	522	163	31	7	9	82	46	.312	.450
1987	158	635	198	25	9	21	99	103	.312	.479
1988	162	621	190	38	**11**	13	92	91	.306	.465
1989	160	614	195	38	9	21	101	103	.318	.511
1990	158	587	145	17	5	17	98	77	.247	.380
1991	130	503	131	20	4	10	66	77	.260	.376
1992	150	557	147	40	3	8	71	77	.264	.390
1993	127	454	117	25	3	8	62	51	.258	.379
Totals	2,856	11,008	3,142	583	126	251	1,632	1,406	.285	.430

Notes: Boldface indicates statistical leader. GP = games played; AB = at bats; 2B = doubles; 3B = triples; HR = home runs; RBI = runs batted in; BA = batting average; SA = slugging average

Robin was still developing as a player during his first four seasons with the Brewers. He batted better than .250 each year and had a strong .288 in 1977. Although he made 44 errors in 1975, he had clearly improved as a fielder three years later.

In 1978, Robin was faced with the most crucial decision of the year. Dissatisfied with his hitting and stricken with tendinitis in his ankles, he was not sure that he wanted to sign his contract in the spring. He was also tempted to move to California so that he could be with his girlfriend, Michelle. It was only when she agreed to marry him later that year that he decided to continue his baseball career.

The Emerging Champion

Robin has always enjoyed playing baseball, but he admits that he had the most fun in the major leagues in 1982. In that year, he hit 29 home runs and won the American League most valuable player award. Robin also helped the Brewers win the division title by hitting two home runs in the fourth game of the playoffs. Even though the Brewers eventually lost the World Series to the St. Louis Cardinals, Robin has fond memories of the spirit of camaraderie that held the team together. To Robin, who has always been a team player, the 1982 Brewers was the ideal team.

After the 1982 World Series, Robin was well on his way to becoming one of the best all-around shortstops in baseball. In 1984 and 1985, however, he suffered two shoulder injuries that almost ended his career. Robin returned to baseball after surgery but was told that his arm would never be strong enough for him to play shortstop again. Robin resisted the temptation to quit playing entirely; instead, he moved to center field where he became a superb defensive player. He learned to live with the harsh reality of never being able to play his favorite position again.

Despite his injuries, Robin still believed that he could be a productive batter, and he proved that he was in 1987. By the end of August, he was batting .312 and had driven in 103 runs. He was the first Brewers player to have 100 runs batted in since 1983. He also hit 21 homers, his highest total since 1982. He left no doubt at the end of what became one of his best seasons that he was still physically able to do the job.

Continuing the Story

Miraculously, Robin has managed to remain humble even as he continues to break records well into his thirties. After hitting his 945th RBI

HONORS AND AWARDS

1980, 1982-83	American League All-Star Team
1982, 1989	American League most valuable player
1982	*Sporting News* Major League Player of the Year American League Gold Glove Award Seagram's Seven Crowns of Sports Award
1999	Inducted into National Baseball Hall of Fame Uniform number 19 retired by Milwaukee Brewers

and breaking the Brewers' old record of 944, Robin could not understand why his teammates wanted him to keep the ball. He was more pleased with giving the Brewers a needed run than with setting a record. Then, in 1989, he became the fifth-youngest player to reach 2,500 hits. Robin told reporters afterward that the hit was important because it drove in two runs. Personal statistics are not important to Robin. He has been able to get that many hits, he says, only because he has played a long time.

Although Robin has tended to downplay his own accomplishments, the baseball world has not. In 1989, he was once again selected as the most valuable player (MVP) in the American League, joining Stan Musial and Hank Greenberg as the only players ever to win the MVP award at two positions. In typical fashion, though, Robin insisted that the award also belonged to his teammates, the Brewers organization, and his fans.

As Robin approached the end of his career, his primary goal was not to break any more records or win any more awards. His fondest wish was to play in the World Series once more before he retired. In fact, in 1989, he filed for free agency and would have left the Brewers if he thought his chances of playing in another World Series would improve by going elsewhere. Meanwhile, Robin was content to occupy himself by giving 100 percent to his game and riding dirt bikes in his spare time.

In 1992, Robin became the seventeenth player in baseball history to pass the 3,000-hit mark. He played one more season with the Brewers in 1993 and then retired. Robin's relentless dedication to baseball culminated in his induction into baseball's Hall of Fame in 1999.

Summary

Robin Yount proved to be one of the Milwaukee Brewers' most consistent performers after making the club as an eighteen-year-old shortstop in 1973. Former Brewers manager Tom Trebelhorn wanted every one of his players to be like Robin. Unlike many players, who long to be standouts, Robin was happy to be a team player and was concerned foremost with living up to his own high standards of performance. He may not have been as entertaining as some of the more flamboyant players, but he was indispensable to his team.

Alan Brown

Additional Sources:

Adelson, Bruce. "Robin Yount: He Has a Hall of Fame Approach to Baseball." *Baseball Digest* 51, no. 9 (1992).

Haudricourt, Tom. "Robin Yount Was Admired for His Work Ethic." *Baseball Digest* 58, no. 11 (1999).

Libman, Gary. *Robin Yount.* Mankato, Minn.: Creative Education, 1983.

Van Dyck, Dave. "Robin Yount: A Future Hall of Famer Bows out Quietly." *Baseball Digest* 53, no. 5 (1994).

STEVE YZERMAN

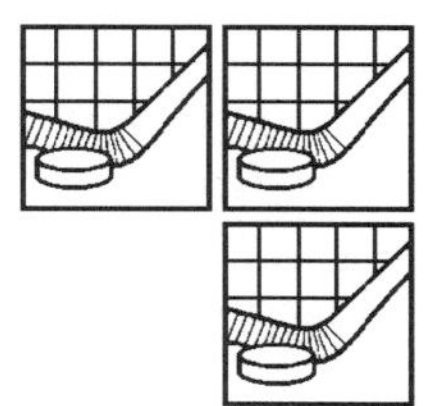

Sport: Ice hockey

Born: May 9, 1965
Cranbrook, British Columbia, Canada

Early Life

Steven Yzerman was the third child of five born to Ron Yzerman, an employee of the Canadian government's health and welfare department, in a suburb of Vancouver. Steve was nine years old when his family moved across the country to Nepean, a suburb of Ottawa. When Ron was offered a chance to coach a hockey team, he agreed on the condition that the league waive its age requirement to let Steve play a year early; thus his son got a head start on most other players.

Steve's childhood idols included Gordie Howe, Mike Bossy, and Bryan Trottier. He chose to wear number 19 because that was Trottier's number for the New York Islanders. At age eleven, Steve began five years of playing for the Junior A Nepean Raiders. At sixteen, he went into major juniors, playing for the Peterborough Petes of the Ontario Hockey League (OHL).

The Road to Excellence

As of 1983, the Detroit Red Wings had missed the playoffs in eleven of their past thirteen seasons. Steve was relatively small, and his numbers with the Petes were not outstanding, but the Red Wings saw something they liked and made him their first draft pick, fourth overall. A few months after his eighteenth birthday, he went straight to the National Hockey League (NHL) without spending any time in the professional minor leagues.

The Red Wings hoped he would help them get back onto a winning track, and he did. In Steve's first game, he scored a goal and an assist against the Winnipeg Jets. Just three weeks later, he scored his first game-winning goal, against the Buffalo Sabres, with only 22 seconds left in overtime. That season, he became the youngest player to play in the NHL All-Star game. By season's end, he had played in all eighty games and scored 39 goals and 48 assists. He was runner-up

AP/Wide World Photos

Steve Yzerman of the Red Wings in October, 2000.

STATISTICS

Season	GP	G	Ast.	Pts.	PIM
1983-84	80	39	48	87	33
1984-85	80	30	59	89	58
1985-86	51	14	28	42	16
1986-87	80	31	59	90	43
1987-88	64	50	52	102	44
1988-89	80	65	90	155	61
1989-90	79	62	65	127	79
1990-91	80	51	57	108	34
1991-92	79	45	58	103	64
1992-93	84	58	79	137	44
1993-94	58	24	58	82	36
1994-95	47	12	26	38	40
1995-96	80	36	59	95	64
1996-97	81	22	63	85	78
1997-98	75	24	45	69	46
1998-99	80	29	45	74	42
1999-00	78	35	44	79	34
2000-01	54	18	34	52	18
Totals	1,310	645	969	1,614	834

Notes: GP = games played; G = goals; Ast. = assists; Pts. = points; PIM = penalties in minutes

for the Calder Trophy, awarded to the league's best rookie.

The Emerging Champion

By the end of 1986, he was named captain of the Red Wings, and coach Jacques Demers had nicknamed him "Stevie Wonder." At age twenty-one, Steve was the youngest captain in the NHL. His captaincy set an NHL record for its longevity.

In the 1987-1988 season, Steve was scoring prolifically. February found him past the 100-point mark, among the league leaders in scoring. In the same game in which he scored his fiftieth goal of the season, he suffered a serious knee injury. "It went from the happiest moment of my life to the scariest," he said later. He missed the rest of the season but made it back onto the ice in time for the playoffs, leading the Red Wings to the conference finals, where they lost to the Edmonton Oilers.

Continuing the Story

Steve's scoring numbers declined in the 1993-1994 season, due to changes in the way the game is played in the NHL and changes in the Red Wings organization in particular. Scotty Bowman came to coach the Red Wings in 1993 and encouraged Steve's transition toward defensive hockey. Steve enjoyed six straight 45-goal, 100-point seasons, with 58 goals and 137 points in 1992-1993, but the new coach's system meant that even the forwards had to have a hand in the defense, so Steve's goal totals plummeted. He continued to be the team leader, though, changing his style to match Bowman's system and bring his team up in the standings. "It's amazing how it's changed," Steve said six years later. "Not only do opponents play differently against you, but your own team plays more defensively. The game isn't as wide open."

In February, 1997, Steve played in his one thousandth regular-season game. He had scored more than 1,300 career points by then. A few months later, at age thirty-two, he won his first Stanley Cup ring. The Red Wings beat the St. Louis Blues in six games, swept the Anaheim Mighty Ducks in four games, then took the Colorado Avalanche in six games. In the finals against the Philadelphia Flyers, the Red Wings swept the series to win the team's first Stanley Cup since 1955.

The next season, 1997-1998, had its ups and downs for Steve. He was on the Olympic team but returned from the Games without a medal. His NHL scoring totals were down, he had not been in the All-Star game, and he was left out of *The*

RECORDS AND MILESTONES

1984	Became youngest player to appear in an NHL All-Star game Set Detroit Red Wings records for most goals (39) and most points (87) in a rookie season
1989	Set Detroit records for goals (65), assists (90), and points (155) in a single season
1993	Recorded 1,000th point; he reached this height in 737 games—just eight players have recorded 1,000 points in fewer games
1998	Recorded 1,400th career point
1996	Scored 500th goal
2000	Set record as longest-serving captain for 12 years with the Red Wings

Hockey News's top fifty. It ended well, though, as the Red Wings swept the Washington Capitals to win their second consecutive Stanley Cup.

Summary

On the ice, Steve Yzerman was known for having great balance and quick feet. Off the ice, his modesty, kindness to his fans, and caring toward those less fortunate stood out. In renaming the Nepean Sportsplex the Steve Yzerman Arena, his hometown cited not only his "stellar achievements as a professional hockey player," but also his active support of charitable causes.

Among the diminishing number of players who have spent their entire career with one NHL team, he set league records for serving the most years as captain, scoring the most goals, and scoring the most points. In 1989, his fellow NHL players voted to honor him with the Lester B. Pearson Award as the league's outstanding player. Also in 1988, he won the Conn Smythe trophy as most valuable player of the playoffs.

J. Edmund Rush

HONORS AND AWARDS

1984	*Sporting News* NHL Rookie of the Year NHL All-Rookie Team
1984, 1988-1993, 1997	NHL All-Star Team
1989	Lester B. Pearson Award *Hockey News* NHL Player of the Year
1998	Conn Smythe Trophy, as most valuable player of the playoffs Team Canada member
1999-2000	Frank J. Selke Trophy

Additional Sources:

Deacon, James. "The Modest Man from Motown." *Maclean's*, February 7, 2000, 46-47.

Dryden, Steve, ed. *The Top 100 NHL Players of All Time.* Toronto: The Hockey News, 1999.

Farber, Michael. "Follow the Leader." *Sports Illustrated*, May 17, 1999, 58-60.

Hollander, Zander, ed. *The Complete Encyclopedia of Hockey.* 4th ed. Detroit, Mich.: Visible Ink Press, 1993.

BABE DIDRIKSON ZAHARIAS

Sport: Track and field, Golf, Basketball, and Softball

Born: June 26, 1914
Port Arthur, Texas
Died: September 27, 1956
Galveston, Texas

Early Life

Mildred Ella Didriksen was born on June 26, 1914, in Port Arthur, Texas. She was the sixth of seven children born to Ole and Hannah Didriksen (she changed the "e" in her parents' Norwegian name to an "o" later in her life).

Mildred's parents were poor but strict. Her father had worked as a cabinetmaker on ships at sea while in Norway but now made a meager wage as a furniture refinisher. Her mother was a housekeepr and took in washing and ironing from neighbors to help the family survive. The family moved to Beaumont, Texas, when Mildred was three years old.

Courtesy of Amateur Athletic Foundation of Los Angeles

Mildred's father was a fitness fanatic. He required each of his seven children to exercise and to play sports. Her mother had been one of the best skaters and skiers while in Norway. Mildred's father built playing fields and exercise equipment of all kinds for his children. With four brothers and two sisters plus many neighbor boys and girls in the yard at all times, Mildred learned to compete against boys in numerous sports.

Some reports claim Mildred was called Babe because she was the baby of the family. Others say it was because she hit a baseball like Babe Ruth.

The Road to Excellence

Through her years at Magnolia Grade School, Babe competed on even terms with the boys. She also played the harmonica for three years on a weekly radio show and was an excellent student. She won first prize at the Texas State Fair for a dress she made.

While at South Junior High School, Babe decided she wanted to become the greatest athlete who ever lived, and while playing basketball for Beaumont Senior High School, she made All-City and All-State.

MAJOR CHAMPIONSHIPS

Year	Competition	Event	Place	Time/Distance/ Height
1930	National AAU Outdoor Championships	Javelin throw	1st	133′ 3″
1931	National AAU Outdoor Championships	80-meter hurdles	1st	12.1
		Long jump	1st	17′ 11½″
1932	Olympic Games	80-meter hurdles	Gold	11.7 OR
		High jump	Silver	5′ 5″
		Javelin throw	Gold	143′ 4″ WR, OR
	National AAU Outdoor Championships	80-meter hurdles	1st	12.1
		High jump	1st	5′ 3¾″ WR
		Shot put	1st	39′ 6¼″
		Javelin throw	1st	139′ 3″ WR

Notes: OR = Olympic Record; WR = World Record

Colonel Melvin J. McCombs, the coach of one of the best women's amateur basketball teams in the nation, convinced Babe to play for his team, the Golden Cyclone Athletic Club, which was sponsored by the Employers Casualty Company of Dallas. The Employers Casualty Company hired Babe as a typist and to play on their basketball, track, and other sport teams. She became an All-American in basketball while leading the team to the national championship. She also won medals in ice skating and swimming.

The Emerging Champion

In the spring of 1929, Babe talked Mr. McCombs into starting an Employers Casualty Company track team because she wanted to try track. She threw herself into practice in the afternoon and again at night. She wanted to try every event. In 1929, track competitors were allowed to enter as many events as they desired. By this time Babe had grown into a 5-foot 4-inch, 105-pound, well-muscled athlete.

Babe won eight of the ten events she entered in the Texas State Track and Field Championships. In 1929, she broke the world javelin record with a throw of 133 feet 3¼ inches. In 1930, her baseball throw of 296 feet set a women's record.

In 1932, Babe became the best female track and field athlete in the United States and then in the world. The National Championships and the 1932 Olympic trials were combined into one meet held at Northwestern University.

Babe entered the meet as a one-woman team representing the Employers Casualty Company. She entered eight of the ten events, winning five and placing in two others. She set world records in the hurdles (12.1 seconds) and the javelin (139 feet 3 inches) and tied Jean Shiley with a world-record high jump (5 feet 3¾ inches). Babe scored 30 points and won the meet by herself, beating the second-place team (twenty-two women representing the Illinois Athletic Club) by 8 points.

Continuing the Story

A few weeks later, Babe was off to Los Angeles for the 1932 Olympics. In 1932, women's Olympic track and field consisted of only five individual events. Each person was allowed to enter no more than three of the events. Babe chose the javelin, the hurdles, and the high jump.

Babe's first throw in the javelin was a world record (143 feet 4 inches). In the 80-meter hurdles, she broke a second world record (11.7 seconds). In the high jump, she tied for first place at a world record height (5 feet 5 inches). A judge disqualified her from first place, contending that her head passed over the bar before the rest of her body, which was not allowed in those days. She settled for the silver medal.

Babe's great dedication to practice, determination to succeed, and athletic ability resulted in her winning her first of six Associated Press Female Athlete of the Year Awards. She had become a star.

MAJOR CHAMPIONSHIP VICTORIES (GOLF)

1940, 1944-45, 1950	Western Open
1946	U.S. Women's Amateur
1947	British Open Amateur Championship
1947, 1950, 1952	Titleholders Championship
1948, 1950, 1954	U.S. Women's Open

OTHER NOTABLE VICTORIES

1940, 1944, 1951-52	Texas Open
1948, 1950-51, 1954	All-American Open
1948, 1951	World Championship
1949	Eastern Open
1953	Babe Zaharias Open

HONORS, AWARDS, AND RECORDS

1929	Set world record in the javelin throw (133' 3¼")
1932, 1945-47, 1950, 1954	Associated Press Female Athlete of the Year
1950	Associated Press Outstanding Female Athlete of the Half-Century
1951	Inducted into LPGA Hall of Fame
1954	GWAA Ben Hogan Award GWAA Richardson Award LPGA Vare Trophy
1957	USGA Bobby Jones Award
1974	Inducted into National Track and Field Hall of Fame Inducted into PGA/World Golf Hall of Fame
1977	Inducted into PGA Golf Hall of Fame
1980	Inducted into Sudafed International Women's Sports Hall of Fame Pioneer
1983	Inducted into U.S. Olympic Hall of Fame

MILESTONES

LPGA leading moneywinner four consecutive years (1948-51)

First American golfer to capture the British Open Amateur Championship since it began in 1893

Garnered thirty-one victories out of one hundred twenty-eight LPGA events during her eight-year career

Founder and Charter Member of the LPGA

Named "Golfer of the Decade" (1948-57) by *Golf* magazine

At first, Babe tried many different activities, attempting to cash in on her Olympic fame. She is said to be the greatest woman athlete of all time. She toured the country with Babe Didrikson's All-Americans, a basketball team. She was the only woman on the team. She traveled with the bearded House of David baseball team. She was a pitcher and the only woman on the team. She pitched in a major league baseball exhibition game during spring training.

After the Olympics, Babe decided to become a golfer. She practiced and practiced, sometimes for as many as ten hours a day. Often her hands would bleed, and she would bandage them and keep practicing. She was a long hitter from the beginning, often out-driving men players. Her short game needed a great amount of practice, and she was determined to become a good player around the greens and to control her tee shots.

Babe entered her first golf tournament in 1934, shooting a 77 to win first place. During the next twenty years, Babe would win fifty-three major golf tournaments all over the world. Between 1946 and 1947, she won seventeen straight titles, a record no one else has come close to before or since.

In 1938, Babe met and married a wrestler, George Zaharias. He gave up his career to help Babe continue her golf career.

Babe was voted the Outstanding Female Athlete of the first half of the twentieth century. In 1953, she learned that she had cancer. Through several cancer operations, she fought the disease valiantly. She won the United States Women's Open and four other golf tournaments in 1954. After a courageous fight, Babe Didrikson Zaharias died of cancer on September 27, 1956.

Summary

Babe Didrikson Zaharias became an outstanding athlete because of her intense desire to be the best woman athlete in the world. Her parents gave her a good foundation and, using her great competitive desire, she achieved her goal.

Walter R. Schneider

Additional Sources:

Cayleff, Susan E. *Babe: The Life and Legend of Babe Didrikson Zaharias.* Urbana: University of Illinois Press, 1995.

Johnson, William O., and Nancy P. Williamson. *Whatta-Gal!: The Babe Didrikson Story.* Boston: Little, Brown, 1977.

Miller, Helen M. *Striving to Be Champion: Babe Didrikson Zaharias.* Chicago: Kingston House, 1961.

Tricard, Louise M. *American Women's Track and Field: A History, 1895 Through 1980.* Jefferson, N.C.: McFarland, 1996.

Zaharias, Babe Didrikson, and Harry T. Paxton. *This Life I've Led: My Autobiography.* New York: A. S. Barnes, 1955.

EMIL ZATOPEK

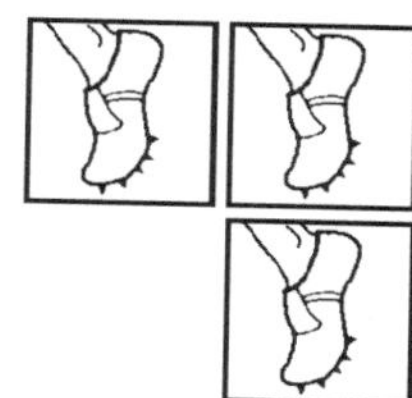

Sport: Track and field (long-distance runs and marathon)

Born: September 19, 1922
Koprivnice, Moravia, Czechoslovakia
(now Czech Republic)
Died: November 21, 2000
Prague, Czech Republic

Early Life

Emil Zatopek was born on September 19, 1922, in Koprivnice, Moravia, in the northern part of Czechoslovakia. His father worked as a carpenter in a local shoe factory. The family was so poor that when Emil was a child, his father would scold him for running because running wore his shoes out faster than if he walked.

AP/Wide World Photos

Emil Zatopek crossing the marathon finish line to take the gold at the 1952 Olympics.

After graduating from secondary school, Emil considered applying to the teacher's training school, but the competition to get in was so great that he felt he would not be accepted. Therefore, he went to work in a shoe factory in Zlin and attended night classes at the Zlin Technical School. Originally, his job was to attach rubber soles to tennis shoes, but he was transferred to another department in which he ground silica to dust. This left him covered with the dust, which he would breathe into his lungs. Aware that this could be harmful to his health, Emil applied for a transfer, but it was denied.

The Road to Excellence

At first, Emil did not wish to be a runner. When his employer entered him in a race sponsored by the shoe factory, Emil tried to hide in the library to avoid having to run. When he was spotted and forced to race, he remembered his father's motto: "A thing worth doing, is worth doing well." Therefore, he did his best and came in second in the race. This display of talent so impressed his employer that he was entered in other races and his career as a runner was under way.

After the Germans were driven out of Czechoslovakia at the end of World War II, Emil enlisted in the Czech army and entered officer training school. While the other cadets were relaxing during their free time, Emil used every available moment to train. He was so determined not to miss his workouts that he would run in the rain or through snow if necessary; sometimes it became dark before he finished and he had to use a flashlight to see the path he used for running.

Emil was one of the pioneers of a new type of training for distance running: interval training.

MAJOR CHAMPIONSHIPS

Year	Competition	Event	Place	Time
1948	Olympic Games	5,000 meters	Silver	14:17.8
		10,000 meters	Gold	29:59.6 OR
1950	European Championships	5,000 meters	1st	14:03.0
		10,000 meters	1st	29:12.0
1952	Olympic Games	5,000 meters	Gold	14:06.6 OR
		10,000 meters	Gold	29:17.0 OR
		Marathon	Gold	2:23:03.2 WR, OR
1954	European Championships	5,000 meters	3d	—
		10,000 meters	1st	28:58.0

Notes: OR = Olympic Record; WR = World Record

Instead of doing long, slow runs in practice to demonstrate that he could complete the distance of the race, he did repeats of very short distances at the pace he hoped to run in the race or faster.

The Emerging Champion

Although his time in the 10,000 meters was less than 2 seconds off the world record, Emil was not the favorite in that event at the 1948 Olympic Games. Because he lived in a country behind the Iron Curtain, his times were not widely known outside Czechoslovakia. His first-place finish in the 10,000-meter race in an Olympic record time at the 1948 Olympics changed that. When he followed this with a close second-place finish in the 5,000-meter race, he was recognized as one of the world's best runners.

At the Olympics, Emil met the woman who would become his wife. Dana Ingrova, representing Czechoslovakia, placed seventh in the Olympic women's javelin throw. Less than two months after the Olympic Games concluded, they were married.

Although Emil was the best distance runner in the world by 1952, he did not expect to do well at the 1952 Olympic Games because he had been ill with influenza and had not been able to train properly. During the early stages of the 10,000-meter race, he stayed at the back, far behind the leaders, but when he surged to the front during the second half of the race, he left the other runners far behind and won in the Olympic record time of 29 minutes 17 seconds. In the 5,000 meters, Emil appeared to have been beaten until he put on a determined kick in the last 100 meters, which brought him into first place.

Emil's performance in the marathon was the most amazing of all. He had never run the event, he was tired from having run in two events already, and he had to compete against the world record holder, Jim Peters. During the race, Emil was so uncertain as to what pace he should run that he asked Peters if the pace was too fast. Hoping that Emil would speed up and wear himself out, Peters tried to trick Emil by telling him the pace was too slow. Emil did increase his speed but surprised Peters by maintaining the faster pace until the finish. In his first attempt at the distance, Emil not only won an Olympic gold medal, he also set an Olympic record of 2 hours, 23 minutes, and 3 seconds.

Continuing the Story

In the years immediately following the 1952 Olympics, Emil continued to dominate distance running, setting world records at every distance from 3 miles to the marathon. Younger runners, however, imitated his training methods and by 1954 were beginning to defeat Emil, especially at shorter distances. Although he had set a world record in the 5,000 meters earlier in the year in 13 minutes 57.2 seconds, Emil only managed third place in the 1954 European Championships. After having been first in the world at

RECORDS

World record at 5,000 meters in 1954 (13:57.2)

Five world records at 10,000 meters: 1949 (29:28.2), 1949 (29:21.2), 1950 (29:02.6), 1953 (29:01.6), and 1954 (28:54.2)

World record at 6 miles in 1954 (27:59.2)

Set 18 world records ranging from 5,000 meters to 30,000 meters

National champion 8 times at 5,000 meters and twice at 10,000 meters

HONORS AND AWARDS

1949 World Trophy

10,000 meters for seven years, he was ranked only fourth in 1955.

Emil responded to his decline by training even harder. He ran as many as ninety repeats of his 400-meter runs in a day. He even tried to strengthen his leg muscles by running with his wife, Dana, on his shoulders. This plan proved disastrous, as he developed a hernia and could not run for several months. Yet the incident was typical of Emil's willingness to experiment with new training methods in order to improve himself.

Summary

Emil Zatopek was famous for his awkward, ungainly running style. Yet by training harder than his opponents and by using the new interval method of training, he became one of the greatest distance runners of all time.

Harold L. Smith

Additional Sources:

"Emil Zatopek: The Indefatigable Czech." Sports Publishing Online. http://www.sportspublishinginc.com/Titles/The-Sports-100-Online/html/Emil-Zatopek.html. 1999.

Henderson, Joe. "Hero of the Half-Century." *Runner's World* 35 (January, 2000): 14.

Kozík, Frantisek. *Zatopek, the Marathon Victor.* Translated by Jean Layton. Prague: Artia, 1954.

Montville, Leigh. "A Winner at the Finish." *Sports Illustrated* 93 (December 4, 2000): R8.

JAN ZELEZNY

Sport: Track and field (javelin throw)

Born: June 16, 1966
Mlada Boleslav, Czechoslovakia (now Czech Republic)

Early Life

Jan Zelezny was born on June 16, 1996, two months prematurely. Long before he began competing in the javelin throw, his family had already established their own dominance in the sport. Jan's father threw competitively, with a career best in 1969 of 68.46 meters. Jan's brother, Petr, set a personal best in 1972 by throwing 72.12 meters, and Jan's mother once held the Czechoslovakian junior record with a throw of 44 meters. As a child, Jan threw wooden javelins carved from tree branches.

Until he was fifteen, Jan played a number of sports, including soccer, ice hockey, and handball. He gave up handball after injuring a goalkeeper during a game. The unfortunate goalie had to be rushed to the hospital with a concussion after Jan hit him in the head with the ball. At that moment Jan decided to follow the family tradition and turned to the javelin.

The Road to Excellence

He displayed a natural ease with the javelin and earned a bronze medal at the 1987 World Championships. His training and talent helped land him a spot on the 1988 Czechoslovakian Olympic Team. Although at 6 feet, 1 inch he was considered too slight to be a threat, he had a powerful arm. He seemed to be assured of the gold medal when his throw set an Olympic record. Unfortunately for Jan, Finland's Tapio Korjus bested his throw by just 16 centimeters. In his first Olympics Jan brought home a bronze medal.

The year following the Olympics was a difficult one for Jan, who had to undergo surgery for a cracked vertebra. Jan's coach, 1976 gold medalist Miklos Nemeth, pushed him back into training once he had recovered from the surgery. Although he was unable to qualify for the 1991 World Championships, Jan slowly attained his

AP/Wide World Photos

Czech Jan Zelezny in the 2000 Olympic javelin competition, which he won.

past form and distance. Nemeth also created a special javelin for Jan, containing a graphite fiber. With this javelin not only did Jan set a new record in Olso, Norway, but he also created a controversy. The Finns contested his win and the new javelin.

The Emerging Champion

Jan arrived in Barcelona for the 1992 Olympics with this controversy hanging over his head. The controversy was not enough, however, to rattle him. He entered the stadium the world record holder and left the gold medalist. That year he also won the World Cup Championships. In 1993 he once again won the World Championships, setting a world record with a distance of 95.44 meters. Jan returned to his training schedule, training south of the equator during several harsh European winters, with his eye on the 1996 Olympic Games in Atlanta. Prior to the Olympics, however, Jan set another world record with a throw of 98.48 meters.

In Atlanta Jan added another Olympic gold medal to his collection. Though in Atlanta for the Olympics, he took the opportunity to attempt another sport. Four days after winning the gold medal, he picked up a baseball rather than a javelin. The Atlanta Braves had asked him to consider changing careers and becoming a pitcher. Jan knew nothing about baseball but decided to give it a try. Pitching Coach Leo Mazzone instructed Jan in the fundamentals. He got a few over the plate, as well as one over the head of the bullpen catcher and one into the stands, scattering the photographers who had come to see him. After about twenty-five minutes of pitching, with some pitches reaching 80 miles per hour, Jan called it a day. Before leaving, however, he used his javelin technique to throw one ball over a wall 275 feet away and out of the park. The Braves offered him an invitation to participate in spring training. Jan turned the offer down, in favor of sticking with the javelin.

After Atlanta he returned to competition. Between 1991 and 1997 he won 91 of the 109 events he entered. In 1998, however, he missed the entire season after injuring his right shoulder. The injury could have ended his career, as the surgery was considered risky, but he underwent the operation and recovered.

MAJOR CHAMPIONSHIPS

Year	Competition	Place	Distance in meters
1987	World Championships	3d	82.20
1988	Olympic Games	Silver	84.12
1992	6th IAAF World Cup in Athletics	1st	88.26
	Olympic Games	Gold	89.66
1993	9th IAAF/Mobil Grand Prix Final	1st	88.28
	World Championships	1st	95.44 WR
1995	IAAF/Mobil Grand Prix Final	1st	92.28
	World Championships	1st	89.58
1996	Olympic Games	Gold	88.16
1997	13th IAAF Grand Prix Final	1st	89.58
	World Championships	9th	82.04
1999	World Championships	3d	87.67
2000	Olympic Games	Gold	90.17

Continuing the Story

As soon as he was properly healed, Jan began training once again. During 1999 he slowly began coming back and late in the year took the bronze medal in the World Championships in Seville, Spain. He was ranked number two in the world that year.

Though he had been expected to retire after his shoulder surgery, in 2000 he again participated in the Olympics. He was unable to train properly due to a rib injury but still wanted to compete. Defying age and injury, Jan achieved the unprecedented when he again won the Olympic gold. Never before had anyone won three Olympic gold medals in the javelin throw.

Summary

A restauranteur, an army colonel, and a father of two, Jan Zelezny did what no other athlete in the javelin throw had been able to accomplish. Initially considered too small to be a world-class javelin thrower, he proved his detractors wrong by setting record after record in his sport. At the same time he battled back against debilitating injuries to become a part of Olympic history by winning three gold medals and one bronze. Once quoted as saying, "In sports, one day you're famous, and the next day you're cursed. You can't think about that," Jan has only been blessed.

Deborah Service

Additional Sources:

"Braves Try Out Olympian." *Orange County Register,* August 8, 1996, p. D6.

Hersh, Philip. "Javelin Thrower Nearly an Immortal." *Chicago Tribune,* September 25, 2000, p. Sports 13.

_______. "Would-Be Pitcher Takes Third Gold in a Row." *Chicago Tribune,* September 24, 2000, p. Sports 15.

Rosenberg, I. J. "Javelin Champ Makes His Pitch to Play Baseball." *The Atlanta Journal-Constitution,* August 8, 1996, p. C1.

KIM ZMESKAL

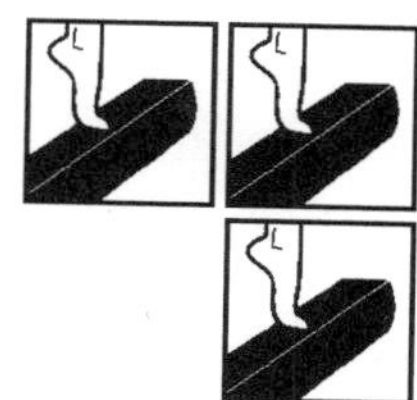

Sport: Gymnastics

Born: February 6, 1976
Houston, Texas

Early Life

Kimberly Lynn Zmeskal was born on February 6, 1976, in Houston, Texas, to David Zmeskal, a welding equipment salesman, and Clarise Zmeskal, a contract analyst. When Kim was six years old, she went with a friend to the Sundance Athletic Club near her home. There, she first experienced the floor exercises, balance beam, vault, and uneven parallel bars that together make up the sport of women's gymnastics.

The club's owner, Romanian immigrant Bela Karolyi, invited Kim to begin learning gymnastics. Karolyi and his wife, Martha, had coached several Olympic champions, including Nadia Comăneci and Mary Lou Retton. Kim was fortunate to have a master coach such as Karolyi in her hometown. Unlike some athletes who leave their families in order to study with prominent trainers, Kim was able to live at home with her parents and younger sister and brother.

The Road to Excellence

Beginning with two classes a week, Kim was among many young girls hoping to be chosen as "Karolyi Kids." This group received special attention as future competitors. Kim was not singled out as part of this elite club until 1988, but she was well known at the gym for her hard work. She developed strong nerves and a competitive spirit, two qualities that helped her climb to the top.

Kim's training schedule gradually increased to two sessions a day, six days a week. In 1989, halfway through the seventh grade, she left school in order to focus all of her energy on competing. Kim spent almost eight hours each day in intense training with Karolyi, who demanded perfection and total concentration from his students.

Kim's dedication led to impressive victories, including the all-around title at the 1989 junior girls championship. (The "all-around" title and gold medal are given to the athlete who displays the best overall performance in the four categories of women's gymnastics.) Victories in Europe followed as well. One year later, the petite four-

AP/Wide World Photos

American Kim Zmeskal performs her balance beam routine at the 1992 Olympics.

teen-year-old won the prestigious McDonald's American Cup. At the 1990 Goodwill Games, she earned two third-place bronze medals. At the United States Championships that same year, Kim surprised audiences and teammates by winning the all-around title among senior, or adult, women. This victory made Kim the youngest U.S. champion ever, male or female.

The Emerging Champion

The following year brought Kim's second national gold medal and title, earned at the 1991 U.S. National Championships. Her determination and spirit were evident at international competitions, as well. At the nine-day 1991 World Gymnastics Championships, in Indianapolis, Indiana, the 4-feet 7-inch, 80-pound athlete received much attention.

As a member of the U.S. women's team, Kim helped to capture its first medal ever in the world championship, a second-place silver. (The gold medal went to the Soviet team, which dominated the sport of gymnastics for many years because of the country's demanding training techniques.) During the team competition, Kim became the only athlete at the meet to receive a perfect score, 10.0, which was awarded to her for a difficult vault. In addition, she received a bronze medal for her floor exercise, an event that combines high-speed tumbling and acrobatics with dance-like grace.

Even more significant, Kim won the prestigious title of 1991 world gymnastics women's all-around champion. She was the first American gymnast ever to receive this top honor at a world competition, earning a total score of 39.848 out of a possible 40. No American woman had ever before finished higher than seventh place.

Kim's victory, however, was controversial. The Soviets complained that Kim won because she was in her own country, not because she was the best athlete. Her routines were criticized for lacking the level of difficulty that other competitors achieved. Despite this ill will, Kim graciously offered her hand to Svetlana Boginskaya, her chief rival from the Soviet team and the previous year's all-around champion. Boginskaya refused to shake.

With characteristic willpower, Kim decided to disprove any speculation that her world title was

MAJOR CHAMPIONSHIPS

Year	Competition	Event	Place	Event	Place
1990	American Cup	All-Around Uneven parallel bars Vault	1st 1st 1st	Balance beam Floor exercise	1st 1st
	U.S. National Championships	All-Around Uneven parallel bars Vault	1st 2d 5th	Balance beam Floor exercise	2d 2d
	Goodwill Games	All-Around Uneven parallel bars	6th 3d	Team Floor exercise	3d 3d
1991	American Cup	All-Around	2d		
	U.S. National Championships	All-Around Floor exercise	1st 1st	Balance beam	2d
	World Championships	All-Around Floor exercise	1st 3d	Team Vault	2d 7th
1992	American Cup	All-Around	1st		
	Olympic Games	All-Around Floor exercise	10th 6th	Team Vault	Bronze 8th
	World Championships	Balance beam	1st	Floor exercise	1st
	U.S. National Championships	All-Around Uneven parallel bars Vault	1st 2d 2d	Balance beam Floor exercise	1st 1st
1998	U.S. Gymnastics Championships	All-Around	1st	Floor exercise	13th
1998	U.S. Gymnastics Championships	Uneven parallel bars Balance beam	22d 4th	Vault	5th

HONORS AND AWARDS

1990	Women's Sports Foundation Up and Coming Award
1991	March of Dimes' Athlete of the Year U.S. Olympic Committee Sportswoman of the Year ABC *Wild World of Sports* Athlete of the Year

accidental. Over the next few months, she increased the difficulty of her routines and faced Boginskaya again at the 1992 World Championships in Paris. There, Kim earned gold medals in the balance beam and floor exercise, the only competitor to win two events. Boginskaya received one medal, a silver in the vault event.

Back at home, Kim again won the national champion title for 1992. Clearly proving her ability to the world and her country, she became the popular favorite for the upcoming Olympic Games in Barcelona, Spain.

As was expected, the Olympic trials earned Kim a place on the U.S. team; however, she did not expect to be outscored by another American gymnast, Shannon Miller. One year younger than Kim, Miller leapt out of the shadows and positioned herself as a challenger for Kim's expected Olympic triumphs.

The Olympic Games were filled with falls and frustrations for Kim. On the first day of the team competition, she lost her balance during her first move and fell off the beam. She recovered quickly, but she was badly shaken. Still, the U.S. team took third place, its first team medal in Olympic competition against the Soviet Union (the Soviets had boycotted the 1984 Olympic Games). The Unified Team, made up of members of the former Soviet Union—including Boginskaya—captured the gold medal in the team competition.

Kim was unable to recover her perfect form for the all-aroud competition and did not place. She stepped out of bounds during her floor exercise, an error for which the judges automatically penalized her. On the apparatus, Kim crash-landed during a vault. She finished in tenth place in the all-around.

Like many athletes, Kim found that Olympic competition was extremely stressful. "I have never been under so much pressure," she said, "but it was a pretty strong effort." Kim's largest reward from the Olympics was learning to live with imperfection, but she vowed never to stop striving for excellence. "I've learned that you don't have to be first place to win," she said.

Continuing the Story

After her disappointment at the Olympics, Kim decided to greatly reduce her training schedule and enjoy a "normal" high school routine. It did not take too long before she realized how much she missed the gym, training, and competition. Two years later, she returned to Karolyi's gym and to top-level competition, but a knee injury dashed her hopes of being a part of the 1996 Olympic squad. She remained an audience favorite while on tour, in exhibitions, and at professional-format meets. She still loved the sport and competition.

In 1998, she moved to Cincinnati and quietly started serious training again, with coach Mary Lee Tracy. Against all odds, she made the national team in 1998. She married her longtime boyfriend, Chris Burdette, in October, 1999. Her hopes of making the 2000 Olympic team, however, were ended when recurring injuries forced her into retirement in January, 2000.

Summary

Kim Zmeskal's determination and competitive spirit led to three national titles and two world titles in women's gymnastics. As a member of the 1992 U.S. Olympic team, she helped win the country's first team medal in an Olympic competition that included the Soviets.

Alecia C. Townsend Beckie

Additional Sources:

Johnson, Anne Janette. "Kim Zmeskal." In *Great Women in Sports.* Detroit, Mich.: Visible Ink Press, 1996.

Quiner, Krista. *Kim Zmeskal: Determination to Win, a Biography.* East Hanover, N.J.: Bradford, 1995.

Smolowe, Jill. "Don't Call Them Pixies!" *Time,* July 27, 1992, 56-60.

Williams, Susan. "On with the Show." *International Gymnast,* March, 2000, 16-20.

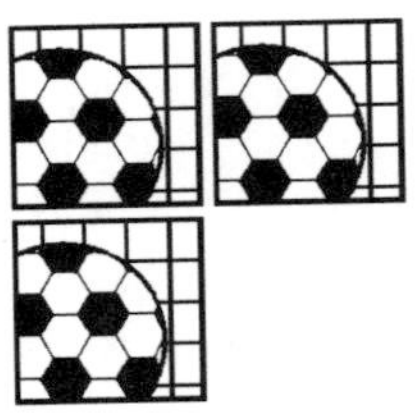

STEVE ZUNGUL

Sport: Soccer

Born: July 28, 1954
Split, Dalmatia, Yugoslavia (now Croatia)

Early Life

Slavisa "Steve" Zungul was born on July 28, 1954, in the coastal city of Split in Dalmatia, Yugoslavia. His father was a semiretired army instructor who was also a commercial fisherman. Steve's talent for soccer was evident when he was very young, and when he was eleven a document was forged to give his age as fifteen so he could play in a youth tournament.

Sometimes Steve would fish with his father on the Adriatic Sea from midnight until five in the morning. At school in the mornings he learned auto mechanics, but nothing could replace his love of soccer, to which he devoted his afternoons and evenings. When he was fifteen, he ran away from home to play in a soccer match. He was gone for a week, to the anger of his family. His mother locked him in his room and told him that there would be no more soccer, but he climbed down two stories on a rope and went to practice.

AP/Wide World Photos

Indoor soccer star Steve Zungul in 1981.

The Road to Excellence

When Steve was seventeen, he was signed by Hajduk Split, a team in Yugoslavia's first division. Yugoslavia was the only Eastern European country that permitted professional soccer, and Steve was soon making his mark in the game. He scored 250 goals in 350 games with Hajduk Split, helping them to three league championships in six years. In 1978, he was named by *France Football* magazine as one of the six best forwards in Europe. At the time he was also the leading scorer for the Yugoslav national team.

In 1978, Steve was due to report for eighteen months of military service. He decided to leave Hajduk Split and travel to the United States. There he met Don Popovic, who was coach of the New York Arrows in the Major Indoor Soccer League (MISL), which was about to commence its first season. Popovic was also a Yugoslav and a former Hajduk Split player, and he offered Steve a chance to play in a few exhibition games. Steve jumped at the opportunity and quickly made an impact in a new type of soccer, very different from the outdoor game to which he was accustomed. The exhibition games led to a longer stay, and at the end of the 1978-1979 season, Steve had scored 43 goals in eighteen games. He was only two goals short of being the league's scoring champion.

The Emerging Champion

Steve's phenomenal goal-scoring feats helped the New York Arrows to dominate the MISL in its early years. Steve led them to four successive championships, in 1979, 1980, 1981, and 1982. He became the MISL's all-time leading scorer, with 419 goals and 222 assists. On one occasion he scored three times in 37 seconds. In 1980, he won the league's Triple Crown for most goals, assists, and points. He did it again in 1981-1982 and 1984-1985.

In addition to his immense natural ability, Steve owed his success to his constant practice and his will to win. He once told a reporter, "I hate to lose; I hate to be beaten at anything. *How* I score goals I cannot tell you; it happens in a dream. It comes from God. But *why* is easy—I will not lose. It hurts me physically to be defeated." Steve was a hard competitor; he knew that he might come in for some rough treatment from the opposition, but when felled he would simply get up and get on with the game. In his goal scoring, he was just as lethal with either foot, and his positioning was almost perfect, which enabled him to take advantage of rebounds. Steve was a thinker, too. He once said to a young player that when a game was over it was not only the body but also the brain that should be tired.

Steve owed a lot of his success to Arrows coach Don Popovic. Steve regarded him as the best coach in the game. It was a stormy relationship between two outspoken men, but each had confidence in the other.

Steve loved his new home of New York, and the Arrows' fans took him to their hearts. He was known admiringly as the "Lord of All Indoors" and was once described as the Pelé of indoor soccer. "ZSHUN-gul, ZSHUN-gul" the crowd would chant when the Arrows needed a goal. The strategy of the whole team was geared to Steve, and it was quite simple: Get the ball to Steve and let him finish off the move with a goal.

During his years with the Arrows, Steve became a celebrity around New York. Some of the publicity concentrated on his fondness for fast cars and the New York nightlife. It was on the soccer field, however, that he earned his glory.

Continuing the Story

In 1983, Steve was traded to the Golden Bay Earthquakes of the North American Soccer League (NASL). The move gave Steve a chance to play outdoor soccer for the first time in nearly five years. After a few months at Golden Bay, he teamed up again with Popovic, who was hired as coach.

The Golden Bay franchise soon folded, though, so Steve took his talents to the San Diego Sockers, one of the most formidable teams in the MISL. He made a typically dramatic impact, scoring five times in his first match in a 10-2 victory. He also helped the Sockers to the MISL championship in 1985.

After that success, Steve was traded to the Tacoma Stars, where he won his sixth MISL scoring title in 1986. In 1988, Steve was back with San Diego, helping them to win the championship for a record fifth time in 1989. The win was Steve's seventh championship. After helping the Sockers to repeat the feat in 1989-1990—although he played in only sixteen games—Steve announced his retirement. During his career he had scored a record 652 goals in the MISL.

Summary

Steve Zungul was the most successful and celebrated player in the history of the MISL. His goal-scoring was prolific: He rarely missed a chance, and he had an almost uncanny knack of knowing in advance where the ball would be. "He's the

MILESTONES

MISL all-time high scorer (652 goals, 1,123 points)

HONORS AND AWARDS

1971, 1974-75	Yugoslavian League champion
1972-77	Yugoslavian League Cup champion
1975	Yugoslavian League Cup most valuable player
1979-82, 1985, 1989-90	MISL champion
1979-82, 1985, 1986	MISL most valuable player
1980, 1982, 1985	MISL Playoff most valuable player MISL Triple Crown winner
1984	NASL most valuable player

Nureyev of soccer," said one soccer coach, referring to the great Russian ballet dancer. Like Rudolf Nureyev, Steve was a supreme artist in his chosen profession.

Bryan Aubrey

Additional Sources:

Henshaw, Richard. *The Encyclopedia of World Soccer.* Washington, D.C.: New Republic Books, 1979.

Hollander, Zander. *The American Encyclopedia of Soccer.* New York: Everett House, 1980.

PIRMIN ZURBRIGGEN

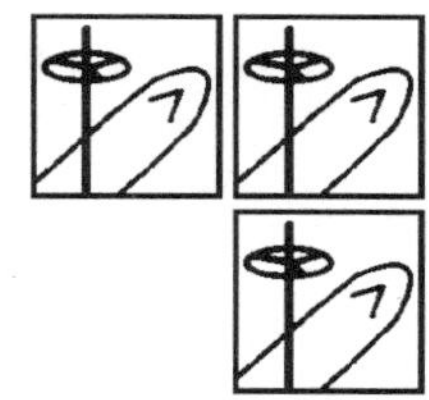

Sport: Skiing

Born: February 4, 1963
Saas-Almagell, Valais, Switzerland

Early Life

Pirmin Zurbriggen was born on February 4, 1963, in the small town of Saas-Almagell, in the canton of Valais, in alpine Switzerland.

Situated near the Italian border, high amid the slopes and pasturelands of the southern Alps, Saas-Almagell is a resort village catering to the tourist crowds that flock to the Alps every year in search of perfect winter sport conditions.

The Zurbriggen name, a common one in the Saas-Valley, has been associated with the hotel trade for generations, and Pirmin's parents were no exception to this tradition. For more than thirty years, Alois and Ida Zurbriggen owned and operated a small sport hotel called the Lärchenhof.

As a young boy and teenager helping in his parents' hotel, Pirmin learned both the respect that alpiners have for the mountains and the sense of tradition that binds families for many years to their villages.

Mike Powell/Allsport

Pirmin Zurbriggen during the World Ski Championships in 1989.

The Road to Excellence

Because the ski trails that snake through his mountain village started not more than a few yards from his front door, Pirmin developed his enthusiasm for speed skiing at an early age.

Every young person taking up a sport has heroes, foretunners who influence the young athlete by their example. Among Pirmin's were the great Italian skier Gustavo Thoeni, his own countryman Bernhard Russi, and Sweden's legendary Ingemar Stenmark, winner of more than eighty-five World Cup medals. These heroes were to serve Pirmin well on his road to excellence in the demanding alpine disciplines.

Young Pirmin did not have to look very far for the practical encouragement he needed to excel, though. His father, Alois, was a ski racer himself, and although Alois had lost a younger brother in a tragic skiing accident and had never raced after that, he was instrumental in coaching young Pirmin to take up the sport seriously.

With his family's encouragement and his own strong sense of commitment to the challenge of competition, Pirmin excelled from the very beginning.

In 1973, at the age of ten, Pirmin entered his first major competitive event, finishing fourth in the Topolino youth races (Marc Girardelli, later to become his rival in World Cup slalom events, finished second). Two years later, Pirmin won the Ovo Grand Prix and subsequently skied his way to becoming Swiss and European junior downhill champion.

The Emerging Champion

A great honor came to the young skier in 1977 when, at age fourteen, he joined the Swiss B team and came under the coaching of Sepp Stadler. After four years spent developing his skills in the second string, Pirmin moved up to the A team and into the mainstream of World Cup competition. He saw his first World Cup downhill race at Val d'Isere in December, 1980, and later that season he won his first points in the giant slalom at Morzine, France, where he finished seventh.

In World Cup competition, skiers earn points for their position in the finals of a particular event. At the end of each season, points are tallied up, and the World Cup is awarded to the skier amassing the greatest number of points.

The years following his entry into international competition saw Pirmin advancing steadily in the standings. He finished eleventh in overall points in 1982 and sixth in 1983.

In 1984, Pirmin traveled with the Swiss team to Sarajevo, Yugoslavia, for the Olympic Winter Games. At the Games, Pirmin was competitive in only one event, the downhill, where he finished fourth, just out of medal reach. Upset by this loss, he failed to win medals in any other Olympic event. He recovered substantially, however, and went on to earn a stunning World Cup championship later that year when he finished first in overall points.

At twenty-one, Pirmin had clearly demonstrated that he was a world-class skier capable of dominating a field of diverse and talented competitors.

Continuing the Story

In both the 1985 and 1986 seasons, despite minor injuries, Pirmin skied to second-place finishes in the World Cup overall points standings.

The next year he triumphed over strong international competition to win his second overall World Cup. With this crucial victory, Pirmin solidified his reputation as a master all-event skier, one who excels at all of the alpine disciplines: slalom, giant slalom, super-giant slalom, and downhill.

Pirmin has been hailed by his coaches and peers as one of the finest downhill technicians in the history of the sport. Beyond an excellent technique, however, Pirmin possessed an acute sense of concentration. On the slopes, the mild, congenial young man was able to block out all distractions. That concentration earned Pirmin many of his victories.

MAJOR CHAMPIONSHIPS

Year	Competition	Event	Place
1981	World Cup	Overall	31st
		Giant slalom	17th
1982	World Cup	Overall	11th
		Giant slalom	6th
		Slalom	33d
1983	World Cup	Overall	6th
		Giant slalom	4th
		Slalom	21st
		Downhill	26th
1984	Olympic Games	Downhill	4th
	World Cup	Overall	1st
		Giant slalom	2d
		Slalom	24th
		Downhill	10th
		Combined	2d
1985	World Championships	Giant slalom	2d
		Downhill	1st
		Combined	1st
	World Cup	Overall	2d
		Giant slalom	2d
		Slalom	14th
		Downhill	5th
		Combined	9th
1986	World Cup	Overall	2d
		Giant slalom	10th
		Super-giant slalom	2d
		Slalom	6th
		Downhill	11th
		Combined	3d
1987	World Championships	Giant slalom	1st
		Super-giant slalom	1st
		Downhill	2d
		Combined	2d
	World Cup	Overall	1st
		Giant slalom	1st
		Super-giant slalom	1st
		Slalom	21st
		Downhill	1st
		Combined	1st
1988	Olympic Games	Giant slalom	Bronze
		Downhill	Gold
	World Cup	Overall	1st
1989	World Cup	Overall	2d
1990	World Cup	Overall	1st

With two World Cup titles behind him, the twenty-five-year-old was a serious contender for as many as five gold medals at the 1988 Olympics held in Calgary, Canada. (To the four traditional events a fifth had been added, a two-day combined, which took an average score of two separate downhill and slalom races.) Pirmin easily won the downhill gold, flashing across the finish line a full half-second faster than the silver medal winner, his teammate Peter Mller.

Hopes for a record-setting Olympic medal win were dashed, however, when Pirmin fell in the combined slalom race. He took third place in the giant slalom and finished out of medal reach in the other events.

Following his return to the international circuit, he went on to win his third overall World Cup crown. The next season he finished second in overall points.

The following year, 1990, proved to be the pinnacle of Pirmin's career. After a season of outstanding finishes in all disciplines, he skied to his fourth overall World Cup championship, becoming (after his early hero Gustavo Thoeni) only the second man in history to have accomplished this feat. Then, at the age of twenty-seven, and at the absolute height of his career, Pirmin Zurbriggen declared his retirement from the world of competitive skiing.

RECORD
Tied the world record for the most overall World Cup championships (4)

Summary

Through his dazzling record as a competitive racer, Pirmin Zurbriggen joined an elite group of skiing superstars. He became part of a tradition of excellence that persists not only in the record books, but everywhere young athletes train in hope of victory.

To Pirmin, however, there was another tradition, equally strong, that he knew someday would draw him to it. He always stated that after his skiing days were over he would return to Saas-Almagell to help his parents run their hotel. Now that tradition has claimed him, too.

Tony Abbott

Additional Sources:

Levinson, David, and Karen Christenson, eds. *Encyclopedia of World Sport: From Ancient to Present.* Santa Barbara, Calif.: ABC-CLIO, 1996.

Wallechinsky, David. *The Complete Book of the Olympics.* Boston: Little, Brown and Company, 1991.

RESOURCES

SELECT BIBLIOGRAPHY OF NOTABLE SPORTS BOOKS

General

Aymar, Brandt, ed. *Men in Sports: Great Sports Stories of All Time from the Greek Olympic Games to the American World Series.* New York: Crown Publishers, 1994.

Brown, Gerry, and Michael Morrison, eds. *2000 ESPN Information Please Sports Almanac.* New York: Hyperion, 1999.

Crothers, Tim. *Greatest Teams: The Most Dominant Powerhouses in Sports.* New York: Bishop Books, 1998.

Drummond, Siobhan, and Elizabeth Rathburn, eds. *Grace and Glory: A Century of Women in the Olympics.* Chicago: Triumph Books, 1996.

Fortin, Francois. *Sports: The Complete Visual Reference.* Buffalo, N.Y.: Firefly Books, 2000.

Friedlander, Noam, ed. *The Mammoth Book of World Sports.* New York: Carroll and Graf, 1999.

Hickok, Ralph. *The Encyclopedia of North American Sports History.* New York: Facts on File, 1992.

———. *A Who's Who of Sports Champions: Their Stories and Records.* Boston: Houghton Mifflin, 1995.

Kirsch, George B., Othello Harris, and Claire E. Nolte, eds. *Encyclopedia of Ethnicity and Sports in the United States.* Westport, Conn.: Greenwood Press, 2000.

Levinson, David, and Karen Christensen, eds. *Encyclopedia of World Sport: From Ancient Times to the Present.* 3 vols. Santa Barbara, Calif.: ABC-CLIO, 1996.

MacCambridge, Michael, ed. *ESPN SportsCentury.* New York: Hyperion/ESPN Books, 1999.

McComb, David G. *Sports: An Illustrated History.* New York: Oxford University Press, 1998.

Macy, Sue. *Winning Ways: A Photohistory of American Women in Sports.* New York: Henry Holt, 1996.

Macy, Sue, and Jane Gottesman, eds. *Play Like a Girl: A Celebration of Women in Sports.* New York: Henry Holt, 1999.

Markel, Robert, Susan Waggoner, and Marcella Smith, eds. *The Women's Sports Encyclopedia.* New York: Henry Holt, 1997.

The Olympic Games: Athens 1896-Sydney 2000. New York: Dorling Kindersley Publishing, 2000.

Pearson, Michael G., ed. *The Sports 100: The One Hundred Greatest Athletes of the Twentieth Century and Their Greatest Career Moments.* Champaign, Ill.: Sports Publishing, 1999.

Pollak, Mark. *Sports Leagues and Teams: An Encyclopedia, 1871 Through 1996.* Jefferson, N.C.: McFarland, 1998.

Radar, Benjamin G. *American Sports: From the Age of Folk Games to the Age of Televised Sports.* 4th ed. Upper Saddle River, N.J.: Prentice Hall, 1999.

Ryan, Joan. *Little Girls in Pretty Boxes: The Making and Breaking of Elite Gymnasts and Figure Skaters.* New York: Warner Books, 2000.

Smith, Lissa, ed. *Nike Is a Goddess: The History of Women in Sports.* New York: Atlantic Monthly, 1998.

Sports Illustrated, editors of. *The Sports Illustrated 2000 Sports Almanac.* New York: Bishop Books, 1999.

Wallechinsky, David. *The Complete Book of the Summer Olympics.* Woodstock, N.Y.: Overlook Press, 2000.

———. *The Complete Book of the Winter Olympics.* Woodstock, N.Y.: Overlook Press, 1998.

Woolum, Janet. *Outstanding Women Athletes: Who They Are and How They Influenced Sports in America.* 2d ed. Phoenix: Oryx, 1998.

Auto Racing

Jones, Bruce. *The Complete Encyclopedia of Formula One: The Bible of Motorsport.* Rev. ed. London: Carlton Books, 2000.

Latford, Bob. *Built for Speed: The Ultimate Guide to Stock Car Racetracks, a Behind-the-Wheel View of the Winston Cup Circuit.* Philadelphia, Pa.: Courage Books, 1999.

Sowers, Richard. *The Complete Statistical History of Stock Car Racing: Records, Streaks, Oddities, and Trivia.* Phoenix: David Bull, 2000.

Stewart, Mark. *Auto Racing: A History of Fast Cars and Fearless Drivers.* New York: Franklin Watts, 1998.

Baseball

DeMarco, Tony. *The Sporting News Selects Fifty Greatest Sluggers.* St. Louis, Mo.: The Sporting News, 2000.

James, Bill, ed. *Bill James Presents: STATS All-Time Major League Handbook.* 2d ed. Morton Grove, Ill.: STATS Publishing, 2000.

Neft, David S., Richard M. Cohen, and Michael L. Neft. *The Sports Encyclopedia: Baseball.* 20th ed. New York: St. Martin's Griffin, 2000.

Nemec, David. *Baseball Chronology.* Lincolnwood, Ill.: Publications International, 2000.

Pietrusza, David, Matthew Silverman, and Michael Gershman, eds. *Baseball: The Biographical Encyclopedia.* Kingston, N.Y.: Total Sports Illustrated, 2000.

Porter, David L., ed. *Biographical Dictionary of American Sports: Baseball.* Rev. ed. 3 vols. Westport, Conn.: Greenwood Press, 2000.

Thorn, John, and Pete Palmer, eds. *Total Baseball.* 7th ed. New York: Total Sports, 2001.

Vancil, Mark, and Peter Hirdt, eds. *All Century Team.* Chicago: Rare Air Books, 1999.

Basketball

Carter, Craig, and John Hareas, eds. *Official NBA Guide.* 2000-2001 ed. St. Louis, Mo.: NBA Properties, 2000.

Hubbard, Jan, ed. *The Official NBA Encyclopedia.* 3d ed. New York: Doubleday, 2000.

Mallozzi, Vincent M. *Basketball: The Legends and the Game.* Willowdale, Canada: Firefly Books, 1998.

Smith, Ron. *The Ultimate Encyclopedia of Basketball: The Definitive Illustrated Guide to the NBA.* 3d ed. London: Carlton Books, 1999.

Stewart, Mark. *Basketball: A History of Hoops.* New York: Franklin Watts, 1998.

Bodybuilding

Hughes, Mary. *The Composite Guide to Bodybuilding.* Philadelphia, Pa.: Chelsea House, 2000.

Schwarzenegger, Arnold, with Bill Dobbins. *The New Encyclopedia of Modern Bodybuilding.* New York: Simon and Schuster, 1998.

Boxing

Mullan, Harry. *The World Encyclopedia of Boxing: The Definitive Illustrated Guide.* London: Carlton, 1999.

Myler, Patrick. *A Century of Boxing Greats: Inside the Ring with the Hundred Best Boxers.* New York: Robson/Parkwest, 1997.

Roberts, James B., and Alexander G. Skutt. *The Boxing Register: International Hall of Fame Official Record Book.* 2d ed. Ithaca, N.Y.: McBooks Press, 1999.

Cycling

Fife, Graeme. *Tour de France: The History, the Legend, the Riders.* Updated. Edinburgh, Scotland: Mainstream, 1999.

Perry, David B. *Bike Cult: The Ultimate Guide to Human-Powered Vehicles.* New York: Four Walls Eight Windows, 1995.

Startt, James. *Tour de France, Tour de Force: A Visual History of the Greatest Bicycle Race in the World.* San Francisco: Chronicle Books, 2000.

Woodland, Les. *The Unknown Tour de France: The Many Faces of the World's Biggest Bicycle Race.* San Francisco: Van der Plas, 2000.

Figure Skating

Malone, John Williams. *The Encyclopedia of Figure Skating.* New York: Facts on File, 1998.

Milton, Steve. *Skate: One Hundred Years of Figure Skating.* North Pomfret, Vt.: Trafalgar Square, 1996.

Wilner, Barry. *The Composite Guide to Figure Skating.* Philadelphia, Pa.: Chelsea House, 2000.

Football

Carroll, Bob, Michael Gershman, David Neft, and John Thorn, eds. *Total Football II: The Official Encyclopedia of the National Football League.* Rev. ed. New York: HarperCollins, 1999.

Neft, David S., Richard M. Cohen, and Rick Korch. *The Sports Encyclopedia: Pro Football, the Modern Era, 1974-1998.* 17th ed. New York: St. Martin's Griffin, 1999.

Official National Football League 2000 Record and Fact Book. New York: Workman, 2000.

Roberts, Brendan, and David Walton, eds. *Pro Football Register.* Rev. ed. St. Louis, Mo.: The Sporting News, 2000.

Ross, Charles K. *Outside the Lines: African Americans and the Integration of the National Football League.* New York: New York University Press, 1999.

Vancil, Mark, ed. *ABC Sports College All-Time All-America Team.* New York: Hyperion, 2000.

Golf

Barrett, Ted, and Michael Hobbs. *The Complete Book of Golf: The Definitive Illustrated Guide to World Golf.* London: Sevenoaks, 1997.

Feinstein, John. *The Majors: In Pursuit of Golf's Holy Grail.* Boston: Little, Brown, 1999.

Lawrenson, Derek. *The Complete Encyclopedia of Golf.* London: Carlton Books, 1999.

Williams, Jackie. *Playing from the Rough: The Women of the LPGA Hall of Fame.* Las Vegas: Women of Diversity Productions, 2000.

Gymnastics

Cohen, Joel H. *Superstars of Women's Gymnastics.* Philadelphia, Pa.: Chelsea House, 1998.

Huff, Richard. *The Composite Guide to Gymnastics.* Philadelphia, Pa.: Chelsea House, 2000.

Page, Jason. *Gymnastics: The Balance Beam, Floor, Rings, Team Events, and Lots, Lots More.* Minneapolis: LernerSports, 2000.

Horse Racing

Hotaling, Edward. *The Great Black Jockeys: The Lives and Times of the Men Who Dominated America's First National Sport.* Rocklin, Calif.: Forum, 1999.

Von Borries, Philip. *Racelines: Observations on Horse Racing's Glorious History.* Lincolnwood, Ill.: Masters Press, 1999.

Ice Hockey

Diamond, Dan, ed. *Total Hockey: The Official Encyclopedia of the National Hockey League.* Kingston, N.Y.: Total Sports, 2000.

Stewart, Mark. *Hockey: A History of the Fastest Game on Ice.* New York: Franklin Watts, 1998.

Walton, David, ed. *Hockey Register.* 2000-2001 ed. St. Louis, Mo.: The Sporting News, 2000.

Martial Arts

Gaines, Ann Graham. *The Composite Guide to Martial Arts.* Philadelphia, Pa.: Chelsea House, 2000.

Metil, Luana, and Jace Townsend. *The Story of Karate: From Buddhism to Bruce Lee.* Minneapolis: Lerner Publishing, 1995.

Smith, Robert W. *Martial Musings: A Portrayal of the Martial Arts in the Twentieth Century.* Erie, Pa.: Via Media, 1999.

Powerboat Racing

David Greene's Statistical History of Major League Boat Racing. Seattle, Wash.: David Greene, 1993.

Hunn, Peter. *The Golden Age of the Racing Outboard.* Marblehead, Mass.: Devereux Books, 2000.

Skiing

Barnes, Bob. *The Complete Encyclopedia of Skiing.* 3d ed. Silverthorne, Colo.: The Snowline Press, 1999.

Soccer

Longman, Jere. *The Girls of Summer: The U.S. Women's Soccer Team and How It Changed the World.* New York: HarperCollins, 2000.

Radnedge, Keir. *The Complete Encyclopedia of Soccer: The Bible of World Soccer.* Rev. ed. London: Carlton Books, 2000.

Rutledge, Rachel. *The Best of the Best in Soccer.* Brookfield, Conn.: Millbrook Press, 1999.

Schoff, Jill Potvin. *Women's Soccer Scrapbook: The Ultimate Insider's Guide.* New York: Somerville House, 2000.

Stewart, Mark. *Soccer: A History of the World's Most Popular Game.* New York: Franklin Watts, 1998.

Surfing

Finney, Ben, and James D. Houston. *Surfing: A History of the Ancient Hawaiian Sport.* Rev. ed. San Francisco: Pomegranate Artbooks, 1996.

Gabbard, Andrea. *Girl in the Curl: A Century of Women in Surfing.* Seattle: Seal Press, 2000.

Kampion, Drew. *Stoked: A History of Surf Culture.* Santa Monica, Calif.: General Publishing Group, 1997.

Warshaw, Matt. *Surfriders: In Search of the Perfect Wave.* New York: Collins, 1997.

Young, Nat, with Craig McGregor and Rod Holmes. *The History of Surfing.* Rev. ed. Angourie, Australia: Palm Beach Press, 1994.

Swimming

Gonsalves, Kelly, and Susan LaMondia. *First to the Wall: One Hundred Years of Olympic Swimming.* East Longmeadow, Mass.: FreeStyle, 1999.

Tennis

Collins, Bud, and Zander Hollander, eds. *Bud Collins' Tennis Encyclopedia*. 3d ed. Detroit: Visible Ink Press, 1997.

Flink, Steve. *The Greatest Tennis Matches of the Twentieth Century*. Danbury, Conn.: Rutledge Books, 1999.

Parsons, John. *The Ultimate Encyclopedia of Tennis: The Definitive Illustrated Guide to World Tennis*. London: Carlton/Hodder and Stoughton, 1999.

Track and Field

Macht, Norman L. *The Composite Guide to Track and Field*. Philadelphia, Pa.: Chelsea House, 1999.

Olson, Leonard T. *Masters of Track and Field: A History*. Jefferson, N.C.: McFarland, 2001.

Watman, Mel. *American Track and Field Presents History of Olympic Track and Field Athletics*. Madison, Wis.: Athletics International, 2000.

Triathlon

Tinley, Scott. *Triathlon: A Personal History*. Boulder, Colo.: Velo Press, 1998.

Volleyball

Huff, Richard. *The Composite Guide to Volleyball*. Philadelphia, Pa.: Chelsea House, 2000.

Shewman, Byron. *Volleyball Centennial: The First One Hundred Years*. Indianapolis, Ind.: Masters Press, 1995.

Wrestling

Gallagher, Jim. *The Composite Guide to Wrestling*. Philadelphia, Pa.: Chelsea House, 1999.

Petrov, Raiko. *One Hundred Years of Olympic Wrestling*. Lausanne, Switzerland: FILA, 1997.

Jeffry Jensen

SPORTS RESOURCES ON THE WORLD WIDE WEB

Web sites listed here include general sports sites, magazines, sports wire services, and television networks that broadcast sporting events. Additional on-line resources and more specialized information may be found in the sections entitled "Additional Sources" in the individual essays in the main text.

1. General Sites 3159
2. Auto Racing 3161
3. Baseball 3161
4. Basketball 3162
5. Bowling 3162
6. Boxing 3162
7. Figure Skating 3162
8. Football 3162
9. Golf 3162
10. Gymnastics 3163
11. Horse Racing 3163
12. Ice Hockey 3163
13. Martial Arts 3163
14. Skiing 3163
15. Soccer 3163
16. Surfing 3164
17. Swimming 3164
18. Tennis 3164
19. Track and Field 3164
20. Triathlon 3164
21. Volleyball 3164

1. General Sites

ABC Sports
http://www.abcsports.com

AllSports
http://www.allsports.com/

Ancient Olympics
http://www.upenn.edu/museum/Olympics/olympicintro.html

Athletics **(magazine)**
http://www.io.org

Ballparks
http://www.ballparks.com/

Black College Sports Review **(magazine)**
http://www.black-sports.com

Bloomberg Personal (sports wire service)
http://www.bloomberg.com

Broadcast Sports
http://www.broadcastsports.com

BroadcastAmerica
http://sports.broadcastamerica.com/

Cable News Network (CNN)/Sports Illustrated (SI)
http://sportsillustrated.cnn.com/

Canada's Sports Hall of Fame
http://www.inforamp.net/~cshof

Canadian Broadcasting Corporation (CBC) Sports
http://cbc.ca/sports/

CBS SportsLine
http://cbs.sportsline.com/

Citysports Magazine
http://www.athand.com

College Athletics World Wide Web Pages
http://www.users.nwark.com/~bryan/Colleges/index.html

CollegeSportsNews
http://www.collegesportsnews.com/

DBC Sports Online
http://sports.dbc.com/

Empire Sports Network
http://www.empiresports.com/

ESPN
http://espn.go.com/

ESPN–The Magazine
http://espn.go.com/magazine/

Excite: Sports
http://sports.excite.com/

Express Sport Live (European Sporting News)
http://www.sportslive.net/

FOXSports
http://www.foxsports.com/

Hickok's Sports History
http://www.ultranet.com/~rhickok/

History of Women in Sports Timeline
http://www.northnet.org/stlawrenceaauw/timeline.htm

Home Box Office (HBO) Sports
http://www.hbo.com/realsports/

International Olympic Committee (IOC)
http://www.olympic.org/

iWon-Sports
http://www.iwon.com/home/sports/sports_overview/0,11766,,00.html

Live Internet Sports Radio Stations
http://www.csi.ukns.com/radios.html

Madison Square Garden Network
http://www.msgnetwork.com/msgframes.html

MSNBC Sports
http:///www.msnbc.com/news/SPT_Front.asp?a

Nando Sports Server
http://www.SportServer.com

National Broadcasting Company (NBC) Sports
http://www.nbci.com/main/channel/0,2,home-sp,00.html?st.sn.fd.t.sp

National Collegiate Athletic Association (NCAA) Online
http://www.ncaa.org/

New England Sports Network
http://www.nesn.com/

Olympic Movement
http://www.olympic.org/

Olympics Through Time
http://sunsite.sut.ac.jp/olympics/

One on One Sports Online
http://www.1on1sports.com

PioneerPlanet: Sports
http://www.pioneerplanet.com/sports/

Real Fans Sports Network
http://www.realfans.com/

Rivals
http://www.rivals.com/

Sport Science
http://www.exploratorium.edu/sports/index.html

The Sporting Life
http://www.sporting-life.com/

Sporting News
http://www.sportingnews.com/

***Sporting News* (magazine)**
http://tsn.sportingnews.com/

***Sports Illustrated* (magazine)**
http://www.pathfinder.com/si

Sports Illustrated for Kids
http://www.sikids.com/

The Sports Library
http://www.thesportslibrary.com/

Sports Network
http://www.sportsnetwork.com/home.asp

Sports Schedules as You Like 'Em
http://www.cs.rochester.edu/u/ferguson/schedules/

SportsArena
http://www.awa.com/arena

SportsCable
http://www.sportscable.com

SportsFan Radio Network
http://www.sportsfanradio.com

SportsFeed (sports wire service)
http://www.sportsfeed.com/

SportsLine USA
http://www.sportsline.com/

SportsServer
http://www.sportserver.com/

SportsSLEUTH
http://www.sports.sleuth.com/

Sportsworld
http://www.sportsworld.com/

Stadiums and Arenas
http://www.wwcd.com/stadiums.html

Summer Olympics–2004
http://www.athens2004.net/

Sydney 2000 Olympic Games
http://www.olympics.com/eng/

TBS Sports
http://www.superstation.com/sports/index.htm

Total College Sports Network
http://www.totalcollegesports.com/

Tuneinsports
http://www.tuneinsports.com/

Turner Network Television (TNT) Sports
http://tnt.turner.com/sports/

United States Olympic Committee (USOC) Online
http://www.usoc.org/

USA Network Sports
http://www.usanetwork.com/sports/index.html

USA Today-Sports
http://www.usatoday.com/

Virgin Net Sport (British Sporting News)
http://www.virgin.net/sport/news/index.html

WANSports (African Sporting News)
http://www.wansports.com/

Wide Web of Sports
http://tns-www.lcs.mit.edu/cgi-bin/sports

Winter Olympics–2002
http://www.SLC2002.org/

World Wide Web Virtual Library: Sports
http://www.justwright.com/sports/

Yahoo! Sports
http://dir.yahoo.com/recreation/sports/

2. Auto Racing

The Auto Channel: Motorsports
http://www.theautochannel.com/

CART Online
http://www.cart.com/

Formula One
http://www.formula1.com/

Goracing
http://www.goracing.com/

MotoWorld
http://www.motoworld.com/

NASCAR Online
http://www.nascar.com/

RaceWire
http://www.racewire.com/

SpeedFX
http://www.speedfx.com/

Turner National Network (TNN) Motorsports
http://www.tnnracing.com/

3. Baseball

Baseball Almanac
http://baseball-almanac.com/

Baseball-Reference
http://www.baseball-reference.com/

Bigleaguers
http://www.bigleaguers.com/

Fastball
http://www.fastball.com/

Minor League Baseball
http://www.minorleaguebaseball.com/

National Baseball Hall of Fame
http://www.baseballhalloffame.org/

Nationalpastime
http://www.nationalpastime.com/

Negro Baseball Leagues
http://www.blackbaseball.com/

Official Site of Major League Baseball
http://www.majorleaguebaseball.com/

Total Baseball
http://www.totalbaseball.com/

Yahoo! Major League Baseball
http://baseball.yahoo.com/mlb/

4. Basketball

All-Time Great NBA Players
http://www.nba.com/history/index_player.html

Basketball Hall of Fame
http://www.hoophall.com/index.cfm

Final Four
http://www.finalfour.net

History of College Basketball
http://www.desktopnet.com/cbask/index2.htm

HoopLife
http://www.hooplife.com/

National Basketball Association (NBA)
http://www.nba.com/index.html

National Collegiate Athletic Association (NCAA) Basketball
http://www.ncaabasketball.net/

***SLAM* (magazine)**
http://www.slamonline.com

***Women's Basketball* (magazine)**
http://www.wbmagazine.com/

Women's National Basketball Association (WNBA)
http://www.wbna.com/

5. Bowling

Bowling World
http://www.bowlingworld.com/

Bowlingzone
http://www.bowlingzone.com/

Professional Bowlers Association (PBA) Online
http://www.pbatour.com

Professional Women's Bowling Association (PWBA) Online
http://www.pwba.com

6. Boxing

BoxingOnline
http://www.boxingonline.com/index.shtml

Fighters
http://www.fighters.com/

Home Box Office (HBO) Boxing
http://www.hbo.com/boxing/

International Boxing Hall of Fame (IBHOF)
http://www.ibhof.com/

Showtime Championship Boxing
http://www.showtimeonline.com/scboxing/

Women's Boxing on the Web
http://femboxer.com/

Yahoo! Boxing
http://dir.yahoo.com/Recreation/Sports/Boxing/

7. Figure Skating

Figure Skating Internet Radio
http://Skate-Radio.com/

International Figure Skating Online
http://www.ifsmagazine.com/

SkateWeb
http://frog.simplenet.com/skateweb/

8. Football

The Football Archive
http://library.thinkquest.org/12590/

National Football League (NFL)
http://www.nfl.com/

Pro Football Hall of Fame
http://www.profootballhof.com/

Super Bowl-SportsLine-NFL
http://www.sportsline.com/u/football/nfl/superbowl/

SuperBowl
http://www.superbowl.com/

9. Golf

Golf
http://www.golf.com/

Golf Around the World
http://www.worldgolf.com/

The Golf Channel
http://www.thegolfchannel.com/

Golf Digest **(magazine)**
http://www.golfworld.com/

Golf Magazine
http://www.golfonline.com

Golf Online
http://www.golfonline.com/

Golf World (magazine)
http://www.golfworld.com/

GolfWeb
http://www.golfweb.com/

Ladies Professional Golf Association
http://www.lpga.com

The Masters
http://www.masters.org/

Professional Golfers' Association (PGA) of America
http://www.pgaonline.com/

PGA Tour
http://www.pgatour.com/

Ryder Cup
http://www.rydercup.com/

United States Golf Association
http://www.usga.org/

10. Gymnastics

International Gymnast **(magazine)**
http://www.intlgymnast.com/

International Gymnastics Hall of Fame
http://www.int-gym-hof.org/

USA Gymnastics Online
http://www.usa-gymnastics.org/

11. Horse Racing

American Turf Monthly **(magazine)**
http://www.winsports.com

Daily Racing Form
http://www.drf.com/index.html

National Thoroughbred Racing Association (NTRA) Online
http://www.ntraracing.com/

United States Trotting Association (USTA) Online
http://www.ustrotting.com/

12. Ice Hockey

A to Z Encyclopedia of Ice Hockey
http://www.azhockey.com/

Hockey Hall of Fame
http://www.hhof.com/index.htm

The Hockey News **(magazine)**
http://www.thn.com/hockey

Hockey Player Magazine
http://www.enews.com

Internet Hockey Database
http://www.hockeydb.com/

National Hockey League (NHL)
http://www.nhl.com/

13. Martial Arts

Black Belt Magazine
http://www.blackbeltmag.com

14. Skiing

Ski Magazine
http://www.skinet.com

SkiCentral
http://skicentral.com/

Skiing Magazine
http://www.skinet.com/skiing

SkiNet
http://www.skinet.com/

US Ski Team Online
http://www.usskiteam.com/

15. Soccer

Euro 2000 UEFA (European Soccer Championships)
http://www.euro2000.org/

Major League Soccer
http://www.mlsnet.com/

Soccer Magazine
http://www.webzone.com/shutterbug

Soccer Times
http://www.soccertimes.com/

SoccerAge
http://www.soccerage.com/en/33/00001.html

World Cup Soccer
http://www.fifa.com/index.html

World Soccernet
http://soccernet.com/

16. Surfing

International Surfing Museum
http://www.surfingmuseum.org/

Legendary Surfers
http://www.legendarysurfers.com/

***Surfer* (magazine)**
http://www.surfermag.com

SurfLine
http://surfline.swell.com/

17. Swimming

International Swimming Hall of Fame (ISHOF)
http://www.ishof.org/

Swimnews Online
http://www.swimnews.com/

Synchronized Swimming
http://www.usasynchro.org/

USA Swimming
http://www.usa-swimming.org/

18. Tennis

Association of Tennis Professionals (ATP) Tour
http://www.atptour.com/

Australian Open
http://www.ausopen.org/

French Open
http://www.frenchopen.org/

***International Tennis* (magazine)**
http://www.atptour.com

International Tennis Hall of Fame
http://www.tennisfame.org/

Tennis Magazine
http://www.tennis.com/

Tennis Server
http://www.tennisserver.com/

U.S. Open
http://www.usopen.org/

Wimbledon
http://www.wimbledon.org/

Women's Tennis Association (WTA)
http://www.wtatour.com/

Worldwide Senior Tennis Circuit
http://www.seniortenniscircuit.com/

19. Track and Field

***American Runner* (magazine)**
http://www.americanrunner.com

Cool Running
http://www.coolrunning.com/

***Runner's World* (magazine)**
http://www.runnersworld.com

***Running Times* (magazine)**
http://www.runningtimes.com/

Track and Field News
http://www.trackandfieldnews.com/

20. Triathlon

***Inside Triathlon* (magazine)**
http://www.greatoutdoors.com/auto_docs/insidetri/

***Triathlete* (magazine)**
http://www.triathletemag.com/

21. Volleyball

Association of Volleyball Professionals
http://www.volleyball.org/avp

AVP Tour
http://www.avptour.com/

Coppertone
http://www.volleyball.org/coppertone/index.html

***Volleyball* (magazine)**
http://www.volleyballmag.com

Volleyball World Wide
http://www.volleyball.org/Index.html

Jeffry Jensen

TIMELINE

Born	Name	Sport	Country
March 29, 1867	Cy Young	Baseball	United States
April 2, 1867	Eugen Sandow	Bodybuilding	Germany
May 9, 1870	Harry Vardon	Golf	England
March 3, 1872	Willie Keeler	Baseball	United States
October 14, 1873	Ray Ewry	High jump, Long jump, Triple jump	United States
February 24, 1874	Honus Wagner	Baseball	United States
September 5, 1874	Nap Lajoie	Baseball	United States
October 13, 1876	Rube Waddell	Baseball	United States
September 9, 1877	Frank Chance	Baseball	United States
January 1, 1878	Bobby Walthour	Cycling	United States
January 29, 1878	Barney Oldfield	Auto racing	United States
March 31, 1878	Jack Johnson	Boxing	United States
November 26, 1878	Major Taylor	Cycling	United States
May, 1880	Willie Anderson	Golf	Scotland
August 12, 1880	Christy Mathewson	Baseball	United States
July 21, 1881	Johnny Evers	Baseball	United States
May 5, 1883	Chief Bender	Baseball	United States
December 18, 1886	Ty Cobb	Baseball	United States
December 20, 1886	Hazel Wightman	Tennis	United States
February 26, 1887	Grover Alexander	Baseball	United States
May 2, 1887	Eddie Collins	Baseball	United States
July 16, 1887	Shoeless Joe Jackson	Baseball	United States
November 6, 1887	Walter Johnson	Baseball	United States
April 4, 1888	Tris Speaker	Baseball	United States
May 22, 1888	Jim Thorpe	Track and field, Football, Baseball	United States
July 22, 1888	Floretta Doty McCutcheon	Bowling	United States
July 13, 1889	Stan Coveleski	Baseball	United States
October 4, 1889	John Kelly, Sr.	Rowing	United States
October 9, 1889	Rube Marquard	Baseball	United States
July 30, 1890	Casey Stengel	Baseball	United States
August 26, 1890	Duke Kahanamoku	Swimming, Surfing	United States
March 4, 1891	Dazzy Vance	Baseball	United States
December 21, 1892	Walter Hagen	Golf	United States
February 10, 1893	Bill Tilden	Tennis	United States
March 24, 1893	George Sisler	Baseball	United States
May 8, 1893	Francis D. Ouimet	Golf	United States
August 18, 1893	Burleigh Grimes	Baseball	United States
January 27, 1894	Fritz Pollard	Football	United States
June 9, 1894	Nedo Nadi	Fencing	Italy
February 6, 1895	Babe Ruth	Baseball	United States
February 18, 1895	George Gipp	Football	United States
June 24, 1895	Jack Dempsey	Boxing	United States
September 24, 1895	Tommy Armour	Golf	Scotland
April 27, 1896	Rogers Hornsby	Baseball	United States

Born	Name	Sport	Country
October 14, 1896	Oscar Charleston	Baseball	United States
April 26, 1897	Eddie Eagan	Boxing, Bobsledding	United States
June 13, 1897	Paavo Nurmi	Long-distance runs, Steeplechase	Finland
April 9, 1898	Paul Robeson	Baseball	United States
May 25, 1898	Gene Tunney	Boxing	United States
August 13, 1898	Jean Borotra	Tennis	France
October 30, 1898	Bill Terry	Baseball	United States
May 24, 1899	Suzanne Lenglen	Tennis	France
November 11, 1899	Pie Traynor	Baseball	United States
December 15, 1899	Harold Abrahams	Sprints, Long jump	England
January 18, 1900	George Charles Calnan	Fencing	United States
March 6, 1900	Lefty Grove	Baseball	United States
March 8, 1900	Anne Barton Townsend	Field hockey	United States
April 12, 1900	Joe Lapchick	Basketball	United States
April 26, 1900	Hack Wilson	Baseball	United States
May 9, 1900	Bob Askin	Rodeo	United States
May 24, 1900	Lionel Conacher	Ice hockey	Canada
August 11, 1900	Charles Paddock	Sprints	United States
October 20, 1900	Judy Johnson	Baseball	United States
December 20, 1900	Gabby Hartnett	Baseball	United States
April 1, 1901	Johnny Farrell	Golf	United States
September 21, 1901	Learie Constantine	Cricket	Trinidad
December 14, 1901	Henri Cochet	Tennis	France
January 16, 1902	Eric Liddell	Sprints	China, Scotland
February 27, 1902	Ethelda Bleibtrey	Swimming	United States
February 27, 1902	Gene Sarazen	Golf	United States
March 17, 1902	Bobby Jones	Golf	United States
April 6, 1903	Mickey Cochrane	Baseball	United States
May 11, 1903	Charlie Gehringer	Baseball	United States
May 17, 1903	James "Cool Papa" Bell	Baseball	United States
May 22, 1903	Al Simmons	Baseball	United States
June 11, 1903	Ernie Nevers	Football	United States
June 13, 1903	Red Grange	Football	United States
June 19, 1903	Lou Gehrig	Baseball	United States
June 20, 1903	Glenna Collett Vare	Golf	United States
June 22, 1903	Carl Hubbell	Baseball	United States
July 3, 1903	Irvine "Ace" Bailey	Ice hockey	Canada
June 2, 1904	Johnny Weissmuller	Swimming	United States
May 3, 1905	Red Ruffing	Baseball	United States
July 2, 1905	René Lacoste	Tennis	France
September 28, 1905	Max Schmeling	Boxing	Germany
October 6, 1905	Helen Wills Moody	Tennis	United States
July ?, 1906	Satchel Paige	Baseball	United States
October 11, 1906	Dutch Clark	Football	United States
October 23, 1906	Gertrude Ederle	Swimming	United States
February 14, 1907	Johnny Longden	Horse racing	England
September 6, 1907	Johnny Kelley	Marathon	United States
September 8, 1907	Buck Leonard	Baseball	United States
October 22, 1907	Jimmie Foxx	Baseball	United States
January 20, 1908	Martha Norelius	Swimming	Sweden, United States

Born	Name	Sport	Country
February 17, 1908	Buster Crabbe	Swimming	United States
August 20, 1908	Al Lopez	Baseball	United States
August 27, 1908	Donald G. Bradman	Cricket	Australia
September 29, 1908	Eddie Tolan	Sprints	United States
November 3, 1908	Bronko Nagurski	Football	Canada, United States
November 26, 1908	Lefty Gomez	Baseball	United States
February 11, 1909	Max Baer	Boxing	United States
March 2, 1909	Mel Ott	Baseball	United States
April 2, 1909	Luke Appling	Baseball	United States
May 18, 1909	Fred Perry	Tennis	England
May 25, 1910	Jimmy Demaret	Golf	United States
June 23, 1910	Lawson Little	Golf	United States
October 14, 1910	John Wooden	Basketball	United States
January 1, 1911	Hank Greenberg	Baseball	United States
January 16, 1911	Dizzy Dean	Baseball	United States
June 24, 1911	Juan Manuel Fangio	Auto racing	Argentina
November 24, 1911	Joe Medwick	Baseball	United States
December 21, 1911	Josh Gibson	Baseball	United States
February 4, 1912	Byron Nelson	Golf	United States
April 8, 1912	Sonja Henie	Figure skating	Norway
May 27, 1912	Sam Snead	Golf	United States
June 5, 1912	Lee Petty	Auto racing	United States
August 13, 1912	Ben Hogan	Golf	United States
December 12, 1912	Henry Armstrong	Boxing	United States
January 7, 1913	Johnny Mize	Baseball	United States
January 13, 1913	Don Hutson	Football	United States
June 27, 1913	Willie Mosconi	Billiards	United States
September 12, 1913	Jesse Owens	Sprints, Long jump	United States
September 28, 1913	Alice Marble	Tennis	United States
December 13, 1913	Archie Moore	Boxing	United States
March 17, 1914	Sammy Baugh	Football	United States
May 13, 1914	Joe Louis	Boxing	United States
June 26, 1914	Babe Didrikson Zaharias	Track and field, Golf, Basketball, Softball	United States
August 1, 1914	Lloyd Mangrum	Golf	United States
October 30, 1914	Marion Ladewig	Bowling	United States
November 25, 1914	Joe DiMaggio	Baseball	United States
February 1, 1915	Sir Stanley Matthews	Soccer	England
June 13, 1915	Don Budge	Tennis	United States
June 22, 1915	Cornelius Warmerdam	Pole vault	United States
February 19, 1916	Eddie Arcaro	Horse racing	United States
June 16, 1916	Hank Luisetti	Basketball	United States
November 21, 1916	Sid Luckman	Football	United States
June 8, 1917	Byron "Whizzer" White	Football	United States
October 8, 1917	Billy Conn	Boxing	United States
February 3, 1918	Helen Stephens	Track and field	United States
February 13, 1918	Patty Berg	Golf	United States
February 25, 1918	Bobby Riggs	Tennis	United States
March 4, 1918	Margaret Osborne duPont	Tennis	United States
April 26, 1918	Fanny Blankers-Koen	Sprints, Jumps, Heptathlon	Netherlands

Born	Name	Sport	Country
August 30, 1918	Ted Williams	Baseball	United States
November 3, 1918	Bob Feller	Baseball	United States
January 31, 1919	Jackie Robinson	Baseball	United States
February 11, 1919	Gretchen Fraser	Skiing	United States
July 20, 1919	Sir Edmund Hillary	Mountaineering	New Zealand
September 28, 1919	Tom Harmon	Football	United States
December 19, 1919	Herb Dudley	Softball	United States
January 6, 1920	Early Wynn	Baseball	United States
January 15, 1920	Bob Davies	Basketball	United States
January 22, 1920	Alf Ramsey	Soccer	England
March 3, 1920	Julius Boros	Golf	United States
June 5, 1920	Marion Motley	Football	United States
July 26, 1920	Bob Waterfield	Football	United States
August 1, 1920	Sammy Lee	Diving	United States
September 6, 1920	Dave Freeman	Badminton	United States
September 22, 1920	Bob Lemon	Baseball	United States
November 21, 1920	Stan Musial	Baseball	United States
December 28, 1920	Steve Van Buren	Football	Honduras, United States
January 12, 1921	John Davis	Weightlifting	United States
March 14, 1921	Lis Hartel	Equestrian	Denmark
April 23, 1921	Warren Spahn	Baseball	United States
May 3, 1921	Sugar Ray Robinson	Boxing	United States
May 3, 1921	Goose Tatum	Basketball	United States
August 1, 1921	Jack Kramer	Tennis	United States
August 4, 1921	Maurice "Rocket" Richard	Ice hockey	Canada
August 8, 1921	Betty Shellenberger	Field hockey	United States
August 28, 1921	Wendell Scott	Auto racing	United States
October 26, 1921	Joe Fulks	Basketball	United States
November 9, 1921	Victor Tchoukarine	Gymnastics	Soviet Union, Ukraine
November 19, 1921	Roy Campanella	Baseball	United States
December 6, 1921	Otto Graham	Football	United States
January 1, 1922	Rocky Graziano	Boxing	United States
September 19, 1922	Emil Zatopek	Long-distance runs, Marathon	Czechoslovakia
October 27, 1922	Ralph Kiner	Baseball	United States
December 14, 1922	Charley Trippi	Football	United States
June 17, 1923	Elroy "Crazylegs" Hirsch	Football	United States
July 8, 1923	Harrison Dillard	Hurdles	United States
July 26, 1923	Hoyt Wilhelm	Baseball	United States
August 8, 1923	Esther Williams	Swimming	United States
August 30, 1923	Vic Seixas	Tennis	United States
September 1, 1923	Rocky Marciano	Boxing	United States
November 9, 1923	Alice Coachman	Sprints, High jump	United States
January 25, 1924	Lou Groza	Football	United States
February 6, 1924	Billy Wright	Soccer	England
March 13, 1924	Bertha Tickey	Softball	United States
June 18, 1924	George Mikan	Basketball	United States
October 11, 1924	Mal Whitfield	Middle-distance runs	United States
November 16, 1924	Mel Patton	Sprints	United States
December 11, 1924	Doc Blanchard	Football	United States

Born	Name	Sport	Country
December 13, 1924	Larry Doby	Baseball	United States
December 23, 1924	Bob Kurland	Basketball	United States
December 26, 1924	Glenn Davis	Football, Track and field	United States
January 4, 1925	Johnny Lujack	Football	United States
February 8, 1925	Raimondo d'Inezeo	Equestrian	Italy
March 26, 1925	Eddie Feigner	Softball	United States
March 29, 1925	Emlen Tunnell	Football	United States
May 1, 1925	Chuck Bednarik	Football	United States
May 12, 1925	Yogi Berra	Baseball	United States
July 18, 1925	Shirley Strickland-de la Hunty	Sprints, Hurdles	Australia
July 29, 1925	Ted Lindsay	Ice hockey	Canada
October 22, 1925	Slater Martin	Basketball	United States
January 21, 1926	Steve Reeves	Bodybuilding	United States
January 23, 1926	Jerry Kramer	Football	United States
February 10, 1926	Danny Blanchflower	Soccer	Northern Ireland
February 20, 1926	Bob Richards	Pole vault, Decathlon	United States
March 15, 1926	Norm Van Brocklin	Football	United States
March 25, 1926	Laszlo Papp	Boxing	Hungary
April 2, 1926	Ferenc Puskas	Soccer	Hungary
May 25, 1926	Bill Sharman	Basketball	United States
July 4, 1926	Alfredo di Stefano	Soccer	Argentina
July 24, 1926	Hans Winkler	Equestrian	Germany
July 29, 1926	Don Carter	Bowling	United States
September 19, 1926	Duke Snider	Baseball	United States
September 30, 1926	Robin Roberts	Baseball	United States
October 3, 1926	Marques Haynes	Basketball	United States
October 24, 1926	Y. A. Tittle	Football	United States
December 6, 1926	Andy Robustelli	Football	United States
December 19, 1926	Bobby Layne	Football	United States
January 1, 1927	Doak Walker	Football	United States
January 2, 1927	Gino Marchetti	Football	United States
August 25, 1927	Althea Gibson	Tennis	United States
September 17, 1927	George Blanda	Football	United States
February 25, 1928	Paul Elvstrøm	Yachting	Denmark
March 31, 1928	Gordie Howe	Ice hockey	Canada
April 9, 1928	Paul Arizin	Basketball	United States
April 16, 1928	Dick "Night Train" Lane	Football	United States
May 9, 1928	Pancho Gonzales	Tennis	United States
May 13, 1928	Jim Shoulders	Rodeo	United States
May 19, 1928	Dolph Schayes	Basketball	United States
August 9, 1928	Bob Cousy	Basketball	United States
October 21, 1928	Whitey Ford	Baseball	United States
December 31, 1928	Hugh McElhenny	Football	United States
January 17, 1929	Jacques Plante	Ice hockey	Canada
March 5, 1929	Casey Tibbs	Rodeo	United States
March 24, 1929	Roger Bannister	Middle-distance runs	England
May 14, 1929	Gump Worsley	Ice hockey	Canada
July 18, 1929	Dick Button	Figure skating	United States
August 14, 1929	Dick Tiger	Boxing	Nigeria
September 7, 1929	Clyde Lovellette	Basketball	United States
September 10, 1929	Arnold Palmer	Golf	United States

Born	Name	Sport	Country
October 22, 1929	Lev Yashin	Soccer	Soviet Union
November 24, 1929	John Henry Johnson	Football	United States
December 23, 1929	Dick Weber	Bowling	United States
December 28, 1929	Terry Sawchuk	Ice hockey	Canada
May 8, 1930	Doug Atkins	Football	United States
May 12, 1930	Pat McCormick	Diving	United States
June 27, 1930	Tommy Kono	Weightlifting, Bodybuilding	United States
August 16, 1930	Frank Gifford	Football	United States
November 17, 1930	Bob Mathias	Decathlon	United States
January 31, 1931	Ernie Banks	Baseball	United States
February 16, 1931	Bernie Geoffrion	Ice hockey	Canada
April 13, 1931	Dan Gurney	Auto racing	United States
May 6, 1931	Willie Mays	Baseball	United States
June 24, 1931	Billy Casper	Golf	United States
July 13, 1931	Frank Ramsey	Basketball	United States
August 1, 1931	Harold Connolly	Hammer throw	United States
August 19, 1931	Willie Shoemaker	Horse racing	United States
August 31, 1931	Jean Beliveau	Ice hockey	Canada
October 3, 1931	Glenn Hall	Ice hockey	Canada
October 13, 1931	Eddie Mathews	Baseball	United States
October 20, 1931	Mickey Mantle	Baseball	United States
December 4, 1931	Alex Delvecchio	Ice hockey	Canada
December 9, 1931	Cliff Hagan	Basketball	United States
January 14, 1932	Don Garlits	Auto racing	United States
January 18, 1932	Joe Schmidt	Football	United States
January 27, 1932	Boris Shakhlin	Gymnastics	Soviet Union, Russia
January 28, 1932	Parry O'Brien	Shot put	United States
February 6, 1932	Jim Poole	Badminton	United States
April 19, 1932	Andrea Mead Lawrence	Skiing	United States
May 25, 1932	K. C. Jones	Basketball	United States
July 16, 1932	Oleg Protopopov	Figure skating	Soviet Union, Russia
August 7, 1932	Abebe Bikila	Marathon	Ethiopia
October 2, 1932	Maury Wills	Baseball	United States
October 17, 1932	Paul Anderson	Weightlifting	United States
November 9, 1932	Frank Selvy	Basketball	United States
November 13, 1932	Olga Connolly	Discus throw	Czechoslovakia
November 21, 1932	Jim Ringo	Football	United States
December 9, 1932	Bill Hartack	Horse racing	United States
December 12, 1932	Bob Pettit	Basketball	United States
January 13, 1933	Tom Gola	Basketball	United States
February 27, 1933	Raymond Berry	Football	United States
February 28, 1933	Chuck Vinci	Weightlifting	United States
March 23, 1933	Hayes Jenkins	Figure skating	United States
May 7, 1933	Johnny Unitas	Football	United States
June 24, 1933	Sam Jones	Basketball	United States
October 18, 1933	Forrest Gregg	Football	United States
October 28, 1933	Garrincha	Soccer	Brazil
November 23, 1933	Carmen Salvino	Bowling	United States
November 25, 1933	Lenny Moore	Football	United States

Born	Name	Sport	Country
January 9, 1934	Bart Starr	Football	United States
February 5, 1934	Hank Aaron	Baseball	United States
February 12, 1934	Bill Russell	Basketball	United States
February 20, 1934	Bobby Unser	Auto racing	United States
April 3, 1934	Jim Parker	Football	United States
May 11, 1934	Jack Twyman	Basketball	United States
August 18, 1934	Roberto Clemente	Baseball	Puerto Rico
August 23, 1934	Sonny Jurgensen	Football	United States
August 26, 1934	Tom Heinsohn	Basketball	United States
September 10, 1934	Roger Maris	Baseball	United States
September 16, 1934	Elgin Baylor	Basketball	United States
September 17, 1934	Maureen Connolly	Tennis	United States
October 4, 1934	Sam Huff	Football	United States
October 28, 1934	Jim Beatty	Middle- and long-distance runs	United States
November 2, 1934	Ken Rosewall	Tennis	Australia
November 23, 1934	Lew Hoad	Tennis	Australia
December 19, 1934	Al Kaline	Baseball	United States
December 22, 1934	David Pearson	Auto racing	United States
December 27, 1934	Larisa Latynina	Gymnastics	Soviet Union, Ukraine
January 4, 1935	Floyd Patterson	Boxing	United States
January 16, 1935	A. J. Foyt	Auto racing	United States
January 25, 1935	Don Maynard	Football	United States
February 14, 1935	Mickey Wright	Golf	United States
May 8, 1935	Jack Charlton	Soccer	England
June 20, 1935	Len Dawson	Football	United States
July 18, 1935	Tenley Albright	Figure skating	United States
July 19, 1935	George Breen	Swimming	United States
August 18, 1935	Rafer Johnson	Decathlon	United States
August 31, 1935	Frank Robinson	Baseball	United States
September 20, 1935	Jim Taylor	Football	United States
October 15, 1935	Willie O'Ree	Ice hockey	Canada
October 15, 1935	Bobby Joe Morrow	Sprints	United States
November 1, 1935	Gary Player	Golf	South Africa
November 5, 1935	Lester Piggott	Horse racing	England
November 9, 1935	Bob Gibson	Baseball	United States
November 17, 1935	Toni Sailer	Skiing	Austria
November 22, 1935	Ludmila Protopopov	Figure skating	Soviet Union, Russia
December 23, 1935	Paul Hornung	Football	United States
December 30, 1935	Sandy Koufax	Baseball	United States
February 17, 1936	Jim Brown	Football	United States
February 26, 1936	Buddy Werner	Skiing	United States
March 14, 1936	Jim Clark	Auto racing	Scotland
June 26, 1936	Hal Greer	Basketball	United States
June 29, 1936	David Jenkins	Figure skating	United States
June 29, 1936	Harmon Killebrew	Baseball	United States
July 23, 1936	Don Drysdale	Baseball	United States
August 21, 1936	Wilt Chamberlain	Basketball	United States
September 19, 1936	Al Oerter	Discus throw	United States
November 3, 1936	Roy Emerson	Tennis	Australia

Born	Name	Sport	Country
December 12, 1936	Iolanda Balas	High jump	Romania
December 23, 1936	Willie Wood	Football	United States
December 29, 1936	Ray Nitschke	Football	United States
February 12, 1937	Charley Dumas	High jump	United States
March 18, 1937	Mark Donohue	Auto racing	United States
May 10, 1937	Tamara Press	Track and field	Ukraine, Soviet Union
July 2, 1937	Richard Petty	Auto racing	United States
August 25, 1937	Lones Wigger	Shooting	United States
September 4, 1937	Dawn Fraser	Swimming	Australia
September 16, 1937	Alexander Medved	Wrestling	Ukraine
October 11, 1937	Bobby Charlton	Soccer	England
October 20, 1937	Juan Marichal	Baseball	Dominican Republic
October 28, 1937	Lenny Wilkens	Basketball	United States
December 3, 1937	Bobby Allison	Auto racing	United States
December 30, 1937	Gordon Banks	Soccer	England
December 30, 1937	Jim Marshall	Football	United States
January 5, 1938	Jim Otto	Football	United States
January 10, 1938	Willie McCovey	Baseball	United States
January 18, 1938	Curt Flood	Baseball	United States
February 25, 1938	Herb Elliott	Middle-distance runs	Australia
March 7, 1938	Janet Guthrie	Auto racing	United States
March 10, 1938	Ron Mix	Football	United States
March 12, 1938	Johnny Rutherford	Auto racing	United States
March 24, 1938	Larry Wilson	Football	United States
March 31, 1938	Jimmy Johnson	Football	United States
April 20, 1938	Betty Cuthbert	Sprints	Australia
April 27, 1938	Earl Anthony	Bowling	United States
May 28, 1938	Jerry West	Basketball	United States
June 15, 1938	Billy Williams	Baseball	United States
June 30, 1938	Billy Mills	Long-distance runs	United States
August 9, 1938	Rod Laver	Tennis	Australia
August 19, 1938	Valentin Mankin	Yachting	Soviet Union, Ukraine
September 15, 1938	Gaylord Perry	Baseball	United States
October 17, 1938	Evel Knievel	Stunt driving	United States
November 19, 1938	Ted Turner	Yachting	United States
November 24, 1938	Oscar Robertson	Basketball	United States
December 9, 1938	Deacon Jones	Football	United States
December 13, 1938	Gus Johnson	Basketball	United States
December 15, 1938	Bob Foster	Boxing	United States
December 17, 1938	Peter Snell	Middle-distance runs	New Zealand
January 3, 1939	Bobby Hull	Ice hockey	Canada
January 6, 1939	Murray Rose	Swimming	England
January 10, 1939	Bill Toomey	Decathlon	United States
March 4, 1939	JoAnne Carner	Golf	United States
March 10, 1939	Irina Press	Track and field	Ukraine, Soviet Union
March 27, 1939	Cale Yarborough	Auto racing	United States
May 9, 1939	Ralph Boston	Long jump	United States
May 29, 1939	Al Unser	Auto racing	United States

Born	Name	Sport	Country
June 8, 1939	Herb Adderley	Football	United States
June 11, 1939	Jackie Stewart	Auto racing	Scotland
June 18, 1939	Lou Brock	Baseball	United States
July 26, 1939	Bob Lilly	Football	United States
August 16, 1939	Tony Trabert	Tennis	United States
August 22, 1939	Carl Yastrzemski	Baseball	United States
September 22, 1939	Junko Tabei	Mountaineering	Japan
September 27, 1939	Kathy Whitworth	Golf	United States
October 11, 1939	Maria Bueno	Tennis	Brazil
October 18, 1939	Mike Ditka	Football	United States
December 1, 1939	Lee Trevino	Golf	United States
December 14, 1939	Ernie Davis	Football	United States
January, 1940	Kip Keino	Long-distance runs	Kenya
January 20, 1940	Carol Heiss	Figure skating	United States
January 21, 1940	Jack Nicklaus	Golf	United States
February 3, 1940	Fran Tarkenton	Football	United States
February 24, 1940	Denis Law	Soccer	Scotland
February 28, 1940	Mario Andretti	Auto racing	United States
March 30, 1940	Jerry Lucas	Basketball	United States
April 8, 1940	John Havlicek	Basketball	United States
May 10, 1940	Sadaharu Oh	Baseball	Japan
May 20, 1940	Stan Mikita	Ice hockey	Czechoslovakia, Slovakia, Canada
June 11, 1940	Johnny Giles	Soccer	Ireland
June 19, 1940	Shirley Muldowney	Auto racing	United States
June 23, 1940	Wilma Rudolph	Sprints	United States
July 18, 1940	Joe Torre	Baseball	United States
July 20, 1940	Tony Oliva	Baseball	Cuba
August 3, 1940	Lance Alworth	Football	United States
August 18, 1940	Joan Joyce	Softball	United States
September 10, 1940	Buck Buchanan	Football	United States
September 15, 1940	Merlin Olsen	Football	United States
October 16, 1940	Dave DeBusschere	Basketball	United States
October 23, 1940	Pelé	Soccer	Brazil
November 27, 1940	Bruce Lee	Gung-fu	Hong Kong
December 15, 1940	Nick Buoniconti	Football	United States
January 12, 1941	Chet Jastremski	Swimming	United States
March 6, 1941	Willie Stargell	Baseball	United States
April 6, 1941	Don Prudhomme	Auto racing	United States
April 12, 1941	Bobby Moore	Soccer	England
April 14, 1941	Pete Rose	Baseball	United States
July 25, 1941	Nate Thurmond	Basketball	United States
December 8, 1941	Geoff Hurst	Soccer	England
January 7, 1942	Vasily Alexeyev	Weightlifting	Russia, Soviet Union
January 15, 1942	Carl Eller	Football	United States
January 17, 1942	Muhammad Ali	Boxing	United States
January 25, 1942	Eusebio	Soccer	Mozambique
February 5, 1942	Roger Staubach	Football	United States
February 20, 1942	Phil Esposito	Ice hockey	Canada
April 15, 1942	Walt Hazzard	Basketball	United States

Born	Name	Sport	Country
May 3, 1942	Vera Čáslavská	Gymnastics	Czechoslovakia
May 14, 1942	Valery Brumel	High jump	Soviet Union, Russia
May 14, 1942	Tony Perez	Baseball	Cuba
May 21, 1942	John Konrads	Swimming	Latvia
June 25, 1942	Willis Reed	Basketball	United States
July 4, 1942	Floyd Little	Football	United States
July 7, 1942	Connie Hawkins	Basketball	United States
July 16, 1942	Margaret Court	Tennis	Australia
September 4, 1942	Ray Floyd	Golf	United States
September 28, 1942	Charley Taylor	Football	United States
November 8, 1942	Angel Cordero, Jr.	Horse racing	Puerto Rico
November 28, 1942	Paul Warfield	Football	United States
December 9, 1942	Billy Bremner	Soccer	Scotland
December 9, 1942	Dick Butkus	Football	United States
December 20, 1942	Bob Hayes	Sprints, Football	United States
February 23, 1943	Fred Biletnikoff	Football	United States
March 1, 1943	Akinori Nakayama	Gymnastics	Japan
March 9, 1943	Bobby Fischer	Chess	United States
April 13, 1943	Billy Kidd	Skiing	United States
April 23, 1943	Gail Goodrich	Basketball	United States
May 11, 1943	Nancy Greene	Skiing	Canada
May 30, 1943	Gale Sayers	Football	United States
May 31, 1943	Joe Namath	Football	United States
June 3, 1943	Billy Cunningham	Basketball	United States
June 8, 1943	Willie Davenport	Hurdles	United States
July 10, 1943	Arthur Ashe	Tennis	United States
July 28, 1943	Bill Bradley	Basketball	United States
August 30, 1943	Jean-Claude Killy	Skiing	France
September 16, 1943	Dennis Conner	Yachting	United States
September 19, 1943	Joe Morgan	Baseball	United States
September 22, 1943	Jimmie Heuga	Skiing	United States
November 21, 1943	Larry Mahan	Rodeo	United States
November 22, 1943	Billie Jean King	Tennis	United States
November 24, 1943	Dave Bing	Basketball	United States
January 17, 1944	Joe Frazier	Boxing	United States
March 28, 1944	Rick Barry	Basketball	United States
May 23, 1944	John Newcombe	Tennis	Australia
June 5, 1944	Tommie Smith	Sprints	United States
July 26, 1944	Micki King	Diving	United States
November 12, 1944	Ken Houston	Football	United States
November 17, 1944	Tom Seaver	Baseball	United States
November 21, 1944	Earl Monroe	Basketball	United States
December 22, 1944	Steve Carlton	Baseball	United States
February 3, 1945	Bob Griese	Football	United States
February 18, 1945	Judy Rankin	Golf	United States
February 28, 1945	Bubba Smith	Football	United States
March 5, 1945	Randy Matson	Shot put	United States
March 29, 1945	Walt Frazier	Basketball	United States
April 2, 1945	Don Sutton	Baseball	United States
May 12, 1945	Alan Ball	Soccer	England
June 3, 1945	Hale Irwin	Golf	United States

Born	Name	Sport	Country
June 12, 1945	Pat Jennings	Soccer	Northern Ireland
June 17, 1945	Eddy Merckx	Cycling	Belgium
July 10, 1945	Virginia Wade	Tennis	England
August 7, 1945	Alan Page	Football	United States
August 15, 1945	Gene Upshaw	Football	United States
August 29, 1945	Wyomia Tyus	Sprints	United States
September 11, 1945	Franz Beckenbauer	Soccer	Germany
October 1, 1945	Rod Carew	Baseball	Panama
October 15, 1945	Jim Palmer	Baseball	United States
November 11, 1945	Gerd Müller	Soccer	Germany
November 17, 1945	Elvin Hayes	Basketball	United States
December 25, 1945	Ken Stabler	Football	United States
March 6, 1946	Gerry Lindgren	Long-distance runs	United States
March 14, 1946	Wes Unseld	Basketball	United States
April 8, 1946	Catfish Hunter	Baseball	United States
April 30, 1946	Don Schollander	Swimming	United States
May 18, 1946	Reggie Jackson	Baseball	United States
May 22, 1946	George Best	Soccer	Northern Ireland
May 24, 1946	Irena Szewinska	Track and field	Soviet Union, Russia
August 29, 1946	Bob Beamon	Long jump, Triple jump	United States
September 10, 1946	Jim Hines	Sprints, Football	United States
September 24, 1946	Joe Greene	Football	United States
October 11, 1946	Sawao Kato	Gymnastics	Japan
October 17, 1946	Bob Seagren	Pole vault	United States
November 26, 1946	Art Shell	Football	United States
December 12, 1946	Emerson Fittipaldi	Auto racing	Brazil
December 14, 1946	Stan Smith	Tennis	United States
December 25, 1946	Larry Csonka	Football	United States
December 29, 1946	Laffit Pincay, Jr.	Horse racing	Panama, United States
January 31, 1947	Nolan Ryan	Baseball	United States
February 6, 1947	Charlie Hickcox	Swimming	United States
February 25, 1947	Lee Evans	Middle-distance runs	United States
March 6, 1947	Dick Fosbury	High jump	United States
April 16, 1947	Kareem Abdul-Jabbar	Basketball	United States
April 25, 1947	Johan Cruyff	Soccer	Netherlands
April 26, 1947	Donna de Varona	Swimming	United States
April 29, 1947	Jim Ryun	Middle-distance runs	United States
June 22, 1947	Pete Maravich	Basketball	United States
July 3, 1947	Mike Burton	Swimming	United States
July 9, 1947	O. J. Simpson	Football	United States
July 30, 1947	Arnold Schwarzenegger	Bodybuilding	Austria, United States
August 8, 1947	Ken Dryden	Ice hockey	Canada
August 12, 1947	Linda Metheny	Gymnastics	United States
September 29, 1947	Corky Carroll	Surfing	United States
October 6, 1947	Klaus Dibiasi	Diving	Italy
October 31, 1947	Frank Shorter	Long-distance runs, Marathon	United States
November 1, 1947	Ted Hendricks	Football	United States
December 7, 1947	Johnny Bench	Baseball	United States

Born	Name	Sport	Country
December 22, 1947	Mitsuo Tsukahara	Gymnastics	Japan
December 23, 1947	Bill Rodgers	Long-distance runs, Marathon	United States
January 22, 1948	George Foreman	Boxing	United States
March 20, 1948	Bobby Orr	Ice hockey	Canada
June 4, 1948	Sandra Post	Golf	Canada
July 27, 1948	Peggy Fleming	Figure skating	United States
September 2, 1948	Nate Archibald	Basketball	United States
September 2, 1948	Terry Bradshaw	Football	United States
September 10, 1948	Bob Lanier	Basketball	United States
October 25, 1948	Dave Cowens	Basketball	United States
October 25, 1948	Dan Gable	Wrestling	United States
October 25, 1948	Dan Issel	Basketball	United States
November 7, 1948	Ivan Yarygin	Wrestling	Soviet Union
December 22, 1948	Steve Garvey	Baseball	United States
December 23, 1948	Jack Ham	Football	United States
December 26, 1948	Carlton Fisk	Baseball	United States
February 22, 1949	Niki Lauda	Auto racing	Austria
April 3, 1949	Lyle Alzado	Football	United States
July 22, 1949	Lasse Viren	Long-distance runs	Finland
August 4, 1949	John Riggins	Football	United States
August 13, 1949	Bobby Clarke	Ice hockey	Canada
August 18, 1949	Rudy Hartono	Badminton	Indonesia
September 4, 1949	Tom Watson	Golf	United States
September 9, 1949	John Curry	Figure skating	England
September 12, 1949	Irina Rodnina	Figure skating	Russia, Soviet Union
September 18, 1949	Peter Shilton	Soccer	England
September 21, 1949	Artis Gilmore	Basketball	United States
September 27, 1949	Mike Schmidt	Baseball	United States
October 20, 1949	Valeri Borzov	Sprints	Soviet Union, Ukraine
October 28, 1949	Bruce Jenner	Decathlon	United States
November 3, 1949	Larry Holmes	Boxing	United States
December 9, 1949	Tom Kite	Golf	United States
December 22, 1949	Ray Guy	Football	United States
February 10, 1950	Mark Spitz	Swimming	United States
February 22, 1950	Julius Erving	Basketball	United States
March 7, 1950	Franco Harris	Football	United States
May 12, 1950	Renate Stecher	Sprints	Germany
May 18, 1950	Rod Milburn	Hurdles	United States
July 27, 1950	Reggie McKenzie	Football	United States
August 5, 1950	Rosi Mittermaier	Skiing	Germany
August 27, 1950	Cynthia Potter	Diving	United States
October 14, 1950	Sheila Young	Speed skating, Cycling	United States
November 8, 1950	Chris Kinard	Badminton	United States
November 13, 1950	Gil Perreault	Ice hockey	Canada
November 15, 1950	Mac Wilkins	Discus throw	United States
November 17, 1950	Roland Matthes	Swimming	Germany
December 20, 1950	Tom Ferguson	Rodeo	United States
December 25, 1950	Kyle Rote, Jr.	Soccer	United States

Born	Name	Sport	Country
January 12, 1951	Bill Madlock	Baseball	United States
January 25, 1951	Steve Prefontaine	Long-distance runs	United States
February 14, 1951	Kevin Keegan	Soccer	England
February 25, 1951	Donald Quarrie	Sprints	Jamaica
March 24, 1951	Pat Bradley	Golf	United States
April 4, 1951	John Hannah	Football	United States
May 23, 1951	Anatoly Karpov	Chess	Soviet Union, Russia
June 16, 1951	Roberto Duran	Boxing	Panama
July 5, 1951	Rich Gossage	Baseball	United States
July 31, 1951	Evonne Goolagong	Tennis	Australia
August 3, 1951	Marcel Dionne	Ice hockey	Canada
September 20, 1951	Guy Lafleur	Ice hockey	Canada
September 25, 1951	Bob McAdoo	Basketball	United States
September 30, 1951	Catie Ball	Swimming	United States
October 3, 1951	Dave Winfield	Baseball	United States
December 3, 1951	Alberto Juantorena	Middle-distance runs	Cuba
December 3, 1951	Rick Mears	Auto racing	United States
December 17, 1951	Tatyana Kazankina	Middle-distance runs	Soviet Union, Russia
January 11, 1952	Ben Crenshaw	Golf	United States
January 12, 1952	John Walker	Middle-distance runs	New Zealand
March 7, 1952	Lynn Swann	Football	United States
March 29, 1952	Teófilo Stevenson	Boxing	Cuba
April 16, 1952	Peter Westbrook	Fencing	United States
April 19, 1952	Alexis Arguello	Boxing	Nicaragua, United States
April 25, 1952	Vladislav Tretiak	Ice hockey	Soviet Union, Russia
April 27, 1952	George Gervin	Basketball	United States
April 29, 1952	Dale Earnhardt	Auto racing	United States
June 16, 1952	Alexander Zaitsev	Figure skating	Russia, Soviet Union
July 8, 1952	Jack Lambert	Football	United States
July 15, 1952	John Stallworth	Football	United States
August 14, 1952	Debbie Meyer	Swimming	United States
August 17, 1952	Guillermo Vilas	Tennis	Argentina
September 2, 1952	Jimmy Connors	Tennis	United States
October 4, 1952	Anita DeFrantz	Rowing	United States
October 7, 1952	Ludmila Turishcheva	Gymnastics	Soviet Union, Russia
October 14, 1952	Nikolai Andrianov	Gymnastics	Russia, Soviet Union
November 5, 1952	Bill Walton	Basketball	United States
December 12, 1952	Cathy Rigby	Gymnastics	United States
January 10, 1953	Bobby Rahal	Auto racing	United States
January 15, 1953	Randy White	Football	United States
February 17, 1953	Pertti Karppinen	Rowing	Finland
March 27, 1953	Annemarie Moser-Proell	Skiing	Austria
April 6, 1953	Janet Lynn	Figure skating	United States
May 13, 1953	Henry Rono	Long-distance runs, Steeplechase	Kenya

Born	Name	Sport	Country
May 15, 1953	George Brett	Baseball	United States
August 8, 1953	Nigel Mansell	Auto racing	England
August 30, 1953	Robert Parish	Basketball	United States
October 1, 1953	Greta Waitz	Marathon	Norway
October 13, 1953	Pat Day	Horse racing	United States
December 3, 1953	Franz Klammer	Skiing	Austria
December 6, 1953	Dwight Stones	High jump	United States
January 4, 1954	Dave Scott	Triathlon	United States
January 5, 1954	Alex English	Basketball	United States
February 10, 1954	Dave Villwock	Hydroplane racing	United States
March 8, 1954	David Wilkie	Swimming	Scotland
April 7, 1954	Tony Dorsett	Football	United States
April 8, 1954	Gary Carter	Baseball	United States
May 23, 1954	Marvin Hagler	Boxing	United States
July 1, 1954	Chip Hanauer	Powerboat racing	United States
July 10, 1954	Andre Dawson	Baseball	United States
July 25, 1954	Walter Payton	Football	United States
July 28, 1954	Steve Zungul	Soccer	Croatia
July 29, 1954	Flo Hyman	Volleyball	United States
August 21, 1954	Archie Griffin	Football	United States
September 28, 1954	Steve Largent	Football	United States
October 3, 1954	Dennis Eckersley	Baseball	United States
November 14, 1954	Bernard Hinault	Cycling	France
December 21, 1954	Chris Evert	Tennis	United States
December 26, 1954	Susan Butcher	Sled dog racing	United States
December 26, 1954	Ozzie Smith	Baseball	United States
1955	Liem Swie-King	Badminton	Indonesia
January 30, 1955	Curtis Strange	Golf	United States
February 10, 1955	Greg Norman	Golf	Australia
February 24, 1955	Alain Prost	Auto racing	France
March 23, 1955	Moses Malone	Basketball	United States
March 26, 1955	Ann Meyers	Basketball	United States
March 27, 1955	Chris McCarron	Horse racing	United States
March 29, 1955	Earl Campbell	Football	United States
April 26, 1955	Mike Scott	Baseball	United States
May 16, 1955	Olga Korbut	Gymnastics	Soviet Union, Belarus
June 7, 1955	Bill Koch	Skiing	United States
June 21, 1955	Michel Platini	Soccer	France
August 13, 1955	Betsy King	Golf	United States
August 31, 1955	Edwin Moses	Hurdles	United States
September 16, 1955	Robin Yount	Baseball	United States
September 25, 1955	Karl-Heinz Rummenigge	Soccer	Germany
October 9, 1955	Steve Ovett	Middle-distance runs	England
January 3, 1956	Willy T. Ribbs	Auto racing	United States
January 20, 1956	John Naber	Swimming	United States
February 24, 1956	Eddie Murray	Baseball	United States
March 11, 1956	Willie Banks	Triple jump	United States
March 12, 1956	Dale Murphy	Baseball	United States
March 18, 1956	Ingemar Stenmark	Skiing	Sweden
March 21, 1956	Ingrid Kristiansen	Middle- and long-distance runs	Norway

Born	Name	Sport	Country
March 29, 1956	Kurt Thomas	Gymnastics	United States
May 5, 1956	Steve Scott	Middle-distance runs	United States
May 17, 1956	Sugar Ray Leonard	Boxing	United States
June 5, 1956	Björn Borg	Tennis	Sweden
June 11, 1956	Joe Montana	Football	United States
July 18, 1956	Bryan Trottier	Ice hockey	Canada
July 26, 1956	Dorothy Hamill	Figure skating	United States
August 14, 1956	Rusty Wallace	Auto racing	United States
September 29, 1956	Sebastian Coe	Middle-distance runs	England
October 18, 1956	Martina Navratilova	Tennis	Czechoslovakia, United States
October 23, 1956	Darrell Pace	Archery	United States
October 27, 1956	Patty Sheehan	Golf	United States
November 18, 1956	Warren Moon	Football	United States
November 23, 1956	Shane Gould	Swimming	Australia
December 7, 1956	Larry Bird	Basketball	United States
December 24, 1956	Lee Kemp	Wrestling	United States
January 2, 1957	Lynne Cox	Swimming	United States
January 6, 1957	Nancy Lopez	Golf	United States
January 22, 1957	Mike Bossy	Ice hockey	Canada
January 28, 1957	Nick Price	Golf	South Africa
January 30, 1957	Payne Stewart	Golf	United States
January 31, 1957	Shirley Babashoff	Swimming	United States
February 19, 1957	Dave Stewart	Baseball	United States
February 26, 1957	Connie Carpenter	Cycling	United States
April 2, 1957	Brad Parks	Tennis, Track and field	United States
April 9, 1957	Seve Ballesteros	Golf	Spain
April 15, 1957	Evelyn Ashford	Sprints	United States
May 7, 1957	Sinjin Smith	Volleyball	United States
May 10, 1957	Phil Mahre	Skiing	United States
May 16, 1957	Joan Benoit	Marathon	United States
July 18, 1957	Nick Faldo	Golf	England
July 26, 1957	Jeff Blatnick	Wrestling	United States
August 7, 1957	Alexander Dityatin	Gymnastics	Soviet Union, Russia
August 17, 1957	Robin Cousins	Figure skating	England
August 27, 1957	Bernhard Langer	Golf	Germany
October 7, 1957	Jayne Torvill	Figure skating	England
December 19, 1957	Kevin McHale	Basketball	United States
1958	Yasuhiro Yamashita	Judo	Japan
January 23, 1958	Sergei Litvinov	Hammer throw	Russia, Soviet Union
March 28, 1958	Bart Conner	Gymnastics	United States
June 14, 1958	Eric Heiden	Speed skating	United States
June 15, 1958	Wade Boggs	Baseball	United States
June 25, 1958	Debbie Green	Volleyball	United States
July 1, 1958	Nancy Lieberman-Cline	Basketball	United States
July 27, 1958	Christopher Dean	Figure skating	England
July 30, 1958	Daley Thompson	Decathlon	England
August 4, 1958	Mary Decker-Slaney	Middle- and long-distance runs	United States
August 4, 1958	Greg Foster	Hurdles	United States

Born	Name	Sport	Country
August 7, 1958	Alberto Salazar	Marathon	Cuba
August 24, 1958	Craig Buck	Volleyball	United States
August 28, 1958	Scott Hamilton	Figure skating	United States
September 16, 1958	Orel Hershiser	Baseball	United States
October 1, 1958	Bill Bowness	Waterskiing	United States
October 9, 1958	Mike Singletary	Football	United States
October 18, 1958	Thomas Hearns	Boxing	United States
October 25, 1958	Kornelia Ender	Swimming	Germany
October 31, 1958	Jeannie Longo	Cycling	France
November 29, 1958	Steve Timmons	Volleyball	United States
December 2, 1958	Randy Gardner	Figure skating	United States
December 25, 1958	Rickey Henderson	Baseball	United States
February 4, 1959	Lawrence Taylor	Football	United States
February 16, 1959	John McEnroe	Tennis	United States
March 24, 1959	Renaldo Nehemiah	Hurdles, Football	United States
April 2, 1959	Brian Goodell	Swimming	United States
April 19, 1959	Scott Schulte	Water Polo	United States
May 8, 1959	Ronnie Lott	Football	United States
July 24, 1959	Eddie Liddie	Judo	France
August 12, 1959	Lynette Woodard	Basketball	United States
August 14, 1959	Magic Johnson	Basketball	United States
August 21, 1959	Jim McMahon	Football	United States
September 13, 1959	Kathy Johnson	Gymnastics	United States
September 16, 1959	Tim Raines	Baseball	United States
September 18, 1959	Ryne Sandberg	Baseball	United States
September 23, 1959	Hortencia Marcari	Basketball	Brazil
October 3, 1959	Fred Couples	Golf	United States
October 6, 1959	Walter Ray Williams, Jr.	Bowling, Horseshoe pitching	United States
December 2, 1959	Greg Barton	Canoeing/Kayaking	United States
December 21, 1959	Florence Griffith-Joyner	Sprints	United States
January 12, 1960	Dominique Wilkins	Basketball	United States
January 29, 1960	Greg Louganis	Diving	United States
January 29, 1960	Steve Sax	Baseball	United States
February 14, 1960	Jim Kelly	Football	United States
March 7, 1960	Ivan Lendl	Tennis	Czechoslovakia, United States
March 21, 1960	Ayrton Senna	Auto racing	Brazil
March 26, 1960	Marcus Allen	Football	United States
May 9, 1960	Tony Gwynn	Baseball	United States
May 10, 1960	Merlene Ottey	Sprints	Jamaica
May 21, 1960	Vladimir Salnikov	Swimming	Soviet Union, Russia
June 28, 1960	John Elway	Football	United States
July 6, 1960	Valerie Brisco-Hooks	Sprints	United States
August 19, 1960	Morten Andersen	Football	United States, Denmark
August 24, 1960	Cal Ripken, Jr.	Baseball	United States
September 2, 1960	Eric Dickerson	Football	United States
September 17, 1960	Damon Hill	Auto racing	England
September 22, 1960	Tai Babilonia	Figure skating	United States
October 30, 1960	Diego Maradona	Soccer	Argentina

Born	Name	Sport	Country
November 1, 1960	Fernando Valenzuela	Baseball	Mexico
November 2, 1960	Said Aouita	Middle-distance runs	Morocco
November 3, 1960	Karch Kiraly	Volleyball	United States
November 29, 1960	Howard Johnson	Baseball	United States
November 30, 1960	Gary Lineker	Soccer	England
December 28, 1960	Ray Bourque	Ice hockey	Canada
January 18, 1961	Mark Messier	Ice hockey	Canada
January 26, 1961	Wayne Gretzky	Ice hockey	Canada, United States
February 20, 1961	Steve Lundquist	Swimming	United States
February 27, 1961	James Worthy	Basketball	United States
March 14, 1961	Kirby Puckett	Baseball	United States
April 20, 1961	Don Mattingly	Baseball	United States
April 30, 1961	Isiah Thomas	Basketball	United States
May 13, 1961	Dennis Rodman	Basketball	United States
May 19, 1961	Lisa Wagner	Bowling	United States
May 27, 1961	Jon Lugbill	Canoeing/Kayaking	United States
May 27, 1961	Jill Sterkel	Swimming	United States
June 3, 1961	Peter Vidmar	Gymnastics	United States
June 26, 1961	Greg LeMond	Cycling	United States
July 1, 1961	Carl Lewis	Long jump, Sprints	United States
July 4, 1961	Connie Paraskevin-Young	Cycling	United States
September 15, 1961	Dan Marino	Football	United States
October 11, 1961	Steve Young	Football	United States
November 12, 1961	Nadia Comăneci	Gymnastics	Romania
December 19, 1961	Reggie White	Football	United States
January 12, 1962	Gunde Svan	Skiing	Sweden
January 18, 1962	David O'Connor	Equestrian	United States
March 3, 1962	Jackie Joyner-Kersee	Heptathlon, Hurdles, Long jump	United States
March 3, 1962	Herschel Walker	Football	United States
March 12, 1962	Darryl Strawberry	Baseball	United States
March 23, 1962	Steven Redgrave	Rowing	England
March 26, 1962	John Stockton	Basketball	United States
April 17, 1962	Nancy Hogshead	Swimming	United States
June 2, 1962	Paula Newby-Fraser	Triathlon	Zimbabwe
June 22, 1962	Clyde Drexler	Basketball	United States
July 12, 1962	Julio César Chávez	Boxing	Mexico
July 17, 1962	Jay Barrs	Archery	United States
August 4, 1962	Roger Clemens	Baseball	United States
August 5, 1962	Patrick Ewing	Basketball	Jamaica, United States
August 26, 1962	Roger Kingdom	Hurdles	United States
October 13, 1962	Jerry Rice	Football	United States
October 16, 1962	Tamara McKinney	Skiing	United States
October 19, 1962	Evander Holyfield	Boxing	United States
October 23, 1962	Doug Flutie	Football	United States
November 30, 1962	Bo Jackson	Baseball, Football	United States
December 12, 1962	Tracy Austin	Tennis	United States
January 2, 1963	David Cone	Baseball	United States
January 2, 1963	Edgar Martinez	Baseball	United States
January 11, 1963	Petra Schneider	Swimming	Germany

Born	Name	Sport	Country
January 21, 1963	Hakeem Olajuwon	Basketball	Nigeria, United States
February 4, 1963	Tracie Ruiz-Conforto	Synchronized swimming	United States
February 4, 1963	Pirmin Zurbriggen	Skiing	Switzerland
February 17, 1963	Michael Jordan	Basketball	United States
February 20, 1963	Charles Barkley	Basketball	United States
March 6, 1963	Tori Murden	Rowing	United States
March 20, 1963	Diana Golden	Skiing	United States
March 27, 1963	Randall Cunningham	Football	United States
April 13, 1963	Garry Kasparov	Chess	Soviet Union, Azerbaijan
April 14, 1963	Cynthia Cooper	Basketball	United States
June 18, 1963	Bruce Smith	Football	United States
July 17, 1963	Matti Nykänen	Ski jumping	Finland
July 24, 1963	Julie Krone	Horse racing	United States
July 24, 1963	Karl Malone	Basketball	United States
July 30, 1963	Chris Mullin	Basketball	United States
September 10, 1963	Randy Johnson	Baseball	United States
October 1, 1963	Mark McGwire	Baseball	United States
October 22, 1963	Brian Boitano	Figure skating	United States
November 10, 1963	Mike Powell	Long jump	United States
November 13, 1963	Vinny Testaverde	Football	United States
December 14, 1963	Sergei Bubka	Pole vault	Soviet Union, Ukraine
January 3, 1964	Cheryl Miller	Basketball	United States
February 7, 1964	Cynthia Woodhead	Swimming	United States
March 13, 1964	Will Clark	Baseball	United States
March 18, 1964	Bonnie Blair	Speed skating	United States
April 11, 1964	Bret Saberhagen	Baseball	United States
June 8, 1964	Butch Reynolds	Middle-distance runs	United States
July 2, 1964	José Canseco	Baseball	Cuba
July 3, 1964	Tom Curren	Surfing	United States
July 16, 1964	Miguel Indurain	Cycling	Spain
July 24, 1964	Barry Bonds	Baseball	United States
August 22, 1964	Mats Wilander	Tennis	Sweden
October 27, 1964	Mary T. Meagher	Swimming	United States
October 31, 1964	Marco van Basten	Soccer	Netherlands
November 16, 1964	Dwight Gooden	Baseball	United States
December 5, 1964	Pablo Morales	Swimming	United States
December 16, 1964	Heike Dreschler	Long jump	Germany
January 29, 1965	Dominik Hasek	Ice hockey	Czechoslovakia
May 9, 1965	Steve Yzerman	Ice hockey	Canada
June 17, 1965	Dan Jansen	Speed skating	United States
July 3, 1965	Greg Vaughn	Baseball	United States
August 6, 1965	David Robinson	Basketball	United States
August 9, 1965	John Smith	Wrestling	United States
August 24, 1965	Reggie Miller	Basketball	United States
September 2, 1965	Lennox Lewis	Boxing	England, Canada
September 25, 1965	Scottie Pippen	Basketball	United States
October 5, 1965	Mario Lemieux	Ice hockey	Canada
October 5, 1965	Patrick Roy	Ice hockey	Canada
October 8, 1965	Matt Biondi	Swimming	United States

Born	Name	Sport	Country
October 11, 1965	Julianne McNamara	Gymnastics	United States
October 28, 1965	Martin Potter	Surfing	England
December 3, 1965	Katarina Witt	Figure skating	Germany
January 19, 1966	Stefan Edberg	Tennis	Sweden
February 1, 1966	Michelle Akers	Soccer	United States
February 7, 1966	Kristin Otto	Swimming	Germany
March 5, 1966	Michael Irvin	Football	United States
March 25, 1966	Tom Glavine	Baseball	United States
April 14, 1966	Greg Maddux	Baseball	United States
May 16, 1966	Thurman Thomas	Football	United States
June 16, 1966	Randy Barnes	Shot put	United States
June 16, 1966	Jan Zelezny	Javelin throw	Czechoslovakia
June 25, 1966	Dikembe Mutombo	Basketball	Congo
June 30, 1966	Mike Tyson	Boxing	United States
July 18, 1966	Dan O'Brien	Decathlon	Unknown
July 22, 1966	Tim Brown	Football	United States
August 25, 1966	Albert Belle	Baseball	United States
August 27, 1966	Deena Wigger	Shooting	United States
September 1, 1966	Tim Hardaway	Basketball	United States
November 19, 1966	Gail Devers	Sprints, Hurdles	United States
November 21, 1966	Troy Aikman	Football	United States
December 19, 1966	Alberto Tomba	Skiing	Italy
January 1, 1967	Derrick Thomas	Football	United States
January 23, 1967	Naim Suleymanoglu	Weightlifting	Bulgaria
February 4, 1967	Sergei Grinkov	Figure skating	Soviet Union, Russia
February 21, 1967	Leroy Burrell	Sprints, Long jump	United States
April 15, 1967	Dara Torres	Swimming	United States
June 2, 1967	Sissi	Soccer	Brazil
June 3, 1967	Tamas Darnyi	Swimming	Hungary
August 9, 1967	Deion Sanders	Football, Baseball	United States
August 10, 1967	Riddick Bowe	Boxing	United States
September 13, 1967	Michael Johnson	Sprints	United States
September 19, 1967	Jim Abbott	Baseball	United States
September 19, 1967	Aleksandr Karelin	Wrestling	Russia, Soviet Union
September 27, 1967	Felix Savon	Boxing	Cuba
October 13, 1967	Javier Sotomayor	High jump	Cuba
November 22, 1967	Boris Becker	Tennis	Germany
December 15, 1967	Mo Vaughn	Baseball	United States
December 16, 1967	Donovan Bailey	Sprints	Canada, Jamaica
January 24, 1968	Mary Lou Retton	Gymnastics	United States
February 3, 1968	Vlade Divac	Basketball	Yugoslavia
February 5, 1968	Roberto Alomar	Baseball	United States
May 27, 1968	Jeff Bagwell	Baseball	United States
May 27, 1968	Frank Thomas	Baseball	United States
June 26, 1968	Shannon Sharpe	Football	United States
July 16, 1968	Barry Sanders	Football	United States
July 21, 1968	Brandi Chastain	Soccer	United States
July 23, 1968	Gary Payton	Basketball	United States
September 4, 1968	Mike Piazza	Baseball	United States
September 18, 1968	Toni Kukoc	Basketball	Yugoslavia, Croatia

Born	Name	Sport	Country
September 28, 1968	Mika Häkkinen	Auto racing	Finland
November 12, 1968	Sammy Sosa	Baseball	Dominican Republic, United States
January 3, 1969	Michael Schumacher	Auto racing	Germany
January 16, 1969	Roy Jones, Jr.	Boxing	United States
February 17, 1969	David Douillet	Judo	France
February 21, 1969	Petra Kronberger	Skiing	Austria
March 14, 1969	Larry Johnson	Basketball	United States
May 8, 1969	Akebono	Sumo wrestling	United States
May 15, 1969	Emmitt Smith	Football	United States
June 7, 1969	Eric Fonoimoana	Beach volleyball	United States
June 14, 1969	Steffi Graf	Tennis	Germany
July 13, 1969	Akakios Kakiasvilis	Weightlifting	Georgia, Soviet Union
August 13, 1969	Midori Ito	Figure skating	Japan
October 10, 1969	Brett Favre	Football	United States
October 11, 1969	Ty Murray	Rodeo	United States
October 13, 1969	Nancy Kerrigan	Figure skating	United States
October 16, 1969	Juan Gonzalez	Baseball	Puerto Rico
November 21, 1969	Ken Griffey, Jr.	Baseball	United States
December 13, 1969	Sergei Fedorov	Ice hockey	Russia
February 8, 1970	Alonzo Mourning	Basketball	United States
February 20, 1970	Noureddine Morceli	Long-distance runs	Algeria
April 29, 1970	Andre Agassi	Tennis	United States
May 16, 1970	Gabriela Sabatini	Tennis	Argentina
June 4, 1970	Deborah Compagnoni	Skiing	Italy
June 16, 1970	Cobi Jones	Soccer	United States
July 9, 1970	Gao Min	Diving	China
August 17, 1970	Jim Courier	Tennis	United States
October 9, 1970	Annika Sorenstam	Golf	Sweden
October 12, 1970	Charlie Ward	Basketball	United States
November 30, 1970	Natalie Williams	Basketball, Volleyball	United States
December 12, 1970	Wilson Kipketer	Long-distance runs	Kenya, Denmark
February 22, 1971	Lisa Fernandez	Softball	United States
March 25, 1971	Stacy Dragila	Pole vault	United States
March 25, 1971	Sheryl Swoopes	Basketball	United States
April 3, 1971	Picabo Street	Skiing	United States
April 9, 1971	Jacques Villeneuve	Auto racing	Canada
May 20, 1971	Tony Stewart	Auto racing	United States
May 28, 1971	Ekaterina Gordeeva	Figure skating	Soviet Union, Russia
June 12, 1971	Kristi Yamaguchi	Figure skating	United States
June 22, 1971	Kurt Warner	Football	United States
July 18, 1971	Penny Hardaway	Basketball	United States
July 22, 1971	Kristine Lilly	Soccer	United States
August 4, 1971	Jeff Gordon	Auto racing	United States
August 12, 1971	Pete Sampras	Tennis	United States
August 16, 1971	Rulon Gardner	Wrestling	United States
August 28, 1971	Janet Evans	Swimming	United States
September 7, 1971	Briana Scurry	Soccer	United States
September 18, 1971	Lance Armstrong	Cycling	United States

Born	Name	Sport	Country
October 25, 1971	Pedro Martinez	Baseball	Dominican Republic
November 6, 1971	Laura Flessel-Colovic	Fencing	France, Guadeloupe
November 13, 1971	Pyrros Dimas	Weightlifting	Albania, Greece
November 16, 1971	Aleksandr Popov	Swimming	Russia, Soviet Union
November 21, 1971	Dain Blanton	Beach volleyball	United States
December 9, 1971	Nick Hysong	Pole vault	United States
December 18, 1971	Arantxa Sanchez-Vicario	Tennis	Spain
January 13, 1972	Vitaly Scherbo	Gymnastics	Belarus, Soviet Union
February 14, 1972	Drew Bledsoe	Football	United States
February 15, 1972	Jaromir Jagr	Ice hockey	Czeckoslovakia
February 22, 1972	Michael Chang	Tennis	United States
March 6, 1972	Shaquille O'Neal	Basketball	United States
March 17, 1972	Mia Hamm	Soccer	United States
May 10, 1972	Tara Nott	Weightlifting	United States
October 5, 1972	Grant Hill	Basketball	United States
October 27, 1972	Maria Mutola	Middle-distance runs	Mozambique
October 28, 1972	Terrell Davis	Football	United States
December 7, 1972	Hermann Maier	Skiing	Austria
January 10, 1973	Felix Trinidad	Boxing	Puerto Rico
February 4, 1973	Oscar de la Hoya	Boxing	United States
February 9, 1973	Svetlana Boginskaya	Gymnastics	Soviet Union, Belarus
February 14, 1973	Steve McNair	Football	United States
February 15, 1973	Amy Van Dyken	Swimming	United States
February 16, 1973	Cathy Freeman	Sprints	Australia
February 26, 1973	Marshall Faulk	Football	United States
February 26, 1973	Jenny Thompson	Swimming	United States
February 28, 1973	Eric Lindros	Ice hockey	Canada
March 1, 1973	Chris Webber	Basketball	United States
March 23, 1973	Jason Kidd	Basketball	United States
April 6, 1973	Sun Wen	Soccer	China
April 18, 1973	Haile Gebreselassie	Long-distance runs	Ethiopia
July 23, 1973	Nomar Garciaparra	Baseball	United States
August 2, 1973	Susan O'Neill	Swimming	Australia
August 24, 1973	Inge De Bruijn	Swimming	Netherlands
October 6, 1973	Rebecca Lobo	Basketball	United States
December 2, 1973	Monica Seles	Tennis	Yugoslavia, United States
December 12, 1973	Denise Parker	Archery	United States
December 30, 1973	Ato Boldon	Sprints	Trinidad
January 14, 1974	Nancy Johnson	Shooting	United States
June 26, 1974	Derek Jeter	Baseball	United States
July 23, 1974	Maurice Greene	Sprints	United States
August 16, 1974	Krisztina Egerszegi	Swimming	Hungary
September 14, 1974	Hicham El Guerrouj	Middle-distance runs	Morocco
January 15, 1975	Mary Pierce	Tennis	Canada, France
May 16, 1975	Simon Whitfield	Triathlon	Canada
June 7, 1975	Allen Iverson	Basketball	United States

Born	Name	Sport	Country
July 27, 1975	Alex Rodriguez	Baseball	United States
September 6, 1975	Ryoko Tamura	Judo	Japan
September 28, 1975	Lenny Krayzelburg	Swimming	Ukraine, United States
October 12, 1975	Marion Jones	Sprints, Long jump	United States
December 30, 1975	Tiger Woods	Golf	United States
February 6, 1976	Kim Zmeskal	Gymnastics	United States
March 24, 1976	Peyton Manning	Football	United States
March 29, 1976	Jennifer Capriati	Tennis	United States
April 25, 1976	Tim Duncan	Basketball	Virgin Islands
May 19, 1976	Kevin Garnett	Basketball	United States
May 28, 1976	Alexei Nemov	Gymnastics	Russia
June 8, 1976	Lindsay Davenport	Tennis	United States
August 27, 1976	Carlos Moya	Tennis	Spain
August 30, 1976	Lu Li	Gymnastics	China
September 5, 1976	Tatiana Gutsu	Gymnastics	Ukraine, Soviet Union
September 18, 1976	Ronaldo	Soccer	Brazil
October 7, 1976	Charles Woodson	Football	United States
October 21, 1976	Lavinia Milosovici	Gymnastics	Romania
January 26, 1977	Vince Carter	Basketball	United States
February 13, 1977	Randy Moss	Football	United States
March 10, 1977	Shannon Miller	Gymnastics	United States
May 21, 1977	Ricky Williams	Football	United States
August 9, 1977	Chamique Holdsclaw	Basketball	United States
September 28, 1977	Se Ri Pak	Golf	South Korea
November 17, 1977	Laura Wilkinson	Diving	United States
November 19, 1977	Kerri Strug	Gymnastics	United States
December 15, 1977	Gong Zhichao	Badminton	China
March 14, 1978	Pieter van den Hoogenband	Swimming	Netherlands
August 1, 1978	Edgerrin James	Football	United States
August 16, 1978	Fu Mingxia	Diving	China
August 23, 1978	Kobe Bryant	Basketball	United States
November 9, 1978	Steven Lopez	Tae Kwon Do	United States
January 19, 1979	Svetlana Khorkina	Gymnastics	Soviet Union
June 17, 1980	Venus Williams	Tennis	United States
July 7, 1980	Michelle Kwan	Figure skating	United States
September 30, 1980	Martina Hingis	Tennis	Slovakia, Czechoslovakia
September 26, 1981	Serena Williams	Tennis	United States
June 10, 1982	Tara Lipinski	Figure skating	United States
October 13, 1982	Ian Thorpe	Swimming	Australia

GLOSSARY

ace: Tennis or volleyball serve delivered so effectively that the opponent cannot even hit it and that scores a point for the server; or a point scored on such a serve.

aft: Toward or near the rear of a boat or ship; also known as the stern.

air rifle: Shoulder weapon with a stock and a long barrel and that shoots a small projectile by means of compressed air or carbon dioxide.

All-American: Nationwide honor awarded yearly to the best high school and college athletes in a number of different sports. All-American honors are awarded by a variety of organizations and publications, and their prestige varies.

all-around: Category of gymnastics competition requiring the performance of routines in all of the individual events. The male and female gymnasts who accumulate the most points at the end are awarded the all-around title, indicative of overall superiority and versatility. Internationally, the men's six events are the floor exercises, the stationary rings, the vault, the pommel horse, the horizontal bar, and the parallel bars. The women's four events are the floor exercises, the balance beam, the vault, and the uneven parallel bars. Competitors are judged on originality, execution, form, artistry, continuity, and degree of difficulty.

All-Star game: In team sports, an annual game between the best players from the various leagues or conferences within a sport. Major League Baseball, the National Basketball Association, and the National Hockey League sponsor official All-Star games; the National Football League's version is the Pro Bowl game. Major news services such as the Associated Press select their own yearly all-star teams, but these selections usually do not involve specially held games.

alley (bowling): Bowling lane.

alley (tennis): Designated area that extends the boundary for doubles matches. In a singles match, hitting the ball into the alley is considered out of bounds.

alpine skiing: Competitive events consisting of downhill, slalom, giant slalom, and super-giant slalom (super-G) ski racing.

amateur: Athlete who competes for honors rather than tangible prizes or money, and who does not attain professional status. In world-class modern sports, however, the distinction between amateur and professional has almost disappeared.

America's Cup: International series of yacht races, and one of the most prestigious events of its kind. Boats in this class must be 75-foot monohulls with 110-foot masts, and are essentially longer and lighter than the previously used twelve-meter sloops. The races are of two types: match races, which involve only two boats at a time, and fleet races, for all entrants in a round-robin competition. The Cup is defended about every three to four years, and the winner selects the next race location. The America's Cup originated in 1851, in England. The entry from the United States New York Yacht Club (NYYC) won the race. Sometime thereafter, the owners gave the trophy to the NYYC with the requirement that it be defended whenever challenged, and the trophy was renamed the America's Cup.

anchor leg: Final leg of a relay race; or the athlete who runs this leg.

arrows (archery): Projectiles shot from a bow. Arrows have slender shafts and pointed tips.

arrows (bowling): Seven triangular marks set into the lane just beyond the foul line, which the bowler uses as target points for releasing the ball.

artistic gymnastics: International Olympic category of events for male and female gymnasts, who compete according to rules prescribed by the International Gymnastics Federation. The men's six events are the floor exercises, the horizontal bar, the parallel bars, the stationary rings, the pommel horse, and the long-horse vault. The women's four events are the floor exercises, the balance beam, the uneven parallel bars, and the side-horse vault.

assist (baseball): Throwing the ball to a teammate on a play that results in a putout.

assist (basketball): Pass completed to a teammate who immediately scores a field goal. In basketball, only one assist can be credited on a scoring play.

assist (hockey): Passing the puck to a teammate who immediately scores a goal, or passing to a teammate who immediately passes the puck to the eventual goal scorer. In ice hockey, a maximum of two assists can be credited on one scoring play.

assist (soccer): Pass completed to a teammate who scores a goal almost immediately.

association football: Term by which most of the world knows "soccer," which derives from the word "association." Association football arose in England, where its name distinguished it from rugby football.

attack: In cycling, a sudden attempt to break away from the peloton, the main group of cyclists, in order to seize the lead.

audible: Offensive football tactic in which the quarterback, after reading the defensive alignment, verbally modifies the offensive play at the line of scrimmage.

axel jump: Figure skating maneuver achieved by jumping off the forward outside edge of one skate, turning one and one-half times in the air, and landing on the backward outside edge of the other skate. Named for its creator, Norwegian skater Axel Paulsen.

backhand: In tennis or badminton, a stroke that originates from the side of the body opposite the racket hand, or forehand side. As the ball (or shuttlecock) is hit, the back of the racket hand is facing the net.

backspin: Backward rotation on a tennis ball imparted by sweeping the racket face down and under the ball at the point of contact.

backstretch: On a racetrack, the straightaway on the side opposite the homestretch and the finish line.

backstroke: Swimming stroke that requires flutter kicks and alternating pulls with both arms moving up and over the head. Performed on the back.

backward dive: In competitive diving, a maneuver in which the diver stands on the edge of the platform or springboard, facing away from the water, then leaps into the air and rotates backward.

bail: In cricket, one of the two short wooden cylindrical pegs set across the tops of the three stumps that together form the wicket. The batsman is out once the bails are dislodged during play.

balance: As used in bodybuilding, a term that describes a well-proportioned physique. The various muscle groups are in even and pleasing proportion to one another. Among competitive bodybuilders, an especially desirable quality.

balance beam: Event in women's gymnastics involving a combination of dance and tricks (tumbling moves) performed back and forth on the balance beam. The beam itself is sixteen feet long, four inches wide, and raised about four feet off the ground. The exercise lasts from 80 to 105 seconds.

barbell: Steel bar five to seven feet long to which iron weighted plates are attached and securely held by removable metal collars.

bareback riding: Rodeo competition that involves riding an unsaddled wild, bucking horse for eight seconds, using only one hand to grip a strap attached to the horse's torso. Riders are judged on their control during the ride and how hard the horse bucks. Said to be comparable to riding a jackhammer with one hand.

barnstorm: Series of exhibition games played by traveling teams from any number of cities or countries.

base stealing: Movement by the base runner in an attempt to catch the defense off guard, and advance from one base to the next without being thrown out. In the event of a hit or error, the advancing runner cannot be credited with a stolen base.

baseline: Back boundary of a tennis court.

baseline player: Tennis player whose game strategy is to stay back at the baseline to hit ground strokes, rarely moving to the net.

bases loaded: Situation in a baseball or softball game in which runners occupy first, second, and third base at the same moment.

baton: Hollow cylinder passed in a relay race from one runner to the next upon the completion of each leg except for the final leg.

batsman: Cricket player positioned next to one of the two wickets who tries to hit bowled balls and score runs by advancing from one wicket to the other as many times as possible without being put out.

batting average: Statistical indication of a batter's hitting record. In baseball, softball, and cricket, a player's average is figured by dividing the total number of hits by the total number of official times at bat. In baseball and softball, batters are not charged with an official "at bat" when they reach base on a walk or are hit by a pitch.

batting order: Sequence in which members of a baseball or softball team take their turns at bat.

belt: Cloth belt of varying colors worn to indicate a particular level of achievement in judo and other martial arts. In judo, the efficiency grades are of two types: kyu (pupil) and dan (master), the highest grade. Starting with the beginner level, the colors won in judo are white, yellow, orange, green, blue, brown, and black, which signifies the dan or master grade and is itself divided into ten degrees. Sixth-, seventh-, and eighth-degree black belts have the option of wearing a red and white belt; ninth- and tenth-degree black belts may choose a solid red belt.

bench press: In weightlifting, a lift made while lying back on a weight bench and pushing the barbell up from the chest to an overhead position, then lowering it.

bicycle kick: Spectacular soccer maneuver that involves falling backward, to an almost upside-down vertical position, while using an overhead scissors-like leg motion to kick the ball.

big-bore: In shooting sports, a term that refers to large-caliber firearms; or a caliber larger than .22.

birdie: Finishing a golf hole at 1 stroke under par for that hole. *See also* bogey, eagle.

blade (fencing): Section of the sword extending from the guard to the tip of the weapon.

blade (rowing): Oar or paddle, or the flat or curved portion of the oar.

bob and weave: Boxer's defensive tactic of rocking his head and torso up and down and back and forth in order to present a moving target that is harder for his opponent to hit.

bobsled: Large, longer racing sled supported underneath by two pairs of runners in tandem, and room for two to four riders. A steering wheel is attached by wires to the two movable front runners. The front rider controls the steering, while the rear rider operates the hand brake.

bobsled run: Narrow, ice-covered chute with high curved walls and numerous banked turns that form the race course in bobsled competition.

body checking: In hockey, to use the body, principally the arms and shoulders, aggressively to block the progress of an opposing puckcarrier or to prevent him from reaching the puck.

bogey: Finishing a golf hole at 1 stroke over par for that hole. *See also* birdie, double bogey.

bomb: Long football pass play, particularly one that scores a touchdown.

bore: Diameter of the inside of the barrel of a pistol or rifle.

bout: Boxing match. In competition, most bouts are between three and twelve rounds. Each round is three minutes long, with a one-minute rest period in between rounds. How many rounds a bout lasts depends on weight classification and whether the match is amateur or professional.

bow (archery): Shooting device used in archery to propel an arrow. Consists of a long, slender strip of flexible material such as fiberglass or wood, the ends of which are connected by a cord drawn tightly enough to bend the strip.

bow (canoeing/kayaking, yachting): Front of a ship or racing shell.

bowler: Cricket player whose position is similar to that of a baseball pitcher. The bowler takes a running start and, using an overhead windmill delivery, hurls the ball at the opposite wicket in an attempt to put out the batsman by dislodging the bail. The bowler is required to keep the throwing arm straight at all times during the delivery.

breakaway: Rider or group of cyclists that has begun an attack by riding away from another, larger group of cyclists.

breaststroke: Swimming stroke that begins with simultaneous pulls with both arms from in front of the head down to the thighs, a frog kick executed just after the arm pulls end, and a glide through the water with a straight full-body extension. Performed on the stomach.

broad jump: Former term for long jump.

broken-field runner: In football, a ballcarrier skilled at avoiding opponents in the open field without the usual benefit of teammates blocking for him.

brush back pitch: High, inside baseball pitch, the only purpose of which is to move the batter away from the plate. An intimidation pitch.

bull riding: Rodeo competition that involves riding a twisting, jumping bull for eight seconds, using only one hand to grip a strap attached to the bull's torso. In major competition, the biggest and fastest bulls weigh more than a ton.

bull's-eye: Center of a target. In archery or shooting sports, hitting the bull's-eye scores the most points.

bully: In field hockey, putting the ball in play by having two opposing players face each other and grapple for possession of it. Similar to the face-off in ice hockey. *See also* face-off.

butterfly: Swimming stroke that requires dolphin kicks and simultaneous pulls with both arms moving up over the head and down under the water. Performed on the stomach.

caliber: Diameter of the inside of the barrel of a pistol or rifle (the bore) measured in hundredths (.22, .44) or thousandths (.357) of an inch.

camel: Skating maneuver performed by spinning the body while in the arabesque position.

canoe: Narrow, lightweight boat that has a pointed bow and stern and is propelled by paddles. Wider than a kayak.

cap: Unofficial honor awarded to a soccer player representing his or her country in an international game. The number of "caps" a player has earned represents the number of international matches the player has appeared in.

catch-as-catch-can wrestling: *See* freestyle (wrestling).

century: Score of at least one hundred runs accumulated by a batsman in the space of one innings in a cricket match.

change-up: Baseball or softball pitch that to the batter appears to be a fastball but is actually much slower. A deception pitch used to interrupt the batter's timing.

checkered flag: Flag with black and white squares that is waved to signal the end of an auto race and to indicate the winner.

chip shot: Golf shot that puts the ball onto the green from a point just off the green. Shorter shots of this type are called chip shots. Longer shots are called pitches.

chute (bobsledding): Bobsled run—a narrow, ice-covered passageway with high curved walls and numerous banked turns.

chute (rodeo): Narrow holding pen adjacent to the rodeo arena, used to restrain an animal so that the rider can mount it. As the ride begins, a gate opens into the arena, releasing the animal.

circuit: In sports such as auto racing or cycling, the race course itself. Can also refer to an organized athletic league or conference or a set of leagues or conferences.

classics: Oldest and most important road races of the cycling season. The typical classic race course may be from city to city or point to point and is much shorter in length and duration than the multistage tours.

clean and jerk: In weightlifting, a lift performed by first pulling the barbell up to shoulder level, then pushing it up and over the head and locking the elbows. In the second segment of the lift, the legs are used not only to help hoist the weight but also to lower the body slightly, enabling the lifter to get beneath the barbell.

cleanup hitter: Baseball or softball player who bats fourth in the lineup and who generally is expected to hit well enough to drive in one or more of the three base runners who preceded him in the batting order.

clutch hitter: Baseball or softball batter who is able to get hits and drive in runners, especially at critical times during a game. In general, a "clutch player" in any team sport can perform at the top of his or her game while under intense pressure.

combination: Flurry of different punches thrown rapidly and successively, usually as part of a practiced plan of attack during a boxing match.

completion: Football pass successfully caught by a receiver on the same team.

compulsory figures (equestrian): Series of competitive exercises that involve guiding the horse through turns, changes of lead, and tight circles. Also called school figures.

compulsory figures (figure skating): Series of prescribed geometric patterns that a skater must trace with as much precision and grace as possible; these figures (from which figure skating got its name) were dropped from the scoring process in 1990. Also called school figures.

Copa Libertadores: Yearly international soccer tournament among the champions and runners-up from leagues in South American countries to determine the best South American club team.

corner kick: Restart in a soccer game in which the attacking team is awarded a free kick from the corner of the field on the opposing team's goal line after the opposing team touches a ball that goes out of play over the goal line. *See also* free kick (soccer), penalty kick.

count: Number of seconds called off by a referee over a fallen boxer. Once the count has begun, the boxer has ten seconds to get back on his feet or the match is over and the opponent wins by a knockout.

counterpunch: To answer or respond immediately to an opponent's lead punch or jab with a punch or a jab during a boxing match.

coxswain: In rowing, a nonrowing crew member who is responsible for setting the rowing pace and maintaining speed and rhythm.

crawl: Swimming stroke that requires flutter kicks and alternating pulls with both arms moving up over the head and down under the water. The fastest of the basic strokes. Performed on the stomach.

crew: Members of a rowing race team, the oarsmen and the coxswain, or any of those who operate a racing shell or a yacht.

criterium: Cycling race of a specified number of laps over a closed course or around an oval track.

cross-country (equestrian): Endurance event in which horse and rider, at various intervals, traverse a course mapped out across the countryside and try to jump over a series of obstacles.

cross-country (skiing): Long-distance races across snow-covered terrain. An event in the Nordic skiing category, which also includes ski jumping.

cross-country (track and field): Long-distance running across dirt roads, wooded areas, grassy fields, and hills. In the United States, cross-country races are generally held in the fall, while regular track and field meets are held in the spring and summer. Many distance runners compete in both.

crossover step: Skating technique used to gain additional thrust while rounding a turn. The skater begins by crossing the outer skate in front of the inner skate, then swinging the inner skate back around and onto the ice while using the outer (first) skate to push off powerfully into the turn.

cup: Small cylindrical chamber into which the golf ball is deposited. Also called the hole.

curveball: Baseball or softball pitch that veers or breaks downward and to the side. A curveball thrown by a right-handed pitcher will move away from a right-handed batter.

cut: In sabre fencing, a scoring hit accomplished by striking the opponent with the edge of the weapon.

cut shot: Tactical, deceptive shot used in volleyball by a hitter to misdirect the flight of the ball.

Cy Young Award: Highest distinction a major league baseball pitcher can receive. Presented annually to the best pitcher in both the National and the American Leagues, as determined by the Baseball Writers Association of America. Named in honor of Hall of Fame pitcher Cy Young, who, with 511 victories, is still professional baseball's all-time wins leader.

dash: Sprint race other than a hurdles or a relay race. In the Olympics, the dashes for both men and women are at distances of 100 meters, 200 meters, and 400 meters.

Davis Cup: Annual international men's tennis tournament between the top sixteen national teams of two to four players each, in both singles and doubles competition. The tournament is played out over the course of a year. Named for American player Dwight Davis.

dead ball: Term used in many sports for a ball that goes out of play, because it either leaves the field of play or is dead by rule. For example, a dropped forward pass in football is a dead ball.

dead lift: In weightlifting, a lift performed by using the lower back and leg muscles to bring the barbell up to around hip level and then down again.

decathlon: Track and field event lasting two days and including ten events: 100- and 400-meter dashes, 1,500-meter run, 110-meter hurdles, long jump, high jump, shot put, discus and javelin throws, and pole vault. Points are awarded for performance in each event, and the athlete with the most points wins the competition. The most prestigious competition is the Olympic decathlon, whose champion is typically declared the "world's greatest athlete." *See also* heptathlon, pentathlon.

decision: Boxing match won on the basis of points scored or the number of rounds won.

defense: In various sports, the attempt to prevent the opposing team from advancing the ball or puck and/or from scoring points, runs, or goals. Playing defense also involves the endeavor to take possession of the ball away from the opponent so that one's own team can advance the ball score. Defense can also refer to the specific game plan used by the team not in possession of the ball. A term used mostly in the context of certain team sports.

definition: As used by bodybuilders, the term means the distinctness or clarity of outline and detail of the exercised muscles. A well-defined bodybuilder will have so little body fat that even the very fine grooves or "striations" of the major muscle groups will be clearly visible.

dig: Successful defensive recovery of a forceful spike or other high-velocity attacking shot in volleyball.

discus throw: Field event that involves throwing a discus for distance. A discus is a heavy disk made of wood or rubber that is thicker at the center than at the perimeter, and about nine inches in diameter and two inches thick at the center.

dog sled racing: *See* Iditarod Trail Sled Dog Race

dojo: In Japanese, *dojo* means "the place of the way." A gymnasium or school where martial arts are taught and practiced.

double: In baseball or softball, a hit that allows the batter to reach second base.

double bogey: Finishing a golf hole at 2 strokes over par for that hole. *See also* bogey.

double eagle: Finishing a golf hole at 3 strokes under par for that hole. *See also* birdie, eagle.

double fault: In a tennis match, the act of committing two foot faults (a foot fault is an illegal placement of at least one of the server's feet) in a row while serving from the same court. A server who commits a double fault loses the point.

double play: In baseball or softball, a defensive move in which two base runners are put out in one play. Perhaps the most frequent double play combination occurs when the shortstop fields a ground ball and tosses it to the second baseman, who touches the base with a foot to put out a runner advancing from first base and then throws the ball to first base for the second out.

double-team: In various team sports, to guard or defend an opponent with two opposing players simultaneously.

down: Unit of offensive play in football. When a team gains possession of the ball, it is permitted four downs to gain 10 yards. Each time the team gains the 10 yards, it is immediately awarded a new first down, which gives it another four downs. In most situations, a team that does not gain the 10 yards during the first three downs of a series punts the ball away on the fourth down to avoid the risk of turning over possession of the ball where it is. *See also* first down.

downhill skiing: Gliding down mountain slopes, whether in competition or merely for recreation. Generally, a downhill racer will ski straight down the fall line—the natural slope of the mountain and the shortest distance from point to point—in order to go as fast as possible. The fastest speed event in the Alpine skiing category, which also includes slalom, giant slalom, and super-giant slalom ski racing.

draft: Method by which professional sports teams annually select new players. Usually the teams with the previous season's worst records are accorded the right to choose first. Many teams trade or sell their draft picks to other teams.

drafting: Particularly in auto racing and cycling, the tactic of driving or riding just behind and very close to another car or cyclist in order to take advantage of the slipstream—the tunnel or pocket of reduced air resistance and forward suction created by the moving object in front. Slipstreaming allows the second rider to maintain a certain speed while expending less energy or fuel. *See also* slipstreaming.

dressage: Equestrian event that puts horse and rider through a series of different maneuvers (such as changing gait or walking sideways) to test the horse's ability, training, and obedience and the cooperation between horse and rider. The signals from the rider to the horse should be virtually imperceptible.

dribble (basketball): Bouncing of the ball on floor of the court using only one hand at a time. Basketball players controlling the ball are not allowed to move without dribbling the ball.

dribble (soccer): Advancing of the ball with the feet, which are generally used to tap it in a left-right alternation.

drive (basketball): To move rapidly and aggressively with the ball off the dribble, especially as a move toward the baseline or the basket.

drive (golf): Generally, a long-yardage shot hit for distance and accuracy, as from the tee to any place on the fairway and occasionally to the green.

eagle: Finishing a golf hole at 2 strokes under par for that hole. *See also* birdie, double eagle.

earned run: From the baseball or softball pitcher's standpoint, a run scored but not as the result of a defensive error. A statistic credited to the pitcher.

earned run average (ERA): Statistical category that indicates how many earned runs a baseball or softball pitcher allows for each 9 innings pitched. ERA is figured by dividing the total number of earned runs by the total number of innings pitched, and multiplying the quotient by 9. The result is the pitcher's ERA for one 9-inning game.

eights: Rowing event for racing shells powered by eight oars.

elite: Oarsman who has rowed on a winning boat or racing shell in a championship race. Can also refer to a competition for crews made up of elite-class oarsmen. Generally can refer to the top athletes in a sport.

end zone: Enclosed areas at each end of a football field into which the offensive team must advance the ball to score a touchdown. Also, the area where the goalpost is located.

entry: Last phase of a dive, when the diver enters the water. The less splash created, the better the entry and the higher the final score.

épée fencing: One of the three styles of fencing, in which the épée is used. An épée is a sword equipped with a guard shaped like a small bowl and a fairly rigid blade with a blunted tip and no cutting edge. A thrusting weapon, similar to the foil. *See also* foil fencing, sabre fencing.

equestrian: Horseback riding and competitive events in riding and handling horses such as dressage, cross-country, and show jumping. An equestrian is a person who participates in these sports.

error: Baseball and softball term for a misplay of a batted or thrown ball that is otherwise considered playable that allows a base runner to advance or prevent a putout.

European Cup: Yearly and prestigious international men's tournament between the national soccer champions from all European countries.

even keel: Nautical phrase that describes an evenly balanced boat or ship.

extra-point conversion: Bonus play allowed after each touchdown in football that gives the scoring team a chance to kick a short field goal (good for 1 extra point) or run or pass the ball into the end zone (good for 2 extra points).

face-off: In hockey, the referee's act of starting or resuming play by dropping the puck between two opposing players, who then try to control the puck or tip it to a teammate. *See also* bully.

fairway: Expansive, well-maintained portion of a golf course situated between the tee and the putting green, but not including water hazards and sand traps.

fall-away jumper: In basketball, a shot attempted while deliberately moving away from the basket, as opposed to jumping straight up and releasing the shot. *See also* jump shot.

fast break: Basketball play that emphasizes getting the basketball downcourt as fast as possible and anticipating the easy basket while denying the other team the chance to set up defensively. This type of game plan requires strong rebounding, skillful passing, and cooperation from all five players.

fastball: Powerful high-velocity baseball pitch capable of rising or dipping on its way to the plate. The best major league pitchers can throw fastballs 90 to 100 miles per hour.

Federation Cup: Davis Cup of women's tennis, started in 1963 by the International Lawn Tennis Federation. Unlike Davis Cup teams, however, Federation Cup teams compete at one location to decide the Cup winner in one week's time. *See also* Davis Cup.

field archery: Series of competitive events set in wooded areas to approximate hunting conditions.

field events: Track and field events that involve skills other than, or additional to, running or walking. These include the high jump, long jump, triple jump, pole vault, shot put, discus throw, javelin throw, and hammer throw.

field goal (basketball): Shot, other than a free throw, that falls through the rim. Good for 2 points if shot in front of the 3-point circle, and 3 points if shot from behind the circle.

field goal (football): Three-point scoring play made by place-kicking (not punting) the ball from behind the line of scrimmage across the goalpost crossbars.

fielding: In field hockey, stopping the ball and controlling it.

fielding average: Statistical category that indicates how effectively a baseball fielder performs on defense. Fielding average is figured by dividing the total number of errorless plays by the total number of chances, or attempts.

first-class cricket: Highest level of play in British cricket. Cricket played between the best teams in various countries and universities in the British Commonwealth, each country having its own version of a national championship. The top players from one nation combine to compete against similar teams from other nations in international first-class test matches.

first down: In football, the first of four downs or possessions of the ball by the offensive team. Also, the team in possession of the ball is awarded a "first down" (another four downs) after successfully advancing the ball at least 10 yards. In the late 1990's, television broadcasts of football games began inserting electronically drawn yellow lines on fields to indicate how far the ball must be moved to make first downs.

fixed-gear cycling: Track cycling event involving bicycles equipped with only one speed. These bicycles travel only as fast as the cyclist can pedal.

flight shooting: Archery competition that involves shooting arrows for distance rather than at targets.

floor exercise: Event in which a gymnast performs a combination of dance, acrobatic, and tumbling moves utilizing as much as possible of the area of a forty-two-foot square mat. Women's floor exercise routines are set to music. Men's routines last fifty to seventy seconds and women's routines last sixty to ninety seconds.

flying camel: Skating maneuver that requires the execution of a flying jump, followed by an airborne camel spin, and a landing that completes the rotation in the camel position. *See also* camel.

foil fencing: One of the three styles of fencing. A foil is a sword equipped with a guard shaped like a small bowl and a flexible blade with a blunted tip and no cutting edge. A thrusting weapon, similar to the épée. *See also* épée fencing, sabre fencing.

forcing the pace: In cycling, to increase the pace to the point that the other cyclists find it hard to keep up.

fore: Toward the front, or the bow, of a boat or ship.

forehand: In tennis or badminton, a stroke that originates from the same side of the body as the racket hand. As the ball is hit, the palm is facing the net.

Formula One: Highest and fastest level of racing competition on the Grand Prix circuit. Formula One cars are open-wheeled and seat only one driver. They must be built according to "formulas" or specifications that govern details such as engine size, weight, and design which are set by the Fédération Internationale de'l Automobile, the worldwide sanctioning body of auto racing. These cars frequently average speeds well above 100 miles per hour in competition.

forward dive: In competitive diving, a maneuver in which the diver stands on the edge of the platform or springboard, facing the water, then springs into the air away from the edge and rotates forward.

forward pass: In a football game, a pass thrown in the direction of the opposing end zone. A forward pass that hits the ground is a dead ball. *See also* lateral.

fours: Rowing event for racing shells powered by four oars.

frame: One of the ten periods or units into which a game of bowling is divided.

free agent: Athlete not under contract to any team who is therefore at liberty to negotiate with any team or organization. A free agent can be a professional athlete whose contract has expired or who has been waived or cut from a team, or an amateur athlete looking to sign with a professional team.

free kick (football): Kick made to restart a game after a safety is scored. A team that gives up the safety may place-kick or punt the ball to the other team from its own twenty-yard line.

free kick (soccer): Restart in a game when one team is allowed to kick the ball into play, without obstruction from the opposing team, after the other team commits a foul on the field. A direct free kick, which is awarded for certain kinds of major fouls, may be kicked directly into the opposing goal for a score. An indirect free kick, which is awarded for certain technical fouls, must touch another player (of either team) before entering a goal to score. *See also* corner kick, penalty kick.

free skating: Long or short skating program consisting of jumps, spirals, dance movements, and other elements designed and choreographed specifically for and/or by the skater. Set to music.

free throw: In basketball, an uncontested shot taken from the free throw line, and which is worth 1 point per shot made. The result of a personal or technical foul by the opposing team.

freestyle (archery): Target competition in which the archer uses an aiming or sighting device such as a rangefinder or bowsight.

freestyle (skiing): Competition in which the skier is judged in three different events: downhill skiing over rough terrain (mogul), artistic, stylized movements along a gradual slope (ballet), and acrobatic stunts and jumps (aerial).

freestyle (surfing): Event that allows each surfer to select the stunts or maneuvers performed.

freestyle (swimming): Race (such as the 200-meter freestyle) in which the swimmer chooses the stroke to be used. This is almost always the forward crawl, since it is the fastest known stroke. In the individual medley and team relay, the final leg of the race is always designated as freestyle—the swimmer can select any stroke except the butterfly, backstroke, or breaststroke. Freestyle also commonly refers to the forward crawl.

freestyle (wrestling): Event that allows the combatants to use any legal and nondangerous wrestling holds. One of two styles of wrestling featured in the Olympics, the other being Greco-Roman wrestling.

funny car: Highly modified top fuel dragster fitted with a late-model production car body usually made of fiberglass. Nearly as fast as the standard top fuel dragsters, funny cars are powered by a similar type of engine that is mounted in the front and that also runs on nitromethane fuel. Can reach speeds in the range of 290 miles per hour. *See also* top fuel.

furlong: On a horse racing track, a measurement of one-eighth of a mile.

gate: General term for the money generated by ticket sales at a sporting event.

gate (horse racing): Movable steel contraption the width of the track and fitted with a row of narrow stalls occupied by the horse and jockey at the start of a race. The starting line.

gate (kayaking, skiing, waterskiing, yachting): Markers, poles, or buoys through or around which competitors must pass on their way to the finish line.

giant slalom: Similar to the slalom, a skiing race that involves negotiating as fast as possible the downhill weaving pattern of the course. The giant slalom ski run is longer and steeper than that used in slalom; however, the gates used are fewer and spread farther apart. As a result, the run is substantially faster. An event in the Alpine skiing category, which also includes downhill skiing, slalom, and super-giant slalom. A race against the clock.

goal (hockey): Netted cage into which the puck must enter for the attacking team to score. The standard goal frame is four feet high and six feet wide. "Goal" is also the term used for the score itself.

goal (soccer): Upright frame, enclosed by a net, through which the ball must pass for the attacking team to score. The standard goal is eight feet high and twenty-four yards wide. "Goal" is also the term used for the score itself.

goal area: Lined area directly in front of each goal on a soccer field; the area is twenty yards wide and six yards deep. Its sole purpose is to delimit the area from which a goal kick may be made. *See also* penalty area.

goal kick: Restart in soccer in which the defending team puts the ball back into play after it goes over the goal line (and not into the goal) when the attacking team is last to touch. Any defending player may take the kick, which must be made from within the goal area and must clear the penalty area.

goalkeeper: Soccer player who is accorded special privileges while protecting his or her team's goal. Goalkeepers wear jerseys of colors different from those of their teams so they can be readily identified. In contrast to all other players, they can handle the ball with their hands—but only within their own penalty areas. They can also go anywhere on the field and do anything that any other player is permitted to do. Also known as keeper.

goaltender: Hockey player who protects the goal. Goaltenders wear special protective equipment and are allowed to handle the puck with their glove. Also known as goalie.

goaltending: Illegal physical interference with a field goal attempt in a basketball game. Both offensive and defensive players can be penalized for this infraction.

Gold Glove Award: Annual distinction given to the best baseball players at each defensive position from both the National and the American Leagues.

Golden Gloves: Nationwide series of amateur boxing elimination tournaments. Regional champions are qualified to compete for the title in their respective weight classifications at the annual Golden Gloves National Championship Tournament.

Grand Prix (auto racing): Most elite series of races in international auto racing competition. A class of races for formula cars. These championship events are now held almost exclusively on specially mapped-out city streets. The driver who accumulates the most points on the Grand Prix circuit is awarded the World Championship of Drivers title at the end of the racing season.

grand prix (equestrian): Expert level of competition at national and international dressage and jumping events. Involves both individual and team competition.

grand slam (baseball and softball): Home run hit with runners on first, second, and third base, with the result of 4 runs being scored.

Grand Slam (golf): Four major golf tournaments; or the feat of winning them all in the same year. For the men, they are the Masters, the U.S. Open, the British Open, and the Professional Golfers Association (PGA) Championship. For the women, they are the Ladies Professional Golf Association (LPGA) Championship, the U.S. Women's Open, the Nabisco-Dinah Shore, and the du Maurier Classic.

Grand Slam (tennis): Four major tennis tournaments; or the feat of winning them all in the same year. They are the same for both men and women: the Australian Open, the French Open, the Wimbledon Championships, and the U.S. Open.

Greco-Roman wrestling: One of two styles of wrestling featured in the Olympics, the other being freestyle wrestling. An event in which the combatants cannot apply holds below the waist and cannot use their legs to apply holds or to effect a takedown or a pin.

green: Smooth, usually well-manicured portion of a golf course where the hole is located and where putting is necessary.

ground strokes: Tennis stroke executed by using the racket to strike the ball after it has bounced on the return. Ground strokes are usually hit from the backcourt area or from just beyond the baseline.

half volley: Tennis stroke made by using the racket to strike the ball the instant it bounces up from the ground on the return.

Hall of Fame: Memorial established to recognize athletes, coaches, and other individuals who have excelled in a particular sport or who have made meritorious contributions to a sport. Most professional Halls of Fame require that athletes be retired for certain periods of time before they are eligible for induction. Sports Halls of Fame are maintained by amateur and professional sports leagues, cities, colleges and universities, and other organizations.

hammer throw: Field event that involves throwing a 16-pound metal ball attached to a steel wire with a handle at the end. Because of the long distances that the hammer is thrown and the danger of its being released in the wrong direction, hammer throw competitions are often held at venues separated from those of other track and field events.

handicap: Numerical rating system used as a means of evening out the range of abilities or skill levels among competitors at certain sports events. In golf, the handicap is the number of strokes a player may legitimately deduct from his or her scorecard after finishing a round or a tournament, as compensation for playing against a better golfer.

harness racing: Form of horse racing in which jockeys ride two-wheel carts pulled by the horses.

hat trick (cricket): Feat accomplished when the bowler dismisses or retires three batsmen on three consecutive balls.

hat trick (ice hockey, soccer): Three goals in one game scored by the same player. The term was originally applied to the feat of scoring three consecutive, unanswered goals.

heading: Using the head to shoot a soccer ball toward the goal, pass the ball to a teammate, or clear the ball away from one's own goal. Heading is generally done from a spot just above the forehead.

head-of-the-river race: Rowing event in which the participants start the race at different intervals along the course.

heat: Preliminary race used to narrow down the field of competitors to the designated number of finalists.

heavyweight (boxing): Weight classification in professional boxing for athletes weighing more than 190 pounds. In amateur boxing, the maximum is 200 pounds.

heavyweight (judo): International weight classification for athletes weighing more than 209 pounds.

heavyweight (weightlifting): International weight classification with 242-pound maximum.

Heisman Trophy: Yearly award presented to the nation's best college football player as determined by sports journalists from across the country. Named in honor of former college football coach John W. Heisman and sponsored by the Downtown Athletic Club of New York. The most coveted individual distinction in college football, this award almost always goes to offensive players—particularly quarterbacks and running backs.

helmsman: In rowing, the crew member who steers the boat or ship by operating the wheel or the tiller.

heptathlon: Individual women's field competition that includes seven events: 100- and 200-meter dashes, 800-meter run, high jump, long jump, shot put, and javelin throw. The Olympic heptathlon replaced the five-event pentathlon in 1984. *See also* decathlon.

high bar: *See* horizontal bar.

high jump: Field event in which the athlete tries to jump over (or clear) a horizontal crossbar set between two upright supports. The object is to clear the greatest height in the fewest attempts, with a maximum of three tries at each height.

high-powered rifle: Big-bore military or big-game hunting rifle that shoots a bullet with a muzzle velocity of at least two thousand feet per second.

hill climb: Auto race up a hill, one car at a time, in a race against the clock.

hit for the cycle: Hitting a single, a double, a triple, and a home run in the same baseball game.

hitter: In volleyball, a player in position to spike or forcefully return the volleyball after being set up by the setter; or the player so designated by his or her immediate line position (front row or back row) on the court.

hole: Generally refers to a unit of the golf course that includes a tee, fairway, and green; used as in a nine-hole golf course or a 4-par hole. *See also* cup.

home plate: Five-sided rubber slab set into the dirt at one corner of a baseball diamond. The pitcher throws toward it, the batter stands over it, and the base runner must cross it successfully to score a run. The object of every runner is to "reach home."

home run: Any hit that enables the baseball or softball batter to round all four bases and score a run in one continuous play before another player comes to bat. Home runs, or "homers," can be balls hit over the fence and out of the park, or balls that stay inside the park. Inside-the-park home runs are common in youth leagues but are rare in major league baseball.

homestretch: On a race track, the length of track between the final turn and the finish line.

hook shot: One-handed shot in which the body is turned sideways to the basket, the outside shooting arm is extended overhead, and the ball is released into an arc with a flick of the wrist. One of the hardest shots for a defender to block.

hop, step, and jump: *See* triple jump.

horizontal bar: Sturdy but pliant metal bar, about one inch in diameter, and about eight feet long, horizontally positioned about eight feet off the floor. It is used by the gymnast to execute swinging, looping and release-regrasp movements. A men's event.

hurdles: Sprint races that involves jumping over series of metal or wooden obstacles (resembling gates) set up along the racetrack. The three standard types of hurdles races are high, intermediate, and low hurdles, at distances of 100 meters (for women), 110 meters (for men), and 400 meters (for both men and women).

hypertrophy: Scientific term that essentially means larger and stronger muscles. Bodybuilders and weightlifters work to induce hypertrophy by overloading the exercised muscles, forcing them to lift more weight than they can normally handle. The result is increased strength and muscle mass.

I-formation: In football, an offensive setup that positions the fullback and the tailback in a line several yards directly behind the quarterback.

Iditarod Trail Sled Dog Race: 1,158-mile sled dog racing endurance test. The Iditarod is an annual event that starts in Anchorage, Alaska, and ends in Nome. First held in 1973, it commemorates a well-known attempt in the winter of 1925 to rush emergency medicines and other supplies to Nome, which was fighting a diphtheria epidemic. The sport's longest and most prestigious event.

indirect free kick: *See* free kick (soccer).

individual medley: Individual swimming race requiring that each leg, or quarter, of the race be completed using a different stroke, typically in the following order: butterfly, backstroke, breaststroke, and freestyle.

Indy car: Car that outwardly resembles a Formula One car but is several hundred pounds heavier, boosted for greater horsepower, and faster. These cars frequently reach speeds well above 200 miles per hour on a straightaway. The only type of race cars allowed on the Championship Auto Racing Teams (CART) circuit, which includes the popular Indianapolis 500.

inning (badminton): Length of time that a player or a team holds service.

inning (baseball, softball): Unit into which a game is divided. There are 9 innings in a regulation baseball game; there are 7 innings in a men's and women's softball game.

innings (cricket): Unit into which a cricket match is divided. Matches are played in durations of 1 or 2 innings per team (each team has 1 or 2 innings to bat). As soon as ten of a team's eleven batsmen have been dismissed (put out), an innings is completed. Since an innings can continue for up to a full day, matches include breaks for meals and rest. Also means a turn at bat in a match, which for the batsman continues until he has been put out.

interception: In football, forward pass caught ("intercepted") by an opposing player.

inward dive: In competitive diving, a maneuver in which the diver stands on the edge of the platform or springboard, facing away from the water, then springs backward but rotates forward.

jab: Type of boxing punch that is a sharp, rapid snap of the arm, and which is thrown a short distance, often directly at the head or face.

jackknife: Forward dive performed by jumping off the springboard into the air, momentarily assuming a jackknife or pike pose (body bent at the waist and hands touching the ankles in a V shape), then straightening the body so as to enter the water headfirst.

javelin throw: Field event that involves throwing the javelin for distance. The javelin is a long, tapered spear with a pointed tip. The men's javelin is about eight and a half feet long; the women's javelin is a few inches over seven feet long.

jockey: Professional rider of race horses.

jump serve: High-velocity volleyball serve in which the server strikes the ball after first taking a running jump from just behind the service line.

jump shot: Generally, a two-handed overhead shot in which the shooter releases the basketball at the top of the jump. Good rotation is imparted by a firm snap of the wrist.

jump ski: Waterskiing event that involves skiing up and over an inclined ramp.

kayak: Narrow, lightweight racing shell, the edges of which are tapered to a point at both the bow and the stern, and which is propelled through the water by a single long paddle with blades at either end. The top of the kayak is entirely covered except for the small cockpit reserved for the kayaker. More slender than a canoe.

kill: Unhittable or unreturnable attacking shot, such as in badminton, tennis, or volleyball, that scores the point for the hitter.

knockout: Victory scored by a boxer who is able to render his opponent unconscious or otherwise unable to continue the match. Following a knockdown, the fallen boxer has ten seconds to get back on his feet or the fight is declared over.

knuckleball: Slow baseball pitch thrown with little or no rotation, and which, as a result, moves around unpredictably as it approaches the plate.

lap: One complete trip around a race track or up and back the length of a pool.

lateral: Football pass that does not move in a forward direction. In contrast to a forward pass, a lateral pass that hits the ground is a live ball that any player can pick up and carry.

layup: Basketball shot in which the ball is released near the rim and at the top of the jump, and frequently off the backboard. Layups are often the end result of a drive to the basket.

leg: In a relay race, that length of the track or pool that each member of the team must complete in order to finish the race. In Olympic swimming and track and field, team relays consist of four legs, as does swimming's individual medley event.

light heavyweight (boxing): Weight classification in professional boxing with a 175-pound maximum. In amateur boxing, the maximum is 178 pounds.

light heavyweight (weightlifting): International weight classification with a 181 ¾-pound maximum.

lightweight (boxing): Weight classification in professional boxing with a 135-pound maximum. In amateur boxing, the maximum is 132 pounds.

lightweight (judo): International weight classification with a 156-pound maximum.

lightweight (weightlifting): International weight classification with a 148 ¾-pound maximum.

line bowling: Style of bowling that involves rolling the ball along an imaginary line from the point of release to the target point.

line of scrimmage: Imaginary line parallel to the goal lines of a football field and extending the width of the field. It marks the position of the football and is reestablished as necessary after each completed play. From the offensive team's point of view, the line extends across the tip of the ball that points toward it. No player may cross the line until the ball is snapped (except for the center, whose fingers may cross the line in order to grip the ball). Forward passes can be thrown only from behind the line of scrimmage.

lock: Wrestling hold that completely prevents the opponent from moving whichever part of his body is being held.

long-distance running: Footrace longer than 1 mile.

long-distance swimming: Open-water event longer than 1 mile.

long-horse vault: *See* vault.

long jump: Field event that involves sprinting toward a sand pit and jumping for distance. Formerly known as the broad jump. *See also* triple jump.

luge: French word for "sled." A small racing sled that seats one or two people. During competition, the luge athlete assumes the most aerodynamically efficient position possible, lying far back on the sled, head held up just enough to see the course. Steering is done by shifting the weight and manipulating the twin metal runners beneath the sled.

lunge: Classic fencing technique of attacking an opponent by stepping forward with the front foot (the foot on the same side of the body as the sword arm) while keeping the back foot planted and extending the sword arm.

mainsail: Principal sail on a ship having several sails.

majority decision: Victory scored by a boxer after two of the ring officials declare him the winner while the third official declares a draw.

man-to-man defense: In various team sports, a strategy in which each defensive player is assigned to guard an opposing player, instead of an area. In professional basketball, man-to-man defense is mandatory. *See also* zone defense.

mandatory eight-count: Boxing rule specifying that once a knockdown occurs, the referee's count must automatically reach eight before the match can resume, if indeed it can resume. Used to allow the fallen boxer a few extra seconds to regain his composure before continuing the fight.

marathon: Footrace of 26 miles and 385 yards, run through public thoroughfares off-limits to traffic. The race was instituted in the modern Olympic Games to commemorate an event in ancient Greek history when a soldier ran a similar distance to deliver a message at a place called Marathon.

master: Title given to a martial artist who has achieved an advanced ranking after many years of study. *See also* belt.

match sprint: 1,000-meter cycling race around a velodrome track. Only the last 200 meters are timed. During the first 800 meters, the cyclists try to position themselves for the final 200-meter rush to the finish line.

middle-distance running: Track event involving races whose length can be anywhere from 800 meters to 1 mile.

middleweight (boxing): Weight classification in professional boxing with a 160-pound limit. In amateur boxing, the limit is 165 pounds.

middleweight (judo): International weight classification with a 189-pound maximum.

middleweight (weightlifting): International weight classification with a 181 ¾-pound maximum.

military press: In weightlifting, a lift made from a standing position and in which the barbell is pushed upward from shoulder level to an overhead position, and then lowered.

Mr./Ms. America: U.S. amateur title awarded to the male and female champions in the Mr./Ms. America bodybuilding competition. Entrants compete for the title in three divisions, according to their height: tall, medium, and short. Sanctioned by the Amateur Athletic Union.

Mr./Ms. Olympia: World professional title awarded to the male and female champions in the Mr. and Ms. Olympia bodybuilding competitions. Entrants compete for the title in a number of weight classifications. Sanctioned by the International Federation of Bodybuilding.

Mr./Ms. Universe: World amateur title awarded to the male and female champions in the Mr./Ms. Universe bodybuilding competition. Entrants compete for the title in a number of weight classifications. Sanctioned by the International Federation of Bodybuilding.

modified stock car: Standard assembly-line car whose power and efficiency have been boosted for greater performance, such as through improvements in the engine, the transmission, the suspension, and the fuel-injection system.

most valuable player awards: Any number of annual distinctions given to the most outstanding athletes in various team sports. The most valuable players are usually those who have done the most to help their teams win games. Among the more popular sports, award recipients are often named at several levels of play within a particular sport: championship series, playoff series, and regular season. Generally speaking, the winning candidates (for the official league award) are determined by the votes of selected sports media associations.

motor-paced cycling: Cycling time trial in which a car or motorcycle is used to cut wind resistance for the cyclist, who rides just behind and very close to the vehicle in front in order to ride in the slipstream created by the vehicle. The reduced air resistance ensures the possibility of reaching higher speeds with less effort.

muscle mass: Relative size of a muscle, a muscle group, or of the physique as a whole. Along with clear definition and well-balanced proportion, muscle mass is a desirable quality among bodybuilders.

natatorium: Building that contains a swimming pool and facilities for holding aquatic competitions.

National Association for Stock Car Auto Racing (NASCAR): Professional stock car-racing circuit that stages competitions in thirteen separate vehicle divisions at tracks throughout the United States. Its premier circuit is the Winston Cup series, in which vehicles with engines as large as 750 horsepower reach speeds as high as 200 miles per hour.

Negro leagues: Series of professional leagues in the United States organized for African American baseball players—largely, if not solely, the result of major league baseball's refusal to integrate. The situation began to change in 1947, the year that Jackie Robinson became the modern major league's first black player. By the late 1940's, the popularity of the Negro leagues had fallen as black players joined major league teams.

nelson: Wrestling hold that involves using the arms and hands to apply pressure to the opponent's head and upper arms. The quarter nelson, half nelson, and full nelson are variations of this type of hold.

Nordic skiing: Competitive events consisting of cross-country skiing and ski jumping.

offense: Term used in many team sports for the side attempting to advance the ball or puck or to score points, runs, or goals against an opponent's defense. The term is also applied to specific game plans used by the team controlling the ball, as well as to the productivity of the offensive team—which might be measured in scores, yards gained, or attempts to score.

offsides (football): Violation committed by any player who starts to cross the line of scrimmage before the ball is snapped.

offsides (soccer): Moment when one or more attacking (offensive) players advance too far upfield. Players can be offsides only when they are in the opponents' half of the field and when fewer than two opposing players are closer to the goal line than they are. Referees signal offside violations only at the moment when the attacking team passes or shoots the ball, and only when they judge an offside player to be gaining an advantage.

Olympic Games: World's most elite international amateur sports exhibition, held every four years in a different host country and open to athletes from virtually every nation. The modern Summer Olympic Games began in Athens, Greece, in 1896. The Winter Games began in France in 1924. From that year until 1992, the Games were divided into Summer and Winter cycles. In 1994 the Winter Games began a separate four-year cycle. Since then, the Winter and Summer Games have alternated every two years. The Olympics were first held at Olympia in ancient Greece at four-year intervals from 776 B.C.E. to 393 C.E., when they were abolished by the Roman government. The earliest Games lasted only one day and consisted of a single footrace the length of the stadium—very roughly, about 200 meters. Other sports, such as chariot racing, boxing, and the pentathlon, were eventually added, extending the festival (which also included religious celebrations) to seven days. The modern Games were resurrected in Athens, Greece, in 1896, mostly through the efforts of French educator and scholar Baron Pierre de Coubertin. His purpose was to revive the Greek tradition of a periodic sports festival and to promote international good will. In modern times, participating athletes engage in many different sports, with new sports being added at virtually every Olympiad. Each Olympics may also include demonstration sports (the 1988 Games, for example, featured baseball and tennis). The Olympic Games are governed by the International Olympic Committee, headquartered in Lausanne, Switzerland.

Olympic lifting: Category of weightlifting events featured at the Olympic Games. Includes the clean and jerk and the snatch.

omnium: Event in track cycling that involves a series of races, each at distances ranging from one-quarter mile to two miles.

overhead smash: Tennis or badminton stroke that is hit from overhead with great force and power. Similar in motion to the serve. An effective put-away shot.

overtime: Period of extended play used when a game is tied at the end of regulation. In some sports, such as basketball, overtime periods are of fixed duration and are played out to the end, with additional overtime periods added when scores remain tied. In other sports, such as football, games may end the moment one team scores. *See also* sudden-death overtime.

pairs: In figure skating competition, a program performed by two skaters, one male and one female, skating in tandem. The programs consist of dancing, jumps, turns, spins, lifts, and throws, among others. Set to music.

par: Number of strokes that expert golfers are expected to take to finish a hole or a course in ordinary weather conditions. Par for one hole is determined by allowing a certain number of strokes from the tee to the green (considering the distance between the two) and allotting 2 strokes for putting. Results of golf matches are typically expressed in strokes over or under par for the entire matches.

parallel bars: Gymnastics apparatus consisting of two parallel oval-shaped wooden or fiberglass poles approximately eleven and a half feet long and five and a half feet off the ground and set as far apart as the gymnast prefers. Used to perform routines that require balancing and swinging movements, for example. A men's event.

parry: Fencer's use of the sword to deflect an opponent's blade.

passing shot: In a tennis match, a ball that is hit past and outside the reach of an opponent who is positioned in the frontcourt or midcourt area.

peloton: French word that means the "pack." The main group of cyclists in a race, typically near the front of the field of competitors.

penalty area: Demarcated part of a soccer field directly in front of each goal, measuring forty-four yards wide and eighteen yards deep. The area delimits the space within which a goalkeeper can handle the ball with his or her hands. Defensive fouls which would result in direct free kicks for a fouled team outside the penalty area result in penalty kicks for the attacking team if they are committed by the defending within its own area. *See also* goal area.

penalty box: In ice hockey, a designated area off the ice in which a penalized player must wait for the penalty minutes to expire before being allowed to resume play. Until that time, that player's team will continue the game shorthanded. Penalizations create opportunities for power plays. *See also* power play.

penalty kick: Free kick awarded to a soccer team when the opposing team commits a major foul within the penalty area. All players but the defending goalkeeper and the designated kicker must be outside the penalty area when the referee signals for the kick to be made. The ball is placed on the marked "penalty spot," twelve yards in front of the goal line, on which the goalkeeper must have his or her feet at the moment the ball is kicked. *See also* corner kick, free kick (soccer).

pennant: Honor accorded to the winning teams in baseball's National and the American League Championship Series. Both pennant champions advance to the World Series to decide major league baseball's overall season champion. In a more general sense, the term "pennant winner" is applied to the champion of any organized sports league

pentathlon: Term for any five-event competition. The modern Olympic pentathlon for men consists of fencing, pistol shooting, freestyle swimming, cross-country running, and horsemanship. The Olympic track and field pentathlon for women was replaced by the heptathlon in 1984.

perfect game (baseball): No-hit game in which a pitcher does not allow a single runner to reach first base under any circumstance. In contrast to other kinds of no-hitters, a perfect game is always a shutout.

perfect game (bowling): Scoring 300, the maximum number of points in a single game. A 300 game requires twelve consecutive strikes.

pike: Position in which a diver or gymnast shapes his or her body like a V, with the body bent at the waist and the arms held straight out and to the sides or touching the feet or the backs of the knees; the legs are straight.

pin (bowling): One of the ten wooden figures that make up the target.

pin (golf): Metal upright flagstaff that indicates where the hole is.

pin (wrestling): Pushing the opponent's shoulder blades to the mat. In Olympic freestyle and Greco-Roman wrestling, the match is over (and won) the moment both blades are touching the mat.

pin bowling: Style of bowling that involves rolling the ball directly toward either a single pin or a specific pocket.

pistol: Handgun that can be aimed and fired with one hand.

pit stop: Leaving the auto raceway for an off-track area to change tires, refuel, or have repairs done.

pitch (baseball): Ball thrown from pitcher to batter.

pitch (golf): Shot that puts the ball onto the green from a point just off the green. Shorter shots of this type are called chip shots.

pitch (soccer): British term for a soccer playing field.

platform diving: Competitive event involving dives off a fixed, nonflexible surface. The platform is set 10 meters above the water in Olympic diving. Divers are judged on such elements as takeoff, execution, form, and entry. The degree of difficulty of each dive is also taken into account.

playoff: Generally, a series of games held at the end of the regular season to determine the finalists for a subsequent championship game or series (as in the Super Bowl or the World Series). "Playoff" may also mean a period of extended play when a game is tied after regulation play has ended, as in a sudden-death playoff in a golf match.

pocket (bowling): For a right-hander, the small space between the headpin (1-pin) and the 3-pin; for a left-hander, between the headpin and the 2-pin. The likelihood of rolling a strike is greatest at these target points. The ten bowling pins are assembled in the shape of a triangle. The topmost pin closest to the bowler is the headpin, or 1-pin. The very next row, left to right, includes the 2-pin and the 3-pin, then come the 4-, the 5-, and the 6-pins, and finally pins 7, 8, 9, and 10.

pocket (football): Area several yards behind the line of scrimmage in which the quarterback sets up to throw a pass. The pocket offers the quarterback the best possible pass protection. Once the ball is snapped, the pocket forms as the offensive line drops back to create this U-shaped barrier.

point: Unit of scoring in any game or contest.

point-of-aim: Point at which the archer sets the line of sight in order to calculate the best elevation for the flight of the arrow.

pole position: In auto racing, the innermost front-row position on the starting line. An advantage awarded to the driver with the fastest times in qualifying time trials held prior to the main racing event.

pole vault: Men's field event that involves using a long fiberglass or wooden pole to lift the body up and over a horizontally positioned crossbar set between two upright supports. The object is to clear (or go over) the crossbar at a height greater than the other competitors and in fewer tries.

pommel horse: Men's event that involves performing any number of balancing and swinging gymnastics moves, while moving back and forth across the top the horse, using both the pommels and the top of the horse and not letting one's legs touch the horse. The horse is a rectangular apparatus approximately five feet long and one foot wide and covered with padded leather. Two pommels, or handles, are set on top and parallel to each other. Also called a side horse.

post: Offensive position occupied by a basketball player just outside the lane, either down close to the basket (the low post) or up around the free throw line (the high post).

post up: On offense in basketball, to set up in a low-post position in order to gain a scoring advantage against a shorter basketball player or an opponent who is in foul trouble.

power lifting: Category of weightlifting competition involving the bench press, the dead lift, and the squat. Both men and women are allowed to participate in a variety of weight classes. Not an Olympic category. *See also* Olympic lifting.

power play: Situation in a hockey game in which one team outnumbers the other on the ice because of players in the penalty box. The first team's numerical advantage generally means greater scoring opportunities against a shorthanded team. Often the team with the advantage will send its fastest skaters and best scorers into the game in an effort to overwhelm the opponent.

press: Defensive strategy in basketball that involves applying intense man-to-man pressure against the opposing team from the moment the ball is inbounded (full-court press) or just after the ball crosses the half-court line (half-court press).

professional: Generally, one who competes for prize money or who is paid to play.

puck: Hard-rubber pellet used as the object that ice hockey teams move around the rink and attempt to place in the opposing teams' goals in order to score. The standard puck is one inch thick and five and a half inches in diameter.

pull: To ride at the front of a group of cyclists, where the wind resistance is greatest and where the lead cyclist is without the benefit of a slipstream. Instead, the leader creates the drafting effect for the others. The members of a cycling team are expected to take turns pulling the others during a race in order to allow every member a chance to conserve energy yet maintain speed.

pumping iron: Slang phrase that means exercising with weights (such as barbells and dumbbells).

pursuit: Track cycling event in which individuals or teams of riders start the race at opposite ends of the track and try to catch up to the opposing side.

put-away: Similar to a kill shot, an unhittable or unreturnable shot that scores a point for the hitter in volleyball, tennis, or badminton.

putt: Golf stroke made with the ball on the green.

putting green: *See* green.

qualifying: For an individual athlete or a team of athletes, the act of becoming eligible for a particular game or tournament by fulfilling certain requirements. Qualifying can arise through a variety of ways, such as through preliminary heats or through individual statistics or through team win-loss records.

quarterback: Position on a football team that has central responsibility for running the team's offensive plays. The quarterback issues instructions to fellow players and throws most of the passes. In the past, quarterbacks called all their own plays; in modern football most plays are called by coaches, who relay their instructions to the quarterbacks on the field.

racing shell: Lightweight and usually very narrow racing boat pulled by oars.

randori: Japanese word that means "free exercise." Judo sparring sessions designed to develop strength, speed, stamina, and technique.

rangefinder: Archer's device that helps in estimating the distance to the target or in locating the point-of-aim.

reading the green: Setting up a golf putt by first studying closely the slope and the surface of the green.

rebound (basketball): Unsuccessful shot that caroms off the backboard or the rim; or the act of gaining possession of such a shot attempt.

rebound (ice hockey): Pass or a shot attempt that caroms off the boards encompassing the ice; or the act of gaining possession of such a pass or shot attempt.

referee's decision: Victory scored by a boxer who has been declared the winner by the referee while the two ring judges have each declared a draw.

regatta: Series of races involving rowboats, sailboats, or speedboats.

relay: Team race, such as in swimming and track events, that requires each team member to complete one leg (of which there are usually four) of the race, one competitor at a time. In swimming, a leg is complete as each swimmer touches the wall. In track, this occurs when the baton is passed from one runner to another (except on the final leg).

reverse dive: Maneuver in which the diver faces the water, jumps up off the board, rotates backward, and enters the water headfirst, facing the board, or feetfirst, facing away from the board.

rhythmic gymnastics: International and Olympic (as of 1984) category of events for female gymnasts, who compete according to rules prescribed by the International Gymnastics Federation (IGF). In individual competition, the gymnasts perform choreographed routines using one of the following objects in each routine: a ribbon, a hoop, a ball, a rope, or clubs. Every two years, the IGF selects four of the five apparatus to be used in routines for the next two years. The routines are performed on a forty-by-forty-foot floor areas, are set to music, last sixty to ninety seconds, and the gymnast and apparatus must be moving at all times. Although not yet an Olympic event, group competition consists of synchronized routines performed by six gymnasts at once.

rifle: Shoulder weapon with a stock and a long barrel with spiral grooves cut into the inside, and which shoots a bullet.

rings: *See* stationary rings.

round (boxing): Three-minute periods into which a boxing match is divided. A one-minute rest period separates each round. The number of rounds in a match depends on whether the event is amateur or professional.

round (golf): Eighteen holes of a golf course. May also simply mean a game of golf; to play a "round" of golf is to play a game of eighteen holes.

routine: Set of graceful movements, difficult stunts, or other elements or tricks performed on a gymnastics apparatus or in floor exercises.

run (baseball): Point scored whenever an offensive player successfully crosses home plate.

run (bobsledding, skiing): Inclined course traversed by the participant.

run (cricket): Point scored whenever the two batsmen successfully exchange wickets (run from one wicket to the other) during a play.

run batted in (RBI): In baseball and softball, a statistic credited to a batter who gets a hit and causes a base runner to score a run. Even if the batter flies out or is thrown out on the play, the run will count unless the third out results. A batter can also be credited with an RBI by being walked by the pitcher and forcing home the runner.

rush: Act of advancing the football by running with it on a play from scrimmage. Also, the defense's attempt to penetrate the offensive backfield in order to get to the ball.

Ryder Cup: Series of men's golf tournaments between professional teams from the United States and various European countries. Begun in 1927 by British businessman Samuel Ryder for competition between professional golfers from the United States and Great Britain. Held every odd-numbered year.

sabre fencing: One of the three styles of fencing. A sabre is a sword with a curved guard protecting the back of the hand and a fairly rigid blade with a blunted tip. A cutting and thrusting weapon. *See also* épée fencing, foil fencing.

sack: Statistic credited to a defender who manages to tackle the quarterback behind the line of scrimmage in a football game.

saddle bronc riding: Rodeo competition that involves riding a saddled wild, bucking horse for eight seconds using one hand to grip a strap attached to the saddle. Riders are judged on how well they ride and how hard the horse bucks. Rodeo's classic event has its roots in the Old West, when restless ranch hands would compete to see who was the best at riding wild horses.

safety (football): Scoring play, good for 2 points, that occurs when the defending team forces the opposing team to end its play within, or behind, its own end zone. Safeties are usually scored when ballcarriers are tackled within, or forced out of, their own end zones, players fumble the ball out of their end zones, or centers snap the ball out of their end zones. "Safety" is also the name of a defensive backfield position.

sail: Large, billowing expanse of fabric, such as cotton or polyester, used on ships to harness the wind and propel the ship forward.

salchow: Figure skating maneuver achieved by jumping from the back inside edge of one skate, turning once in the air, and landing on the back outside edge of the second skate. Named for its inventor, Swedish skater Ulrich Salchow, who in 1908 won the first gold medal awarded in men's Olympic figure skating, which was then a Summer Games event.

sand trap: Depression filled with loose sand and usually set near the green on a golf course.

save (baseball): Statistic credited to a relief pitcher who enters the game with his team ahead and preserves the victory. To earn the save, the reliever must generally come into a situation in which he faces a potentially tying run, while protecting a lead of from one to three runs. On the other hand, a reliever who enters the game with the team behind or tied but pitches a victory will be credited with a win.

save (ice hockey): Statistic credited to a goalie who deflects a shot on goal or otherwise prevents a goal from being scored.

school figures: *See* compulsory figures.

schooner: Fore-and-aft rigged ship equipped with two or more masts. Rigging refers to the lines of rope stretching from the tops of the masts to the deck and which are used for support.

schussing: Skiing at high speed straight down the mountain's natural slope—the steepest and fastest line of descent.

scissors volley: Soccer maneuver that involves leaping up and, from a horizontal position, kicking the ball using a scissors-like leg motion.

screwball: Reverse curveball. A baseball pitch that veers or breaks in the direction opposite that of a curveball. A screwball thrown by a right-handed pitcher will break down and toward a right-handed batter.

sculls: Rowing sport in which two oars mounted in fixed positions on either side of the racing shell are pulled at the same time to propel the boat in one direction.

sensei: Japanese word meaning "teacher" or "instructor." A title accorded to instructors in the martial arts such as judo.

serve and volley player: Tennis player whose game strategy is to rush the net aggressively after serving the ball, anticipating the volley or the put-away.

setter: Volleyball player who occupies the middle front row position. He or she must put the ball up into the air near the net so that the hitter can spike it.

shoot the tube: To ride a surfboard into the hollow tunnel of water created by the curl of an ocean wave.

shot put: Field event that involves heaving the shot for distance. A shot is an iron or brass ball weighing from 8 to 16 pounds (16 in Olympic competition).

shotgun formation: In football, an offensive formation used to give the quarterback more time to pass. The quarterback lines up several yards behind the center, while the running backs position themselves farther out as flankers or blockers.

show jumping: Equestrian event in which horse and rider attempt to jump over a succession of fences at varying distances within a prescribed time limit. Held in an arena.

shutout: Statistic credited to a baseball or softball pitcher who does not allow the opposition to score any runs in a game. More generally, a shutout occurs when one team fails to score a point in any sporting event.

shuttlecock: Lightweight, conical object volleyed back and forth in badminton.

sidehorse: *See* pommel horse.

side-horse vault: *See* vault.

single: In baseball or softball, a hit that allows the batter to reach first base.

single wing: In football, an offensive formation with an emphatic strong side (the side that has more players lined up either left or right of the center, thus making that side "stronger"). In the single wing, the tailback lines up about 4 to 5 yards directly behind the center and receives the snap. On the strong side, the fullback lines up about a yard ahead of and just to the side of the tailback, and can also receive the snap. The quarterback positions himself as a blocking back a few yards away from the center, again on the strong side. The fourth back, the wingback, lines up behind and just outside the offensive end on the strong side.

sit-ski: Much-wider-than-normal water ski with a seat affixed to the top. Invented especially for disabled athletes who are paralyzed from the waist down.

ski jumping: Competitive distance event that involves gliding straight down an upward curling ramp or hill without help from ski poles, taking off into air, and trying to achieve the greatest distance possible before landing. A event in Nordic skiing, which also includes cross-country skiing.

skipper: Person in charge of a ship.

sky hook: High-arching hook shot taken from far above the rim of a basketball hoop. Popularized by former NBA star Kareem Abdul-Jabbar, for whom the phrase was coined.

slalom (skiing): Race that involves negotiating as fast as possible the downhill zigzag pattern of the course. This design forces the skier to execute a number of turns through gates set up at different distances and angles. A race against the clock. An event in the Alpine skiing category, which also includes downhill, giant slalom, and super-giant slalom ski racing.

slalom (waterskiing): Event that involves zigzagging through a line of buoys set out lengthwise across the water. One of three basic water skiing events, the others being jump skiing and trick riding.

slam dunk: Especially forceful and intimidating basketball scoring move in which the ball is stuffed or pushed through the rim rather than shot.

slap shot: High-velocity hockey shot in which the shooter takes the hockey stick all the way back for increased power and then propels the puck at speeds that are often well above 100 miles per hour.

slider: Baseball pitch that is thrown like a fastball but moves like a curveball, except that it breaks slightly later than a curve, just as it crosses the plate.

slingshotting: Maneuver in auto racing and cycling in which the slipstreaming car or cyclist uses the power and energy conserved to shoot past the lead racer.

slipstreaming: Riding in the slipstream, the pocket of reduced air resistance and forward suction behind a rapidly moving object, such as a lead race car, a lead cyclist, or a motorcycle, in order to conserve energy while maintaining speed. *See also* drafting.

slugging percentage: Statistical category that indicates a baseball batter's ability to get extra-base hits (doubles, triples, and home runs). Figured by dividing the total number of bases reached safely on hits by the total number of at bats.

small-bore: In shooting sports, a term that refers to small-caliber firearms, in the .22 range.

snatch: In weightlifting, a lift performed by pulling the barbell off the floor and in one continuous motion bringing it to rest in an overhead position.

somersault: Maneuver in which the body is turned one full revolution, either forward or backward. The head and feet rotate up and over each other. Frequently used in diving and gymnastics. Often called a "flip" when executed completely in the air.

spare: In bowling, the feat of knocking down all ten pins with both balls in a single frame.

spike: To hit the volleyball downward into the opposite court with as much velocity as possible. The spiker often tries to jump high up over the net because the added height creates a better hitting angle.

spitball: Baseball pitch that moves unpredictably, the result of spit, sweat, petroleum jelly, or some other substance having been applied to the ball. Illegal since the 1920's.

split decision: Victory scored by a boxer after two of the ring officials declare him the winner while the third official votes for his opponent.

split-fingered fastball: Baseball pitch thrown with the same arm motion and speed as a fastball but with the index and middle fingers spread more widely apart. The ball tends to dip sharply just as it reaches the plate.

spot bowling: Style of bowling that involves rolling the ball across a specific marker—such as one of the seven triangular arrows set into the line just beyond the foul line—as the target point for releasing the ball.

spread eagle: One of the basic movements of free skating, in which the skater performs smooth glides through large circles or straight lines. To do this, both skates must be turned outward from each other in a line (right toes pointing directly right, left toes point directly left) and the heels spread apart a little more than hip distance.

springboard diving: Competitive event involving dives off a springboard. A springboard is a flat and flexible board mounted at one end and positioned over a fulcrum. The diver uses the board as a launching pad, attaining the height necessary to perform the dive. Olympic competition consists of the 1-meter and 3-meter dives (the springboards are set 1 and 3 meters above the water). Divers are judged on such elements as takeoff, execution, form, and entry. The degree of difficulty of each dive is also taken into account.

sprint: All-out race to the finish line. Sprint events occur in such sports as cycling, speed skating, and track and field.

squat: Weightlifting exercise or a competitive event that involves balancing the barbell behind the head and atop the shoulders, then squatting down and rising to a standing position.

stage race: Cycling race divided into a succession of individual stages or segments. Each stage is really only a shorter race, and the distance of each race will vary, sometimes greatly. The cyclist who wins the entire race is the one with the lowest overall time after his or her times for all the stages are added together. The Tour de France is the world's longest and most famous stage race.

Stanley Cup: End-of-season tournament that determines the National Hockey League champion team. The preliminary rounds lead up to final best-of-seven-games Stanley Cup Championship Series between the Wales and the Campbell Conference champions. The cup was first awarded to amateur champions in the late nineteenth century.

stationary rings: Men's gymnastics event performed while hanging from two rings suspended from above by long straps. Each ring is approximately seven and one-half inches in diameter and positioned about eight feet off the floor. Routines on the rings combine swinging, balancing movements such as handstands and crosses (where the body is held vertically and the arms are fully extended in the shape of a cross) and are a test of strength and stamina. In competition, the rings should remain stationary.

steeplechase (horse racing): Event that takes place on a steeplechase course consisting of obstacles such as fences, water jumps, and open ditches.

steeplechase (track and field): Race in which competitors encounter a series of rigid hurdles and water jumps. A standard steeplechase race, which is an Olympic event, is 3,000 meters long.

stern: Rear of a ship or boat. Also called aft.

steroids: Class of natural and artificial organic chemical substances with significant applications in medicine, biology, and chemistry. Various types of artificial steroids are used therapeutically for such reasons as fighting inflammation of tissues or stimulating physical growth. Anabolic steroids are synthetically derived from the male hormone testosterone. They have often been taken by athletes in training to build up the size of their muscles or to help their injuries heal faster. Because of the dangerous side effects associated with using steroids, however, many of the organizations and national governing bodies that regulate various worldwide sports have banned them, imposing suspensions, fines, or other penalties if their use is detected during drug testing. Drug testing has become common at a number of international sporting events such as the Olympic Games and the World Championships.

stock car: Technically speaking, an unmodified race car that resembles its standard assembly-line model. In actuality, however, the likeness ends with the visible similarities. For the purposes of competition, stock cars are always modified to some degree to ensure peak performance. Alterations are often made to the engine and other critical components—whatever will make the car go faster.

stolen base: *See* base stealing.

strike (baseball): Pitch that the batter swings at but misses, or hits into foul territory for strikes one or two, or lets pass through the strike zone without swinging (a called strike). Three strikes and the batter is out.

strike (bowling): Knocking down all ten pins on the first roll in a single frame.

strikeout: Statistic credited to a pitcher every time a batter is retired solely on strikes. Credited also to the batter.

striker: On a soccer team, the offensive player who occupies the central forward position and who has a major responsibility to score goals.

stroke (golf): Unit of scoring in golf, one stroke being charged to a player for each shot taken, including penalty strokes. Or the controlled swing used to hit the ball.

stroke (rowing): Crew member who sits in the rear of the racing shell and who is responsible for setting the rowing pace for the oarsmen. Or this crew member's act of setting the pace ("setting the stroke"). Also, the rower's use of an oar to pull the shell through the water.

stroke (swimming): Any of several popular swimming styles involving the arms, hands, and feet. Also, the swimmer's controlled use of the arms and legs to move through the water.

stroke (tennis): Any of several popular methods of hitting the ball, such as the forehand and the backhand. Also, the controlled swing used to hit the ball.

sudden-death overtime: Method for determining the winner of a game still tied at the end of regulation play. Ordinarily, the first player or team to score a numerical advantage wins. In professional football, for example, the team that scores first in the fifteen-minute overtime period wins the game.

Super Bowl: Yearly postseason January spectacle between the conference champions of the National Football League (NFL). The game that decides the overall NFL champion, it is the single most-watched sporting event in North America and is often among the most-watched television broadcasts each year.

super heavyweight (boxing): Weight classification in Olympic (amateur) boxing for athletes weighing more than 200 pounds.

super heavyweight (weightlifting): International weight classification for athletes weighing more than 242 pounds.

super set: In weightlifting sports, a set of exercises for one group of muscles that is performed just before a set for an opposing muscle group, followed by a normal rest interval.

swan dive: Front dive in which the body is fully extended, the back is arched, the arms are outstretched, and the entry into the water is head first.

sweeper: On a soccer team, a defensive player who is free to roam in front of or behind his or her team's rear defensive line.

T-formation: Early offensive formation in football, which has been modified several times over the years, that positions the backfield players into roughly the shape of a T. The quarterback lines up directly over the center, the fullback sets up several yards right behind the quarterback, and the two halfbacks position themselves on either side and slightly ahead of the fullback. The modern T, or pro set, removes the third halfback. Another variation, the split T, removes the middle back and spreads the offensive linemen a little farther apart along the line of scrimmage.

take a wicket: In cricket, the act of putting out the batsman by throwing the ball at the wicket and dislodging at least one of the bails.

takedown: Controlling an opponent and forcing him to the wrestling mat.

target archery: Shooting at targets placed at varying distances.

technical foul: Basketball rules violation that arises principally in the instance of flagrant and unsportsmanlike conduct on or off the court and before or after play has stopped. Such behavior is most often directed at an opponent or a referee. The nonoffending team can be awarded free throws and possession of the ball.

technical knockout (TKO): Victory scored by a boxer after the referee has stopped the match because the other boxer cannot continue fighting or cannot really defend himself, or because that boxer has indicated that he wants to stop.

test match cricket: International first-class match in which the best players from one country team up to compete against similar players from other countries. Test matches often take as long as five days to complete the required 2 innings per team.

thoroughbreds: Race horses bred for speed and stamina. Descended from Arabian stallions that were brought over to England between 1690 and 1730 and crossed with English racing mares. These sensitive, spirited animals have delicate heads, slender bodies, and long muscles and legs.

time trial: Form of cycling competition in which riders start the race at intervals of several minutes apart from each other. The cyclist with the best time wins.

TKO: *See* technical knockout.

toe loop jump: Skating maneuver achieved by jumping off the back outside edge of one skate after having planted the toe of the other skate into the ice (to assist takeoff), turning once in the air, and landing on the outside edge of the first skate.

top fuel: Category of professional drag racing called the top fuel eliminators, featuring dragsters that burn a potent blend of methanol and nitromethane fuel. Top fuel vehicles are of two types—funny cars and top fuel dragsters—and are the most powerful piston-driven machines in the world. The driver relies primarily on a hand-activated parachute to stop the car, a process that can take as much as twelve hundred feet. Top fuel competition involves a series of elimination heats, two cars per heat. These cars are built with a lightweight tubular frame, wide rear tires, and a powerful engine placed front (funny cars) or back (top fuel dragsters) of the frame; they often reach speeds in the range of 290 miles per hour over the one-quarter-mile course. *See also* funny car.

topspin: Forward rotation of a tennis ball imparted by sweeping the racket face up and over the ball at the point of contact.

touchdown: In football, a scoring play of 6 points that are earned by successfully advancing the football across the opposing goal line and into the end zone. Passing, rushing, and recovering a fumble are various ways of scoring a touchdown.

tours: Most important and usually the longest stage races of the international cycling season. A tour is won by completing all of the stages in the shortest amount of time. The most famous of these is the approximately 2,200-mile-long Tour de France.

track events: "Track" is often used loosely for "track and field"; however, in its narrower sense, it applies only to running and walking events: dashes, middle- and long-distance runs, hurdle races, the steeplechase, and walking races.

trampoline: Gymnastics apparatus in which a rectangular canvas cover or webbing is attached by springs to a surrounding metal frame. The trampoline's canvas cover normally stands about three to four feet above the ground. Used to perform a variety of jumping, somersaulting, and other acrobatic elements. Not a standard event in artistic gymnastic competitions.

trim: To adjust the sails of a ship in order to keep the ship on course.

triple: In baseball or softball, a hit that allows the batter to reach third base.

triple bogey: Finishing a golf hole at 3 strokes over par for that hole.

Triple Crown (baseball): Unofficial championship title awarded to the major league baseball players who at the end of the regular season lead their leagues (National and American) in home runs, batting average, and runs batted in.

Triple Crown (general): Those events or tournaments in a particular sport that are considered to be the three major ones; or the feat of winning all three of them in a single season or year.

Triple Crown (horse racing): Unofficial championship title awarded to the horse that wins the Kentucky Derby, the Preakness Stakes, and the Belmont Stakes in the same season.

triple jump: Field event similar to the long jump that involves jumping for distance. The mechanics, however, differ greatly. The triple jumper is allowed to take three sequential jumps following a running start. The first landing is made on the takeoff foot, the second landing on the other foot, and the third and final landing on both feet. Also called the hop, step, and jump after the three basic movements required. The top distances in this event are about double the top distances in the long jump.

tuck: Diving and gymnastic position in which the knees are bent, the thighs are held tightly against the chest, and the hands are wrapped around the lower legs.

tumbling: Gymnastics event performed down a large floor mat and in which the gymnast executes handsprings, twists, rolls, somersaults, and other acrobatic moves in a continuous series. Not a standard event in artistic gymnastic competitions.

turnover: Term used in many team sports for a play in which one team loses possession of the ball to the other. In football, most turnovers are the result of fumbles or intercepted passes.

twist: Dive that requires twisting the body sideways, in a half-twist, a full-twist, or more before entering the water. In gymnastics, twists are added to flips to increase the difficulty of the trick.

unanimous decision: Victory scored by a boxer after all three of the ring officials (the two ring judges and the referee) have declared him the winner.

unassisted goal (hockey): Scoring play by a player who wins possession of the puck without the assistance of a teammate.

uneven parallel bars: Women's gymnastics event in which the gymnast performs a variety of continuous swinging and balancing tricks, moving between and around both bars. The apparatus consists of two wooden or fiberglass rails affixed to metal supports and set at different heights. The bars are parallel to each other and, in competition, are set at seven and one-half feet and five feet off the floor.

vault: Gymnastics event that involves vaulting over a padded, rectangular, leather covered apparatus a little more than five feet one inch long, slightly more than one foot wide, and raised about four and one-half feet high for men and three and one-half feet high for women, called a horse. Gymnasts start by running toward the horse, then jump off a springboard, place their hands on the horse, and shove off, landing feet first on the other side. While in the air either before or after hitting the horse, the gymnast often performs acrobatic somersaults or other movements that raise his or her score. Men vault over the horse lengthwise, from end to end (also called long-horse vault), and women vault over the side, widthwise (also called side-horse vault).

velodrome: Cycling racetrack with banked turns and usually made of wood or concrete.

victory lap: Extra lap taken by the winning driver, cyclist, or runner once the race is over. A gesture of celebration between athlete and spectator.

volley: In badminton, tennis, or volleyball, to hit the shuttlecock or the ball while it is airborne and before it has touched the court; or hitting the ball back and forth in continuous play.

walk: Statistic credited to a baseball or softball pitcher for throwing four "balls"—pitches outside the strike zone—thereby sending the batter to first base. Credited also to the batter.

water hazard: Any body of standing water, such as a lake, a pond, or a stream, set within the boundaries of the golf course. Does not include "casual water," water that accumulates on the course such as from rain.

welterweight: Weight classification in professional and amateur boxing with a 147-pound maximum.

white-water racing: Race, or that portion of a race, that takes place through the white water, or the rapids, of a river or waterway.

wicket: In cricket, one of the two frames consisting of three wooden stumps, each twenty-eight inches high, atop which are set two bails. The bowler hurls the ball at the wicket and tries to dislodge the bails. If that happens, the batsman is out. Also refers to a batsman's turn at bat during an innings.

Wimbledon: Oldest and most highly regarded international tennis event in the world. This annual Grand Slam tournament is officially called "The Lawn Tennis Championships" at the All-England Club in Church Road, Wimbledon, England.

wind-aided time: In certain track events, a performance time that has been assisted favorably by wind blowing generally in the direction of the race or finish line at a predetermined velocity. Wind-aided times are not counted as official records because of the advantage that is said to have occurred. The International Amateur Athletic Federation, which governs track and field, does not recognize as world or national records times in sprints and horizontal jumps set with a tailwind in excess of 2.0 meters per second.

windmill delivery: Softball pitching delivery that requires rapidly rotating the pitching arm in a circular underhand direction. A windmill windup allows the pitcher to generate as much velocity as possible prior to releasing the ball. The cricket bowler also uses a windmill-style delivery, but in an overhand direction.

winner's circle: Section away from a racetrack's finish line where the winning jockey and horse are officially awarded.

World Cup (golf): Yearly international four-day tournament in which thirty-two two-person teams from more than fifty countries compete in stroke play matches.

World Cup (skiing): Annual series of international Alpine skiing events for amateurs. The World Cup is awarded to the male and female winners.

World Cup (soccer): Perhaps the single most-popular sports competition in the world, soccer's World Cup tournament features the best teams from thirty-two countries, selected during a two-year elimination tournament sponsored by the International Federation of Football Association (FIFA). The World Cup in men's soccer began in Uruguay in 1930 and has been held every four years—except during World War II. Competition in the women's World Cup began in 1991.

World Series: Championship best-of-seven-games baseball series between the pennant winners from the National League and the American League played each October. Determines major league baseball's overall season champion. Originated in 1903, when the National League's Pittsburgh Pirates played the American League's Boston Red Sox in a best-of-nine-games series. Boston won, five games to three.

wrist shot: Ice hockey shot delivered with a quick snap of the wrists. The shooter uses the blade of the hockey stick to flip the puck toward the goal. Unlike the faster, more powerful slap shot, no backswing is involved,

zone defense (basketball): Defensive strategy in which each player is assigned to a specified zone or area around the basket being defended, and must therefore guard any opposing player who invades that zone. Almost the opposite of the man-to-man defense, in which each defender must guard a specific opponent.

zone defense (football): Same idea as in basketball's zone defense. Each member of the defensive secondary, and often each of the linebackers, must defend a specified zone on the field and cover any opposing player who invades that zone.

ALL-TIME GREAT ATHLETES LISTS

AP Top Athletes of the Twentieth Century

The most outstanding athletes of the twentieth century, as voted by a sixteen-member panel assembled by the Associated Press (AP) in 1999. The athletes are listed in descending order of the numbers of votes they received. All these names, except a racehorse, are included in *Great Athletes, Revised.*

1. Babe Ruth, baseball
2. Michael Jordan, basketball
3. Jim Thorpe, track and field; football
4. Muhammad Ali, boxing
5. Wayne Gretzky, ice hockey
6. Jim Brown, football
7. Joe Louis, boxing
8. Jesse Owens, track and field
9. Babe Didrikson Zaharias, track and field; tennis; golf
10. Wilt Chamberlain, basketball
11. Willie Mays, baseball
12. Jack Nicklaus, golf
13. Ted Williams, baseball
14. Ty Cobb, baseball
15. Pelé, soccer
16. Bill Russell, basketball
17. Lou Gehrig, baseball
18. Hank Aaron, baseball
19. Joe DiMaggio, baseball
20. Martina Navratilova, tennis
21. Carl Lewis, track and field
22. Gordie Howe, ice hockey
23. Sugar Ray Robinson, boxing
24. Larry Bird, basketball
25. Ben Hogan, golf
26. Oscar Robertson, basketball
27. Red Grange, football
28. Walter Payton, football
29. Jackie Robinson, baseball
30. Rod Laver, tennis
31. Kareem Abdul-Jabbar, basketball
32. Magic Johnson, basketball
33. Arnold Palmer, golf
34. Sandy Koufax, baseball
35. Mickey Mantle, baseball
35. Mark Spitz, swimming
37. Joe Montana, football
38. Jack Dempsey, boxing
39. Bobby Orr, ice hockey
40. Jackie Joyner-Kersee, track and field
41. Billie Jean King, tennis
42. Walter Johnson, baseball
43. Sammy Baugh, football
44. Rocky Marciano, boxing
44. Johnny Unitas, football
46. Stan Musial, basketball
47. Bobby Jones, tennis
48. Rogers Hornsby, baseball
49. Honus Wagner, baseball
50. Jerry Rice, football
51. Pete Sampras, tennis
52. Nadia Comăneci, gymnastics
53. Bill Tilden, tennis
54. Don Hutson, football
55. Chris Evert, tennis
56. Cy Young, baseball
57. Julius Erving, basketball
58. Tiger Woods, golf
59. Roger Bannister, track and field
60. Jerry West, basketball
61. Rafer Johnson, track and field
62. Maurice Richard, ice hockey
63. Eric Heiden, speed skating
64. Lawrence Taylor, football
65. Jean-Claude Killy, skiing
66. Edwin Moses, track and field
67. Nolan Ryan, baseball
68. Steffi Graf, tennis
69. Paavo Nurmi, track and field
70. Bobby Hull, ice hockey
71. Bob Mathias, track and field
72. Christy Mathewson, baseball
72. Bronco Nagurski, football
74. Elgin Baylor, basketball
75. Sam Snead, golf
76. Sonja Henie, figure skating
76. Wilma Rudolph, track and field
78. Dick Butkus, football
79. Bob Cousy, basketball
80. Willie Shoemaker, horse racing
81. *Secretariat*, racehorse

82. Cal Ripken, Jr., baseball
83. Althea Gibson, tennis
84. Mark McGwire, baseball
85. John McEnroe, tennis
86. Otto Graham, football
87. O. J. Simpson, football
88. Pete Rose, baseball
89. Roger Staubach, football
90. Don Budge, tennis
91. Eddie Arcaro, horse racing
91. Juan Manuel Fangio, auto racing
93. Henry Armstrong, boxing
94. Mario Lemieux, ice hockey
95. Sugar Ray Leonard, boxing
96. Mario Andretti, auto racing
97. Emil Zatopek, track and field
98. Josh Gibson, baseball
99. Warren Spahn, baseball
100. Roberto Clemente, baseball
100. Bob Gibson, baseball

ESPN SportsCentury 100 Greatest Athletes of the Twentieth Century

The greatest athletes who competed in the United States and Canada during the twentieth century, as selected by ESPN as part of the SportsCentury retrospective in 1999. The athletes are listed in descending order of the numbers of votes they received. All these names, except three racehorses, are covered in *Great Athletes, Revised.*

1. Michael Jordan, basketball
2. Babe Ruth, baseball
3. Muhammad Ali, boxing
4. Jim Brown, football
5. Wayne Gretzky, ice hockey
6. Jesse Owens, track and field
7. Jim Thorpe, track and field; football
8. Willie Mays, baseball
9. Jack Nicklaus, golf
10. Babe Didrikson Zaharias, track and field; tennis; golf
11. Joe Louis, boxing
12. Carl Lewis, track and field
13. Wilt Chamberlain, basketball
14. Hank Aaron, baseball
15. Jackie Robinson, baseball
16. Ted Williams, baseball
17. Magic Johnson, basketball
18. Bill Russell, basketball
19. Martina Navratilova, tennis
20. Ty Cobb, baseball
21. Gordie Howe, ice hockey
22. Joe DiMaggio, baseball
23. Jackie Joyner-Kersee, track and field
24. Sugar Ray Robinson, boxing
25. Joe Montana, football
26. Kareem Abdul-Jabbar, basketball
27. Jerry Rice, football
28. Red Grange, football
29. Arnold Palmer, golf
30. Larry Bird, basketball
31. Bobby Orr, ice hockey
32. Johnny Unitas, football
33. Mark Spitz, swimming
34. Lou Gehrig, baseball
35. *Secretariat*, racehorse
36. Oscar Robertson, basketball
37. Mickey Mantle, baseball
38. Ben Hogan, golf
39. Walter Payton, football
40. Lawrence Taylor, football
41. Wilma Rudolph, track and field
42. Sandy Koufax, baseball
43. Julius Erving, basketball
44. Bobby Jones, golf
45. Bill Tilden, tennis
46. Eric Heiden, speed skating
47. Edwin Moses, track and field
48. Pete Sampras, tennis
49. O. J. Simpson, football
50. Chris Evert, tennis
51. Rocky Marciano, boxing
52. Jack Dempsey, boxing
53. Rafer Johnson, track and field
54. Greg Louganis, diving
55. Mario Lemieux, ice hockey
56. Pete Rose, baseball
57. Willie Shoemaker, horse racing
58. Elgin Baylor, basketball
59. Billie Jean King, tennis
60. Walter Johnson, baseball
61. Stan Musial, baseball
62. Jerry West, basketball
63. Satchel Paige, baseball
64. Sammy Baugh, football
65. Althea Gibson, tennis
66. Eddie Arcaro, horse racing
67. Bob Gibson, baseball
68. Al Oerter, track and field
69. Bonnie Blair, speed skating
70. Dick Butkus, football
71. Roberto Clemente, baseball
72. Bo Jackson, football; baseball
73. Josh Gibson, baseball
74. Deion Sanders, football; baseball
75. Dan Marino, football
76. Barry Sanders, football
77. Cy Young, baseball

78. Bob Mathias, track and field
79. Gale Sayers, football
80. A. J. Foyt, auto racing
81. Jimmy Connors, tennis
82. Bobby Hull, ice hockey
83. Honus Wagner, baseball
84. *Man o' War,* racehorse
85. Maurice Richard, ice hockey
86. Otto Graham, football
87. Henry Armstrong, boxing
88. Joe Namath, football
89. Rogers Hornsby, baseball
90. Richard Petty, auto racing
91. Bob Beamon, track and field
92. Mario Andretti, auto racing
93. Don Hutson, football
94. Bob Cousy, basketball
95. George Blanda, football
96. Michael Johnson, track and field
97. *Citation,* racehorse
98. Don Budge, tennis
99. Sam Snead, golf
100. Jack Johnson, boxing

Major League Baseball's All-Time Team

Players were voted in by a panel of thirty-six members of the Baseball Writers' Association of America for the Classic Sports Network just before the 1997 All-Star game.

Catcher
Johnny Bench

First base
Lou Gehrig

Second base
Rogers Hornsby

Shortstop
Honus Wagner

Third base
Mike Schmidt

Left field
Ted Williams

Center field
Willie Mays

Right field
Babe Ruth

Designated hitter
Paul Molitor

Right-handed pitcher
Walter Johnson

Left-handed pitcher
Sandy Koufax

Relief pitcher
Dennis Eckersley

Manager
Casey Stengel

National Basketball Association's Fifty Greatest Players

The fifty greatest players in NBA history were chosen by the league in 1996 to celebrate the league's first half-century. They appear in alphabetical order.

Kareem Abdul-Jabbar
Nate Archibald
Paul Arizin
Charles Barkley
Rick Barry
Elgin Baylor
Dave Bing
Larry Bird
Wilt Chamberlain
Bob Cousy
Dave Cowens
Billy Cunningham
Dave DeBusschere
Clyde Drexler
Julius Erving
Patrick Ewing
Walt Frazier
George Gervin
Hal Greer
John Havlicek
Elvin Hayes
Magic Johnson
Sam Jones
Michael Jordan
Jerry Lucas
Kevin McHale
Karl Malone
Moses Malone
Pete Maravich
George Mikan
Earl Monroe
Hakeem Olajuwon
Shaquille O'Neal
Robert Parish
Bob Pettit
Scottie Pippen
Willis Reed
Oscar Robertson
David Robinson
Bill Russell
Dolph Schayes
Bill Sharman
John Stockton
Isiah Thomas
Nate Thurmond
Wes Unseld
Bill Walton
Jerry West
Lenny Wilkens
James Worthy

ATHLETE-OF-THE-YEAR AWARDS

ABC *Wide World of Sports* Athlete of the Year

The top athletes have been selected annually by the producers of ABC Sports since 1962. One award goes to both men and women.

1962 Jim Beatty, track and field
1963 Valery Brumel, track and field
1964 Don Schollander, swimming
1965 Jim Clark, auto racing
1966 Jim Ryun, track and field
1967 Peggy Fleming, figure skating
1968 Bill Toomey, track and field
1969 Mario Andretti, auto racing
1970 Willis Reed, basketball
1971 Lee Trevino, golf
1972 Olga Korbut, gymnastics
1973 O. J. Simpson, football
Jackie Stewart, auto racing
1974 Muhammad Ali, boxing
1975 Jack Nicklaus, golf
1976 Nadia Comăneci, gymnastics
1977 Steve Cauthen, horse racing
1978 Ron Guidry, baseball
1979 Willie Stargell, baseball
1980 U.S. Olympic hockey team
1981 Sugar Ray Leonard, boxing
1982 Wayne Gretzky, hockey
1983 *Australia II* crew, yachting
1984 Edwin Moses, track and field
1985 Pete Rose, baseball
1986 Debi Thomas, figure skating
1987 Dennis Conner, yachting
1988 Greg Louganis, diving
1989 Greg LeMond, cycling
1990 Greg LeMond, cycling
1991 Carl Lewis, track and field
Kim Zmeskal, gymnastics
1992 Bonnie Blair, speed skating
1993 Evander Holyfield, boxing
1994 Al Unser, auto racing
1995 Miguel Indurain, cycling
1996 Michael Johnson, track and field
1997 Tiger Woods, golf
1998 Mark McGwire, baseball
1999 Lance Armstrong, cycling

Associated Press Athlete of the Year

The top men and top women athletes have been selected annually by Associated Press newspaper sports editors since 1931.

Men

1931 Pepper Martin, baseball
1932 Gene Sarazen, golf
1933 Carl Hubbell, baseball
1934 Dizzy Dean, baseball
1935 Joe Louis, boxing
1936 Jesse Owens, track and field
1937 Don Budge, tennis
1938 Don Budge, tennis
1939 Nile Kinnick, college football
1940 Tom Harmon, college football
1941 Joe DiMaggio, baseball
1942 Frank Sinkwich, college football
1943 Gunder Haegg, track and field
1944 Byron Nelson, golf
1945 Byron Nelson, golf
1946 Glenn Davis, college football
1947 Johnny Lujack, college football
1948 Lou Boudreau, baseball
1949 Leon Hart, college football
1950 Jim Konstanty, baseball
1951 Dick Kazmaier, college football
1952 Bob Mathias, track and field
1953 Ben Hogan, golf
1954 Willie Mays, baseball
1955 Hopalong Cassady, college football
1956 Mickey Mantle, baseball
1957 Ted Williams, baseball
1958 Herb Elliott, track and field
1959 Ingemar Johansson, boxing
1960 Rafer Johnson, track and field
1961 Roger Maris, baseball
1962 Maury Wills, baseball
1963 Sandy Koufax, baseball
1964 Don Schollander, swimming
1965 Sandy Koufax, baseball
1966 Frank Robinson, baseball
1967 Carl Yastrzemski, baseball
1968 Denny McLain, baseball
1969 Tom Seaver, baseball
1970 George Blanda, pro football
1971 Lee Trevino, golf
1972 Mark Spitz, swimming
1973 O. J. Simpson, pro football
1974 Muhammad Ali, boxing
1975 Fred Lynn, baseball
1976 Bruce Jenner, track and field
1977 Steve Cauthen, horse racing
1978 Ron Guidry, baseball
1979 Willie Stargell, baseball
1980 U.S. Olympic hockey team
1981 John McEnroe, tennis
1982 Wayne Gretzky, hockey
1983 Carl Lewis, track and field
1984 Carl Lewis, track and field
1985 Dwight Gooden, baseball
1986 Larry Bird, pro basketball
1987 Ben Johnson, track and field
1988 Orel Hershiser, baseball
1989 Joe Montana, pro football
1990 Joe Montana, pro football
1991 Michael Jordan, pro basketball
1992 Michael Jordan, pro basketball
1993 Michael Jordan, pro basketball
1994 George Foreman, boxing
1995 Cal Ripken, Jr., baseball
1996 Michael Johnson, track and field
1997 Tiger Woods, golf
1998 Mark McGwire, baseball
1999 Tiger Woods, golf
2000 Tiger Woods, golf

Women

1931 Helene Madison, swimming
1932 Babe Didrikson, track and field
1933 Helen Jacobs, tennis
1934 Virginia Van Wie, golf
1935 Helen Wills Moody, tennis
1936 Helen Stephens, track and field
1937 Katherine Rawls, swimming
1938 Patty Berg, golf
1939 Alice Marble, tennis
1940 Alice Marble, tennis
1941 Betty Hicks Newell, golf

GREAT ATHLETES

ASSOCIATED PRESS ATHLETE OF THE YEAR

1942 Gloria Callen, swimming
1943 Patty Berg, golf
1944 Ann Curtis, swimming
1945 Babe Didrikson Zaharias, golf
1946 Babe Didrikson Zaharias, golf
1947 Babe Didrikson Zaharias, golf
1948 Fanny Blankers-Koen, track and field
1949 Marlene Bauer, golf
1950 Babe Didrikson Zaharias, golf
1951 Maureen Connolly, tennis
1952 Maureen Connolly, tennis
1953 Maureen Connolly, tennis
1954 Babe Didrikson Zaharias, golf
1955 Patty Berg, golf
1956 Pat McCormick, diving
1957 Althea Gibson, tennis
1958 Althea Gibson, tennis
1959 Maria Bueno, tennis
1960 Wilma Rudolph, track and field
1961 Wilma Rudolph, track and field
1962 Dawn Fraser, swimming
1963 Mickey Wright, golf
1964 Mickey Wright, golf
1965 Kathy Whitworth, golf
1966 Kathy Whitworth, golf
1967 Billie Jean King, tennis
1968 Peggy Fleming, skating
1969 Debbie Meyer, swimming
1970 Chi Cheng, track and field
1971 Evonne Goolagong, tennis
1972 Olga Korbut, gymnastics
1973 Billie Jean King, tennis
1974 Chris Evert, tennis
1975 Chris Evert, tennis
1976 Nadia Comăneci, gymnastics
1977 Chris Evert, tennis
1978 Nancy Lopez, golf
1979 Tracy Austin, tennis
1980 Chris Evert Lloyd, tennis
1981 Tracy Austin, tennis
1982 Mary Decker Tabb, track and field
1983 Martina Navratilova, tennis
1984 Mary Lou Retton, gymnastics
1985 Nancy Lopez, golf
1986 Martina Navratilova, tennis
1987 Jackie Joyner-Kersee, track and field
1988 Florence Griffith Joyner, track and field
1989 Steffi Graf, tennis
1990 Beth Daniel, golf
1991 Monica Seles, tennis
1992 Monica Seles, tennis
1993 Sheryl Swoopes, basketball
1994 Bonnie Blair, speed skating
1995 Rebecca Lobo, college basketball
1996 Amy Van Dyken, swimming
1997 Martina Hingis, tennis
1998 Se Ri Pak, golf
1999 U.S. Soccer Team
2000 Marion Jones, track and field

CNN/*Sports Illustrated* Sportsman of the Year

The top athletes have been selected annually by the editors of *Sports Illustrated* magazine since 1954. One award goes to both men and women.

1954 Roger Bannister, track and field
1955 Johnny Podres, baseball
1956 Bobby Morrow, track and field
1957 Stan Musial, baseball
1958 Rafer Johnson, track and field
1959 Ingemar Johansson, boxing
1960 Arnold Palmer, golf
1961 Jerry Lucas, basketball
1962 Terry Baker, football
1963 Pete Rozelle, pro football
1964 Ken Venturi, golf
1965 Sandy Koufax, baseball
1966 Jim Ryun, track and field
1967 Carl Yastrzemski, baseball
1968 Bill Russell, basketball
1969 Tom Seaver, baseball
1970 Bobby Orr, hockey
1971 Lee Trevino, golf
1972 Billie Jean King, tennis;
John Wooden, basketball
1973 Jackie Stewart, auto racing
1974 Muhammad Ali, boxing
1975 Pete Rose, baseball
1976 Chris Evert, tennis
1977 Steve Cauthen, horse racing
1978 Jack Nicklaus, golf
1979 Terry Bradshaw, football;
Willie Stargell, baseball
1980 U.S. Olympic hockey team
1981 Sugar Ray Leonard, boxing
1982 Wayne Gretzky, hockey
1983 Mary Decker, track and field
1984 Mary Lou Retton, gymnastics;
Edwin Moses, track and field
1985 Kareem Abdul-Jabbar, basketball
1986 Joe Paterno, football
1987 "8 Athletes Who Care":
Bob Bourne, hockey;
Kip Keino, track and field;
Judi Brown King, track and field;
Dale Murphy, baseball;
Chip Rives, football;
Patty Sheehan, golf;
Rory Sparrow, basketball;
Reggie White, football
1988 Orel Hershiser, baseball
1989 Greg LeMond, cycling
1990 Joe Montana, football
1991 Michael Jordan, basketball
1992 Arthur Ashe, tennis
1993 Don Shula, football
1994 Johan Olav Koss, speed skating;
Bonnie Blair, speed skating
1995 Cal Ripken, Jr., baseball
1996 Tiger Woods, golf
1997 Dean Smith, college basketball
1998 Mark McGwire, baseball;
Sammy Sosa, baseball
1999 U.S. Women's World Cup Soccer Team
2000 Tiger Woods, golf

ESPY Outstanding Athlete of the Year

The ESPY awards were created by ESPN and are given for excellence in sports performance in more than thirty categories. The top men and top women athletes have been selected yearly by the ESPY Finalist Committee, made up of top athletes and coaches along with ESPN/ABC personnel, since 1993.

Men

1993 Michael Jordan, basketball
1994 Barry Bonds, baseball
1995 Steve Young, football
1996 Cal Ripken, Jr., baseball
1997 Michael Johnson, track and field
1998 Ken Griffey, Jr., baseball
Tiger Woods, golf
1999 Mark McGwire, baseball
2000 Tiger Woods, golf

Women

1993 Monica Seles, tennis
1994 Julie Krone, horse racing
1995 Bonnie Blair, speed skating
1996 Rebecca Lobo, basketball
1997 Amy Van Dyken, swimming
1998 Mia Hamm, soccer
1999 Chamique Holdsclaw, basketball
2000 Mia Hamm, soccer

James E. Sullivan Memorial Award

Selected by the Amateur Athletic Union since 1930, this award goes to each year's outstanding male or female amateur athlete.

1930 Bobby Jones, golf
1931 Barney Berlinger, track and field
1932 Jim Bausch, track and field
1933 Glenn Cunningham, track and field
1934 Bill Bonthron, track and field
1935 Lawson Little, golf
1936 Glenn Morris, track and field
1937 Don Budge, tennis
1938 Don Lash, track and field
1939 Joe Burk, rowing
1940 Greg Rice, track and field
1941 Leslie MacMitchell, track and field
1942 Cornelius Warmerdam, track and field
1943 Gilbert Dodds, track and field
1944 Ann Curtis, swimming
1945 Doc Blanchard, football
1946 Arnold Tucker, football
1947 John B. Kelly, Jr., rowing
1948 Bob Mathias, track and field
1949 Dick Button, skating
1950 Fred Wilt, track and field
1951 Bob Richards, track and field
1952 Horace Ashenfelter, track and field
1953 Sammy Lee, diving
1954 Mal Whitfield, track and field
1955 Harrison Dillard, track and field
1956 Pat McCormick, diving
1957 Bobby Morrow, track and field
1958 Glenn Davis, track and field
1959 Parry O'Brien, track and field
1960 Rafer Johnson, track and field
1961 Wilma Rudolph, track and field
1962 Jim Beatty, track and field
1963 John Pennel, track and field
1964 Don Schollander, swimming
1965 Bill Bradley, basketball
1966 Jim Ryun, track and field
1967 Randy Matson, track and field
1968 Debbie Meyer, swimming
1969 Bill Toomey, track and field
1970 John Kinsella, swimming
1971 Mark Spitz, swimming
1972 Frank Shorter, track and field
1973 Bill Walton, basketball
1974 Rich Wohlhuter, track and field
1975 Tim Shaw, swimming
1976 Bruce Jenner, track and field
1977 John Naber, swimming
1978 Tracy Caulkins, swimming
1979 Kurt Thomas, gymnastics
1980 Eric Heiden, speed skating
1981 Carl Lewis, track and field
1982 Mary Decker, track and field
1983 Edwin Moses, track and field
1984 Greg Louganis, diving
1985 Joan B. Samuelson, track and field
1986 Jackie Joyner-Kersee, track and field
1987 Jim Abbott, baseball
1988 Florence Griffith-Joyner, track and field
1989 Janet Evans, swimming
1990 John Smith, wrestling
1991 Mike Powell, track and field
1992 Bonnie Blair, speed skating
1993 Charlie Ward, football
1994 Dan Jansen, speed skating
1995 Bruce Baumgartner, wrestling
1996 Michael Johnson, track and field
1997 Peyton Manning, football
1998 Chamique Holdsclaw, basketball
1999 Kelly Miller, basketball
Coco Miller, basketball
2000 Rulon Gardner, Greco-Roman wrestling

Jesse Owens International Trophy

Selected annually by the International Amateur Athletic Association since 1981.

1981 Eric Heiden, speed skating
1982 Sebastian Coe, track and field
1983 Mary Decker, track and field
1984 Edwin Moses, track and field
1985 Carl Lewis, track and field
1986 Said Aouita, track and field
1987 Greg Louganis, diving
1988 Ben Johnson, track and field
1990 Roger Kingdom, track and field
1991 Greg LeMond, cycling
1992 Mike Powell, track and field
1993 Vitaly Scherbo, gymnastics
1994 Wang Junxia, track and field
1995 Johan Olva Koss, speed skating
1996 Michael Johnson, track and field
1997 Michael Johnson, track and field
1998 Haile Gebreselassie, track and field
1999 Marion Jones, track and field
2000 Lance Armstrong, cycling

Sporting News Sportsman of the Year

The year's best athlete has been selected by the editors of *Sporting News* since 1968. The name of the award was changed from "Man of the Year" to "Sportsman of the Year" in 1993.

1968 Denny McLain, baseball
1969 Tom Seaver, baseball
1970 John Wooden, basketball
1971 Lee Trevino, golf
1972 Charles O. Finley, baseball
1973 O. J. Simpson, pro football
1974 Lou Brock, baseball
1975 Archie Griffin, football
1976 Larry O'Brien, basketball
1977 Steve Cauthen, horse racing
1978 Ron Guidry, baseball
1979 Willie Stargell, baseball
1980 George Brett, baseball
1981 Wayne Gretzky, hockey
1982 Whitey Herzog, baseball
1983 Bowie Kuhn, baseball
1984 Peter Ueberroth, baseball
1985 Pete Rose, baseball
1986 Larry Bird, pro basketball
1987 (*No award*)
1988 Jackie Joyner-Kersee, track and field
1989 Joe Montana, football
1990 Nolan Ryan, baseball
1991 Michael Jordan, basketball
1992 Mike Krzyzewski, college basketball
1993 Cito Gaston, baseball
Pat Gillick, baseball
1994 Emmitt Smith, pro football
1995 Cal Ripken, Jr., baseball
1996 Joe Torre, baseball
1997 Mark McGwire, baseball
1998 Mark McGwire, baseball
Sammy Sosa, baseball
1999 New York Yankees, baseball
2000 Kurt Warner, football
Marshall Faulk, football

USOC Sportsman and Sportswoman of the Year

Selected annually by members of the national media, USOC board of directors, and Athletes' Advisory Council. Inductees include outstanding overall male and female athletes from within the U.S. Olympic Committee member organizations.

Men

1974 Jim Bolding, track and field
1975 Clint Jackson, boxing
1976 John Naber, swimming
1977 Eric Heiden, speed skating
1978 Bruce Davidson, equestrian
1979 Eric Heiden, speed skating
1980 Eric Heiden, speed skating
1981 Scott Hamilton, figure skating
1982 Greg Louganis, diving
1983 Rick McKinney, archery
1984 Edwin Moses, track and field
1985 Willie Banks, track and field
1986 Matt Biondi, swimming
1987 Greg Louganis, diving
1988 Matt Biondi, swimming
1989 Roger Kingdom, track and field
1990 John Smith, wrestling
1991 Carl Lewis, track and field
1992 Pablo Morales, swimming
1993 Michael Johnson, track and field
1994 Dan Jansen, speed skating
1995 Michael Johnson, track and field
1996 Michael Johnson, track and field
1997 Pete Sampras, tennis
1998 Jonny Moseley, skiing
1999 Lance Armstrong, cycling
2000 Rulon Gardner, Greco-Roman wrestling

Women

1974 Shirley Babashoff, swimming
1975 Kathy Heddy, swimming
1976 Sheila Young, speed skating
1977 Linda Fratianne, figure skating
1978 Tracy Caulkins, swimming
1979 Sippy Woodhead, swimming
1980 Beth Heiden, speed skating
1981 Sheila Ochowicz, speed skating and cycling
1982 Melanie Smith, equestrian
1983 Tamara McKinney, skiing
1984 Tracy Caulkins, swimming
1985 Mary Decker-Slaney, track and field
1986 Jackie Joyner-Kersee, track and field
1987 Jackie Joyner-Kersee, track and field
1988 Florence Griffith-Joyner, track and field
1989 Janet Evans, swimming
1990 Lynn Jennings, track and field
1991 Kim Zmeskal, gymnastics
1992 Bonnie Blair, speed skating
1993 Gail Devers, track and field
1994 Bonnie Blair, speed skating
1995 Picabo Street, skiing
1996 Amy Van Dyken, swimming
1997 Tara Lipinski, figure skating
1998 Picabo Street, skiing
1999 Jenny Thompson, swimming
2000 Marion Jones, track and field

HALLS OF FAME

Hockey Hall of Fame

Established in 1945 by the National Hockey League. Nominees must be retired for three years, but exceptions are occasionally made. Inductees are voted in by a fifteen-member panel of hockey personalities and media representatives. The years of induction are given in parentheses.

Sid Abel (1969)
Jack Adams (1959)
Syl Apps (1961)
George Armstrong (1975)
Irvine "Ace" Bailey (1975)
Dan Bain (1945)
Hobey Baker (1945)
Bill Barber (1990)
Marty Barry (1965)
Andy Bathgate (1978)
Bobby Bauer (1996)
Jean Beliveau (1972)
Clint Benedict (1965)
Doug Bentley (1964)
Max Bentley (1966)
Toe Blake (1966)
Leo Boivin (1986)
Dickie Boon (1952)
Mike Bossy (1991)
Butch Bouchard (1966)
Frank Boucher (1958)
George Boucher (1960)
Johnny Bower (1976)
Dubbie Bowie (1945)
Frank Brimsek (1966)
Punch Broadbent (1962)
Turk Broda (1967)
John Bucyk (1981)
Billy Burch (1974)
Harry Cameron (1962)
Gerry Cheevers (1985)
King Clancy (1958)
Dit Clapper (1947)
Bobby Clarke (1987)
Sprague Cleghorn (1958)
Neil Colville (1967)
Charlie Conacher (1961)
Lionel Conacher (1994)
Roy Conacher (1998)
Alex Connell (1958)
Bill Cook (1952)
Bun Cook (1995)
Art Coulter (1974)
Yvan Cournoyer (1982)
Bill Cowley (1968)
Rusty Crawford (1962)
Jack Darragh (1962)
Scotty Davidson (1950)
Hap Day (1961)
Alex Delvecchio (1977)
Cy Denneny (1959)
Marcel Dionne (1992)
Gordie Drillon (1975)
Graham Drinkwater (1950)
Ken Dryden (1983)
Woody Dumart (1992)
Tommy Dunderdale (1974)
Bill Durnan (1964)
Red Dutton (1958)
Babe Dye (1970)
Phil Esposito (1984)
Tony Esposito (1988)
Arthur Farrel (1965)
Fernie Flaman (1990)
Frank Foyston (1958)
Frank Fredrickson (1958)
Bill Gadsby (1970)
Bob Gainey (1992)
Chuck Gardiner (1945)
Herb Gardiner (1958)
Jimmy Gardner (1962)
Bernie Geoffrion (1972)
Eddie Gerard (1945)
Eddie Giacomin (1987)
Rod Gilbert (1982)
Billy Gilmour (1962)
Moose Goheen (1952)
Ebbie Goodfellow (1963)
Michel Goulet (1998)
Mike Grant (1950)
Shorty Green (1962)
Wayne Gretzky (1999)

Si Griffis (1950)
George Hainsworth (1961)
Glenn Hall (1975)
Joe Hall (1961)
Doug Harvey (1973)
George Hay (1958)
Riley Hern (1962)
Bryan Hextall (1969)
Hap Holmes (1972)
Tom Hooper (1962)
Red Horner (1965)
Tim Horton (1977)
Gordie Howe (1972)
Syd Howe (1965)
Harry Howell (1979)
Bobby Hull (1983)
Bouse Hutton (1962)
Harry Hyland (1962)
Dick Irvin (1958)
Busher Jackson (1971)
Ching Johnson (1958)
Ernie Johnson (1952)
Tom Johnson (1970)
Aurel Joliat (1947)
Duke Keats (1958)
Red Kelly (1969)
Ted Kennedy (1966)
Dave Keon (1986)
Elmer Lach (1966)
Guy Lafleur (1988)
Newsy Lalonde (1950)
Jacques Laperriere (1987)
Guy Lapointe (1993)
Edgar Laprade (1993)
Jack Laviolette (1962)
Hughie Lehman (1958)
Jacques Lemaire (1984)
Mario Lemieux (1997)
Percy LeSueur (1961)
Herbie Lewis (1989)
Ted Lindsay (1966)
Harry Lumley (1980)
Lanny McDonald (1992)
Frank McGee (1945)
Billy McGimsie (1962)
Mickey MacKay (1952)
George McNamara (1958)
Frank Mahovlich (1981)
Joe Malone (1950)
Sylvio Mantha (1960)
Jack Marshall (1965)
Fred Maxwell (1962)
Stan Mikita (1983)
Dickie Moore (1974)
Paddy Moran (1958)
Howie Morenz (1945)
Bill Mosienko (1965)
Joseph Mullen (2000)
Frank Nighbor (1947)
Reg Noble (1962)
Buddy O'Connor (1988)
Harry Oliver (1967)
Bert Olmstead (1985)
Bobby Orr (1979)
Bernie Parent (1984)
Brad Park (1988)
Lester Patrick (1947)
Lynn Patrick (1980)
Gilbert Perreault (1990)
Tom Phillips (1945)
Pierre Pilote (1975)
Didier Pitre (1962)
Jacques Plante (1978)
Denis Potvin (1991)
Babe Pratt (1966)
Joe Primeau (1963)
Marcel Pronovost (1978)
Bob Pulford (1991)
Harvey Pulford (1945)
Bill Quackenbush (1976)
Frank Rankin (1961)
Jean Ratelle (1985)
Chuck Rayner (1973)
Kenny Reardon (1966)
Henri Richard (1979)
Maurice Richard (1961)
George Richardson (1950)
Gordie Roberts (1971)
Larry Robinson (1995)
Art Ross (1945)
Blair Russel (1965)
Ernie Russell (1965)
Jack Ruttan (1962)
Borje Salming (1996)
Denis Savard (2000)
Serge Savard (1986)
Terry Sawchuk (1971)
Fred Scanlan (1965)
Milt Schmidt (1961)
Sweeney Schriner (1962)

Earl Seibert (1963)
Oliver Seibert (1961)
Eddie Shore (1947)
Steve Shutt (1993)
Babe Siebert (1964)
Joe Simpson (1962)
Darryl Sittler (1989)
Alf Smith (1962)
Billy Smith (1993)
Clint Smith (1991)
Hooley Smith (1972)
Tommy Smith (1973)
Allan Stanley (1981)
Barney Stanley (1962)
Peter Stastny (1998)
Jack Stewart (1964)
Nels Stewart (1962)
Bruce Stuart (1961)
Hod Stuart (1945)
Cyclone Taylor (1947)
Tiny Thompson (1959)
Vladislav Tretiak (1989)
Harry Trihey (1950)
Bryan Trottier (1997)
Norm Ullman (1982)
Georges Vezina (1945)
Jack Walker (1960)
Marty Walsh (1962)
Harry (Moose) Watson (1962)
Harry Percival Watson (1994)
Cooney Weiland (1971)
Harry Westwick (1962)
Fred Whitcroft (1962)
Phat Wilson (1962)
Gump Worsley (1980)
Roy Worters (1969)

International Boxing Hall of Fame

Established in 1989, the Boxing Hall of Fame uses a panel of Boxing Writers' Association members and boxing historians to select inductees. Nominees must be retired from competitive boxing for five years. The years of induction are given in parentheses.

Muhammad Ali (1990)
Sammy Angott (1998)
Alexis Arguello (1992)
Henry Armstrong (1990)
Carmen Basilio (1990)
Wilfred Benitez (1996)
Nino Benvenuti (1992)
Jackie "Kid" Berg (1994)
Jimmy Bivins (1999)
Joe Brown (1996)
Ken Buchanan (2000)
Charley Burley (1992)
Miguel Canto (1998)
Jimmy Carter (2000)
Marcel Cerdan (1991)
Antonio Cervantes (1998)
Jeff Chandler (2000)
Ezzard Charles (1990)
Billy Conn (1990)
Flash Elorde (1993)
Bob Foster (1990)
Joe Frazier (1990)
Gene Fullmer (1991)
Khaosai Galaxy (1999)
Kid Gavilan (1990)
Joey Giardello (1993)
Wilfredo Gomez (1995)
Billy Graham (1992)
Rocky Graziano (1991)
Emile Griffith (1990)
Marvin Hagler (1993)
"Fighting" Harada (1995)
Beau Jack (1991)
Lew Jenkins (1999)
Eder Jofre (1992)
Harold Johnson (1993)
Jake LaMotta (1990)
Sugar Ray Leonard (1997)
Sonny Liston (1991)
Joe Louis (1990)
Rocky Marciano (1990)
Joey Maxim (1994)
Bob Montgomery (1995)
Carlos Monzon (1990)
Archie Moore (1990)
Matthew Saad Muhammad (1998)
Jose Napoles (1990)
Ken Norton (1992)
Ruben Olivares (1991)
Bobo Olson (2000)
Carlos Ortiz (1991)
Manuel Ortiz (1996)
Floyd Patterson (1991)
Eusebio Pedroza (1999)
Willie Pep (1990)
Pascual Perez (1995)
Aaron Pryor (1996)
Sugar Ray Robinson (1990)
Luis Rodriguez (1997)
Sandy Saddler (1990)
Vicente Saldivar (1999)
Salvador Sanchez (1991)
Max Schmeling (1992)
Michael Spinks (1994)
Dick Tiger (1991)
Jose Torres (1997)
Jersey Joe Walcott (1990)
Ike Williams (1990)
Chalky Wright (1997)
Tony Zale (1991)
Carlos Zarate (1994)
Fritzie Zivic (1993)

International Gymnastics Hall of Fame

Publisher Glenn Sundby founded the Gymnastics Hall of Fame, for which inductees are selected by volunteers with backgrounds in gymnastics and business. The years of induction are given in parentheses.

Frank Bare (1999)
Vera Čáslavská (1998)
Miroslav Cerar (1999)
Nadia Comăneci (1993)
Bart Conner (1997)
Yukio Endo (1999)
Arthur Gander (1997)
Savino Guglielmetti (1998)
Jack Gunthard (1997)
Bela Karolyi (1997)
Nelli Kim (1999)
Olga Korbut (1988)
Eugen Mack (1999)
Mary Lou Retton (1997)
Cathy Rigby (1997)
Leon Stukelj (1997)
Larisa Latynina (1998)
Takashi Ono (1998)
Masao Takemoto (1997)
Yuri Titov (1999)
Ludmila Turishcheva (1998)
Peter Vidmar (1998)

International Soccer Hall of Champions

The International Soccer Hall of Champions was established in 1998 by the Féderation Internationale de Football Association (FIFA), soccer's international governing body. Nominees for induction must be retired from competition for five years and are voted in by a panel of soccer journalists. The years of induction are given in parentheses.

Franz Beckenbauer (1998)
Sir Bobby Charlton (1998)
Johan Cruyff (1998)
Alfredo Distefano (1998)
Eusebio (1998)
Just Fontaine (1999)
Garrincha (1999)
Sir Stanley Matthews (1998)
Bobby Moore (1999)
Gerd Müller (1999)
Pelé (1998)
Michel Platini (1998)
Ferenc Puskas (1998)
Lev Yashin (1998)

International Swimming Hall of Fame

The International Swimming Hall of Fame was established in 1965 by the U.S. College Coaches' Swim Forum. The 270 American inductees of the nearly 500 members are listed here. The years of induction are given in parentheses.

U.S. Men

Miller Anderson (1967)
Mike Barrowman (1997)
William Phillips Berge (1997)
Matt Biondi (1997)
Phil Boggs (1985)
Walter Brack (1997)
George Breen (1975)
Skippy Browning (1975)
Mike Bruner (1988)
Mike Burton (1977)
Tedford Cann (1967)
Rick Carey (1993)
Earl Clark (1972)
Steve Clark (1966)
Dick Cleveland (1991)
Robert Clotworthy (1980)
Buster Crabbe (1965)
Charlie Daniels (1965)
Dick Degener (1971)
Rick DeMont (1990)
Frank Dempsey (1996)
Pete Desjardins (1966)
David Edgar (1996)
John Faricy (1990)
Jeff Farrell (1968)
Peter Fick (1978)
Ralph Flanagan (1978)
Alan Ford (1966)
Bruce Furniss (1987)
Rowdy Gaines (1995)
Tim Garton (1997)
Harrison Glancy (1990)
Budd Goodwin (1971)
Jed Graef (1988)
George Haines (1977)
Gary Hall (1981)
Bruce Harlan (1973)
Harry Hebner (1968)
John Hencken (1988)
Charles Hickcox (1976)
John Higgins (1971)
Harry Holiday (1991)
Tom Jager (2001)
Chet Jastremski (1977)
Duke Kahanamoku (1965)
Warren Kealoha (1968)
Adolph Kiefer (1965)
John Kinsella (1986)
George Kojac (1968)
Ford Konno (1972)
Stubby Kruger (1986)
Louis Kuehn (1988)
Ludy Langer (1988)
Lance Larson (1980)
Sammy Lee (1968)
Kelley Lemmons (1999)
Harry LeMoyne (1988)
Greg Louganis (1993)
Steve Lundquist (1990)
Pat McCormick (1965)
Turk McDermott (1969)
Perry McGillivray (1981)
Don McKenzie (1989)
Frank McKinney (1975)
Jimmy McLane (1970)
Thompson Mann (1984)
Jack Medica (1966)
Jim Montgomery (1986)
Bill Mullikan (1984)
John Naber (1982)
Keo Nakama (1975)
Wally O'Connor (1966)
Yoshi Oyakawa (1979)
Al Patnik (1969)
Mickey Riley (1977)
Wally Ris (1966)
Carl Robie (1976)
Gail Roper (1997)
Clarence Ross (1988)
Norman Ross (1967)
Dick Roth (1987)

Jeff Rouse (2001)
Joe Ruddy (1986)
Doug Russell (1985)
Roy Saari (1976)
E. Carroll Schaeffer (1968)
Clarke Scholes (1980)
Don Schollander (1965)
Tim Shaw (1989)
George Sheldon (1989)
Robert Skelton (1988)
Bill Smith (1966)
Dutch Smith (1979)
Jimmy Smith (1992)
R. Jackson Smith (1983)
Mark Spitz (1977)
Allen Stack (1979)
Ted Stickles (1995)
Tom Stock (1989)
Juno Irwin Stover (1980)
Clyde Swendsen (1991)
Gary Tobian (1978)
Mike Troy (1971)
Albert Vande Weghe (1990)
Jesse Vassallo (1997)
Joe Verdeur (1966)
Matt Vogel (1996)
Hal Vollmer (1990)
Marshall Wayne (1981)
Bob Webster (1970)
Johnny Weissmuller (1965)
Al White (1965)
Bernie Wrightson (1984)
Bill Yorzyk (1971)

U.S. Women

Terry Anderson (1986)
Sue Atwood (1992)
Shirley Babashoff (1982)
Kristen Babb-Sprigue (1999)
Catie Ball (1976)
Sybil Bauer (1967)
Dawn Pawson Bean (1996)
Melissa Belote (1983)
Ethelda Bleibtrey (1967)
Charlotte Boyle (1988)
Lynne Burke (1978)
Lesley Bush (1986)
Gloria Callen (1984)
Patty Caretto (1987)
Cathy Carr (1988)
Tracy Caulkins (1990)
Florence Chadwick (1970)
Jennifer Chandler (1987)
Tiffany Cohen (1996)
Georgia Coleman (1966)
Carin Cone (1984)
Candy Costie (1995)
Lynne Cox (2000)
Helen Crlenkovich (1981)
Ann Curtis (1966)
Ellie Daniel (1997)
Penny Dean (1996)
Donna de Varona (1969)
Olga Dorfner (1970)
Vickie Draves (1969)
Ginny Duenkel (1985)
Barbara Dunbar (2000)
Gertrude Ederle (1965)
Kathy Ellis (1991)
Janet Evans (2001)
Cathy Ferguson (1978)
Sharon Finneran (1985)
Claire Galligan (1970)
Eleanor Garatti-Seville (1992)
Marjorie Gestring (1976)
Sue Gossick (1988)
Irene Guest (1990)
Kaye Hall (1979)
Jan Henne (1979)
Eleanor Holm (1966)
Virginia Hunt-Newman (1993)
Gail Johnson (1983)
Karen Josephson (1997)
Sarah Josephson (1997)
Marion Kane (1981)
Beth Kaufman (1967)
Lenore Kight (1981)
Micki King (1978)
Claudia Kolb (1975)
Ethel Lackie (1969)
Kim Linehan (1997)
Alice Landon Lord (1993)
Kelly McCormick (1999)
Margo McGrath (1989)
Josephine McKim (1991)
Helene Madison (1966)
Shelly Mann (1966)
Mary T. Meagher (1993)
Helen Meany (1971)
Maxine Merlino (1999)

Debbie Meyer (1977)
Michele Mitchell (1995)
Karen Moe (1992)
Pam Morris (1965)
Sandra Neilson (1986)
Megan Neyer (1997)
Martha Norelius (1967)
Zoe-Ann Olsen (1989)
Heidi O'Rourke (1980)
Albina Osipowich (1986)
Susan Pedersen (1995)
Betty Becker Pinkston (1967)
Paula Jean Meyers Pope (1979)
Cynthia Potter (1987)
Dorothy Poynton (1968)
Katherine Rawls (1965)
Carol Redmond (1989)
Aileen Riggin (1967)
Anne Ross (1984)
Keena Rothammer (1991)
Tracie Ruiz-Conforto (1993)
Sylvia Ruuska (1976)
Carolyn Schuler (1989)
Peg Seller (1988)
Caroline Smith (1988)
Carrie Steinseifer (1999)
Sharon Stouder (1972)
Vee Toner (1995)
Kay Vilen (1978)
Chris Von Saltza (1966)
Oho Wahle (1996)
Helen Wainwright (1972)
Lillian Watson (1984)
Mary Wayte (2000)
Mariechen Wehselau (1989)
Kim Welshons (1988)
Sharon Wichman (1991)
Esther Williams (1966)
Margaret Woodbridge (1989)
Wendy Wyland (2001)

International Tennis Hall of Fame

Established in 1953 by James Van Alan and sanctioned by the U.S. Tennis Association in 1954, the International Tennis Hall of Fame was known as the National Tennis Hall of Fame until 1976. Nominees must be retired from significant competition for five years and are voted in by the international tennis media. The years of induction are given in parentheses.

Pauline Betz Addie (1965)
George Adee (1964)
Fred Alexander (1961)
Wilmer Allison (1963)
Manuel Alonso (1977)
Malcolm Anderson (2000)
Arthur Ashe (1985)
Juliette Atkinson (1974)
H. W. "Bunny" Austin (1997)
Tracy Austin (1992)
Lawrence Baker, Sr. (1975)
Maude Barger-Wallach (1958)
Angela Mortimer Barrett (1993)
Karl Behr (1969)
Björn Borg (1987)
Jean Borotra (1976)
Lesley Turner Bowrey (1997)
John Bromwich (1984)
Norman Brookes (1977)
Mary K. Browne (1957)
Jacques Brugnon (1976)
Don Budge (1964)
Maria Bueno (1978)
May Sutton Bundy (1956)
Mabel Cahill (1976)
Oliver Campbell (1955)
Rosemary "Rosie" Casals (1996)
Malcolm Chace (1961)
Dorothea Douglass Chambers (1981)
Philippe Chatrier (1992)
Louise Brough Clapp (1967)
Clarence Clark (1983)
Joseph Clark (1955)
William Clothier (1956)
Henri Cochet (1976)
Arthur W. "Bud" Collins, Jr. (1994)
Maureen Connolly (1968)
Jimmy Connors (1998)
Ashley Cooper (1991)
Margaret Court (1979)
Jack Crawford (1979)
Joseph F. Cullman III (1990)
Allison Danzig (1968)
Sarah Palfrey Danzig (1963)
Herman David (1998)
Dwight Davis (1956)
Lottie Dod (1983)
John Doeg (1962)
Lawrence Doherty (1980)
Reginald Doherty (1980)
Jaroslav Drobny (1983)
Margaret Osbourne duPont (1967)
James Dwight (1955)
Roy Emerson (1982)
Pierre Etchebaster (1978)
Chris Evert (1995)
Bob Falkenburg (1974)
Neale Fraser (1984)
Shirley Fry-Irvin (1970)
Charles Garland (1969)
Althea Gibson (1971)
Kathleen McKane Godfree (1978)
Pancho Gonzalez (1968)
Evonne Goolagong (1988)
Bryan Grant (1972)
David Gray (1985)
Clarence Griffin (1970)
King Gustav V of Sweden (1980)
Harold Hackett (1961)
Ellen Hansell (1965)
Darlene Hard (1973)
Doris Hart (1969)
Gladys Heldman (1979)
W. E. "Slew" Hester (1981)
Bob Hewitt (1992)
Lew Hoad (1980)
Harry Hopman (1978)
Fred Hovey (1974)
Joe Hunt (1966)
Lamar Hunt (1993)

Frank Hunter (1961)
Helen Hull Jacobs (1962)
Bill Johnston (1958)
Ann Haydon Jones (1985)
Perry Jones (1970)
Robert Kelleher (2000)
Billie Jean King (1987)
Jan Kodes (1990)
Jack Kramer (1968)
René Lacoste (1976)
Al Laney (1979)
William Larned (1956)
Art Larsen (1969)
Rod Laver (1981)
Suzanne Lenglen (1978)
Dorothy Round Little (1986)
George Lott (1964)
John McEnroe (1999)
Ken McGregor (1999)
Chuck McKinley (1986)
Maurice McLoughlin (1957)
Frew McMillan (1992)
Don McNeill (1965)
Gene Mako (1973)
Molla Bjurstedt Mallory (1958)
Hana Mandlikova (1994)
Alice Marble (1964)
Alastair Martin (1973)
William McChesney Martin (1982)
Dan Maskell (1996)
Helen Wills Moody (1959)
Elisabeth Moore (1971)
Gardnar Mulloy (1972)
R. Lindley Murray (1958)
Julian Myrick (1963)
Ilie Nastase (1991)
Martina Navratilova (2000)
John Newcombe (1986)
Arthur Nielsen (1971)
Alex Olmedo (1987)
Rafael Osuna (1979)
Mary Outerbridge (1981)
Frank Parker (1966)
Gerald Patterson (1989)
Budge Patty (1977)
Theodore Pell (1966)
Fred Perry (1975)
Tom Pettitt (1982)
Nicola Pietrangeli (1986)
Adrian Quist (1984)
Dennis Ralston (1987)
Ernest Renshaw (1983)
William Renshaw (1983)
Vincent Richards (1961)
Bobby Riggs (1967)
Tony Roche (1986)
Ellen Roosevelt (1975)
Ken Rosewall (1980)
Elizabeth Ryan (1972)
Manuel Santana (1984)
Dick Savitt (1976)
Ted Schroeder (1966)
Eleonora Sears (1968)
Richard Sears (1955)
Frank Sedgman (1979)
Pancho Segura (1984)
Vic Seixas (1971)
Frank Shields (1964)
Betty Nuthall Shoemaker (1977)
Henry Slocum (1955)
Stan Smith (1987)
Fred Stolle (1985)
Bill Talbert (1967)
Bill Tilden (1959)
Lance Tingay (1982)
Ted Tinling (1986)
Bertha Townsend Toulmin (1974)
Tony Trabert (1970)
James Van Alen (1965)
John Van Ryn (1963)
Guillermo Vilas (1991)
Ellsworth Vines (1962)
Gottfried Von Cramm (1977)
Virginia Wade (1989)
Marie Wagner (1969)
Holcombe Ward (1956)
Watson Washburn (1965)
Malcolm Whitman (1955)
Hazel Wightman (1957)
Anthony Wilding (1978)
Richard N. Williams 2nd (1957)
Walter Clopton Wingfield (1997)
Sidney Wood (1964)
Robert Wrenn (1955)
Beals Wright (1956)

International Women's Sports Hall of Fame

Established in 1980 by the Women's Sports Foundation. The years of induction are given in parentheses.

Alpine Skiing

Christl Cranz (1991)
Diana Golden (1997)
Andrea Mead Lawrence (1983)
Annemarie Moser-Proell (1982)

Auto Racing

Janet Guthrie (1980)

Aviation

Bessie Coleman (1992)
Amelia Earhart (1980)
Marie Marvingt (1987)

Badminton

Judy Devlin Hashman (1995)

Baseball

Toni Stone (1993)

Basketball

Ann Meyers (1985)
Cheryl Miller (1991)

Bowling

Marion Ladewig (1984)

Cycling

Connie Carpenter (1990)

Diving

Micki King (1983)
Pat McCormick (1984)
Aileen Riggin (1988)

Equestrian

Lis Hartel (1994)

Fencing

Ilona Schacherer-Elek (1989)

Figure Skating

Tenley Albright (1983)
Theresa Weld Blanchard (1989)
Peggy Fleming (1981)
Carol Heiss Jenkins (1992)
Sonja Henie (1982)
Ludmila Protopopov (1992)
Irina Rodnina (1988)
Barbara Ann Scott-King (1997)

Golf

Patty Berg (1980)
JoAnne Carner (1987)
Betty Hicks (1995)
Carol Mann (1982)
Betsy Rawls (1986)
Louise Suggs (1987)
Glenna Collett Vare (1981)
Kathy Whitworth (1984)
Mickey Wright (1981)

Golf/Track and Field

Babe Didrikson Zaharias (1980)

Gymnastics

Vera Čáslavská (1991)
Nadia Comăneci (1990)
Olga Korbut (1982)
Larysa Latynina (1985)
Mary Lou Retton (1993)
Ludmila Turishcheva (1987)

Orienteering

Annichen Kringstad (1995)

Shooting

Margaret Murdock (1988)

Softball

Joan Joyce (1989)

Speed Skating

Kit Klein Outland (1993)
Sheila Young (1981)

Swimming

Tracy Caulkins (1986)
Florence Chadwick (1996)
Ann Curtis Cuneo (1985)
Donna de Varona (1983)
Gertrude Ederle (1980)
Dawn Fraser (1985)
Eleanor Holm (1980)
Mary T. Meagher (1993)
Debbie Meyer-Reyes (1987)

Tennis

Maureen Connolly (1987)
Margaret Court (1986)
Charlotte Dod (1986)
Margaret Osbourne duPont (1998)
Chris Evert (1981)
Althea Gibson (1980)
Evonne Goolagong (1989)
Billie Jean King (1980)
Suzanne Lenglen (1984)
Martina Navratilova (1984)
Eleanora Sears (1984)
Hazel Wightman (1986)

Track and Field

Evelyn Ashford (1997)
Joan Benoit (1999)
Fanny Blankers-Koen (1982)
Chi Cheng (1994)
Alice Coachman (1991)
Florence Griffith-Joyner (1998)
Madeline Manning Mims (1987)
Wilma Rudolph (1980)
Aeriwentha Mae Faggs Star (1996)
Helen Stephens (1983)
Shirley Strickland-de la Hunty (1998)
Irena Szewinska (1992)
Wyomia Tyus (1981)
Grete Waitz (1995)
Willye White (1988)

Volleyball

Flo Hyman (1986)

Naismith Memorial Basketball Hall of Fame

Named after James Naismith, the inventor of basketball, the Naismith Memorial Basketball Hall of Fame was established in 1949 by the National Association of Basketball Coaches. Nominees must be retired for five years and are voted in by a twenty-four-member committee of media representatives, Hall of Fame members, and trustees. Players only are listed here; their years of induction are given in parentheses.

Kareem Abdul-Jabbar (1995)
Nate Archibald (1991)
Paul Arizin (1977)
Thomas Barlow (1980)
Rick Barry (1987)
Elgin Baylor (1976)
John Beckman (1972)
Walter Bellamy (1993)
Sergei Belov (1992)
David Bing (1990)
Larry Bird (1998)
Carol Blazejowski (1994)
Bernard Borgmann (1961)
Bill Bradley (1982)
Joe Brennan (1974)
Al Cervi (1984)
Wilt Chamberlain (1978)
Charles Cooper (1976)
Kresimir Cosic (1996)
Bob Cousy (1970)
Dave Cowens (1991)
Joan Crawford (1997)
Billy Cunningham (1986)
Denise Curry (1997)
Bob Davies (1969)
Forrest DeBernardi (1961)
David DeBusschere (1982)
Henry Dehnert (1968)
Anne Donovan (1995)
Paul Endacott (1971)
Alex English (1997)
Julius Erving (1993)
Harold Foster (1964)
Walter Frazier (1987)
Max Friedman (1971)
Joe Fulks (1977)
Harry Gallatin (1991)
William Gates (1989)
George Gervin (1996)
Thomas Gola (1975)
Gail Goodrich (1996)
Harold Greer (1981)
Robert Gruenig (1963)
Cliff Hagan (1977)
Victor Hanson (1960)
Lucy Harris (1992)
John Havlicek (1983)
Cornelius Hawkins (1992)
Elvin Hayes (1990)
Marques Haynes (1998)
Thomas Heinsohn (1986)
Nat Holman (1964)
Robert Houbregs (1987)
Bailey Howell (1997)
Charles Hyatt (1959)
Danl Issel (1993)
Harry "Buddy" Jeannette (1994)
William Johnson (1976)
Neil Johnston (1990)
K. C. Jones (1989)
Sam Jones (1983)
Edward Krause (1975)
Bob Kurland (1961)
Bob Lanier (1992)
Joe Lapchick (1966)
Nancy Lieberman-Cline (1996)
Clyde Lovellette (1988)
Jerry Lucas (1979)
Angelo Luisetti (1959)
Bob McAdoo (2000)
Edward Macauley (1960)
Branch McCracken (1960)
Jack McCracken (1962)
Robert McDermott (1988)
Richard McGuire (1993)
Kevin McHale (1999)

Moses Malone (2001)
Pete Maravich (1987)
Slater Martin (1981)
Ann Meyers (1993)
George Mikan (1959)
Vern Mikkelsen (1995)
Cheryl Miller (1995)
Earl Monroe (1990)
Calvin Murphy (1993)
Charles Murphy (1960)
Harlan Page (1962)
Bob Pettit (1970)
Andy Phillip (1961)
James Pollard (1977)
Frank Ramsey (1981)
Willis Reed (1981)
Arnie Risen (1998)
Oscar Robertson (1979)
John Roosma (1961)
Bill Russell (1964)
John Russell (1974)
Dolph Schayes (1972)
Ernest Schmidt (1973)
John Schommer (1959)
Barney Sedran (1962)
Juliana Semenova (1993)
Bill Sharman (1975)
Christian Steinmetz (1961)
Isiah Thomas (2000)
David Thompson (1996)
John Thompson (1962)
Nate Thurmond (1984)
Jack Twyman (1982)
Wes Unseld (1988)
Robert Vandivier (1974)
Edward Wachter (1961)
Bill Walton (1993)
Robert Wanzer (1987)
Jerry West (1979)
Nera White (1992)
Lenny Wilkens (1989)
John Wooden (1960)
George Yardley (1996)

National Baseball Hall of Fame

The National Baseball Hall of Fame was established in 1935 by Major League Baseball. Nominees must have played for at least part of ten seasons and be retired for five years; inductees are voted in by the Baseball Writers' Association of America. Players only are listed here; their years of induction are given in parentheses.

Hank Aaron (1982)
Pete Alexander (1938)
Cap Anson (1939)
Luis Aparicio (1984)
Luke Appling (1964)
Richie Ashburn (1995)
Earl Averill (1975)
Home Run Baker (1955)
Dave Bancroft (1971)
Ernie Banks (1977)
Jake Beckley (1971)
James "Cool Papa" Bell (1974)
Johnny Bènch (1989)
Chief Bender (1953)
Yogi Berra (1972)
Jim Bottomley (1974)
Lou Boudreau (1970)
Roger Bresnahan (1945)
George Brett (1999)
Lou Brock (1985)
Dan Brouthers (1945)
Mordecai Brown (1949)
Jim Bunning (1996)
Jesse Burkett (1946)
Roy Campanella (1969)
Rod Carew (1991)
Max Carey (1961)
Steve Carlton (1994)
Orlando Cepeda (1999)
Frank Chance (1946)
Oscar Charleston (1976)
Jack Chesbro (1946)
Fred Clarke (1945)
John Clarkson (1963)
Roberto Clemente (1973)
Ty Cobb (1936)
Mickey Cochrane (1947)
Eddie Collins (1939)
Jimmy Collins (1945)
Earle Combs (1970)
Roger Connor (1976)
Stan Coveleski (1969)
Sam Crawford (1957)
Joe Cronin (1956)
Kiki Cuyler (1968)
Ray Dandridge (1987)
George Davis (1998)
Leon Day (1995)
Dizzy Dean (1953)
Ed Delahanty (1945)
Bill Dickey (1954)
Martín Dihigo (1977)
Joe DiMaggio (1955)
Larry Doby (1998)
Bobby Doerr (1986)
Don Drysdale (1984)
Hugh Duffy (1945)
Johnny Evers (1946)
Buck Ewing (1939)
Red Faber (1964)
Bob Feller (1962)
Rick Ferrell (1984)
Rollie Fingers (1992)
Carlton Fisk (2000)
Elmer Flick (1963)
Whitey Ford (1974)
Bill Foster (1996)
Rube Foster (1981)
Nellie Fox (1997)
Jimmie Foxx (1951)
Frankie Frisch (1947)
Pud Galvin (1965)
Lou Gehrig (1939)
Charlie Gehringer (1949)
Bob Gibson (1981)
Josh Gibson (1972)
Lefty Gomez (1972)
Goose Goslin (1968)
Hank Greenberg (1956)
Burleigh Grimes (1964)

Lefty Grove (1947)
Chick Hafey (1971)
Jesse Haines (1970)
Billy Hamilton (1961)
Gabby Hartnett (1955)
Harry Heilmann (1952)
Billy Herman (1975)
Harry Hooper (1971)
Rogers Hornsby (1942)
Waite Hoyt (1969)
Carl Hubbell (1947)
Catfish Hunter (1987)
Monte Irvin (1973)
Reggie Jackson (1993)
Travis Jackson (1982)
Fergie Jenkins (1991)
Hugh Jennings (1945)
Judy Johnson (1975)
Walter Johnson (1936)
Addie Joss (1978)
Al Kaline (1980)
Tim Keefe (1964)
Willie Keeler (1939)
George Kell (1983)
Joe Kelley (1971)
George Kelly (1973)
King Kelly (1945)
Harmon Killebrew (1984)
Ralph Kiner (1975)
Chuck Klein (1980)
Sandy Koufax (1972)
Nap Lajoie (1937)
Tony Lazzeri (1991)
Bob Lemon (1976)
Buck Leonard (1972)
Fred Lindstrom (1976)
Pop Lloyd (1977)
Ernie Lombardi (1986)
Ted Lyons (1955)
Tommy McCarthy (1946)
Willie McCovey (1986)
Joe McGinnity (1946)
Bill McKechnie (1962)
Bid McPhee (2000)
Mickey Mantle (1974)
Heinie Manush (1964)
Rabbit Maranville (1954)
Juan Marichal (1983)
Rube Marquard (1971)
Eddie Mathews (1978)
Christy Mathewson (1936)
Willie Mays (1979)
Joe Medwick (1968)
Johnny Mize (1981)
Joe Morgan (1990)
Stan Musial (1969)
Hal Newhouser (1992)
Kid Nichols (1949)
Phil Niekro (1997)
Jim O'Rourke (1945)
Mel Ott (1951)
Satchel Paige (1971)
Jim Palmer (1990)
Herb Pennock (1948)
Tony Perez (2000)
Gaylord Perry (1991)
Eddie Plank (1946)
Kirby Puckett (2001)
Charley Radbourn (1939)
Pee Wee Reese (1984)
Sam Rice (1963)
Eppa Rixey (1963)
Phil Rizzuto (1994)
Robin Roberts (1976)
Brooks Robinson (1983)
Frank Robinson (1982)
Jackie Robinson (1962)
Bullet Rogan (1998)
Edd Roush (1962)
Red Ruffing (1967)
Amos Rusie (1977)
Babe Ruth (1936)
Nolan Ryan (1999)
Ray Schalk (1955)
Mike Schmidt (1995)
Red Schoendienst (1989)
Tom Seaver (1992)
Joe Sewell (1977)
Al Simmons (1953)
George Sisler (1939)
Enos Slaughter (1985)
Duke Snider (1980)
Warren Spahn (1973)
Tris Speaker (1937)
Willie Stargell (1988)
Turkey Stearnes (2000)
Don Sutton (1998)
Bill Terry (1954)
Sam Thompson (1974)
Joe Tinker (1946)

Pie Traynor (1948)
Dazzy Vance (1955)
Arky Vaughan (1985)
Rube Waddell (1946)
Honus Wagner (1936)
Bobby Wallace (1953)
Ed Walsh (1946)
Lloyd Waner (1967)
Paul Waner (1952)
John Ward (1964)
Mickey Welch (1973)
Willie Wells (1997)
Zack Wheat (1959)
Hoyt Wilhelm (1985)
Billy Williams (1987)
Joe Williams (1999)
Ted Williams (1966)
Vic Willis (1995)
Hack Wilson (1979)
Dave Winfield (2001)
Early Wynn (1972)
Carl Yastrzemski (1989)
Cy Young (1937)
Ross Youngs (1972)
Robin Yount (1999)

National Track and Field Hall of Fame

The National Track and Field Hall of Fame was established in 1974 by The Athletics Congress (now USA Track & Field). Nominees must be retired for three years and are voted in by an eight-hundred-member panel made up of Hall of Fame and USA Track & Field officials, Hall of Fame members, current U.S. champions, and members of the Track & Field Writers of America. The years of induction are given in parentheses.

Men

Dave Albritton (1980)
Horace Ashenfelter (1975)
Willie Banks (2000)
James Bausch (1979)
Bob Beamon (1977)
Jim Beatty (1990)
Greg Bell (1988)
Dee Boeckmann (1976)
Ralph Boston (1974)
Don Bragg (1996)
Lee Calhoun (1974)
Milt Campbell (1989)
Henry Carr (1997)
Ellery Clark (1991)
Harold Connolly (1984)
Tom Courtney (1978)
Glenn Cunningham (1974)
William Curtis (1979)
Willie Davenport (1982)
Glenn Davis (1974)
Harold Davis (1974)
Harrison Dillard (1974)
Charley Dumas (1990)
Larry Ellis (2000)
Lee Evans (1983)
Barney Ewell (1986)
Ray Ewry (1974)
John Flanagan (1975)
Dick Fosbury (1981)
Greg Foster (1998)
Fortune Gordien (1979)
Charlie Greene (1992)
Archie Hahn (1983)
Glenn Hardin (1978)
Bob Hayes (1976)
Bud Held (1987)
Jim Hines (1979)
Bud Houser (1979)
DeHart Hubbard (1979)
Charlie Jenkins (1992)
Bruce Jenner (1980)
Cornelius Johnson (1994)
Rafer Johnson (1974)
Hayes Jones (1976)
John Kelley (1980)
Abel Kiviat (1985)
Alvin Kraenzlein (1974)
Ron Laird (1986)
Don Lash (1995)
Henry Laskau (1997)
Marty Liquori (1995)
Dallas Long (1996)
Joe McCluskey (1996)
Bob Mathias (1974)
Randy Matson (1984)
Earle Meadows (1996)
Ted Meredith (1982)
Ralph Metcalfe (1975)
Rod Milburn (1993)
Billy Mills (1976)
Charles Moore (2000)
Tom Moore (1988)
Bobby Morrow (1975)
Jess Mortensen (1992)
Edwin Moses (1994)
Lawrence Myers (1974)
Renaldo Nehemiah (1997)
Parry O'Brien (1974)
Al Oerter (1974)
Harold Osborn (1974)
Jesse Owens (1974)
Charley Paddock (1976)
Mel Patton (1985)
Eulace Peacock (1987)
Steve Prefontaine (1976)
Joie Ray (1976)
Greg Rice (1977)

Bob Richards (1975)
Bill Rodgers (2000)
Ralph Rose (1976)
Jim Ryun (1980)
Jackson Scholz (1977)
Bob Schul (1991)
Bob Seagren (1986)
Mel Sheppard (1976)
Martin Sheridan (1988)
Frank Shorter (1989)
Jay Silvester (1998)
Dave Sime (1981)
Robert Simpson (1974)
Tommie Smith (1978)
Andy Stanfield (1977)
Les Steers (1974)
Dwight Stones (1998)
Walter Tewksbury (1996)
John Thomas (1985)
Earl Thomson (1977)
Jim Thorpe (1975)
Eddie Tolan (1982)
Bill Toomey (1975)
Forrest Towns (1976)
Cornelius Warmerdam (1974)
Mal Whitfield (1974)
Mac Wilkins (1993)
Archie Williams (1992)
Rick Wohlhuter (1990)
John Woodruff (1978)
Dave Wottle (1982)
Frank Wykoff (1977)
George Young (1981)

Women

Evelyn Ashford (1997)
Valerie Brisco-Hooks (1995)
Alice Coachman (1975)
Lillian Copeland (1994)
Mae Faggs (1976)
Barbara Ferrell (1988)
Florence Griffith-Joyner (1995)
Evelyne Hall Adams (1988)
Doris Brown Heritage (1990)
Nell Jackson (1989)
Mildred McDaniel (1983)
Edith McGuire (1979)
Madeline Manning (1984)
Jean Shiley Newhouse (1993)
Louise Ritter (1995)
Betty Robinson (1977)
Wilma Rudolph (1974)
Kate Schmidt (1994)
Francie Larrieu Smith (1998)
Helen Stephens (1975)
Wyomia Tyus (1980)
Stella Walsh (1975)
Martha Watson (1987)
Willye White (1981)
Babe Didrikson Zaharias (1974)

Pro Football Hall of Fame

Established in 1963 by the National Football League. Nominees must be retired for five years and are voted in by a thirty-six-member panel of media representatives, one PFWA representative, and five selectors-at-large. Players only are listed here; their years of induction are given in parentheses.

Herb Adderley (1980)
Lance Alworth (1978)
Doug Atkins (1982)
Morris "Red" Badgro (1981)
Lem Barney (1992)
Cliff Battles (1968)
Sammy Baugh (1963)
Chuck Bednarik (1967)
Bobby Bell (1983)
Raymond Berry (1973)
Fred Biletnikoff (1988)
George Blanda (1981)
Mel Blount (1989)
Terry Bradshaw (1989)
Jim Brown (1971)
Roosevelt Brown (1975)
Willie Brown (1984)
Buck Buchanan (1990)
Dick Butkus (1979)
Earl Campbell (1991)
Tony Canadeo (1974)
Guy Chamberlin (1965)
Jack Christiansen (1970)
Dutch Clark (1963)
George Connor (1975)
Jimmy Conzelman (1964)
Lou Creekmur (1996)
Larry Csonka (1987)
Willie Davis (1981)
Len Dawson (1987)
Eric Dickerson (1999)
Dan Dierdorf (1996)
Mike Ditka (1988)
Art Donovan (1968)
Tony Dorsett (1994)
Paddy Driscoll (1965)
Bill Dudley (1966)
Albert Glen "Turk" Edwards (1969)
Tom Fears (1970)
Ray Flaherty (1976)
Len Ford (1976)
Dan Fortmann (1965)
Dan Fouts (1993)
Frank Gatski (1985)
Bill George (1974)
Frank Gifford (1977)
Otto Graham (1965)
Red Grange (1963)
Joe Greene (1987)
Forrest Gregg (1977)
Bob Griese (1990)
Lou Groza (1974)
Joe Guyon (1966)
George Halas (1963)
Jack Ham (1988)
John Hannah (1991)
Franco Harris (1990)
Mike Haynes (1997)
Ed Healey (1964)
Mel Hein (1963)
Ted Hendricks (1990)
Wilbur "Pete" Henry (1963)
Arnie Herber (1966)
Bill Hewitt (1971)
Clarke Hinkle (1964)
Elroy Hirsch (1968)
Paul Hornung (1986)
Ken Houston (1986)
Cal Hubbard (1963)
Sam Huff (1982)
Don Hutson (1963)
Jimmy Johnson (1994)
John Henry Johnson (1987)
Charlie Joiner (1996)
Deacon Jones (1980)
Stan Jones (1991)
Henry Jordan (1995)
Sonny Jurgensen (1983)
Leroy Kelly (1994)
Walt Kiesling (1966)
Frank "Bruiser" Kinard (1971)
Paul Krause (1998)

Curly Lambeau (1963)
Jack Lambert (1990)
Dick "Night Train" Lane (1974)
Jim Langer (1987)
Willie Lanier (1986)
Steve Largent (1995)
Yale Lary (1979)
Dante Lavelli (1975)
Bobby Layne (1967)
Alphonse "Tuffy" Leemans (1978)
Bob Lilly (1980)
Larry Little (1993)
Howie Long (2000)
Ronnie Lott (2000)
Link Lyman (1964)
George McAfee (1966)
Mike McCormack (1984)
Tommy McDonald (1998)
Hugh McElhenny (1970)
Tom Mack (1999)
John Mackey (1992)
John "Blood" McNally (1963)
Gino Marchetti (1972)
Ollie Matson (1972)
Don Maynard (1987)
Mike Michalske (1964)
Wayne Millner (1968)
Bobby Mitchell (1983)
Ron Mix (1979)
Joe Montana (2000)
Lenny Moore (1975)
Marion Motley (1968)
Anthony Muñoz (1998)
George Musso (1982)
Bronko Nagurski (1963)
Joe Namath (1985)
Ernie Nevers (1963)
Ozzie Newsome (1999)
Ray Nitschke (1978)
Leo Nomellini (1969)
Merlin Olsen (1982)
Jim Otto (1980)
Steve Owen (1966)
Alan Page (1988)
Clarence "Ace" Parker (1972)
Jim Parker (1973)
Walter Payton (1993)
Joe Perry (1969)
Pete Pihos (1970)
Mel Renfro (1996)
John Riggins (1992)
Jim Ringo (1981)
Andy Robustelli (1971)
Bob St. Clair (1990)
Gale Sayers (1977)
Joe Schmidt (1973)
Lee Roy Selmon (1995)
Billy Shaw (1999)
Art Shell (1989)
O. J. Simpson (1985)
Mike Singletary (1998)
Jackie Smith (1994)
Bart Starr (1977)
Roger Staubach (1985)
Ernie Stautner (1969)
Jan Stenerud (1991)
Dwight Stephenson (1998)
Ken Strong (1967)
Joe Stydahar (1967)
Fran Tarkenton (1986)
Charley Taylor (1984)
Jim Taylor (1976)
Lawrence Taylor (1999)
Jim Thorpe (1963)
Y. A. Tittle (1971)
George Trafton (1964)
Charley Trippi (1968)
Emlen Tunnell (1967)
Clyde "Bulldog" Turner (1966)
Johnny Unitas (1979)
Gene Upshaw (1987)
Norm Van Brocklin (1971)
Steve Van Buren (1965)
Doak Walker (1986)
Paul Warfield (1983)
Bob Waterfield (1965)
Mike Webster (1997)
Arnie Weinmeister (1984)
Randy White (1994)
Dave Wilcox (2000)
Bill Willis (1977)
Larry Wilson (1978)
Kellen Winslow (1995)
Alex Wojciechowicz (1968)
Willie Wood (1989)
Jack Youngblood (2001)

U.S. Olympic Hall of Fame

Established in 1983 by the United States Olympic Committee. Nominees must be retired from competition for five years. Inductees have been voted in by the National Sportscasters and Sportswriters Association, Hall of Fame members, and the USOC board of directors, but voting was ultimately suspended in 1993. The years of induction are given in parentheses.

Alpine Skiing

Phil Mahre (1992)

Bobsled

Eddie Eagan (1983)

Boxing

Muhammad Ali (1983)
Eddie Eagan (1983)
George Foreman (1990)
Joe Frazier (1989)
Sugar Ray Leonard (1985)
Floyd Patterson (1987)

Cycling

Connie Carpenter (1992)

Diving

Micki King (1992)
Sammy Lee (1990)
Greg Louganis (1985)
Pat McCormick (1985)

Figure Skating

Tenley Albright (1988)
Dick Button (1983)
Peggy Fleming (1983)
Dorothy Hamill (1991)
Scott Hamilton (1990)

Gymnastics

Bart Conner (1991)
Mary Lou Retton (1985)
Peter Vidmar (1991)

Rowing

John Kelly, Sr. (1990)

Speed Skating

Eric Heiden (1983)

Swimming

Shirley Babashoff (1987)
Tracy Caulkins (1990)
Charles Daniels (1988)
Donna de Varona (1987)
Duke Kahanamoku (1984)
Helene Madison (1992)
Debbie Meyer (1986)
John Naber (1984)
Don Schollander (1983)
Mark Spitz (1983)
Johnny Weissmuller (1983)

Track and Field

Bob Beamon (1983)
Ralph Boston (1985)
Lee Calhoun (1991)
Milt Campbell (1992)
Willie Davenport (1991)
Glenn Davis (1986)
Harrison Dillard (1983)
Lee Evans (1989)
Ray Ewry (1983)
Dick Fosbury (1992)
Bruce Jenner (1986)
Rafer Johnson (1983)
Alvin Kraenzlein (1985)
Carl Lewis (1985)
Bob Mathias (1983)
Billy Mills (1984)
Bobby Morrow (1989)
Edwin Moses (1985)
Parry O'Brien (1984)
Al Oerter (1983)
Jesse Owens (1983)
Charley Paddock (1991)
Bob Richards (1983)
Wilma Rudolph (1983)
Mel Sheppard (1989)
Frank Shorter (1984)

Jim Thorpe (1983)
Bill Toomey (1984)
Wyomia Tyus (1985)
Mal Whitfield (1988)
Frank Wykoff (1984)
Babe Didrikson Zaharias (1983)

Weightlifting
John Davis (1989)
Tommy Kono (1990)

Wrestling
Dan Gable (1985)

World Golf Hall of Fame

Established in 1974. Nominees must have ten victories in approved tournaments, be at least forty years old, and have been members of the PGA or LPGA tour for ten years. The years of induction are given in parentheses.

Amy Alcott (1999)
Willie Anderson (1975)
Tommy Armour (1976)
John Ball, Jr. (1977)
Seve Ballesteros (1999)
Jim Barnes (1989)
Patty Berg (1974)
Julius Boros (1982)
Pat Bradley (1991)
James Braid (1976)
Jack Burke, Jr. (2000)
William C. Campbell (1990)
JoAnne Carner (1985)
Billy Casper (1978)
Harry Cooper (1992)
Henry Cotton (1980)
Beth Daniel (2000)
Jimmy Demaret (1983)
Roberto De Vicenzo (1989)
Chick Evans (1975)
Nick Faldo (1998)
Ray Floyd (1989)
Ralph Guldahl (1981)
Walter Hagen (1974)
Sandra Haynie (1977)
Harold Hilton (1978)
Ben Hogan (1974)
Dorothy Campbell Hurd Howe (1978)
Juli Inkster (2000)
Hale Irwin (1992)
Betty Jameson (1951)
Bobby Jones (1974)
Betsy King (1995)
Lawson Little (1980)
Gene Littler (1990)
Bobby Locke (1977)
Nancy Lopez (1989)
Lloyd Mangrum (1999)
Carol Mann (1977)
Cary Middlecoff (1986)
Johnny Miller (1998)
Tom Morris, Jr. (1975)
Tom Morris, Sr. (1976)
Byron Nelson (1974)
Jack Nicklaus (1974)
Francis Ouimet (1974)
Arnold Palmer (1974)
Gary Player (1974)
Judy Rankin (2000)
Betsy Rawls (1987)
Chi Chi Rodriguez (1992)
Paul Runyan (1990)
Gene Sarazen (1974)
Patty Sheehan (1993)
Horton Smith (1990)
Sam Snead (1974)
Louise Suggs (1979)
John Taylor (1975)
Peter Thomson (1988)
Jerome Travers (1976)
Walter Travis (1979)
Lee Trevino (1981)
Harry Vardon (1974)
Glenna Collett Vare (1975)
Tom Watson (1988)
Joyce Wethered (1975)
Kathy Whitworth (1982)
Mickey Wright (1976)
Babe Didrikson Zaharias (1974)

World Skating Hall of Fame

The World Skating Hall of Fame was established in 1976. Nominees must be retired for five years and are voted in by World Skating Hall of Fame electors, composed of former champions, judges, and skating officials. The years of induction are given in parentheses.

Tenley Albright (1976)
Jeannette Altwegg (1993)
Ernst Baier (1979)
Willy Boeckl (1977)
Brian Boitano (1996)
Norris Bowden (1984)
Pierre Brunet (1976)
Dick Button (1976)
Herbert Clark (1996)
Cecelia Colledge (1980)
Tom Collins (1998)
John Curry (1991)
Frances Dafoe (1984)
Christopher Dean (1989)
Lawrence Demmy (1977)
Richard Dwyer (1993)
Paul Falk (1993)
Ria Baran Falk (1993)
Carlo Fassi (1997)
Jacques Favart (1993)
Peggy Fleming (1976)
Bernard Ford (1993)
Willie Frick (1981)
Sheldon Galbraith (1996)
Arnold Gerschwiler (1985)
Jacques Gerschwiler (1976)
Ekaterina Gordeeva (1995)
Alexander Gorshkov (1988)
Gillis Grafstrom (1976)
Sergei Grinkov (1995)
Werner Groebi (1984)
Jackson Haines (1976)
Scott Hamilton (1990)
Georg Hasler (1993)
Carol Heiss Jenkins (1976)
Sonja Henie (1976)
Maxi Herber (1979)
William Hickok (1981)
Donald Jackson (1977)
David Jenkins (1976)
Hayes Jenkins (1976)
Andree Joly (1976)
Courtney Jone (1986)
Felix Kaspar (1998)
James Koch (1994)
Lily Kronberger (1997)
Gustave Lussi (1976)
Howard Nicholson (1976)
Charlotte Oelschlagel (1985)
Liudmila Pakhomova (1988)
Robert Paul (1980)
Alex Paulsen (1976)
Ludmila Protopopov (1978)
Oleg Protopopov (1978)
T. D. Richardson (1976)
Ronald Robertson (1993)
Irina Rodnina (1989)
Louis Rubenstein (1984)
Ulrich Salchow (1976)
Karl Schafer (1976)
Edi Scholdan (1976)
Barbara Ann Scott (1979)
F. Ritter Shumway (1986)
Herma Szabo Stark (1982)
Madge Syers (1981)
Jayne Torvill (1989)
Dianne Towler (1993)
William Thayer Tutt (1995)
Barbara Wagner (1980)
Jean Westwood (1977)
Reginald Wilkie (1976)
Montgomery Wilson (1976)
Katarina Witt (1995)
Benjamin Wright (1997)
Kristi Yamaguchi (1998)

GREAT ATHLETES

Sport Index

ARCHERY
Jay Barrs 1-165
Darrell Pace 6-2114
Denise Parker 6-2143

AUTO RACING
Bobby Allison 1-46
Mario Andretti 1-67
Jim Clark 2-461
Mark Donohue 2-688
Dale Earnhardt 2-731
Juan Manuel Fangio 2-802
Emerson Fittipaldi 3-836
A. J. Foyt 3-871
Don Garlits 3-911
Jeff Gordon 3-995
Dan Gurney 3-1060
Janet Guthrie 3-1063
Mika Häkkinen 3-1085
Damon Hill 3-1182
Niki Lauda 4-1564
Nigel Mansell 5-1771
Rick Mears 5-1851
Shirley Muldowney 5-1964
Barney Oldfield 6-2072
David Pearson 6-2164
Lee Petty 6-2185
Richard Petty 6-2188
Alain Prost 6-2244
Don Prudhomme 6-2251
Bobby Rahal 6-2263
Willy T. Ribbs 6-2291
Johnny Rutherford 6-2397
Michael Schumacher 7-2483
Wendell Scott 7-2498
Ayrton Senna 7-2518
Jackie Stewart 7-2652
Tony Stewart 7-2658
Al Unser 8-2853
Bobby Unser 8-2856
Jacques Villeneuve 8-2902
Rusty Wallace 8-2937
Cale Yarborough 8-3107

BADMINTON
Dave Freeman 3-890
Gong Zhichao 3-971
Rudy Hartono 3-1128
Chris Kinard 4-1459
Jim Poole 6-2217
Liem Swie-King 7-2695

BASEBALL
Hank Aaron 1-1
Jim Abbott 1-4
Grover Alexander 1-32
Roberto Alomar 1-49
Luke Appling 1-79
Jeff Bagwell 1-128
Ernie Banks 1-147
James "Cool Papa" Bell 1-199
Albert Belle 1-202
Johnny Bench 1-205
Chief Bender 1-208
Yogi Berra 1-218
Wade Boggs 1-270
Barry Bonds 1-282
George Brett 1-330
Lou Brock 1-337
Roy Campanella 1-388
José Canseco 1-394
Rod Carew 2-400
Steve Carlton 2-403
Gary Carter 2-418
Vince Carter 2-421
Wilt Chamberlain 2-433
Frank Chance 2-437
Oscar Charleston 2-443
Will Clark 2-464
Roger Clemens 2-470
Roberto Clemente 2-473
Ty Cobb 2-479
Mickey Cochrane 2-485
Eddie Collins 2-491
David Cone 2-503
Cynthia Cooper 2-531
Bob Cousy 2-549
Stan Coveleski 2-552
Dave Cowens 2-555
Billy Cunningham 2-573
Andre Dawson 2-612
Dizzy Dean 2-622
Joe DiMaggio 2-665
Larry Doby 2-685
Don Drysdale 2-709
Dennis Eckersley 2-734
Johnny Evers 2-787
Bob Feller 3-820
Carlton Fisk 3-833
Curt Flood 3-844
Whitey Ford 3-853
Jimmie Foxx 3-868
Nomar Garciaparra 3-905
Steve Garvey 3-920
Lou Gehrig 3-926
Charlie Gehringer 3-929
Bob Gibson 3-941
Josh Gibson 3-945
Tom Glavine 3-959
Lefty Gomez 3-968
Juan Gonzalez 3-977
Dwight Gooden 3-983
Rich Gossage 3-998
Hank Greenberg 3-1018
Ken Griffey, Jr. 3-1042
Burleigh Grimes 3-1051
Lefty Grove 3-1054
Tony Gwynn 3-1072
Gabby Hartnett 3-1125
Rickey Henderson 3-1165
Orel Hershiser 3-1173
Rogers Hornsby 4-1223
Carl Hubbell 4-1235
Catfish Hunter 4-1244
Bo Jackson 4-1277
Reggie Jackson 4-1280
Shoeless Joe Jackson 4-1283
Derek Jeter 4-1310
Howard Johnson 4-1316
Judy Johnson 4-1328
Randy Johnson 4-1349
Walter Johnson 4-1352
Al Kaline 4-1399
Willie Keeler 4-1423
Harmon Killebrew 4-1453
Ralph Kiner 4-1462
Sandy Koufax 4-1502
Nap Lajoie 4-1540
Bob Lemon 4-1585
Buck Leonard 4-1597
Al Lopez 5-1657
Willie McCovey 5-1712
Mark McGwire 5-1723
Greg Maddux 5-1744
Bill Madlock 5-1747
Mickey Mantle 5-1774
Juan Marichal 5-1795
Roger Maris 5-1801
Rube Marquard 5-1804
Edgar Martinez 5-1813

Pedro Martinez **5**-1816
Eddie Mathews **5**-1819
Christy Mathewson **5**-1822
Don Mattingly **5**-1837
Willie Mays **5**-1843
Joe Medwick **5**-1856
Johnny Mize **5**-1906
Joe Morgan **5**-1938
Dale Murphy **5**-1976
Eddie Murray **5**-1979
Stan Musial **5**-1985
Sadaharu Oh **6**-2065
Tony Oliva **6**-2075
Mel Ott **6**-2093
Satchel Paige **6**-2123
Jim Palmer **6**-2132
Tony Perez **6**-2170
Gaylord Perry **6**-2179
Mike Piazza **6**-2191
Kirby Puckett **6**-2254
Tim Raines **6**-2266
Cal Ripken, Jr. **6**-2314
Robin Roberts **6**-2317
Brooks Robinson **6**-2326
Frank Robinson **6**-2333
Jackie Robinson **6**-2336
Alex Rodriguez **6**-2355
Pete Rose **6**-2367
Red Ruffing **6**-2382
Babe Ruth **6**-2393
Nolan Ryan **6**-2400
Bret Saberhagen **6**-2410
Ryne Sandberg **6**-2431
Deion Sanders **6**-2438
Steve Sax **7**-2454
Mike Schmidt **7**-2472
Mike Scott **7**-2492
Tom Seaver **7**-2506
Al Simmons **7**-2549
George Sisler **7**-2558
Ozzie Smith **7**-2574
Duke Snider **7**-2592
Sammy Sosa **7**-2598
Warren Spahn **7**-2604
Tris Speaker **7**-2607
Willie Stargell **7**-2619
Casey Stengel **7**-2634
Dave Stewart **7**-2649
Darryl Strawberry **7**-2669
Don Sutton **7**-2686
Bill Terry **7**-2727
Frank Thomas **7**-2735
Jim Thorpe **7**-2756
Joe Torre **7**-2789
Pie Traynor **7**-2804
Fernando Valenzuela **8**-2862
Dazzy Vance **8**-2875
Greg Vaughn **8**-2890
Mo Vaughn **8**-2893
Rube Waddell **8**-2914
Honus Wagner **8**-2920
Hoyt Wilhelm **8**-3012
Billy Williams **8**-3029
Ted Williams **8**-3043
Maury Wills **8**-3051
Hack Wilson **8**-3054
Dave Winfield **8**-3059
Early Wynn **8**-3098
Carl Yastrzemski **8**-3116
Cy Young **8**-3119
Robin Yount **8**-3128

BASKETBALL

Kareem Abdul-Jabbar **1**-7
Nate Archibald **1**-85
Paul Arizin **1**-92
Charles Barkley **1**-159
Rick Barry **1**-168
Elgin Baylor **1**-178
Dave Bing **1**-232
Larry Bird **1**-239
Bill Bradley **1**-312
Kobe Bryant **1**-349
Bob Davies **2**-597
Dave DeBusschere **2**-629
Vlade Divac **2**-682
Clyde Drexler **2**-702
Tim Duncan **2**-718
Alex English **2**-768
Julius Erving **2**-771
Patrick Ewing **2**-793
Walt Frazier **3**-883
Joe Fulks **3**-896
Kevin Garnett **3**-914
George Gervin **3**-935
Artis Gilmore **3**-953
Tom Gola **3**-962
Gail Goodrich **3**-986
Hal Greer **3**-1030
Cliff Hagan **3**-1076
Penny Hardaway **3**-1108
Tim Hardaway **3**-1111
John Havlicek **3**-1134
Connie Hawkins **3**-1138
Elvin Hayes **3**-1144
Marques Haynes **3**-1147
Walt Hazzard **3**-1149
Tom Heinsohn **3**-1159
Grant Hill **3**-1185
Chamique Holdsclaw **3**-1212
Dan Issel **4**-1268
Allen Iverson **4**-1274
Gus Johnson **4**-1313
Larry Johnson **4**-1334
Magic Johnson **4**-1337
K. C. Jones **4**-1364
Sam Jones **4**-1373
Michael Jordan **4**-1376
Jason Kidd **4**-1450
Toni Kukoc **4**-1522
Bob Kurland **4**-1525
Bob Lanier **4**-1552
Joe Lapchick **4**-1555
Nancy Lieberman-Cline **4**-1616
Rebecca Lobo **5**-1648
Clyde Lovellette **5**-1675
Jerry Lucas **5**-1681
Hank Luisetti **5**-1691
Bob McAdoo **5**-1703
Kevin McHale **5**-1726
Karl Malone **5**-1757
Moses Malone **5**-1760
Pete Maravich **5**-1780
Hortencia Marcari **5**-1786
Slater Martin **5**-1810
Ann Meyers **5**-1871
George Mikan **5**-1874
Cheryl Miller **5**-1883
Reggie Miller **5**-1886
Earl Monroe **5**-1909
Alonzo Mourning **5**-1959
Chris Mullin **5**-1970
Dikembe Mutombo **5**-1992
Hakeem Olajuwon **6**-2068
Shaquille O'Neal **6**-2081
Robert Parish **6**-2140
Gary Payton **6**-2158
Bob Pettit **6**-2182
Scottie Pippen **6**-2202
Frank Ramsey **6**-2272
Willis Reed **6**-2281
Oscar Robertson **6**-2320
Paul Robeson **6**-2323
David Robinson **6**-2329
Dennis Rodman **6**-2349
Bill Russell **6**-2390
Dolph Schayes **7**-2460
Frank Selvy **7**-2515
Bill Sharman **7**-2524
John Stockton **7**-2660
Sheryl Swoopes **7**-2697
Goose Tatum **7**-2710
Isiah Thomas **7**-2738
Nate Thurmond **7**-2759
Jack Twyman **7**-2837
Wes Unseld **7**-2850
Bill Walton **8**-2943
Charlie Ward **8**-2947
Chris Webber **8**-2964
Jerry West **8**-2976
Lenny Wilkens **8**-3015
Dominique Wilkins **8**-3021
Natalie Williams **8**-3035
Lynette Woodard **8**-3070
John Wooden **8**-3073

James Worthy 8-3089
Babe Didrikson Zaharias 8-3134

BEACH VOLLEYBALL
Dain Blanton 1-259
Eric Fonoimoana 1-259

BILLIARDS
Willie Mosconi 5-1944

BOBSLEDDING
Eddie Eagan 2-728

BODYBUILDING
Tommy Kono 4-1494
Steve Reeves 6-2284
Eugen Sandow 6-2442
Arnold Schwarzenegger 7-2486

BOWLING
Earl Anthony 1-73
Don Carter 2-415
Marion Ladewig 4-1534
Floretta Doty McCutcheon 5-1715
Carmen Salvino 6-2422
Lisa Wagner 8-2923
Dick Weber 8-2967
Walter Ray Williams, Jr. 8-3049

BOXING
Muhammad Ali 1-38
Alexis Arguello 1-88
Henry Armstrong 1-98
Max Baer 1-125
Riddick Bowe 1-306
Julio César Chávez 2-454
Billy Conn 2-506
Oscar de la Hoya 2-638
Jack Dempsey 2-648
Roberto Duran 2-724
Eddie Eagan 2-728
George Foreman 3-856
Bob Foster 3-862
Joe Frazier 3-880
Rocky Graziano 3-1012
Marvin Hagler 3-1082
Thomas Hearns 3-1152
Larry Holmes 4-1215
Evander Holyfield 4-1219
Jack Johnson 4-1319
Roy Jones, Jr. 4-1370
Sugar Ray Leonard 4-1600
Lennox Lewis 4-1607
Joe Louis 5-1671
Rocky Marciano 5-1792
Archie Moore 5-1923
Laszlo Papp 6-2135
Floyd Patterson 6-2152
Sugar Ray Robinson 6-2339
Felix Savon 7-2448
Max Schmeling 7-2466
Teófilo Stevenson 7-2646
Dick Tiger 7-2768
Felix Trinidad 7-2813
Gene Tunney 7-2828
Mike Tyson 7-2840

CANOEING/KAYAKING
Greg Barton 1-172
Jon Lugbill 5-1688

CHESS
Bobby Fischer 3-829
Anatoly Karpov 4-1405
Garry Kasparov 4-1411

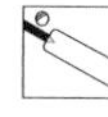
CRICKET
Donald G. Bradman 1-318
Learie Constantine 2-528

CYCLING
Lance Armstrong 1-102
Connie Carpenter 2-409
Bernard Hinault 3-1191
Miguel Indurain 4-1259
Greg LeMond 4-1588
Jeannie Longo 5-1654
Eddy Merckx 5-1859
Connie Paraskevin-Young 6-2137
Major Taylor 7-2721
Bobby Walthour 8-2940
Sheila Young 8-3122

DECATHLON
Bruce Jenner 4-1304
Rafer Johnson 4-1346
Bob Mathias 5-1825
Dan O'Brien 6-2053
Bob Richards 6-2300
Daley Thompson 7-2747
Jim Thorpe 7-2756
Bill Toomey 7-2786

DISCUS THROW
Olga Connolly 2-522
Al Oerter 6-2062
Mac Wilkins 8-3024

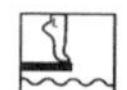
DIVING
Klaus Dibiasi 2-657
Fu Mingxia 3-893
Gao Min 3-902
Micki King 4-1471
Sammy Lee 4-1579
Greg Louganis 5-1668
Pat McCormick 5-1709
Cynthia Potter 6-2226
Laura Wilkinson 8-3027

EQUESTRIAN
Raimondo D'Inezeo 2-671
Lis Hartel 3-1123
David O'Connor 6-2059
Hans Winkler 8-3062

FENCING
George Charles Calnan 1-385
Laura Flessel-Colovic 3-842
Nedo Nadi 5-1998
Peter Westbrook 8-2979

FIELD HOCKEY
Betty Shellenberger 7-2535
Anne Barton Townsend 7-2798

FIGURE SKATING
Tenley Albright 1-29
Tai Babilonia 1-122
Brian Boitano 1-277
Dick Button 1-382
Robin Cousins 2-546
John Curry 2-582
Christopher Dean 7-2794
Peggy Fleming 3-839
Randy Gardner 1-122
Ekaterina Gordeeva 3-992
Sergei Grinkov 3-992
Dorothy Hamill 3-1093
Scott Hamilton 3-1096
Carol Heiss 3-1162
Sonja Henie 3-1170
Midori Ito 4-1271
David Jenkins 4-1298
Hayes Jenkins 4-1301
Nancy Kerrigan 4-1441
Michelle Kwan 4-1528

Tara Lipinski **5**-1637
Janet Lynn **5**-1700
Ludmila Protopopov **6**-2247
Oleg Protopopov **6**-2247
Irina Rodnina **6**-2352
Jayne Torvill **7**-2794
Katarina Witt **8**-3065
Kristi Yamaguchi **8**-3101
Alexander Zaitsev **6**-2352

FOOTBALL

Herb Adderley **1**-14
Troy Aikman **1**-20
Marcus Allen **1**-42
Lance Alworth **1**-52
Lyle Alzado **1**-55
Morten Andersen **1**-58
Doug Atkins **1**-114
Sammy Baugh **1**-175
Chuck Bednarik **1**-193
Raymond Berry **1**-221
Fred Biletnikoff **1**-229
Doc Blanchard **1**-246
George Blanda **1**-252
Drew Bledsoe **1**-265
Terry Bradshaw **1**-321
Jim Brown **1**-340
Tim Brown **1**-343
Buck Buchanan **1**-355
Nick Buoniconti **1**-367
Dick Butkus **1**-379
Earl Campbell **1**-391
Dutch Clark **2**-458
Larry Csonka **2**-570
Randall Cunningham **2**-576
Ernie Davis **2**-600
Glenn Davis **2**-603
Terrell Davis **2**-609
Len Dawson **2**-615
Eric Dickerson **2**-659
Mike Ditka **2**-676
Tony Dorsett **2**-691
Carl Eller **2**-750
John Elway **2**-759
Marshall Faulk **3**-808
Brett Favre **3**-811
Doug Flutie **3**-850
Frank Gifford **3**-948
George Gipp **3**-956
Otto Graham **3**-1006
Red Grange **3**-1009
Joe Greene **3**-1021
Forrest Gregg **3**-1033
Bob Griese **3**-1039
Archie Griffin **3**-1045
Lou Groza **3**-1057
Ray Guy **3**-1069
Jack Ham **3**-1091
John Hannah **3**-1105
Tom Harmon **3**-1114
Franco Harris **3**-1117
Bob Hayes **3**-1141
Ted Hendricks **3**-1168
Jim Hines **3**-1194
Elroy "Crazylegs" Hirsch **3**-1200
Paul Hornung **4**-1226
Ken Houston **4**-1229
Sam Huff **4**-1238
Don Hutson **4**-1250
Michael Irvin **4**-1262
Bo Jackson **4**-1277
Edgerrin James **4**-1289
Jimmy Johnson **4**-1322
John Henry Johnson **4**-1325
Deacon Jones **4**-1361
Sonny Jurgensen **4**-1390
Jim Kelly **4**-1432
Jerry Kramer **4**-1508
Jack Lambert **4**-1543
Dick "Night Train" Lane **4**-1546
Steve Largent **4**-1558
Bobby Layne **4**-1573
Bob Lilly **4**-1619
Floyd Little **5**-1640
Ronnie Lott **5**-1666
Sid Luckman **5**-1685
Johnny Lujack **5**-1694
Hugh McElhenny **5**-1717
Reggie McKenzie **5**-1729
Jim McMahon **5**-1735
Steve McNair **5**-1738
Peyton Manning **5**-1768
Gino Marchetti **5**-1789
Dan Marino **5**-1798
Jim Marshall **5**-1807
Don Maynard **5**-1840
Ron Mix **5**-1903
Joe Montana **5**-1912
Warren Moon **5**-1919
Lenny Moore **5**-1929
Randy Moss **5**-1953
Marion Motley **5**-1956
Bronko Nagurski **5**-2000
Joe Namath **5**-2006
Renaldo Nehemiah **5**-2014
Ernie Nevers **5**-2022
Ray Nitschke **6**-2035
Merlin Olsen **6**-2078
Jim Otto **6**-2099
Alan Page **6**-2120
Jim Parker **6**-2146
Walter Payton **6**-2161
Fritz Pollard **6**-2215
Jerry Rice **6**-2294
John Riggins **6**-2306
Jim Ringo **6**-2312
Andy Robustelli **6**-2343
Barry Sanders **6**-2435
Deion Sanders **6**-2438
Gale Sayers **7**-2457
Joe Schmidt **7**-2469
Shannon Sharpe **7**-2527
Art Shell **7**-2533
O. J. Simpson **7**-2552
Mike Singletary **7**-2555
Bruce Smith **7**-2564
Bubba Smith **7**-2566
Emmitt Smith **7**-2568
Ken Stabler **7**-2613
John Stallworth **7**-2616
Bart Starr **7**-2622
Roger Staubach **7**-2625
Lynn Swann **7**-2692
Fran Tarkenton **7**-2707
Charley Taylor **7**-2712
Jim Taylor **7**-2715
Lawrence Taylor **7**-2718
Vinny Testaverde **7**-2730
Derrick Thomas **7**-2732
Thurman Thomas **7**-2744
Jim Thorpe **7**-2756
Y. A. Tittle **7**-2777
Charley Trippi **7**-2816
Emlen Tunnell **7**-2825
Johnny Unitas **7**-2847
Gene Upshaw **8**-2859
Norm Van Brocklin **8**-2869
Steve Van Buren **8**-2872
Doak Walker **8**-2928
Herschel Walker **8**-2931
Paul Warfield **8**-2950
Kurt Warner **8**-2955
Bob Waterfield **8**-2958
Byron "Whizzer" White **8**-2981
Randy White **8**-2984
Reggie White **8**-2987
Ricky Williams **8**-3038
Larry Wilson **8**-3057
Willie Wood **8**-3068
Charles Woodson **8**-3083
Steve Young **8**-3125

GOLF

Willie Anderson **1**-64
Tommy Armour **1**-95
Seve Ballesteros **1**-144
Patty Berg **1**-214
Julius Boros **1**-288
Pat Bradley **1**-315
JoAnne Carner **2**-406
Billy Casper **2**-427
Fred Couples **2**-536
Ben Crenshaw **2**-564

Jimmy Demaret **2**-645
Nick Faldo **2**-799
Johnny Farrell **3**-805
Ray Floyd **3**-847
Walter Hagen **3**-1079
Ben Hogan **3**-1206
Hale Irwin **4**-1265
Bobby Jones **4**-1355
Betsy King **4**-1465
Tom Kite **4**-1482
Bernhard Langer **4**-1549
Lawson Little **5**-1643
Nancy Lopez **5**-1660
Lloyd Mangrum **5**-1763
Byron Nelson **5**-2017
Jack Nicklaus **5**-2031
Greg Norman **6**-2041
Francis D. Ouimet **6**-2105
Se Ri Pak **6**-2126
Arnold Palmer **6**-2128
Gary Player **6**-2212
Sandra Post **6**-2223
Nick Price **6**-2241
Judy Rankin **6**-2275
Gene Sarazen **7**-2445
Patty Sheehan **7**-2530
Sam Snead **7**-2586
Annika Sorenstam **7**-2595
Payne Stewart **7**-2655
Curtis Strange **7**-2666
Lee Trevino **7**-2810
Harry Vardon **8**-2884
Glenna Collett Vare **8**-2887
Tom Watson **8**-2961
Kathy Whitworth **8**-2996
Tiger Woods **8**-3079
Mickey Wright **8**-3095
Babe Didrikson Zaharias **8**-3134

GYMNASTICS

Nikolai Andrianov **1**-70
Svetlana Boginskaya **1**-273
Vera Čáslavská **2**-424
Nadia Comăneci **2**-495
Bart Conner **2**-510
Alexander Dityatin **2**-679
Tatiana Gutsu **3**-1066
Kathy Johnson **4**-1331
Sawao Kato **4**-1414
Svetlana Khorkina **4**-1444
Olga Korbut **4**-1499
Larisa Latynina **4**-1561
Lu Li **5**-1678
Julianne McNamara **5**-1741
Linda Metheny **5**-1865
Shannon Miller **5**-1889
Lavinia Milosovici **5**-1896
Akinori Nakayama **5**-2003
Alexei Nemov **5**-2020
Mary Lou Retton **6**-2286
Cathy Rigby **6**-2303
Vitaly Scherbo **7**-2463
Boris Shakhlin **7**-2521
Kerri Strug **7**-2678
Victor Tchoukarine **7**-2724
Kurt Thomas **7**-2741
Mitsuo Tsukahara **7**-2822
Ludmila Turishcheva **7**-2831
Peter Vidmar **8**-2896
Kim Zmeskal **8**-3143

HAMMER THROW

Harold Connolly **2**-516
Sergei Litvinov **5**-1645

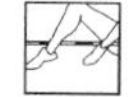

HEPTATHLON

Fanny Blankers-Koen **1**-256
Jackie Joyner-Kersee **4**-1384

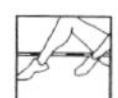

HIGH JUMP

Iolanda Balas **1**-136
Valery Brumel **1**-346
Alice Coachman **2**-476
Charley Dumas **2**-715
Ray Ewry **2**-796
Dick Fosbury **3**-859
Javier Sotomayor **7**-2601
Dwight Stones **7**-2663

HORSE RACING

Eddie Arcaro **1**-82
Angel Cordero, Jr. **2**-534
Pat Day **2**-619
Bill Hartack **3**-1120
Julie Krone **4**-1519
Johnny Longden **5**-1651
Chris McCarron **5**-1706
Lester Piggott **6**-2197
Laffit Pincay, Jr. **6**-2200
Willie Shoemaker **7**-2540

HURDLES

Willie Davenport **2**-594
Glenn Davis **2**-603
Gail Devers **2**-654
Harrison Dillard **2**-662
Greg Foster **3**-865
Jackie Joyner-Kersee **4**-1384
Roger Kingdom **4**-1474
Rod Milburn **5**-1880
Edwin Moses **5**-1950
Renaldo Nehemiah **5**-2014
Shirley Strickland-de la Hunty **7**-2675

HYDROPLANE RACING

Dave Villwock **8**-2905

ICE HOCKEY

Irvine "Ace" Bailey **1**-134
Jean Beliveau **1**-196
Mike Bossy **1**-297
Ray Bourque **1**-303
Bobby Clarke **2**-467
Lionel Conacher **2**-500
Alex Delvecchio **2**-642
Marcel Dionne **2**-673
Ken Dryden **2**-706
Phil Esposito **2**-775
Sergei Fedorov **3**-814
Bernie Geoffrion **3**-932
Wayne Gretzky **3**-1035
Glenn Hall **3**-1088
Dominik Hasek **3**-1131
Gordie Howe **4**-1232
Bobby Hull **4**-1241
Jaromir Jagr **4**-1286
Guy Lafleur **4**-1537
Mario Lemieux **4**-1582
Eric Lindros **5**-1628
Ted Lindsay **5**-1631
Mark Messier **5**-1862
Stan Mikita **5**-1877
Willie O'Ree **6**-2087
Bobby Orr **6**-2090
Gil Perreault **6**-2173
Jacques Plante **6**-2206
Maurice "Rocket" Richard **6**-2297
Patrick Roy **6**-2376
Terry Sawchuk **7**-2451
Vladislav Tretiak **7**-2807
Bryan Trottier **7**-2819
Gump Worsley **8**-3086
Steve Yzerman **8**-3131

JAVELIN THROW

Jan Zelezny **8**-3140

JUDO

David Douillet **2**-694
Eddie Liddie **4**-1613
Ryoko Tamura **7**-2704
Yasuhiro Yamashita **8**-3104

LONG-DISTANCE RUNS

Jim Beatty **1**-185
Mary Decker-Slaney **2**-632
Haile Gebreselassie **3**-923
Kip Keino **4**-1426
Wilson Kipketer **4**-1477
Ingrid Kristiansen **4**-1513
Gerry Lindgren **5**-1625
Billy Mills **5**-1893
Noureddine Morceli **5**-1935
Paavo Nurmi **6**-2047
Steve Prefontaine **6**-2235
Bill Rodgers **6**-2346
Henry Rono **6**-2361
Frank Shorter **7**-2543
Lasse Viren **8**-2911
Emil Zatopek **8**-3137

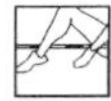

LONG JUMP

Harold Abrahams **1**-11
Bob Beamon **1**-181
Ralph Boston **1**-300
Leroy Burrell **1**-370
Heike Drechsler **2**-699
Ray Ewry **2**-796
Marion Jones **4**-1367
Jackie Joyner-Kersee **4**-1384
Carl Lewis **4**-1604
Jesse Owens **6**-2111
Mike Powell **6**-2232

MARATHON

Joan Benoit **1**-211
Abebe Bikila **1**-226
Johnny Kelley **4**-1429
Bill Rodgers **6**-2346
Alberto Salazar **6**-2416
Frank Shorter **7**-2543
Greta Waitz **8**-2925
Emil Zatopek **8**-3137

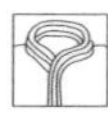

MARTIAL ARTS

Bruce Lee **4**-1576
Steven Lopez **5**-1663

MIDDLE-DISTANCE RUNS

Said Aouita **1**-76
Roger Bannister **1**-156
Jim Beatty **1**-185
Sebastian Coe **2**-488
Mary Decker-Slaney **2**-632
Hicham El Guerrouj **2**-747
Herb Elliott **2**-753
Lee Evans **2**-784
Alberto Juantorena **4**-1387
Tatyana Kazankina **4**-1417
Ingrid Kristiansen **4**-1513
Maria Mutola **5**-1989
Steve Ovett **6**-2108
Butch Reynolds **6**-2289
Jim Ryun **6**-2404
Steve Scott **7**-2495
Peter Snell **7**-2589
John Walker **8**-2934
Mal Whitfield **8**-2990

MOUNTAINEERING

Sir Edmund Hillary **3**-1188
Junko Tabei **7**-2701

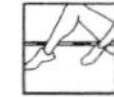

PENTATHLON

Jim Thorpe **7**-2756

POLE VAULT

Sergei Bubka **1**-352
Stacy Dragila **2**-696
Nick Hysong **4**-1256
Bob Richards **6**-2300
Bob Seagren **7**-2503
Cornelius Warmerdam **8**-2953

POWERBOAT RACING

Chip Hanauer **3**-1102

RODEO

Bob Askin **1**-111
Tom Ferguson **3**-823
Larry Mahan **5**-1750
Ty Murray **5**-1982
Jim Shoulders **7**-2546
Casey Tibbs **7**-2762

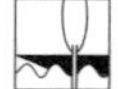

ROWING

Anita DeFrantz **2**-635
Pertti Karppinen **4**-1408
John Kelly, Sr. **4**-1435
Tori Murden **5**-1973
Steven Redgrave **6**-2278

SHOOTING

Nancy Johnson **4**-1343
Deena Wigger **8**-2999
Lones Wigger **8**-3002

SHOT PUT

Randy Barnes **1**-162
Randy Matson **5**-1828
Parry O'Brien **6**-2056

SKI JUMPING

Matti Nykänen **6**-2050

SKIING

Deborah Compagnoni **2**-498
Gretchen Fraser **3**-877
Diana Golden **3**-965
Nancy Greene **3**-1027
Jimmie Heuga **3**-1176
Billy Kidd **4**-1447
Jean-Claude Killy **4**-1456
Franz Klammer **4**-1485
Bill Koch **4**-1491
Petra Kronberger **4**-1516
Tamara McKinney **5**-1732
Phil Mahre **5**-1752
Hermann Maier **5**-1755
Andrea Mead Lawrence **5**-1846
Rosi Mittermaier **5**-1900
Annemarie Moser-Proell **5**-1947
Toni Sailer **6**-2413
Ingemar Stenmark **7**-2637
Picabo Street **7**-2672
Gunde Svan **7**-2689
Alberto Tomba **7**-2783
Buddy Werner **8**-2973
Pirmin Zurbriggen **8**-3149

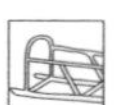

SLED DOG RACING

Susan Butcher **1**-376

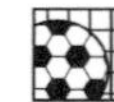

SOCCER

Michelle Akers **1**-26
Alan Ball **1**-139
Gordon Banks **1**-150
Franz Beckenbauer **1**-188
George Best **1**-224
Danny Blanchflower **1**-249
Billy Bremner **1**-327
Bobby Charlton **2**-446
Jack Charlton **2**-449
Brandi Chastain **2**-452
Johan Cruyff **2**-567
Eusebio **2**-778
Garrincha **3**-917
Johnny Giles **3**-951
Mia Hamm **3**-1099
Geoff Hurst **4**-1247
Pat Jennings **4**-1307

Cobi Jones **4**-1358
Kevin Keegan **4**-1420
Denis Law **4**-1570
Kristine Lilly **4**-1622
Gary Lineker **5**-1634
Diego Maradona **5**-1777
Sir Stanley Matthews **5**-1834
Bobby Moore **5**-1926
Gerd Müller **5**-1967
Pelé **6**-2167
Michel Platini **6**-2209
Ferenc Puskas **6**-2257
Alf Ramsey **6**-2269
Ronaldo **6**-2358
Kyle Rote, Jr. **6**-2373
Karl-Heinz Rummenigge **6**-2388
Briana Scurry **7**-2500
Peter Shilton **7**-2538
Sissi **7**-2561
Alfredo di Stefano **7**-2631
Sun Wen **7**-2684
Marco van Basten **8**-2866
Billy Wright **8**-3092
Lev Yashin **8**-3113
Steve Zungul **8**-3146

SOFTBALL
Herb Dudley **2**-712
Eddie Feigner **3**-817
Lisa Fernandez **3**-826
Joan Joyce **4**-1381
Bertha Tickey **7**-2765
Babe Didrikson Zaharias **8**-3134

SPEED SKATING
Bonnie Blair **1**-243
Eric Heiden **3**-1156
Dan Jansen **4**-1292
Sheila Young **8**-3122

SPRINTS
Harold Abrahams **1**-11
Evelyn Ashford **1**-108
Donovan Bailey **1**-131
Fanny Blankers-Koen **1**-256
Ato Boldon **1**-280
Valeri Borzov **1**-294
Valerie Brisco-Hooks **1**-334
Leroy Burrell **1**-370
Alice Coachman **2**-476
Betty Cuthbert **2**-585
Gail Devers **2**-654
Cathy Freeman **3**-887
Maurice Greene **3**-1024
Florence Griffith-Joyner **3**-1048
Bob Hayes **3**-1141
Jim Hines **3**-1194
Michael Johnson **4**-1341
Marion Jones **4**-1367
Carl Lewis **4**-1604
Eric Liddell **4**-1610
Bobby Joe Morrow **5**-1941
Merlene Ottey **6**-2096
Jesse Owens **6**-2111
Charles Paddock **6**-2117
Mel Patton **6**-2155
Donald Quarrie **6**-2260
Wilma Rudolph **6**-2379
Tommie Smith **7**-2583
Renate Stecher **7**-2628
Shirley Strickland-de la Hunty **7**-2675
Eddie Tolan **7**-2780
Wyomia Tyus **7**-2844

STEEPLECHASE
Paavo Nurmi **6**-2047
Henry Rono **6**-2361

STUNT DRIVING
Evel Knievel **4**-1488

SUMO WRESTLING
Akebono **1**-23

SURFING
Corky Carroll **2**-412
Tom Curren **2**-579
Duke Kahanamoku **4**-1393
Martin Potter **6**-2229

SWIMMING
Shirley Babashoff **1**-120
Catie Ball **1**-142
Matt Biondi **1**-235
Ethelda Bleibtrey **1**-267
George Breen **1**-324
Mike Burton **1**-373
Tracy Caulkins **2**-430
Lynne Cox **2**-558
Buster Crabbe **2**-561
Tamas Darnyi **2**-588
Inge De Bruijn **2**-626
Donna de Varona **2**-651
Gertrude Ederle **2**-741
Krisztina Egerszegi **2**-744
Kornelia Ender **2**-765
Janet Evans **2**-781
Dawn Fraser **3**-874
Brian Goodell **3**-980
Shane Gould **3**-1001
Charlie Hickcox **3**-1179
Nancy Hogshead **3**-1209
Chet Jastremski **4**-1295
Duke Kahanamoku **4**-1393
John Konrads **4**-1497
Lenny Krayzelburg **4**-1510
Steve Lundquist **5**-1697
Roland Matthes **5**-1831
Mary T. Meagher **5**-1848
Debbie Meyer **5**-1868
Pablo Morales **5**-1932
John Naber **5**-1995
Martha Norelius **6**-2038
Susan O'Neill **6**-2084
Kristin Otto **6**-2102
Aleksandr Popov **6**-2220
Murray Rose **6**-2364
Vladimir Salnikov **6**-2419
Petra Schneider **7**-2475
Don Schollander **7**-2477
Mark Spitz **7**-2610
Jill Sterkel **7**-2643
Jenny Thompson **7**-2750
Ian Thorpe **7**-2753
Dara Torres **7**-2792
Pieter van den Hoogenband **8**-2878
Amy Van Dyken **8**-2881
Johnny Weissmuller **8**-2970
David Wilkie **8**-3018
Esther Williams **8**-3032
Cynthia Woodhead **8**-3076

SYNCHRONIZED SWIMMING
Tracie Ruiz-Conforto **6**-2385

TENNIS
Andre Agassi **1**-17
Arthur Ashe **1**-105
Tracy Austin **1**-117
Boris Becker **1**-190
Björn Borg **1**-285
Jean Borotra **1**-291
Don Budge **1**-361
Maria Bueno **1**-364
Jennifer Capriati **2**-397
Michael Chang **2**-440
Henri Cochet **2**-482
Maureen Connolly **2**-519
Jimmy Connors **2**-525
Jim Courier **2**-539
Margaret Court **2**-542
Lindsay Davenport **2**-591
Margaret Osborne duPont **2**-721

Stefan Edberg **2**-738
Roy Emerson **2**-762
Chris Evert **2**-790
Althea Gibson **3**-938
Pancho Gonzales **3**-974
Evonne Goolagong **3**-989
Steffi Graf **3**-1003
Martina Hingis **3**-1197
Lew Hoad **3**-1203
Billie Jean King **4**-1468
Jack Kramer **4**-1505
René Lacoste **4**-1531
Rod Laver **4**-1567
Ivan Lendl **4**-1591
Suzanne Lenglen **4**-1594
Carl Lewis **4**-1604
Eric Liddell **4**-1610
John McEnroe **5**-1720
Alice Marble **5**-1783
Helen Wills Moody **5**-1916
Carlos Moya **5**-1962
Martina Navratilova **5**-2010
John Newcombe **5**-2028
Brad Parks **6**-2149
Fred Perry **6**-2176
Mary Pierce **6**-2194
Bobby Riggs **6**-2309
Ken Rosewall **6**-2370
Gabriela Sabatini **6**-2407
Pete Sampras **6**-2425
Arantxa Sanchez-Vicario **6**-2428
Vic Seixas **7**-2509
Monica Seles **7**-2512
Stan Smith **7**-2580
Bill Tilden **7**-2771
Tony Trabert **7**-2801
Guillermo Vilas **8**-2899
Virginia Wade **8**-2917
Hazel Wightman **8**-3006
Mats Wilander **8**-3009
Serena Williams **8**-3040
Venus Williams **8**-3046

TRACK AND FIELD

Harold Abrahams **1**-11
Said Aouita **1**-76
Evelyn Ashford **1**-108
Donovan Bailey **1**-131
Iolanda Balas **1**-136
Willie Banks **1**-153
Roger Bannister **1**-156
Randy Barnes **1**-162
Bob Beamon **1**-181
Jim Beatty **1**-185
Joan Benoit **1**-211
Abebe Bikila **1**-226
Fanny Blankers-Koen **1**-256
Ato Boldon **1**-280
Valeri Borzov **1**-294
Ralph Boston **1**-300
Valerie Brisco-Hooks **1**-334
Valery Brumel **1**-346
Sergei Bubka **1**-352
Leroy Burrell **1**-370
Alice Coachman **2**-476
Sebastian Coe **2**-488
Harold Connolly **2**-516
Olga Connolly **2**-522
Betty Cuthbert **2**-585
Willie Davenport **2**-594
Glenn Davis **2**-603
Mary Decker-Slaney **2**-632
Gail Devers **2**-654
Harrison Dillard **2**-662
Stacy Dragila **2**-696
Heike Dreschler **2**-699
Charley Dumas **2**-715
Hicham El Guerrouj **2**-747
Herb Elliott **2**-753
Lee Evans **2**-784
Ray Ewry **2**-796
Dick Fosbury **3**-859
Greg Foster **3**-865
Cathy Freeman **3**-887
Haile Gebreselassie **3**-923
Maurice Greene **3**-1024
Florence Griffith-Joyner **3**-1048
Bob Hayes **3**-1141
Jim Hines **3**-1194
Nick Hysong **4**-1256
Bruce Jenner **4**-1304
Michael Johnson **4**-1341
Rafer Johnson **4**-1346
Marion Jones **4**-1367
Jackie Joyner-Kersee **4**-1384
Alberto Juantorena **4**-1387
Tatyana Kazankina **4**-1417
Kip Keino **4**-1426
Johnny Kelley **4**-1429
Roger Kingdom **4**-1474
Wilson Kipketer **4**-1477
Ingrid Kristiansen **4**-1513
Gerry Lindgren **5**-1625
Sergei Litvinov **5**-1645
Bob Mathias **5**-1825
Randy Matson **5**-1828
Rod Milburn **5**-1880
Billy Mills **5**-1893
Noureddine Morceli **5**-1935
Bobby Joe Morrow **5**-1941
Edwin Moses **5**-1950
Maria Mutola **5**-1989
Renaldo Nehemiah **5**-2014
Paavo Nurmi **6**-2047
Dan O'Brien **6**-2053
Parry O'Brien **6**-2056
Al Oerter **6**-2062
Merlene Ottey **6**-2096
Steve Ovett **6**-2108
Jesse Owens **6**-2111
Charles Paddock **6**-2117
Brad Parks **6**-2149
Mel Patton **6**-2155
Mike Powell **6**-2232
Steve Prefontaine **6**-2235
Irina Press **6**-2238
Tamara Press **6**-2238
Donald Quarrie **6**-2260
Butch Reynolds **6**-2289
Bob Richards **6**-2300
Bill Rodgers **6**-2346
Henry Rono **6**-2361
Wilma Rudolph **6**-2379
Jim Ryun **6**-2404
Alberto Salazar **6**-2416
Steve Scott **7**-2495
Bob Seagren **7**-2503
Frank Shorter **7**-2543
Tommie Smith **7**-2583
Peter Snell **7**-2589
Javier Sotomayor **7**-2601
Renate Stecher **7**-2628
Helen Stephens **7**-2640
Dwight Stones **7**-2663
Shirley Strickland-de la Hunty **7**-2675
Irena Szewinska **7**-2699
Daley Thompson **7**-2747
Jim Thorpe **7**-2756
Eddie Tolan **7**-2780
Bill Toomey **7**-2786
Wyomia Tyus **7**-2844
Lasse Viren **8**-2911
Greta Waitz **8**-2925
John Walker **8**-2934
Cornelius Warmerdam **8**-2953
Mal Whitfield **8**-2990
Mac Wilkins **8**-3024
Babe Didrikson Zaharias **8**-3134
Emil Zatopek **8**-3137
Jan Zelezny **8**-3140

TRIATHLON

Paula Newby-Fraser **5**-2025
Dave Scott **7**-2489
Simon Whitfield **8**-2993

TRIPLE JUMP

Willie Banks **1**-153
Bob Beamon **1**-181
Ray Ewry **2**-796

VOLLEYBALL

Craig Buck **1**-358
Debbie Green **3**-1015
Flo Hyman **4**-1253
Karch Kiraly **4**-1479
Sinjin Smith **7**-2577
Steve Timmons **7**-2774

WATER POLO

Scott Schulte **7**-2480

WATERSKIING

Bill Bowness **1**-309

WEIGHTLIFTING

Vasily Alexeyev **1**-35
Paul Anderson **1**-61
John Davis **2**-606
Pyrros Dimas **2**-668
Akakios Kakiasvilis **4**-1396
Tommy Kono **4**-1494
Tara Nott **6**-2044
Naim Suleymanoglu **7**-2681
Chuck Vinci **8**-2908

WRESTLING

Jeff Blatnick **1**-262
Dan Gable **3**-899
Rulon Gardner **3**-908
Aleksandr Karelin **4**-1402
Lee Kemp **4**-1438
Alexander Medved **5**-1853
John Smith **7**-2571
Ivan Yarygin **8**-3110

YACHTING

Dennis Conner **2**-513
Paul Elvstrøm **2**-756
Valentin Mankin **5**-1766
Ted Turner **7**-2834

Country Index

This index lists athletes by the countries—including some dependencies—with which they are most closely associated by virtue of their citizenship, residence, or membership on national teams. Many names are listed under more than one country, but some athletes are not listed under the countries in which they were born because they have no other meaningful ties with those countries. The index is intended to serve only as a guide and not be a definitive list of nationalities or birthplaces.

ALBANIA
Pyrros Dimas **2**-668

ALGERIA
Noureddine Morceli **5**-1935

ARGENTINA
Juan Manuel Fangio **2**-802
Diego Maradona **5**-1777
Gabriela Sabatini **6**-2407
Alfredo di Stefano **7**-2631
Guillermo Vilas **8**-2899

AUSTRALIA
Donald G. Bradman **1**-318
Margaret Court **2**-542
Betty Cuthbert **2**-585
Herb Elliott **2**-753
Roy Emerson **2**-762
Dawn Fraser **3**-874
Cathy Freeman **3**-887
Evonne Goolagong **3**-989
Shane Gould **3**-1001
Lew Hoad **3**-1203
Rod Laver **4**-1567
John Newcombe **5**-2028
Greg Norman **6**-2041
Susan O'Neill **6**-2084
Ken Rosewall **6**-2370
Shirley Strickland-de la Hunty **7**-2675
Ian Thorpe **7**-2753

AUSTRIA
Franz Klammer **4**-1485
Petra Kronberger **4**-1516
Niki Lauda **4**-1564
Hermann Maier **5**-1755
Annemarie Moser-Proell **5**-1947
Toni Sailer **6**-2413
Arnold Schwarzenegger **7**-2486

AZERBAIJAN. *See also* SOVIET UNION
Garry Kasparov **4**-1411

BELARUS. *See also* SOVIET UNION
Svetlana Boginskaya **1**-273
Olga Korbut **4**-1499
Vitaly Scherbo **7**-2463

BELGIUM
Eddy Merckx **5**-1859

BRAZIL
Maria Bueno **1**-364
Emerson Fittipaldi **3**-836
Garrincha **3**-917
Hortencia Marcari **5**-1786
Pelé **6**-2167
Ronaldo **6**-2358
Ayrton Senna **7**-2518
Sissi **7**-2561

BULGARIA
Naim Suleymanoglu **7**-2681

CANADA
Donovan Bailey **1**-131
Irvine "Ace" Bailey **1**-134
Jean Beliveau **1**-196
Mike Bossy **1**-297
Ray Bourque **1**-303
Bobby Clarke **2**-467
Lionel Conacher **2**-500
Alex Delvecchio **2**-642
Marcel Dionne **2**-673
Ken Dryden **2**-706
Phil Esposito **2**-775
Bernie Geoffrion **3**-932
Nancy Greene **3**-1027
Wayne Gretzky **3**-1035
Glenn Hall **3**-1088
Gordie Howe **4**-1232
Bobby Hull **4**-1241
Guy Lafleur **4**-1537
Mario Lemieux **4**-1582
Lennox Lewis **4**-1607
Eric Lindros **5**-1628
Ted Lindsay **5**-1631
Mark Messier **5**-1862
Stan Mikita **5**-1877
Bronko Nagurski **5**-2000
Willie O'Ree **6**-2087
Bobby Orr **6**-2090
Gil Perreault **6**-2173
Mary Pierce **6**-2194
Jacques Plante **6**-2206
Sandra Post **6**-2223
Maurice "Rocket" Richard **6**-2297
Patrick Roy **6**-2376
Terry Sawchuk **7**-2451
Bryan Trottier **7**-2819
Jacques Villeneuve **8**-2902
Simon Whitfield **8**-2993
Gump Worsley **8**-3086
Steve Yzerman **8**-3131

CHINA. *See also* HONG KONG
Fu Mingxia **3**-893
Gao Min **3**-902
Gong Zhichao **3**-971
Lu Li **5**-1678
Sun Wen **7**-2684

CONGO
Dikembe Mutombo **5**-1992

CROATIA. *See also* YUGOSLAVIA
Toni Kukoc **4**-1522
Steve Zungul **8**-3146

CUBA
José Canseco **1**-394
Alberto Juantorena **4**-1387
Tony Oliva **6**-2075
Tony Perez **6**-2170
Alberto Salazar **6**-2416
Felix Savon **7**-2448
Javier Sotomayor **7**-2601
Teófilo Stevenson **7**-2646

CZECHOSLOVAKIA. *See also* SLOVAKIA
Vera Čáslavská **2**-424
Olga Connolly **2**-522
Dominik Hasek **3**-1131
Martina Hingis **3**-1197
Jaromir Jagr **4**-1286
Ivan Lendl **4**-1591
Stan Mikita **5**-1877
Martina Navratilova **5**-2010
Emil Zatopek **8**-3137
Jan Zelezny **8**-3140

DENMARK
Morten Andersen **1**-58
Paul Elvstrøm **2**-756
Lis Hartel **3**-1123
Wilson Kipketer **4**-1477

DOMINICAN REPUBLIC
Juan Marichal **5**-1795
Pedro Martinez **5**-1816
Sammy Sosa **7**-2598

ENGLAND. *See also* SCOTLAND
Harold Abrahams **1**-11
Alan Ball **1**-139
Gordon Banks **1**-150
Roger Bannister **1**-156
Bobby Charlton **2**-446
Jack Charlton **2**-449
Sebastian Coe **2**-488
Robin Cousins **2**-546
John Curry **2**-582
Christopher Dean **7**-2794
Nick Faldo **2**-799
Damon Hill **3**-1182
Geoff Hurst **4**-1247
Kevin Keegan **4**-1420
Lennox Lewis **4**-1607
Gary Lineker **5**-1634
Johnny Longden **5**-1651
Nigel Mansell **5**-1771
Stanley Matthews **5**-1834
Bobby Moore **5**-1926
Steve Ovett **6**-2108
Fred Perry **6**-2176
Lester Piggott **6**-2197
Martin Potter **6**-2229
Alf Ramsey **6**-2269
Steven Redgrave **6**-2278
Murray Rose **6**-2364
Peter Shilton **7**-2538
Daley Thompson **7**-2747
Jayne Torvill **7**-2794
Harry Vardon **8**-2884
Virginia Wade **8**-2917
Billy Wright **8**-3092

ETHIOPIA
Abebe Bikila **1**-226
Haile Gebreselassie **3**-923

FINLAND
Mika Häkkinen **3**-1085
Pertti Karppinen **4**-1408
Paavo Nurmi **6**-2047
Matti Nykänen **6**-2050
Lasse Viren **8**-2911

FRANCE
Jean Borotra **1**-291
Henri Cochet **2**-482
David Douillet **2**-694
Laura Flessel-Colovic **3**-842
Bernard Hinault **3**-1191
Jean-Claude Killy **4**-1456
René Lacoste **4**-1531
Suzanne Lenglen **4**-1594
Eddie Liddie **4**-1613
Jeannie Longo **5**-1654
Mary Pierce **6**-2194
Michel Platini **6**-2209
Alain Prost **6**-2244

GEORGIA. *See also* SOVIET UNION
Akakios Kakiasvilis **4**-1396

GERMANY
Franz Beckenbauer **1**-188
Boris Becker **1**-190
Heike Dreschler **2**-699
Kornelia Ender **2**-765
Steffi Graf **3**-1003
Bernhard Langer **4**-1549
Roland Matthes **5**-1831
Rosi Mittermaier **5**-1900
Gerd Müller **5**-1967
Kristin Otto **6**-2102
Karl-Heinz Rummenigge **6**-2388
Eugen Sandow **6**-2442
Max Schmeling **7**-2466
Petra Schneider **7**-2475
Michael Schumacher **7**-2483
Renate Stecher **7**-2628
Hans Winkler **8**-3062
Katarina Witt **8**-3065

GREECE
Pyrros Dimas **2**-668

GUADELOUPE
Laura Flessel-Colovic **3**-842

HONDURAS
Steve Van Buren **8**-2872

HONG KONG
Bruce Lee **4**-1576

HUNGARY
Tamas Darnyi **2**-588
Krisztina Egerszegi **2**-744
Laszlo Papp **6**-2135
Ferenc Puskas **6**-2257

INDONESIA
Rudy Hartono **3**-1128
Liem Swie-King **7**-2695

IRELAND. *See also* NORTHERN IRELAND
Johnny Giles **3**-951

ITALY
Deborah Compagnoni **2**-498
Klaus Dibiasi **2**-657
Raimondo D'Inezeo **2**-671
Nedo Nadi **5**-1998
Alberto Tomba **7**-2783

JAMAICA
Donovan Bailey **1**-131
Patrick Ewing **2**-793
Merlene Ottey **6**-2096
Donald Quarrie **6**-2260

JAPAN
Midori Ito **4**-1271
Sawao Kato **4**-1414
Akinori Nakayama **5**-2003
Sadaharu Oh **6**-2065
Junko Tabei **7**-2701
Ryoko Tamura **7**-2704
Mitsuo Tsukahara **7**-2822
Yasuhiro Yamashita **8**-3104

KENYA
Kip Keino **4**-1426
Wilson Kipketer **4**-1477
Henry Rono **6**-2361

LATVIA. *See also* SOVIET UNION
John Konrads **4**-1497

MEXICO
Julio César Chávez **2**-454
Fernando Valenzuela **8**-2862

MOROCCO
Said Aouita **1**-76
Hicham El Guerrouj **2**-747

MOZAMBIQUE
Eusebio **2**-778
Maria Mutola **5**-1989

NETHERLANDS
Fanny Blankers-Koen **1**-256
Johan Cruyff **2**-567
Inge De Bruijn **2**-626
Marco van Basten **8**-2866
Pieter van den Hoogenband **8**-2878

NEW ZEALAND
Sir Edmund Hillary **3**-1188
Peter Snell **7**-2589
John Walker **8**-2934

NICARAGUA
Alexis Arguello **1**-88

NIGERIA
Hakeem Olajuwon **6**-2068
Dick Tiger **7**-2768

NORTHERN IRELAND
George Best **1**-224
Danny Blanchflower **1**-249
Pat Jennings **4**-1307

NORWAY
Sonja Henie **3**-1170
Ingrid Kristiansen **4**-1513
Greta Waitz **8**-2925

PANAMA
Rod Carew **2**-400
Roberto Duran **2**-724
Laffit Pincay, Jr. **6**-2200

PUERTO RICO
Roberto Clemente **2**-473
Angel Cordero, Jr. **2**-534
Juan Gonzalez **3**-977
Felix Trinidad **7**-2813

ROMANIA
Iolanda Balas **1**-136
Nadia Comăneci **2**-495
Lavinia Milosovici **5**-1896

RUSSIA. *See also* SOVIET UNION
Vasily Alexeyev **1**-35
Nikolai Andrianov **1**-70
Valery Brumel **1**-346
Alexander Dityatin **2**-679
Sergei Fedorov **3**-814
Ekaterina Gordeeva **3**-992
Sergei Grinkov **3**-992
Aleksandr Karelin **4**-1402
Anatoly Karpov **4**-1405
Tatyana Kazankina **4**-1417
Sergei Litvinov **5**-1645
Alexei Nemov **5**-2020
Aleksandr Popov **6**-2220
Oleg Protopopov **6**-2247
Ludmila Protopopov **6**-2247
Irina Rodnina **6**-2352
Vladimir Salnikov **6**-2419
Boris Shakhlin **7**-2521
Irena Szewinska **7**-2699
Vladislav Tretiak **7**-2807
Ludmila Turishcheva **7**-2831
Alexander Zaitsev **6**-2352

SCOTLAND
Willie Anderson **1**-64
Tommy Armour **1**-95
Billy Bremner **1**-327
Jim Clark **2**-461
Denis Law **4**-1570
Eric Liddell **4**-1610
Jackie Stewart **7**-2652
David Wilkie **8**-3018

SLOVAKIA. *See also* CZECHOSLOVAKIA
Martina Hingis **3**-1197
Stan Mikita **5**-1877

SOUTH AFRICA
Gary Player **6**-2212
Nick Price **6**-2241

SOUTH KOREA
Se Ri Pak **6**-2126

SOVIET UNION. *See also names of former Soviet republics*
Vasily Alexeyev **1**-35
Nikolai Andrianov **1**-70
Svetlana Boginskaya **1**-273
Valeri Borzov **1**-294
Valery Brumel **1**-346
Sergei Bubka **1**-352
Alexander Dityatin **2**-679
Ekaterina Gordeeva **3**-992
Sergei Grinkov **3**-992
Tatiana Gutsu **3**-1066
Akakios Kakiasvilis **4**-1396
Aleksandr Karelin **4**-1402
Anatoly Karpov **4**-1405
Garry Kasparov **4**-1411
Tatyana Kazankina **4**-1417
Svetlana Khorkina **4**-1444
Olga Korbut **4**-1499
Larisa Latynina **4**-1561
Sergei Litvinov **5**-1645
Valentin Mankin **5**-1766
Aleksandr Popov **6**-2220
Irina Press **6**-2238
Tamara Press **6**-2238
Oleg Protopopov **6**-2247
Ludmila Protopopov **6**-2247
Irina Rodnina **6**-2352
Vladimir Salnikov **6**-2419
Vitaly Scherbo **7**-2463
Boris Shakhlin **7**-2521
Irena Szewinska **7**-2699
Victor Tchoukarine **7**-2724
Vladislav Tretiak **7**-2807
Ludmila Turishcheva **7**-2831

Ivan Yarygin **8**-3110
Lev Yashin **8**-3113
Alexander Zaitsev **6**-2352

SPAIN
Seve Ballesteros **1**-144
Miguel Indurain **4**-1259
Carlos Moya **5**-1962
Arantxa Sanchez-Vicario **6**-2428

SWEDEN
Björn Borg **1**-285
Stefan Edberg **2**-738
Martha Norelius **6**-2038
Annika Sorenstam **7**-2595
Ingemar Stenmark **7**-2637
Gunde Svan **7**-2689
Mats Wilander **8**-3009

SWITZERLAND
Pirmin Zurbriggen **8**-3149

TRINIDAD AND TOBAGO
Ato Boldon **1**-280
Learie Constantine **2**-528

TURKEY
Naim Suleymanoglu **7**-2681

UKRAINE. *See also* SOVIET UNION
Valeri Borzov **1**-294
Sergei Bubka **1**-352
Tatiana Gutsu **3**-1066
Lenny Krayzelburg **4**-1510
Larisa Latynina **4**-1561
Valentin Mankin **5**-1766
Alexander Medved **5**-1853
Irina Press **6**-2238
Tamara Press **6**-2238
Victor Tchoukarine **7**-2724

UNITED KINGDOM. *See also* ENGLAND; SCOTLAND; NORTHERN IRELAND

UNITED STATES
Hank Aaron **1**-1
Jim Abbott **1**-4
Kareem Abdul-Jabbar **1**-7
Herb Adderley **1**-14
Andre Agassi **1**-17
Troy Aikman **1**-20
Akebono **1**-23
Michelle Akers **1**-26
Tenley Albright **1**-29
Grover Alexander **1**-32
Muhammad Ali **1**-38
Marcus Allen **1**-42
Bobby Allison **1**-46
Roberto Alomar **1**-49
Lance Alworth **1**-52
Lyle Alzado **1**-55
Morten Andersen **1**-58
Paul Anderson **1**-61
Mario Andretti **1**-67
Earl Anthony **1**-73
Luke Appling **1**-79
Eddie Arcaro **1**-82
Nate Archibald **1**-85
Alexis Arguello **1**-88
Paul Arizin **1**-92
Henry Armstrong **1**-98
Lance Armstrong **1**-102
Arthur Ashe **1**-105
Evelyn Ashford **1**-108
Bob Askin **1**-111
Doug Atkins **1**-114
Tracy Austin **1**-117
Shirley Babashoff **1**-120
Tai Babilonia **1**-122
Max Baer **1**-125
Jeff Bagwell **1**-128
Catie Ball **1**-142
Ernie Banks **1**-147
Willie Banks **1**-153
Charles Barkley **1**-159
Randy Barnes **1**-162
Jay Barrs **1**-165
Rick Barry **1**-168
Greg Barton **1**-172
Sammy Baugh **1**-175
Elgin Baylor **1**-178
Bob Beamon **1**-181
Jim Beatty **1**-185
Chuck Bednarik **1**-193
James "Cool Papa" Bell **1**-199
Albert Belle **1**-202
Johnny Bench **1**-205
Chief Bender **1**-208
Joan Benoit **1**-211
Patty Berg **1**-214
Yogi Berra **1**-218
Raymond Berry **1**-221
Fred Biletnikoff **1**-229
Dave Bing **1**-232
Matt Biondi **1**-235
Larry Bird **1**-239
Bonnie Blair **1**-243
Doc Blanchard **1**-246
George Blanda **1**-252
Dain Blanton **1**-259
Jeff Blatnick **1**-262
Drew Bledsoe **1**-265
Ethelda Bleibtrey **1**-267
Wade Boggs **1**-270
Brian Boitano **1**-277
Barry Bonds **1**-282
Julius Boros **1**-288
Ralph Boston **1**-300
Riddick Bowe **1**-306
Bill Bowness **1**-309
Bill Bradley **1**-312
Pat Bradley **1**-315
Terry Bradshaw **1**-321
George Breen **1**-324
George Brett **1**-330
Valerie Brisco-Hooks **1**-334
Lou Brock **1**-337
Jim Brown **1**-340
Tim Brown **1**-343
Kobe Bryant **1**-349
Buck Buchanan **1**-355
Craig Buck **1**-358
Don Budge **1**-361
Nick Buoniconti **1**-367
Leroy Burrell **1**-370
Mike Burton **1**-373
Susan Butcher **1**-376
Dick Butkus **1**-379
Dick Button **1**-382
George Charles Calnan **1**-385
Roy Campanella **1**-388
Earl Campbell **1**-391
Jennifer Capriati **2**-397
Steve Carlton **2**-403
JoAnne Carner **2**-406
Connie Carpenter **2**-409
Corky Carroll **2**-412
Don Carter **2**-415
Gary Carter **2**-418
Vince Carter **2**-421
Billy Casper **2**-427
Tracy Caulkins **2**-430
Wilt Chamberlain **2**-433
Frank Chance **2**-437
Michael Chang **2**-440
Oscar Charleston **2**-443
Brandi Chastain **2**-452
Dutch Clark **2**-458
Will Clark **2**-464
Roger Clemens **2**-470
Alice Coachman **2**-476
Ty Cobb **2**-479
Mickey Cochrane **2**-485
Eddie Collins **2**-491
David Cone **2**-503
Billy Conn **2**-506
Bart Conner **2**-510

Dennis Conner **2**-513
Harold Connolly **2**-516
Maureen Connolly **2**-519
Jimmy Connors **2**-525
Cynthia Cooper **2**-531
Fred Couples **2**-536
Jim Courier **2**-539
Bob Cousy **2**-549
Stan Coveleski **2**-552
Dave Cowens **2**-555
Lynne Cox **2**-558
Buster Crabbe **2**-561
Ben Crenshaw **2**-564
Larry Csonka **2**-570
Billy Cunningham **2**-573
Randall Cunningham **2**-576
Tom Curren **2**-579
Lindsay Davenport **2**-591
Willie Davenport **2**-594
Bob Davies **2**-597
Ernie Davis **2**-600
Glenn Davis **2**-603
John Davis **2**-606
Terrell Davis **2**-609
Andre Dawson **2**-612
Len Dawson **2**-615
Pat Day **2**-619
Dizzy Dean **2**-622
Dave DeBusschere **2**-629
Mary Decker-Slaney **2**-632
Anita DeFrantz **2**-635
Oscar de la Hoya **2**-638
Jimmy Demaret **2**-645
Jack Dempsey **2**-648
Donna de Varona **2**-651
Gail Devers **2**-654
Eric Dickerson **2**-659
Harrison Dillard **2**-662
Joe DiMaggio **2**-665
Mike Ditka **2**-676
Larry Doby **2**-685
Mark Donohue **2**-688
Tony Dorsett **2**-691
Stacy Dragila **2**-696
Clyde Drexler **2**-702
Don Drysdale **2**-709
Herb Dudley **2**-712
Charley Dumas **2**-715
Margaret Osborne duPont **2**-721
Eddie Eagan **2**-728
Dale Earnhardt **2**-731
Dennis Eckersley **2**-734
Gertrude Ederle **2**-741
Carl Eller **2**-750
John Elway **2**-759
Alex English **2**-768
Julius Erving **2**-771
Janet Evans **2**-781
Lee Evans **2**-784
Johnny Evers **2**-787
Chris Evert **2**-790
Patrick Ewing **2**-793
Ray Ewry **2**-796
Johnny Farrell **3**-805
Marshall Faulk **3**-808
Brett Favre **3**-811
Eddie Feigner **3**-817
Bob Feller **3**-820
Tom Ferguson **3**-823
Lisa Fernandez **3**-826
Bobby Fischer **3**-829
Carlton Fisk **3**-833
Peggy Fleming **3**-839
Curt Flood **3**-844
Ray Floyd **3**-847
Doug Flutie **3**-850
Eric Fonoimoana **1**-259
Whitey Ford **3**-853
George Foreman **3**-856
Dick Fosbury **3**-859
Bob Foster **3**-862
Greg Foster **3**-865
Jimmie Foxx **3**-868
A. J. Foyt **3**-871
Gretchen Fraser **3**-877
Joe Frazier **3**-880
Walt Frazier **3**-883
Dave Freeman **3**-890
Joe Fulks **3**-896
Dan Gable **3**-899
Nomar Garciaparra **3**-905
Randy Gardner **1**-122
Rulon Gardner **3**-908
Don Garlits **3**-911
Kevin Garnett **3**-914
Steve Garvey **3**-920
Lou Gehrig **3**-926
Charlie Gehringer **3**-929
George Gervin **3**-935
Althea Gibson **3**-938
Bob Gibson **3**-941
Josh Gibson **3**-945
Frank Gifford **3**-948
Artis Gilmore **3**-953
George Gipp **3**-956
Tom Glavine **3**-959
Tom Gola **3**-962
Diana Golden **3**-965
Lefty Gomez **3**-968
Pancho Gonzales **3**-974
Brian Goodell **3**-980
Dwight Gooden **3**-983
Gail Goodrich **3**-986
Jeff Gordon **3**-995
Rich Gossage **3**-998
Otto Graham **3**-1006
Red Grange **3**-1009
Rocky Graziano **3**-1012
Debbie Green **3**-1015
Hank Greenberg **3**-1018
Joe Greene **3**-1021
Maurice Greene **3**-1024
Hal Greer **3**-1030
Forrest Gregg **3**-1033
Wayne Gretzky **3**-1035
Bob Griese **3**-1039
Ken Griffey, Jr. **3**-1042
Archie Griffin **3**-1045
Florence Griffith-Joyner **3**-1048
Burleigh Grimes **3**-1051
Lefty Grove **3**-1054
Lou Groza **3**-1057
Dan Gurney **3**-1060
Janet Guthrie **3**-1063
Ray Guy **3**-1069
Tony Gwynn **3**-1072
Cliff Hagan **3**-1076
Walter Hagen **3**-1079
Marvin Hagler **3**-1082
Jack Ham **3**-1091
Dorothy Hamill **3**-1093
Scott Hamilton **3**-1096
Mia Hamm **3**-1099
Chip Hanauer **3**-1102
John Hannah **3**-1105
Penny Hardaway **3**-1108
Tim Hardaway **3**-1111
Tom Harmon **3**-1114
Franco Harris **3**-1117
Bill Hartack **3**-1120
Gabby Hartnett **3**-1125
John Havlicek **3**-1134
Connie Hawkins **3**-1138
Bob Hayes **3**-1141
Elvin Hayes **3**-1144
Marques Haynes **3**-1147
Walt Hazzard **3**-1149
Thomas Hearns **3**-1152
Eric Heiden **3**-1156
Tom Heinsohn **3**-1159
Carol Heiss **3**-1162
Rickey Henderson **3**-1165
Ted Hendricks **3**-1168
Orel Hershiser **3**-1173
Jimmie Heuga **3**-1176
Charlie Hickcox **3**-1179
Grant Hill **3**-1185
Jim Hines **3**-1194
Elroy "Crazylegs" Hirsch **3**-1200
Ben Hogan **3**-1206
Nancy Hogshead **3**-1209
Chamique Holdsclaw **3**-1212
Larry Holmes **4**-1215
Evander Holyfield **4**-1219
Rogers Hornsby **4**-1223
Paul Hornung **4**-1226
Ken Houston **4**-1229

Carl Hubbell 4-1235
Sam Huff 4-1238
Catfish Hunter 4-1244
Don Hutson 4-1250
Flo Hyman 4-1253
Nick Hysong 4-1256
Michael Irvin 4-1262
Hale Irwin 4-1265
Dan Issel 4-1268
Allen Iverson 4-1274
Bo Jackson 4-1277
Reggie Jackson 4-1280
Shoeless Joe Jackson 4-1283
Edgerrin James 4-1289
Dan Jansen 4-1292
Chet Jastremski 4-1295
David Jenkins 4-1298
Hayes Jenkins 4-1301
Bruce Jenner 4-1304
Derek Jeter 4-1310
Gus Johnson 4-1313
Howard Johnson 4-1316
Jack Johnson 4-1319
Jimmy Johnson 4-1322
John Henry Johnson 4-1325
Judy Johnson 4-1328
Kathy Johnson 4-1331
Larry Johnson 4-1334
Magic Johnson 4-1337
Michael Johnson 4-1341
Nancy Johnson 4-1343
Rafer Johnson 4-1346
Randy Johnson 4-1349
Walter Johnson 4-1352
Bobby Jones 4-1355
Cobi Jones 4-1358
Deacon Jones 4-1361
K. C. Jones 4-1364
Marion Jones 4-1367
Roy Jones, Jr. 4-1370
Sam Jones 4-1373
Michael Jordan 4-1376
Joan Joyce 4-1381
Jackie Joyner-Kersee 4-1384
Sonny Jurgensen 4-1390
Duke Kahanamoku 4-1393
Al Kaline 4-1399
Willie Keeler 4-1423
Johnny Kelley 4-1429
Jim Kelly 4-1432
John Kelly, Sr. 4-1435
Lee Kemp 4-1438
Nancy Kerrigan 4-1441
Billy Kidd 4-1447
Jason Kidd 4-1450
Harmon Killebrew 4-1453
Chris Kinard 4-1459
Ralph Kiner 4-1462
Betsy King 4-1465
Billie Jean King 4-1468
Micki King 4-1471
Roger Kingdom 4-1474
Karch Kiraly 4-1479
Tom Kite 4-1482
Evel Knievel 4-1488
Bill Koch 4-1491
Tommy Kono 4-1494
Sandy Koufax 4-1502
Jack Kramer 4-1505
Jerry Kramer 4-1508
Lenny Krayzelburg 4-1510
Julie Krone 4-1519
Bob Kurland 4-1525
Michelle Kwan 4-1528
Marion Ladewig 4-1534
Nap Lajoie 4-1540
Jack Lambert 4-1543
Dick "Night Train" Lane 4-1546
Bob Lanier 4-1552
Joe Lapchick 4-1555
Steve Largent 4-1558
Bobby Layne 4-1573
Sammy Lee 4-1579
Bob Lemon 4-1585
Greg LeMond 4-1588
Ivan Lendl 4-1591
Buck Leonard 4-1597
Sugar Ray Leonard 4-1600
Carl Lewis 4-1604
Nancy Lieberman-Cline 4-1616
Bob Lilly 4-1619
Kristine Lilly 4-1622
Gerry Lindgren 5-1625
Tara Lipinski 5-1637
Floyd Little 5-1640
Lawson Little 5-1643
Rebecca Lobo 5-1648
Al Lopez 5-1657
Nancy Lopez 5-1660
Steven Lopez 5-1663
Ronnie Lott 5-1666
Greg Louganis 5-1668
Joe Louis 5-1671
Clyde Lovellette 5-1675
Jerry Lucas 5-1681
Sid Luckman 5-1685
Jon Lugbill 5-1688
Hank Luisetti 5-1691
Johnny Lujack 5-1694
Steve Lundquist 5-1697
Janet Lynn 5-1700
Bob McAdoo 5-1703
Chris McCarron 5-1706
Pat McCormick 5-1709
Willie McCovey 5-1712
Floretta Doty McCutcheon 5-1715
Hugh McElhenny 5-1717
John McEnroe 5-1720
Mark McGwire 5-1723
Kevin McHale 5-1726
Reggie McKenzie 5-1729
Tamara McKinney 5-1732
Jim McMahon 5-1735
Steve McNair 5-1738
Julianne McNamara 5-1741
Greg Maddux 5-1744
Bill Madlock 5-1747
Larry Mahan 5-1750
Phil Mahre 5-1752
Karl Malone 5-1757
Moses Malone 5-1760
Lloyd Mangrum 5-1763
Peyton Manning 5-1768
Mickey Mantle 5-1774
Pete Maravich 5-1780
Alice Marble 5-1783
Gino Marchetti 5-1789
Rocky Marciano 5-1792
Dan Marino 5-1798
Roger Maris 5-1801
Rube Marquard 5-1804
Jim Marshall 5-1807
Slater Martin 5-1810
Edgar Martinez 5-1813
Eddie Mathews 5-1819
Christy Mathewson 5-1822
Bob Mathias 5-1825
Randy Matson 5-1828
Don Mattingly 5-1837
Don Maynard 5-1840
Willie Mays 5-1843
Andrea Mead Lawrence 5-1846
Mary T. Meagher 5-1848
Rick Mears 5-1851
Joe Medwick 5-1856
Linda Metheny 5-1865
Debbie Meyer 5-1868
Ann Meyers 5-1871
George Mikan 5-1874
Rod Milburn 5-1880
Cheryl Miller 5-1883
Reggie Miller 5-1886
Shannon Miller 5-1889
Billy Mills 5-1893
Ron Mix 5-1903
Johnny Mize 5-1906
Earl Monroe 5-1909
Joe Montana 5-1912
Helen Wills Moody 5-1916
Warren Moon 5-1919
Archie Moore 5-1923
Lenny Moore 5-1929
Pablo Morales 5-1932
Joe Morgan 5-1938
Bobby Joe Morrow 5-1941
Willie Mosconi 5-1944
Edwin Moses 5-1950

Randy Moss **5**-1953
Marion Motley **5**-1956
Alonzo Mourning **5**-1959
Shirley Muldowney **5**-1964
Chris Mullin **5**-1970
Tori Murden **5**-1973
Dale Murphy **5**-1976
Eddie Murray **5**-1979
Ty Murray **5**-1982
Stan Musial **5**-1985
John Naber **5**-1995
Bronko Nagurski **5**-2000
Joe Namath **5**-2006
Martina Navratilova **5**-2010
Renaldo Nehemiah **5**-2014
Byron Nelson **5**-2017
Ernie Nevers **5**-2022
Jack Nicklaus **5**-2031
Ray Nitschke **6**-2035
Martha Norelius **6**-2038
Tara Nott **6**-2044
Dan O'Brien **6**-2053
Parry O'Brien **6**-2056
David O'Connor **6**-2059
Al Oerter **6**-2062
Hakeem Olajuwon **6**-2068
Barney Oldfield **6**-2072
Merlin Olsen **6**-2078
Shaquille O'Neal **6**-2081
Mel Ott **6**-2093
Jim Otto **6**-2099
Francis D. Ouimet **6**-2105
Jesse Owens **6**-2111
Darrell Pace **6**-2114
Charles Paddock **6**-2117
Alan Page **6**-2120
Satchel Paige **6**-2123
Arnold Palmer **6**-2128
Jim Palmer **6**-2132
Connie Paraskevin-Young **6**-2137
Robert Parish **6**-2140
Denise Parker **6**-2143
Jim Parker **6**-2146
Brad Parks **6**-2149
Floyd Patterson **6**-2152
Mel Patton **6**-2155
Gary Payton **6**-2158
Walter Payton **6**-2161
David Pearson **6**-2164
Gaylord Perry **6**-2179
Bob Pettit **6**-2182
Lee Petty **6**-2185
Richard Petty **6**-2188
Mike Piazza **6**-2191
Mary Pierce **6**-2194
Laffit Pincay, Jr. **6**-2200
Scottie Pippen **6**-2202
Fritz Pollard **6**-2215
Jim Poole **6**-2217
Cynthia Potter **6**-2226
Mike Powell **6**-2232
Steve Prefontaine **6**-2235
Don Prudhomme **6**-2251
Kirby Puckett **6**-2254
Bobby Rahal **6**-2263
Tim Raines **6**-2266
Frank Ramsey **6**-2272
Judy Rankin **6**-2275
Willis Reed **6**-2281
Steve Reeves **6**-2284
Mary Lou Retton **6**-2286
Butch Reynolds **6**-2289
Willy T. Ribbs **6**-2291
Jerry Rice **6**-2294
Bob Richards **6**-2300
Cathy Rigby **6**-2303
John Riggins **6**-2306
Bobby Riggs **6**-2309
Jim Ringo **6**-2312
Cal Ripken, Jr. **6**-2314
Robin Roberts **6**-2317
Oscar Robertson **6**-2320
Paul Robeson **6**-2323
Brooks Robinson **6**-2326
David Robinson **6**-2329
Frank Robinson **6**-2333
Jackie Robinson **6**-2336
Sugar Ray Robinson **6**-2339
Andy Robustelli **6**-2343
Bill Rodgers **6**-2346
Dennis Rodman **6**-2349
Alex Rodriguez **6**-2355
Pete Rose **6**-2367
Kyle Rote, Jr. **6**-2373
Wilma Rudolph **6**-2379
Red Ruffing **6**-2382
Tracie Ruiz-Conforto **6**-2385
Bill Russell **6**-2390
Babe Ruth **6**-2393
Johnny Rutherford **6**-2397
Nolan Ryan **6**-2400
Jim Ryun **6**-2404
Bret Saberhagen **6**-2410
Carmen Salvino **6**-2422
Pete Sampras **6**-2425
Ryne Sandberg **6**-2431
Barry Sanders **6**-2435
Deion Sanders **6**-2438
Gene Sarazen **7**-2445
Steve Sax **7**-2454
Gale Sayers **7**-2457
Dolph Schayes **7**-2460
Joe Schmidt **7**-2469
Mike Schmidt **7**-2472
Don Schollander **7**-2477
Scott Schulte **7**-2480
Arnold Schwarzenegger **7**-2486
Dave Scott **7**-2489
Mike Scott **7**-2492
Steve Scott **7**-2495
Wendell Scott **7**-2498
Briana Scurry **7**-2500
Bob Seagren **7**-2503
Tom Seaver **7**-2506
Vic Seixas **7**-2509
Monica Seles **7**-2512
Frank Selvy **7**-2515
Bill Sharman **7**-2524
Shannon Sharpe **7**-2527
Patty Sheehan **7**-2530
Art Shell **7**-2533
Betty Shellenberger **7**-2535
Willie Shoemaker **7**-2540
Frank Shorter **7**-2543
Jim Shoulders **7**-2546
Al Simmons **7**-2549
O. J. Simpson **7**-2552
Mike Singletary **7**-2555
George Sisler **7**-2558
Bruce Smith **7**-2564
Bubba Smith **7**-2566
Emmitt Smith **7**-2568
John Smith **7**-2571
Ozzie Smith **7**-2574
Sinjin Smith **7**-2577
Stan Smith **7**-2580
Tommie Smith **7**-2583
Sam Snead **7**-2586
Duke Snider **7**-2592
Sammy Sosa **7**-2598
Warren Spahn **7**-2604
Tris Speaker **7**-2607
Mark Spitz **7**-2610
Ken Stabler **7**-2613
John Stallworth **7**-2616
Willie Stargell **7**-2619
Bart Starr **7**-2622
Roger Staubach **7**-2625
Casey Stengel **7**-2634
Helen Stephens **7**-2640
Jill Sterkel **7**-2643
Dave Stewart **7**-2649
Payne Stewart **7**-2655
Tony Stewart **7**-2658
John Stockton **7**-2660
Dwight Stones **7**-2663
Curtis Strange **7**-2666
Darryl Strawberry **7**-2669
Picabo Street **7**-2672
Kerri Strug **7**-2678
Don Sutton **7**-2686
Lynn Swann **7**-2692
Sheryl Swoopes **7**-2697
Fran Tarkenton **7**-2707
Goose Tatum **7**-2710
Charley Taylor **7**-2712
Jim Taylor **7**-2715

Lawrence Taylor **7**-2718
Major Taylor **7**-2721
Bill Terry **7**-2727
Vinny Testaverde **7**-2730
Derrick Thomas **7**-2732
Frank Thomas **7**-2735
Isiah Thomas **7**-2738
Kurt Thomas **7**-2741
Thurman Thomas **7**-2744
Jenny Thompson **7**-2750
Jim Thorpe **7**-2756
Nate Thurmond **7**-2759
Casey Tibbs **7**-2762
Bertha Tickey **7**-2765
Bill Tilden **7**-2771
Steve Timmons **7**-2774
Y. A. Tittle **7**-2777
Eddie Tolan **7**-2780
Bill Toomey **7**-2786
Joe Torre **7**-2789
Dara Torres **7**-2792
Anne Barton Townsend **7**-2798
Tony Trabert **7**-2801
Pie Traynor **7**-2804
Lee Trevino **7**-2810
Charley Trippi **7**-2816
Emlen Tunnell **7**-2825
Gene Tunney **7**-2828
Ted Turner **7**-2834
Jack Twyman **7**-2837
Mike Tyson **7**-2840
Wyomia Tyus **7**-2844
Johnny Unitas **7**-2847
Wes Unseld **7**-2850
Al Unser **8**-2853
Bobby Unser **8**-2856
Gene Upshaw **8**-2859
Norm Van Brocklin **8**-2869
Steve Van Buren **8**-2872
Dazzy Vance **8**-2875
Amy Van Dyken **8**-2881
Glenna Collett Vare **8**-2887
Greg Vaughn **8**-2890
Mo Vaughn **8**-2893
Peter Vidmar **8**-2896
Dave Villwock **8**-2905
Chuck Vinci **8**-2908
Rube Waddell **8**-2914
Honus Wagner **8**-2920
Lisa Wagner **8**-2923
Doak Walker **8**-2928
Herschel Walker **8**-2931
Rusty Wallace **8**-2937
Bobby Walthour **8**-2940
Bill Walton **8**-2943
Charlie Ward **8**-2947
Paul Warfield **8**-2950
Cornelius Warmerdam **8**-2953
Kurt Warner **8**-2955
Bob Waterfield **8**-2958
Tom Watson **8**-2961
Chris Webber **8**-2964
Dick Weber **8**-2967
Johnny Weissmuller **8**-2970
Buddy Werner **8**-2973
Jerry West **8**-2976
Peter Westbrook **8**-2979
Byron "Whizzer" White **8**-2981
Randy White **8**-2984
Reggie White **8**-2987
Mal Whitfield **8**-2990
Kathy Whitworth **8**-2996
Deena Wigger **8**-2999
Lones Wigger **8**-3002
Hazel Wightman **8**-3006
Hoyt Wilhelm **8**-3012
Lenny Wilkens **8**-3015
Dominique Wilkins **8**-3021
Mac Wilkins **8**-3024
Laura Wilkinson **8**-3027
Billy Williams **8**-3029
Esther Williams **8**-3032
Natalie Williams **8**-3035
Ricky Williams **8**-3038
Serena Williams **8**-3040
Ted Williams **8**-3043
Venus Williams **8**-3046
Walter Ray Williams, Jr. **8**-3049
Maury Wills **8**-3051
Hack Wilson **8**-3054
Larry Wilson **8**-3057
Dave Winfield **8**-3059
Willie Wood **8**-3068
Lynette Woodard **8**-3070
John Wooden **8**-3073
Cynthia Woodhead **8**-3076
Tiger Woods **8**-3079
Charles Woodson **8**-3083
James Worthy **8**-3089
Mickey Wright **8**-3095
Early Wynn **8**-3098
Kristi Yamaguchi **8**-3101
Cale Yarborough **8**-3107
Carl Yastrzemski **8**-3116
Cy Young **8**-3119
Sheila Young **8**-3122
Steve Young **8**-3125
Robin Yount **8**-3128
Babe Didrikson Zaharias **8**-3134
Kim Zmeskal **8**-3143

VIRGIN ISLANDS

Tim Duncan **2**-718

YUGOSLAVIA

Vlade Divac **2**-682
Toni Kukoc **4**-1522
Monica Seles **7**-2512
Steve Zungul **8**-3146

ZIMBABWE

Paula Newby-Fraser **5**-2025

Name Index

Aaron, Hank **1**-1
Abbott, Jim **1**-4
Abdul-Jabbar, Kareem **1**-7
Abrahams, Harold **1**-11
Adderley, Herb **1**-14
Agassi, Andre **1**-17
Aikman, Troy **1**-20
Akebono **1**-23
Akers, Michelle **1**-26
Albright, Tenley **1**-29
Alcindor, Ferdinand Lewis, Jr. *See* Abdul-Jabbar, Kareem
Alexander, Grover **1**-32
Alexeyev, Vasily **1**-35
Ali, Muhammad **1**-38
Allen, Marcus **1**-42
Allison, Bobby **1**-46
Alomar, Roberto **1**-49
Alworth, Lance **1**-52
Alzado, Lyle **1**-55
Andersen, Greta. *See* Waitz, Greta
Andersen, Morten **1**-58
Anderson, Paul **1**-61
Anderson, Willie **1**-64
Andretti, Mario **1**-67
Andrianov, Nikolai **1**-70
Anthony, Earl **1**-73
Aouita, Said **1**-76
Appling, Luke **1**-79
Arcaro, Eddie **1**-82
Archibald, Nate **1**-85
Arguello, Alexis **1**-88
Arizin, Paul **1**-92
Armour, Tommy **1**-95
Armstrong, Henry **1**-98
Armstrong, Lance **1**-102
Ashe, Arthur **1**-105
Ashford, Evelyn **1**-108
Askin, Bob **1**-111
Atkins, Doug **1**-114
Austin, Tracy **1**-117

Babashoff, Shirley **1**-120
Babilonia, Tai **1**-122
Baer, Max **1**-125
Bagwell, Jeff **1**-128
Bailey, Donovan **1**-131
Bailey, Irvine "Ace" **1**-134
Balas, Iolanda **1**-136
Ball, Alan **1**-139
Ball, Catie **1**-142
Ballesteros, Seve **1**-144
Banks, Ernie **1**-147
Banks, Gordon **1**-150
Banks, Willie **1**-153
Bannister, Roger **1**-156
Barbella, Thomas Rocco. *See* Graziano, Rocky
Barkley, Charles **1**-159
Barnes, Randy **1**-162
Barrs, Jay **1**-165
Barrow, Joseph Louis. *See* Louis, Joe
Barry, Rick **1**-168
Barton, Greg **1**-172
Baugh, Sammy **1**-175
Baylor, Elgin **1**-178
Beamon, Bob **1**-181
Beatty, Jim **1**-185
Beckenbauer, Franz **1**-188
Becker, Boris **1**-190
Bednarik, Chuck **1**-193
Beliveau, Jean **1**-196
Bell, James "Cool Papa" **1**-199
Belle, Albert **1**-202
Belousova, Ludmila. *See* Protopopov, Ludmila
Bench, Johnny **1**-205
Bender, Chief **1**-208
Benoit, Joan **1**-211
Berg, Patty **1**-214
Berra, Yogi **1**-218
Berry, Raymond **1**-221
Best, George **1**-224
Bikila, Abebe **1**-226
Biletnikoff, Fred **1**-229
Bing, Dave **1**-232
Biondi, Matt **1**-235
Bird, Larry **1**-239
Blair, Bonnie **1**-243
Blanchard, Doc **1**-246
Blanchflower, Danny **1**-249
Blanda, George **1**-252
Blankers-Koen, Fanny **1**-256
Blanton, Dain **1**-259
Blatnick, Jeff **1**-262
Bledsoe, Drew **1**-265
Bleibtrey, Ethelda **1**-267
Boggs, Wade **1**-270
Boginskaya, Svetlana **1**-273
Boitano, Brian **1**-277
Boldon, Ato **1**-280
Bonds, Barry **1**-282
Borg, Björn **1**-285
Boros, Julius **1**-288
Borotra, Jean **1**-291
Borzov, Valeri **1**-294
Bossy, Mike **1**-297
Boston, Ralph **1**-300
Bourque, Ray **1**-303
Bowe, Riddick **1**-306
Bowness, Bill **1**-309
Bradley, Bill **1**-312
Bradley, Pat **1**-315
Bradman, Donald G. **1**-318
Bradshaw, Terry **1**-321
Breen, George **1**-324
Bremner, Billy **1**-327
Brett, George **1**-330
Brisco-Hooks, Valerie **1**-334
Brock, Lou **1**-337
Brown, Jim **1**-340
Brown, Tim **1**-343
Brumel, Valery **1**-346
Bryant, Kobe **1**-349
Bubka, Sergei **1**-352
Buchanan, Buck **1**-355
Buck, Craig **1**-358
Budge, Don **1**-361
Bueno, Maria **1**-364
Buoniconti, Nick **1**-367
Burrell, Leroy **1**-370
Burton, Mike **1**-373
Butcher, Susan **1**-376
Butkus, Dick **1**-379
Button, Dick **1**-382

Calnan, George Charles **1**-385
Campanella, Roy **1**-388
Campbell, Earl **1**-391
Canseco, José **1**-394
Capriati, Jennifer **2**-397
Carew, Rod **2**-400
Carlton, Steve **2**-403
Carner, JoAnne **2**-406
Carpenter, Connie **2**-409
Carroll, Corky **2**-412
Carter, Don **2**-415
Carter, Gary **2**-418
Carter, Vince **2**-421
Čáslavská, Vera **2**-424
Casper, Billy **2**-427
Caulkins, Tracy **2**-430
Chamberlain, Wilt **2**-433
Chance, Frank **2**-437
Chang, Michael **2**-440
Charleston, Oscar **2**-443
Charlton, Bobby **2**-446
Charlton, Jack **2**-449
Chastain, Brandi **2**-452

Chávez, Julio César **2**-454
Clark, Dutch **2**-458
Clark, Jim **2**-461
Clark, Will **2**-464
Clarke, Bobby **2**-467
Clay, Cassius Marcellus, Jr. *See* Ali, Muhammad
Clemens, Roger **2**-470
Clemente, Roberto **2**-473
Coachman, Alice **2**-476
Cobb, Ty **2**-479
Cochet, Henri **2**-482
Cochrane, Mickey **2**-485
Coe, Sebastian **2**-488
Collett, Glenna. *See* Vare, Glenna Collet
Collins, Eddie **2**-491
Comăneci, Nadia **2**-495
Compagnoni, Deborah **2**-498
Conacher, Lionel **2**-500
Cone, David **2**-503
Conn, Billy **2**-506
Conner, Bart **2**-510
Conner, Dennis **2**-513
Connolly, Harold **2**-516
Connolly, Maureen **2**-519
Connolly, Olga **2**-522
Connors, Jimmy **2**-525
Constantine, Learie **2**-528
Cooper, Cynthia **2**-531
Cordero, Angel, Jr. **2**-534
Couples, Fred **2**-536
Courier, Jim **2**-539
Court, Margaret **2**-542
Cousins, Robin **2**-546
Cousy, Bob **2**-549
Coveleski, Stan **2**-552
Cowens, Dave **2**-555
Cox, Lynne **2**-558
Crabbe, Buster **2**-561
Crenshaw, Ben **2**-564
Cruyff, Johan **2**-567
Csonka, Larry **2**-570
Cunningham, Billy **2**-573
Cunningham, Randall **2**-576
Curren, Tom **2**-579
Curry, John **2**-582
Cuthbert, Betty **2**-585

Darnyi, Tamas **2**-588
Davenport, Lindsay **2**-591
Davenport, Willie **2**-594
Davies, Bob **2**-597
Davis, Ernie **2**-600
Davis, Glenn **2**-603
Davis, John **2**-606
Davis, Terrell **2**-609
Dawson, Andre **2**-612
Dawson, Len **2**-615
Day, Pat **2**-619
Dean, Christopher **7**-2794
Dean, Dizzy **2**-622
De Bruijn, Inge **2**-626
DeBusschere, Dave **2**-629
Decker-Slaney, Mary **2**-632
DeFrantz, Anita **2**-635
De la Hoya, Oscar **2**-638
Delvecchio, Alex **2**-642
Demaret, Jimmy **2**-645
Dempsey, Jack **2**-648
De Varona, Donna **2**-651
Devers, Gail **2**-654
Dibiasi, Klaus **2**-657
Dickerson, Eric **2**-659
Didriksen, Mildred Ella. *See* Zaharias, Babe Didrikson
Dillard, Harrison **2**-662
DiMaggio, Joe **2**-665
Dimas, Pyrros **2**-668
D'Inezeo, Raimondo **2**-671
Dionne, Marcel **2**-673
Diryi, Larisa Semyenovna. *See* Latynina, Larisa
Ditka, Mike **2**-676
Dityatin, Alexander **2**-679
Divac, Vlade **2**-682
Doby, Larry **2**-685
Donohue, Mark **2**-688
Dorsett, Tony **2**-691
Douillet, David **2**-694
Dragila, Stacy **2**-696
Dreschler, Heike **2**-699
Drexler, Clyde **2**-702
Dryden, Ken **2**-706
Drysdale, Don **2**-709
Dudley, Herb **2**-712
Dumas, Charley **2**-715
Duncan, Tim **2**-718
DuPont, Margaret Osborne **2**-721
Duran, Roberto **2**-724

Eagan, Eddie **2**-728
Earnhardt, Dale **2**-731
Eckersley, Dennis **2**-734
Edberg, Stefan **2**-738
Ederle, Gertrude **2**-741
Egerszegi, Krisztina **2**-744
El Guerrouj, Hicham **2**-747
Eller, Carl **2**-750
Elliott, Herb **2**-753
Elvstrøm, Paul **2**-756
Elway, John **2**-759
Emerson, Roy **2**-762
Ender, Kornelia **2**-765
English, Alex **2**-768
Erving, Julius **2**-771
Esposito, Phil **2**-775
Eusebio **2**-778
Evans, Janet **2**-781
Evans, Lee **2**-784
Evers, Johnny **2**-787
Evert, Chris **2**-790
Ewing, Patrick **2**-793
Ewry, Ray **2**-796

Faldo, Nick **2**-799
Fangio, Juan Manuel **2**-802
Farrell, Johnny **3**-805
Faulk, Marshall **3**-808
Favre, Brett **3**-811
Fedorov, Sergei **3**-814
Feigner, Eddie **3**-817
Feller, Bob **3**-820
Ferguson, Tom **3**-823
Fernandez, Lisa **3**-826
Fikotová, Olga. *See* Connolly, Olga
Fischer, Bobby **3**-829
Fisk, Carlton **3**-833
Fittipaldi, Emerson **3**-836
Fleming, Peggy **3**-839
Flessel-Colovic, Laura **3**-842
Flood, Curt **3**-844
Floyd, Ray **3**-847
Flutie, Doug **3**-850
Fonoimoana, Eric **1**-259
Ford, Whitey **3**-853
Foreman, George **3**-856
Fosbury, Dick **3**-859
Foster, Bob **3**-862
Foster, Greg **3**-865
Foxx, Jimmie **3**-868
Foyt, A. J. **3**-871
Fraser, Dawn **3**-874
Fraser, Gretchen **3**-877
Frazier, Joe **3**-880
Frazier, Walt **3**-883
Freeman, Cathy **3**-887
Freeman, Dave **3**-890
Fu Mingxia **3**-893
Fulks, Joe **3**-896

Gable, Dan **3**-899
Gao Min **3**-902
Garciaparra, Nomar **3**-905
Gardner, Randy **1**-122
Gardner, Rulon **3**-908
Garlits, Don **3**-911
Garnett, Kevin **3**-914
Garrincha **3**-917
Garvey, Steve **3**-920
Gebreselassie, Haile **3**-923
Gehrig, Lou **3**-926
Gehringer, Charlie **3**-929
Geoffrion, Bernie **3**-932
Gervin, George **3**-935
Gibson, Althea **3**-938
Gibson, Bob **3**-941

Gibson, Josh **3**-945
Gifford, Frank **3**-948
Giles, Johnny **3**-951
Gilmore, Artis **3**-953
Gipp, George **3**-956
Glavine, Tom **3**-959
Gola, Tom **3**-962
Golden, Diana **3**-965
Gomez, Lefty **3**-968
Gong Zhichao **3**-971
Gonzales, Pancho **3**-974
Gonzalez, Juan **3**-977
Goodell, Brian **3**-980
Gooden, Dwight **3**-983
Goodrich, Gail **3**-986
Goolagong, Evonne **3**-989
Gordeeva, Ekaterina **3**-992
Gordon, Jeff **3**-995
Gossage, Rich **3**-998
Gould, Shane **3**-1001
Graf, Steffi **3**-1003
Graham, Otto **3**-1006
Grange, Red **3**-1009
Graziano, Rocky **3**-1012
Green, Debbie **3**-1015
Greenberg, Hank **3**-1018
Greene, Joe **3**-1021
Greene, Maurice **3**-1024
Greene, Nancy **3**-1027
Greer, Hal **3**-1030
Gregg, Forrest **3**-1033
Gretzky, Wayne **3**-1035
Griese, Bob **3**-1039
Griffey, Ken, Jr. **3**-1042
Griffin, Archie **3**-1045
Griffith-Joyner, Florence **3**-1048
Grimes, Burleigh **3**-1051
Grinkov, Sergei **3**-992
Grove, Lefty **3**-1054
Groza, Lou **3**-1057
Gunderson, JoAnne. *See* Carner, JoAnne
Gurney, Dan **3**-1060
Guthrie, Janet **3**-1063
Gutsu, Tatiana **3**-1066
Guy, Ray **3**-1069
Gvoth, Stanislaus. *See* Mikita, Stan
Gwynn, Tony **3**-1072

Hagan, Cliff **3**-1076
Hagen, Walter **3**-1079
Hagler, Marvin **3**-1082
Häkkinen, Mika **3**-1085
Hall, Glenn **3**-1088
Ham, Jack **3**-1091
Hamill, Dorothy **3**-1093
Hamilton, Scott **3**-1096
Hamm, Mia **3**-1099
Hanauer, Chip **3**-1102
Hannah, John **3**-1105
Hardaway, Penny **3**-1108
Hardaway, Tim **3**-1111
Harmon, Tom **3**-1114
Harris, Franco **3**-1117
Hartack, Bill **3**-1120
Hartel, Lis **3**-1123
Hartnett, Gabby **3**-1125
Hartono, Rudy **3**-1128
Hasek, Dominik **3**-1131
Havlicek, John **3**-1134
Hawkins, Connie **3**-1138
Hayes, Bob **3**-1141
Hayes, Elvin **3**-1144
Haynes, Marques **3**-1147
Hazzard, Walt **3**-1149
Hearns, Thomas **3**-1152
Heiden, Eric **3**-1156
Heinsohn, Tom **3**-1159
Heiss, Carol **3**-1162
Henderson, Rickey **3**-1165
Hendricks, Ted **3**-1168
Henie, Sonja **3**-1170
Hershiser, Orel **3**-1173
Heuga, Jimmie **3**-1176
Hickcox, Charlie **3**-1179
Hill, Damon **3**-1182
Hill, Grant **3**-1185
Hillary, Sir Edmund **3**-1188
Hinault, Bernard **3**-1191
Hines, Jim **3**-1194
Hingis, Martina **3**-1197
Hirsch, Elroy "Crazylegs" **3**-1200
Hoad, Lew **3**-1203
Hogan, Ben **3**-1206
Hogshead, Nancy **3**-1209
Holdsclaw, Chamique **3**-1212
Holmes, Larry **4**-1215
Holst, Lis. *See* Hartel, Lis
Holyfield, Evander **4**-1219
Hornsby, Rogers **4**-1223
Hornung, Paul **4**-1226
Hotchkiss, Hazel Virginia. *See* Wightman, Hazel
Houston, Ken **4**-1229
Howe, Gordie **4**-1232
Hubbell, Carl **4**-1235
Huff, Sam **4**-1238
Hull, Bobby **4**-1241
Hunter, Catfish **4**-1244
Hurst, Geoff **4**-1247
Hutson, Don **4**-1250
Hyman, Flo **4**-1253
Hysong, Nick **4**-1256

Ihetu, Richard. *See* Tiger, Dick
Indurain, Miguel **4**-1259
Irvin, Michael **4**-1262
Irwin, Hale **4**-1265
Issel, Dan **4**-1268
Ito, Midori **4**-1271
Iverson, Allen **4**-1274

Jackson, Bo **4**-1277
Jackson, Henry. *See* Armstrong, Henry
Jackson, Reggie **4**-1280
Jackson, Shoeless Joe **4**-1283
Jagr, Jaromir **4**-1286
James, Edgerrin **4**-1289
Jansen, Dan **4**-1292
Jastremski, Chet **4**-1295
Jenkins, David **4**-1298
Jenkins, Hayes **4**-1301
Jenner, Bruce **4**-1304
Jennings, Pat **4**-1307
Jeter, Derek **4**-1310
Johnson, Gus **4**-1313
Johnson, Howard **4**-1316
Johnson, Jack **4**-1319
Johnson, Jimmy **4**-1322
Johnson, John Henry **4**-1325
Johnson, Judy **4**-1328
Johnson, Kathy **4**-1331
Johnson, Larry **4**-1334
Johnson, Magic **4**-1337
Johnson, Michael **4**-1341
Johnson, Nancy **4**-1343
Johnson, Rafer **4**-1346
Johnson, Randy **4**-1349
Johnson, Walter **4**-1352
Jones, Bobby **4**-1355
Jones, Cobi **4**-1358
Jones, Deacon **4**-1361
Jones, K. C. **4**-1364
Jones, Marion **4**-1367
Jones, Roy, Jr. **4**-1370
Jones, Sam **4**-1373
Jordan, Michael **4**-1376
Joyce, Joan **4**-1381
Joyner-Kersee, Jackie **4**-1384
Juantorena, Alberto **4**-1387
Jurgensen, Sonny **4**-1390

Kahanamoku, Duke **4**-1393
Kakiasvilis, Akakios **4**-1396
Kaline, Al **4**-1399
Karelin, Aleksandr **4**-1402
Karpov, Anatoly **4**-1405
Karppinen, Pertti **4**-1408
Kasparov, Garry **4**-1411
Kato, Sawao **4**-1414
Kazankina, Tatyana **4**-1417
Keegan, Kevin **4**-1420
Keeler, Willie **4**-1423
Keino, Kip **4**-1426
Keller, Patricia Joan. *See* McCormick, Pat

Kelley, Johnny **4**-1429
Kelly, Jim **4**-1432
Kelly, John, Sr. **4**-1435
Kemp, Lee **4**-1438
Kerrigan, Nancy **4**-1441
Khorkina, Svetlana **4**-1444
Kidd, Billy **4**-1447
Kidd, Jason **4**-1450
Killebrew, Harmon **4**-1453
Killy, Jean-Claude **4**-1456
Kinard, Chris **4**-1459
Kiner, Ralph **4**-1462
King, Betsy **4**-1465
King, Billie Jean **4**-1468
King, Micki **4**-1471
King, Myrle Vernon. *See* Feigner, Eddie
Kingdom, Roger **4**-1474
Kipketer, Wilson **4**-1477
Kiraly, Karch **4**-1479
Kite, Tom **4**-1482
Klammer, Franz **4**-1485
Knievel, Evel **4**-1488
Koch, Bill **4**-1491
Kono, Tommy **4**-1494
Konrads, John **4**-1497
Korbut, Olga **4**-1499
Koufax, Sandy **4**-1502
Kowalewski, Stanislaus. *See* Coveleski, Stan
Kramer, Jack **4**-1505
Kramer, Jerry **4**-1508
Krayzelburg, Lenny **4**-1510
Kristiansen, Ingrid **4**-1513
Kronberger, Petra **4**-1516
Krone, Julie **4**-1519
Kukoc, Toni **4**-1522
Kunigk, Gretchen Claudia. *See* Fraser, Gretchen
Kurland, Bob **4**-1525
Kurniawan, Rudy Hartono. *See* Hartono, Rudy
Kwan, Michelle **4**-1528

Lacoste, René **4**-1531
Ladewig, Marion **4**-1534
Lafleur, Guy **4**-1537
Lajoie, Nap **4**-1540
Lambert, Jack **4**-1543
Lane, Dick "Night Train" **4**-1546
Langer, Bernhard **4**-1549
Lanier, Bob **4**-1552
Lapchick, Joe **4**-1555
Largent, Steve **4**-1558
Latynina, Larisa **4**-1561
Lauda, Niki **4**-1564
Laver, Rod **4**-1567
Law, Denis **4**-1570
Layne, Bobby **4**-1573
Lee, Bruce **4**-1576
Lee, Sammy **4**-1579
Lee Jun Fan. *See* Lee, Bruce
Lemieux, Mario **4**-1582
Lemon, Bob **4**-1585
LeMond, Greg **4**-1588
Lendl, Ivan **4**-1591
Lenglen, Suzanne **4**-1594
Leonard, Buck **4**-1597
Leonard, Sugar Ray **4**-1600
Lewis, Carl **4**-1604
Lewis, Lennox **4**-1607
Liddell, Eric **4**-1610
Liddie, Eddie **4**-1613
Lieberman-Cline, Nancy **4**-1616
Lilly, Bob **4**-1619
Lilly, Kristine **4**-1622
Lindgren, Gerry **5**-1625
Lindros, Eric **5**-1628
Lindsay, Ted **5**-1631
Lineker, Gary **5**-1634
Lipinski, Tara **5**-1637
Little, Floyd **5**-1640
Little, Lawson **5**-1643
Litvinov, Sergei **5**-1645
Lobo, Rebecca **5**-1648
Longden, Johnny **5**-1651
Longo, Jeannie **5**-1654
Lopez, Al **5**-1657
Lopez, Nancy **5**-1660
Lopez, Steven **5**-1663
Lott, Ronnie **5**-1666
Louganis, Greg **5**-1668
Louis, Joe **5**-1671
Lovellette, Clyde **5**-1675
Lu Li **5**-1678
Lucas, Jerry **5**-1681
Luckman, Sid **5**-1685
Lugbill, Jon **5**-1688
Luisetti, Hank **5**-1691
Lujack, Johnny **5**-1694
Lundquist, Steve **5**-1697
Lynn, Janet **5**-1700

McAdoo, Bob **5**-1703
McCarron, Chris **5**-1706
McCormick, Pat **5**-1709
McCovey, Willie **5**-1712
McCutcheon, Floretta Doty **5**-1715
McElhenny, Hugh **5**-1717
McEnroe, John **5**-1720
McGwire, Mark **5**-1723
McHale, Kevin **5**-1726
McKenzie, Reggie **5**-1729
McKinney, Tamara **5**-1732
McMahon, Jim **5**-1735
McNair, Steve **5**-1738
McNamara, Julianne **5**-1741
Maddux, Greg **5**-1744
Madlock, Bill **5**-1747
Mahan, Larry **5**-1750
Mahre, Phil **5**-1752
Maier, Hermann **5**-1755
Malone, Karl **5**-1757
Malone, Moses **5**-1760
Mangrum, Lloyd **5**-1763
Mankin, Valentin **5**-1766
Manning, Peyton **5**-1768
Mansell, Nigel **5**-1771
Mantle, Mickey **5**-1774
Maradona, Diego **5**-1777
Maravich, Pete **5**-1780
Marble, Alice **5**-1783
Marcari, Hortencia **5**-1786
Marchegiano, Rocco Francis. *See* Marciano, Rocky
Marchetti, Gino **5**-1789
Marciano, Rocky **5**-1792
Marichal, Juan **5**-1795
Marino, Dan **5**-1798
Maris, Roger **5**-1801
Marquard, Rube **5**-1804
Marshall, Jim **5**-1807
Martin, Slater **5**-1810
Martinez, Edgar **5**-1813
Martinez, Pedro **5**-1816
Mathews, Eddie **5**-1819
Mathewson, Christy **5**-1822
Mathias, Bob **5**-1825
Matson, Randy **5**-1828
Matthes, Roland **5**-1831
Matthews, Sir Stanley **5**-1834
Mattingly, Don **5**-1837
Maynard, Don **5**-1840
Mays, Willie **5**-1843
Mead Lawrence, Andrea **5**-1846
Meagher, Mary T. **5**-1848
Mears, Rick **5**-1851
Medved, Alexander **5**-1853
Medwick, Joe **5**-1856
Meisner, Renate. *See* Stecher, Renate
Merckx, Eddy **5**-1859
Messier, Mark **5**-1862
Metheny, Linda **5**-1865
Meyer, Debbie **5**-1868
Meyers, Ann **5**-1871
Mikan, George **5**-1874
Mikita, Stan **5**-1877
Milburn, Rod **5**-1880
Miller, Cheryl **5**-1883
Miller, Reggie **5**-1886
Miller, Shannon **5**-1889
Mills, Billy **5**-1893
Milosovici, Lavinia **5**-1896
Mittermaier, Rosi **5**-1900
Mix, Ron **5**-1903
Mize, Johnny **5**-1906

Moffitt, Billie Jean. *See* King, Billie Jean
Monroe, Earl **5**-1909
Montana, Joe **5**-1912
Moody, Helen Wills **5**-1916
Moon, Warren **5**-1919
Moore, Archie **5**-1923
Moore, Bobby **5**-1926
Moore, Lenny **5**-1929
Morales, Pablo **5**-1932
Morceli, Noureddine **5**-1935
Morgan, Joe **5**-1938
Morrow, Bobby Joe **5**-1941
Mosconi, Willie **5**-1944
Moser-Proell, Annemarie **5**-1947
Moses, Edwin **5**-1950
Moss, Randy **5**-1953
Motley, Marion **5**-1956
Mourning, Alonzo **5**-1959
Moya, Carlos **5**-1962
Muldowney, Shirley **5**-1964
Müller, Friedrich Wilhelm. *See* Sandow, Eugen
Müller, Gerd **5**-1967
Mullin, Chris **5**-1970
Murden, Tori **5**-1973
Murphy, Dale **5**-1976
Murray, Eddie **5**-1979
Murray, Ty **5**-1982
Musial, Stan **5**-1985
Mutola, Maria **5**-1989
Mutombo, Dikembe **5**-1992

Naber, John **5**-1995
Nadi, Nedo **5**-1998
Nagurski, Bronko **5**-2000
Nakayama, Akinori **5**-2003
Namath, Joe **5**-2006
Nascimento, Edson Arantes do. *See* Pelé
Navratilova, Martina **5**-2010
Nehemiah, Renaldo **5**-2014
Nelson, Byron **5**-2017
Nemov, Alexei **5**-2020
Nevers, Ernie **5**-2022
Newby-Fraser, Paula **5**-2025
Newcombe, John **5**-2028
Nicklaus, Jack **5**-2031
Nitschke, Ray **6**-2035
Norelius, Martha **6**-2038
Norman, Greg **6**-2041
Nott, Tara **6**-2044
Nowicki, Janet Lynn. *See* Lynn, Janet
Nurmi, Paavo **6**-2047
Nykänen, Matti **6**-2050

O'Brien, Dan **6**-2053
O'Brien, Parry **6**-2056
O'Connor, David **6**-2059
Oerter, Al **6**-2062
Oh, Sadaharu **6**-2065
Olajuwon, Hakeem **6**-2068
Oldfield, Barney **6**-2072
Oliva, Tony **6**-2075
Olsen, Merlin **6**-2078
O'Neal, Shaquille **6**-2081
O'Neill, Susan **6**-2084
O'Ree, Willie **6**-2087
Orr, Bobby **6**-2090
Osborne, Margaret. *See* duPont, Margaret Osborne
Ott, Mel **6**-2093
Ottey, Merlene **6**-2096
Otto, Jim **6**-2099
Otto, Kristin **6**-2102
Ouimet, Francis D. **6**-2105
Ovett, Steve **6**-2108
Owens, Jesse **6**-2111

Pace, Darrell **6**-2114
Paddock, Charles **6**-2117
Page, Alan **6**-2120
Paige, Satchel **6**-2123
Pak, Se Ri **6**-2126
Palmer, Arnold **6**-2128
Palmer, Jim **6**-2132
Papp, Laszlo **6**-2135
Paraskevin-Young, Connie **6**-2137
Parish, Robert **6**-2140
Parker, Denise **6**-2143
Parker, Jim **6**-2146
Parks, Brad **6**-2149
Patterson, Floyd **6**-2152
Patton, Mel **6**-2155
Payton, Gary **6**-2158
Payton, Walter **6**-2161
Pearson, David **6**-2164
Pelé **6**-2167
Perez, Tony **6**-2170
Perreault, Gil **6**-2173
Perry, Fred **6**-2176
Perry, Gaylord **6**-2179
Petinak, Bertha. *See* Tickey, Bertha
Pettit, Bob **6**-2182
Petty, Lee **6**-2185
Petty, Richard **6**-2188
Piazza, Mike **6**-2191
Pierce, Mary **6**-2194
Piggott, Lester **6**-2197
Pincay, Laffit, Jr. **6**-2200
Pippen, Scottie **6**-2202
Plante, Jacques **6**-2206
Platini, Michel **6**-2209
Player, Gary **6**-2212
Pollard, Fritz **6**-2215
Poole, Jim **6**-2217
Popov, Aleksandr **6**-2220
Post, Sandra **6**-2223
Potter, Cynthia **6**-2226
Potter, Martin **6**-2229
Powell, Mike **6**-2232
Prefontaine, Steve **6**-2235
Press, Irina **6**-2238
Press, Tamara **6**-2238
Price, Nick **6**-2241
Proell, Annemarie. *See* Moser-Proell, Annemarie
Prost, Alain **6**-2244
Protopopov, Ludmila **6**-2247
Protopopov, Oleg **6**-2247
Prudhomme, Don **6**-2251
Puckett, Kirby **6**-2254
Puskas, Ferenc **6**-2257

Quarrie, Donald **6**-2260

Rahal, Bobby **6**- 2263
Raines, Tim **6**- 2266
Ramsey, Alf **6**- 2269
Ramsey, Frank **6**- 2272
Rankin, Judy **6**- 2275
Redgrave, Steven **6**- 2278
Reed, Willis **6**- 2281
Reeves, Steve **6**- 2284
Retton, Mary Lou **6**- 2286
Reynolds, Butch **6**- 2289
Ribbs, Willy T. **6**- 2291
Rice, Jerry **6**- 2294
Richard, Maurice "Rocket" **6**- 2297
Richards, Bob **6**- 2300
Rigby, Cathy **6**- 2303
Riggins, John **6**- 2306
Riggs, Bobby **6**- 2309
Ringo, Jim **6**- 2312
Ripken, Cal, Jr. **6**- 2314
Roberts, Robin **6**- 2317
Robertson, Oscar **6**- 2320
Robeson, Paul **6**- 2323
Robinson, Brooks **6**- 2326
Robinson, David **6**- 2329
Robinson, Frank **6**- 2333
Robinson, Jackie **6**- 2336
Robinson, Sugar Ray **6**- 2339
Robustelli, Andy **6**- 2343
Rodgers, Bill **6**- 2346
Rodman, Dennis **6**- 2349
Rodnina, Irina **6**- 2352
Rodriguez, Alex **6**- 2355
Ronaldo **6**- 2358
Rono, Henry **6**- 2361
Rose, Murray **6**- 2364
Rose, Pete **6**- 2367
Rosewall, Ken **6**- 2370
Rote, Kyle, Jr. **6**- 2373
Rowan, Chad. *See* Akebono
Roy, Patrick **6**- 2376
Rudolph, Wilma **6**- 2379

Ruffing, Red **6**- 2382
Ruiz-Conforto, Tracie **6**- 2385
Rummenigge, Karl-Heinz **6**- 2388
Russell, Bill **6**- 2390
Ruth, Babe **6**- 2393
Rutherford, Johnny **6**- 2397
Ryan, Nolan **6**- 2400
Ryun, Jim **6**- 2404

Sabatini, Gabriela **6**- 2407
Saberhagen, Bret **6**- 2410
Sailer, Toni **6**- 2413
Salazar, Alberto **6**- 2416
Salnikov, Vladimir **6**- 2419
Salvino, Carmen **6**- 2422
Sampras, Pete **6**- 2425
Sanchez-Vicario, Arantxa **6**- 2428
Sandberg, Ryne **6**- 2431
Sanders, Barry **6**- 2435
Sanders, Deion **6**- 2438
Sandow, Eugen **6**- 2442
Santos, Manuel Francisco dos. *See* Garrincha
Saraceni, Eugenio. *See* Sarazen, Gene
Sarazen, Gene **7**-2445
Savon, Felix **7**-2448
Sawchuk, Terry **7**-2451
Sax, Steve **7**-2454
Sayers, Gale **7**-2457
Schayes, Dolph **7**-2460
Scherbo, Vitaly **7**-2463
Schmeling, Max **7**-2466
Schmidt, Joe **7**-2469
Schmidt, Mike **7**-2472
Schneider, Petra **7**-2475
Schollander, Don **7**-2477
Schulte, Scott **7**-2480
Schumacher, Michael **7**-2483
Schwarzenegger, Arnold **7**-2486
Scott, Dave **7**-2489
Scott, Mike **7**-2492
Scott, Steve **7**-2495
Scott, Wendell **7**-2498
Scurry, Briana **7**-2500
Seagren, Bob **7**-2503
Seaver, Tom **7**-2506
Seixas, Vic **7**-2509
Seles, Monica **7**-2512
Selvy, Frank **7**-2515
Senna, Ayrton **7**-2518
Shakhlin, Boris **7**-2521
Sharman, Bill **7**-2524
Sharpe, Shannon **7**-2527
Sheehan, Patty **7**-2530
Shell, Art **7**-2533
Shellenberger, Betty **7**-2535
Shilton, Peter **7**-2538
Shoemaker, Willie **7**-2540
Shorter, Frank **7**-2543
Shoulders, Jim **7**-2546
Simmons, Al **7**-2549
Simpson, O. J. **7**-2552
Singletary, Mike **7**-2555
Sisler, George **7**-2558
Sissi **7**-2561
Smith, Bruce **7**-2564
Smith, Bubba **7**-2566
Smith, Emmitt **7**-2568
Smith, John **7**-2571
Smith, Margaret. *See* Court, Margaret
Smith, Ozzie **7**-2574
Smith, Sinjin **7**-2577
Smith, Stan **7**-2580
Smith, Tommie **7**-2583
Smith, Walker, Jr. *See* Robinson, Sugar Ray
Snead, Sam **7**-2586
Snell, Peter **7**-2589
Snider, Duke **7**-2592
Sorenstam, Annika **7**-2595
Sosa, Sammy **7**-2598
Sotomayor, Javier **7**-2601
Spahn, Warren **7**-2604
Speaker, Tris **7**-2607
Spitz, Mark **7**-2610
Stabler, Ken **7**-2613
Stallworth, John **7**-2616
Stargell, Willie **7**-2619
Starr, Bart **7**-2622
Staubach, Roger **7**-2625
Stecher, Renate **7**-2628
Stefano, Alfredo di **7**-2631
Stengel, Casey **7**-2634
Stenmark, Ingemar **7**-2637
Stephens, Helen **7**-2640
Sterkel, Jill **7**-2643
Stevenson, Teófilo **7**-2646
Stewart, Dave **7**-2649
Stewart, Jackie **7**-2652
Stewart, Payne **7**-2655
Stewart, Tony **7**-2658
Stockton, John **7**-2660
Stones, Dwight **7**-2663
Strange, Curtis **7**-2666
Strawberry, Darryl **7**-2669
Street, Picabo **7**-2672
Strickland-de la Hunty, Shirley **7**-2675
Strug, Kerri **7**-2678
Suleimanov, Naim. *See* Suleymanoglu, Naim
Suleymanoglu, Naim **7**-2681
Sun Wen **7**-2684
Sutton, Don **7**-2686
Svan, Gunde **7**-2689
Swann, Lynn **7**-2692
Swie-King, Liem **7**-2695
Swoopes, Sheryl **7**-2697
Szewinska, Irena **7**-2699
Szymanski, Aloysius Harry. *See* Simmons, Al

Tabei, Junko **7**-2701
Tamura, Ryoko **7**-2704
Tarkenton, Fran **7**-2707
Tatum, Goose **7**-2710
Taylor, Charley **7**-2712
Taylor, Jim **7**-2715
Taylor, Lawrence **7**-2718
Taylor, Major **7**-2721
Tchoukarine, Victor **7**-2724
Terry, Bill **7**-2727
Testaverde, Vinny **7**-2730
Thomas, Derrick **7**-2732
Thomas, Frank **7**-2735
Thomas, Isiah **7**-2738
Thomas, Kurt **7**-2741
Thomas, Thurman **7**-2744
Thompson, Daley **7**-2747
Thompson, Jenny **7**-2750
Thorpe, Ian **7**-2753
Thorpe, Jim **7**-2756
Thurmond, Nate **7**-2759
Tibbs, Casey **7**-2762
Tickey, Bertha **7**-2765
Tiger, Dick **7**-2768
Tilden, Bill **7**-2771
Timmons, Steve **7**-2774
Tittle, Y. A. **7**-2777
Tolan, Eddie **7**-2780
Tomba, Alberto **7**-2783
Toomey, Bill **7**-2786
Torluemke, Judith. *See* Rankin, Judy
Torre, Joe **7**-2789
Torres, Dara **7**-2792
Torvill, Jayne **7**-2794
Townsend, Anne Barton **7**-2798
Trabert, Tony **7**-2801
Traynor, Pie **7**-2804
Tretiak, Vladislav **7**-2807
Trevino, Lee **7**-2810
Trinidad, Felix **7**-2813
Trippi, Charley **7**-2816
Trottier, Bryan **7**-2819
Tsukahara, Mitsuo **7**-2822
Tunnell, Emlen **7**-2825
Tunney, Gene **7**-2828
Turishcheva, Ludmila **7**-2831
Turner, Ted **7**-2834
Twyman, Jack **7**-2837
Tyson, Mike **7**-2840
Tyus, Wyomia **7**-2844

Unitas, Johnny **7**-2847
Unseld, Wes **7**-2850

Unser, Al **8**-2853
Unser, Bobby **8**-2856
Upshaw, Gene **8**-2859

Valenzuela, Fernando **8**-2862
Van Basten, Marco **8**-2866
Van Brocklin, Norm **8**-2869
Van Buren, Steve **8**-2872
Vance, Dazzy **8**-2875
Van den Hoogenband, Pieter **8**-2878
Van Dyken, Amy **8**-2881
Van Oosten, Marion. *See* Ladewig, Marion
Vardon, Harry **8**-2884
Vare, Glenna Collett **8**-2887
Vaughn, Greg **8**-2890
Vaughn, Mo **8**-2893
Vidmar, Peter **8**-2896
Vilas, Guillermo **8**-2899
Villeneuve, Jacques **8**-2902
Villwock, Dave **8**-2905
Vinci, Chuck **8**-2908
Viren, Lasse **8**-2911

Waddell, Rube **8**-2914
Wade, Virginia **8**-2917
Wagner, Honus **8**-2920
Wagner, Lisa **8**-2923
Waitz, Greta **8**-2925
Walker, Doak **8**-2928
Walker, Herschel **8**-2931
Walker, John **8**-2934
Wallace, Rusty **8**-2937
Walthour, Bobby **8**-2940
Walton, Bill **8**-2943
Ward, Charlie **8**-2947
Warfield, Paul **8**-2950
Warmerdam, Cornelius **8**-2953
Warner, Kurt **8**-2955
Waterfield, Bob **8**-2958
Watson, Tom **8**-2961
Webber, Chris **8**-2964
Weber, Dick **8**-2967
Weissmuller, Johnny **8**-2970
Werner, Buddy **8**-2973
West, Jerry **8**-2976
Westbrook, Peter **8**-2979
White, Byron "Whizzer" **8**-2981
White, Randy **8**-2984
White, Reggie **8**-2987
Whitfield, Mal **8**-2990
Whitfield, Simon **8**-2993
Whitworth, Kathy **8**-2996
Wigger, Deena **8**-2999
Wigger, Lones **8**-3002
Wightman, Hazel **8**-3006
Wilander, Mats **8**-3009
Wilhelm, Hoyt **8**-3012
Wilkens, Lenny **8**-3015
Wilkie, David **8**-3018
Wilkins, Dominique **8**-3021
Wilkins, Mac **8**-3024
Wilkinson, Laura **8**-3027
Williams, Billy **8**-3029
Williams, Esther **8**-3032
Williams, Natalie **8**-3035
Williams, Ricky **8**-3038
Williams, Serena **8**-3040
Williams, Ted **8**-3043
Williams, Venus **8**-3046
Williams, Walter Ray, Jr. **8**-3049
Wills, Helen Newington. *See* Moody, Helen Wills
Wills, Maury **8**-3051
Wilson, Hack **8**-3054
Wilson, Larry **8**-3057
Winfield, Dave **8**-3059
Winkler, Hans **8**-3062
Witt, Katarina **8**-3065
Wood, Willie **8**-3068
Woodard, Lynette **8**-3070
Wooden, John **8**-3073
Woodhead, Cynthia **8**-3076
Woods, Tiger **8**-3079
Woodson, Charles **8**-3083
Worsley, Gump **8**-3086
Worthy, James **8**-3089
Wright, Archibald Lee. *See* Moore, Archie
Wright, Billy **8**-3092
Wright, Mickey **8**-3095
Wynn, Early **8**-3098

Yamaguchi, Kristi **8**-3101
Yamashita, Yasuhiro **8**-3104
Yarborough, Cale **8**-3107
Yarygin, Ivan **8**-3110
Yashin, Lev **8**-3113
Yastrzemski, Carl **8**-3116
Young, Cy **8**-3119
Young, Sheila **8**-3122
Young, Steve **8**-3125
Yount, Robin **8**-3128
Yzerman, Steve **8**-3131

Zaharias, Babe Didrikson **8**-3134
Zaitsev, Alexander **6**- 2352
Zatopek, Emil **8**-3137
Zelezny, Jan **8**-3140
Zmeskal, Kim **8**-3143
Zungul, Steve **8**-3146
Zurbriggen, Pirmin **8**-3149